Lecture Notes in Computer Science

Lecture Notes in Artificial Intelligence   13496

Founding Editor

Jörg Siekmann

Series Editors

Randy Goebel, *University of Alberta, Edmonton, Canada*
Wolfgang Wahlster, *DFKI, Berlin, Germany*
Zhi-Hua Zhou, *Nanjing University, Nanjing, China*

The series Lecture Notes in Artificial Intelligence (LNAI) was established in 1988 as a topical subseries of LNCS devoted to artificial intelligence.

The series publishes state-of-the-art research results at a high level. As with the LNCS mother series, the mission of the series is to serve the international R & D community by providing an invaluable service, mainly focused on the publication of conference and workshop proceedings and postproceedings.

Qi Su · Ge Xu · Xiaoyan Yang
Editors

Chinese Lexical Semantics

23rd Workshop, CLSW 2022
Virtual Event, May 14–15, 2022
Revised Selected Papers, Part II

 Springer

Editors
Qi Su ⓘ
Peking University
Beijing, China

Ge Xu
Minjiang University
Fuzhou, China

Xiaoyan Yang
Minjiang University
Fuzhou, China

ISSN 0302-9743 ISSN 1611-3349 (electronic)
Lecture Notes in Artificial Intelligence
ISBN 978-3-031-28955-2 ISBN 978-3-031-28956-9 (eBook)
https://doi.org/10.1007/978-3-031-28956-9

LNCS Sublibrary: SL7 – Artificial Intelligence

This Springer imprint is published by the registered company Springer Nature Switzerland AG
The registered company address is: Gewerbestrasse 11, 6330 Cham, Switzerland

CLSW 2022 Preface

The 2022 Chinese Lexical Semantics Workshop (CLSW 2022) was the 23th annual meeting in a series that began in 2000, and the series has been hosted in Beijing, Hong Kong, Taipei, Singapore, Xiamen, Hsin Chu, Yantai, Suzhou, Wuhan, Zhengzhou, Macao, Leshan, and Chia-Yi, etc. The Chinese Lexical Semantics Workshop (CLSW) is well known for both linguists and computer science academics reporting and discussing their thoughts. Theoretical and applied linguistics, computational linguistics, information processing, and computational lexicography are some of its topics. CLSW serves as one of the most prominent gatherings in Asia for Chinese Lexical Semantics, having a great impact on as well as promoting academic research and application development in those topics.

CLSW 2022 was hosted by Minjiang University (MJU for short), Fuzhou, China, on May 14–15, 2022. 214 papers were submitted to the conference; at least two independent reviewers conducted a double-blind review of each submission. Of all submissions, we were only able to accommodate 42.99% (92 papers) as oral presentations and 24.77% (53 papers) as poster presentations. Among accepted papers, selected English papers are included in Springer's LNAI series. They are organized in topical sections covering all major topics of lexical semantics, semantic resources, corpus linguistics, and natural language processing, etc.

We heartily thank the invited speakers for their excellent keynote addresses. Furthermore, we are very appreciative to the conference chairs on behalf of the Program Committee: Zonghua Wang (President of MJU) and Houfeng Wang (Peking University), honorary members of the Advisory Committee: Shiwen Yu (Peking University), Chin-Chuan Cheng (National Taiwan Normal University), Benjamin Ka Yin T'sou (The Education University of Hong Kong), and other members of the Advisory Committee for their guidance in supporting the conference. Also, we would like to acknowledge the chairs of the Organization Committee: Ge Xu (MJU), Guomei Cai (MJU), Xiaoyan Yang (MJU), Hua Zhong (Fujian Normal University) and Xiangwen Liao (Fuzhou University).

Thanks should also be given to the student volunteers of Minjiang University for their tremendous contribution in this event. We appreciate the time and effort put forth by the Program Chairs: Jia-fei Hong (National Taiwan Normal University), Peng Jin (Leshan Normal University), and Jingxia Lin (Nanyang Technological University), as well as the entire Program Committee, and all the reviewers in order to have the submitted papers properly evaluated. We are pleased that the accepted English papers are published by Springer as part of their Lecture Notes in Artificial Intelligence (LNAI) series and are indexed by EI and SCOPUS.

Last but not least, we would like to express our gratitude to all authors and attendees for their scholarly work and cooperation in making CLSW 2022 a success.

January 2023   Zonghua Wang

Organization

General Chairs

Wang, Zonghua   Minjiang University
Wang, Houfeng   Peking University

Steering Committee Honorary Members

Cheng, Chin-Chuan   Taiwan Normal University
T'sou, Ka Yin Benjamin   The Education University of Hong Kong
Yu, Shiwen   Peking University

Steering Committee Members

Diao, Yanbin   Beijing Normal University
Hong, Jia-Fei   Taiwan Normal University
Hsieh, Shu-Kai   Taiwan University
Huang, Chu-Ren   Hong Kong Polytechnic University
Ji, Donghong   Wuhan University
Jin, Peng   Leshan Normal University
Jing-Schmidt, Zhuo   University of Oregon
Liu, Meichun   City University of Hong Kong
Lu, Qin   The Hong Kong Polytechnic University
Lua, Kim-Teng   National University of Singapore
Qu, Weiguang   Nanjing Normal University
Su, Xinchun   Xiamen University
Sui, Zhifang   Peking University
Wu, Jiun-Shiung   Taiwan Chung Cheng University
Xu, Jie   University of Macau
Zan, Hongying   Zhengzhou University
Zhang, Yangseng   Beijing Information Science & Technology University

Program Committee Chairs

Hong, Jia-Fei	Taiwan Normal University
Jin, Peng	Leshan Normal University
Lin, Jingxia	Nanyang Technological University

Organization Chairs

Cai, Guomei	Minjiang University
Liao, Xiangwen	Fuzhou University
Xu, Ge	Minjiang University
Yang, Xiaoyan	Minjiang University
Zhong, Hua	Fujian Normal University

Publication Chairs

Su, Qi	Peking University
Tang, Xuri	Huazhong University of Science and Technology

Contents – Part II

General Linguistics, Lexical Resources

Corpus Linguistics

Semantic Prosody: The Study of Gei in BA and BEI Constructions

Xiaolong Lu[✉] [iD]

Department of East Asian Studies, The University of Arizona, Tucson, USA
charmander@arizona.edu

Abstract. The spoken word *gei* in Chinese is often used in the disposal and passive contexts to construct two types of patterns: (i) *ba* NP *gei* VP, (ii) and *bei* NP *gei* VP. By comparing the distribution of the semantic prosody of the two patterns in corpora, I found that the pattern *ba* NP *gei* VP is more likely to be used in positive contexts than the pattern *bei* NP *gei* VP, but a negative semantic prosody is dominant in both patterns. The reason is that the meaning of *bei* NP *gei* VP as a passive construction was highly associated with negative interpretation in the historical development of BA constructions. The negative meaning of *ba* NP *gei* VP emerged late, but "causality" as its constructional meaning gives the negative interpretation in the corpus. From diachronic and synchronic perspectives, I suggest that the study of semantic prosody in Chinese should widen traditional discussions by transferring from synonym comparison to the investigation of widely used phrases or sentence patterns.

Keywords: *Gei* · BA construction · BEI construction · Semantic prosody

1 Introduction

Gei (给) is one of the most commonly used verbs in modern Chinese. When *gei* serves as a preposition, it can not only be used to mark the goal of the transaction named by the verb but also introduce recipients denoted by the benefactive noun phrases [1]. Lü [2] also mentioned the preverbal *gei* as a particle is often used with BA and BEI constructions, creating a colloquial style in Chinese. The study aims to examine the particle *gei* in Mandarin Chinese. To be specific, the syntactic function of *gei* allows it to be preverbal to form a *gei* VP construction. Although the *gei* VP construction does not constitute a complete sentence, it is frequently used in modern Chinese[1]. The VP is often composed of a verb-resultative or verb-directional construction, or a single verb. Consider the following examples:

(1) 他把茶杯给摔破了。(VP = verb-resultative)
     Ta ba chabei gei shuai-po le.

---

[1] The use of *gei* as a particle has 63103 cases in the spoken Chinese database of the BCC corpus (http://bcc.blcu.edu.cn/zh/search/3/%E7%BB%99v). Our intuition shows that VP following the word *gei* is often used as a colloquial pattern.

Q. Su et al. (Eds.): CLSW 2022, LNAI 13496, pp. 3–15, 2023.
https://doi.org/10.1007/978-3-031-28956-9_1

3SG[2] BA teacup PART throw-break PFV
'He broke the teacup.'
(2) 椅子被老李给搬进来了。(VP = verb-directional)
Yizi bei Lao Li gei ban-jinlai le.
chair PASS PN DISP carry-enter PERF
'The chair was carried in by Lao Li.'
(3) 空调坏了，我们给修。(VP = a single verb)
Kongtiao huai le, women gei xiu.
Air conditioner broken PERF 2PL DISP repair
'If the air conditioner is broken, we repair it.'

Li and Thompson [2] also argued that the preverbal *gei* in the BA construction can highlight the disposal interpretation. Notice that in modern Chinese, the markers showing the meaning of disposal include *jiang* (将) and *ba* (把), and the disposal construction is mostly represented by the BA construction. In contrast, the markers indicating passivity consist of *rang* (让), *jiao* (叫), *bei* (被) and the like, and the typical passive construction is the BEI construction. *Gei* as a colloquial word often occurs in BA and BEI constructions, resulting in the following patterns, with forms and meanings described below:

A. *Ba* NP *gei* VP (Disposal: the agent acts on the recipient by doing sth.)
B. *Bei* NP *gei* VP (Passive: the recipient is affected by the agent who did sth.)

Based on my native speaker intuition and analysis of the BCC corpus, we know that the two constructions are commonly used and the words *ba* and *bei* can be optionally omitted. The goal of this paper is to investigate the syntactic and semantic behaviors of the particle *gei* in disposal and passive contexts (i.e., BA and BEI constructions), and to explore the semantic prosody of *gei* in the two constructions through corpus analysis.

2   Literature Review

The particle *gei* and its related constructions have been hotly discussed in Chinese linguistic studies since the 1990s. Standing from different perspectives, previous studies have discussed the syntactic and semantic characteristics of *gei* VP in Chinese causative and passive sentences. For example, Xu [3] studied Chinese dialects in which the word *gei* can be used in BA and BEI constructions. Wang [4] examined how the disposal meaning is related to the *gei*-related constructions from a diachronic perspective. Based on pragmatic function, Wen and Fan [5] argued that the word *gei* is a type of natural focus marker. Moreover, Xiong [6] as well as Ye and Pan [7] analyzed the syntactic

---

[2] The following abbreviations are used in this paper: 1SG = 1st person singular; 1PL = 1st person plural; 2SG = 2nd person singular; 2PL = 2nd person plural; 3SG = 3rd person singular; 3PL = 3rd person plural; ATTR = Attributive *de*; C = Complementizer *de*; COMP = Postverbal complement marker *de*; CL = Classifier; CP = Clause; EM = Emphasis marker; NEG = Negator; NP = Noun phrase; PART = particle *gei*; PERF: perfective/ perfect marker *le*; PREP = Preposition; PST = Past tense; S = Sentence final *de*; VP = Verb phrase; DISP = disposal marker *ba*; PASS = passive marker *bei*; PREP = Preposition *zai*; PN = proper name.

distribution and semantic features of *gei* by adopting a generative approach. Huang [8] employed the subjective concept of empathy to account for the syntactic and semantic behaviors of *gei*, along with the existence of gei in BA and BEI constructions.

In details, Wang [9] primarily examined the pattern *Ba...gei* VP and he found that the semantics of this construction focuses on a resultative interpretation. From a pragmatic perspective, the construction is used to indicate a complaint or warning, and usually occurs at the end of topic chains. Additionally, the use of *gei* as a particle can stress a sense of unpredicted result and topic closure denoted by BA constructions. Li [10] provided historical evidence to demonstrate that the *ba...gei* VP construction originated earlier than the *bei...gei* VP construction. He also found the particle *gei* occurs mostly in the speech of Northern Chinese, represented by the Beijing dialect. In another dialectal study, Shi [11] pointed out that the word *gei* has double duty in the spoken Beijing dialect, i.e., serving as both passive marker and disposal marker. Similarly, Li and Chen [12] historically investigated the *gei* VP construction in the Beijing dialect, showing the passive *gei* can be replaced with *bei*, the disposal *gei* can be substituted with *ba*, and beneficiary *gei* can be interchanged to *wei* (为) and *ti* (替). Meanwhile, they found the ratios of beneficiary, disposal, and passive interpretations in the *gei* VP construction are 32:25:41 in data from Chinese novels, suggesting that the passive interpretation outweighs the other readings. Regarding the semantics of *gei*-related constructions, Huang [8] stressed the fact that the verbs following the word *gei* usually have a sense of losing or suffering. Because of unexpected and unfortunate events in our life, the use of *gei* can better reflect the effect of empathy in speakers' feelings. Kou and Yuan [13] in their discourse analysis argued that the word *gei* is a subjective marker, emphasizing the reason why *gei* VP indicates counter expectation and resultative interpretation is associated with the speakers. They found that the use of *gei* suggests a high degree of subjectivity, empathy, and cognitive salience. Their findings are consistent with the discussion of *gei* within the empathy theory in Huang [8], as well as Wen and Fan [5], who argued that the preverbal *gei* is a focus marker to make the natural focus become the resultative focus.

Above all, the studies reviewed so far indicated the use of the particle *gei* in Chinese BA and BEI constructions often denotes counter expectation and resultative readings. In certain Chinese dialects, particularly northern dialects, the word *gei* can serve as a grammatical marker. However, some issues remain unclear. For instance, Huang [8] postulated that the post-*gei* verbs are mostly negative but she did not provide data to prove her argument. Also, through the data analysis of novels, Li and Chen [12] concluded that *gei* VP has a passive reading in a majority of cases. However, the genres of their corpus are not diverse, and they did not provide the exact percentages for the different readings. Given this, this study aims to fill a gap by examining different genres within the BCC corpus to investigate the frequency and semantic prosody of *gei* in BA and BEI constructions. My research questions are directed by the above discussions: (i) How often does *gei* occur in BA and BEI constructions, and (ii) how does the semantic prosody of *gei* emerge in different genres of the Chinese corpus?

3 Research Methodology

To measure the distribution of semantic prosody, I checked against different kinds of databases in the BCC corpus [14], including magazines, weblogs, technology writings, literature, and multi-source databases (http://bcc.blcu.edu.cn/). The sample size for each database is relatively balanced. The query for searching *gei* in BA and BEI constructions was 把N给V and 被N给V, respectively. The date for my initial corpus search was on July 5th, 2021. The semantic prosody of *gei* was measured by considering contexts and verbs. If both contexts and verbs had negative meanings, then the word *gei* was taken to indicate a negative reading. If both contexts and verbs were positive, then *gei* indicated a positive reading. If both contexts and verbs were neutral, then *gei* had a neutral reading. Take some sentences in BCC for example:

(4) 弟把车给弄丢了, 老爸老妈肯定心疼死了。
     Di ba che gei <u>nongdiu</u> le, <u>lao ba lao ma kending</u>
     younger.brother DISP car PART get.lost PREF old papa old mom surely
     <u>xinteng si le.</u>
     distressed death PERF
     'My younger brother lost his car, our old papa and mom will surely be distressed to death.' (both underlined context and verb are negative)

(5) <u>我这边有几个自行车友坚持骑自行车</u>, 结果把肩周炎给治好了。
     <u>Wo zhebian you jige zixingche you jianchi qi zixingche</u>, jieguo
     1SG here have several bike friend keep ride bike consequently
     ba jianzhouyan gei <u>zhi hao le.</u>
     DISP periarthritis of shoulder PART cure well PERF
     'On my side, there are a few bike lovers insisting on riding bikes, consequently their periarthritis of shoulder has been cured.' (both underlined context and verb are positive)

(6) …<u>不过一边讲也就顺便把作文给背</u>了。
     …<u>buguo yibian jiang yejiu shunbian</u> ba zuowen gei <u>bei</u> le.
     but simultaneously speak then by.the.way DISP essay PART recite PERF
     '(s/he) spoke but simultaneously recited the essay.' (both underlined context and verb are neutral)

4   The Semantic Prosody of G*ei*

4.1   Semantic Prosody

Semantic prosody or evaluative prosody is one of the key constructs in corpus linguistics. Louw [15] initially proposed semantic prosody in the study of irony as a rhetorical device in English texts. He argued that the study of semantic prosody of a linguistic structure is closely associated with its collocation with other constituents in corpora. Therefore, the judgment of semantic prosody does not only depend on speakers' subjective intuition or introspection. We need to see how semantic prosody emerges from usages in objective contexts. Sinclair [16] and Stubbs [17] further developed the idea of semantic prosody, showing that semantic prosody has been assigned a discourse function under the influence of contexts. Hunston and Thompson [18] defined semantic prosody as "the speaker or writer's attitude or stance towards, viewpoint or feelings about the entities and propositions that he or she is talking about" (p. 5). This shows that speakers with different backgrounds have different attitudes or evaluations towards topics in discourse.

The study of semantic prosody in Chinese emerged late but has played a crucial role in the development of lexical semantics studies. For example, Tao [19] proposed the "emergent lexical semantics", using the theory of semantic prosody to account for the semantic and pragmatic differences among a group of Chinese synonyms, such as *chuxian* 'emerge', *chansheng* 'produce', and *fasheng* 'happen'. By comparing English with Chinese, Xiao and McEnery [20] found that the English noun *consequence* has the same semantic prosody as *houguo* 'consequence' in Chinese, and the noun *result* or *outcome* corresponds to *jieguo* 'result' in Chinese. Moreover, they examined the distribution of different verbs that can be collocated with these nouns in the corpus. Their findings suggest that semantic prosody, based on a functional approach, centers on the semantic preferences of words and phrases in different contexts. It is through big data that we can dig into the semantic prosody of different constituents in a language, and this contributes to the knowledge of the semantic features of Chinese lexicon. In what follows, I will adopt the theory of semantic prosody to summarize and analyze the distribution of *gei* in BA and BEI constructions.

4.2 Semantic Prosody of *Gei*

In Table 1, horizontally speaking, the existence of the particle *gei* is dominant in BA constructions with all kinds of genres, including formal genres (e.g., magazine, technology, literature) and informal genres (e.g., weblog). For instance, the *ba* NP *gei* VP construction amounts to 86.6% in the technology database, and the percentage is far higher than that of *bei* NP *gei* VP (13.4%). Viewed vertically from the table, the number of cases for the two constructions is the highest (5595), surpassing the total sum (1390) of cases in magazine, technology, and literature genres. However, the frequency of *gei* in BA constructions is much higher than that in BEI constructions. This result shows that the two constructions have a higher frequency in informal or spoken contexts (e.g., weblog) whereas have a lower frequency in written or formal contexts (e.g., technology, magazine).

Table 1. The frequency of the two constructions in BCC

BCC databases Frequency Constructions	Magazine	Weblog	Technology	Literature
ba NP gei VP	426 (88.2%)	4035 (72.1%)	306 (86.6%)	407 (73.4%)
bei NP gei VP	57 (11.8%)	1560 (27.9%)	47 (13.4%)	147 (26.6%)
Sum	483	5595	353	554

Regarding the semantic prosody of *gei* in BA and BEI constructions, I searched the BCC multi-domain database (with different genres) to calculate the distribution of semantic prosody in the two constructions. The results are summarized in Table 2.

From above we know that although the word *gei* in BA constructions can occur in positive and neutral contexts, this possibility is only realized 28.6% of the time. In example (7), the VP *gei zhihao* 'got cured' denotes a positive context, whereas *gei xi le*

Table 2. The semantic prosody of the two constructions in BCC (multi-domain database)

Constructions Distribution Semantic prosody	ba NP gei VP	bei NP gei VP
Positive or neutral	1159 (28.6%)	12 (0.9%)
Negative	2894 (71.4%)	1269 (99.1%)
Sum	4053	1281

'got washed' in example (8) and *gei guo le* 'have spent' in example (9) both have neutral readings.

(7)   罗松巴登一连跑了七次, 把病给治好了。
       Luosongbadeng yilian pao le qi ci, ba bing gei zhidao le.
       3SG at.a.stretch run PERF seven times DISP illness PART cure PERF
       'Luosongbadeng ran for seven times at a stretch, which cured his illness.'
(8)   明天无论如何把车给洗了去!让你们再嘲笑我的车脏!
       Mingtian wulunruhe ba che gei xi le qu! Rang nimen zai
       tomorrow in.any.case DISP car PART wash PERF go let 2PL again
       chaoxiao wo de che zang!
       make.fun.of 1SG ATTR car dirty
       'In any case (I) will go and wash my car tomorrow! (Don't) Let you guys make fun of my dirty car again!'
(9)   今天提前把生日给过了, 明天出差。
       Jintian tiqian ba shengri gei guo le, mingtian
       Today in.advance DISP birthday PART spend PERF tomorrow
       chuchai.
       take.business.trip
       'Today (I) spent my birthday in advance, (so that) I can take my business trip tomorrow.'

Instead, the word *gei* in BA constructions occurs mostly in negative contexts (71.4%). The frequent VPs that are collocated with *gei* are ranked as: *gua shang* 'hang up' (76 cases), *shuo wan/ chu* 'finish telling/ speak out' (34 cases), *xia si/pao/huai* 'scare to death/ scare to run/ freak out' (20 cases), *mie le/ diao* 'destroy' (19 cases), *wai le* 'twisted' (19 cases), *jie le* 'abstained' (18 cases), *shan le* 'sprained' (18 cases), *niu le* 'twisted' (17 cases), *xian le/ fan* 'turned over' (14 cases), and *wang le* 'forgot' (10 cases). We see that most of VPs and verb resultative constructions can create negative contexts where the construction *ba NP gei VP* occurs frequently. For example, *gei nong shang* 'got hurt' in (10), *gei qi si* 'got pissed off' in (11), and *gei mie diao* 'got destroyed' in (12) all have negative meanings. Another evidence is to see how the word *gei* is used in BA constructions to generalize negative readings in most contexts, as shown in Fig. 1 below:

(10)   昨天练瑜珈, 动作幅度太大, 把腰给弄伤了。
       Zuotian lian yujia, dongzuo fudu taida, ba yao gei nongshang le.

yesterday practice yoga movement range too big DISP waist PART hurt PERF
'Yesterday (I) practiced yoga, I hurt my waist due to my large movement range.'

(11) 结果有一位才子听写出来的让全班笑得东倒西歪，一塌糊涂，活活把老师给气死。
Jieguo you yi-wei caizi tingxie chulai de rang quanban
Consequently there.be one-CL talented.person dictate out C make whole.class
xiao-de dongdaoxiwai, yitahutu, huohuo ba laoshi
laugh-COMP lying.on.all.sides in.a.complete.mess actually DISP teacher
gei qisi.
PART piss.off.
'Consequently, there was a talented person whose dictated work made the whole class laugh so as to lie on all sides, such a complete mess, which actually got the teacher pissed off.'

(12) 每个月总有那么几天想把主人给灭掉。
Mei-ge yue zong you name jitian xiang ba zhuren gei miediao.
every-CL month always have those days want DISP owner PART destroy
'Every month, there are always a few days when (he) wants to destroy his owner.'

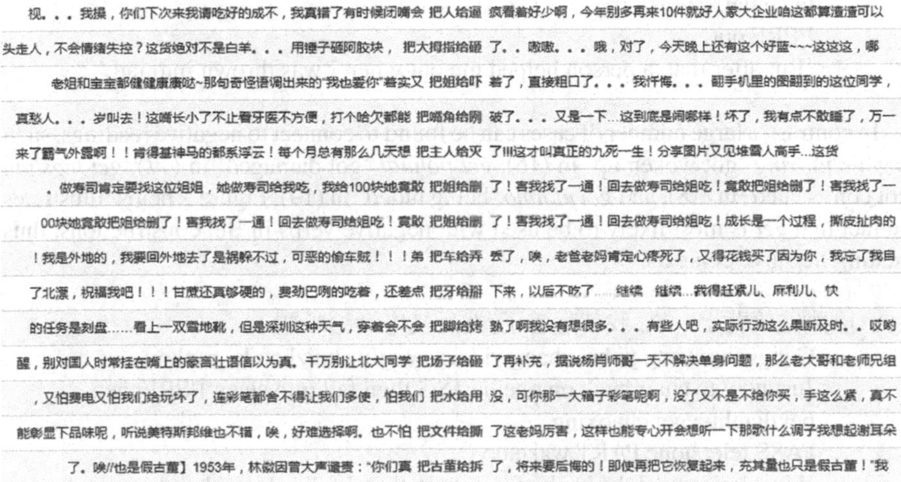
视。。。我操，你们下次来我请吃好的成不，我真错了有时候闭嘴会 把人给逼 疯看着好少啊，今年别多再来10件就好人家大企业咱这都算渣渣可以
头走人，不会情绪失控？这货绝对不是白羊。。。用锤子砸阿胶块， 把大拇指给砸 了。。嗷嗷。。。哦，对了，今天晚上还有这个好蓝~~~这这这，哪
老姐和宝宝都健健康康哒~那句奇怪语调出来的"我也爱你"着实又 把姐给吓 着了，直接粗口了。。。我忏悔。。。翻手机里的图翻到的这位同学，
真愁人。。。岁叫去！这嘴长小了不止看牙医不方便，打个哈欠都能 把嘴角给撕 破了。。。又是一下...这到底是闹哪样！坏了，我有点不敢睡了，万一
来了霸气外露啊！！肯得基神马的都系浮云！每个月总有那么几天想 把主人给灭 了!!!这才叫真正的九死一生！分享图片又见堆雪人高手...这货
。做寿司肯定要找这位姐姐，她做寿司给我吃，我给100块她竟敢 把姐给删 了！害我找了一通！回去做寿司给姐吃！竟敢把姐给删了！害我找了一
00块她竟敢把姐给删了！害我找了一通！回去做寿司给姐吃！竟敢 把姐给删 了！害我找了一通！回去做寿司给姐吃！成长是一个过程，撕皮扯肉的
！我是外地的，我要回外地去了是祸躲不过，可恶的偷车贼！！！弟 把车给弄 丢了，唉，老爸老妈肯定心疼死了，又得花钱买了因为你，我忘了我自
了北漂，祝福我吧！！！甘蔗还真够硬的，费劲巴咧的吃着，还差点 把牙给掰 下来，以后不吃了..... 继续 继续...我得赶紧儿、麻利儿、快
的任务是刻盘......看上一双雪地靴，但是深圳这种天气，穿着会不会 把脚给烤 熟了啊我没有想很多。。。有些人吧，实际行动这么果断及时。。哎哟
醒，别对国人时常挂在嘴上的豪言壮语信以为真。千万别让北大同学 把场子给砸 了再补充，据说杨肖师哥一天不解决单身问题，那么老大哥和老师兄组
，又怕费电又怕我们给玩坏了，连彩笔都舍不得让我们多使，怕我们 把水给用 没，可你那一大箱子彩笔呢啊，没了又不是不给你买，手这么紧，真不
能彰显下品味呢，听说美特斯邦维也不错，唉，好难选择啊。也不怕 把文件给撕 了这老妈厉害，这样也能专心开会想听一下那歌什么调子我想起谢耳朵
了。唉//也是假古董】1953年，林徽因曾大声谴责："你们真 把古董给拆 了，将来要后悔的！即使再把它恢复起来，充其量也只是假古董！"我

Fig. 1. Screenshot of *ba* NP *gei* VP construction in BCC

Meanwhile, *gei* collocating with BEI constructions is overwhelmingly dominant in negative contexts (99.1%), far outweighing the frequency in BA constructions. Those VPs which can be frequently used with *gei* include: *chui mie/ zou* 'blow out/ blow away' (10 cases), *ji le* 'squeezed' (6 cases), *pian le* 'being cheated', *hui le* 'destroyed' (5 cases), *ran hong* 'reddened' (5 cases), *pi si/ zhong* 'struck/ struck to death' (5 cases), *zhuang si* 'knocked down to death' (4 cases), *sha le* 'killed' (4 cases), *chao xing* 'wake up' (4 cases), *dian wu le* 'tarnished' (4 cases). From these VPs we know that there is a limited number of cases showing positive readings, but 12 examples were found to indicate positive contexts. For instance, *gei shouyang* 'got adopted' in (13), *gei jiejue* 'got solved' in (14), and *gei jiule chulai* 'got helped out' in (15) all concern positive readings.

(13) 记得那年我们楼道也有5只被遗弃的小狗, 后来都被好心人给收养了。
      Jide na nian women loudao ye you wu zhi bei yiqi de
      remember that year 2PL stairway also have five CL PASS abandon ATTR
      xiaogou houlai dou bei haoxin ren gei shouyang le.
      puppy later.on all PASS warm.heart person PART adopt PERF
      'Remember in that year there were also five puppies being abandoned in our
      stairway. Later on, they were all adopted by people with warm hearts.'

(14) 困扰我多年的耳朵问题今天被老公给解决了!
      Kunrao wo duonian de erduo wenti jintian bei laogong gei jiejue le!
      Trouble 1SG years ATTR ear issue today PASS husband PART solve PERF
      'The ear issue that had troubled me for many years was solved by my husband
      today!'

(15) 但是后来, 身陷囹圄的我却被人给救了出来。
      Danshi houlai, shen-xian-ling-yu de wo que bei ren gei jiu
      but after.that be.thrown.into.jail ATTR 1SG EM PASS person PART rescue
      le chulai.
      PERF out
      'But after that, a person helped me out when I was thrown into jail.'

In contrast, a large number of cases can be found to connect to negative readings, such as *gei chaoxing* 'got woken up' in (16), *gei pohuai* 'got damaged' in (17), *gei moshou* 'got confiscated' in (18), and *gei maimo* 'being hided' in (19). Figure 2 below illustrates the fact that *gei* is most likely to be used with negative verbs in Bei constructions, thus creating negative contexts.

(16) 刚刚往椅背上一靠, 我就睡着了, 然后被电话给吵醒。
      Ganggang wang yi bei shang yi kao, wo jiu shuizhao le, ranhou
      Just.now to chair back on one lie 1SG then fall.into.sleep PERF then
      bei dianhua gei chaoxing.
      PASS telephone PART wake.up
      'I just lay toward the back of the chair, then I fell asleep, then I was woken up
      by the telephone.'

(17) 本来美好的一天都被一个人给破坏了。
      Benlai meihao de yi-tian dou bei yi-ge-ren gei pohuai
      Originally wonderful ATTR one-day EM PASS one-CL-person PART ruin.
      le.
      PERF
      'Originally my wonderful day has been ruined by one person.'

(18) 昨天买了个三国杀, 我连碰都没碰今天就被班主任给没收了。

Zuotian mai le ge San-guo-sha, wo lian peng dou

Yesterday buy PERF CF Killers.of.the.Three.Kingdoms 1SG even touch

mei peng jiu bei banzhuren gei moshou le.

NEG touch then PASS head.teacher PART confiscate PERF

'Yesterday (I) purchased a set of Killers of the Three Kingdoms, the head teacher confiscated the board game today even though I did not touch it at all.'

(19) 摄影的根源到底还是一门艺术, 不能完全被商业给埋没了自己的灵性。

Sheying de genyuan daodi haishi yi-men yishu, bu neng wanquan

photography ATTR nature actually still one-CL art NEG can purely

bei shangye gei maimo le ziji de lingxing.

PASS business PART sacrifice PERF self ATTR intelligence

'(I realized that) The nature of photography is purely a type of art, so I cannot sacrifice my intelligence of photograpy to pursue the business.'

百是官场倾压互斗。这个倒霉鬼, 有可能也是个政治争斗的可怜虫。被政敌给整 的吧, 要不, "天上人间"享乐的视频, 怎么会被拍到?难道不是有目

方面跟年纪真没关系。拉丿, 卧室里被打死老。萨达姆老在家呆着, 被人给弄 个死老。卡扎菲, 下水道做游戏被弄死了。所以得出一结论: 宅男是没

为最后的段子是北京朋友朗诵的, 那一段朗诵了小半个小时, 最后是 被服务员给打住了。北京的朋友姓陈, 6岁开始读莎诗, 他父亲是一个著名的翻译家。

也不知道怎么办好。。。《因为爱情》很有难度啊。一大清早的, 就 被阳光给吵 醒了。又睡到大餐啦!!!我到底要不要去呢!很搞笑啊, 太强大了。

那24K黄金狗眼长屁股上了是吧···爷都说了不发了···微博都 被管理员给删 了你还找我要···还是你看不懂字啊·要不要我一个字念给你听啊

啊。。知道分别点的是什么嘛?立等, 一个人吃面。过分!好男人都 被猪给拱 了!不是2B就是同志!!!看的我梗到了!!!这肯定是个在发春的

yFM城市之音至尊金榜投票1/3)投给"周笔畅对唱"我擦···· 被梦给吐 醒了我参加了投票《二十首2011华语新歌你最喜欢哪首?》投给"

有我这么无语·····你是呆去哪里啦??那么多天都不见你!!不会是 被芒果给淹死 了吧!!你说是吧?辛苦辛苦!!~要转。我在, 曬曬法学院外联部给

ndle快点到货吧。好冷好冷啊, 求团购热水袋。很多年醒的故事 被文字给美化··让人进以接受事实··甚至会嘲笑。·但是那才是故事本身今天去

opping!我听到他声音额抖了·····回复好啊, 就是风燕的孩子 被皇后给打 掉了, 然后那个皇后就陷害风燕还有飞鸿说他们通奸, 然后那个狗帝就

今天把好久没用的加湿器给派上用场了!吹的我好冷!可恶得是竟然 被蚊子给咬 了!唉!毛的办公室啊!!真心期待我在"钻石小屋免费送帖石吊坠啦

7!走到哪儿都是榜首。英年早逝我就听的有点蒜了了···今年确实 被LMFAO给洗 脑了。各种神曲啊。···你心中的Top10是怎样排列的呢?明天

了六次牌, 最后才发现捕了一根方块J在地上, TMD, 切切实实是 被牌给整 了·······呜呜······一个学期又这样结束了······还有几个学期···

地方就是··当你那个的时候会被压住你懂的上床那么纠结得东西···别 被整倒给玷污 了!对对对最烦那些虚伪的人了我还是觉得英语是坑爹明明是一门语言

Fig. 2. Screenshot of *bei* NP *gei* VP construction in BCC

4.3 Explanations of Semantic Prosody

From Table 2 we know that the probability of being negative in the construction *ba* NP *gei* VP approximates 71.4% while the percentage of being negative in the construction *bei* NP *gei* VP reaches almost 99.1%. This shows that the passive reading emerges mostly in the BEI constructions rather than the BA constructions. Literally, the use of the word *bei* can denote a sense of mischance and oppression, but it can also show something positive, as indicated in examples from (13) to (15). Furthermore, whether the word *gei* is used in the BA constructions or BEI constructions, the contexts in which it occurs tend to be negative in most cases. The reason probably lies in the historical development of the two constructions. First, the negative meaning associated with the BEI constructions is traditionally dominant. Zhang [21] examined the historical literary works, showing that from classical Chinese to modern Chinese, the semantic color of the BEI constructions has been changed from passive to neutral, then to positive reading. This shows that the BEI construction has been developed into a semantic network prioritizing a passive reading while absorbing positive and neutral meanings. Second, modern Chinese provided an environment for the extension of passive meaning in the construction *bei* NP *gei* VP. The passive reading can be increasingly found in some social media catchphrases, such as the wide use of the passive construction *bei* X (X = VP/AP/NP) in 2009. For example, the occurrences of *bei jiuye* 'be said to be employed', *bei xingfu* 'be said to be happy', *bei zisha* 'unwillingly suicided' can reflect speakers' strong sense of resistance and sarcasm to social conflicts and injustice. Except for the BEI constructions, the word *gei* can also appear in passive readings. For instance, *gei gui le*[3] 'give me a break' as an online buzzword in 2012 is still widely used to self-deprecate by surrendering to somebody or something. Compared with BEI constructions, BA constructions firstly emerged in the Tang Dynasty (618–907AD) and became popular in the Ming and Qing Dynasties (1368–1912AD). Compared with the BEI constructions, the BA constructions appeared late, and their passive readings have not been further developed, thus positive and neutral readings exist in historical BA constructions. Based on intuition, we also know that there is no dominant reading in the Ba constructions. Instead, different semantic prosodies become possible in different contexts.

Additionally, I agree with Huang's [8] empathy theory, which can be used to account for the subjective empathy reflected in BA and BEI constructions. Another explanation for the passive reading in the *ba* NP *gei* VP construction, however, is that the causativity denoted by the BA construction interacts with the meaning of *gei*, leading to a negative semantic prosody. This hypothesis echoes Zhang's [22] argument, showing that the basic meaning of the BA constructions denotes a causal relation instead of the traditionally called "disposal relation" [23]. For example, *ba dian nao gei nong diu le* 'got computer lost' tends to show the agent caused the computer to get lost instead of actively throwing (disposal) the computer away. The corpus analysis suggested that causativity often gives rise to a passive reading. The grammatical meaning of *ba* NP *gei* VP thus relies on the meaning of VP to emphasize that an agent acts on a recipient to produce a causative and passive result. It is worth mentioning the fact that the causativity meaning in BA constructions and the "unfortunate" meaning in BEI constructions both belong to passive readings, which provided a semantic context where the two meanings are compatible. There are a limited number of cases but the mixture of BA constructions and BEI constructions contributes to structural simplification (economy) and expressive effect to show passivity caused by the VPs. For example, *bei ta pian qu* 'be cheated by him' in (20) and *bei jianboqi zha shang* 'be punctured and injured by the radio detector' in (21) both stress the serious consequences after the actions denoted by VPs.

(20) 奉劝世间的嫖客及早回头, 不可被戏文小说引偏了心, 把血汗钱被他骗去。
      Fengquan shijian de piaoke jizao huitou, bu

---

[3] See: https://en.wiktionary.org/wiki/%E7%B5%A6%E8%B7%AA%E4%BA%86#Chinese.

kindly.suggest world ATTR prostitution.client ASAP mend.one's.ways NEG
ke bei xiwen xiaoshuo yin pian le xin, ba xuehanqian
can PASS dramas novels tempt mislead PERF heart DISP hard-earned.money
bei ta pian qu.
PASS 3SG cheat away
'Kindly suggest the prostitution clients in the world should mend their ways as soon as possible. Don't be tempted and misled by his dramas and novels, thus being cheated out of hard-earned money.'

(21) 排列撒线人员田进和, 在撒线作业时不慎把脚被检波器扎伤。
Pailie saxian renyuan Tian Jinhe, zai saxian zuoye shi bushen
arrange release.wire staff PN PREP release.wire work time inadvertent
ba jiao bei jianboqi zha shang.
DISP leg PASS radiodetector puncture injured
'Tian Jinhe, the staff for wire arrangement and release, was punctured and injured his legs with the radio detector when he was releasing wires.'

5 Concluding Remarks

Grounded in the context of BA and BEI constructions, this study investigated the semantic prosody of the particle *gei* collocating with VPs in Chinese. The results reveal that the *gei* VP construction prefers a negative interpretation in different genres of texts. I hope the study can benefit other studies on the semantic prosody of collocations. The study also implies that research on semantic prosody calls for a transition from traditional synonym comparison to similar phrases and sentence patterns. As Partington [24] contended, "prosodies are not a property of words: they are a property of groups of recurring, inter-collocating words and phrases." (p. 287). Also, he argued that "the distribution of evaluative meaning can spread across words and phrases both synchronically and diachronically" (p. 295). Therefore, I suggest the study of semantic prosody in the future should take different types of phrases into consideration. For instance, the verbal phrase V *lai* V *qu* 'doing something back and forth' might have negative interpretation in some contexts [25], and the same goes with the nominal phrase *zheyang nayang* 'such-and-such things'[4]. Some sentence patterns, including comparative constructions, *lian* constructions (连字句), and exclamations, might also bear negative meanings. Another important research area is to quantitatively examine the semantic prosody of Chinese idioms as fixed phrases. For example, the idiom *an tu suo ji* (按图索骥) has two contrasting meanings; one is to show inflexibility in dealing with something (negative), whereas another is to indicate using clues to find something valuable (positive). The idiom *hu feng huan yu* (呼风唤雨) can be used to not only denote seditious activities (negative) but also express the power of humans over nature (positive). The idiom *qi wen gong shang* (奇文共赏) is used to mean a wonderful essay is appreciated by all (positive), but it can also be used to indicate a joint critique of problematic essays (negative). The

---

[4] 难怪街上这么吵闹, 原来是你们这些家伙到处走来走去。(No wonder such a noisy street, it is you guys who <u>walk back and forth</u> on the street.)一身白得象灰面, 松塌塌的, 一点儿无意思, 还装模作态, <u>这样那样</u>。(The guy's whole body looks like a block of grey flour, loose and languid, but he behaves in an affected way, <u>doing such-and-such things</u>.)(c.f. BCC).

frequencies of these idioms in our life are not as high as that of some synonyms, so we cannot easily judge whether they are negative or positive based only on our own knowledge and intuition. Only in a large number of collocations can we find semantic prosodies of these expressions, emerging from the speakers' discourses. It is therefore believed that phrases and sentence patterns with positive and negative meanings in modern Chinese should receive more attention, with the goal of exploring their semantic preferences developed in different periods of time. The proportion of being positive and negative in lexical semantics can perhaps uncover the social cognition and rules of historical changes behind language use.

References

1. Li, C., Thompson, S.A.: Functional Reference Grammar of Mandarin Chinese. University of California Press, Berkeley (1981)
2. Lü, S.: Modern Chinese Eight Hundred Words. The Commercial Press, Beijing (1999). (in Chinese)
3. Xu, D.: Grammatical marker gei in Beijing dialect. Dialect 1, 54–60 (1992). (in Chinese)
4. Wang, J.: The origin of disposal gei constructions. Linguist. Res. 93(4), 9–13 (2004). (in Chinese)
5. Wen, S., Fan, Q.: Gei as a natural-focus marker in contemporary spoken Chinese. Stud. Chin. Lang. 1, 19–25+95 (2006). (in Chinese)
6. Xiong, Z.: The syntactic-semantic properties of the passive category gei. Mod. Foreign Lang. 34(2), 119–126+218 (2011). (in Chinese)
7. Ye, K., Pan, H.: The syntactic nature of gei in the Ba construction. Foreign Lang. Teach. Res. 46(5), 656–665+799 (2014). (in Chinese)
8. Huang, B.: Gei as subjectivity marker: remarks on the deficiencies of gei as syntactic marker. Linguist. Sci. 83(4), 377–390 (2016). (in Chinese)
9. Wang, Y.: The conditions required and the expressive function of gei in the sentence pattern of ba…gei V. Lang. Teach. Linguist. Stud. 2, 64–70 (2001). (in Chinese)
10. Li, W.: The auxiliary word gei in reinforcing the disposition/passive voice. Lang. Teach. Linguist. Stud. 1, 55–61 (2004). (in Chinese)
11. Shi, Y.: Gei: its double functions as passive and disposal markers. Chin. Teach/ World 69(3), 15–26+2 (2004). (in Chinese)
12. Li, Y., Chen, Q.: The status and development of the passive gei construction in Beijing dialect. Dialect. 4, 289–297 (2005). (in Chinese)
13. Kou, X., Yuan, Y.: Transitivity and some problems with the gei-VP construction in Mandarin. Chin. Lang. Learn. 6, 12–20 (2017). (in Chinese)
14. Xun, E., Rao, G., Xiao, X., Zang, J.: The construction of the BCC Corpus in the age of Big Data. Corpus Linguist. 3(1), 93–109 (2016). (in Chinese)
15. Louw, B.: Irony in the text or insincerity in the writer? The diagnostic potential of semantic prosodies. Text and Technology: In Honour of John Sinclair, pp. 157–176 (1993)
16. Sinclair, J.: The search for units of meaning. The Search for Units of Meaning, pp. 1000–1032 (1996)
17. Stubbs, M.: Words and Phrases: Corpus Studies of Lexical Semantics. Blackwell Publishers, Oxford (2001)
18. Hunston, S., Thompson, G. (eds.): Evaluation in Text: Authorial Stance and the Construction of Discourse: Authorial Stance and the Construction of Discourse. OUP, Oxford (2000)
19. Tao, H.: Toward an emergent view of lexical semantics. Lang. Linguist. 4(4), 837–856 (2003)

20. Xiao, R., McEnery, T.: Collocation, semantic prosody, and near synonymy: a cross-linguistic perspective. Appl. Linguis. **27**(1), 103–129 (2006). https://doi.org/10.1093/applin/ami045
21. Zhang, Y.: A Historical Study of Chinese Passive Constructions. China Social Sciences Press, Beijing (2010). (in Chinese)
22. Zhang, B.: On the sentence meaning of Ba constructions. Stud. Lang. Linguist. **38**(1), 28–40 (2000). (in Chinese)
23. Wang, L.: Modern Chinese Grammar. Zhonghua Bookstore, Beijing (1943). (in Chinese)
24. Partington, A.: Evaluative prosody. In: Aijmer, K., Rühlemann, C. (eds.) Corpus Pragmatics: A Handbook, pp. 279–303. Cambridge University Press (2014). https://doi.org/10.1017/CBO 9781139057493.015
25. Lu, X.: A cognitive study on modern Chinese construction "V-lai-V-qu." In: Hong, J.-F., Qi, S., Wu, J.-S. (eds.) Chinese Lexical Semantics: 19th Workshop, CLSW 2018, Chiayi, Taiwan, May 26–28, 2018, Revised Selected Papers, pp. 202–224. Springer International Publishing, Cham (2018). https://doi.org/10.1007/978-3-030-04015-4_18

Corpus-Based Lexical Features and Thematic Analysis of CHina's Five-Year Plan for the 21st Century

Lulu Gu[1], Lili Gu[2], and Pengyuan Liu[1,3](✉)

[1] Department of Information Science, Beijing Language and Culture University, 15th Xue Yuan Road, Haidian District, Beijing 100083, China
liupengyuan@pku.edu.cn
[2] School of Public Administration, Zhejiang Gongshang University, Xiasha University Town, No. 18, Xuezheng Street, Hangzhou 310018, Zhejiang, China
[3] Center of National Language Recourse and Monitoring Research Print Media Branch, Beijing Language and Culture University, 15th Xue Yuan Road, Haidian District, Beijing 100083, China

Abstract. The Five-Year Plan is one of the typical symbols and representations of the socialist system with Chinese characteristics, and its interpretation is of far-reaching significance. This paper selects the five Five-Year Plans of China since the 21st century to build a corpus. It was found by high-frequency words, keywords, LDA topic, and systematic clustering analysis that the words "发展 (develop)" and "建设 (construct)" are not absent in the Five-Year Plan of different stages. Although national economic and social development are shared topics, the Five-Year Plans focus on different topics in detail according to the different stages and requirements. Among those topics, three topics are emphasized, namely, optimizing industrial structure, promoting trade cooperation, and securing resource expansion, which are very different from each other and each covers a wide range of concerns respectively. Generally Speaking, the five Five-Year Plans can be divided into two categories, "Solid Advancement Type" and "Quality Expansion Type", which have their own characteristics in four aspects: stability, balance, sustainability, and fairness.

Keywords: Five-Year Plan · Corpus · Lexical features · LDA · Systematic clustering

1 Introduction

Xi Jinping once said: historical development has its own laws, but people are not completely passive in it. As long as we grasp the general trend of historical development, seize the moment of historical change, be vigorous and enterprising, human society will be better. The world is in the midst of a major change unprecedented in the century today. The international economic situation is not optimistic, and economic globalization is experiencing headwinds. It is also a critical period for China to move forward

Q. Su et al. (Eds.): CLSW 2022, LNAI 13496, pp. 16–33, 2023.
https://doi.org/10.1007/978-3-031-28956-9_2

from building a moderately prosperous society to the basic realization of socialist modernization. Therefore, the Chinese Communist Party prefers to take a full approach to strategic planning in governing the country, and the Five-Year Plan is an adequate example of this. Five-Year Plan, the full name of *Outline of the Five-Year Plan for National Economic and Social Development of the People's Republic of China*, publishing every five years since 1953, is the feedback survey on China's national conditions and regional development from Central Committee of the Communist Party of China, an important regulatory tool for China's macro socialist market economy and the grand blueprint and action program for the cause of socialism with Chinese characteristics [1]. The content of the Five-year Plan spans politics, economics, military, education and many other aspects.

At present, the research on the Five-year Plan is still in its infancy. The research methods are mostly focused on simple qualitative methods, and the research content is limited to the management and economic fields. It is lack of creative combination of macro-overarching and language processing. Based on the fields of computer science and artificial intelligence, Natural Language Processing (NLP) is one of the common operating techniques across disciplines and domains [2]. This paper analyzes and processes text content from different perspectives of documents, knowledge, paragraphs, sentences, and vocabulary with natural language technology. The paper selects the five Five-Year Plan outlines formulated by the new China since the 21st century and uses Python and SPSS to explore the texts. Furthermore, by constructing a corpus, China's development positioning and goals under the trend of globalization is further analyzed. The research questions of this paper are listed as follows.

(1) How are high-frequency words distributed within the text? Is this linked to particular social events?
(2) What are the specific key words within the text? How do they vary? What does it mean?
(3) How many topics can the five Five-Year Plan outlines be divided into? What areas of development are emphasized more? How are they related?
(4) How are the five Five-Year Plans classified? What are the characteristics of each of them? Are they linked to historical background or events?

2   Research Methodology

In order to deeply study the economic and social development since the founding of New China, this paper establishes five corpora of the Five-Year Plan for National Economic and Social Development of the People's Republic of China from 2000 to 2021 issued by the National People's Congress respectively. High-frequency words, keyword variation analysis, LDA topic model analysis and systematic clustering analysis were conducted respectively. As an important factor in language, vocabulary has become the fastest and most prominent aspect in the development process [3], so this paper uses it to deeply explore the internal structure and external connections.

High-frequency word change analysis is commonly used in NLP text analysis, using Jieba[1] to de-separate Chinese words and remove deactivated words to generate the

---

[1] https://github.com/fxsjy/jieba.

vocabulary of each text and rank them by frequency, and the top 10 are high-frequency words, which can reflect the irreproducibility of the text to some extent [4] and show the objects, attitudes, connotations and future plans that point to.

Keyword variation analysis is one of the most commonly used methods in natural language processing (NLP), referring to words whose frequency is significantly higher or significantly lower than the frequency of their counterparts in the reference corpus [5]. For the predicted direction of national development under study, unsupervised keyword extraction is used based on our self-built corpus. Ten keywords were extracted using the textrank algorithm in the Jieba toolkit to provide a reference for the study of future national economic development priorities.

LDA topic model analysis is commonly used in NLP analysis of various policy documents, and refers to the clustering of terms within a text according to different topics based on relevance and similarity, which are represented as bubbles in a horizontal and vertical coordinate plot. Also, the overall term frequencies in the corpus and the estimated term frequencies within the selected topics are displayed, i.e., the keywords within each topic are scored and ranked. After adjusting and comparing the relevance indicators, the most appropriate and accurate λ is selected to determine the specific content of each topic. Generally speaking, LDA topic model analysis is divided into three main types, namely topic intensity distribution, topic domain analysis and topic structure analysis [6]. In this paper, for practical purposes, two perspectives are considered: subject area analysis and subject architecture analysis.

Systematic cluster analysis is one of the hierarchical clustering methods commonly used for text classification. The distance of a given data object is calculated, and the layers are cycled for aggregation and categorization until each data object has a corresponding category. The data within each category has a greater similarity, while the data between different classes have less similarity [7]. In this paper, after normalizing and standardizing the number of real words, we use SPSS to calculate the similarity of corresponding nodes and obtain the clustering results through a longitudinal tree diagram. Unlike the LDA topic model analysis, where systematic clustering emphasizes the division of the five Five-Year Plans separately, the latter integrates the texts and focuses on the classification of topics.

3   Analysis Based on High Frequency Word Variations

3.1   Five-Year Plan

Five groups of 10 high-frequency words were generated for the five corpus, as shown in Table 1, and the 12 words "发展 (develop)" "建设 (construct)" "推进 (advance)" "完善 (perfect)" "体系 (system)" "加强 (strengthen)" "加快 (accelerate)" "制度 (system)" "服务 (service)" "提高 (improve)" "社会 (social)" and "经济 (economic)" were used throughout the text of the five-year outline plan for China's national economic and social development over the past 25 years. That is, in terms of content, the Five-Year Plan has not deviated from the original intent of the national economic plan, always making economic and social development the top priority of all work, and constantly maintaining a forward-looking, positive attitude toward development. Further, the word "发展 (develop)" has the highest number of occurrences, nearly 1.5 times more than the word "建设 (construct)". This is the eternal purpose of China since it entered the 21st century. It is a kind of recognition of "being beaten if you fall behind" and a summary of the blueprint for future development.

Excluding the same words in the top 10 of the corpus, the main words that are important for the development and construction of the national economy are "市场 (market)" "企业 (enterprise)" and "社会 (society)". It emphasizes the profound significance of adherence to China's socialist economic system, especially the existence of a socialist social economy. Secondly, the words "制度(system)" "体系 (system)" "改革 (reform)" and "创新 (innovation)" imply that CCCPC attaches great importance to the construction of economic development system, and only by continuously promoting economic transformation and upgrading and accelerating structural optimization can we maintain sustainable economic growth. At the same time, the words "资源 (resource)" and "服务 (service)" fully illustrate the unique position of the resource economy in the international trend of economic globalization, i.e., to a certain extent, the growth of the economy depends on the ability to occupy, dominate resources and services as well as the position of both. In addition, from the 10th Five-Year Plan "市场 (market)" and "社会 (society)", to the 11th Five-Year Plan "区域 (region)" "农村 (rural)" and "社会 (society)", to the 12th Five-Year Plan "社会 (society)", to the 14th Five-Year Plan "国家 (country)" and "健全 (sound)", it can be seen that China's Five-Year Plan has moved from the monolithic and modular economic development to regionalization, following the development vein of economic globalization and making great strides toward national and international integration, and emphasizing that the forces driving national economic growth are different in different stages of development.

Table 1. Five-Year Plan High-frequency Words.

Strategic Planning	The 10th Five-Year Plan	Amount	The 11th Five-Year Plan	Amount	The 12th Five-Year Plan	Amount	The 13th Five-Year Plan	Amount	The 14th Five-Year Plan	Amount
Word 1	Develop 发展	220	Develop 发展	256	Develop 发展	434	Develop 发展	500	Develop 发展	487
Word 2	Construct 建设	150	Construct 建设	156	Construct 建设	267	Construct 建设	258	Construct 建设	458
Word 3	Strengthen 加强	134	Develop 开发	82	Strengthen 加强	229	Advance 推进	266	Advance 推进	289
Word 4	Improve 提高	111	Strengthen 加强	75	Advance 推进	207	Strengthen 加强	256	Perfect 完善	285
Word 5	Economy 经济	104	Region 区域	72	Perfect 完善	202	Perfect 完善	245	System 体系	262
Word 6	Perfect 完善	76	Rural 农村	70	Accelerate 加快	169	Accelerate 加快	204	Strengthen 加强	252
Word 7	Enterprise 企业	72	Improve 提高	70	Improve 提高	151	Innovation 创新	194	Promote 推动	197
Word 8	Society 社会	70	Advance 推进	62	System 制度	133	System 制度	192	Country 国家	195
Word 9	Market 市场	62	Economy 经济	61	Service 服务	133	System 体系	177	Enhance 提升	178
Word 10	Reform 改革	60	Resource 资源	53	Society 社会	129	Service 服务	173	Sound 健全	178

3.2 The 14th Five-Year Plan

Based on the high-frequency word analysis of five corpora, this paper calculates the top 50 high-frequency words from the 14th Five-Year Plan text by Python, further analyzes the change trend of each word within the text, and generates the word cloud diagram shown in Fig. 1. In the face of unprecedented opportunities and challenges in the " international" environment and the huge impact of the new epidemic on the real sector, "创新 (innovation)" "科技 (technology)" "服务 (service)" "企业 (enterprise)" "资源 (resource)" "产业 (industry)" "文化 (culture)" and "城市 (city)" are the focus of the 14th Five-Year Plan, with a greater tendency to "optimize" the development of "security" in all "fields in a more "comprehensive" manner which means more emphasis on the influence of mixed internal and external factors in the process of governance.

Grounding on reality and giving overall consideration, the 14th Five-Year Plan was formed after a full investigation of the real environment. On the one hand, it clarifies the areas that need to be further strengthened and improved in the reform process to cope with China's changing reform and development environment, and allows governments at all levels to better reduce the uncertainties brought about by society by setting interval ranges while setting targets, which is conducive to responding to various risk challenges more actively and calmly and enhancing the flexibility and adaptability of development. On the other hand, unlike the previous quantitative GDP indicators. The 14th Five-Year Plan adopts the method of qualitative indicator description, and in terms of target setting, the pursuit of growth quality replaces the pursuit of quantity, emphasizing the unity of value and common priority of economic development, efficiency feedback,and ecological environment, which is not only more rational but also more conducive to guiding all parties to focus their efforts on improving the quality and efficiency of development, i.e., changing from the pursuit of high economic growth to high-quality development and enhancing the efficiency with high standards.

Fig. 1. The first 50 Words of the 14th Five-Year Plan Word Cloud.

To verify the historical background and specific reasons for the shift from high-speed to high-quality development in the 14th Five-Year Plan, this paper examines its relationship with a major global public health event (COVID-19). Using the official World Bank GDP data from 2019 to 2020 as the basis, the mean value test of the annual GDP per capita growth rate in China was done by SPSS, and the following

Table 2 and 3 were generated. Before the epidemic, the mean annual GDP per capita growth rate in China was 6.1915, and after the epidemic, it showed 1.9792, which shows that the post-epidemic data is significantly lower than the pre-epidemic data, i.e. the economic development after the epidemic sluggish, but whether the difference is statistically significant or not requires further results to be seen below.

Table 2. One of the Results of the Mean Test for the Annual Growth Rate of GDP per Capita in China: Case Processing Summary.

Case Processing Summary						
	Case					
	Included		Excluded		Total	
	N	Percentage	N	Percentage	N	Percentage
VAR00003*VAR00001	6	28.60%	15	71.40%	21	100.00%

Table 3. Results of the Mean Test for the Annual Growth rate of GDP per Capita in China II: Case Processing Report.

Report					
VAR00003					
VAR00001	Average	N	Standard Deviation (SD)	Minimum	Maxima
After COVID-19	1.9792	1		1.98	1.98
Before COVID-19	6.1915	5	0.35901	5.57	6.5
Total	5.4894	6	1.74939	1.98	6.5

As can be seen in Table 4, the significance level in the ANOVA table is 4.30545289E−4, which is less than 0.05, indicating that the difference between the change in the annual growth rate of GDP per capita of China and COVID-19 is statistically significant. As can be seen in Table 5, the Eta coefficient of 0.983 and the Eta square of 0.966 are both large, with values close to 1 indicating a high correlation, and further indicating that the change in the annual growth rate of GDP per capita in China is significantly correlated with COVID-19. Therefore, it is concluded that the growth rate of China's economy was directly or indirectly affected by COVID-19, an international social event, China's economic growth was affected by the event and the growth rate was reduced, and more prudent economic measures were taken to cope with the growing uncertainties, thus further stabilizing the national economy in the context of the normalization of epidemic prevention and control.

Table 4. ANOVA on the Difference between the Change in Annual Growth rate of per Capita GDP in China and COVID-19.

ANOVA Table (a)		Sum of Squares	df	Mean Square	F	Significance
VAR00003*VAR00001	Intergroup	14.786	1	14.786	114.724	4.3E-4
	Within the group	0.516	4	0.129		
	Total	15.302	5			

Table 5. Correlation Metrics between the Change in Annual Growth rate of per Capita GDP in China and COVID-19.

Correlation Metric	Eta	Eta Squared
VAR00003 * VAR00001	0.983	0.966

4 Analysis Based on Keyword Changes

After keyword extraction based on word graph model in Python, the top 10 keywords that best reflect the central content of the text in the Five-Year Plan corpus from 2000 to 2021 are generated to form a summary table. As shown in Table 6, it can be seen that the top 10 keywords of the Five-Year Plan as a whole still revolve around the national economic planning of China's economy, and are largely similar to the top 10 high-frequency words in terms of content, only with some words differing in ranking, which is closely related not only to the calculation formula of the Python in extracting high-frequency words and keywords, but also to the specific use of words pointing to the Five-Year Plan text.

In the Tenth Five-Year Plan, the words "经济 (economy)" "市场 (market)" and "改革 (reform)" imply that in the face of the severe international and domestic situation at the beginning of the 21st century, where opportunities and challenges coexist. CCCPC continues to insist on giving full play to the special advantages of a socialist market economy, effectively allocating the various resources needed for development, effectively improving the efficiency of business operations, and establishing a long-term and stable network of business relationships in the course of reform. At the same time, the words "社会 (society)" and "提高 (improve)" indicate the importance of coordinated development of social development and economic improvement, enriching the supply of diversified goods for enterprises, improving the production structure, promoting the growth rate of economic volume, and striving to meet the growing material and cultural needs of the general public.

In the 11th Five-Year Plan, the words "区域 (region)" "农村 (rural)" "经济 (economy)" show that between 2006 and 2010, the country has given more prominence to the key point of coordinated development of urban and rural areas. It contributed to the issuance and implementation of *the Outline of the National Land Use Master Plan (2006–2020)* to promote the joint progress of urban and rural areas in infrastructure development, education, economy, culture, and other fields. At the same time, another perspective of urban-rural coordination is the progress of the countryside, which strives to build its own characteristic industrial structure, realize its own blood supply cycle, stimulate endogenous power to promote sustainable development, and lay a solid foundation for the formal introduction of the "rural revitalization" strategy at the 19th Party Congress in 2017.

In the 12th Five-Year Plan, which covers the period from 2011 to 2015, is a critical period for building a moderately prosperous society, and a period for deepening reform and opening up and accelerating the transformation of the economic development mode. Therefore, in the process of field research, analysis and special discussion, CCCPC has put more emphasis on meeting the needs of the people for "students have access to education, employees to pay, patients to medical treatments, elders to good care and residents to housing". In Table 6, nouns such as "制度 (system)" and "社会 (society)" are linked with verbs such as "加快 (accelerate)" and "推进 (advance)", and a great deal of ink is devoted to describing how to consolidate the national economic system, promote social stability, increase the employment rate of the people, and further ensure the harmony and order of society at large.

In the 13th Five-Year Plan, the word "创新 (innovation)" is the overall keynote of the national economic and social development from 2016 to 2020. We vigorously implement the innovation-driven development strategy, find the jumping lever of science and technology innovation, cultivate innovative talents in the new era, and further build an interactive platform for organic integration, so that the power of science and technology can replace excessive energy consumption while maximizing the utilization of resources to achieve sustainable development. Meanwhile, on the basis of the 11th and the 12th Five-Year Plans, we will solidify the cornerstone of comprehensive development in urban and rural areas, and continuously implement the development concepts of innovation, coordination, green, openness and sharing to achieve a pattern of internalization in the heart and externalization in action.

In the 14th Five-Year Plan, words such as "治理 (governance)" and "完善 (perfect)" express the determination of CCCPC to face the unpredictable domestic and international situation under the new crown epidemic, to firmly develop the existing achievements and turn quantity into quality. We try to continue the momentum of steady development and seize the opportunity of the times to enhance manufacturing productivity and thus improve the spatial structure. For example, during the 14th Five-Year Plan period, we should emphasize a high-quality people-centered approach, with a particular focus on cultural construction. On the basis of building green, smart, innovative, cultural and compact cities, we should pay more attention to building healthy cities, consumer cities and resilient cities to build a overrall well-off society that benefits more people [8].

Table 6. Five-Year Plan Keywords.

Strategic Planning	The 10th Five-Year Plan	The 11th Five-Year Plan	The 12th Five-Year Plan	The 13th Five-Year Plan	The 14th Five-Year Plan
Keyword1	Develop 发展1.00	Develop 发展1.00	Develop 发展1.00	Develop 发展1.00	Develop 发展1.00
Keyword2	Construct 建设0.71	Construct 建设0.82	Construct 建设0.67	Construct 建设0.79	Construct 建设0.94
Keyword3	Strengthen 加强0.60	Develop 开发0.61	Strengthen加强0.56	Promote 推进0.70	Country 国家0.64
Keyword4	Improve 提高0.52	Strengthen 加强0.61	Promote 推进0.54	Strengthen 加强0.57	System 体系0.63
Keyword5	Economy 经济0.44	Improve 提高0.57	Perfect 完善0.52	Perfect 完善0.47	Advance 推进0.54
Keyword6	Perfect 完善0.40	Region 区域0.46	Accelerate 加快0.42	System 制度0.42	Economy 经济0.52
Keyword7	Enterprise 企业0.40	Rural 农村0.45	Improve 提高0.40	Accelerate 加快0.34	Governance 治理0.42
Keyword8	Society 社会0.37	Economy 经济0.41	System 制度0.33	Innovation 创新0.34	Society 社会0.40
Keyword9	Market 市场0.34	Advance 推进0.38	Service 服务0.32	Service 服务0.31	Strengthen 加强0.37
Keyword10	Reform 改革0.32	Resource 资源0.37	Society 社会0.31	Implement 实施0.30	Perfect 完善0.36

5   LDA Topic Analysis

5.1   Topic Area Analysis

The five Five-Year Plan texts are placed in a text, and the texts are quantified by Python's topic-based division formula to generate the LDA topic area distribution of the five total five-year plan texts. As shown in Fig. 2, which is the intra-topic distance diagram after multi-dimensional scaling, the bubbles in the diagram indicate the topics formed by clustering, the number of bubbles is the number of topics, the size of bubbles represents the number of times the topics are presented and the importance of the policy issuing department, and the interval between centers means the similarity degree among topics. As can be seen from Fig. 2, the total text of the five Five-Year Plans can be divided into three topics, and each of the three topics is distributed in different dimensions, with Topic 1 mainly spanning the upper left and lower left, Topic 2 rooted in the lower right, and Topic 3 concentrated in the upper right. The centers of the three thematic bubbles are far apart, which indicates a low level of proximity between the three topics and a concentration of content in three scattered areas.

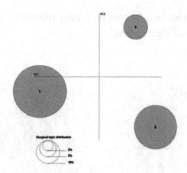

Fig. 2. Intersubject distance map (by multidimensional scaling).

The texts of the five Five-Year Plans were integrated, and the high-frequency words and corresponding word frequency numbers of the total texts were generated by using Jieba to de-separate Chinese words and remove deactivated words, then we make a word cloud map as shown in Fig. 3. Meanwhile, the top 10 high-frequency words of the total text and their corresponding word frequencies are derived as shown in Table 7. It can be found that, among the top 10 high-frequency words in the total text, the first 6 high-frequency words such as "发展 (develop)" "建设 (construct)" "加强 (strengthen)" and "提高 (improve)" are verbs of emphasis and do not have domain-oriented meanings, while the high-frequency words "制度(system)" "体系 (system)" and "经济(economy)" have a clearer directional meaning. It mainly refers to the top-level design aspect to ensure the system is reasonable and complete, and the procedure is correct, thus ensuring the solidity of the economy, and the specific field definition and interpretation still need to be confirmed through other high frequency words.

Table 7. High Frequency Words in the Total Text.

Keyword	Word Frequency	Keyword	Word Frequency
Develop发展	1897	Accelerate加快	644
Construct建设	1388	System体系	620
Strengthen加强	946	Improve提高	599
Advance推进	883	System制度	554
Perfect完善	848	Economy经济	546

Combined with Table 7 and Fig. 3, the top 50 high-frequency words are mainly "产业(industry)" "企业(enterprise)" "贸易(trade)" "合作(cooperation)" "粮食(food)" "保障(guarantee)", etc. This can be inferred that since the 21st century, CCCPC has paid more attention to industrial structure, trade cooperation, resource security, etc., but fewer words are mentioned in the fields of science and technology, environment, stock market, engineering and construction safety, scientific research, etc. This may be due to the different focus of development in different five-year planning stages, but it is impossible to avoid reflecting the lack of macro-level.

Fig. 3. Word Cloud of the General Text of the Five-Year Plan.

5.2 Topic Area Analysis

After analyzing the LDA topic model of the total text by Python and comprehensive testing of the relevance index, we chose $\lambda = 0.1$ to analyze the top 30 most relevant words of the three topics, indicating the fusion of the two attributes, that is, the frequency of words and the uniqueness of words, as shown in Fig. 4 below, and what we got is the top 30 most relevant words of topic one. The specific contents was obtained by in-depth categorization of the most relevant words for the three topics.

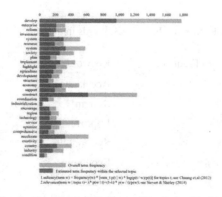

Fig. 4. Top 30 Most Relevant Words for Topic 1.

After removing meaningless words, importance assessment and screening, and manual judgment on the first 30 most relevant words of the three topics, the three topics are finally defined as optimizing industrial structure, promoting trade cooperation, and securing resource expansion. In other words, China's national economic and social development since entering the 21st century has covered the above three areas from the beginning to the end, which are the core and focus of development, and strengthened support for other industry areas on these three core surfaces, and this part of the support will change with the changing times and the trend of national conditions.

From the top 30% of high-frequency words, topic 1 "Optimizing Industrial Structure" is 51.9%, more than half, occupying the absolute core position, indicating that over the past 25 years, the Chinese government has attached great importance to the development and progress of this field. Topic 2 "Promoting Trade Cooperation" is 36.6%, 15.3% different from the former, ranking second., belongs to the direction that CCCPC and the State Council care more about and vigorously promote. Topic 3, "Securing Resource Expansion", is 11.4%, lower than the former 25.2%, with the least attention. The focus is narrower and more marginal in the long term, but still part of the overall development, with a constant investment of resources.

Optimizing Industrial Structure. The top 30 most relevant terms in Topic 1 include "企业 (enterprise)" "改革 (reform)" "投资 (investment)" "开发(develop)" "结构(structure)" "经济 (economy)" "协调 (coordination)" "产业化(industrialization)" "区域(region)" "产业 (industry)" "条件 (condition)" and each with rich connotation. As we enter the 21st century, it is difficult to adapt to the requirements of the new era and meet the growing needs of the people for a better life, and to gain advantages in the competitive international market environment. Therefore, the main goal orientation of long-term optimization of industrial structure is to promote high-quality development, which is a typical symbol and expression of endogenous sustainable development capacity. Of course, the field of optimizing industrial structure encompasses many aspects, such as continuously promoting the independent innovation of enterprises to force green transformation and development, steadily expanding effective investment in the market and developing comprehensive long-term projects, comprehensively coordinating the proportion of the three major industries to stimulate economic growth effects; strengthening the synergy of industrialization and regionalization to provide value shaping conditions.

Promoting Trade Cooperation. The first 30 most relevant words in Topic 2 include "推进 (promote)" "能源 (energy)" "合作 (cooperation)" "提升 (enhance)" "project (工程)" "格局 (pattern)" "工作 (work)" "强化 (strengthen)" "线 (line)" "基础 (foundation)" "行业 (industry)" and "创新 (innovation)", which have profound meanings. The promotion of trade cooperation consists of two main aspects. On the one hand, it strengthens domestic cross-regional exchange and cooperation, with the government as the main body, based on improving economic policies, enhancing information disclosure, expanding informed coverage of enterprises, and increasing employment rates. At the same time, the differences in resources and development advantages between regions are used to trade on commodities, narrowing the differences in economic income between regions and achieving efficiency and equity. On the other hand, to further promote international trade cooperation, General Secretary Xi stressed that "COVID-19 has dealt a full blow to global production and demand, and every country should join hands to increase macro policy hedging efforts to prevent the world economy from falling into recession" and urged "G20 member countries to cut tariffs, eliminate barriers and promote trade".

Securing Resource Expansion. The first 30 most relevant words in Topic 3 include "生态 (ecology)" "财政 (finance)" "粮食 (food)" "保障 (guarantee)" "拓展 (expansion)"

"水资源 (water resources)" "高标准 (high standard)" "养老 (pension)" "城市 (city)" "工程(project)" "补齐 (complement)". In the process of economic growth and social development, resources have always been the top priority. Especially in the context of urban-rural integration, finance is the root of the economic market to leverage capital. "水资源 (water resources)" is the prerequisite for the good life of the people, "粮食 (food)" is the basic life of the proletariat, "城市 (city)" "工程(project)" is the key to the rational use of geographical resources, "高标准 (high standard)" "养老 (pension)" is the essence of the re-use of the elderly force resources. At the same time, under the regular management of the new crown epidemic, there is still a huge gap to be filled for living materials, medical supplies, and distribution personnel, which also tests China's resource allocation capacity to a certain extent. Therefore, through 25 years of policy emphasis, the government has sought to set a direction to continuously strengthen the integration of resources, including land, labor, capital, technology, data, etc., and promote the use of digitalization and technology, as well as timely government information disclosure and stabilization of the people, so as to build a new development pattern of a large national unified market and a national chessboard.

6   Systematic Clustering Analysis

The number of times all the real words in the Five-Year Plan – noun (n), verb (v), adjective (a), pronoun (r), number (m), measure (q), orientation (f), place (s), time (t), and distinguishing word (b) - are used in the five corpora and normalized [9].

As can be seen in Fig. 5, the number of nouns occupies the first place in all five corpora, the number of verbs ranks second, followed by adjectives with the number of times occupying a relatively large number, showing a fluctuating upward trend with the growth of time, and the total number of their words also climbs, while the number of all other lexical properties is smaller, which is mainly influenced by the text focus and utterance usage.

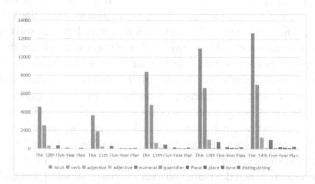

Fig. 5. Five-Year Plan all Real Words Statistics Bar Chart.

By using SPSS, the results of the data normalized in Fig. 5 were analyzed by hierarchical clustering, selecting "systematic clustering" and "intergroup association", which is an appropriate way to judge the distance of the data objects, which can reduce the influence of errors caused by extreme high and low data values on the discrimination of classification distance[10], and Table 8 was obtained, which is rich in content. The "order" represents the first aggregation and categorization, the "cluster combination" means the aggregation of two data objects "cluster 1" and "cluster 2", the "factor" means the distance of the data objects, the "first order cluster" symbolizes the proximity of two aggregation types "cluster 1" and "cluster 2", and the "next order" symbolizes the level at which this step of aggregation and categorization is used again. For example, in the first step, No. 1 (The 15th Five-Year Plan) and No. 3 (The 12th Five-Year Plan) are clustered into one category, and the individual distance is almost 0. The aggregation and categorization of this subcategory will be applied in the clustering of the 2nd step, and all other clusters can be inferred from this, as shown in Fig. 6, showing the distance and joint relationship between each subcategory.

Table 8. Cohesive State Table for Hierarchical Cluster Analysis.

Order	Cluster Combination		Coefficient	First appearance of order clusters		Next Order
	Cluster 1	Cluster 2		Cluster 1	Cluster 2	
1	1	3	0	0	0	3
2	2	5	0.001	0	0	4
3	1	4	0.001	1	0	4
4	1	2	0.001	3	2	0

Based on the international pattern and domestic development process, the five corpora are classified into multiple types according to the clustering in Table 8 to determine their development characteristics, point out the development direction and focus, and better promote China's overall quality development. From Fig. 6, there are three planning classifications. With the guideline that the clustering volume is moderate and clearly shows the planning focus area, we divided the cross-section of the number of clusters into two categories[11]. The 10th Five-Year Plan, the 12th Five-Year Plan and the 13th Five-Year Plan are individually called "Solid Advancement Type". The 11th Five-Year Plan and the 14th Five-Year Plan are closer in the same dimension and are regarded as "Quality Expansion Type".

Solid Advancement Type. The plan was developed at a time of significant domestic and international events that affected domestic economic growth. During the planning period, the Key Economic Development Areas (KEDAs) concentrated their resources on "more" development, trying to make the pilot more, farther and wider, to reach a level where external funding is no longer needed to sustain development and raise the economic level. It is less balanced and only a part of the regional economy develops first. With the tilting of funds, the gap between regions, industries and fields may become bigger and bigger, which is manifested in several aspects, including the economic growth rate, the number of infrastructure inputs, and the ratio of capital input to output. It is less sustainable, and rapid economic development may come at the cost of massive resource consumption and pollution, even exchanging the environment for development and touching the ecological red line, which requires technological transformation at a later stage. It is more equitable and these plans are equivalent to supporting the first rich in some regions, which lacks equity in a short time and ignore the advantages and importance of other regions, projects, industries, etc., but in the long run, it is a balance of opportunities and crises.

The 10th Five-Year Plan was based on multiple historical events, such as in 1978, China began to implement a policy of internal reform and external opening. In 1997, the Asian financial crisis raised the risk of financial security in the market. In 1999, 13 countries in NATO, led by the U.S., launched air strikes against the FRY, igniting the Kosovo War and bombing the Chinese Embassy in the center of Belgrade. In 2001, China joined the World Trade Organization, further integrating China into the general environment of economic globalization.

The 12th Five-Year Plan gradually adjusted the domestic and international development approach. In 2010, the strongest earthquake in history occurred in Yushu, Qinghai, a mudslide disaster occurred in Zhouqu, Gansu, China successfully held the Shanghai World Expo, a cross-strait economic cooperation framework agreement was signed, and the China-ASEAN FTA (Free Trade Agreement) came into force. CCCPC has proposed the basic orientation of macroeconomic policy of "active and stable, prudent and flexible".

The 13th Five-Year Plan faced a more complex international environment. In 2016, Republican Donald Trump was elected as the 45th president of the United States, a civil war broke out in Syria, the United Kingdom decided to leave the European Union in a referendum on "Brexit", the 11th summit of the leaders of the Group of 20 (G20) was held in Hangzhou, China, and China decided to build seven new pilot free trade zones in Zhejiang Province and Liaoning Province on the basis of the success of the free trade zones in Shanghai, Guangdong, Tianjin and Fujian.

Quality Expansion Type. This type prefers to promote successful pilot projects to the whole country, but due to the diversity of regions and changes in the epidemic, the pilot projects have different feedback and less stability, which is a breakthrough and self-challenge in a stable international situation, but higher stability is also one of the goals during the planning period. It is more balanced, with the first rich driving the latter rich, narrowing the gap between the rich and the poor in various fields and regions with coordinated urban and rural development and rural revitalization strategies, and gaining higher national satisfaction. It is more sustainable, focusing on promoting high quality across the board, injecting scientific and technological innovation into various fields, bringing clean and efficient new power, and improving the capacity structure. It is fairer, promoting social equity with common prosperity, and strives to meet the contradiction between people's growing need for a better life and unbalanced and insufficient development.

The 11th Five-Year Plan faces a more stable international background, the 10th Five-Year Plan has laid a good foundation, and China's national economic growth has entered a new round of stability. China's exports are facing "new trade barriers" and do not meet multiple international standards and certifications, such as green standards, commodity standards, etc., and need to further improve quality. China's internal ecological environment is poor, with high levels of pollution and increasing pressure on resources, including major water pollution incidents in the Songhua River, the dead fish incident in Baiyangdian in Hebei, water pollution in Taihu Lake, and cyanobacteria outbreaks in Chaohu and Dianchi.

The 14th Five-Year Plan emphasizes the transition from high-speed growth to high-quality development, alleviating the huge conflict in the national economy caused by COVID-19, and helping China to cross the middle-income trap and avoid going astray. In 2021, General Secretary Xi solemnly declared at the congress celebrating the 100th anniversary of the founding of the Communist Party of China that "through the sustained struggle of the entire Party and the people of all ethnic groups, we have achieved the first hundred-year goal, built a moderately prosperous society on the Chinese land, historically solved the problem of absolute poverty, and are marching with vigor toward the second hundred-year goal of fully building a socialist modern power". Therefore, the 14th Five-Year Plan period aims to start a new journey of building a modern socialist country, marching towards the second-century goal and striving to achieve the great rejuvenation of the Chinese nation.

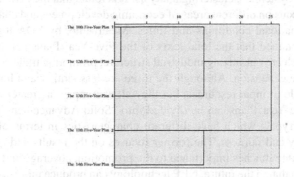

Fig. 6. Hierarchical Clustering Analysis Tree Diagram.

As shown in Fig. 6, the five Five-year plans since the 21st century can be categorized into two types, "Solid Advancement Type" and "Quality Expansion Type", which show different characteristics in four major dimensions: stability, balance, sustainability and fairness, and a visualization of the characteristics of the Five-Year Plans is shown in Fig. 7. Based on the types of the Five-Year Plans, CCCPC at all levels can clearly see the more focused levels and perspectives of planning according to the types of Five-Year Plans they are in, and make planning texts for the current period and the next round by combining the types of planning texts with advantageous levels, and after integrating special social events, international situations and other realities, make targeted development strategies to further promote the process of high speed and quality growth of the national economy.

Fig. 7. Planning Category Feature Visualization.

7 Conclusion

China's Five-Year Plans are the requirements and directions for national economic and social development in the next five years. In this paper, the five Five-Year Plans since the 21st century were processed by different NLP methods, including high-frequency words, keyword changes and systematic clustering analysis. It is found that the Five-Year Plans of different periods focus on different areas of economic development and changes with the development of national conditions and times. Meanwhile, by LDA topic model analysis, it can be obtained that the total texts of the Five-Year Plans can be divided into three topics, which are optimizing industrial structure, promoting trade cooperation and securing resource expansion. Although the three are less similar and have greater differences in the scale of input resources, but they all encompass a greater number of aspects. The five Five-Year Plans can be divided into "Solid Advancement Type" and "Quality Expansion Type", which have different characteristics in terms of stability, balance, sustainability and fairness. The former focuses on the results and quantity of the pilot, while the latter attaches importance to the promotion, coverage and quality of the pilot. It is believed that in the future, NLP technology can produce more constructive research conclusions and suggestions in national policy research.

Acknowledgements. This work was supported by Science Foundation of Beijing Language and Culture University (supported by "the Fundamental Research Funds for the Central Universities") (21YJ040005)).

References

1. Hu, A., Liu, M., Zhao, H.: An important way of governing in China: five-year planning practice (1953–2020). J. Beijing Univ. Technol. (Soc. Sci. Edn.) **22**(03), 1–22 (2022). (in Chinese)
2. Li, D., Li, L., Li. D.: The public opinion effect and revelation of the introduction of the three-child policy–Analysis of network big data based on NLP. China Youth Stud. **308**(10), 46–53 (2021). (in Chinese)

3. Wang, S., Wang, X.: The attention to safety issues from mainland China and Taiwan. In: Hong, J.-F., Su, Q., Wu, J.-S. (eds.) CLSW 2018. LNCS (LNAI), vol. 11173, pp. 801–818. Springer, Cham (2018). https://doi.org/10.1007/978-3-030-04015-4_69

4. Zhang, J., Zhu, Y.: A comparison of translators' styles of Hosseini's novels - a parallel corpus perspective. Foreign Lang. (J. Shanghai Foreign Lang. Univ.) **44**(05), 102–114 (2021). (in Chinese)

5. Li, B.W.: An analysis of the difference between Chinese and American attitudes toward China's military culture construction–a comparative analysis based on the corpus of China's Military Power Report and China's Defense White Paper J. Henan Normal Univ. (Philos. Soc. Sci. Edn.) **41**(02), 26–30 (2014). (in Chinese)

6. Li, L., Li, Z.: Clustering analysis of FTA governance policy texts based on LDA topic model–Liaoning FTA as an example. J. Jishou Univ. (Soc. Sci. Edn.) **42**(02), 23–34 (2021). (in Chinese)

7. Yang, Y.J., Feng, X., Wang, Y.L., Qh, K.: An improved H-K clustering algorithm for news text topic extraction. J. Nanjing Univ. Posts Telecommun. (Nat. Sci. Edn.) **40**(01), 82–88 (2020). (in Chinese)

8. Yang, K.: The paths to improve china's urbanization strategy. Chin. J. Urban Env. Stud. **09**(01), 2175001 (2021)

9. Xiao, T., Liu, Y.: Analysis of the words and N meta-grammar of Dream of the Red Chamber. Mod. Libr. Inform. Technol. **257**(04), 50–57 (2015). (in Chinese)

10. Zhang, T., Luan, C., Over, S.: Co-term clustering analysis of research on public cultural service provision in China. Intell. Sci. **33**(04), 104–109 (2015). (in Chinese)

11. Wu, J.: The disciplinary layout of top global young universities and their strategic choices–and the institutional space for building world-class disciplines in post-haircut countries. Chin. High. Educ. Res. **285**(05), 68–75 (2017). (in Chinese)

Corpus Construction for Generating Knowledge Graph of Sichuan Cuisine

Xia Yang[✉], Siyuan Jing, Xingyuan Chen, and Peng Jin

Laboratory of Intelligent Information Processing and Application, Leshan Normal University, Leshan, China
Xia_yang113@163.com, siyuan-jing@lsnu.edu.cn, jandp@pku.edu.cn

Abstract. Sichuan cuisine and its culture play an important role in Chinese food culture. Unfortunately, people can only learn Sichuan cuisine through traditional ways such as the Web and books. To address the problem, we developed the annotation system of Sichuan cuisine and designed the annotation schemes of named entities and entity relations under the guidance of Sichuan cuisine masters. There are 220,000 words in the corpus that was annotated and proofread manually by an annotation system. We constructed a corpus of named entities and entity relations of Sichuan cuisine. It contains 691 kinds of Sichuan cuisine recipes, including 8,683 entities and 8,700 entity relations. The consistency of multiple-around annotation is 0.94 and 0.93, respectively. Based on the corpus, a knowledge graph of Sichuan cuisine was constructed and will be used to develop the tourism QA system in the future.

Keywords: Sichuan Cuisine · Corpus · Knowledge Graph · Named Entity · Entity Relation

1 Introduction

Knowledge Graph [1] was formally proposed by Google in 2012 [2], which aims to describe various entities and their relationships in the real world. According to the coverage and different fields of knowledge, the knowledge graph can be divided into the general knowledge graph and the domain knowledge graph. The general knowledge graph is not limited to specific domains. It is often based on encyclopedia knowledge and is large-scale, including DBpedia [3], KnowItAll [4], NELL [5], YAGO [6], and Google Knowledge Vault [7]. The creation of the domain knowledge graph is domain-oriented and based on industry data. It has performed well in solving problems in various fields, and it has been deeply studied and explored in the medical (Chinese Medical Knowledge Map CMeKG [8]), social(Kinship [9]), bioscience (Bio2RDF [10]), and other domains [11]. However, we did not find a knowledge graph of cuisine. Although Meituan did make the food knowledge graph for takeout, it was only for dishes and shops.

Food influences human history and has become an indispensable part of tourism. Food tourism is also becoming a new form of tourism. As one of the eight major cuisines in China, Sichuan cuisine with strong local characteristics occupies an important place

Q. Su et al. (Eds.): CLSW 2022, LNAI 13496, pp. 34–42, 2023.
https://doi.org/10.1007/978-3-031-28956-9_3

in the history of Chinese cuisine and forms a unique Sichuan cuisine culture. However, there is no relevant research on the knowledge graph of Sichuan cuisine at present. Without exception, the intelligentization of the food field also needs a knowledge graph to realize. The gastronomic knowledge graph can provide diners with more accurate, richer, and more personalized services. Constructing the knowledge graph corpus of Sichuan dishes is also one of the key technologies of the tourism QA system. It is also a work of great significance for artificial intelligence to help regional development. Therefore, it is necessary to construct a professional Sichuan cuisine knowledge graph corpus.

The rest of this paper is organized as follows. Section 2 describes the data source and pretreatment. Section 3 introduces the standardization of the corpus annotation system. In Sect. 4, we propose a method of corpus construction. Section 5 shows the annotation consistency results. Section 6 is the conclusion of this paper.

2 Data Source and Preprocessing

Although there are many books and online data on Sichuan cuisine, it is easier for the public to accept classic books written by authoritative experts because of their professionalism and preciseness. Therefore, this paper takes Sichuan Cuisine Cooking Dictionary (Revised Version) as the primitive corpus to create a Sichuan cuisine corpus. Through an in-depth analysis of the literature and considering the suggestions of Sichuan cuisine masters, we divided entities into 13 categories. We choose Chapter IV technical terms and Chapter VII famous dishes as the original data. So far, we have completed the annotation work of 220,000 words, including 691 dishes, 8,683 named entities, and 8700 entity relations. The construction of the Sichuan cuisine knowledge graph requires reliable data support, which comes from a discussion on corpus labeling standards and the construction of Sichuan cuisine named entities and relations annotation corpus. In the original corpus, the "cuisine" and "main ingredient categories" do not appear in the introduction of each dish, so the annotation effect is not ideal. Therefore, we pre-add "cuisine" and "main ingredient categories" to each dish.

3 Standardization of Corpus Annotation System

There are some methods for named entity recognition and relationship extraction: such as traditional rules and templates [12], statistical machine learning [13], and deep learning [14], etc. Because of the authority of the primitive corpus, we adopt a method based on traditional rules to extract named entities and relationships. Sichuan cuisine corpus is a labeling system with dishes as the center, containing 13 entities and 23 relationships. The named entities are shown in Table 1.

According to the characteristics of Sichuan cuisine, we have formulated the following rules about named entities.

1. No overlap. The same string cannot be marked as two different entities.
2. No nesting. One entity cannot contain another entity.

Table 1. Entities of Sichuan cuisine.

No	Entity(abbreviation)	Chinese Label	Example
1	Dish (Ds)	菜	"Mapo Tofu"
2	Cuisine (Cs)	菜系	"Sichuan cuisine"
3	Main ingredient Category (MiC)	主料类别	"Poultry eggs"
4	Dish Category (DC)	菜品类别	"Hot Dishes", "Cold dishes"
5	Dish Subcategory (DSc)	菜品子类别	"Soup dish" belong to "Hot Dishes"
6	Ingredient (Id)	食材	"Beef", "Sichuan Pepper"
7	Main ingredient (Mi)	主料	"Chicken" in "saute diced chicken with hot peppers"
8	Auxiliary ingredient (Ai)	辅料	"Scallion"
9	Seasoning (Sn)	调料	"Sugar" in "Sweet skin duck"
10	Dipping (Dp)	蘸料	"Sesame paste disc"
11	Flavor type (Ft)	味型	The flavor type of "twice-cooked pork" is "Homely flavor"
12	Cooking (Ck)	烹饪方式	The cooking method of "Spicy Chicken" is "fry"
13	Cooking subclass (CkS)	烹饪子类	The cooking method of "Fish Flavored pork" is "Stir-frying", and "Stir-frying" is the subclass of "fry"

3. Entity does not contain punctuation as much as possible, but there are exceptions, such as "口袋豆腐(之二)".
4. Entity strings extract long words instead of short ones, such as "白皮肥子公鸡", should be marked as "白皮肥子公鸡", rather than "公鸡" or "子公鸡".
5. If the same ingredients appear more than once in the same dish, we only annotate the entity appearing for the first time. However, if an ingredient appears in different cooking steps, it should be annotated separately.
6. If a dish does not strictly distinguish the main ingredients, auxiliary ingredients, and seasonings, we annotate them as ingredients without manual distinction. For example, "芹菜肉末 芹菜择去叶洗净, 切成粗粒, 入筲箕撒盐渍入味, 挤尽水分。牛肉剁成细末……". In this sentence, celery and beef do not specify whether they are main ingredients or auxiliary ingredients, so we all mark them as ingredients.

Annotation principle of entity relation: entity relation can be labeled when two entities come from the same dish. Table 2 shows the rules of the entity relation.

Table 2. Entity relation of Sichuan cuisine.

No	Triples	Label	Chinese Label	Note
1	< Ds R Cs >	Is a case of	菜系	<鱼香肉丝 菜系 川菜>
2	<Ds R MiC>	Is a case of	主料类别	<百花江团 主料类别 鱼鲜>
3	<Ds R DC>	Is a case of	菜品类别	<百花江团 菜品类别 热菜>
4	<Ds R DSc>	Is a case of	菜品类别	<百花江团 菜品类别 半汤菜>
5	<DC R DSc>	Is a kind of	子类	<热菜 子类 半汤菜>
6	<Ds R Id>	Has ingredients	包含食材	<夫妻肺片 包含食材 芹菜>
7	<Ds R Mi>	Has key ingredient	包含主料	<夫妻肺片 包含主料 猪瘦肉>
8	<Ds R Ai>	Has Auxiliary material	包含辅料	<夫妻肺片 包含辅料 芹菜>
9	<Ds R Sn>	Has seasoning	包含调料	<夫妻肺片 包含配料 红油>
10	<Id R Id>	Has ingredient	食材组成	<高汤 食材组成 老母鸡>
11	<Ds R Ft>	Has flavor type	味型	<白油肝片 味型 咸鲜味>
12	<Ds R Ck>	Be cooking	烹饪方式	<五香仔鸭 烹饪方式 卤>
13	<Ds R CkS>	Be cooking	烹饪子方式	<鱼香肉丝 烹饪子方式 滑炒>
14	<Ck R CkS>	Has cooking	子类	<炒 子类 滑炒>
15	<Sn R Ft>	Has flavor type	调料味型	<郫县豆瓣 配料味型 家常味>
16	<Ds R Ds>	Goes with	搭配菜	<樟茶鸭子 搭配菜 荷叶饼>
17	<Ds R Dp>	Has dipping	蘸料	<清蒸江团 蘸料 毛姜醋碟>
18	<Dp R Ft>	Has flavor type	蘸碟味型	<味碟 蘸料味型 椒麻>
19	<Dp R Id>	Has ingredient	蘸料食材	<味碟 蘸料食材 味精>
20	<CkS R CkS>	Has another name	烹饪别称	<酒腌 烹饪别称 酒醉>
21	<Ck R Ck>	Has another name	子类别称	<糖粘 子类别称 挂霜>
22	<Ds R Ds>	Has another name	菜名别称	<盐煎肉 菜名别称 生爆盐煎肉>
23	<Id R Id>	Has another name	食材别称	<吊汤 食材别称 坠汤>

4   Corpus Construction Method

The core work of corpus construction is to annotate the corpus according to the annotation specification. Based on the named entity and entity relation annotation specification formulated in Sect. 2, this paper adopts the model of group annotation and domain experts. Four experts in the field of Sichuan cuisine and artificial intelligence and two undergraduates participated in the corpus annotation of 691 Sichuan dishes. To improve the annotation efficiency, we used the entity and entity relation annotation tool developed by the natural language processing laboratory of Zhengzhou University, as shown in Fig. 1.

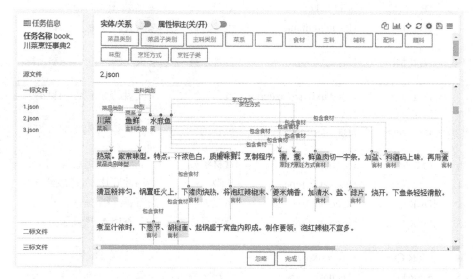

Fig. 1. Entity & relationship annotation tool

It requires professional knowledge to formulate the specification of named entities and entity relations for annotations of Sichuan cuisine. We analyzed the characteristics of the primitive corpus, referred to many Sichuan cuisine books and online data, discussed with Sichuan cuisine masters, and formulated a preliminary specification. Finally, we adopt the multi-round iteration mode to update the annotation specification and annotation work. Figure 2 shows the process.

In the first stage, named entities and entity relationships are determined. Under the guidance of the Sichuan cuisine master, we analyzed the corpus and the characteristics of Sichuan cuisine in detail and formulated the specification V1.0. The annotation tool is the annotation system developed by Zhengzhou University. We pre-annotated to verify the feasibility of the specification.

The second stage is formal annotation. For the accuracy and consistency of manual annotation, each text is annotated independently by two annotators. First, when annotator A completes the annotation, annotator B reannotates the same corpus. Second, we record the inconsistency or uncertainty between the two rounds, and discuss and find out the

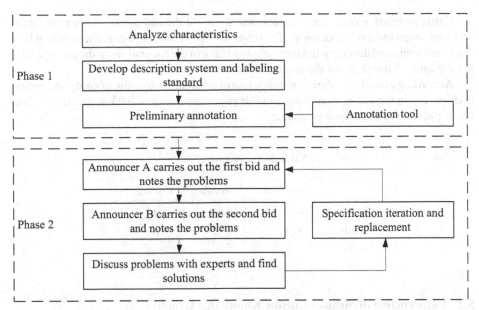

Fig. 2. Annotation process.

solution. Finally, annotator A revises it again to get the final annotation result. In the process, we constantly revise the annotation specification to make it closer to the corpus. So far, there are more than ten editions of the annotation specification.

5 Annotation Results

5.1 Evaluation Method and Results

Inter-annotator agreement (IAA) is the degree of agreement between two independent annotators on the annotating results [15]. In this paper, annotation result B is regarded as a gold-standard annotation, and we calculate the precision (P), recall (R), and f1-score (F) of annotation result A.

$$P = \frac{Number\ of\ A\ and\ B\ consistent}{Total\ of\ A} \tag{1}$$

$$R = \frac{Number\ of\ A\ and\ B\ consistent}{Total\ of\ B} \tag{2}$$

$$F = \frac{2 \times P \times R}{P + R} \tag{3}$$

Entity annotation consistency is recognized only if the entity text, entity type label, and start-stop position are identical. The relationship annotation is consistent only when the relationship and the entity and the start-stop place of the two entities in the relationship are the same. Table 3 shows the results.

According to statistics, the consistency rate of artificial annotation of entity and entity relationship in the corpus constructed in this paper are 0.94 and 0.93, respectively. The result proves that the corpus is reliable.

Table 3. Results for IAA

	Precision	Recall	F-score
Entity	94.7	93.6	94.1
Relation	94.1	92.8	93.4

5.2 Construction of Sichuan Cuisine Knowledge Graph

The corpus contains 691 kinds of dishes, 8,683 kinds of entities, and 8,700 relations. Triples are stored in JSON files. The statistics of entity quantity and entity relation quantity in the annotation results are shown in Table 4.

Table 4. Statistics of entity and entity relationship

Entity	Quantity	Entity Relation	Quantity
Ingredient	4,775	Dish – Ingredient	5011
Dish	691	Dish – Cooking	852
Cooking method	661	Dish – Dish_Category	650
Main ingredient category	581	Dish – Cuisine	645
Cuisine	578	Dish – Main_ingredient_Category	634
Dish Category	514	Dish – Flavor type	476
The others	883	The others	432
Total	8,683	Total	8,700

Visualization of Sichuan cuisine knowledge graph used by ECharts and Fig. 3 is effect diagram.

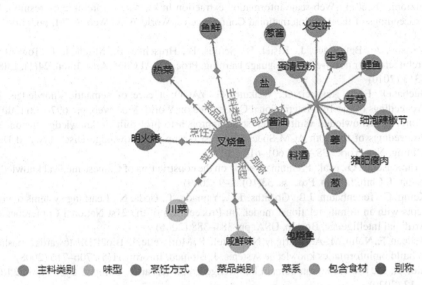

Fig. 3. Example of knowledge graph

6   Conclusions and Future Works

This paper introduces a corpus for a knowledge graph of Sichuan cuisine and explains the annotating process. We have completed a corpus of 200000 words, including 691 kinds of dishes, 8683 kinds of named entities, and 8700 entity relations. Based on this corpus, the knowledge graph of Sichuan cuisine is constructed and will be used to develop a tourism Knowledge Q & A system in the future. Next, we will enrich and improve the corpus, add online shop information and other authoritative books to expand it, and provide users with fuller food information.

Acknowledgments. This work is supported partly by Science And Technology Bureau Of LeShan Town (No. 21GZD008).

References

1. Zhao, J., Liu, K., He, S., et al.: Knowledge Graph, pp. 7–10. Higher Education Press, Beijing (2018)
2. Amit, S.: Introducing the Knowledge Graph: Things, Not Strings. Official Blog of Google, America (2012)

3. Auer, S., Bizer, C., Kobilarov, G., Lehmann, J., Cyganiak, R., Ives, Z.: DBpedia: a nucleus for a web of open data. In: Aberer, K., et al. (eds.) ASWC/ISWC -2007. LNCS, vol. 4825, pp. 722–735. Springer, Heidelberg (2007). https://doi.org/10.1007/978-3-540-76298-0_52

4. Etzioni, O., et al.: Web-scale information extraction in knowitall: (preliminary results). In: Proceedings of the 13th International Conference on World Wide Web. ACM, pp. 100–110 (2004)

5. Carlson, A., Betteridge, J., Kisiel, B., Settles, B., Hruschka, E., Mitchell, T.: Toward an architecture for never-ending language learning. Proc. AAAI Conf. Artif. Intell. **24**(1), 1306–1313 (2010)

6. Suchanek, F.M., Kasneci, G., Weikum, G. YAGO: a core of semantic knowledge. In: Proceedings of the 16th International Conference on World Wide Web, pp. 697–706 (2007)

7. Dong, X.: Knowledge vault: a web-scale approach to probabilistic knowledge fusion. In: Proceedings of the 20th ACM Special Interest Group on Knowledge Discovery and Data Mining. New York, USA, pp. 601–610 (2014)

8. Byambasuren, O., et al.: Preliminary study on the construction of Chinese medical knowledge graph. J. Chin. Inform. Process. **33**(10), 1–9 (2019)

9. Kemp, C., Tenenbaum, J.B., Griffiths, T.L., Yamada, T., Ueda, N.: Learning systems of concepts with an infinite relational model. In: Proceedings of the 21st National Conference on Artificial Intelligence. Boston, USA, pp. 381–388 (2006)

10. Belleau, F., Nolin, M.-A., Tourigny, N., Rigault, P., Morissette, J.: Bio2RDF: towards a mashup to build bioinformatics knowledge systems. J. Biomed. Inform. **41**(5), 706–716 (2008)

11. Liu, Y., Li, H.: Survey on domain knowledge graph research. Comput. Syst. Appl. **29**(6), 1–12 (2020)

12. Humphreys, K., et al.: University of sheffield: description of the LaSIE-II system as used for MUC-7. Association for Computational Linguistics (1998)

13. Guodong, Z., Jie, Z., Jian, S., Dan, S., Chew, L.T.: Recognizing names in biomedical texts: a machine learning approach. Bioinformatics **20**(7), 1178–1190 (2004)

14. Ronan, C., Jason, W., Leon, B., Michael, K., Koray, K., Pavel, K.: Natural Language Processing (Almost) from Scratch. J. Mach. Learn. Res. **12**(Aug), 2493–2537 (2011)

15. Hripcsak, G., Rothschild, A.S.: Agreement, the f-measure, and reliability in information retrieval. J. Am. Med. Inform. Assoc. **12**(3), 296–298 (2005)

Building a Semantically Annotated Corpus of Chinese Directional Complements

Byeongkwu Kang[1] and Sukyong Yu[2(✉)]

[1] Sogang University, 35 Baekbeom-Ro, Mapo-Gu, Seoul 04107, Korea
kbg43@sogang.ac.kr
[2] Yeungnam University, 280 Daehak-Ro, Gyeongsan, Gyeongbuk, Korea
yousk@yu.ac.kr

Abstract. In this study, we build a semantically annotated corpus of Chinese directional complements, conduct Chinese linguistic analysis using them, and propose an application plan for NLP and Teaching Chinese as a Second Language (TCSL). This study particularly focuses on the four directional complements *shang*, *qilai*, *xiaqu*, and *xialai*, which function as grammatical markers. This study utilizes a semantically annotated corpus for Chinese linguistic analysis. We classify the directional complements according to semantic features, quantitatively analyze the classified semantic types, and conduct a network analysis. The semantically annotated corpus from this study can be utilized in various fields in the future. It can be used to improve the performance of word sense disambiguation in the field of NLP. It will also be actively used for TCSL. If our corpus is properly utilized, it will be possible to provide learners and instructors with a variety of essential information on directional complements.

Keywords: directional complement · semantically annotated corpus · semantic type · network analysis · word sense disambiguation · TCSL

1 Introduction

This paper presents a semantically annotated corpus that more fully explains the Chinese directional complement (CDC) for linguistic analysis. The paper defines the guidelines, and textual data are designed for automatic semantic classification, machine translation, and Teaching Chinese as a Second Language (TCSL). The importance of the chosen subject is highlighted for Chinese grammar research and TCSL.

The directional complement is a sentence component that follows a verb to indicate directional movement (*zhan-qilai*), the resultative (*zhong-qilai*), the inceptive (*xiao-qilai*), and the estimative (*kan-qilai*). It displays high-frequency usage and represents a variety of meanings from lexical to grammatical. Despite the directional complement's significance in Chinese grammar research and language education, only theoretical analysis or partial quantitative analysis have been attempted. Thence, we propose this paper in order to build a semantically annotated corpus that compensates for the deficiencies in previous studies. Quantitative and qualitative analysis will be then conducted on both

© The Author(s), under exclusive license to Springer Nature Switzerland AG 2023
Q. Su et al. (Eds.): CLSW 2022, LNAI 13496, pp. 43–57, 2023.
https://doi.org/10.1007/978-3-031-28956-9_4

the meaning and function of directional complements, followed by the use of textual data.

In the field of NLP, the detailed meanings and interpretations in an annotated corpus provide information necessary for increasing the accuracy of semantic analysis and machine translation. For machine translation systems, such concepts are difficult for an accurate translation. There are various types of directional complement in Chinese, and most of them are omitted when translated into other languages like English and Korean. A big problem is the difficulty in a directional complement's appropriate expression when translating foreign languages into Chinese. An example is the frequent omission of directional complements in Korean and English translations made through Google, Baidu, and Naver Translator. Examples below provide evidence of such discussed notions with improper understanding of meanings.

(1) a. Source sentence: (Korean) Mo-du-deul i-ya-gi-leul deud-go us-gi si-jag-haess-eo-yo.

(Everyone started laughing when they heard the story.)

b. Target sentence: *Ting wan zhe ge gushi, dajia dou xiao__le.* (Google translation).

(Chinese) → Dajia tingle gushi, dou xiao-<u>qilai</u> le. (Human translation)

(2) a. Source sentence: (Korean) Mang-go-leul meog-go ib-sul-i bu-eo-ol-lass-da.

(My lips are swollen after eating mango.)

b. Target sentence: *Wo chi le mangguo hou zuicun zhong__le.* (Baidu translation)

(Chinese) → Wo chi le mangguo, zuicun Zhong-<u>qilai</u> le. (Human translation)

(3) a. Source sentence: (Korean) Eom-ma-ga a-i-leul kkog kkyeo-an-ass-da.

(The mother hugged the child tightly.)

b. Target sentence: *Muqin jinjindi bao<u>zhe</u> haizi.* (Naver translation).

(Chinese) → Mama ba haizi jinjindi bao-<u>qilai</u> le. (Human translation)

Directional complements are used in various ways in Mandarin Chinese. However, corresponding expressions are seldom used in languages like English, Korean, and Japanese. Therefore, it is very difficult for foreign learners to fully understand the directional complement and translate it accurately. As previously mentioned, directional complements are misused by most second language learners. And the presented annotated Chinese directional complement (CDC) corpus solves such problems. Meanings and functions in directional complements can be either 'simple' or 'complex'. Meanings for complements with simple functions are relatively easy to classify.

This semantic annotation study was performed by selecting complements with more complex functions, preferably four complements in consideration of both research time and capacity. The selected complements semantically express symmetrical directions of upward—*shang*; *qilai*—and downward—*xialai*; *xiaqu*. And expressed directional complements are divided into three or more semantic categories [1] with a grammatical function similar to an aspect marker [2]. According to TCSC studies [3], these complements are often missed by students in the process of learning Chinese. In our study, we constructed 20,000 sentence data with semantic information on these four complements.

2 Semantic Annotation Criteria for Directional Complements

2.1 Review of Previous Research

2.1.1 Literature Review and Theoretical Background

Previous studies included many references that outline the meaning of all directional complements to explain the semantic relationship as a mechanism of metaphor and derivation.

A representative study was conducted by Liu [1]. She divided the meanings of complements into three categories: directional movement, resultative, and change of state. Her classification method was used in many subsequent studies. Although this classification is systematic, it still lacked validity in the explanations because they tried to include all meanings within the concept of directional complements. In addition, the core meaning was not revealed—only a simple description of the three semantic types of directional complement, which does not help understand the core.

Later studies focused on some directional complements with complex functions, and some scholars have approached them with a linguistic perspective for the complement's explanation.

Specifically, Lu [2], Chen [4], and Yu [5] analyzed the semantic functions of complements with complex functions (qilai, xialai, xiaqu) by arguing the aspectual semantic features within these complements. The recent increase in research on language acquisition and TCSL is also noteworthy. Again, this paper focuses on difficult-to-understand directional complements and their proper usage by foreign learners, despite their frequency, dealing in particular with an analysis of learners' misuse and more effective learning methods [3, 6].

2.1.2 Problems and Limitations in Previous Semantic Classification Studies

Previous semantic classification studies mainly focused on the function of a single directional complement and a semantic comparison between two directional complements with symmetrical structures. Although these studies help to understand the meaning of individual directional complements, they did not provide empirical information based on a large corpus. Another problem not considered is the semantic system of the overall directional complements, or the relationship between each meaning. In addition, since the meanings of directional complements with complex functions are presented simply, there is a lack of understanding about the main function of these directional complements and their characteristics. As a result, Chinese learners are accustomed to having a shallow understanding of the significant meanings of directional complements.

Some functions of directional complements need to be analyzed with grammatical markers outside of the complement category. For example, *shang*, *qilai*, *xiaqu*, and *xialai* have aspectual semantic features. Although studies on the aspectual properties of directional complements have been published recently, they are descriptive studies based on a small corpus without an empirical analysis based on quantitative analysis.

This study basically annotated all directional complements semantically, and intensively analyzed the lexical and functional meanings of directional complements with some complex functions.

2.2 Semantic Classification Criteria for CDC

In this section, semantic classification criteria and examples are presented focusing on *shang*, *qilai*, *xiaqu*, and *xialai*. Chinese directional complements follow a verb, and they express a state resulting from a single event that took place, which is a typical characteristic. *Shang*, *qilai*, *xiaqu*, and *xialai* also have this aspectual property (change of state). Based on this property, all directional complements express movement in the direction each complement signifies. This is the movement meaning, that is, *shang*1 and *qilai*1 in Table 1 represent a change of position in an upward movement, and *xiaqu*1 and *xialai*1 in Table 2 express a change of position in a downward movement.

As the semantic features of movement and direction are weakened, the directional complements express only the resulting state (the resultative meaning), not the movement. Differences in the resultative meaning of each complement exist due to derivation from basic meanings that represent different directions (upward and downward). Examples are *shang*2, *shang*3, *qilai*2, *xiaqu*2, and *xialai*2 Table 1 and 2.

During grammaticalization, some of the resultative meanings develop into grammatical functions, such as aspect markers or discourse markers. Such a process is called the unidirectionality of grammaticalization. However, the grammatical functions differ from each other because they are also influenced by the direction of the directional complements. *Shang*4 expresses the completive and the beginning of continuation; *qilai*3 has the inceptive function; *xiaqu*3 expresses continuation from the present to the future based on the speaker's viewpoint; and *xialai*3 represents the completion of a stable state. In addition, *qilai*4 has an estimative function, whereas *xialai*4 and *xiaqu*4 function as discourse continuative markers.

As such, we classified the sub-meanings of *shang*, *qilai*, *xiaqu*, and *xialai* as shown in Tables 1 and 2 below. The classified meanings were used to build the semantic annotation corpus.

Table 1. The semantic classes of –*shang* and –*qilai*

Semantic Feature	V-shang				V-qilai			
	shang1	shang2	shang3	shang4	qilai1	qilai2	qilai3	qilai4
Change of state	+	+	+	+	+	+	+	−
Movement	+	±	−	−	+	−	−	−
Upward	±	−	−	−	+	−	−	−
Resultative	−	+	−	−	−	+	−	−
Completive	−	−	+	−	−	−	−	−
Continuative-A/S*	−	−	−	−	−	−	+	−
Continuative-R**	−	−	−	+	−	−	−	−
Beginning	−	−	−	+	−	−	+	−
Discourse	−	−	−	−	−	−	−	+
Example	pao-shang	tie-shang	mai-shang	ai-shang	zhan-qilai	zhong-qilai	xiao-qilai	kan-qilai

* Continuative-Activity/State
** Continuative-Result State

Table 2. The semantic classes of -*xialai* and -*xiaqu*

Semantic Feature	V- *xialai*				V- *xiaqu*			
	*xialai*1	*xialai*2	*xialai*3	*xialai*4	*xiaqu*1	*xiaqu*2	*xiaqu*3	*xiaqu*4
Change of state	+	+	+	−	+	+	−	−
Movement	+	±	−	−	+	±	−	−
Downward	±	−	−	−	±	−	−	−
Resultative	−	+	−	−	−	+	−	−
Completive	−	+	−	−	−	−	−	−
Continuative-A/S*	−	−	+	−	−	−	+	−
Continuative-R**	−	−	+	−	−	−	+	−
Beginning	−	−	−	−	−	−	−	−
Discourse	−	−	−	+	−	−	−	+
Example	*zou-xialai*	*xie-xialai*	*ting-xialai*	*jie-xialai*	*fei-xiaqu*	*zhai-xiaqu*	*shuo-xiaqu*	*jie-xiaqu*

* Continuative-Activity/State
** Continuative-Result State

3 Quantitative Analysis of the Semantically Annotated Corpus

3.1 Semantic Annotation Corpus for CDCs

The CDC semantic annotation corpus consists of 20,825 sentences with directional complements, which we collected from 5,475 literary works, 108 broadcast scripts, and 290 Chinese textbooks [7]. This corpus contains 5,605 sentences with shang, 5,024 sentences with qilai, 5,100 sentences with xialai, and 5,096 sentences with xiaqu. The sources were chosen to meet our project's overall goal to provide unbiased and sufficient data.

The extracted directional complement sentences were manually classified according to the semantic classification criteria established in this study (see Sect. 2.2), and then, semantic annotations were added to construct the corpus.

Based on the semantic annotation corpus, this study conducted a survey of the semantic class ratio for each directional complement (explained in Sect. 3.2 below), a semantic network analysis of complements (in Sect. 3.3), and statistical analysis of verbs combined with directional complements (Sect. 3.4).

3.2 The Distribution of Semantic Classes

See (Tables 3, 4, 5 and 6)

The above analysis confirmed two aspects as follows: first, the relationship between the semantic classes of each directional complement, and second, the comparison of semantic classes between different directional complements.

It is necessary to change the perception of the core meaning of the directional complement. According to the analysis, the semantic classes with the highest token frequency are *shang*2 (47.87%), *qilai*3 (52.29%), *xialai*2 (37.18%), and *xiaqu*3 (63.11%). The meanings are relative in the grammatical functions, expressing the resulting state of the action, the beginning, and the continuative meaning of an action or state.

Table 3. The distribution of semantic classes for *shang*

	*shang*1	*shang*2	*shang*3	*shang*4
Quantity	1,148	2,683	1,209	565
Ratio	20.48%	47.87%	21.57%	10.08%

Table 4. The distribution of semantic classes for *qilai*

	*qilai*1	*qilai*2	*qilai*3	*qilai*4
Quantity	1,295	586	2,627	516
Ratio	25.77%	11.66%	52.29%	10.28%

Table 5. The distribution of semantic classes for *xialai*

	*xialai*1	*xialai*2	*xialai*3	*xialai*4
Quantity	1,787	1,896	1,104	313
Ratio	35.04%	37.18%	21.65%	6.13%

Table 6. The distribution of semantic classes for *xiaqu*

	*xiaqu*1	*xiaqu*2	*xiaqu*3	*xiaqu*4
Quantity	1,437	323	3,217	119
Ratio	28.21%	6.34%	63.11%	2.34%

In the past, most scholars focused on the meaning of movement and direction in the directional complements. They defined directional complements as a component used to describe the direction of a verb. However, according to the analysis in this paper, that definition needs to be reconsidered. It is a common linguistic phenomenon for a single linguistic element to derive several meanings from the original meaning. While the original meaning is important, the more commonly used meaning is a considerable factor that leads to frequent errors in machine translations and calls into question which function should be focused on in TCSL. Therefore, this study argues that it is necessary to teach and apply a directional complement based on its actual frequency in TCSL and NLP.

Second, this analysis empirically confirmed that each directional complement has a different degree of grammaticalization. Among the meanings of *shang* and *xialai*, *shang*2 and *xialai*2, which express the resulting state of an action, have the highest frequency. This is the basic meaning of a Chinese complement. On the other hand, among the meanings of *qilai* and *xiaqu*, *qilai*3 and *xiaqu*3, which express the beginning and continuative meanings corresponding to the aspect marker, have the highest frequency. As such, the core meaning of each directional complement is different in the degree of grammaticalization. This means *qilai* and *xiaqu* are more grammaticalized than *shang* and *xialai*. To talk about *shang* and *xialai* again, their semantic classes seem to have almost the same frequency. However, considering the semantic constraint on the collocation verb, *xialai2* has a wider range of collocation verbs than *shang2* (Sect. 3.3 below). In particular, *xialai* expresses a discourse continuous meaning (*xialai4*) with a high degree of grammaticalization, but *shang* does not. It is thus apparent that *xialai* is more grammaticalized than *shang*.

3.3 A Semantic Network of CDCs Based on the Annotated Corpus

Directional complements have different basic meanings, but there are many shared semantic features in derived meanings. The previous section classified the meanings of four complements, *shang*, *qilai*, *xiaqu*, and *xialai*, based on 10 semantic features. Some semantic features are shared by all complements. For example, 'movement' and 'change of state' are semantic features commonly used in *shang*, *qilai*, *xiaqu*, and *xialai*. However, other semantic features appear differently for each directional complement.

The ratio of specific semantic features also depends on the directional complements. For example, the 'change-of-state' feature is 100% in *shang* but only 35% in *xiaqu*. The percentage of 'movement' is high in *shang*, but low in *qilai*. Table 7 examines the ratio of semantic features used in the corpus for each directional complement.

Table 7. The percentage of semantic features in the CDC corpus

	shang	*qilai*	*xialai*	*xiaqu*
Change of state	100%	90%	94%	35%
Movement	68%	26%	72%	35%
Upward	20%	26%	0%	0%
Downward	0%	0%	35%	28%
Resultative	48%	12%	37%	6%
Completive	22%	0%	37%	0%
Continuative-A/S*	0%	52%	22%	63%
Continuative-R**	10%	0%	22%	63%
Beginning	10%	52%	0%	0%
Discourse	0%	10%	6%	2%

* Continuative-Activity/State
** Continuative-Result State

Depending on the usage ratio of semantic features, a semantic network of the directional complements is shown in Fig. 1. In this figure, the central node is configured with four directional complements. The semantic features shared by each complement are represented by small nodes. The thickness of the edge line indicates the strength of the connection between semantic features and complements.

Based on the network analysis, each complement has similar semantic features with distinct significant features.

First, *shang* and *qilai*, which express upward movement from the reference point, are projected from a static state to a dynamic beginning through a metaphorical mechanism, thereby forming a semantic domain of *beginning*. Due to the semantic difference between movements with an end point (*shang*) and without an end point (*qilai*), these two complements have a subtle semantic difference between the onset of a static state and the onset of a dynamic action/state.

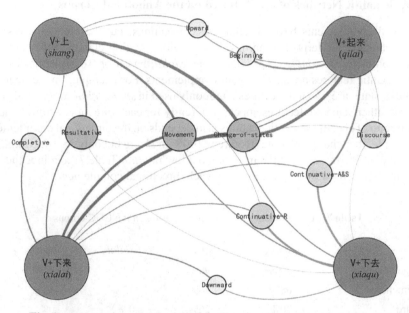

Fig. 1. A semantic network of the four directional complements analyzed

Second, *qilai* and *xiaqu* refer to a movement that clearly highlights the speaker's starting point but possesses a non-explicit end point. The speaker's starting point is projected into the time domain (beginning) while the movement without an end point is projected as an unfinished action. As a result, it develops the continuative meaning.

Third, *shang* and *xialai* refer to movement to an end point or a speaker's position. Through the metaphorical mechanism, the meaning of arrival at this end point is projected into the completive and resultative semantic domains.

3.4   Co-occurrence Restrictions Between Verbs and Directional Complements

In this paper, we investigate co-occurrence restrictions between verbs and directional complements. Table 8 shows the number of verbs with two or more co-occurrence frequencies. As shown in the table, the frequency of the verb type combined with each directional complement shows a different pattern. The complement with the highest frequency is *qilai*. There are 456 verbs that occur with *qilai*. The frequency of verb types in other directional complements is around 320. This result shows that *qilai* has a more diverse distribution than other complements.

Table 8. The frequencies of verbs with directional complements

Directional Complement	Verb Frequency	Average Co-occurrence
shang	313	15.0
qilai	456	8.5
xialai	317	11.9
xiaqu	324	11.9

Table 9. Relations between semantic types of verbs and directional complements

			shang	*qilai*	*xialai*	*xiaqu*
[+telic]			983 (41.8%)	31 (1.7%)	876 (40.1%)	195 (8.9%)
[−telic]	Activity	[+Movement]	594 (25.3%)	248 (13.6%)	236 (10.8%)	231 (10.6%)
		[−Movement]	153 (6.5%)	874 (47.8%)	356 (16.3%)	1,702 (78.0%)
	Activity & result state		545 (23.2%)	638 (34.9%)	446 (20.4%)	0 (0%)
	State		76 (3.2%)	37 (2.0%)	268 (12.3%)	0 (0%)
Total			2,351	1,828	2,182	2,128

Co-occurrence restrictions are the semantic restrictions that a word imposes on the environment in which it occurs. According to our analysis, there is a difference in the co-occurrence type for verbs with each directional complement. Figure 2 shows in network form the verbs frequently co-occurring with complements. The colors of nodes indicate the quantity of directional complements. Purple nodes have the most, indicating verbs co-occurring with only one directional complement. Green nodes indicate verbs co-occurring with two directional complements; blue shows verbs co-occurring with three directional complements, and orange nodes are verbs co-occurring with four directional complements. This verb network shows selected restrictions of directional complements that exhibit the different patterns.

In Fig. 2, it is worth noting that verb nodes associated with two or more directional complements have a common co-occurrence preference for their complements. That is, some verbs co-occurring with different directional complements represent the fact that these directional complements actually have similar meanings.

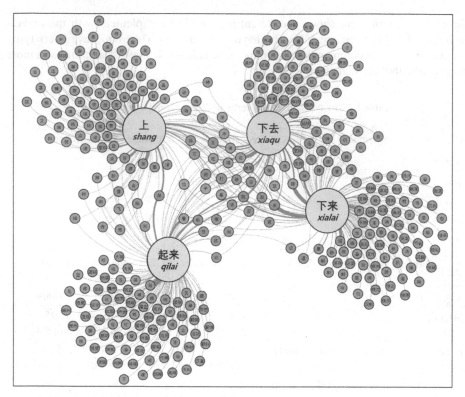

Fig. 2. A verb network of the four directional complements

Most of the verbs shared by four directional complements (orange nodes) show motion (some also include high-frequency action verbs). This shows that motion verbs freely combine with directional complements with a low degree of selectional constraints. The verbs associated with blue nodes (shared by three directional complements) generally indicate dynamic actions. Most of these action verbs are used frequently in the corpus. The directional complement serves to supplement the aspectual information of an action by combining with these verbs. Verb-complement collocations representing aspectual meaning are frequently used. This proves once again that aspectual meaning is the core semantic feature of directional complements.

The verbs from green nodes (shared by two directional complements) are more scattered than verbs in the orange and blue nodes, which are closely related to the semantic characteristics of the connected directional complements. Some directional complement pairs share many verbs, while some do not. For example, verbs co-occurring with *xiaqu* and *xialai* have a relatively large quantity. They also share downward movement and continuative semantic features. The verbs co-occurring with *xiaqu* and *qilai* are action verbs with a process. Their main semantic features are inceptive and continuative. Verbs shared by *shang* and *qilai* usually have attachment or fixation semantic features. This is because the meanings contained in the resultative *shang* and *qilai* are shared. On the other hand, only a few verbs are shared by *shang* & *xiaqu*, *shang* & *xialai*, or *xialai* & *qilai*, and the common semantic features are not clear.

The verb-complement collocation is closely related to the aspectual meaning of the verb. For example, [+telic] verbs with an end point have a high collocation rate with *shang* or *xialai*. On the other hand, [−telic] verbs without an end point are sub-classified by their characteristics and show different collocation patterns. Action verbs without a movement feature tend to have the highest association with *xiaqu* and a relatively high association with *qilai*. This is because the [−telic] and [−movement] features of the verb have an important influence on the choice of directional complement. Activity and resulting-state verbs have two meanings: action and the resulting state of the action. When these verbs are combined with directional complements, the meaning of the action is highlighted. These verbs express completion of an action when combined with *shang* (which refers to completion). However, when combined with other directional complements, they mainly express movement in the corresponding direction. State verbs with [−telic]/[+durative] features show a high combination frequency with *xialai*, describing the durative process. The table below shows the co-occurrence frequency of directional complements according to the semantic type of the verb.

4   How to Use the CDC Semantically Annotated Corpus

4.1   Word Sense Disambiguation with the Annotated Corpus

Our annotated corpus can be utilized in various fields. For example, in the field of natural language processing, it is possible to increase accuracy if there is an annotated corpus of good quality. The annotated corpus was tested with a word sense disambiguation (WSD) task for this paper. In NLP, WSD is a fundamental task assigning appropriate meanings to words in given contexts. Many function words in Chinese are ambiguous because of the multiple meanings that include directional complements. A sufficient amount of the annotated corpus can be useful data for identifying the intended meaning of a directional complement in context.

In an experiment for this paper, we used a manually annotated corpus that is curated by Chinese native speakers and linguists. Our basic assumption is that contextual information from the CDC in the annotated corpus can provide sufficient evidence for disambiguation. Although manual sense annotation is a time-consuming process, small but precise data can produce good performance. In transfer learning, a manually annotated corpus can be used as a seed to increase the performance of a pre-trained language model. Transfer learning is a deep learning technique that increases efficiency by training newly constructed data after pre-training them. Transfer learning tries to improve learners' performance with target domains by transferring knowledge from different but related source domains.

In this study, the transfer learning process was conducted by combining Chinese BERT pre-trained data and the semantically annotated corpus for directional complements. MacBERT-large was our pre-trained language model [8]. It is a modified version of the original BERT classification model, which gained high scores in experiments conducted for various NLP tasks. The learning process is accomplished by learning basic information from large-scale data and then learning target data for semantic classification.

In the fine-tuning process, the BERT classification model was used to properly distinguish multiple meanings of directional complements in context. Used as training data were 5,000 sentences with each directional complement, with 500 sentences for each directional complement used as test data. Each model was trained at a learning rate of 5e-5, a training batch size of 64, and three epochs. The following are the results from predicting a test sentence after finishing the fine-tuning process.

Table 10. Accuracy and F1 score from the semantic classification test

	Accuracy	Precision	Recall	F1 score
shang	91.1%	92.0%	90.2%	91.1%
qilai	96.9%	96.4%	97.9%	97.2%
xialai	94.6%	94.0%	89.9%	91.9%
xiaqu	97.1%	94.0%	97.4%	95.7%

As we can see from Table 10, the accuracy of semantic classification for directional complements is quite high. This result proves the semantically annotated corpus can contribute to resolving semantic ambiguity in directional complements. Through this test, we found that more than 90% of the semantic ambiguity can be resolved accurately using 5,000 sentences of training data for directional complements. This not only represents the quality of the training data that determines the performance of the model but also proves that our training data were of good quality (Table 11).

As shown in the examples above, the computer predicted the meaning of *shang* and *xialai* very accurately after the fine-tuning process. It also can resolve ambiguity in meaning based on the context in which *shang* and *xialai* are used. If there is an annotated corpus of good quality, the same method can be applied to the disambiguation task of other polysemous complements. This will ultimately contribute to improving the performance of the NLP system [9].

4.2   The Semantically Annotated Corpus for CDC Teaching and Learning

Using the semantically annotated corpus to study CDC grammatical functions is meaningful, but it can be more valuable through educational usage. If our corpus is utilized properly, it will help to address the challenges that students and instructors face in learning about and teaching CDCs.

More than 200 universities in Korea provide students with a Chinese language program every year, and more than 100,000 students annually take the HSK (Hanyu shuiping

Table 11. Examples of semantic predictions for directional complements

Tamen jiannandi pa-shang shanling, qianmian de danjiadui dou xiadao banshanpo le. (They climbed up the mountain with difficulty, and the stretcher team in front of them went down half the hillside.)   1 (Upward): 99.88%   2 (Resultative): 0.08%   3 (Completive): 0.02%   4 (Beginning): 0.02%
Wo haipa paosheng, yi tingdao paosheng, jiu ganjin wu-shang erduo. (I was afraid of the gunfire. I immediately covered my ears when I heard the sound of gunfire.)   1 (Upward): 0.07%   **2 (Resultative): 99.88%**   3 (Completive): 0.04%   4 (Beginning): 0.01%
Xiongdi shi pengyou, jiushi tian ta-xialai, ni bangmang cheng yihuir, you suan shenme ne?(Brothers are friends, it is natural to help from the side even if the sky falls.)   **1 (Downward): 99.88%**   2 (Resultative): 0.07%   3 (Continuative): 0.03%   4 (Discourse): 0.03%
Zhe xie xin ruguo baoliu-xialai, rujin chongdu gai duome youqu! (If these letters were kept, how interesting it would be to reread them now!)   1 (Downward): 0.03%   **2 (Resultative): 99.87%**   3 (Continuative): 0.06%   4 (Discourse): 0.03%

kaoshi) Chinese proficiency test. Korea records the highest number of students taking the exam, compared to other countries in the world. Most of the students rely on physical books when learning Chinese or preparing for the HSK exam. However, physical textbooks and reference books do not contain various explanations and examples of Chinese vocabulary and grammar. For instance, the Chinese directional complement is one of the trickiest concepts for Korean students due to its derivative meanings. In particular, *shang, qilai, xialai*, and *xiaqu* are easily confused. Most of the textbooks present only the basic meaning of movement in directional complements, forcing students to guess the derived meaning based on the context. Explanations of the various CDC semantic types are not provided in textbooks. In some cases, even an explanation of a function with high token frequency is not provided. Because there is no proper guidebook, the instructor's explanation is inevitably subjective and not systematic. In this situation, the CDC semantic annotation corpus and the semantic network in this study will play an important role in helping students understand and correctly use the grammatical functions of CDCs.

The positive effects of this study on CDC education are as follows.

First, the instructor can teach the core meaning of each directional complement and its semantic characteristics through the classification of semantic types and the frequency analysis of the directional complements in this study. In fact, meanings with high token frequency must be learned preferentially and intensively in TCSL. In addition, the analysis of token frequency by meaning will be helpful in compiling Chinese textbooks or grammar books.

Second, it is possible to grasp the collocation tendency and understand the mechanism of directional complements throughout the network of directional complements and verbs. Students generally focus on verb phrases to make a sentence. Therefore, information on collocation of verbs and directional complements can provide guidelines for students to select and use the appropriate directional complement in a sentence.

Third, the distribution and sharing of meaning in the directional complement is definable through the semantic network from this study. For example, it is possible to know whether *shang* or *xialai* is expressing continuation of the resulting state, and whether *qilai* or *shang* should be chosen to express the start of an action. This semantic network can be used as a new method to approach semantic classification of directional complements in TCSL and Chinese translation education.

Fourth, the semantic annotation corpus and the analysis from this study will have greater meaning when provided through second-language teaching and learning. Online education is preferred as the current educational method. The demand for education applications is rapidly increasing, in which educational systems based on information and communication technologies (ICT) have appeared rapidly, and the content still needs improvement. Most of the educational applications only provide simple language exercises, such as multiple choice, fill in the blanks, and matching workouts [10]. The convergence of linguistic knowledge and computational knowledge seems very necessary for high-level learning including lessons in an educational application. Only then is it possible to build a language-aware intelligent language education system.

The current representative educational application systems include Computer Assisted Language Learning (CALL). This system attracts a great deal of attention from the field of second-language learning as well as Intelligent Computer Assisted Language Learning (ICALL) that applies computing technology to second-language teaching and learning. ICALL specifically combines artificial intelligence with CALL systems to provide software that interacts with students intelligently, responding flexibly and dynamically to a student's progress. The system allows students to input a sentence from their learning language, and the AI tutor in the system corrects any mistakes. If collocation of directional complements and verbs, semantic types, and analysis results of this study are added to a current system, students will conveniently and efficiently learn more of the various directional complements. In addition, the adjusted system can be used as an example-sentence search tool, a grammar checker, and for automatic writing evaluation.

Overall, the corpus or the analysis from this study can resolve the difficulties in CDC education, and can stimulate students' motivations for learning by utilizing them as meaningful educational materials for instructors. Results of this study are expected to be more effective through an educational application based on ICT.

5   Conclusion

In this study, we built a semantically annotated corpus of Chinese directional complements, then conducted Chinese linguistic analysis using them, and proposed an application plan for NLP and TCSL. This study focused on four directional complements, *shang*, *qilai*, *xiaqu*, and *xialai*, which function as grammatical markers.

First of all, this study utilized the semantically annotated corpus in terms of Chinese linguistic analysis. First, we analyzed the meanings of the four directional complements.

We classified them according to semantic features, and quantitatively analyzed the classified semantic types. Through the analysis in this study, we checked the frequency of each meaning, and identified the core meanings of the four directional complements. Next, we conducted a network analysis considering the semantic features, constructed a semantic network of the four directional complements, and constructed a verb network based on co-occurrence frequency with verbs. We confirmed the semantic features, grammatical functions, and correlations between meanings of *shang*, *qilai*, *xiaqu*, and *xialai*.

The semantically annotated corpus from this study will be utilized in various fields in the future. It can be used to improve the performance of word sense disambiguation in natural language processing. It will also be actively used in TCSL. If our corpus is properly utilized, it will be possible to provide learners and instructors with a variety of essential information on directional complements in learning about and teaching CDCs. Now, online education has become the preferred method. In this situation, if the semantically annotated corpus is effectively used through an educational application, its value will be highly appreciated.

Acknowledgments. This work was supported by the Ministry of Education of the Republic of Korea and the National Research Foundation of Korea (NRF-2020S1A5A2A01045437).

References

1. Liu, Y.: Interpretation of Directional Complement. Beijing Language and Culture University Press, Beijing (1998). (in Chinese)
2. Lu, Y.: On the "duration aspect" in Mandarin Chinese. J. Anhui Normal Univ. **28**, 430–435 (2000). (in Chinese)
3. Xiao, X., Zhuo, W.: The acquisition of directional complement for foreign students in Chinese. Chinese Lang. Learn. **1**, 70–81 (2009). (in Chinese)
4. Chen, Q.: A Typological Perspective on the Study of Chinese Aspectuality. The Commercial Press, Beijing (2008). (in Chinese)
5. Yu, S.: A study on the aspectual function of directional complement: a corpus-based analysis of "xialai", "xiaqu." Korea J. Chin. Linguist. **89**, 159–193 (2020). (in Korean)
6. Liu, L.: Acquisition Error Analysis of Chinese Directional Complement Based on HSK Dynamic Composition Corpus. Anyang Normal University Doctoral dissertation (2016). (in Chinese)
7. Jeong, Y., Li, M., Kang, S., Eum, Y., Kang, B.: Automatic prediction and linguistic interpretation of chinese directional complements based on BERT model. In: Workshop on Chinese Lexical Semantics, pp. 411–422. Springer, Cham (2022)
8. Cui, Y., Che, W., Liu, T., Qin, B., Wang, S., Hu, G.: Revisiting Pre-Trained Models for Chinese Natural Language Processing. arXiv preprint arXiv:2004.13922 (2020)
9. Erk, K., Kowalski, A., Padó, S., Pinkal, M.: Towards a resource for lexical semantics: a large German corpus with extensive semantic annotation. In: Proceedings of the 41st Annual Meeting of the Association for Computational Linguistics (2003)
10. Lee, S.: Establishing a Learner Error Annotated Corpus and Developing Intelligent Learning Tools: New Korean Language Education based on Linguistic Knowledge. Language Facts and Perspectives, vol. 24, pp. 187–220. Institute of Language and Information Studies (2009). (in Korean)

BBAE: A Method for Few-Shot Charge Prediction with Data Augmentation and Neural Network

Yingjie Han[1], Yuke Wang[1], Junyi Chen[1], Ailian Cao[2], and Hongying Zan[1(✉)]

[1] School of Computer and Artificial Intelligence, Zhengzhou University, Zhengzhou, Henan, China
{ieyjhan,iehyzan}@zzu.edu.cn, junyichen_ch@sina.com
[2] School of International Studies, Zhengzhou University, Zhengzhou, Henan, China

Abstract. Charge prediction aims to predict charges from the case descriptions and plays a significant role in legal assistance systems. When we use deep learning methods, prediction on high-frequency charges has achieved promising results, but prediction on few-shot charges is still a challenge. To address this issue, a few-shot charge prediction method with data augmentation and neural network is proposed, named BBAE (BERT-BiGRU-Attention based on easy data augmentation techniques), which can be divided into three layers: data augmentation layer, encoder layer, and output layer. Specifically, the data augmentation layer takes the case description as input and uses EDA (easy data augmentation techniques) to generate synthetic samples biased to few-shot charges based on charge categories. The encoder layer employs the BERT-BiGRU-Attention model to fully extract text features, while the output layer predicts the charge on the basis of text features. Experiments on three public datasets of Chinese criminal cases demonstrate that our method achieves more effective improvements over other baselines. BBAE outperforms state-of-the-art methods by 4.6% and 9.3% under Macro F1 in low-frequency and medium-frequency charges, which indicates that our method is effective in few-shot charge prediction.

Keywords: Charge prediction · Few-shot charge · EDA

1 Introduction

Charge prediction has become an essential sub-task in legal judgment prediction [1]. It aims to automatically predict charges according to a given case description, and its essence is text classification of judgment documents [2]. It not only provides a convenient reference for legal experts but also gives important legal advice to people who are not familiar with legal knowledge [3]. Different from traditional text classification, higher accuracy is required in charge prediction. Automatic charge prediction has been studied for decades. Early research used statistical methods to predict charges [4, 5]. However, it was only effective for small-scale datasets with obvious characteristics, which was difficult to generalize to the general situation. With the application of machine learning methods, researchers can extract more effective features from case descriptions to make predictions [6–9]. In recent years, with the development of deep learning methods, researchers have used neural network models to further improve the accuracy when predicting charges [10–13].

Neural network models usually require huge amounts of data for training, but criminal judgment documents in China present the characteristic of long-tail distribution, that is, some charges have small amounts of data. At present, the high-frequency charge prediction can obtain more than 80% under Macro F1, while the few-shot charge prediction can only obtain about 50% under Macro F1.

To address the above issues, we propose a few-shot prediction method, named BBAE, aiming at improving the few-shot charge prediction performance. In this work, we make two main contributions as follows:

1) To alleviate the imbalance of charges, we propose EDA to generate synthetic samples biased to few-shot charges.
2) We propose a few-shot charge prediction method with data augmentation and neural network, named BBAE. Experiments on three public datasets of Chinese criminal cases demonstrate that our method outperforms other baselines by 4.6% and 9.3% at least for low-frequency and medium-frequency charges, respectively.

2 Related Work

Recently, research on few-shot charge prediction is mostly based on neural network models. He et al. [14] proposed a Sequence Enhanced Capsule model, dubbed as SECaps model to relieve unbalance of charges. Zhang et al. [15] proposed a loss function based on mutual information, which leverages the prior distribution of the charges to tune their weights, so the few-shot charges can contribute more to model optimization. To get more accurate prediction results, researchers have tried to introduce other methods, which can be divided into two categories: the method with **introducing external knowledge** and the method with **data augmentation**.

Some scholars have tried to improve the prediction accuracy of few-shot charges by **introducing external knowledge**. Hu et al. [16] introduced the distinguishing legal attributes of different charges and took these attributes as the internal mapping between case facts and charges. Li et al. [17] proposed a Semi-supervised Learning with BERT-Text-Convolutional neural network method (hereinafter referred to as SLBCNN) for few-shot charge prediction. Zhang et al.[15]introduced a convolutional neural network (CNN) with multiple kernels to extract coarse-grained features and a bilinear CNN to extract fine-grained features from case descriptions, then used the features to enhance the model's capability on representation, based on which the few-shot charges can be better distinguished. Guo et al. [18] proposed a method with auxiliary sentences, which provides better applicability in real-life scenarios. These methods can achieve better few-shot charge prediction effects, but require a lot of human resources.

Different from the above methods, from the perspective of **data augmentation**, Xian et al. [19] proposed a mixup data augmentation strategy that combined category prior knowledge to improve the prediction performance of few-shot charge prediction.

Wang et al. [20] proposed a model with data augmentation and feature augmentation for few-shot charge prediction. Such methods can obtain more training samples without human resources to achieve higher prediction accuracy, but they are time-consuming.

Drawing on previous works, we focus on solving the problem in few-shot charge prediction from data augmentation and neural network models. We propose BBAE, which uses BERT-BiGRU-Attention based on easy data augmentation techniques. Different from Wang et al. [20], we choose an easier augmentation method named EDA, in which the operation is performed on input text rather than on hidden vectors like previous approaches, and synthetic samples can be generated more quickly.

3   Method

As shown in Fig. 1, BBAE can be divided into three parts: data augmentation layer, encoder layer, and output layer. The data augmentation layer takes fact description as input and uses EDA based on charge categories to generate synthetic samples biased to few-shot charges. The encoder layer uses BERT for training word vectors, BiGRU for extracting text features and attention mechanism for focusing on more significant information. The output layer is responsible for classification tasks.

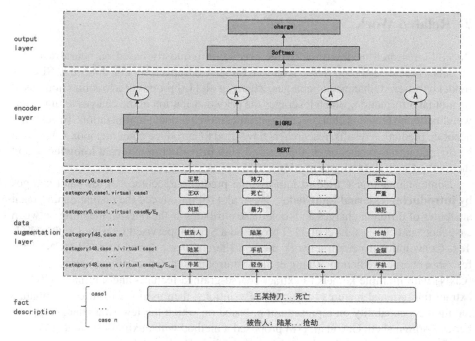

Fig. 1. The structure of BBAE

3.1 Data Augmentation Layer

To alleviate the imbalance of the categories of charges, we propose a data augmentation method with EDA based on charge categories to generate synthetic samples biased to few-shot charges.

Wei et al. [21] proposed EDA for boosting performance on text classification tasks, which consists of four simple but powerful operations: synonym replacement, random insertion, random swap as well as random deletion. They showed that EDA demonstrated particularly strong results for smaller datasets on five text classification tasks.

In data augmentation layer, the sample number of each charge E_i (i represents the charge category, $i \in \{0, 1, ..., 148\}$) is counted. Then EDA is used to make the synthetic sample number generate for each charge as N_i, and the synthetic sample number for each case is N_i/E_i. N_i is calculated by:

$$N_i = N - E_i \tag{1}$$

where $N \in \{1, 2, ...\}$ is adjusting according to the size of the dataset. Through many rounds of experiments, it is found that high N leads to data redundancy, while low N causes data insufficiency. By comparing experimental results, $N = 2000, N = 2200$ and $N = 2500$ are used in Criminal-S, Criminal-M and Criminal-L respectively.

3.2 Encoder Layer

The encoder layer uses BERT-BiGRU-Attention model, in which BERT model employs bidirectional transformers as encoder, fusing the context information of the left and right sides of the current word. Firstly, BERT uses the fine-tuning parameter mechanism to obtain the final word vector c_i of the case description. Then BiGRU is employed to ensure that context information is fully extracted while the training time for that model is greatly reduced, and h_i is obtained. In addition, in order to highlight important words for text classification, the model introduces the attention mechanism to obtain u_i, and gets a normalized importance weight a_i. Finally, we obtain the sentence vector s_i. The specific calculation steps are as follows.

$$h_i = B_i GRU (c_i) \tag{2}$$

$$s_i = \Sigma_{i=1}^{n} a_i h_i \tag{3}$$

$$a_i = \frac{\exp(u_i^T u_w)}{\sum_{i=1}^{n} \exp(u_i^T u_w)} \tag{4}$$

$$u_i = tanh(W_w h_i + b_w) \tag{5}$$

W_w represents weight matrices, and b_w represents bias parameters. The word context vector u_w is randomly initialized and jointly learned during the training process.

3.3 Output Layer

The classification result of the output layer is calculated by using the softmax function on the output of encoder layer, where P is the predicted charge label of the output, and is calculated by:

$$P = softmax(W_v s_i + b_v) \tag{6}$$

Where W_v represents the probability weight assigned by the attention mechanism, and b_v stands for the corresponding offset.

4 Experiments

In order to investigate the effectiveness of BBAE on criminal charges prediction, multiple sets of experiments are conducted on real datasets and compared with several state-of-the-art baseline models as well as ablation experiments to demonstrate the validity of each module in the model.

4.1 Dataset Construction

The available dataset from Hu et al. [16] is used for experiments, which contains real cases for few-shot charges prediction and has three subsets of different sizes, denoted as Criminal-S (small), Criminal-M (medium), and Criminal-L (large). The statistics of Hu's datasets [16] are shown in Table 1.

Table 1. The statistic of Hu's datasets [16]

Dataset	Criminal-S	Criminal-M	Criminal-L
train	61,589	153,521	306,900
test	7,702	19,189	38,368
valid	7,755	19,250	38,429

4.2 Baselines

A basic neural network model and several state-of-the-art models of charge prediction are selected as baselines, and a comparative analysis is used to prove the effectiveness of BBAE. The descriptions of the baseline models are as follows:

① **CNN [22]:** A text classification model based on Multi-core CNN.
② **LSTM [23]:** A two-layer LSTM with a max-pooling layer as the fact encoder.
③ **Fact-Law Attention Model [9]:** An attention-based neural charge prediction model.

④ **Attribute-attentive Charge Prediction Model** [16]: A attribute-attentive charge prediction model, which employs conventional LSTM as the fact encoder and can infer the attributes and charges simultaneously.

⑤ **MFMI** [15]: A framework with multi-grained features and mutual information for few-shot charge prediction, which extracts coarse- and fine-grained features to enhance the model's capability on representation and proposes a loss function based on mutual information.

⑥ **DAFA** [20]: A few-shot charge prediction with data augmentation and feature augmentation proposing a category prior loss function to further alleviate the difficulty of inadequate training for few-shot charge cases, which uses Mixup data enhancement algorithm[24] to generate samples based on word-level and sentence-level BiGRU.

For a fair comparison, a 100×200 fully connected layer is added after the pooling layer in CNN and LSTM, denoted as CNN-200and LSTM-200 [16].

4.3 Experiment Settings and Evaluation Metrics

Due to the input limitation of BERT [25], the maximum document length is set to 512. Adam [26] is used as the optimizer, and the learning rate is set to 1e–5, the dropout rate to 0.5.

For EDA operations consisting of synonym substitution, random insertion, random swap, and random deletion, all the augmentation parameters are set to 0.1 [21].

Accuracy (Acc.), Macro-precision (MP), Macro-recall (MR), and Macro F1 are employed as our evaluation metrics.

4.4 Results and Analysis

The experimental results on three criminal datasets are shown in Table 2. It can be observed that BBAE achieves significant performance on three datasets with 73.6%, 74.2%, and 81.4% respectively under Macro F1, surpassing MFMI and DAFA, especially in Criminal-S, which demonstrates the effectiveness of our method.

As shown in Table 3, following Hu et al. [16], to further verify the advance of BBAE in dealing with few-shot charges, they divide the charges into three categories according to their frequencies. Here, the charges with less than 10 cases are low-frequency, and the charges with more than 100 cases belong to high-frequency. The charge prediction of low-frequency and medium-frequency cases is our main task in few-shot charge prediction.

As shown in Table 3, BBAE has improved charge prediction performance for three datasets of cases at different frequencies, with the highest increase in low-frequency and medium-frequency cases of 4.6% and 9.3% than DAFA under Macro F1 respectively, which demonstrates that BBAE is effective in dealing with few-shot charge prediction.

4.5 Ablation Test

In order to validate different modules, an ablation test is designed as shown in Table 4. We can observe that the performance drops obviously after removing the EDA layer,

Table 2. Charge prediction results of three datasets

Dataset	Criminal-S				Criminal-M				Criminal-L			
Metrics	Acc	MP	MR	F1	Acc	MP	MR	F1	Acc	MP	MR	F1
CNN	91.9	50.5	44.9	46.1	93.5	57.6	48.1	50.5	93.9	66.0	50.3	54.7
CNN-200	92.6	51.5	46.3	47.3	92.8	56.2	50.0	50.8	94.1	61.9	50.0	53.1
LSTM	93.5	59.4	58.6	57.3	94.7	65.8	63.0	62.6	95.5	69.8	67.0	66.8
LSTM-200	92.7	66.0	58.4	57.0	94.4	66.5	62.4	62.7	95.1	72.8	66.7	67.6
Fact-Law Att	92.8	57.0	53.9	53.4	94.7	66.7	60.4	61.8	95.7	73.3	67.1	68.6
Few-Shot Attributes	93.4	66.7	69.2	64.9	94.4	68.3	69.2	67.1	95.8	75.8	73.7	73.1
MFMI	**93.7**	69.3	70.5	68.2	**94.9**	70.2	75.0	71.0	**95.9**	78.7	77.4	76.4
DAFA	93.5	66.2	63.8	62.1	**94.9**	70.3	73.5	70.0	**95.9**	78.6	77.1	76.2
BBAE	**93.7**	**73.7**	**76.9**	**73.6**	94.2	**74.5**	**78.0**	**74.2**	95.8	**80.8**	**85.4**	**81.4**

Table 3. Macro F1 values of various charges on Criminal-S

Charge Type	Low-frequency	Medium-frequency	High-frequency
Charge Number	49	51	49
LSTM-200	32.1	54.5	82.7
Few-Shot Attributes	49.7	60.0	85.2
MFMI	55.9	63.5	85.7
DAFA	55.2	64.1	83.9
BBAE	**59.8**	**73.4**	**87.7**

and the Macro F1 score decreases by at least 25.7%. Therefore, it can be seen that EDA based on charge categories strategy is an important module to improve the model performance. After removing BERT, the Macro F1 score decreases by at least 9.6%, which demonstrates that BERT, as a pre-training model, has strong language representation ability and feature extraction ability, and therefore can learn rich representations from limited data. After removing the attention mechanism, the Macro F1 score decreases by about 1%, which indicates that the attention mechanism can obtain more local features and achieve a better classification effect.

Table 4. Experimental results of ablation test

Dataset	Criminal-S				Criminal-M				Criminal-L			
Metrics	Acc	MP	MR	F1	Acc	MP	MR	F1	Acc	MP	MR	F1
BBAE	**93.7**	**73.7**	**76.9**	**73.6**	**94.2**	**74.5**	**78.0**	**74.2**	**95.8**	**85.4**	**80.8**	**81.4**
-EDA	89.9	48.7	51.9	47.9	89.2	47.8	52.8	44.6	88.7	49.7	45.9	45.8
-BERT	90.8	60.3	64.2	63.8	91.3	64.2	65.5	64.6	92.9	68.4	65.5	66.9
-Attention	92.6	71.8	74.7	72.8	92.3	72.6	77.8	73.1	94.0	83.0	79.3	80.2

5 Conclusion

This work focuses on improving the prediction accuracy of few-shot charges through combing data augmentation and neural network models. To alleviate the lack of few-shot charges, we propose a data augmentation method with EDA based on charge categories, which can generate samples biased to few-shot charges effectively. Moreover, BBAE for few-shot charge prediction with data augmentation and neural network is also proposed. The experimental results prove that BBAE can be effectively applied in the field of few-shot charge prediction.

In the future, we will endeavor to propose better solutions for complex situations such as multiple charges, which is more consistent with the actual situation of Chinese criminal charge prediction.

References

1. Zhong, H., Xiao, C., Tu, C., et al.; How does NLP benefit legal system: a summary of legal artificial intelligence. In: Proceedings of the 58th Annual Meeting of the Association for Computational Linguistics, pp. 5218–5230 (2020)
2. Chen, J., Du, L., Liu, M., et al.: Mulan: a multiple residual article-wise attention network for legal judgment prediction. Trans. Asian Low-Res. Lang. Inf. Process. **21**(4), 1–15 (2022)
3. Zhang, H., Dou, Z.C., Zhu, Y.T., Wen, J.R.: Few-shot charge prediction with multi-grained features and mutual information.In: Proceedings of the 20th Chinese National Conference on Computational Linguistics, Huhhot, China, 22–24 October 2021; pp. 387–403 (2021)
4. Ulmer, S.S.: Quantitative analysis of judicial processes: some practical and theoretical applications. Law Contemp. Probl. **28**(1), 164–184 (1963)
5. Nagel, S.S.: Applying correlation analysis to case prediction. Tex. L. Rev. **42**, 1006 (1963)
6. Lin, W.C., Kuo, T.T., Chang, T.J., et al.: Exploiting machine learning models for Chinese legal documents labeling, case classification, and sentencing prediction. Processdings ROCLING **17**(4), 140 (2012)
7. Lauderdale, B.E., Clark, T.S.: The supreme court's many median justices. Am. Polit. Sci. Rev. **106**(4), 847–866 (2012)
8. Tang, D., Qin, B., Liu, T.: Document modeling with gated recurrent neural network for sentimentclassification. In: Proceedings of EMNLP, pp. 1422–1432 (2015)
9. Katz, D.M., Bommarito, M.J., Blackman, J.: A general approach for predicting the behavior of the supreme court of the united states. PLoS ONE **12**(4), e0174698 (2017)

10. Luo, B., Feng, Y., Xu, J., et al.: Learning to predict charges for criminal cases with legal basis. In: Proceedings of the 2017 Conference on Empirical Methods in Natural Language Processing, pp. 2727–2736 (2017)
11. Jiang, X., Ye, H., Luo, Z., et al.: Interpretable rationale augmented charge prediction system. In: Proceedings of the 27th International Conference on Computational Linguistics: System Demonstrations, pp. 146–151 (2018)
12. Bao, Q., Zan, H., Gong, P., Chen, J., Xiao, Y.: Charge prediction with legal attention. In: Tang, J., Kan, M.-Y., Zhao, D., Li, S., Zan, H. (eds.) NLPCC 2019. LNCS (LNAI), vol. 11838, pp. 447–458. Springer, Cham (2019). https://doi.org/10.1007/978-3-030-32233-5_35
13. Xu, N., Wang, P., Chen, L., et al.: Distinguish confusing law articles for legal judgment prediction. In: Proceedings of the 58th Annual Meeting of the Association for Computational Linguistics, pp. 3086–3095 (2020)
14. He, C., Peng, L., Le, Y., He, J., Zhu, X.: SECaps: a sequence enhanced capsule model for charge prediction. In: Tetko, I.V., Kůrková, V., Karpov, P., Theis, F. (eds.) ICANN 2019. LNCS, vol. 11730, pp. 227–239. Springer, Cham (2019). https://doi.org/10.1007/978-3-030-30490-4_19
15. Zhang, H., Dou, Z., Zhu, Y., Wen, J.: Few-shot charge prediction with multi-grained features and mutual information. In: Li, S., et al. (eds.) CCL 2021. LNCS (LNAI), vol. 12869, pp. 387–403. Springer, Cham (2021). https://doi.org/10.1007/978-3-030-84186-7_26
16. Hu, Z., Li, X., Tu, C., et al.: Few-shot charge prediction with discriminative legal attributes. In: Proceedings of the 27th International Conference on Computational Linguistics, pp. 487–498 (2018)
17. Li, X., Rao, Y., Wang, W., et al.: SLBCNN: a improved deep learning model for few-shot charge prediction. Procedia Comput. Sci. **174**, 32–39 (2020)
18. Guo, J.J., Liu, Z.C., Yu, Z.T., Huang, Y.X., Xiang, Y.: Few shot and confusing charges prediction with the auxiliary sentences of case. Ruan Jian Xue Bao/J. Softw. **32**(10), 3139–3150 (2021)
19. Xian, Y., Chen, W., Yu, Z., Zhang, Y., Wang, H.: Category prior guided mixup data argumentation for charge prediction. Acta Automatica Sinica, 1–11 (2021)
20. Wang, P., Zhang, X., Cao, Z.: Few-shot charge prediction with data augmentation and feature augmentation. Appl. Sci. **11**(22), 10811 (2021)
21. Wei, J., Zou, K.: EDA: easy data augmentation techniques for boosting performance on text classification tasks. In: Proceedings of the 2019 Conference on Empirical Methods in Natural Language Processing and the 9th International Joint Conference on Natural Language Processing (EMNLP-IJCNLP), pp. 6382–6388 (2019)
22. Kim, Y.: Convolutional neural networks for sentence classification. In: Proceedings of the 2014 Conference on Empirical Methods in Natural Language Processing, pp. 1746–1751 (2014)
23. Hochreiter, S., Schmidhuber, J.: Long short-term memory. Neural Comput. **9**(8), 1735–1780 (1997)
24. Zhang, H., Cisse, M., Dauphin, Y.N., et al.: mixup: beyond empirical risk minimization. In: International Conference on Learning Representations (2018)
25. Devlin, J., Chang, M.W., Lee, K., et al.: BERT: pre-training of deep bidirectional transformers for language understanding. In: Proceedings of the 2019 Conference of the North {A}merican Chapter of the Association for Computational Linguistics: Human Language Technologies, vol. 1 (Long and Short Papers) (2019)
26. Kingma, D.P., Ba, J.: Adam: a method for stochastic optimization. Int. Conf. Learn. Representations (2015)

A Preliminary Quantitative Investigation of Chinese Monosyndetic Coordinators

Tsy Yih [ID] and Haitao Liu [✉] [ID]

School of International Studies, Zhejiang University, Yuhangtang Rd. 866, Hangzhou 310058, China
htliu@gmail.com

Abstract. Despite extensive discussion in the traditional linguistic literature, few quantitative data regarding the phenomenon of coordination are known. The present study hence offers an exploratory yet comprehensive quantitative study of the Chinese coordinators using the GSDSimp treebank in the Universal Dependencies (UD) project. The results are many-folded: (1) At the micro level, *hé* is the most frequent overt coordinator in Written Chinese, followed by *jí*, *yǔ*, *bìng*, *huò*. *Gēn* is extremely infrequent despite its reported commonality in the literature. (2) At the macro level, measured by the lexical richness indicator of entropy, Chinese has a rather large inventory of coordinators, at least compared with English. (3) For the syntactic category of coordinands, NP and VP coordinations constitute two largest parts and each have dedicated markers. By contrast, the coordinations of other categories are rather infrequent, mostly without dedicated markers. Specifically, adpositional and sentential coordinations are rarely found in Chinese. The present study also sheds some light on the nature of coordination.

Keywords: Coordinate Constructions · Coordinators · Quantitative Methods · Word Frequency · Form-Meaning Mapping · Functional Typology

1 Introduction

Chinese coordinators are traditionally considered a subclass of conjunctions [1], following the traditional Western grammar [2]. Within the circle of Chinese linguistics, previous studies have paid attention to the boundary between conjunctions and adpositions [3, 4], the historical origins of coordinators [5, 6], the distribution and usage of specific coordinators [7]. Later with the advent of the functional typological approach, researchers also came to study the colexification of different functions of coordinators. However, previous theories of coordination, be it along the formal [8, 9] or functional [10, 11] trend, have been primarily constructed following the mode of English and other European languages. As [12] has shown, only half of the world's languages, including most European languages, commonly co-lexify NP coordination and VP coordination (probably as well as other categories), which leads to the neglect of the fact that the so-called coordination is not a mono-centered category but a bi-centered category [13, 14]. Chinese is among those which distinguish these two functions, one being collection

© The Author(s), under exclusive license to Springer Nature Switzerland AG 2023
Q. Su et al. (Eds.): CLSW 2022, LNAI 13496, pp. 67–82, 2023.
https://doi.org/10.1007/978-3-031-28956-9_6

formation and the other being proposition connection. In addition, previous typological studies are based on a few word-forms (see [Mauri] for her sample), also partially due to the colexification of multiple functions. On the contrary, Chinese has been reported to have a relatively large inventory of coordinators[1] as compared with English [15, 16]. Therefore, Chinese coordinators, being of a different type from the English ones, are worth studying in this respect. Nevertheless, previous studies are mainly intuitionistic and qualitative, and to our knowledge, there are few quantitative studies on Chinese coordinators so far.

The aim of this paper is to conduct a preliminary investigation into Chinese coordinators from various aspects under the setting of functional typology by way of a dependency-annotated treebank. Specifically, we focus on mono-syndetic coordinate constructions, which have exactly one overt coordinator.

2 Literature Review

In the Chinese linguistic literature, coordination is traditionally called *liánhé jiégòu* (联合结构) and more recently *bìngliè jiégòu* (并列结构)[2] [14, 17], whereas coordinators are placed together with subordinators under the rubric of conjunctions in parallel with the traditional Western grammar (see [1] for a discussion of this issue, p. 44). Among those classic Chinese grammars, Chao [15] focused on asyndetic coordination, especially natural coordination, which often functions as a strategy of word-formation. As for overt coordinators, Chao pointed out that *hé*, *gēn*, *tóng*, are prepositional conjunctions, i.e., those lying at the fuzzy boundary between coordinators and adpositions, and that *jí* and *yǔ* are archaic usages. *Gēn* is the commonest overt marker next to the covert juxtaposition strategy in spoken language, while in written language, *hé* prevails. *Tóng* is used more in central and southern dialects. Likewise, Zhu [14] made similar claims (p. 156). More literature on coordination in Chinese can be found in [18, 19]. However, the existing few claims regarding common coordinators are intuitionistic and qualitative.

Another feature of the coordination studies in Chinese literature *and*-type coordinators is not often discussed together with *or*-type coordinators. Zheng & Cao [20] is among the few that conducted quantitative research on coordinators. Nevertheless, they only investigated one historical fiction *Shuihuzhuan* 水浒传 'Water Margin', and the language of the text is Modern Chinese, rather than Contemporary Chinese. They found that *hé* is the commonest coordinator, followed by *bìng* and *yǔ* and a few of *gòng*, *tóng*, and *jí*. Yet most of them conjoin NP rather than VP and other categories. Li & Jin [21] conducted a small-scale corpus survey of *hé* to discover the categories of the coordinands that it combines. 213 out of 300 are NP coordination and the rest 77 are VP coordination. There are also dedicated studies on disjunctive coordinators in Chinese [22]. This is understandable because as the two kinds do not appear in the same context, it seems less meaningful to compare their frequencies. Yet such comparison might also reveal

---

[1] To avoid the ambiguity of the terms 'conjunction/conjuncts' either used in the coordinate constructions of all types or representing the specific *and*-type logical operation between propositions, we follow Haspelmath's more neutral terminology 'coordinator' and 'coordinand'.

[2] This has been fully reflected in the transfer of term usage from *liánhé duǎnyǔ* 联合短语 to 并列短语 *bìngliè duǎnyǔ* in Yunhua Deng's serial works.

what Yih referred to as 'function frequency' [13], which reflects regularities in language use, as opposed to the surface form frequency. Haspelmath [10] and Ohori [23] pointed out that *and*-type words appear more often than *or*-type. Therefore, it is worth testing if that regularity also holds in Chinese, and studying both conjunctive coordinators and disjunctive ones quantitatively.

From the cross-linguistic point of view, Haspelmath [10, 11] proposed a comprehensive typological framework of coordination from various perspectives, and offered examples of a number of world's languages. Mauri [24] conducted a survey based on 37 European languages and 37 non-European languages. Nevertheless, in her sample, each language contained about one to two coordinators for each semantic type alone, which suggests that world's languages generally have a small group of coordinators. In contrast with this finding, Chinese seems to possess a rather large inventory. Therefore, it is worth digging into this question further.

Finally, a major distinction was found to be existing between NP coordination and VP coordination in terms of the syntactic categories being conjoined. Haspelmath found that slightly over half of the world's languages use identical markers for NP and VP coordination (161 out of 301 in his data), while a smaller proportion uses different markers (125 out of 301)[3] [12]. In these languages, they generally use the same form for comitative and NP conjunction, falling under the rubric of the WITH-type of languages following Stassen's terminology [25, 26]. In fact, in addition to comitative markers, in WITH-languages, the NP markers can be used for more case markers [10, 13]. The case of Chinese happens to fall into the second half. In addition, NP coordination and VP coordination have different functional prototypes in parallel. One statement put forth recently is that the so-called coordinate construction should be bi-centered, i.e. having two functional prototypes, rather than mono-centered [13]. One central function is the group formation, primarily encoded by NP coordination, and the other is logical connectives of propositions, which is realized by sentential coordination and its reduced forms. In the latter case, it behaves like a distributive law in a mathematical equation. These two cases happen to correspond to the major syntactic categorical division above. The two cases intersect with each other in the situation where NP coordination has a distributive reading, which might cause ambiguity, as shown in (1a–c). However, it is not necessarily the case, as the collective reading cannot be seen as a subcase of the latter, and the collection it forms (*John and Mary*) does have a unique psychological referent as a group with two persons.

(1a) John and Mary lifted a bucket.

(1b) John and Mary each lifted a bucket.

(1c) John and Mary lifted a bucket together.

Within the Chinese linguistic circle, Zhu [14] also distinguished between two types. Li & Liu [17] wrote a dedicated monograph on coordinative phrases and coordinative complex sentences, where they also drew a similar dichotomy as reflected in the title. In a word, the duality of coordination has been noticed both within the Chinese linguistic circle and the general linguists and especially linguistic typologists. Yet considering the alleged high lexical richness of Chinese coordinators, it is worthwhile to explore their

---

[3] There are also some languages in which juxtaposition is the major strategy (15 out of 301). Li & Jin [21] regard them as a special type of colexification.

difference. One possibility is that Chinese makes finer distinctions between the syntactic categories of coordinands and has dedicated markers for each category.

To fill the abovementioned gaps in the literature, we aim to answer the following research questions:

(1) What are the frequencies of Chinese coordinators?
(2) What is the lexical richness of this functional category in Chinese, compared with that in English?
(3) What are the frequencies of each type of coordinator in terms of the syntactic category being coordinated? Does each of them have a dedicated form in Chinese?

3 Methods

3.1 Corpus

The present study used the GSDSimplified (henceforth GSDSimp) Chinese treebank from the Universal Dependencies (UD) project[4]. We first introduce UD in brief and then report the basic information of GSDSimp.

UD is an initiative which offers various open-access annotated dependency treebanks. It has 217 corpora in 122 languages till the version of 2.9.

A UD treebank is generally represented in.*conllu* format, which is roughly a table containing 10 columns each with a specific sense. Among all the columns, the most important ones are the ID (the index of the token in the sentence), HEAD (the index of its head word), UPOS (universal parts of speech), and DEPREL (dependency relations). The latter two were used as a tool to extract relevant data.

Table 1 shows the.*conllu* format of a sample sentence 我喜欢葡萄、西瓜和草莓 *wǒ xǐhuān pútao, xīguā hé cǎoméi* 'I like grapes, watermelons and strawberries', while Fig. 1 demonstrates its corresponding dependency tree representation.

Specifically, the GSDsimp treebank in UD contains 123,284 tokens cp[5] and 106,193 tokens sp, and consists of one genre, wikipedia. We first merged the three files (the dev, test, and train parts) into one, and then imported it into Microsoft Excel for further processing (data extraction, annotation) and computation with VBA codes.

To answer the second research question, we also consulted an English treebank for comparison. The.*conllu* version of the Georgetown University Multilayer (GUM) corpus was employed as a reference corpus, which contains 135,886 tokens cp and 117,458 tokens sp, roughly comparable to the Chinese GSDsimp. While they differ in the genre since GUM is designed to be a balanced corpus, yet so far they are the largest comparable treebanks that are accessible.

---

[4] https://universaldependencies.org/.

[5] The abbreviation *cp* stands for 'con punctuations' (including punctuations), while *sp* stands for 'sans punctuations' (excluding punctuations).

Table 1. The conllu format of the sample sentence

ID	FORM	LEMMA	UPOS	XPOS	FEAT	HEAD	DEPREL	DEPS	MISC
# text = 我喜欢葡萄、西瓜和草莓。									
1	我	我	PRON	_	_	2	nsubj	_	_
2	喜欢	喜欢	VERB	_	_	0	root	_	_
3	葡萄	葡萄	NOUN	_	_	2	obj	_	_
4	、	、	PUNCT	_	_	5	punct	_	_
5	西瓜	西瓜	NOUN	_	_	3	conj	_	_
6	和	和	CCONJ	_	_	7	cc	_	_
7	草莓	草莓	NOUN	_	_	3	conj	_	_
8	。	。	PUNCT	_	_	2	punct	_	_

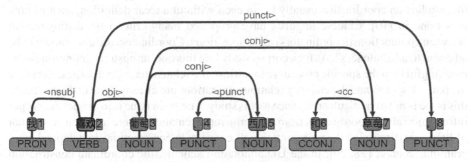

Fig. 1. The dependency tree of the sample sentence

3.2 Metrics

Frequencies are the most direct and apparent metrics for comparing commonness. Yih [13] has distinguished form frequencies, function frequencies, and form-function mapping frequencies (or simply mapping frequencies). Form frequencies are the superficial numbers of certain word types or category types which are abstracted from tokens in texts. Apart from that, function frequencies depend on semantic or other functional annotation of tokens, while mapping frequencies are obtained from the cross-tabulation of two dimensions. For the first question, we compared form frequencies, and for the third question, mapping frequencies were employed. In this research, the various categories of constituents being coordinated are seen as different functions of coordinators.

In addition, to answer the second research question, a quantitative metric, entropy, was used to measure the diversity of coordinators or their lexical richness [27]. Entropy is a comprehensive measure of lexical richness in that it takes into consideration both the number of categories and their proportions. It is insensitive to those categories with small proportions, compared with sensitive measures such as the simple number of word types or relative entropy. In other words, if there are new categories but only with very small frequencies, they will be taken into account but will not affect the metric much. The mathematical properties of the metric guarantee that the more categories there are, the large the metric is, and that the more even the distribution is, the larger the metric is. Therefore, entropy is an appropriate measure for the purpose of our study. Note that in this study, it was used to calculate the lexical richness of a specific word class rather than that of all words in a language. The formula is given as below:

$$\text{Entropy} = -\sum_{i=1}^{V} p_i \log_2 p_i, \tag{1}$$

where V is the number of all categories, i is the index of each category, and p_i is the proportion of that category among all.

3.3 Identification of Coordinators in Corpus

Categorization is always the preliminary step before counting. It is worth noting is that studies on coordination usually begin even without a clear definition, such as how it is done in [10]. Chinese linguists have proposed many criteria for distinguishing between conjunctions(/coordinators) and adpositions. Coordinators are also known to be adjacent to ad-sentences[6]. As for a corpus study like this one, an abstract definition is less meaningful than the specific procedure to retrieve the relative terms in a corpus. Yet since the part-of-speech and dependency relation annotations are already done in the treebank, this issue is not of particular relevance to this study. The main issue is to extract the proper information about coordinators from a specific representation. There has been an amount of literature discussing the representation of coordinate constructions in a dependency-grammar context [28, 29]. In the UD annotation scheme, the coordinate construction is represented as follows. The initial coordinand is regarded as the head of the whole construction, while the non-initial coordinands are labelled with the dependency relation conj, all attached to the first coordinand. As for the coordinators, they have the UPOS label "CCONJ" (coordinate conjunction in traditional terminology) and the DEPREL label cc, depending on the head of the corresponding coordinand[7]. Figure 1 contains the graphical representation of the coordinate construction in UD. The example above also shows the case with more than two coordinands. Therefore, in the GSDSimp with UD annotation, we extracted all those marked with UPOS tag "CCONJ" and DEPREL tag "cc" for a double check.

Finally, we found 1943 coordinators in the GSDSimp treebank. By comparing the relative position of a coordinator and its head, i.e., a non-initial coordinand, a preliminary look shows that all the coordinators in Chinese are prepositive without exception

---

[6] By 'ad-sentences' we refer to what are traditionally called 'sentential adverbs' which appear at the front or the end of the sentence, to distinguish it from the true 'ad-verb'.

[7] Note that this representation is adequate for a prespositive language such as English and Chinese, while it might constitute a problem for a postpositive language such as Japanese and Korean. However, since it is not within the concern of the present paper, we will not delve into this issue here.

(including the correlative parts). In UD, the label for the correlative part of a coordinate construction in a prepositive language is cc:preconj. Only one type, 既 *jì*, is inaccurately annotated simply as *cc*, which was excluded from the scope of the study.

3.4 Annotations

To answer the third research question, we annotated the categories of the coordinands. The identification process was automatically done through a VBA code. All the coordinators and coordinands were first extracted. Since the DEPREL of the non-initial coordinand is conj, the syntactic category was therefore decided by means of the DEPREL of the first coordinand.

Then we distinguished between four levels of syntactic categories, i.e., lexical, phrasal and clausal and sentential. No cases of affixal coordination, such as *intra-and cross-linguistic*, are identified in Chinese because there is no auxiliary tool such as hyphen. By sentential coordination, we mean two matrix clauses with full features such as mood and overt linkers (otherwise, those with no covert linkers are annotated with the relation parataxis in UD). As for clausal coordination, we referred to the coordination of subordinate clauses. Phrasal coordination primarily includes VP coordination, NP coordination, and predicate adjectival coordination. Finally, lexical coordination includes the coordination of adnominal adjectives, verbs, adverbs, and auxiliaries.

A problem is that the categories of the coordinands might be different or even non-constituent, which is often reported in the literature [30]. We compared the UPOS label of initial and non-initial coordinands, and only 3.5% (68 out of 1875) are of different categories. This ensures that our method of extraction is effective to a large extent.

4 Results and Discussion

4.1 The Frequencies of Chinese Coordinators

Table 2 shows the frequency distribution of Chinese coordinators, from which much information can be read. First, with regard to the number of each word type, *hé* takes the largest proportion, which corroborates Chao [15] and Zhu [14]'s observation that *hé* is the commonest overt marker in written language, since the genre of GSDSimp is wiki. However, although the corpus investigated is not a spoken one, the number of *gēn* is extremely small, which is close to zero. On the contrary, although Chao claims that *jí* and *yǔ* are archaic usages, the authentic text data shows that they are not really uncommon, at least in written language. It is reasonable since spoken language is generally more formal but they are no doubt part of Contemporary Chinese and do not sound like archaic usage, which is reflected by their high frequencies.

Second, bisyllabic or trisyllabic coordinators are less common than monosyllabic ones. This is manifested in two ways. On the one hand, the proportion of the former is much smaller than the latter on the whole. On the other hand, multisyllabic coordinators generally have monosyllabic counterparts, such as *huòzhě* and *huò* [31], while the former is obviously less frequent than the latter. This phenomenon conforms to the principle of economy [32]. Then why does Chinese need these bisyllabic coordinators

Table 2. The frequencies of coordinators in GSDsimp Chinese treebank

Forms	En	Frequencies	Forms	En	Frequencies
和 hé	And	769	并且 bìngqiě	and	5
及 jí	and	254	比 bǐ	to	5
与 yǔ	and	243	暨 jì	also as	3
并 bìng	and	224	甚至 shènzhì	even	2
或 huò	or	161	连同 liántóng	as well as	2
以及 yǐjí	and	82	而是 érshì	but	2
至 zhì	to	74	又或 yòuhuò	or	1
到 dào	to	28	以至 yǐzhì	so as to	1
或者 huòzhě	or	19	而非 érfēi	but not	1
而 ér	while	14	甚至是 shènzhìshì	even	1
或是 huòshì	or	11	而且 érqiě	and	1
又 yòu	and	8	加 jiā	plus	1
且 qiě	and	8	乃至 nǎizhì	even	1
兼 jiān	also as	7	而又 éryòu	but	1
也 yě	also	7	同 tóng	and	1
还是 háishì	or	5	跟 gēn	and	1

at all? One possible explanation is to think of them and their monosyllabic counterparts as dialectal, stylistic or prosodic variants. For instance, bisyllabic coordinators might express emphatic uses as they are more marked (having more syllables or being longer in terms of the number of syllables) than monosyllabic ones. In addition, a bisyllabic coordinator is more likely to be used as an ad-sentence and followed by a pause for prosodic reasons. Yet such explanations call for further exploration.

Third, the number of *and*-type coordinators is much more than that of *or*-type ones ($1626/197 = 8.25$), which supports Haspelmath [10] and Ohori [23]'s claim. Table 3 shows the distribution of each semantic type of coordinators. The classification is rough and based on word types[8]. Note that the *and*-type can be further divided into two types, since NP conjunction and VP conjunction denote two semantic prototypes (collection formation and logical conjunction) [13]. Also note that a third *but*-type is rare in our sample, of which the reason might be two-fold. In one respect, the sentential *but* is more likely to be encoded as an ad-sentence in Chinese. On the other, an NP adversative use of English *but* is expressed by *érshì* in Chinese, which may indeed have a low function frequency.

In addition, there are several special types of compounding strategy, which are generally ignored in the previous literature on coordinate structures based on the English

---

[8] That is, each word type is assigned one semantic type based on their major usage, regardless of the real context in text.

Table 3. The frequencies of each semantic type of coordinators

Meaning	Frequencies
NP and	1358
VP and	268
or	197
(from) ... to ...	102
also known as	10
even	5
but	3

language. These conclude比 *bǐ*, forming a score in a game, 到 *dào* /至 *zhì*, constituting a range in time or space, and 暨 *jì*/兼 *jiān*, which means 'also known as, also being'. A special use of 又 *yòu* also forms a mixed fraction in mathematics, such as 九又四分之三 *jiǔ yòu sì-fēnzhī-sān* 'nine and three-fourths'[9]. By introspection, an additional type could also be thought of, which is *duì* 对 'versus'. These findings show us more cases of coordination, which were ignored in the literature [10]. In addition, the findings might give us some ideas about the nature of NP conjunction, which might not only be collection formation, but also forming a new concept by conjoining two NPs. This is parallel to the so-call co-compound or natural coordination insofar as the latter is generally marked with a covert coordinator [33]. The findings further support that what is traditionally called coordination is in essence bi-centered [13, 14], and show that the functions around the NP-coordination center are also diverse in themselves.

Finally, from a quantitative and synergetic linguistic perspective, the coordinators constitute a subsystem of the whole lexicon of Chinese. The rank-frequency distribution follows a Zipf-like function [34–36], having a long tail and a number of hapaxes, which behaves like an open category. This is against the general understanding that the coordinator is a closed word class. We infer the result is closely related to the relatively small size of the treebank. If the corpus size goes up to the magnitude of million or more, the number of coordinators will grow rather slowly. In the BCC corpus[10] of Modern Chinese whose size is 15 billion, there are only 219 conjunctions, which contain not only coordinate conjunction, but also the correlative parts and the subordinate conjunctions. In addition, the number of coordinator hapaxes in BCC is also small, which indicates that their nature is not temporarily or newly created words. Zhou [37] has compared several dictionaries and concluded that Zhang [38] contains the most conjunction (194), which also covers both coordinating and subordinating ones. The next section will test how large the group of Chinese coordinators is on earth, especially compared with English coordinators.

---

[9] One example 'Platform Nine and Three-Quarters' is famous in English due to the Harry Potter series.

[10] http://bcc.blcu.edu.cn/.

4.2   The Lexical Richness of Chinese Coordinators

Table 4. The frequencies of coordinators in GUM English treebank

Forms	Frequencies
and	3211
or	483
but	293
&	39
nor	12
yet	6
plus	2
n'	1
slash	1
though	1
versus	1

Next, we compared the lexical richness of coordinators in Chinese and in English. Table 4 shows the frequency distribution of English coordinators. The normalized frequency of overt coordinators in Chinese is 18.3 per thousand words (= 1,943 × 1,000/106,193), about half of that in English (34.5 = 4,050 × 1,000/117,458), while the entropy of Chinese coordinators is 2.856, higher than that of English coordinators (1.026). This result reflects that although there are many items in Chinese with low frequency, the lexical richness of its coordinators is still much higher than that of the English ones[11]. In other words, Chinese has a very large inventory of coordinators, which seems to be larger than what are collected in the literature for most languages[12] [24]. It also supports [39]'s claim that 'languages with a written tradition tend to develop a richer set of conjunctions than languages with an oral tradition', as the Chinese language has a rather long history. The bisyllabic forms in Table 3 originate from the monosyllabic ones over time through the bisyllabification process.

However, although it might be understandable in one sense since Chinese marks different categories by means of different markers, the number is still quite large. For instance, Ohori [23] lists about seven forms of coordinators in Japanese, which is already a large number, while Chinese possesses much more. The number of 32 is larger than that in most languages which distinguish between NP coordination and VP coordination [12, 24]. Does that mean Chinese has a finer classification for distinguishing the syntactic

---

[11] Note that even symbols are counted in for the case of English.

[12] The data of traditional typological research is generally based on reference grammars. They might only enumerate a few examples rather than give the whole list of relevant expressions in that language. Hence in fact we do not have an idea about the whole, clear picture in those languages as the previous research was not conducted on corpora.

categories being coordinated and possesses a dedicated coordinator for each category? We will explore that in the following section.

4.3 The Frequencies of Categories of Coordinands

Table 5. The frequencies of coordinands of each syntactic category

Syntactic Categories	Frequencies
NP	1419
VP	440
A (mod)	40
N (pred)	10
Adv	8
V	7
Subordinate clause	6
A (pred)	5
S	5
Aux	3
Sum	1943

Table 5 first shows the frequencies of each category being coordinated in Chinese. The NP coordination constitutes overwhelmingly the largest part and next follows VP coordination. The rest categories take up only a little of real language use[13]. As we have pointed out, an NP conjunction could be ambiguous. Although the addressor generally intends to express a unique meaning, rather than causing ambiguity, it needs further discerning for the analysts if there are no collective or distributive operators as an auxiliary tool for disambiguition.

It can be noticed that two categories are almost missing. First, there are few adpositional phrase coordinations detected in Chinese despite that we have presupposed the category. One possible reason might be due to the annotation, as many Chinese adpositions are deverbal and might be classified as verbs. Second, there are few cases of sentential coordination in authentic data. A closer look at the data even reveals that even the existent ones might be mis-annotated by the automatic process. In other words, when sentences are combined, the human language tends to either share a common part, or otherwise have a connective with other meanings, such as being causal, adversative, progressive or sequential/simultaneous in time. These markers are generally realized as

---

[13] Yet this does not mean the true occurrences of other kinds are that rare, since we only consider coordination with overt markers in the present study. The coordination of adjectives, for instance, might tend to employ the juxtaposition strategy or with the help of commas as an orthographically auxiliary way.

sentential adverbs in Chinese, which fall out of the scope of our definition for coordinators. Those which simply express logical, truth-conditional conjunction are rare, as they might be overridden by other markers. The cases of coordination of all other categories than the collective reading of NP coordination seem to be prepared for ellipsis and sharing. This has to do with economy, i.e., to avoid repeating the same wording, abiding by Zipf's Principle of Least Effort [32]. The shared part could be either topics, generally realized as NPs, or simply a string of words, or even non-constituents.

Table 6. The cross-tabulation of coordinators and coordinand categories

	NP	VP	Amod	Clause	V	S	Aux	Adv	Npred	Apred	Sum
hé	693	56	11	1	1	1	1	1	4	0	769
Jí	211	29	9	2	1	1	0	0	1	0	254
yǔ	218	18	3	0	2	0	0	1	1	0	243
bìng	2	219	0	0	1	2	0	0	0	0	224
huò	101	41	8	1	1	0	1	3	1	4	161
yǐjí	61	17	0	2	1	1	0	0	0	0	82
zhì	70	2	1	0	0	0	0	0	1	0	74
dào	25	3	0	0	0	0	0	0	0	0	28
huòzhě	4	14	0	0	0	0	0	0	1	0	19
ér	0	9	5	0	0	0	0	0	0	0	14
huòshì	5	6	0	0	0	0	0	0	0	0	11
yòu	0	6	1	0	0	0	0	1	0	0	8
qiě	0	5	2	0	0	0	1	0	0	0	8
jiān	7	0	0	0	0	0	0	0	0	0	7
yě	0	6	0	0	0	0	0	0	0	1	7
bìngqiě	0	5	0	0	0	0	0	0	0	0	5
háishì	2	2	0	0	0	0	0	0	1	0	5
bǐ	4	0	0	0	0	0	0	1	0	0	5
Jì	3	0	0	0	0	0	0	0	0	0	3
érshì	1	1	0	0	0	0	0	0	0	0	2
liántóng	2	0	0	0	0	0	0	0	0	0	2
shènzhì	2	0	0	0	0	0	0	0	0	0	2
nǎizhì	1	0	0	0	0	0	0	0	0	0	1
érfēi	1	0	0	0	0	0	0	0	0	0	1
yǐzhì	1	0	0	0	0	0	0	0	0	0	1
éryòu	0	0	0	0	0	0	0	1	0	0	1
jiā	1	0	0	0	0	0	0	0	0	0	1

(*continued*)

Table 6. (*continued*)

	NP	VP	Amod	Clause	V	S	Aux	Adv	Npred	Apred	Sum
tóng	1	0	0	0	0	0	0	0	0	0	1
gēn	1	0	0	0	0	0	0	0	0	0	1
Shènzhìshì	1	0	0	0	0	0	0	0	0	0	1
yòuhuò	1	0	0	0	0	0	0	0	0	0	1
érqiě	0	1	0	0	0	0	0	0	0	0	1
Sum	1419	440	40	6	7	5	3	8	10	5	1943

Next, we do a cross-tabulation between coordinators and coordinand categories (Table 6). For those whose frequencies are over 80, *hé*, *jí*, *yǔ* and *yǐjí* are primarily used with NP coordination, while *bìng* shows a strong tendency for being used with VP coordination. *Huò*, as a special case, has a relatively more balanced proportion of two uses, which implies that disjunction is Chinese do not distinguish between NP and VP coordination. None of the other categories has its own dedicated coordinators. On the one hand, it might be due to the corpus size which is not big enough. On the other, some have been noticed in the literature [15] but are correlative (又... 又... *yòu* ... *yòu* ...), so they are excluded here.

To summarize, although Chinese has a large inventory of coordinators, some of them conjoin the same categories, which means that we have excluded one possibility that the various coordinators, especially those of *and*-type, are dedicated to conjoining each category. In other words, the differences between these forms must lie in other dimensions, which are left for future studies.

5 Conclusions

The present study used a dependency-annotated Chinese treebank GSDSimp under the Universal Dependencies (UD) initiative to investigate several quantitative aspects Chinese coordinators. We found that: (1) At the micro level, *hé* is the most frequent overt coordinator in Written Chinese, followed by *jí*, *yǔ*, *bìng*, *huò*. *Gēn* is extremely infrequent despite its reported commonality in the literature. Several types are NP coordinations are ignored previously in the literature, which forms complex concepts. (2) At the macro level, Chinese has a rather large inventory of coordinators, which is much more diverse at least compared with that in English. (3) For the syntactic categories of coordinands, the NP coordination constitutes the largest part and next follows the VP coordination. The number of coordinations of other categories with overt markers in Chinese is small. Specifically, adpositional and sentential coordination are rarely found in Chinese. In addition, it is not that each category has a dedicated marker despite the large inventory of coordinators in Chinese. For the counterparts of *and*-type in English, four markers (*hé*, *jí*, *yǔ*, and *yǐjí*) are used most for NP coordination and one (*bìng*) for VP coordination. The *or*-type marker, *huò*, has a relatively more balanced distribution. Finally, other types do not have dedicated markers.

We conclude that the definition of coordination has been perplexed by two factors. On the one hand, it is affected by the logical use of 'conjunction', which however is often overridden by other semantic relations between propositions or states of affairs and rarely marked by *and*-forms in natural language expressions. On the other hand, the English colexification of the prototypical uses of *and*, *or*, *but* and other functions also contributes to the confusion of the problem. These all lead us to have another thought about the nature of coordination. Our results support the view that the coordination as traditionally understood has at least two functional prototypes. On one aspect, traditional so-called coordination denotes the formation of new concepts, while on another, it denotes the sharing and ellipsis of at least some words in a pure surface-textual sense to reach the economy of linguistic production.

Hopefully, this study has paved steady ways for future studies. For instance, since there are at least four frequent NP coordinators, the next step might also take into consideration other factors to explain their difference in usage, such as formality, the number and the length of the coordinands. Asyndetic and correlative coordination are also worth investigating with the help of treebanks in the future.

Acknowledgment. This research was funded by the National Social Science Foundation in China (Grant No. 20CYY030).

References

1. Lü, S.: Issues in Analyzing Chinese Grammar. The Commercial Press, Beijing (1979). (in Chinese)
2. Quirk, R., Greenbaum, S., Leech, G., Svartvik, J.: A Comprehensive Grammar of the English Language. Longman, London (1985)
3. Zhang, J., Tao, H.: On combinatory coordinators. Chin. Lang. Learn. 50–52 (1993) (in Chinese)
4. Zhang, Y.: The differentiation between comitative phrases and prepositional-conjunctions. Stud. Chin. Lang. 330–338 (1996) (in Chinese)
5. Liu, J.: On the development of *hé*, as well as *gòng* and *lián*. Stud. Chin. Lang. 447–453 (1989) (in Chinese)
6. Yu, J.: A historical investigation into the *hé*-words in modern chinese. Stud. Chin. Lang. 457–464 (1996) (in Chinese)
7. Peng, X., Zhao, M.: Investigating the usage of conjunction *bìng*. J. Jinan Univ. (Humanit. Soc. Sci.) 107–111 (2004) (in Chinese)
8. Grover, C.: Coordination. In: Asher, R.E., Simpson, J.M.Y. (eds.) The Encyclopedia of Language and Linguistics, pp. 762–768. Pergamon Press, New York (1994)
9. Crysmann, B.: Coordination. In: Brown, K. (ed.) The Encyclopedia of Language and Linguistics (2nd ed.), pp. 183–196. Elsevier, New York (2006)
10. Haspelmath, M.: Coordinating constructions: an overview. In: Haspelmath, M. (ed.) Coordinating Constructions, pp. 3–39. John Benjamins, Amsterdam (2004)
11. Haspelmath, M.: Coordination. In: Shopen, T. (ed.) Language Typology and Syntactic Description (2nd ed.) (Vol. II) Complex Construction, pp. 1–51. Cambridge University Press, Cambridge (2007)
12. Haspelmath, M.: Nominal and verbal conjunction. In: Dryer, M.S., Haspelmath, M. (eds.) The World Atlas of Language Structures Online. Max Planck Institute for Evolutionary Anthropology, Leipzig (Available online at http://wals.info/chapter/64, Accessed 14 Jan 2022

13. Yih, T.S.: Vertex-weighted semantic map: a study of coordination constructions based on the corpus of Mandarin, Shanghainese and English. Master thesis, Shanghai International Studies University (2019) (in Chinese)
14. Zhu, D.: Lectures on Grammar. The Commercial Press, Beijing (1982). (in Chinese)
15. Chao, Y.-R.: A Grammar of Spoken Chinese. University of California Press, Berkeley (1968)
16. Li, Z.: The Typological Studies on Coordinate Constructions. The Commercial Press, Beijing (2019). (in Chinese)
17. Li, J., Liu, S.: Coordinative Phrases and Coordinative Complex Sentences. Shanghai Educational Publishing House (1958/1985) (in Chinese)
18. Meng, F.: The *Hé*-structure in the subject position revisited. In: Hong, J.-F., Zhang, Y., Liu, P. (eds.) CLSW 2019. LNCS (LNAI), vol. 11831, pp. 776–787. Springer, Cham (2020)
19. Wei, M., Zhang, G., Zhou, Q., Wang, Y., Huang, H.: Statistics and analysis of coordination structures in patent text. In: Su, X., He, T. (eds.) CLSW 2014. LNCS (LNAI), vol. 8922, pp. 380–389. Springer, Cham (2014)
20. Zheng, W., Cao, W.: A quantitative investigation of the distribution of coordinators in Shuihuzhuan. J. Changshu Inst. Technol. (Philos. & Soc. Sci.) 94–98 (2007) (in Chinese)
21. Li, Z., Jin, L.: A typological study of coordinators. Minor. Lang. China 23–31 (2012) (in Chinese)
22. Jing-Schmidt, Z., Peng, X.: The emergence of disjunction: a history of constructionalization in Chinese. Cogn. Linguis. **27**, 101–136 (2016)
23. Ohori, T.: Coordination in mentalese. In: Haspelmath, M. (ed.) Coordinating Constructions, pp. 41–66. John Benjamins Publishing Company, Amsterdam (2004)
24. Mauri, C.: Coordination Relations in the Languages of Europe and Beyond. Mouton de Gruyter, Berlin, New York (2008)
25. Stassen, L.: And-languages and with-languages. Linguist. Typology **4**, 1–54 (2000)
26. Stassen, L.: Noun phrase conjunction. In: Dryer, M.S., Haspelmath, M. (eds.) The World Atlas of Language Structures Online. Max Planck Institute for Evolutionary Anthropology, Leipzig (Available online at http://wals.info/chapter/63, (2013). Accessed 14 Jan 2022
27. Popescu, I.-I., Mačutek, J., Altmann, G.: Aspects of Word Frequencies. RAM Verlag, Lüdenscheid (2009)
28. Zhao, Y.: Study on automatic parsing of coordination structure in contemporary Chinese. Master thesis, Communication University of China (2008) (in Chinese)
29. Popel, M., Mareček, D., Štěpánek, J., Zeman, D., Žabokrtský, Z. Coordination structures in dependency treebanks. In: Proceedings of the 51st Annual Meeting of the Association for Computational Linguistics, pp. 517 527 (2013)
30. Patejuk, A., Przepiórkowski, A.: Coordination of unlike grammatical functions. In: DepLing, SyntaxFest, pp. 26–37 (2019)
31. Lü, S.: 800 Words in Modern Chinese. The Commercial Press, Beijing (1980). (in Chinese)
32. Zipf, G.: Human Behavior and the Principle of Least Effort. Addison-Wesley Press, Cambridge (1949)
33. Wälchli, B.: Co-Compounds and Natural Coordination. Oxford University Press (2005)
34. Liu, H.: An Introduction to Quantitative Linguistics. The Commercial Press, Beijing (2017). (in Chinese)
35. Dulan, D.: A study of the polysemy distribution of mongolian. In: Liu, M., Kit, C., Qi, S. (eds.) Chinese Lexical Semantics: 21st Workshop, CLSW 2020, Hong Kong, China, May 28–30, 2020, Revised Selected Papers, pp. 473–481. Springer International Publishing, Cham (2021)
36. Yan, J., Liu, H.: Quantitative analysis of Chinese and English verb valencies based on probabilistic valency pattern theory. In: Dong, M., Yanhui, G., Hong, J.-F. (eds.) Chinese Lexical Semantics: 22nd Workshop, CLSW 2021, Nanjing, China, May 15–16, 2021, Revised Selected Papers, Part II, pp. 152–162. Springer International Publishing, Cham (2022)

37. Zhou, G.: Conjunctions and Related Issues. Anhui Educational Publishing House (2001) (in Chinese)
38. Zhang, B.: A Dictionary of Functional Words in Contemporary Chinese. The Commercial Press, Beijing (2001). (in Chinese)
39. Mauri, C.: Conjunctions. In: Oxford Bibliographies (2017)

Frequency in Chinese Ballad Song Lyrics: A Quantitative Morpheme-Based Study

Xiaojin Zhang[1] ⓘ and Zheyuan Dai[2(✉)] ⓘ

[1] Department of Foreign Languages, North Minzu University, Ningxia 750000, China
[2] College of Foreign Languages, Zhejiang University of Technology, Xihu District, Hangzhou, China
zydai@zju.edu.cn

Abstract. The present study aims to study the non-material heritage – Chinese ballad song lyrics (*Hua'er*) – from the perspective of frequency distribution and the inner structure of the content words as well as the rhymed morphemes. The results yield, first of all, that the rank-frequency of both vocabularies and phonemes in Chinese prosody words can be well captured by the right-truncated modified Zipf-Alekseev distribution. Second, the autosemantics of *Hua'er* vividly depict the local customs and practices of Northwest China. Third, the two most frequently used Chinese compound finals are /an/ and /ɑŋ/. Apart from qualitative analysis, our quantitative study on the content words and phonemes also provides new insight into the field of heritage folk literature.

Keywords: Chinese ballad song lyrics · Quantitative linguistics · Digital humanities · Frequency distribution · Autosemantics · Rhymed morphemes

1 Introduction

Hua'er, a genre of Chinese folksongs in the regions along the Silk Road, has a unique artistic feature that is formed under its unique geographical environment, regional culture, and regional historical inheritance. From the perspective of folk literature, it is a collection of works by many people, and the authors of most works are unknown. Interestingly, it has been hailed as 'the soul of Northwest China', 'the Book of Songs in the Northwest'. Such ballads are registered on the intangible cultural heritage list by UNESCO because of their authentic and oral features in 2009.

Many studies focused on offering qualitative descriptions, concentrating on the analysis of *Hua'er's* classification [1] and origins [2], etc. Having been passed down from generation to generation, *Hua'er* were composed in the countryside by the peasants who sing spontaneously of their daily life and customs, thoughts, and emotions. As for the content, *Hua'er* is rich as it conveys different people's views on social life from house chores, personal emotions, seasonal and traditional festival activities as well as events concerning marriage and life in general. Moreover, as Dégh claims [3: 43], the interchange of the inherited and the cultural elements resulted in the creation of a new version of the national culture. In other words, the national pride was catered to through

Q. Su et al. (Eds.): CLSW 2022, LNAI 13496, pp. 83–95, 2023.
https://doi.org/10.1007/978-3-031-28956-9_7

the definition, propagation, and perpetuation of ethnic values. All in all, as a genre, the theme of *Hua'er* places emphasis on everyday life. To this end, learning the content words may assist in understanding the inner worlds of both the daily lives of ordinary people and ethnic values.

However, some researchers claimed that experts at *Hua'er* faced the challenge of lacking interdisciplinary research in this literary domain [4]. As a breakthrough, Zhang and Liu [5] investigated the quantitative properties of ballad songs along the Silk Road *Hua'er*. Also, they quantitatively studied the color use and color preference of Chinese folksongs, yielding that the self-organization property of the language system plays a role in the selection of color [6]. The previous research also exemplifies the feasibility of quantitatively investigating Chinese ballad songs. For instance, Lin and Liu [7] explored the Chinese Zhuang folksongs by calculating word frequency and found the interrelation between the words and their folk culture.

Ballad songs have the characteristics of being orally traditional. It is thus necessary to explore the rhythmic features, which can be viewed as one of the important mediums for the expression of semantics and cultural connotations. Put simply, rhymes are one of the important factors in the appreciation of literature work. Folksong carries the process of singing which usually occurred without a particular aesthetic objective like the poets and without printed text. Presently, although the repertoire of the *Hua'er* is rather a field of folklore music, the choral tradition has to some extent influenced the overall classical poems production. To this end, the phoneme system is critical in interpreting the poetic aesthetics of the special genre of Chinese *Hua'er*. There have been studies focusing on the quantitative features of Chinese poetic literature. Liu and Pan [8] compared the rhythmic features of Chinese new poetry to Shakespeare's sonnet by extracting the frequency of rhymed morphemes. Though confined to rhymed words, Zhang and Liu [5] provided evidence of increasing disyllables of Chinese folksongs. Phoneme frequency is viewed as being the usual way to capture the phonic phenomena in texts. Moreover, former research on the statistical properties of phonemes in different languages [9–12] has been conducted to investigate not only the frequency of phonemes, and the relations between vowels and consonants, but also the distinctive phonetic features of the given languages as in English, Czech and Slovak. Fry and Denes [13, 14] have well demonstrated that the statistical information of phonemes is indispensable to speech-related technology. In terms of frequency of occurrences and statistical models for frequency distribution, a study of statistical properties of phonemes in Standard Chinese from Deng [15] reports that vowels and nasals are used most frequently and that the top three vowels in Chinese speeches are: /i4/, /a4/ and /ə2/. The previous research sheds light on the quantitative comparison between Chinese ballad songs and foreign songs, which might be helpful to the quantitative investigation into poetic texts and literary studies.

The goal of quantitative linguistics is to discover the underlying language laws and then explore the mechanisms of the language system [9, 16–18]. Popescu et al. [19] applied quantitative parameters to investigate 143 poetry texts by Romanian poet Mihai Eminescu mainly on phonemes and words. Liu and Huang [17] measured the quantitative features of the Chinese pinyin system with POS distribution of the frequency. Moreover, the distribution of the use of the imagery of classic Chinese Tang poems has been verified as conforming to Zipf's law, a long-tail distribution [20]. Above the phonemic level, the corpus-based investigation into the comparison of Tang, Song, Yuan, Ming, and Qing reported the exponential property increases and the declined tendency of the power-law function [21]. Their study mainly focused on compound words and single-character words. Thus, it might be necessary to explore other text genres in Chinese. As mentioned before, though Zhang and Liu [5]'s research quantitatively investigated the color used in *Hua'er*, they have not touched upon content words. Moreover, the question of whether and how frequency distribution reflects the inner phonemic structural features, however, has not been addressed yet. Applying quantitative methods to the study of *Hua'er* may assist in discovering the underlying language laws, and then in exploring the mechanisms of the language system of *Hua'er* [9, 16, 17].

In order to investigate the quantitative properties related to frequency in Chinese poetic texts, we focus on the following three research questions:

(1) What are the features of the content words in Chinese *Hua'er*?
(2) Do the rank-frequency of vocabularies and rhymed morphemes of Chinese *Hua'er* conform to certain linguistic laws?
(3) What are the most frequently used rhymed morphemes in Chinese *Hua'er*?

Our study has implications for quantitative poetic studies and literary research. Based on the quantitative measurement on the level of autosemantics and rhymed morphemes, the findings are beneficial to developing more effective techniques in the analysis of ballads.

The remainder of this paper is organized as follows: Sect. 2 introduces the materials. We present an example of *Hua'er*, which is the key object of analysis in the present paper. In addition, the research methods employed are also presented. Section 3 presents the results and relevant discussion. Specifically, Sect. 3.1 answers question (1) with special attention payed to content words, and Sect. 3.2 focuses on quantitative features of rhymed morphemes of the selected *Hua'er*. At last, Sect. 4 goes with the conclusion.

2 Materials and Method

In the present study, we built a corpus of around 90 *Hua'er* texts (word count: 38633) based on the research in the *General Theory of Chinese Hua'er* [22]. For a better understanding of the ballad songs, we first present an example of *Hua'er* with its Chinese character form, translation, pinyin and phonemes as follows:

Word frequency has been testified as effective in various aspects of linguistic research [23, 24]. For the analysis of the content words, the h-point was calculated on the basis of word frequency. H-point was first introduced into linguistics within Popescu's work [25]. It marks the moment that the rank of a certain word equals its occurrence if we rank the word frequencies of a text in descending order. The computation of the h-point can be expressed as follows:

$$h = \begin{cases} r_i & , \ r = f(r_i) \\ \frac{f(r_i)r_{i+1} - f(r_{i+1})r_i}{r_{i+1} - r_i + f(r_i) - f(r_{i+1})} & , \ r \neq f(r_i) \end{cases} \quad (1)$$

Table 1. An Example of *Hua'er*

	Verse line 1	Verse line 2	Verse line 3	Verse line 4
Character form	诸葛亮/摆/了/个/八卦阵	不/知道/是/阴阵/吗/阳阵?	二/阿哥/充军/去/当兵	不/知道/是/步兵/吗/马兵?
Translation	Zhuge Liang sets up the military tactics of the eight trigrams	We couldn't understand the military tactics	My dear boyfriend attends in the army	Is he a soldier on foot or riding on a horse?
Pinyin	/zhū'gě/ /liàng/ /bǎi/ /le/ /gè/ /bā'guà'zhèn/	/bù/ /zhī'dào/ /shì/ /yīn'zhèn/ /ma/ /yáng'zhèn/	/èr/ /ā'gē/ /chōng'jūn/ /qù/ /dāng'bīng/	/bù/ /zhī'dào/ /shì/ /bù'bīng/ /ma/ /mǎ'bīng/
Phonemes	/ts/ /x/ /u/ /k/ /ɣ/ /l/ /i/ /A̠/ /n/ /g/ /b/ /A̠/ /i/ /l/ /ɣ/ /k/ /ɣ/ /b/ /A̠/ /k/ /u/ /A̠/ /ts/ /x/ /ɣ/ /n/	/b/ /u/ /ts/ /x/ /i/ /d/ /A̠/ /o/ /s/ /x/ i/ /j/ /i/ /n/ /ts/ /x/ /x/ /ɣ/ /n/ /m/ /A̠/ /j/ /A̠/ /n/ /k/ /ts/ /x / /ɣ/ /n/	/ɣ/ / z̠/ /A̠/ /k/ /ɣ/ /ts/ /x/ /o/ /n/ /k/ /j/ /u/ /n/ /q/ /u/ /n/ /d/ /A̠/ /n/ /k/ /b/ /i/ /n/ /k/	/b/ /u/ /ts/ /x/ /i/ /d/ /A̠/ /o/ s/ /x/ /i/ /b/ /u/ /b/ /i/ /n/ /k/ m/ /A̠/ /m/ /A̠/ /b/ /i/ /n/ /k/

H-point fuzzily functions as the cut-off boundary of so-called frequent synsemantics (i.e., pronouns, participles, prepositions, and articles), and autosemantics (i.e., nouns, adjectives, and adverbs) [26]. In this paper, autosemantic words appearing before the *h*-point always play the role of bearers of textual themes. Therefore, only autosemantics are taken into consideration.

As for the rhymed features, based on the self-built corpus, phoneme frequency was extracted and computerized. For the vocalic assonance patterns in Chinese ballad texts, we selected the vocalic phonemes: /a/, /o/, /ə/, /i/, /u/, /y/. To meet the purpose of our investigation, we added two phonemes: /n/ and /ŋ/ that assist in the rhyme expression of Chinese folk songs. Following Popescu's study in 2015 [19], we then tested the individual phoneme cell by calculating *u*, the quantile of the standard normal distribution N(0,1). The *u* values functions similarly as *p* values in a two-sided test. Performing the test for each phoneme of *Hua'er*, we took the value of $u = 1.96$ as a boundary (which is adopted in [19]), corresponding to $p = 0.05$. If $u \geq 1.96$, the text is thought to have a significant pattern. Formula (2) below shows the computation method of *u* values.

$$u = \frac{n_{ij} - \frac{n_i n_j}{n}}{\sqrt{\frac{n_i n_j (n - n_i)(n - n_j)}{n^2 (n-1)}}} \tag{2}$$

The selected phonemes were arranged in an 8×8 contingency table for various combinations (i, j) of Chinese compound finals (See Table 5 in Sect. 3.2). As formula (2) shows, n_{ij} is the frequency in cell (i, j), n_i the sum of row i, n_j the sum of column j, and n the total sum. The expression $n_i n_j / n$ is the expectation for the cell (i, j), and the expression in the denominator is the standard deviation in the cell (i, j). In all, if the *u* value of the tested (i, j) is greater than 1.96, then the frequency of the tested compound finals is significantly high among all the combinations.

3   Results and Discussion

In this section, based on the self-built corpus, in accordance with the data, rank-frequency distribution of content words, frequency of phonemes and compound finals are extracted and then computerized in the present paper.

3.1   Vocabulary Distribution and Content Words

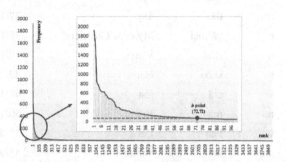

Fig. 1. Rank-Frequency Distribution of Vocabularies in *Hua'er*

    Figure 1 demonstrates the rank-frequency distribution of vocabularies in our self-built *Hua'er* corpus. The x-axis refers to the ranks of vocabularies, and the y-axis is the corresponding frequencies of the vocabularies. The small figure within Fig. 1 shows the enlarged detail, especially the *h*-point where the rank equals the frequency, of the distribution. The distribution of the frequency conforms to the Zipf's Law [27, 28], a long-tailed power-law distribution, indicating that the words of *Hua'er* have reached a balance of homogeneity and diversity in the production of the ballad songs. What's more, the distribution is neither excessively concentrated nor overly dispersed, indiacting that the development of the folk song has its unique "procedural mechanism". Figure 1 also presents the *h*-point of the distribution. As shown in Table 2, content words appearing before the *h*-point would be viewed as autosemantics that bear the themes of the texts.

Table 2. Autosemantics Before *H*-Point in *Hua'er*

Autosemantics	POS	Pinyin	Meaning	Rank/frequency
尕	adj	gǎ	Little (with intimacy)	17/304
阿哥	n	ā'gē	My dear boyfriend	20/249
心	n	xīn	Heart	21/245
花儿	n	huā'er	Hua'er	22/242
想	v	xiǎng	Miss	24/225
人	n	rén	People	25/219

(continued)

Table 2. (*continued*)

Autosemantics	POS	Pinyin	Meaning	Rank/frequency
好	adj	hǎo	Good	27/191
山	n	shān	Mountain	28/190
唱	v	chàng	Sing	29/177
走	v	zǒu	Walk	33/161
花	n	huā	Flower	36/146
天	n	tiān	Sky	37/145
尕妹	n	gǎ'mèi	My dear Girlfriend	38/136
水	n	shuǐ	Water	39/135
手	n	shǒu	Hand	42/123
吃	v	chī	Eat	47/111
马	n	mǎ	Horse	50/102
看	v	kàn	Look	53/99
白	adj	bái	White	55/95
说	v	shuō	Say	56/95
见	v	jiàn	See	57/93
红	adj	hóng	Red	58/89
家	n	jiā	Home	62/83
妹妹	n	mèi'mèi	My beloved	63/82
话	n	huà	Word	66/81
路	n	lù	Road	72/72

Words and their cultural symbols tell each other their history and present. As a genre, the theme of *Hua'er* puts emphasis on everyday life, singing the inner words of ordinary people. The content of *Hua'er* is rich as it conveys different people's perspectives on the social life from farmers, workers, house chores, personal emotions, seasonal and traditional festival activities as well as people's views and events concerning marriage and life in general. As Table 2 shows, the autosemantics appearing before the *h*-point helps to present a lively scroll of the grand natural scenery of the Chinese Northwest. 山 *shān* (mountain), 天 *tiān* (sky) and 水 *shuǐ* (water) are the main natural elements of the Chinese Northwest landscape. The expanse of natural scenery paints the basic color of the scroll, offering space for other related elements. For instance, rolling mountains and mighty rivers make local transportation inconvenient, 马 *mǎ* (horse) becomes one of the important means of transportation. As a saying goes, the mountain dweller lives off the mountain. Village life in the Northwest is an integrated part of farming civilization. 马 *mǎ* (horse) thus also shoulders the responsibility of being helpers of nomads in the Northwest. As a means for interpreting feelings and transmitting messages; in the meantime, the folksongs in fact strengthen the national identity. Wu [22: 339] strongly believed that *Hua'er* reflects the history and reality of ethnic minority groups while singing and transmitting in a way that can be credited as an encyclopedia of folk customs, history, and culture of Northwest China. In all, nature worship expressed through *Hua'er* is deeply engraved in the local souls, demonstrating the harmony between humans and environments.

Folksongs are artistic expressions that are widely used by working people to convey their understanding of nature as well as life. In the preindustrial traditional society, folksongs formed a part of the social communicating system in the community, in the field of folklore, thus its original intangible cultural value functions to tie the traditional rites. Therefore, the cultural connotation of *Hua'er* also penetrates all aspects of social life. Seemingly distinct from classical poetry, *Hua'er* contains its literary charm in metaphorical technique. "Bixing", a metaphor widely employed in the ancient *The Book of Songs*, plays a common but significant role in the creation process of *Hua'er* [29]. 花儿 (*Hua'er*), with an r-colored vowel, is a peculiar pronunciation phenomenon in the oral Chinese dialect. *Hua'er*, as its Chinese character 花儿 reveals, it means flowers at first glance. People of different ethnic groups shared its beautiful music, like Hui, Baoan, Dongxiang, Yugu, Salar, Tu, Zang, Meng, and Han, where the boys and men usually refer to beautiful girls and women who catch their fancy as Hua'er [30: 33]. In a word, it is a metaphor for young beautiful maidens in hometowns and naturally, and it is acknowledged that the name Hua'er is nicknamed by a male for a female he is in love with and intends to pursue. 花儿 *Hua'er* and 少年 *Shaonian* denote the ceaseless passion of a man in pursuit of love at his golden age. It is noted that this pair of using the names has gone beyond the highlighting the stunning beauty of a particular young girl [30: 33]. The vast landscape refers to not only the nature scene but also the hardships and obstacles that lie ahead of the lovers. "人在山西河南哩, 心在花儿门前哩" (I am in the west of the mountain and the south of the river, while the place my lover lives is where my heart belongs.)The geographical limitation promotes the lovesickness between lovers more prosperous. Though thousands of miles apart, the two hearts in love stay close. According to Wu [22: 153], the majority of the traditional *Hua'er* songs collected in Northwest China fall into the category of love songs or romantic *Hua'er*. Apart from telling lovesickness through Bixing euphemistically, the outspoken characteristics of Northwesterners also shape the straightforward way of expression. 想 *xiǎng* (miss) is the most frequent verb in *Hua'er*, which directly describes the romance between the young lovers. 尕 *gǎ* (little), an adjective that depicts an intimate relationship, is a typical dialect at Loess Plateau. 尕妹 *gǎmèi* (my dear girlfriend) and 阿哥 *āgē* (my dear boyfriend), the callings singing the song of love revolve around the sky and earth in the northwest, expressing the fiery love straightforwardly.

3.2 Phoneme Distribution and Rhymed Morphemes

As mentioned in the introduction, rhymed features are critical to the poetic interpretation. As an indispensable component of a language, the phonemic system also features self-organization and the usage of a phoneme is always in a cooperative process with other linguistic properties [31: 761–763]. The phoneme distribution is one of the important ways that may capture the features of poetic texts. Previous studies on phoneme structures have applied a number of models, including the Zipf function/distribution [5, 6, 8, 19].

The rank frequency of Chinese phonemes is listed according to vowel and consonant occurrence in the morphemes of the *Hua'er*. Figure 2 demonstrates the matrix of the four figures fitting each individual verse line to the right-truncated modified Zipf-Alekseev distribution. R^2 refers to the goodness of fit of the rank-frequency distribution to a certain law. What is worth mentioning is that the right-truncated modified Zipf-Alekseev distribution has been testified as being effective in capturing features of various linguistic units [32, 33]. As can be seen from Table 3, therefore, the fitted right-truncated modified Zipf-Alekseev distribution curves can capture the frequency of the phonemes in each verse line of our example in Table 1, especially for the verse line 3.

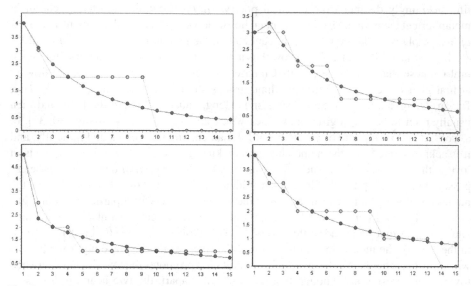

Fig. 2. Matrix of the Four Figures of Fitting the Right-Truncated Modified Zipf-Alekseev Distribution to Each Individual Verse Line

Table 3. Parameters of Fitting the Right-Truncated Modified Zipf-Alekseev Distribution to Individual Lines of the Example

	Verse line 1	Verse line 2	Verse line 3	Verse line 4
a	0.0204	0.3009	0.1703	0.2654
b	0.2861	0.1472	0.1157	0.1299
R^2	0.7585	0.8923	0.9298	0.8340

The single phoneme could be combined to form a single final and compound final in the Chinese pinyin system. Thus, the word length would vary the phoneme segmentation of Chinese words. Wei and Qiu [34] have examined the quantitative relation between the number of senses of polysyllabic words and their word length. Moreover, word length has been measured in terms of syllable numbers and phoneme numbers in Altmann's

2016 study [35]. The following phoneme segmentations shown in Table 4 turn out to be different from the phonemes in Table 1.

Table 4. Phoneme Segmentations of the Example of *Hua'er*

	Verse line 1	Verse line 2	Verse line 3	Verse line 4
Phoneme segmentations	/tʂu/ /kə/ /liaŋ/ /bai/ /lə/ /kə/ /ba/ /kuɑ/ /tʂən/	/bu/ /tʂi/ /dɑu/ /ʂʻi/ /jin/ /tʂən/ /ma/ /jaŋ/ /tʂən/	/era/ /kə/ /tʂʻuŋ/ /juən/ /tɕʻy/ /dɑŋ/ /biŋ/	/bu/ /tʂi/ /dɑu/ /ʂʻ i/ /bu/ /biŋ/ /ma/ /ma/ /biŋ/

Fitting the right-truncated modified Zipf-Alekseev distribution to the rank-frequency of phoneme segmentations in the above four lines, the R^2 is 0.9220 with a value of 0.0233 and b value of 0.0367, demonstrating a high level of goodness of fit. Figure 3 presents the fitted results.

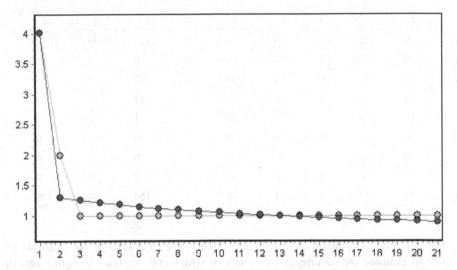

Fig. 3. Fitting the Right-Truncated Modified Zipf-Alekseev Distribution to phoneme sequences of *Hua'er*

The Principle of Least Effort proposed by Zipf explains the minimization of the production effort of *Hua'er* [28]. Human beings tend to choose phonemes that are frequently used. Zhang and Liu [5] also fitted the frequency and probability of words in *Hua'er* with a report on the phenomenon of two-character finals in *Hua'er*, which is also typically in line with the development of modern Chinese characters. Besides, the fitting results confirm the former research, that is, the linguistic features of both the phonemes and the phoneme segmentations of Hua'er can be well captured by the right-truncated modified Zipf-Alekseev distribution. As an indispensable component of a language, the phoneme system also features self-organization and self-regulation, and the usage of a phoneme is always in a cooperative process with other linguistic properties [31].

As mentioned in the introduction, in terms of the frequency of occurrences and statistical models for frequency distribution, a study of statistical properties of phonemes in Standard Chinese from Deng [15] reports that vowels and nasals are used most frequently. For the investigation of vocalic assonance patterns in Chinese poetic texts, we observe the transitions of vowels form in an 8×8 contingency table in the Table 5, which presents the frequency of compound finals the example of *Hua'er* in Table 1. We use the vocalic phonemes: /a/, /o/, /ə/, /i/, /u/, /y/, for the expected assonance distribution, and add another two phonemes: /n/ and /iŋ/ for the purpose of our investigation. The selected six vowels and two consonants could be combined to form different compound finals in Chinese. As mentioned in the introduction, Deng [15] also reports that the top three vowels in Chinese speeches are: /i4/, /a4/ and /ə2/. Our research further finds another two frequently occurring compound finals in Chinese prosody words are /an/ and /aŋ/ with a frequency of 123 and 49, respectively (see Table 5).

Table 5. Frequency of compound finals in the example of *Hua'er*

	a	o	ə	i	u	y	n	ŋ	n_i
a	0	32	0	28	0	0	123	49	232
o	0	0	0	0	28	0	0	0	28
ə	0	0	0	22	0	0	12	9	43
i	14	0	5	0	6	0	14	16	55
u	17	3	2	7	0	0	1	0	30
y	0	0	0	0	0	0	0	0	0
n	0	0	0	0	0	0	0	0	0
ŋ	0	0	0	0	0	0	0	0	0
n_j	31	35	7	57	34	0	150	74	388

We continue to compute the u values of each compound final in our example of *Hua'er* to examine the occurrence frequency of which combinations is significant. In Fig. 4, the u values of /ao/, /ou/, /ai/, /an/, /aŋ/ are greater than 1.96, which means these phoneme combinations are significant pattern. Popescu et al. [19] view the assonance as reminding of an echo, a repetition of a sound sequence in another position of the poem, which may play a certain euphonic role in poetry. Deng [15] also finds that standard Chinese shows a preference for articulation at the back of the tone. The employment of compound finals in *Hua'er* may indicate that though people who produced and sang *Hua'er* might not receive formal training, in the process of production, to pursue the poetic expressions and euphonic experience, they will automatically be affected by its internal mechanism of using content words, as well as rhymed morphemes. To sum up, the phoneme-based study presents two discoveries of Chinses *Hua'er*: First, for phoneme frequency and word frequency, the right-truncated modified Zipf-Alekseev distribution fit them well. Second, Chinese phonemic sequence distribution reflects its euphony on the level of phoneme distribution and word frequency distribution. With the index of the

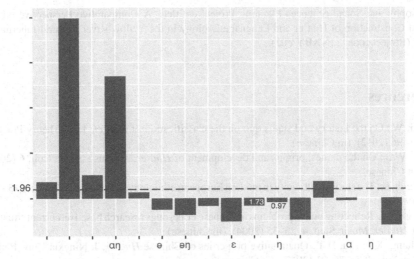

Fig. 4. *U* Statistics of the Vowel Finals in *Hua'er*

u values, we compute the two most frequently used vowel compounds; namely, /an/ and /aŋ/ in Chinese prosodic words.

4   Conclusion

The study of particular folkloristic songs reveals that the functions of the words related to the cultural performance are equivalent on the linguistic level and on the social level. This article studies the rank-frequency distribution of vocabulary and prosody words based on the self-built *Hua'er* corpus. Empirically, we adopted the quantitative features of vocabulary and phoneme distribution. Thus, it yields a rather satisfying and pleasing result on the inner structure of the Chinese folksongs for that the right-truncated modified Zipf-Alekseev distribution may capture the rank-frequency well. The words before *h-point*, namely the thematic words of *Hua'er* provide a linguistic scenery for manifestations of cultural and national identity. Qualitative analysis of autosemantics before the *h*-point demonstrates a scroll of village life in Northwest China as well as the simple but strong emotions between young lovers. Moreover, Chinese phonemic sequence distribution reflects its euphony on the level of phoneme distribution. Comparison among the *u* values, we found out the two most frequently used vowel compounds, i.e., /an/ and /aŋ/. This is useful for the recognition of Chinese phonemes and distinguishing Chinese poetic texts from other genres or languages. Specifically, the distribution of vocabularies and phonemes in the self-built *Hua'er* corpus conforms to the Zipf's Law, which could be further compared to other folksongs as to the underlying self-organization nature of the orally transmitted oral literature.

Acknowledgements. This work was partially funded by the National Social Science Project of China entitled "The Construction of Chinese Folk Song Database and Quantitative Research from the Perspective of Chinese National Community" (Project code: 22BYY084), and Ningxia

Philosophy and Social Sciences Planning Project entitled "A Comparative Perspective on the Digital Construction of Hua'er and Language Ecology in the Yellow River Cultural Inheritance Area" (Project code: 21NXBYY02).

References

1. Li, W.: On the history and status quo on the classification of *Hua'er*. Libr. Theory Pract. **8**, 91–96 (2012). (in Chinese)
2. Ji, W.L.: On the names, origins and development of *Hua'er*. J. Gansu Norm. Coll. **6** (2007) (in Chinese)
3. Dégh, L.: The study of ethnicity in modern European ethnology. J. Folk. Inst. **12**(2/3), 113–129 (1975)
4. Yang, M.: Reflecting on the problems in Chinese Folk songs research based on current situation of *Hua'er*. Music Stud. **4**, 23–35 (2004). (in Chinese)
5. Zhang, X.J., Liu, H.T.: Quantitative properties of Chinese *Hua'er*. J. Ningxia Univ. Philos. Soc. Sci. **39**(5), 76–91 (2017). (in Chinese)
6. Zhang, X.J., Liu, H.T.: Red or white? Color in Chinese folksongs. Digit. Scholarship Human. **36**(1), 225–241 (2021)
7. Lin, Y.N., Liu, H.T.: Rice and rhyme: seeing the zhuang rice-related folklore through their folksongs. Folklore **132**, 34–58 (2021)
8. Liu, H.T., Pan, X.X.: Quantitative properties of Chinese contemporary poetry. J. Shanxi Univ. Philos. Soc. Sci. **2**, 20–27 (2015)
9. Altmann, G.: Science and linguistics. In: Kohler, R., Eieger, B.B. (eds.) Contributions to Quantitative Linguistics, pp. 3–10. Klwer Academic Publishers, Dordrecht (1993)
10. Denes, P.: On the statistics of spoken English. J. Acoust. Soc. Am. **35**, 892–904 (1963)
11. Horecký, J.: The evaluation of three-member consonant. Asian Afr. Stud. **1**, 112–122 (1965)
12. Sabol, J.: Pomer jednotlivych typov konsonantickych skupin [The ratio of the individual types of consonant groups]. SIR **36**, 71–78 (1971)
13. Fry, D.B., Denes, P.: On presenting the output of a mechanical speech recognizer. J. Acoust. Soc. Am. **29**, 364–367 (1957)
14. Fry, D.B., Denes, P.: The solution of some fundamental problems in mechanical speech recognition. Lang. Speech **1**, 35–58 (1958)
15. Deng, Y.: Some statistical properties in standard Chinese. J. Quant. Linguist. **23**, 30–48 (2016)
16. Altmann, G.: The art of quantitative linguistic. J. Quant. Linguist. **1**, 313–322 (1997)
17. Liu, H.T., Huang, W.: Quantitative linguistic: state of the art, theories and methods. J. Zhejiang Univ. Hum. Soc. Sci. **2**, 178–192 (2012). (in Chinese)
18. Dulan, D.: A study of the polysemy distribution of Mongolian. In: Liu, M., et al. (eds.) CLSW 2020, LNAI 12278, pp. 473–481 (2021)
19. Popescu, I.-I., Lupea, M.L., Tatar, D., Altmann, G.: Quantitative Analysis of Poetic Texts. Walter de Gruyter, Berlin, Boston (2015)
20. Hao, X.Y., Ge, S.J., Zhang, Y., Dai, Y.L., Yan, P.Y., Li, B.: The construction and analysis of annotated imagery corpus of three hundred tang poems. In: Hong, J.-F., et al. (eds.) CLSW 2019, LNAI 11831, pp. 517–524 (2020)
21. Chen, Q.H., Guo, J.Z., Liu, Y.F.: A statistical study on Chinese word and character usage in literature from the Tang Dynasty to the present. J. Quant. Linguist. **19**(3), 232–248 (2012)
22. Wu, Y.L.: General Theory of Chinese *Hua'er*. Ningxia people's Publishing House, Yinchuan (2008). (in Chinese)

23. Wan, I.-P., Allassonnière-Tang, M.: The effect of word frequency and position-in-utterance in mandarin speech errors: a connectionist model of speech production. In: Liu, M., et al. (eds.) CLSW 2020, LNAI 12278, pp. 491–500 (2021)
24. Wang, G.R., Rao, G.Q., Xun, E.D.: Resource construction and distribution analysis of internal structure of modern Chinese double-syllable verb. In: Hong, J.-F., et al. (eds.) CLSW 2019, LNAI 11831, pp. 156–164 (2020)
25. Popescu, I.-I.: Text ranking by the weight of highly frequent words. In: Grzybek, P. (ed.) Exact Methods in the Study of Language and Text, pp. 555–566. Mouton de Gruyter, Berlin (2007)
26. Popescu, I.-I., Maþutek, J., Altmann, G.: Aspects of Word Frequencies. RAM, Lüdenscheid (2009)
27. Zipf, G.K.: The Psychobiology of Language. Houghton-Miflin, Boston (1935)
28. Zipf, G.K.: Human Behaviour and the Principle of Least Effort. Addison-Wesley, Cambridge MA (1949)
29. Jin, Y.L.: The special usage of "Bi" in Hehuang *Hua'er*. J. Lanzhou Univ. Soc. Sci. **23** (1995) (in Chinese)
30. Zhang, Y.: A Collection of *Hua'er*. China Federation of Literary and Art Circles Publishing House (1986)
31. Köhler, R.: Synergetic linguistics. In: Köhler, R., Altmann, G., Piotrowski, R.G. (eds.) Quantitative Linguistics. An International Handbook, pp. 760–774. de Gruyter, Berlin (2005)
32. Jiang, J.Y., Liu, H.T.: The effects of sentence length on dependency distance, dependency direction and the implications-based on a parallel English-Chinese dependency treebank. Lang. Sci. **50**, 93–104 (2015)
33. Ouyang, J.H., Jiang, J.Y.: Can the probability distribution of dependency distance measure language proficiency of second language learners? J. Quant. Linguist. **25**(4), 295–313 (2018)
34. Wei, H.F., Qiu, B.: Quantitative relation of the length and the count of senses for Chinese polysyllabic words. In: Dong, M., Lin, J., Tang, X. (eds.) Chinese Lexical Semantics. CLSW 2016, LNAI 10085, pp. 101–109 (2016)
35. Altmann, G.: Types of hierarchies in Language. Glottometrics **34**, 44–55 (2016)

Gender-Related Use of Tonal Patterns in Mandarin Chinese
The Case of Sentence-Final Particle *Ma*

Xin Luo[✉] and Chu-Ren Huang

Department of Chinese and Bilingual Studies, The Hong Kong Polytechnic
University, Hong Kong, China
`xin-tracy.luo@connect.polyu.hk`, `churen.huang@polyu.edu.hk`

Abstract. Gender and language and gendered language are two important topics where linguistic studies have great societal impacts. These two topic have not been well studied in Mandarin Chinese due to its lack of grammatical gender marking. We explore the gendered usage of Mandarin Chinese sentence-final particle (SFP) in casual conversation to address this issue. Previous studies of SPFs focus either on grammatical function or on pragmatic uses of expressing attitude or emotion. This study focuses on the gender-related use of tonal patterns in association with SFP *ma* in Mandarin Chinese. By combining the stance marking of Mandarin Chinese SFPs [13] as well as the attitudinal marking function of prosody to study gendered language patterned in Chinese, the results show that the gender selection of tonal patterns of *ma* in different sentence types seem to vary. We believe that this study will significantly enhance the research on language and gender.

Keywords: Sentence-final particle · Tonal pattern · Gender

1 Introduction

Gender and language and gendered language are two important topics where linguistic studies have great societal impacts [8]. [22] showed that there is a correlation between the use of grammatical gender in a language and the degree of gender equality in the society. [23], noting the lack of grammatical gender in Chinese, uses the markedness of gender modification to study trends and regional variations of professional gender segregation in the past 100 years. In terms of systematic linguistic studies, however, there is a significant gap in Mandarin Chinese as the few past studies tend to use specific lexical items (e.g., [29]) instead of global grammatical feature, partly due to the grammatical gender marking. We propose to combine the stance marking of Mandarin Chinese sentence-final particles [13] as well as the attitudinal marking function of prosody to study gendered language patterned in Chinese. In particular, we study gender related use of tonal patterns in association with sentence-final particle *ma* in Mandarin Chinese.

Q. Su et al. (Eds.): CLSW 2022, LNAI 13496, pp. 96–107, 2023.
https://doi.org/10.1007/978-3-031-28956-9_8

Sentence-final particles abound in the tonal languages (such as Mandarin and Cantonese) and atonal languages (such as English). Traditionally, SFPs refer to elements that 'have little or no lexical meaning but provide a predominantly interpretive cue to reader or hearer' to better understand the sentence or utterance in many languages [2]. Another traditional terms for SFPs is *clitics*. [12] argued that SFPs *ma* and *ne* are sentential clitics occurring at the end of the sentence. Sentence-final particles can occur in monosyllabic forms such as *ma*, *ba* and *ne* as well as disyllabic forms such as *shima*, *dele*. While many existing studies are in monosyllabic SFPs, little attention has been placed on disyllabic ones. In discourse-oriented studies, it is also called *interactional particles* for stance-building in interaction in conversation analytic approach [18]. 句末语气词 and 句末助词 are two widely accepted terms in Chinese. In modern colloquial speech, SFPs can facilitate both conversational interactions and can reflect the speaker's attitudes and emotions (e.g., [6]). In this regard, sentence-final particles are thus an important feature of human language which cannot be overlooked.

The study of sentence-final particles, which has become an indispensable part of linguistic studies, has had a rapid development in the past 50 years. The focus has largely been on semantic and pragmatic accounts. On the contrary, there has been very limited research to date on language and gender concerning tonal patterns. A series of studies related to gender use of sentence-final particles have been conducted by Marjorie Chan (e.g., [3,4]) using transcriptions of conversational data in Cantonese but few studies have been done in Mandarin Chinese. Some SFPs in Mandarin Chinese have received attention in the form of detailed analysis over the past few decades, such as *de*, *le*, and *ne* while SFP *ma* received considerably less attention.

Therefore, this paper sets out to provide a corpus-based investigation of the gender use of SFP *ma* by combining the stance marking of Mandarin Chinese SFPs [13] as well as the attitudinal marking function of prosody to study whether there is gender difference of tonal patterns using conversational data in Mandarin Chinese. In Sect. 2, a brief introduction of the sentence-final particle *ma* and tonal features in Mandarin Chinese are found. Second 3 presents the data and methodology while Sect. 4 provides the findings of the tonal pattern of SFP *ma*, based on a corpus from the transcription of conversational data in Mandarin and discussion of the distribution of SFP *ma* with respect to gender and sentence types. Section 5 presents some conclusions based on the findings and addresses some related issues. Examples given below are excerpted from *Behind the Headline with Wentao* otherwise specified. Keeping in mind gender differences in the amount of talk, we proceed to study the distribution and use of *ma* in the corpus. While the authors understand that there are many variables contributing to the gender difference such as age, nationality and occupation, this study only considers the tonal pattern to avoid confusion.

2   Literature Review

2.1   Stance-Marking of Mandarin Chinese Sentence-Final Particles

Stance refers to speaker's knowledge towards the person or matter being addressed. Different aspects of stance include epistemic state, commitment, judgement, evaluation, perspective, feeling, affect, attitude, subjectivity and intersubjectivity [1]. Researchers of Mandarin Chinese have started to examine stance in interaction through the use of sentence final particles. The existing studies on sentence-final particles has largely been on semantic and pragmatic accounts. For example, [16] found that SFP 了 *le* which appears at the end of the interlocutor's speakership serves as intersubjectivity marker in the conversation to invite the hearer's participation in conversation.

For sentence-final particle 吗 *ma*, it is a marker for the yes-or-no question. Notably, it is generally agree that 嘛 is a graphic variant of 吗 . Phonologically, 吗 *ma1* and 嘛 *ma2* are toneless, unstressed and lacking definite intonation contour (see [5,15]). Pragmatically, [14] treated 吗 *ma1* and 嘛 *ma2* as a single particle for 'high degree either with respect to the speaker's commitment to the assertion or with respect to the speaker's intention to have an action fulfilled' because the two graphics are in complementary distribution. However, there has been very limited research to date concerning the attitudinal marking function of prosody in SFPs especially in Mandarin Chinese.

2.2   Tones and Intonation in Mandarin Chinese

Chao (1968) proposed a 5-point scale to measure tonal pitch. The pitch number represents the pitch register in the scale with 1 being the lowest level and 5 being the highest level. Following Chao, the tonal pitch of the four tones in Mandarin Chinese tone 1 (high level tone), tone 2 (rising tone), tone 3 (falling-rising tone) and tone 4 (falling tone) are measurable in this 5-point scale:

Tone	Pitch	Ending pitch	Ending pitch description
1st tone	55	5	high
2nd tone	35	5	high
3rd tone	214	4	high
4th tone	51	1	low

The neutral tone is a common characteristic in Mandarin Chinese as the neutral tone is not found in some other dialects such as in Cantonese [4]. Although the neutral tone is unstressed, its pronunciation is influenced by the preceding stressed tone [5,32]. Information-seeking questions and rhetorical questions have the normal rising intonation. However, the same intonational features can express neutral, positive or negative attitude depending on prosody, text and context [25]. Therefore, rhetorical question tends to be used to emphasize or challenge, it can be more assertive than information-seeking question because the former is used to emphasize or challenge [30]. [14] proposed that 'a low tone is usually associated with a stronger force of an utterance; a high or rising tone generally convey a weaker force; whereas a mid-level tone is relatively neutral'.

Previous studies found that tones can identify emotion and authorship. On the one hand, [28] suggested that the emotional cues may be lexicalized in lexical tones by measuring the variation in tonal height and slope of the tonal contour of Mandarin emotion words expressing four basic emotion categories (joy, anger, sadness, fear). Specifically, they found that words expressing sadness tended to have a higher tonal level than the other three emotion categories. On the other hand, [11] proposed a successful classification model to discriminate different authors using tone and rimes to represent texts. For the sentence-final particles, [17] proposed that they reflect the speaker's attitude rather than feeling or emotion.

2.3 Attitudinal Marking Function of Prosody in SFPs in Mandarin Chinese

Many studies have documented how prosody can also be used in conjunction with non-lexicalized response tokens or emotional cries of various sorts to convey affective stance. [19] suggested that the intonational and rhythmic features, particularly those features indicating cohesion, are important in determining whether a particular acknowledgement token is used to embody a stance of affiliation or disaffiliation, i.e. whether it contains further commitments or not.

In terms of tonal effect on attitudinal difference, guided by the theoretical and methodological principle of conversation analysis (CA), [10], in his work on acknowledging tokens in face-to-face conversations in English, pointed to a particular difference between *mm* produced with different prosodic shapes contours. *Mm* produced with a falling terminal contour serves mainly to claim agreement and understanding whereas *mm* produced with a fall-rising contour is used primarily as a continuer to return the floor to the prior speaker to explain or clarify. In Chinese, [29] explored the meaning and the social practice of *sajiao* from ethnographic perspective to study gender and language in the cultural context of Taiwan. It is found that the use of sentence final particles can achieve *sajiao* performance. With the non-verbal cues such as rising intonation, the *sajiao* form will be intensified. The results found by [10] can be concluded and further elaborated by Law [14]'s conclusion based on Cantonese data that 'a low tone is usually associated with a stronger force of an utterance; a high or rising tone generally convey a weaker force'.

However, the same intonational features can express neutral, positive or negative attitude depending on prosody, text and context [18]. For example, information-seeking questions and rhetorical questions have the normal rising intonation. The later may be more assertive because rhetorical questions is used to emphasize or challenge [20].

Although sentence final particles have been claimed to be inherently toneless, unstressed and lacking definite intonation contours (e.g., [5,15]), the prosodic features are nonetheless found to be crucial to their intrinsic meanings and highly versatile use for various interactional stance purpose, including doubt, challenge, assertion, among many others.

2.4   Gender Talk and Sentence-Final Particles

One of the focuses of face-to-face conversation is gender talk. Although the face-to-face conversation is constructed jointly over a series of turns by different speakers, [9] observed that males tend to hold the turns and post longer messages (Edelsky's F1 floor type) whereas females exhibit collaborative turn-taking (Edelsky's F2 floor type) in conversation. The gender differences have been observed in many different contexts, such as in the Spanish language classroom [27] and in political interview in Australia [26]. [7] proposed that males tend to maintain self-oriented style to talk about a subject they are an expert on while females tend to maintain interlocutor-oriented collaborative style to minimize social distance.

Gender is also a central variable in sociolinguistic studies of sentence-final particles. Although the meanings of the sentence final particles are vague, their occurrence with certain constructions is not random. There are gendered-linked differences in the choice of particles [4]. Previous studies found that females tend to use more SFPs than males [13]. [24] found that women who work as domestic workers tend to use more *wo33* than men in Cantonese.

3   Data and Method

The data of this study consist of 50 episodes of 20 guest speakers (10 males and 10 females) from the talk show *Behind the Headline with Wentao*. The conversational recordings have been fully transcribed and segmented. In the 50 recordings of this 200,000-word corpus, they were conversations between the host and 2–3 male or female guests. The main characteristic of this corpus is that they are natural colloquial language and highly representative in gender talk. The current study aims to find out whether there is gender difference in tonal patterns in association with sentence-final particle *ma*.

Tonal pattern in this study refers to the tone pitch in the preceding word in association with SFP *ma*. Following tone pitch value in the 5-point scale proposed by [5], there are three tonal patterns in association with sentence-final particle *ma*:

1) high tone (H) + ma (e.g.: 她吗 ta1ma0);
2) low tone (L) + *ma* (e.g.: 是吗 shi4ma0);
3) neutral tone (N) + *ma* (e.g.: 了吗 le0ma0).

These patterns will be named H+*ma*, L+*ma* and N+*ma* in the following sessions. By converting the text into *Pinyin* to represent the sound, the tones were extracted by Python and further analyzed in IBM SPSS Statistics version28.

4   Results and Discussion

The data contains a total of 269 *ma* utterances, of which 75 are produced by female guests and 194 are produced by male guests. This is summarized in Table 1. Overall, male guests produce more utterances than female guests. However, only 1.62% of male sentences (total 11,987) contain SFP *ma*. In contrast, female guests produce only 3,722 sentences in total, out of which 2.02% contain SFP *ma*. Therefore, females produce *ma* proportionately more frequently than males. Previous study observed that females used more Cantonese SFP *wo33* than men at work [24]. Our result showed that female guests' speech has higher frequency of using *ma* than that in male guests' speech in the talk show.

Table 1. Distribution of *ma* sentences across sex.

SFP	Females(n = 3,722)	Males(n = 11,987)	Total(n = 15,710)
ma sentences	75 (2.02%)	194 (1.62%)	269 (1.71%)

4.1   Gender Difference in Tone Choices in Association with *Ma*

With respect to the question of whether there are different tone choices by male and female speakers, Table 2 shows the distribution of *ma* sentences with three different tonal patterns across the male and female guests' speech. It is observed that different tonal patterns (H+*ma*, L+*ma* and N+*ma*) are used during male and female conversation. Among these three types of tonal patterns, H+*ma* tonal pattern is proportionally more frequent than the other two tonal patterns in both male and female guests' speech. H+*ma* tonal pattern have the highest frequency which covers 40.52% of the total frequency. 27 instances (36%) are used in female guests' speech and 82 instances (42.27%) are used male guests' speech respectively. N+*ma* tonal pattern (total 31.60%) is the second most frequent used pattern in both male and female speech followed by L+*ma* which contains 27.88%.

Table 2. Distribution of *ma* sentences with different tonal patterns across sex.

SFP	Females(n = 3,722)	Males(n = 11,987)	Total(n = 15,710)
H+*ma*	27 (36.00%)	82 (42.27%)	109 (40.52%)
N+*ma*	26 (34.67%)	59 (30.41%)	85 (31.60%)
L+*ma*	22 (29.33%)	53 (27.32%)	75 (27.88%)
Total	75 (100.00%)	194 (100.00%)	269 (100.00%)

In previous study, [11] found that the different authors have established his or her own stylometrics rhythms (tones and rimes) of writing. Using support vector machines and random forests, [11] proved that in addition to lexical features such as function words (e.g., [20]), authorship can be identified effectively by non-lexical feature (tones and rimes) which are written unconsciously by authors. Following similar idea of using non-lexical feature to identify authorship, it is observed that male and female guests in the talk show have different preferences of using tonal patterns with *ma*.

First of all, it is observed in Table 2 that three tonal patterns (H+*ma*, L+*ma* and N+*ma*) are used during gendered conversation. For example:

Example 1

a. 她弟弟知情吗?
   ta1   di4di0   zhi1qing2   ma0
   She   brother   know   situation   MA
   'Does her brother know?'
b. 年纪越轻越浪漫嘛 .
   nian2ji4   yue4   qing1   yue4   lang4man4   ma0
   age   more   young   more   romantic   MA
   'The younger you are, the more romantic you are.'
c. 我刚刚不是说了嘛 .
   wo3   gang1gang1   bu2   shi4   shuo1   le0   ma0
   I   just   NEG   be   say   LE   MA
   'I told you just now.'

Secondly, among these three types of tonal patterns, males and females use H+*ma* proportionally more frequent than the other two tonal patterns. The preference of H+*ma* may suggest that this tonal pattern convey certain conceptual meaning which cannot be expressed by L+*ma* and N+*ma*. Generally, a high or rising tone is associated with a weaker force whereas low tone is associated with a stronger force [14]. For instance, Example 1a ends in H+*ma* tonal patterns (qing2 ma0). It shows the speaker has a slight doubt and is seeking confirmation. Compared to Example 1a, 1b ends in L+*ma* tonal pattern (man4 ma0) which shows stronger affirmation whereas Example 1c ends in N+*ma* tonal pattern (le0 ma0) which serves as a reminder to the listener of what is being said.

4.2   Gender Difference of Tonal Pattern in Different Sentence Types

Given the preference of H+*ma* in both male and female speech, there seems to be no gender difference of the choice of tonal patterns. Therefore, further investigation is conducted on the distribution of H+*ma* in different sentence types. The result in repeated measures ANOVA (Table 3) shows that there is an interaction between gender and sentence types and the result is statistically significant ($p = 0.014$). Table 4 and Fig. 1 show that male and female guests used three sentence types (declarative sentences, rhetorical questions and yes-or-no questions) in H+*ma* tonal pattern. In addition, female guests prefer to use H+*ma* tonal pattern in yes-or-no questions (62.96%) whereas male guests prefer to use H+*ma* tonal pattern in declarative sentences (85.11%) and rhetorical questions (91.43%). With respect to the two types of questions, females have a strong preference for using H+*ma* tonal pattern in yes-or-no questions while males prefer to use H+*ma* tonal pattern in rhetorical questions.

Table 3. Tests of Within-Subjects Effects (Measure: Sentence_types).

Source		Type III Sum of Squares	df	Mean Square	F	Sig.	Partial Eta Squared
sentype * Gender	Sphericity Assumed	24.267	2	12.133	4.506	.014	.106

Table 4. Distribution of H+*ma* across sex and sentence types.

SFP	Females(n = 3,722)*	Males(n = 11,987)*	Total(n = 15,710)
Declarative sentences	7 (14.89%)	40 (85.11%)	47 (100.00%)
Rhetorical questions	3 (8.57%)	32 (91.43%)	35 (100.00%)
Yes-or-no questions	17 (62.96%)	10 (37.04%)	27 (100.00%)
Total	27 (24.77%)	82 (75.23%)	109 (100.00%)

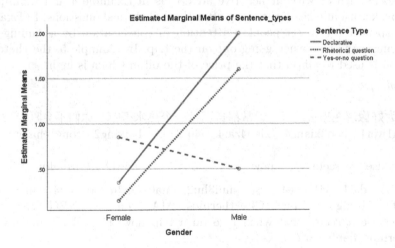

Fig. 1. Distribution of H+*ma* across sex and sentence types.

According to the investigation of [31], the semantic function of *ma* in declarative sentence can provide explanatory information of either cause (e.g., *yin-*

wei...ma (because...MA) or effect (e.g., *suoyi...ma* (so...MA) in causal relation-ship. Example 2 and Example 3 are uttered by males. the use of *ma* in Example 2 explains the reason why Apple only makes a brief reply to customers' complaints whereas *ma* is attached to the effect in the causal relationship in Example 3.

Example 2
因为他不怕你不来嘛，......
yin1wei4 ta1 bu4 pa4   ni3 bu4 lai2   ma0
because   him not afraid you NEG come   MA
'Because he's not afraid if you won't come, ...'

Example 3

......所以基于这样的理由捧出了四大小说出来嘛。 ......
suo3yi3 ji1yu2   zhe4yang4 de0 li3you2 peng3chu1 le0
so   base on   this   DE   reason   make   LE

si4   da4 xiao3shuo1 chu1lai2 ma0
four big novel   out   MA
'So based on this reason, the four classic novels were brought out.'

For questions, the high tone in the final position of an utterance usually marks an ordinary question or rhetorical question [21]. Although a high or rising tone generally conveys a weaker force [14], it is not the case for rhetorical questions. Rhetorical questions are used to either enhance the meaning of the affirmation or negation, or challenge [32]. It is found that males use more rhetorical questions than females in the corpus. For *ma*, the rhetorical question can be used in yes-or-no form with or without negative adverb as in Example 4 and Example 5. The speaker usually keep on talking after these rhetorical questions. In Example 4, the speaker try to get people's attention in conversation by assuming they also bring a thermos when going out on the trip. In Example 5, the rhetorical question is used to affirm that the price of the oil in China is high.

Example 4

因为好像现在出去旅行，通常都自己带一个热水壶嘛，你们不会吗? ......
yin1wei4 hao3xiang4 xian4zai4 chu1qu4 lv3xing2 tong1chang2 dou1
because   seem   now   out   travel   usually   all

zi4ji3 dai4   yi1 ge4 re4 shui3hu2 ma0 ni3men0 bu4 hui4 ma0
self   bring one CL   CL   thermos   MA   you   NEG can   MA
'Because it seems that when I go on a trip now, I usually bring my own thermos, don't you?'

Example 5

你知道它的油多少钱吗? 我们一公升是 9块多人民币，它是 0.05美元， ......
ni3 zhi1dao4 ta1 de0 you2 duo1shao3 qian2 ma0 wo3men0 yi1
you know   it   DE   oil   how much   money MA   Our   one

gong1sheng1   shi4   9   kuai4   duo1   ren2min2bi4   ta1   shi4   0.05
mei3yuan2
liter   is   9   piece   more   RMB   it   is   0.05
dollar
'Do you know how much the oil is? Our one liter is more than 9 yuan, it is
0.05 US dollars (in Venezuela),'

Females have a stronger preference for using yes-or-no questions. In Example
6, the female guest repeatedly asked whether the name is Brooklyn. She posted
a question and was eager to get the confirmation from the listener. This shows
the collaborative conversational style by females to maintain the interaction in
a discussion (Edelsky's F2 floor type). One might also note that the utterance
length in Example 5 which is produced by the female is relatively shorter than
Example 5. The male utterance in Example 5 is 'playing the expert' and holds the
floor to talk about the price of oil which he is familiar with. Such phenomenon is
observed in the utterances made by male speakers in different types of sentences.

Example 6

是叫布鲁克林吗? 是叫布鲁克林吗?
shi4   jiao4   bu4lu3ke4lin2   ma0
is   call   Brooklyn   MA
'Is it Brooklyn? Is it Brooklyn?'

5   Conclusion

In this paper, we propose a new approach to study gender related patterns in
a language without grammatical gender markers. In particular, we focus on the
total pattern used by speakers of in association with SFP *ma*. Our study shows
tonal pattern in association with SFP *ma* may indeed show gender differences.
The SFP *ma* tends to be preceded by words with a higher tone pitch (H+*ma*)
than low and neutral tones in male and female utterances. With respect to
sentence types, H+*ma* has more occurrences in declarative and rhetorical questions in male speech while H+*ma* has more occurrences in yes-or-no questions in
female speech. We believe that this study will significantly enhance the research
on sentence-final particles and language and gender. In future work, we will
extend the research to a larger pool of data and further investigate the tonal
pattern of *ne, ba, le, de* and *a*.

References

1. Alexandre, J.: Introduction: The Sociolinguistics of Stance. In: Stance: Sociolinguistic Perspectives. Oxford University Press (2009)
2. Blakemore, D.: Semantic constraints on relevance (1987)

3. Chan, M.K.: Gender-marked speech in cantonese: the case of sentence-final particles JE and JEK. Stud. Linguist. Sci. **26**(1/2), 1–38 (1996)
4. Chan, M.K.: Particles in cantonese. Gend. Across Lang.: Linguist. Representation Women Men **2**, 57–72 (2002). https://doi.org/10.1075/impact.10.08cha
5. Chao, Y.R., Zhao, Y.: A Grammar of Spoken Chinese. University of California Press, Berkeley, CA (1968)
6. Chappell, H.: Strategies for the assertion of obviousness and disagreement in mandarin: a semantic study of the modal particle me. Aust. J. Linguist. **11**(1), 39–65 (1991). https://doi.org/10.1080/07268609108599451
7. Coates, J.: Women, Men and Everyday Talk, chap. The Organisation of Men's Talk. Palgrave Macmillan UK, One-at-a-Time (2013)
8. Eckert, P., McConnell-Ginet, S.: Language and Gender, 2 edn. Cambridge University Press, Cambridge (2013). https://doi.org/10.1017/CBO9781139245883
9. Edelsky, C.: Who's got the floor? Lang. Soc. **10**(3), 383–421 (1981). http://www.jstor.org/stable/4167262
10. Gardner, R.: The conversation object mm: a weak and variable acknowledging token. Res. Lang. Soc. Interac. **30**(2), 131–156 (1997). https://doi.org/10.1080/07268609108599451
11. Hou, R., Huang, C.R.: Robust stylometric analysis and author attribution based on tones and rimes. Nat. Lang. Eng. **26**(1), 49–71 (2020). https://doi.org/10.1017/S135132491900010X
12. Huang, C.R.: Chinese sentential clitics and theories of cliticization. In: LSA Annual Meeting at Seattle, pp. 247–287 (1989)
13. Jing-Schmidt, Z.: Sentence-final particles: Sociolinguistic and discourse perspectives (2022)
14. Law, S.P.: The syntax and phonology of Cantonese sentence-final particles. Ph.D. thesis, Boston University (1990)
15. Li, C.N., Thompson, S.A.: Mandarin Chinese: A Functional Reference Grammar. University of California Press, Berkeley (1981)
16. Lu, L.W.l., Lily, I., et al.: Speech in interaction: mandarin particle le as a marker of intersubjectivity. Zeitschrift für interkulturellen Fremdsprachenunterricht **14**(1) (2009)
17. Lu, W.Y.: Sentence-final particles as attitude markers in Mandarin Chinese. Ph.D. thesis (2005)
18. Morita, E.: Stance marking in the collaborative completion of sentences: final particles as epistemic markers in Japanese. In: Akatsuka, N.M., Strauss, S. (eds.) Japanese / Korean linguistics, Stanford, Calif, vol. 10, pp. 220–233. Published for the Stanford Linguistics Association by CSLI Publications (2002)
19. Müller, F.E.: Affiliating and disaffiliating with continuers: prosodic aspects of recipiency. In: Couper-Kuhlen, E., Selting, M. (eds.) Prosody in Conversation, pp. 131–176. Cambridge University Press
20. Neal, T., Sundararajan, K., Fatima, A., Yan, Y., Xiang, Y., Woodard, D.: Surveying stylometry techniques and applications. ACM Comput. Surv. **50**(6), 1–36 (2017). https://doi.org/10.1145/3132039
21. Pierrehumbert, Janet; Hirschberg, J.B.: The meaning of intonational contours in the interpretation of discourse. In: Intentions in Communication. The MIT Press (2003)
22. Prewitt-Freilino, J.L., Caswell, T.A., Laakso, E.K.: The gendering of language: a comparison of gender equality in countries with gendered, natural gender, and genderless languages. Sex Roles **66**(3), 268–281 (2012). https://doi.org/10.1007/s11199-011-0083-5

23. Su, Q., Liu, P., Wei, W., Zhu, S., Huang, C.R.: Occupational gender segregation and gendered language in a language without gender: trends, variations, implications for social development in china. Human. Soc. Sci. Commun. **8**(1), 1–10 (2021). https://doi.org/10.1057/s41599-021-00799-6

24. Timothy, L.: On 'de-ing'. Comput. Analy. Asian Afr. Lang. (CAAAL) **19**, 21–49 (1982)

25. Wichmann, A.: The attitudinal effects of prosody, and how they relate to emotion. In: ISCA Tutorial and Research Workshop (ITRW) on Speech and Emotion (2000)

26. Winter, J.: Gender and the political interview in an Australian context. J. Pragmatics **20**(2), 117–139 (1993). https://doi.org/10.1016/0378-2166(93)90079-5. special Issue on ‘Pragmatics in Australia and New Zealand&rsquo

27. Yakushkina, M.: Gender performance through turn-taking organisation in a foreign language classroom. Lang. Learn. J. **49**, 176–188 (2018). https://doi.org/10.1080/09571736.2018.1520915

28. Yao, Y., Lin, J., Ren Huang, C.: Lexicalized emotion? tonal patterns of emotion words in mandarin Chinese (2013)

29. Yueh, H.I.S.: Body performance in gendered language deconstructing the mandarin term Sajiao in the cultural context of Taiwan. Ricerche di Pedagogia e Didattica. J. Theor. Res. Educ. **8**(1), 159–182 (2013). https://doi.org/10.6092/issn.1970-2221/3777

30. Zahner, K., Xu, M., Chen, Y., Dehé, N., Braun, B.: The prosodic marking of rhetorical questions in standard Chinese. In: Proceedings of Speech Prosody, vol. 10, pp. 389–393 (2020). https://doi.org/10.21437/speechprosody.2020-80

31. Zhao, C.L., Yang, C.Y.: On the relevance between cognition and emotion of the sentence-final particle "ma". J. Foreign Lang. **39**(5), 32–45 (2016)

32. Zhu, Y.P., Huang, C.R.: A student grammar of Chinese (2022)

A Quantitative Study on the Low-Degree Adverb *"Shaowei"* – A Stylistic Perspective

Zhong Wu[✉]

Jianghan University, Wuhan 430056, Hubei, China
zhongwu2000@163.com

Abstract. Based on large-scale corpora, this study examines the stylistic charac-teristics of the low-degree adverb *"shaowei"* (稍微'slightly') from three aspects: stylistic distribution, colligation and semantic prosody. It has been found that: 1. The proportion of *"shaowei"* in spoken Chinese is higher than that in written Chinese, but the distribution of *"shaowei"* in different sub-genres varies consid-erably. 2. The proportion of colligation of *"shaowei* + verb phrase" is higher than that of *"shaowei* + adjective phrase". In terms of sub-genres, *"shaowei"* inclines to modify verbs in Translation Works and tends to modify adjectives in CCTV News. 3. *"Shaowei"* has a positive semantic prosody in both written and spoken Chinese, but it is quite different from the dictionary which says *"shaowei"* can only collocate with commendatory words. To be specific, *"shaowei"* shows a neutral semantic prosody in Practical Writing and Learned and a negative one in CCTV News.

Keywords: Quantitative study · Stylistic perspective · *Shaowei*

1 Introduction

Degree adverbs usually act as modifiers before verbs and adjectives. Their complex nature, such as scope, classification, semantic features, grammatical functions, charac-teristics of the sentence pattern and co-occurrence with other components, is always the focus of related research. Till now, low-degree adverbs have received less attention when compared with high-degree adverbs, as the former, with low frequency, have fewer family members. It is known that only through detailed analysis of all members within its scope, can researchers achieve a comprehensive and objective understanding of the degree adverb family. Therefore, the less frequently used low-degree adverbs cannot be neglected in studying the properties of degree adverbs.

"Shaowei", which means "low degree, low quantity, or less time", is a typical member of low-degree adverb family. The current research on *"shaowei"* mainly focus on three aspects, namely, the semantic difference, the syntactic characteristic, and the historical evolvement. Ma, Zhou and Yue conducted comparative researches between *"shaowei"* and other low-degree adverbs with the same function [1–3], while Shi and Pan mainly studied the syntactic and semantic features of *"shaowei"* from the perspec-tive of co-occurrence [4–6]. Xiao also researched the semantic and syntactic features

of *"shaowei"* [7], but his research, mainly by analyzing limited examples, is a qualitative study in nature. Zhang discussed the origin of *"shaowei"* from the perspective of grammaticalization [8].

Up to now, the distribution feature, syntactic characteristics and semantic prosody of *"shaowei"* in different genres have not yet been comprehensively investigated. Therefore, based on large-scale corpora, this article will give a quantitative and detailed description of the stylistic distribution, colligation and semantic prosody of *"shaowei"*, and try to find its grammatical function and semantic features in various genres.

2 Research Design

Genre, a particular category of composition characterized by similarities in form, style, or subject matter, is formed to meet different communication needs [9]. Generally speaking, it can be divided into spoken language and written language and each of them also has various sub-genres. It is universally acknowledged that there are only six sub-genres we use in daily life, including conversational, artistic, scientific, practical, reportorial, and political genres, as well as their variants and integrations [10]. Different genres have their own characteristics in wording and sentence pattern [11].

It can be seen that there is a methodological difference between quantitative research and qualitative one, as the former relies on observation and statistics, while the latter depends on experience and intuition. Thus, a corpus is useful for deepening our understanding of language when quantitative research is taken into consideration. On the basis of two corpora, this research tries to investigate the stylistic differences of *"shaowei"* in different genres. As such, the corpora adopted, research methods and research questions are listed below.

2.1 Corpora

Two comparable corpora, the Modern Chinese Corpus of Peking University (CCL) and the Media Language Corpus (MLC) are adopted in this research. The corpus of CCL, developed by the Center for Chinese Linguistics of Peking University, contains several sub-corpora in different languages style, and among which, Speaking, Practical writing, Newspaper, Learned, Literature and Translation Works represent conversational, practical, reportorial, scientific and artistic genres respectively.

The corpus of MLC is established by the Communication University of China (CUC). In this study, the transcribed texts of *"Xinwen Lianbo"* (CCTV's flagship news program at 7 pm.) are selected as the research objects. Although the genre of *"Xinwen Lianbo"* is controversial, it can be regarded as a standardized spoken language, as well as a variant and integration of spoken and written Chinese.

In summary, CCL and MLC reveal more fine-grained genre distinctions between spoken and written Chinese. Therefore, they are appropriate research objects in the stylistic study.

2.2 Research Design

By searching each sub-corpus of the CCL and MLC, concordances containing the keyword *"shaowei"* are downloaded and numbered. If all downloaded examples in each sub-genre is no more than 100, all of them will serve as the research objects; if there are more than 100 sentences in a certain genre, a software, Randommaker, will be used to randomly select 100 sentences. Then Antconc3.2.4w, a multiplatform tool for carrying out corpus linguistics research and data-driven learning, will be adopted to retrieve the research objects, and the data collected will be used as the original material for further analysis.

2.3 Research Questions

This research tries to answer the following questions:

1. What are the characteristics of the stylistic distribution of *"shaowei"*?
2. What are the characteristics of the colligation of *"shaowei"*?
3. What are the characteristics of the semantic prosody of *"shaowei"*?

3 Results and Discussion

3.1 The Stylistic Distribution of *"Shaowei"*

It is believed that *"shaowei"* is more commonly used in spoken language [12]. However, it is an intuitive conclusion without quantitative support. In this article, the researcher retrieved the keyword *"shaowei"* from the corpora of CCL and MLC, and downloaded all concordances. Then, irrelevant ones were deleted, while the rest, 2471 sentences in total, retained. After careful analysis of the extracted sentences, it is found that the frequency and proportion of *"shaowei"* appearing in different sub-genres vary considerably. Since the size of each sub-corpus is different, the hits of *"shaowei"* in each sub-genre are standardized in the unit of per-million for the convenience of comparison. The statistics are shown in Table 1.

After careful analysis of the data in Table 1, it has been found that the distribution of *"shaowei"* in different sub-genres has following characteristics:

1. There is indeed a great difference in the number and frequency of *"shaowei"* in spoken and written Chinese. In spoken Chinese, the average hits of *"shaowei"* in one million words is 5.45, while in written Chinese, the number is 2.22. In other words, the former is 2.45 times that of the latter, which is a significant difference.

An important reason for the higher proportion of "shaowei" in spoken language is that "shaowei" can be used in both spoken and written language. There are several members having the same function in the "shaowei" family, such as "shao" (稍'slightly'), "lüe"(略'slightly'), "shaoshao"(稍稍'slightly'), and *"lüelüe"*(略略'slightly'). Compared with *"shaowei"*, these words are more common in written language [13], as they have the characteristic of classic Chinese and always form set phrases or four-character phrases. Therefore, *"shaowei"* is more frequently adopted in spoken Chinese.

Table 1. The stylistic distribution of *"shaowei"*

Language Style	Genre	Hits	Overall Size	Per million
Written Chinese	practical writing	221	48, 286, 885	4. 58
	Newspaper	778	839, 973, 730	0. 92
	Literature	449	85, 241, 162	5. 27
	Translation Works	932	90, 046, 147	10. 35
	Learned	22	20, 655, 712	1. 07
	Total	2402	1, 084, 203, 636	2. 22
Spoken Chinese	CCTV News	21	9, 572, 033	2. 19
	Speaking	48	3, 081, 723	15. 58
	Total	69	12, 653, 756	5. 45

2. Even in written Chinese, the frequency of *"shaowei"* varies considerably in sub-genres. It is clear that the hits of *"shaowei"* in the Translation Works are far more frequent than that in Literature and Practical Writing, and the frequency of *"shaowei"* in these two sub-genres is much higher than that in the Learned and Newspaper.

3. In spoken Chinese, *"shaowei"* appears far more frequently in Speaking than it does in CCTV News. The table shows that *"shaowei"* appears 7.11 times more often in Speaking than in CCTV News.

4. Comparison among sub-genres demonstrates that the frequency of *"shaowei"* appearing in Speaking is 7.11 times that of CCTV News, whereas the frequency of *"shaowei"* in CCTV News is 2.38 times that of Newspaper. From the stylistic point of view, "spoken language is formed in people's casual talk" and CCTV News often has the characteristics, to a certain extent, of formal written Chinese in serious conversations [10]. Thus, it emerges as a variety of spoken Chinese in the transition to written Chinese. CCTV News, pursuing universality and popularity, is a kind of news broadcast in the form of spoken Chinese, and has some features of both spoken and written Chinese. To some extent, it can be regarded as a news report in the form of written language. Therefore, a continuum of *"shaowei"* is formed on the basis of frequency in three sub-genres, namely Speaking > CCTV News > Newspaper.

It can be seen from the above analysis that the proportion of *"shaowei"* in spoken Chinese is indeed higher than that in written Chinese. But from the perspective of sub-genres, there are substantial differences. In addition, the distribution of *"shaowei"* in the three sub-genres presents a continuum as CCTV News has the characteristics of both spoken Chinese and written one.

3.2 The Colligation of *"Shaowei"*

Colligation is an abstract representation of combination of word classes, and collocation is the concrete manifestation of colligation [14]. In other words, a colligation represents a class of collocation [15]. For instance, each of the following sentences represents a certain colligation.

Eg.1   严醉 稍微 停 了 一下。(Literature)
       Yanzui **shaowei** ting le yixia.
       Yan Zui paused for a while.
Eg.2   韩玉姬 心里 稍微 踏实 了 些。(Newspaper)
       Hanyuji xinli **shaowei** tashi le xie.
       HanYuji was a little more surefooted.

There is a verb "*ting*"(停'stop') in Eg.1 and an adjective "*tashi*"(踏实'surefooted') in Eg. 2. When colligation is taken into account, the two examples are marked as "*shaowei* + VP" and "*shaowei* + AP*" respectively. In terms of the above principles, the statistics of colligations of "*shaowei*" are given in Table 2:

Table 2. The colligation of "*shaowei*"

Language Style	Sub-genre	VP	AP	PP	ADP
Written Chinese	Practical writing	63/63%	31/31%	3/3%	3/3%
	Newspaper	53/53%	40/40%	2/2%	5/5%
	Literature	54/54%	34/34%	2/2%	10/10%
	Translation Works	73/73%	20/20%	2/2%	5/5%
	Learned	13/59. 1%	9/40. 9%	0/0%	0/0%
	Total	256/60. 7%	134/31.8%	9/2. 13%	23/5. 5%
Spoken Chinese	CCTV News	4/19. 0%	15/71. 4%	0/0%	2/9. 5%
	Speaking	28/58. 3%	17/35. 4%	0/0%	3/6. 3%
	Total	32/46. 4%	32/46. 4%	0/0%	5/7. 3%

Specifically, the proportion of "*shaowei*" modifying verbs in written Chinese is 60.7%, 14.3% higher than that in spoken Chinese, while the proportion of modifying adjectives is 31.8%, 14.6% lower than that in spoken Chinese. That is to say that "*shaowei*" tends to modify verbs in written Chinese.

It can be seen from the table that in both written and spoken genres, the proportion of "*shaowei*" modifying verb phrases is the highest, accounting for 60.7% and 46.4%; and the proportion of modifying adjective phrases ranks the second, accounting for 31.8% and 46.4% respectively. This is also the main function of degree adverb, namely, acting as a modifier before verb and adjective. In addition, "*shaowei*" can also modify certain adverbs, such as the negative adverb "*bu*"(不'not') and degree adverbs "*youdian*"(有点'somewhat') and "*youxie*"(有些'a little').

When sub-genre is taken into consideration, the proportion of "*shaowei*" modifying verb phrases in Translation Works is the highest, reaching 73%, while the proportion of modifying verb phrases in CCTV News is the lowest, only 19.0%; and there is little difference in other sub-genres as all of them are around 60%. On the contrary, the proportion of "*shaowei*" modifying adjective phrases is the highest in CCTV News, reaching 71.4%; and it is only 20% in Translation Works, the lowest in all sub-genres. There are not many differences among the rest of other sub-genres. Therefore, a safe conclusion can be reached that "*shaowei*" inclines to modify verbs in Translation Works, while it tends to modify adjectives in CCTV News.

3.3   The Semantic Prosody of "*Shaowei*"

The traditional view shows that "*shaowei*" exclusively co-occurs with commendatory predicates, and those with negative one cannot collocate with "*shaowei*" [13, 16]. Although there is little objection, no statistics are available to support this conclusion.

To obtain a clearer picture of the attitudinal preference of "*shaowei*", this research introduces semantic prosody, a new perspective to identify the affective meaning of a given word [17]. Theoretically, semantic prosody is defined as "words occur in characteristic collocations, showing the associations and connotations they have and therefore the assumptions which they embody" and generally falls into three categories: positive, neutral and negative [15].

Examples downloaded from corpora were analyzed and counted. Then, the hits and the percent of "*shaowei*" are listed in Table 3.

Table 3. The prosody of "*shaowei*"

Language Style	Genre	Positive		Neutral		Negative	
		Freq	Percent	Freq	Percent	Freq	Percent
Written Chinese	Practical Writing	23	23%	61	61%	16	16%
	Newspaper	51	51%	23	23%	26	26%
	Literature	48	48%	25	25%	27	27%
	Translation Works	38	38%	41	41%	21	21%
	Learned	8	36. 4%	10	45. 5%	4	18. 2%
	Total	168	39. 8%	160	37. 9%	94	22. 3%
Spoken Chinese	CCTV News	6	28. 6%	3	14. 3%	12	57. 1%
	Speaking	23	47. 9%	14	29. 2%	11	22. 9%
	Total	29	42%	17	24. 6%	23	33. 3%

Table 3 illustrates the attitudinal preference of "*shaowei*". According to the table, the positive ratios of "*shaowei*" in written Chinese and spoken Chinese are 39.8% and 42% respectively. It seems that "*shaowei*" has a positive semantic prosody in both genres. However, it also shows in the table that the neutral proportions of "*shaowei*" are 37.9% and 24.6%, and the negative ones are 22.3% and 33.3%. Besides, it has been found in the corpora that "*shaowei*" can modify derogatory predicates, such as "*dayi*"(大意'careless'), "*chihuan*"(迟缓'sluggish'), "*luohou*"(落后'backward'), "*zoushen*"(走神'distracted'), "*baoyuan*"(抱怨'complaining') and neutral words, like "*jiancha*"(检查'check'), "*tingdun*"(停顿'pause'), "*xie*"(写'write'), "*da*"(大'big') and "*xiao*"(小'small'). Based on the authentic-material extracted from large-scale corpora, it can be found that "*shaowei*" can modify neutral words in both written and spoken Chinese. Moreover, the sum of the neutral and negative hits exceeds half of the total, which is the other evidence that "*shaowei*" does not exclusively collocate with commendatory predicts.

The situation is more complicated with respect to various sub-genres. According to Table 3, "*shaowei*" obviously shows a neutral semantic prosody in Practical Writing and Learned. The main reason is that texts in these sub-genres are mainly expository writings, and they are objective and rational in nature. Under this circumstance, "*shaowei*" in these sub-genres are largely neutral.

In CCTV News, "*shaowei*" shows a negative semantic prosody, for the ratio reaches 57.14%; while in Newspaper, it shows a positive one, for the ratio is 51%. Although both sub-genres are news reports, CCTV News, a nationwide program, is directly broadcast to all people every day. As such, low-degree adverbs are needed, on the basis of the Politeness Principle, to modify derogatory words, reducing negative connotations and achieving the purpose of euphemism.

To sum up, although "*shaowei*" has a positive semantic prosody in both written and spoken Chinese, the proportion of "*shaowei*" modifying neutral and derogatory predicates should not be underestimated. In this sense, "*shaowei*" is by no means exclusively able to modify commendatory predicates. In addition, it shows a neutral semantic prosody in Practical Writing and Learned. In order to be objective and euphemistic, it modifies derogatory words in CCTV News, showing a negative semantic prosody.

3.4 Conclusion

"*Shaowei*" is a representative member of low-degree adverbs. Based on two large corpora, CCL and MLC, this research investigates its stylistic characteristics from three aspects: distribution, colligation and semantic prosody. There are three major findings after careful counting and detailed analysis. Firstly, the proportion of "*shaowei*" in spoken Chinese is higher than that in written one. But from the perspective of sub-genre, the distribution of "*shaowei*" varies considerably. Among them, CCTV News has the characteristics of both Speaking and Newspaper, and the distribution of "*shaowei*" in these three sub-genres presents a continuum, namely, Speaking > CCTV News > Newspaper. Secondly, the proportion of colligation of "*shaowei* + verb phrase" is higher than that of "*shaowei* + adjective phrase". With regard to sub-genre, "*shaowei*" is more likely to modify verbs in Translation Works, while in CCTV News, "*shaowei*" tends to modify adjective phrases. Finally, as for attitudinal preference, "*shaowei*" has a positive semantic prosody in both written and spoken Chinese, but the proportion of "*shaowei*" collocating with neutral and derogatory verbs and adjectives should not be underestimated. In terms of sub-genre, "*shaowei*" has a neutral semantic prosody in Practical Writing and Learned, and a negative one in CCTV News.

Acknowledgments. This research was supported by the Humanity and Social Science Project of Hubei Provincial Department of Education (21G079, A Research on Modern Chinese Event Nouns for International Chinese Education).

References

1. Ma, Z.: *Shaowei*" and "*Duoshao*. Lang. Teach. Linguist. Stud. **3**, 30–33 (1985). (in Chinese)
2. Zhou, X.B.: On degree adverbs in modern Chinese. Stud. Chin. Lang. **2**, 100–104 (1995). (in Chinese)
3. Yue, Y.: Chinese adverbs "*Shaowei*"/"*Duoshao*" and the quantity category. Lang. Teach. Linguist. Stud. **5**, 61–71 (2017). (in Chinese)
4. Shi, W.G.: "*Shaowei*" + Adjective + Responding Component. J. Shandong Univ. (Philos. Soc. Sci.) **3**, 51–56 (1996). (in Chinese)
5. Shi, W.G.: "*Shaowei*" + Verb + Response Component. J. Zaozhuang Univ. **4**, 84–90 (1998). (in Chinese)
6. Pan, X.J.: On the usages and collocations of the degree adverbs like "*Shaowei*". J. Yunnan Normal Univ. (Teach. Stud. Chin. Foreign Lang. Ed.) **5**, 76–83 (2008). (in Chinese)
7. Xiao, X.Q.: Analysis of syntax and semantics of relative degree adverb. J. Nanjing Normal Univ. (Soc. Sci.) **6**, 144–150 (2003). (in Chinese)
8. Zhang, Y.S., Pan, X.J.: Diachronic source and development of degree adverbs like "*Shaowei*". J. Xinzhou Teach. Univ. **3**, 55–60 (2007). (in Chinese)
9. Fan, C.: A Corpus-Based Genre and Language Feature Analysis of Chinese and English Linguistics and Literature Article Abstracts. In: Liu, P., Su, Qi. (eds.) CLSW 2013. LNCS (LNAI), vol. 8229, pp. 617–624. Springer, Heidelberg (2013). https://doi.org/10.1007/978-3-642-45185-0_64
10. Wang, D.C., Chen, R.R.: Stylistics. Guangxi Education Publishing House, Nanning (2000). (in Chinese)
11. Niu, G.: A Genre Analysis of Chinese and English Abstracts of Academic Journal Articles: A Parallel-Corpus-Based Study. In: Liu, P., Su, Qi. (eds.) CLSW 2013. LNCS (LNAI), vol. 8229, pp. 603–616. Springer, Heidelberg (2013). https://doi.org/10.1007/978-3-642-45185-0_63
12. Wang, H.: A New Chinese-English Dictionary of Function Words. Sinolingua Press, Beijing (1999). (in Chinese)
13. Zhang, B.: Modern Chinese Dictionary of Function Words. The Commercial Press, Beijing (2005). (in Chinese)
14. Mitchell, T.F.: Principles of Firthian Linguistics. Longman, London (1975)
15. Wei, N.X.: A general introduction of semantic prosody research. Foreign Lang. Teach. Res. (Bimonthly) **4**, 300–307 (2002). (in Chinese)
16. Hou, X.C.: Modern Chinese Dictionary of Function Words. Peking University Press, Beijing (1998). (in Chinese)
17. Wu, Z.: The Semantic Prosody of "*Youyu*": Evidence from Corpora. In: Hong, J., et al. (eds.) Chinese Lexical Semantics, pp. 654–660. Springer, Cham. (2019)

The Relationship of Lexical Richness to the Quality of CSL Writings

Yueming Du[✉]

School of Chinese as a Second Language, Peking University, Beijing, China
ddddym@yeah.net.net

Abstract. The current paper proposed 32 indicators to measure the relationship of lexical richness to the quality of Chinese as a second language (CSL) learners' compositions. The indicators of 6 dimensions-lexical variation, lexical sophistication, lexical density, lexical error, lexical originality, and lexical frequency profile-were automatically extracted with Natural Language Processing techniques and the large-scale Chinese compositions were sampled from HSK Dynamic Composition Corpus. The results demonstrated that 21 indicators were correlated with writing scores. The regression analysis experiment showed that $PLFW_{BCC-T}$ can effectively predict the writing performance and PSW_T is in the second place. TTR, LO and LE1 are also effective indicators to predict the writing quality of CSL learners.

Keywords: Lexical Richness · Writing Quality · CSL Learners · Natural Language Processing

1 Introduction

Lexical knowledge, which has always been regarded as an important component in language acquisition [1], plays a critical role in measuring the language proficiency of second language (L2) learners. A growing body of research has employed quite a few measures to assess the proficiency of L2 learners' lexical usage, but lexical richness seems to be the most popular one over the last decade. As a multidimensional construct, lexical richness can be subdivided into several dimensions- primarily, lexical sophistication (LS), lexical variation (LV), lexical density (LD), lexical error (LE), lexical originality (LO) and lexical frequency profile (LFP) [2–4].

In the field of Chinese as a second language (CSL), researchers have conducted a series of empirical studies on the relationship between lexical richness and writing quality. Li Huang and Xujing Qian [5] investigated the developmental features of lexical richness in CSL learners' writings using lexical variation, lexical sophistication, lexical originality, lexical error and demonstrated that after one semester, the lexical sophistication of CSL learners increased and lexical error decreased, but the other three dimensions did not change significantly. By diving the lexical richness into lexical accuracy, lexical sophistication and variation, Xianwen Cao and Xin Tian [6] compared the writing performance of L1 and L2 students of Chinese. The results revealed that the learners' lexical accuracy was lower than L1 speakers, while the lexical variation was higher. Jifeng Wu [7] examined lexical variation, lexical sophistication, lexical density, and lexical error to assess the developmental features of lexical richness in writing and its relationship with writing quality. He concluded that as the language proficiency improved, L1 speakers' lexical variation and sophistication increased significantly, the formal errors decreased gradually, but the semantic errors increased substantially, and the production lexical was seriously insufficient. Based on this, Yixuan Wang [8] further integrated 27 lexical richness indicators to explore the relationship of each indicator to CSL writing scores. It is found that the proportion of lexical errors and the number of word types, as well as the number of frequently used words, had correlations with writing quality.

Although the previous studies have assessed the lexical richness of CSL learners, there are still several drawbacks: First, from the perspective of the dataset, the existing studies are primarily based on a dataset of small-scale or case studies, as to it is applicable to other learners needs to be further verified. Additionally, most of the studies examining the relationship between lexical richness and writing quality mainly focus on the developmental features of lexical indicators in CSL writings. Secondly, as for the indicators, researchers have adopted fewer indicators compared to the lexical richness studies in EFL. The findings of many studies could not be compared horizontally and lacked a well-accepted lexical richness system in CSL. Last but not least, in terms of the research method, the indicators in many studies still need to be extracted by hand, which is time-consuming.

In light of this, the current paper attempts to use natural language processing techniques to automatically calculate the semantic indicators of Chinese lexical based on a large-scale corpus of Chinese learners' writings. We construct a six-dimensional lexical richness feature system to examine the relationship between different quality of writing scripts and different dimensions of lexical indicators, in order to provide a reference for Chinese lexical acquisition and its related research specifically.

2   Research Design

2.1   Research Questions

The present study investigates the impact of six dimensions of lexical richness (namely, lexical sophistication, lexical variation, lexical density, lexical errors, lexical frequency profile and lexical originality) to the quality of Chinese as a second language (CSL) learners' writing quality. According, this study is guided by the following research questions:

1. What kind of indicators in lexical variation should be selected to evaluate CSL learners' writing texts?
2. What kind of indicators in lexical sophistication should be selected to evaluate the quality of CSL learners' writing texts?
3. What kind of indicators in lexical density should be selected to evaluate the quality of CSL learners' writing texts?
4. What kind of indicators in lexical error should be selected to evaluate the quality of CSL learners' writing texts?

5. What kind of indicators in lexical originality should be selected to evaluate the quality of CSL learners' writing texts?
6. What kind of indicators in lexical frequency profile should be selected to evaluate the quality of CSL learners' writing texts?

2.2 Data Description

The writing samples used for the current study were drawn from HSK Dynamic Composition Corpus[1]. This corpus was compiled by Beijing Language and Culture University, and consists of approximately 10,000 pieces of written texts written by intermediate-advanced non-native Chinese speakers from all over the world in HSK (abbr. of Hànyǔ Shuǐpíng Kǎoshì in Pinyin, or Chinese Proficiency Test). These writing texts in the corpus are rated from 40 points to 95 points with five as an interval. The mean score is 69.49 and the standard deviation is 19.98.

For this research, 1,000 scripts were randomly selected from the corpus as our data set (the total number of tokens is 364,100). Then the essays ranked among 40–55, 60–75 and 80–95 were assigned to Group A, B and C, respectively. The sample size of Group A to C were 396, 336 and 268. As compositions in the data set are manually labeled with different types of writing errors, we carefully remove these annotation tags after retrieving the writing error indicator.

2.3 Feature Selection

Lexical Variation
Lexical variation also known as Lexical diversity [9], generally refers to the variety of unique word types used in a speech or writing sample [10]. There exist several manners to measure lexical variation. One traditional measure is the type-token ratio (TTR), that is, the ratio of the number of different words to the number of words om a text [11], which is widely used in L2 acquisition research. The hypothesis of lexical variation is that higher proficiency language users will use a wider variety of vocabulary items [12]. However, this measure has been widely criticized by many researchers for its sensitivity to text length [13–15].

To overcome this problem, this current paper used another two transformations of TTR, including Uber Indicator (UTTR) [16] and Root TTR [17] (RTTR) to examine lexical variation in the writing samples of CSL learners.

In addition to the two transformations, we also used the number of tokens (NN), the number of types (NT), and TTR to assess the lexical variation more systematically.

Lexical Sophistication
Lexical sophistication is currently by far the most operationalized indicator of lexical richness, which measures the proportion of relatively unusual or advanced words in the learners' writing samples [4]. A well-written text is supposed to involve a few advanced words that fit in with genres [4]. To decide what kind of words could be labelled as 'sophistication' would depend on the researcher's definition [3]. Li Huang and Xujing

---

[1] http://hsk.blcu.edu.cn

Qian [5], who investigated the lexical use in L2 writing texts by Chinese beginning learners, identified the words of level B, level C and level D as sophisticated words in the Syllabus of Chinese Level Vocabulary and Chinese Character Level (Revised Vision,2001) (Syllabus). Yixuan Wang [8] aimed to examine the lexical features of intermediate-advanced CSL learners, therefore defined the words of HSK-3 level to HSK-6 level and the words out of the syllabus as sophisticated words, then calculate the ratio of the number of sophisticated words to the total number of lexical words in a text.

We adopted Yixuan Wang's [8] definition of sophisticated words since both of our data came from HSK Dynamic Composition Corpus. It is also noteworthy that the present paper differed from Yixuan Wang's [8] was we used tokens (N) and types (T) to calculate the values of lexical sophistication. Hence two indicators would be used in this dimension.

Lexical Density

Lexical density typically refers to the ratio of the number of lexical words (i.e., nouns, verbs, adjectives, and adverbs, NLW) to the total number of words (NGW) in a writing manuscript. Ure (1971) [18] found that lexical density in written texts is higher than in spoken texts and Halliday [19] pointed out that lexical density is a useful measure to distinguish levels of texts along the oral-written continuum, Therefore, a text with a higher lexical density is characteristically more written-like, and lexical density will increase if the text moves along the continuum from spoken to written (Zhang et al., 2021). Although the significance of lexical density is generally accepted, there is notable variation in how to calculate this important indicator. Ure (1971) [18] proposed that lexical density was the ratio of the number of lexical words to the number of grammatical words. Based on Ure's definition, Halliday [19] measured lexical density by calculating the ratio of the number of lexical words to the total number of clauses in a text.

For this current study, we used the 6 indicators to investigate the lexical density. Firstly, we calculated the ratio of the number of lexical words to the number of total words (LD1). Secondly, we employed Ure's [18] (1971) and Halliday's [19] methods to assess the lexical density respectively. Yixuan Wang [8] suggested that the low number of grammatical words in the text could affect the writing performance to some extent, so the proportion of grammatical words (LD2) was also included in this study. In addition, the number of lexical words (NLW) and grammatical words (NGW) were applied in our study.

Lexical Errors

The occurrence of errors is a common feature of L2 writing [4] which has been dealt with in studies that cover the whole spectrum of learners' errors and generally far outweigh grammatical ones in second language performance [20]. Yanhui Zhang and Weiping Wu [21] declaimed those lexical errors became conspicuous as quality indicators of CSL learners' written work and as predictors of lexical proficiency. Consequently, lexical errors may obscure the writer's original meaning and hinder the reader's interpretation of the text. The percentage of lexical errors is negatively correlated with L2 writing quality [22].

Jifeng Wu [7] divided lexical errors in CSL learners' writing manuscripts into lexical form errors and semantic errors. Yixuan Wang [8] defined lexical errors as five categories, i.e., word missing (MW), word redundant (RW) and the errors of separable words (SW) as well as borrowed words (BW).

As the writing samples in our study were too many to label multi-granularity lexical errors, we decided to use the error-annotations in HSK Dynamic Composition Corpus. Then we proposed seven indicators to measure CLS lexical errors.

Lexical Originality

Lexical originality assesses the L2 learner's performance relative to the group in which the composition was written [3]. This indicator is generally defined as the percentage of words in a given piece of writing that are used by one particular writer and no one else in the group. However, Laufer and Nation [3] argued that such a measure is not reliable since it is defined not only by the composition in question but by the group factor. Read [4] pointed out that this indicator could not evaluate the development of lexical performance. After that, quite a few studies including ESL and CSL didn't investigate the contribution of lexical originality [7, 23].

However, these conclusions were all based on a small corpus, and whether the argument is reliable or not needs to be further investigated in a large-scale corpus. Consequently, our paper tried to use a larger data set and adopt the formula of Li Huang and Xujing Qian [5] 's research (LO1) to explore if this indicator is effective.

Lexical Frequency Profile

The lexical frequency profile shows the relative proportion of words from different frequency levels [3]. It reflects that an L2 learner with higher lexical proficiency tends to use less frequent words in writing manuscripts. Yixuan Wang [8] defined the words from level 1 to level 4 in the syllabus as the most frequently used words, frequently used words, infrequently used words, and most infrequently used words. Further referred to Read's [4] method, Yixuan Wang [8] calculated the percentage of each category based on token and type respectively in writing samples.

Unlike Yixuan Wang [8] 's research, this work introduced the vocabulary frequency lists of BCC Corpus and the Modern Chinese Corpus (MCC) established by the National Language Commission to describe lexical frequency profiles. The procedure was as follows: first, calculated the average word frequency and standard deviation of the two lexicons separately. Besides that, divided the words into high-frequency words (HFW), intermediate-frequency words (IFW), and low-frequency words (LFW) based on the result of adding or subtracting the standard deviation from the average. Finally, got the number of tokens and types of the three categories of words and then calculate the proportion.

In general, the lexical richness of 32 indicators in 6 dimensions are displayed in Table 1.

Table 1. Measures of 32 indicators in 6 dimensions.

Dimension	Indicator	Code	Formula
Lexical variation (LV)	Number of tokens	NN	/
	Number of types	NT	/
	Type-token ratio	TTR	T/N
	Root TTR	RTTR	$T/\sqrt{N}$
	Unber index	UTTR	LogT/LogN
Lexical sophistication (LS)	The proportion of sophisticated words in terms of tokens	PSW_N	NSW/N
	The proportion of sophisticated words based on Syllabus in terms of types	PSWT	NSW/T
Lexical density (LD)	The ratio of the number of Lexical words to the number of total words	LD1	NLW / N
	The ratio of the number of Lexical words to the number of grammatical words	Ure's	NLW/NGW
	The ratio of the number of Lexical words to the number of clauses	Halliday's	NLW/NC
	The number of lexical words	NLW	/
	The number of grammatical words	NGW	/
	The ratio of the number of grammatical words to the number of total words	LD2	NGW/N
Lexical errors (LE)	The ratio of the number errors in spelling or word-choice (SWC) to the total words	LE_{swc}	SWC/N
	The ratio of the number of errors in separable words (SW) to the total words	LEsw	SW/N
	The ratio of the number missing words (MW) to the total words	LEmw	MW/N
	The ratio of the number redundant words (RW) to the total words	LErw	RW/N
	The ratio of the number of errors of foreign words usage	LE_{fwu}	FWU/N
	The ratio of the number of all errors to the total words	LE1	E/N
Lexical originality (LO)	The ratio of the number of original words to the number of the total words	LO1	NOW/N

(*continued*)

Table 1. (*continued*)

Dimension	Indicator	Code	Formula
Lexical frequency profile (LFP)	The proportion of low-frequency words in BCC in terms of tokens	PLFWBCC-N	LFW_{BCC}/N
	The proportion of low-frequency words in BCC in terms of types	$PLFW_{BCC\text{-}T}$	LFW_{BCC}/T
	The proportion of low-frequency words in MCC in terms of tokens	$PLFW_{MCC\text{-}N}$	LFW_{MCC}/N
	The proportion of low-frequency words in MCC in terms of types	$PLFW_{MCC\text{-}T}$	LFW_{MCC}/T
	The proportion of intermediate-frequency words in BCC in terms of tokens	$PIFW_{BCC\text{-}N}$	IFW_{BCC}/N
	The proportion of intermediate-frequency words in BCC in terms of types	$PIFW_{BCC\text{-}T}$	IFW_{BCC}/T
	The proportion of intermediate-frequency words in MCC in terms of tokens	$PIFW_{MCC\text{-}N}$	IFW_{MCC}/N
	The proportion of intermediate-frequency words in MCC in terms of types	$PIFW_{MCC\text{-}T}$	IFW_{MCC}/T
	The proportion of high-frequency words in BCC in terms of tokens	PHFWBCC-N	HFW_{BCC}/N
	The proportion of high-frequency words in BCC in terms of types	$PHFW_{BCC\text{-}T}$	HFW_{BCC}/T
	The proportion of high-frequency words in MCC in terms of tokens	$PHFW_{MCC\text{-}N}$	HFW_{MCC}/N
	The proportion of high-frequency words in MCC in terms of types	$PHFW_{MCC\text{-}T}$	HFW_{MCC}/T

2.4 Automatic Extraction of Lexical Indicators

Natural language processing techniques were employed in the current work to extract each indicator. We perform word segmentation and POS tagging using Jieba. Then the lexical indicators were extracted automatically and 2 students with backgrounds in linguistics checked and corrected the results. The whole process of this experiment was implemented by Python.

2.5 Evaluation Metrics

The correlation coefficients can be used to determine whether two indicators are correlated and how tightly they are correlated. To investigate the relations between the lexical richness indices and writing quality, we first adopted Pearson Correlations between all lexical variables and the holistic score of writing quality. We then checked all predictor/independent variables for multicollinearity and eliminated collinear indicators. After that, the lexical richness indicators that were most relevant to the writing score could be selected to conduct a multiple linear regression (MLR) model. This analytical approach was utilized to assess the degree to which the chosen lexical variables influence the human-rated holistic writing score since multiple regression demonstrates combined and independent contributions of predictors.

3 Results

3.1 Lexical Variation

The descriptive statistics of lexical variation indicators are shown in Table 2.

Table 2. Means and standard deviations of lexical variation indicators.

Group	T		N		TTR		UTTR		RTTR	
	Mean	SD	Mean	SD	Mean	SD	Mean	SD	Mean	SD
Group A	94.40	23.22	160.44	48.73	0.60	0.08	23.19	5.02	7.52	0.87
Group B	121.32	22.53	207.54	43.13	0.59	0.07	23.14	4.38	8.35	0.90
Group C	143.16	29.33	237.19	49.26	0.61	0.06	25.65	5.78	8.96	1.06

As can be seen from Table 2, the mean values of N, T, UTTR and RTTR in writing samples steadily increased as writing score increased, suggesting that these four indicators were quantitatively positively correlated with writing quality. TTR, on the other hand, displayed a tendency that was independent of writing scores because its mean value first decreased and then increased with the writing score going up. The findings were consistent with Yixuan Wang (2017).

Subsequently, we worked out Pearson correlations between the three groups and the five indicators. The results indicated that four variables had a correlation with writing scores ($r \geq 0.30$), including T ($r = 0.68$), N ($r = 0.61$), UTTR ($r = 0.64$), and RTTR ($r = 0.33$). The correlation coefficients of Pearson revealed that the writing samples are lexically varied. Learners with poor writing performance tend to produce compositions by repeating certain words. However, the students who get a higher score prefer to use more variation words.

3.2 Lexical Sophistication

Table 3 reflects the statistical results of lexical sophistication of CSL learners' written text across different groups. It has been observed that the mean values of PSW_N and PSW_T exhibit an upward trend. This demonstrates that the two lexical sophistication indicators are distributed differently across Group A to Group C and are positively connected with writing quality.

We computed the Pearson correlation to examine the relationship between the three groups and the two indicators mentioned above. A correlation was found between PSW_T and writing performance (r = 0.329), indicating that this indicator is more effective than PSW_N in the task of predicting the learner's writing score.

Table 3. Means and standard deviations of lexical sophistication indicators.

Group	PSWT		PSW$_N$	
	Mean	SD	Mean	SD
Group A	0.112	0.034	0.092	0.035
Group B	0.125	0.034	0.100	0.033
Group C	0.140	0.037	0.111	0.033

3.3 Lexical Density

Our third research question concerned the relationship between lexical density and CSL learners' writing. Limited by the length of this article, Table 4 only provides the mean and standard deviation of N_{lex} and N_{gra}. It is not difficult to discover in Table 4 that as the learners' writing scores improve, the mean values of the number of lexical words and grammatical words rise dramatically.

The results of the Pearson correlation between 4 indicators and writing performance showed that only the N_{lex} and the N_{gra} were significantly correlated with writing scores (r = 0.605 and 0.508, respectively).

Table 4. Means and standard deviations of lexical density indicators.

Group	N_{lex}		N_{gra}	
	Mean	SD	Mean	SD
Group A	115.766	39.496	33.153	11.833
Group B	152.685	32.091	42.746	10.505
Group C	176.839	37.745	48.677	12.693

3.4 Lexical Errors

Table 5 reflects the mean values and the standard deviation of the 7 indicators of lexical errors in different groups. As writing quality moves develops, it is apparent that learners' lexical errors eventually decline. For intermediate-advanced CSL learners, the number of errors in separable words is quite few but the proportion of errors of SWC is highest demonstrating that learners still have difficulty in spelling and word-choice.

Only the proportion of errors of SWC has the strongest correlation with writing scores ($r = 0.566$), indicating that grades of texts are most vulnerable to the impact of the proportion of errors of SWC during the scoring process, while other indicators of lexical errors have a negligible effect on scoring.

Table 5. Means and standard deviations of lexical errors indicators.

Group	LE_{swc}	LEsw	LE_{fwu}	LE_{mw}	LErw	LEn
Group A	0.028	0	0.005	0.010	0.011	0.053
Group B	0.018	0	0.002	0.007	0.008	0.012
Group C	0.016	0	0.001	0.005	0.004	0.027

3.5 Lexical Originality

The statistical results of the correlation between lexical originality and writing quality are presented in Table 6. It can be seen from the mean values in the table that the difference of lexical originality across the different groups is not obvious. However, the Pearson correlation between LO1 and writing scores is 0.44 ($r \geq 0.3$), which indicates that there stands a positive correlation.

The fact reflects that the one who tends to use more original words are easy to get a high score.

Table 6. Means and standard deviations of lexical originality indicators.

Group	Mean	SD
Group A	0.649	0.067
Group B	0.627	0.062
Group C	0.619	0.056

3.6 Lexical Frequency Profile

The mean values of lexical frequency profile are displayed in Table 7 and Table 8, respectively. We found that group B and group CV both utilized more low-frequency words. Generally speaking, it is more challenging to master and comprehend the words which are not used commonly. Therefore, it is easier to get a good grade to use low-frequency items that are relevant to the prompt to convey thoughts. The statistical findings could be verified by the results of lexical sophistication.

Table 7. Means and standard deviations of lexical frequency profile indicators based on BCC.

Group	PLFW$_{BCC-T}$	PIFW$_{BCC-T}$	PHFW$_{BCC-T}$	PLFW$_{BCC-N}$	PIFW$_{BCC-N}$	PHFW$_{BCC-N}$
Group A	0.153	0.032	0.411	0.131	0.031	0.361
Group B	0.190	0.034	0.367	0.156	0.032	0.322
Group C	0.218	0.034	0.033	0.175	0.031	0.293

The correlation coefficients of the 12 lexical frequency profile indicators with the writing scores were all more than 0.3, except the proportion of high frequency words in terms of tokens which is more than 0.5, indicating that the lexical frequency profile based on word frequency can reflect the features of lexical richness and is significantly related to the writing performance.

Table 8. Means and standard deviations of lexical frequency profile indicators based on MCC.

Group	PLFW$_{MCC-T}$	PIFW$_{MCC-T}$	PHFW$_{MCC-N}$	PLFW$_{MCC-N}$	PIFW$_{MCC-N}$	PHFW$_{MCC-N}$
Group A	0.506	0.041	0.326	0.422	0.035	0.443
Group B	0.530	0.038	0.282	0.436	0.035	0.419
Group C	0.524	0.032	0.269	0.429	0.027	0.414

3.7 Multiple Linear Regression Analysis

The current study conducted multiple regression analyses on 32 indicators so as to construct a robust model to further investigate the influence of each indicator on CSL learners' performance. The indicators entered the regression analysis were required to meet the following conditions: firstly, the indicators were significantly correlated with composition scores ($r \geq 0.3$); secondly, the indicators that are collinear should be deleted ($r < 0.3$).

Table 9 presents the 7 indicators that entered the regression analysis and their correlation coefficients with writing quality (in descending order), except for the lexical sophistication dimension, for which only one indicator entered the regression analysis.

We set the above 6 indicators as variables and used the package of statsmodels in python to conduct multiple linear regression analysis. The results are described in Table 10 and the regression coefficients of each indicator are shown in Table 11.

Table 9. Correlations between writing quality and lexical richness indicators.

Dimension	Indicators	Pearson's
LFP	PLFW$_{BCC-T}$	0.706
LR	N	0.676
LD	NLW	0.605
LE	LE1	0.581
LO	LO1	0.439
LS	PSW$_T$	0.329

Table 10. Regression analysis results.

	R^2	Adjusted R^2	Std err
Model-6	0.692	0.686	2.364

According to the calculation, the regression model that incorporates all six indicators has a standard error of the estimate (Std. Error of the Estimate) that is lower than 10.46 (the standard deviation of writing scores). The R2 of the model is 0.692, indicating that 69.2% of the variance in the writing scores can be explained based on lexical richness, which means that the model is effective.

Table 9 demonstrates that, except for the number of lexical words, all five indicators are valid predictors. The regression coefficients show that PLFW$_{BCC-T}$ has a significant effect on writing performance. The second place was PSW$_T$, followed by LE1, LO1 and N.

Finally, we build the regression equation of lexical richness based on the regression coefficients of each indicator, that is:

Writing score $= - 84.4267*$PLFW$_{BCC-T} + 46.4724*$PSW$_T - 0.4909*$LE1$-0.2650*$LO1$ + 0.1172*$N.

Table 11. The summary of regression coefficients.

Dimension	indicators	Coef	Std err	P > |t|
LFP	PLFW$_{BCC-T}$	−84.4267	9.466	0.000
LR	N	0.1172	0.0034	0.001
LD	NLW	0.0423	0.023	0.072
LE	LE1	−0.4909	0.103	0.000
LO	LO1	−0.2650	0.109	0.015
LS	PSW$_T$	46.4724	10.971	0.000

4 Discussion

4.1 The Relationship Between Lexical Richness and Writing Quality

This study examined the relationship between several indicators and writing quality by measuring the lexical richness in learners' writing texts from the perspectives of lexical variation, lexical sophistication, lexical density, lexical errors, lexical originality, and lexical frequency profile. The findings reveal a correlation between the performance of CSL writing and 21 of the 34 lexical richness measures based on 6 dimensions, proving the validity and reliability of the lexical richness indicators developed in this study.

Based on this, we performed a multiple regression analysis to assess how well the lexical richness indicators could predict writing quality. The regression produced a model that include five indicators, i.e., $PLFW_{BCC-T}$, T, LE1, LO1, PSW_T, and explained 69.2% of the variance in holistic scores.

To validate this model, a 5-fold cross validation multiple regression was also conducted using the five variables identified in the previous multiple regression model. The 5-fold cross validation result indicates that the five-variable model was stable across subsections of the data set and generalizable to other populations.

The indicator $PLFW_{BCC-T}$, belonging to the dimension of lexical sophistication, was negatively correlated with writing quality which reflected that the proportion of low-frequency words in Group C was the lowest. Lexical frequency profile is a crucial component of lexical usage, and related works demonstrated that CSL learners were particularly sensitive to word frequency, which is directly related to the reader's capacity for word decoding.

The significance of the indicator PSW_T was second place in the regression model, reporting that the writing texts with high scores tend to convey their thoughts by using more complex and advanced words. it should be noted that the low-frequency terms in this study, which were based on a large L1 corpus, did not overlap with the sophisticated words. High-frequency words that are used frequently by L1 speakers are likewise used frequently by L2 learners, while the complicated words may not be in the same situation among L1 speakers.

The indicator of lexical variation, i.e., T, was strongly connected with the quality of the student's writing, showing that as the writings' scores rose, the diversity of their lexical usage was also increasing. The lexical breadth of writers is related to their lexical size, and the large the lexical size acquired by L2 learners, the broader the variety of words they can use.

The indicator, LE1, which belongs to the dimension of lexical error, and the indicator of lexical originality both have a negative impact on the scores of writings. The former is in line with our perception that high scores of essays typically contain relatively fewer lexical problems. But contrary to what we would expect, the originality of the lexical was lower in the high-score group than in the low-score group. The reason for this may be that the "original words" were a more subjective issue, therefore it was unfair to indicate originality simply by dividing the total number of proper words in the essay by the words that other students did not use; in addition, because of the various subjects of the essay, the writings are easy to include some "unique words" which concerned with the topic, but it is doubtful whether they are novel words or not.

The validity of lexical density has also been criticized [8], and scholars like Read [4], Xiaofei Lu [24], and Jifeng Wu [7] have demonstrated that lexical density does not indicate learners' writing performance, which is doubtful in this study. The number of lexical words, the number of grammatical terms, and the proportion of lexical words were all related with writing quality in this study ($r > 0.3$), even though the indicators based on the lexical density did not enter the final regression equation. Therefore, it is important to explore the issue of whether lexical density and writing quality are correlated or not as more data sets are added.

4.2 Pedagogical Implications

Based on the above findings, we believe that teachers should pay attention to the following issues in teaching Chinese writing.

Based on the aforementioned findings, we think that teachers should pay more attention to the following issues in CSL writing.

First, a variety of instructional techniques should be employed to broaden CSL learners' vocabulary, particularly high-frequency and advanced vocabulary. This study demonstrates how high-frequency words have a significant impact on the writing quality of intermediate-advanced Chinese learners. Therefore, to increase the precision and readability of their writings, students should be encouraged to employ high-frequency terms during the writing process. Additionally, most of the research has demonstrated that the choice of thematically appropriate high-frequency words can raise lexical complexity and hence enhance learners' writing performance, and our study supports those findings.

Second, lexical errors made by learners should be addressed, and specific measures should be employed to overcome this issue. Teachers are encouraged to apply a variety of approaches to assist students to avoid making lexical errors while writing as research has shown that fewer lexical errors occur in high-score essays. For instance, utilizing lexical discrimination to distinguish terms that are similar.

5 Conclusion

This research examined 6 dimensions of lexical richness, including lexical variation, lexical complexity, lexical density, lexical errors, lexical originality, and lexical frequency profile, in Chinese compositions by Chinese intermediate-advanced. By introducing a larger scale of composition data of CSL, we investigated systematically the relationship of 32 indicators of lexical richness to the quality of CSL writings. The statistical findings revealed that, with the exception of the TTR, PSW_N, and the indicators of lexical density, all the indicators left were correlated with writing performance. The findings of the regression analysis indicated that $PLFW_{BCC-T}$ and PSW_T had the strongest significance on writing performance. TTR, LO, and LE1 rank third, fourth, and fifth, respectively.

The relationship between the lexical richness indicators and the quality of CSL writing has been extensively assessed in this work, however, there are still some issues that need to be further investigated. This paper utilized 1000 pieces of HSK writing samples, which is an improvement over previous research in terms of data set size. The HSK writing participants, however, came from a variety of countries and all of them are intermediate-advanced learners. Therefore, more and more compositions written by CSL learners should be introduced in order to construct a rather balanced data set. Second, deep learning techniques could be used to find more indicators of lexical richness as it has achieved state-of-art achievements in many NLP tasks.

Acknowledgements. This study was supported by High-performance Computing Platform of Peking University.

References

1. Shi, G., Yang, C., Li, X.: A study on the idiomatic development of CSL learners' vocabulary collocation knowledge. Int. Chin. Lang. Educ. **6**, 5–12+29 (2021)
2. Batia, L.: The lexical profile of second language writing: does it change over time? RELC J. **25**, 21–33 (1994)
3. Laufer, B., Nation, P.: Vocabulary size and use - lexical richness in L2 written production. Appl. Linguist. **16**, 307–322 (1995). https://doi.org/10.1093/applin/16.3.307
4. Read, J.: Assessing Vocabulary. Cambridge University Press, Cambridge (2000). https://doi.org/10.1017/CBO9780511732942
5. Huang, L., Qian, X.: An Inquiry into Chinese learners' knowledge of productive vocabulary: a quantitative study. Chin. Lang. Learn. **6** (2003)
6. Cao, X., T, X.: The effects of task planning on the lexical richness of foreign students' Chinese oral production. Chinese Lang. Learn. **10** (2020)
7. Wu, J.: Research on lexical richness development in CSL writing by English native Speakers. Chinese teaching in the world. **30**, 129–142 (2016). https://doi.org/10.13724/j.cnki.ctiw.2016.01.013
8. Wang, Y.: The correlation between lexical richness and writing scores of CSL learners-the multivariable linear regression model and equation of writing quality. Appl. Linguist (Chin.) 93–101 (2017). https://doi.org/10.16499/j.cnki.1003-5397.2017.02.011
9. Treffers-Daller, J., Parslow, P., Williams, S.: Back to basics: how measures of lexical diversity can help discriminate between CEFR Levels. Appl. Linguist. amw009 (2016). https://doi.org/10.1093/applin/amw009
10. McCarthy, P.M., Jarvis, S.: MTLD, vocd-D, and HD-D: a validation study of sophisticated approaches to lexical diversity assessment. Behav. Res. Methods. **42**, 381–392 (2010). https://doi.org/10.3758/BRM.42.2.381
11. Templin, M.C.: Certain language skills in children: their development and interrelationships (1957)
12. Eguchi, M., Kyle, K.: Continuing to Explore the Multidimensional Nature of Lexical Sophistication: The Case of Oral Proficiency Interviews. Mod. Lang. J. **104**, 381–400 (2020). https://doi.org/10.1111/modl.12637
13. Arnaud, P.J.L.: Objective lexical and grammatical characteristics of L2 written compositions and the validity of separate-component tests. In: Arnaud, P.J.L., Béjoint, H. (eds.) Vocabulary and Applied Linguistics, pp. 133–145. Palgrave Macmillan, London. (1992). https://doi.org/10.1007/978-1-349-12396-4_13
14. Engber, C.A.: The relationship of lexical proficiency to the quality of ESL compositions. J. Second Lang. Writ. **4**, 139–155 (1995)
15. Richards, B.: Type token ratios - what do they really tell us. J. Child Lang. **14**, 201–209 (1987). https://doi.org/10.1017/S0305000900012885

16. Jarvis, S.: Short texts, best-fitting curves and new measures of lexical diversity. Lang. Test. **19**, 57–84 (2002). https://doi.org/10.1191/0265532202lt220oa

17. Torruella, J., Capsada, R.: Lexical statistics and Tipological structures: a measure of lexical richness. Procedia - Soc. Behav. Sci. **95**, 447–454 (2013)

18. Ure,J.: Lexical density: a computational technique and some findings. In: M. Coultard (Ed.). Talking about text, pp. 27–48. English Language Research, University of Birmingham, Birmingham, England

19. Halliday, M.A.K.: Spoken and Written Language. Oxford University Press, Oxford (1989)

20. Llach, M.P.A.: Lexical errors as writing quality predictors. Stud. Linguist. **61**, 1–19 (2007). https://doi.org/10.1111/j.1467-9582.2007.00127.x

21. Zhang, Y., Wu, W.: How effective are lexical richness measures for differentiations of vocabulary proficiency? A comprehensive examination with clustering analysis. Lang. Test. Asia **11**(1), 1–19 (2021). https://doi.org/10.1186/s40468-021-00133-6

22. Wang, H., Zhou, X.: A longitudinal study on the features of lexical richness in writing by university non-English majors. Foreign Lang. Their Teach. 5 (2012)

23. Zhang, H., Chen, M., Li, X.: Developmental features of lexical richness in English writings by Chinese beginner learners. Front. Psychol. **12**, 665988 (2021). https://doi.org/10.3389/fpsyg.2021.665988

24. Lu, X.: The relationship of lexical richness to the quality of ESL learners' oral narratives. Mod. Lang. J. **96**, 190–208 (2012). https://doi.org/10.1111/j.1540-4781.2011.01232_1.x

Research on Korean "Long-Before-Short" Preference from the Perspective of Dependency Distance

Yingnan Hua, Jiapeng Li, and Yude Bi[(✉)]

Fudan University, Shanghai 200433, China
{20110120015,21110120014,biyude}@fudan.edu.cn

Abstract. The word order of different language types has different syntactic arrangement. Under the framework of dependency syntax, the change of constituent position in a sentence directly affects the size of dependency distance. Based on the general rule of word order in different language types, this paper makes a quantitative analysis of the reasons from the perspective of dependency distance. It is found that: First, the general rule that SVO has a smaller mean dependency distance than SOV cannot be obtained when considering the additional constituent of sentences. Second, in the dative-accusative construction of Korean, the "long-before-short" order is more preferred. Finally, the mean dependency distance has nothing to do with the specific constituents before the root verb, but only with its ordering rules.

Keywords: Korean · dependency distance · word order · long-before-short preferences

1 Introduction

Word order is used to represent the relative positions of language Constituents, and is also one of the most easily observed aspects of human language syntax [1]. The word order of human language can be classified differently according to the Angle of attention. According to the order of the most common subject (S), predicate (V) and object (O), it can be divided into SOV, SVO, VSO, VOS, OSV and OVS, among which the first three word orders are the most common, accounting for about 83% of the total types [2]; According to the word order between the verb and the object, there are only two logical possibilities, either OV or VO [3]. Under the framework of dependency grammar, word order can be divided according to the relative order between the governor and dependent. When the governor comes after the dependent, it is called the head-final language, such as Korean, Japanese, German, etc. When the governor precedes the dependent, it is called the head-initial language, such as Chinese and English. At the same time, a language is said to have a free word order if its dependents are less uniform in their position relative to the governor than those of a language with a fixed word order [4]. The head-final languages generally have rich morphological markers and flexible word order, so they generally also have free word order characteristics.

Q. Su et al. (Eds.): CLSW 2022, LNAI 13496, pp. 132–142, 2023.
https://doi.org/10.1007/978-3-031-28956-9_11

In the framework of dependency grammar, dependency distance represents the linear distance between words. Therefore, different linear ordering rules between words in a sentence will directly affect the dependency distance. A large-scale corpus analyses, computational simulations and psychological experiments have confirmed that, despite the obvious diversity of word order in various language types, there is a general rule of dependency distance minimization. A study of 37 languages by Futrell et al. [5] showed that dependency distance minimization makes the word order of languages tend to minimize permutations.

Although the dependency distance minimization is a general rule of language, there are also certain differences in the specific influence of different language types on the dependency distance due to different word order. Ferrer-i-Cancho [6, 7], Gildea and Temperley [8] found that theoretically SVO has a smaller mean dependency distance (MDD) than SOV. The conclusion can be drawn intuitively from Fig. 1 by simply abstracting the SVO and SOV word order types. For SVO word order languages, the predicate is in the middle of the sentence, and its MDD is 1. The predicate of SOV is at the end of the sentence and MDD is 1.5.

Fig. 1. The dependency distance between SVO and SOV word order

However, the change of word order in human language is very complex in actual use, and in real text, there are very few structures in which SOV or SVO only appear in a simple, fixed order as shown in Fig. 1. Most of human languages add other Constituents on the basis of this basic word order or adopt a more free word order to express richer thoughts and emotions. In addition, previous studies have shown that, in addition to word order, factors such as sentence length, dependency direction, number of long-distance dependencies, annotation scheme and genres will all affect the mean dependency distances. In particular, Hiranuma [9] found that there is no significant difference in dependency distance between Japanese (OV word order) and English (VO word order). Liu [10] conducted an empirical study on 20 languages and found that the MDD of Chinese (VO word order) was generally higher than that of OV languages such as Japanese and Turkish. Gildea and Temperley [8] observed that German tends to have longer dependencies compared to English, which they attributed to the greater freedom of German word order, that is, the freer the word order is, the lower the degree of dependency distance minimization is. Korean is a SOV word order language, and the word order is more flexible. Compared with English and Chinese, which have a relatively fixed word order in SVO, does Korean have a smaller MDD? Therefore, it is necessary to carry out a comparative study of word order for different language types.

Previous studies focused on the question whether the conclusion that SVO languages have smaller MDD than SOV languages is universal. For a single type of language, what is the regularity of SVO or SOV word order? Through a series of corpus analyses, Hawkins

[11, 12] showed that syntactic selection usually places short Constituent closer to the head than long ones, arguing that such ordering makes language comprehension easier. Since this placement minimizes the size of the Constituent Recognition Domain (CRD), it helps the parser identify sub-elements of a larger Constituent earlier and faster. By analyzing English and Japanese corpora, Hawkins confirmed that short-before-long ordering is preferred in English, while long-before-short ordering is indeed preferred in Japanese. Temperley [13, 14] associated this word order preference with dependency distance minimization, arguing that if a head has multiple dependents and their order can be selected, then when the shorter dependent is located closer to the head, it is most beneficial to minimize the dependency distance. And this principle has been verified in the empirical analysis of English and German corpora, the syntactic patterns that conform to this rule are generally superior to the opposite syntactic patterns. Choi [15] used a million-word corpus to examine the word order alternation in the dative-accusative construction in Korean. And it quantitatively testifies to the "long-before-short" preference of the Korean word order. This study provides quantitative support for the preference of "long-before-short" in the OV word order, however, this study only conducts quantitative statistics on the dative-accusative construction in Korean, and does not make in-depth analysis of the reasons for this phenomenon. Dennison [16] confirmed the preference of "long-before-short" in Korean through on-line production experiments and off-line judgment studies, and believed that the order of "long-before-short" reflects the processing strategy, which is beneficial to the production system to reduce the difficulty at the verb positions. In order to make a better quantitative analysis of the Korean word order arrangement, this paper tries to explain the Korean word order preference from the perspective of dependency distance, in order to find out the deep reasons for the Korean word order preference.

2   Resources and Methods

2.1   Corpus

The dependency treebank selected in this paper is the corpus of Surface Syntactic Universal Dependencies in Korean (Sud-Korean). SUD (https://surfacesyntacticud.github. io/data/) adopts the Universal dependency annotation scheme based on surface syntax, which is near-isomorphic to UD (https://universaldependencies.org/introduction.html). So far, the Korean dependency treebanks based on SUD annotation scheme include Google Treebank, Kaist Treebank, and Penn Treebank. The SUD-Korean corpus follows the CONLL-U format, its format and data statistics are shown in Fig. 2 and Table 1, respectively.

In order to enhance the reliability of the research results and reduce the influence of variables such as treebank annotation scheme and genre on the research results, SUD-Korean treebank was uniformly used for research and analysis in this paper.

2.2   Calculation Method of Dependency Distance

Dependency grammar focuses on the relationships between words that form a sentence. According to the theory of dependency grammar, dependency distance indicates the "far

sent_id = M2TA_064-s35↓
text = 이것은 오직 원숙한 문화적 정서로만이 가능하다.

1	이것은	이것+은	PRON	npd+jxt	6	dislocated
2	오직	오직	ADV	mag	5	mod
3	원숙한	원숙+하+ㄴ	VERB	ncps+xsm+etm	5	mod
4	문화적	문화+적	NOUN	ncn+xsn_	5	mod
5	정서로만이	정서+로만+이	NOUN	ncn+jxc+jcs	6	subj
6	가능하다	가능+하+다	VERB	ncps+xsm+ef	0	root
7	.	.	PUNCT	sf	6	punct

Fig. 2. Example of SUD-Kaist dependency treebank

Table 1. Data statistics of SUD-Korean dependency treebank

Treebank	Number of sentences	Tokens	Average sentence length	Genre
GSD	6339	80322	12.67	News, blogs
Kaist	27363	350090	12.79	News
PUD	1000	16584	16.58	News, literature, academic manuscript

or near" of the relationship between the governor and the dependent, and the value is represented by the number of words separated between them. In the process of dependency parsing, the dependents in the sentence are continuously stored in the working memory, and can be deleted only when governor appear. The larger the dependency distance, the longer the word is stored and the more difficult it is to process. Therefore, dependency distance is often used as an important indicator to measure memory burden and syntactic difficulty. We use the dependency distance calculation method proposed in [17], and number the words of the sentence from front to back, then the dependency distance of a sentence can be expressed as:

$$d = \sum_{i=1}^{l} dd_i \tag{1}$$

where, dd_i represents the difference value between the governor minus the dependent (itself) word order number of the i-th word in the sentence, that is, the order number difference between two words in a dependency relationship. The difference value has positive and negative, which are used to indicate the direction of dependency. In order to facilitate statistical analysis and better discover language rules, it is usually necessary to ensure that all differences are positive, so dd_i in Formula (1) needs to take the absolute value of serial number differences. Because there is only one root verb in a sentence, the root verb has no governor or its governor can be considered as itself. Therefore, this paper defines the dependency distance of the root verb as 0, The mean dependence distance $\overline{d}$ of a sentence consisting of l words can be expressed as:

$$\overline{d} = \frac{1}{l-1} \sum_{i=1}^{l} |dd_i| \tag{2}$$

3 Results and Discussion

3.1 The Relationship Between SVO vs SOV Word Order and Dependency Distance Minimization

In this section, the SUD-Kaist treebank and the SUD-PUD treebank are selected as research resources for the study of Korean (SOV) and Chinese (SVO) respectively, in order to reduce the influence of other factors on the solution of dependency distance, we preprocessed the treebank as follows: The genres are all news, the sentence length is 10–20, and the total number of sentences is 370. According to Formula (2) in Sect. 2, MDD of SUD-Kaist and SUD-PUD are calculated respectively, and Combined with the proportion of adjacent dependency, we jointly represent the degree of minimization of the dependency distances of the two word order types. The specific results are shown in Table 2:

Table 2. Statistical results of Chinese and Korean dependency distance minimization

SVO (Chinese)		SOV (Korean)	
Mean dependency distance	3.03	Mean of dependency distance	2.48
The proportion of adjacent dependency	45.38%	The proportion of adjacent dependency	60.52%

As can be seen from Table 2, Korean has a higher proportion of adjacent dependencies and smaller MDD than Chinese. In addition to the basic subject-verb-object constituents, human language also includes other additional constituents, such as attributive and adverbial constituents. In which the attributive modifies the subject and object, and the adverbial modifies the predicate. Theoretically Chinese has a smaller MDD than Korean, but when we verified it based on the corpus, we came to the opposite conclusion that Korean has a smaller MDD. Therefore, we hypothesize that the additional constituents have a significant effect on MDD in Both Chinese and Korean, and the length, order and position of the additional constituents in the sentence will have a significant influence on MDD. Dependency distance represents the linear distance between the governor and the dependent, and the linear distance between the two depends on the relative position between the governor and the dependent, which essentially reveals that the word order (position) of different constituents will have an important influence on the dependency distance. When only S, O, and V constituents are considered, Korean has a larger MDD, but in actual language use, the usage and position of other additional constituents in Korean reduces the overall MDD, achieving a trade-off between the main constituents and additional constituents, and reducing the overall syntactic complexity. The following are examples of attributive constituents added in Chinese and Korean sentences, when attributive that modify objects are added to Chinese and Korean sentences respectively, the typical positions of attributive in each language are shown as follows:

(1) 他戴着（象征忠诚的红色的）帽子。
　　S　V　　　 ATT　　　　　 O
'He wears a red hat that symbolizes loyalty.'
(2) 그는 (충성의 상징인 빨간) 모자를 쓴다.
　　S　　　　 ATT　　　　 O　 V

It can be seen from example sentences (1) and (2) that when a Chinese sentence adds attributive that modify the object, the attributive is located between the predicate and the object. When attributive is added to Korean sentences, they appear before the predicate and object. When calculating the mean dependency distance of two sentences, the dependency structure diagram and the mean dependency distance are as follows:

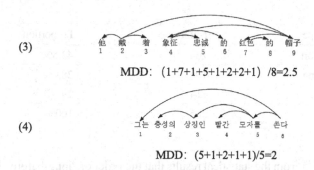

(3)

MDD: (1+7+1+5+1+2+2+1) /8=2.5

(4)

MDD: (5+1+2+1+1)/5=2

It can be seen from the calculation results that when adding the additional constituents of modifying the object, Korean has a smaller MDD than Chinese. Therefore, when we consider the additional constituents of the sentence, we cannot conclude that SVO has a smaller MDD than SOV. The reason is that, on the one hand, the attributive added in Chinese is located between the predicate and the object, and the most significant effect is a significant increase in the dependency distance between the predicate and the object, and the attributive added in Korean caused a significant increase in the dependency distance between the subject and the predicate, but compared with Chinese, the length of the attributive in Korean was shorter, and the increase in the subject-predicate dependency distance was relatively small. On the other hand, compared with Chinese, the proportion of short-distance dependencies, especially the adjacent dependencies, is higher in Korean after adding attributive, thereby reducing the MDD of the entire sentence. It should be noted that the above example only considers the case of adding one additional constituent. When adding two or more additional constituent, how will the position, length of the additional constituent and the proportion of short-distance dependency relations within the additional constituent affect the mean dependency distance? Further analysis and research are required. In addition, this section only illustrates the typical positions of attributive constituent frequently appearing in sentences in Chinese and Korean, and attempts to give a preliminary explanatory analysis of the reasons why Korean has a smaller MDD than Chinese. In order to make the conclusion analysis more scientific and accurate, it is necessary to conduct a detailed statistical analysis of the types of additional constituent of sentences in the whole corpus and their influence on the entire sentence. Due to the limited space of the paper, it is reserved for subsequent research and analysis.

3.2 The Arrangement of Korean Sentence Constituents

Due to the limited space, in order to better illustrate the problem, this paper takes the double-object construction in Korean, namely the dative-accusative construction, as the object of research. A total of 386 sentences containing dative-accusative construction are extracted from the SUD-Korean treebank. The ordering distribution of the lengths of the dative-accusative construction is shown in Table 3:

Table 3. The ordering distribution of dative-accusative construction of Korean in SUD-Korean treebank

The ordering type	Number	Proportion
Long-before-short	164	42.5%
Short-before-long	108	28.0%
Equal	114	29.5%
Total	386	100%

It can be seen from the statistical results that the order of "long-before-short" is more preferred to be used than "short-before-long" in the dative-accusative construction of Korean. This statistical result is consistent with the results of Choi [15] and Dennison [16], and "long-before-short" preference in Korean is again validated quantitatively.

3.3 The Relationship Between "Long-Before-Short" Preference in Korean and MDD

On the basis of Sect. 3.2, in order to further explore the reasons for the "long-before-short" preference in Korean, this paper intends to analyze it from the perspective of dependency distance. It should be noted that, for the sake of simplification, this section only discusses the ordering preference of double-objects construction in Korean, and the positions of other constituents remain unchanged to reduce the influence of interference terms on the calculation results. This paper makes a comparative analysis of the dative-accusative construction of the original word order and the permuted word order in order to find the theoretical support for the ordering preference of Korean subordinate elements. The calculation process is as follows: first, when the dative-accusative construction follows the "long-before-short" order, calculate their MDD. Then, while keeping the position of the root verb unchanged, the order of the long dependent and the short dependent is reversed and the MDD is calculated. Since Korean is a free word order language, changing the order of dative-accusative does not affect the semantics of the sentence. Finally, by comparing the MDD of the two kinds of ordering, it is concluded whether there is a direct relationship between MDD and "long-before-short" preference. Through the above calculation steps, some typical results of MDD are shown in Table 4:

Table 4. MDD of "long-before-short" and corresponding results of "short-before-long" after permuted

Number	Constituent length	Long-before-short (A)	MDD	Short-before-long (A')	MDD
1	(2,1)	자기 자식에게 무엇인가를 남겨준다	1.25	무엇인가를 자기 자식에게 남겨준다	1.5
2	(3,1)	이것이 유익한다는 것을 소농에게 보여준다	1.2	소농에게 이것이 유익한다는 것을 보여준다	1.6
3	(3,2)	지중해 연안의 국가들에게 포도주와 오일을 준다	1.5	포도주와 오일을 지중해 연안의 국가들에게 준다	1.67
4	(4,1)	서쪽으로 이주한 아시아의 투르크족들에게 돌파구를 마련해 주었다	1.29	돌파구를 서쪽으로 이주한 아시아의 투르크족들에게 마련해 주었다	1.71
5	(4,2)	ɴ어난 공적을 세운 이에게 관작과 토지를 주었다	1.43	관작과 토지를 ɴ어난 공적을 세운 이에게 주었다	1.71
6	(4,3)	어린 아이를 많이 낳은 여성에게 여러 가지 혜택을 배푼다	1.5	여러 가지 혜택을 어린 아이를 많이 낳은 여성에게 배푼다	1.63
7	(5,1)	이런 광통신 기술의 빠른 행보를 실수요자에게 돌리다	1.43	실수요자에게 이런 광통신 기술의 빠른 행보를돌리다	2
8	(5,2)	가난하고 헐벗고 굶주린 우리의 이웃에게 따뜻한 사랑을 준다	1.5	따뜻한 사랑을 가난하고 헐벗고 굶주린 우리의 이웃에게 준다	2
9	(6,1)	앞으로의 정보통신에 필요한 모든 고속 대용량정보를 가입자에게 전달한다	1.5	가입자에게 앞으로의 정보통신에 필요한 모든 고속 대용량정보를 전달한다	2.13
10	(6,2)	몽골 제일을 자랑하는 우넨 신문사 부사장에게 그 까닭을 묻다	1.33	몽골 제일을 자랑하는 우넨 신문사 부사장에게 묻다	1.78

(continued)

Table 4. (*continued*)

Number	Constituent length	Long-before-short (A)	MDD	Short-before-long (A')	MDD
11	(6,4)	어쩔 줄 몰라 하는 어린이 시청자들에게 특별한 형태의 센세이션한 프로그램을 제공한다	1.64	특별한 형태의 센세이션한 프로그램을 어쩔 줄 몰라 하는 어린이 시청자들에게 제공한다	1.82

Note: The constituent length column (x, y) represents the length of dative and accusative respectively, and includes all the ordering situations of "long-before-short" in the corpus. Since the annotation unit of SUD is word segment, the constituent length in the table refers to the number of word segment. The wavy line represents the dative and the horizontal line represents the accusative.

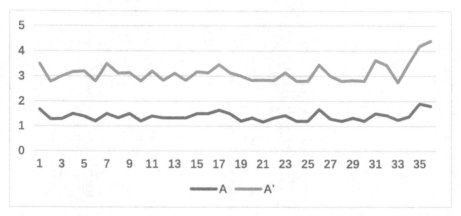

Fig. 3. MDD of "long-before-short" (A) and corresponding results of "short-before-long" (A') after permuted

It can be seen from Table 4 and Fig. 3 that for the same Korean sentence, the MDD of "long-before-short" order is significantly smaller than that of "short-before-long" order. According to the principle of ordered nesting, the sentences in Table 4 are abstracted into Fig. 4 for representation [14].

For the order of "long-before-short" in Fig. 4(a), dependent 1 and 2 depend on root V respectively, and the distance from dependent 1 to V needs to cross over dependent 2, which is relatively short, so the overall dependency distance of the sentence tends to be shorter. On the contrary, for the order of "short-before-long" in Fig. 4(b), the distance from dependent 1 to root V needs to cross the dependent 2, which is relatively long, directly leading to the long-distance dependency between dependent 1 and root V, and finally making the overall MDD of the sentence larger. Furthermore, in Korean, although "long-before-short" order and "short-before-long" order have the same semantics, the information structure meanings of the two word orders are different. When choosing the order of 4(a) to express a sentence, the emphasis at this time is placed on [1, 2, 3, 4], while when choosing the order of 4(b) to express a sentence, the emphasis at this

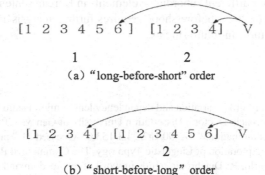

(a) "long-before-short" order

(b) "short-before-long" order

Fig. 4. Ordered nesting representation under different word order

time is placed on [1, 2, 3, 4, 5, 6]. Therefore, the two orders not only bring differences in the processing difficulty of sentences, but also cause differences in the meaning of information structure.

The above analysis shows that, firstly, As SOV language, The root verb is generally located at the end of the sentence, and dative-accusative construction tend to preferred "long-before-short" in order to reduce the overall MDD of Korean. Secondly, through the analysis of the influence of different order on MDD, it is shown that the size of MDD has nothing to do with whether the constituent near the root verb is related to the dative or accusative. As long as the constituent in front of the root verb are ordered to follow the rule of "long-before-short", MDD will be reduced. Finally, from the perspective of cognition, the memory load can be ended only after the governor word is found. When the shorter dependent is close to the root verb, the long dependent can reach the root verb more quickly, thus reducing the memory load. Dependency distance essentially reflects human memory and cognitive load, and the "long-before-short" order is a preference made by humans to reduce memory load.

4 Conclusion

Under the framework of dependency grammar, this paper analyzed the general rules of Korean with SOV word order. First, through a cross-language comparative analysis with Chinese, the results showed that in human language, besides the basic subject-verb-object constituent, the position, length and short-distance dependency proportion of the additional constituent all have a certain influence on MDD. Moreover, when considering the additional constituent, it cannot be concluded that SVO has a smaller MDD than SOV. Secondly, the statistical analysis of the ordering rules of dative-accusative construction in Korean showed that the "long-before-short" is preferred in Korean dative-accusative construction. Finally, through the analysis of the influence of different order on MDD, it is shown that the size of MDD has nothing to do with whether the constituents near the root verb are related to the dative or accusative. As long as the constituents in front of the root verb are ordered to follow the rule of "long-before-short", MDD will be reduced. Due to limited space, this paper only verifies the ordering preference of dative-accusative construction. Whether different subordinate elements in Korean sentences all follow the ordering preference of "long-before-short" requires further analysis and verification on more sentence structures in future studies.

References

1. Gulordava, K.: Word order variation and dependency length minimisation: a cross-linguistic computational approach. Doctoral Dissertation University of Geneva (2018)
2. https://wals.info/combinations/83A_90A#2/24.3/153.0. Accessed 21 Apr 2022
3. Jin, L., et al.: An Exploration of Linguistic Typology. The Commercial Press (2018)
4. Gulordava, K., Merlo, P.: Diachronic trends in word order freedom and dependency length in dependency-annotated corpora of Latin and ancient Greek. In: Proceedings of the Third International Conference on Dependency Linguistics, pp. 121–130 (2015)
5. Futrell, R., Mahowald, K., Gibson, E.: Large scale evidence for dependency length minimization in 37 languages. Proc. Natl. Acad. Sci. U.S.A. 10336–10341 (2015)
6. Ferrer-i-Cancho, R.: Some word order biases from limited brain resources: a mathematical approach. Adv. Complex Syst. 393–414 (2008)
7. Ferrer-i-Cancho, R.: The placement of the head that minimizes online memory: a complex systems approach. Lang. Dyn. Change 114–137 (2015)
8. Gildea, D., Temperley, D.: Do grammars minimize dependency length? Cogn. Sci. 286–310 (2010)
9. Hiranuma, S.: Syntactic difficulty in English and Japanese – a textual study. UCL Working Papers in Linguistics, pp. 309–322 (1999)
10. Liu, H.: Dependency distance as a metric of language comprehension difficulty. J. Cogn. Sci. 159–191 (2008)
11. Hawkins, J.A.: A Performance Theory of Order and Constituency. Cambridge University Press, Cambridge (1994)
12. Hawkins, J.A.: Efficiency and Complexity in Grammars. Oxford University Press, Oxford (2004)
13. Temperley, D.: Minimization of dependency length in written English. Cognition 300–333 (2007)
14. Temperley, D.: Dependency-length minimization in natural and artificial language. J. Quant. Linguist. 256–282 (2008)
15. Choi, H.-W.: Length and order: a corpus study of Korean dative-accusative construction. Speech Cognit. (2007)
16. Dennison: Universal versus language-specific conceptual effects on shifted word-order production in Korean – evidence from bilinguals. Working Papers In Linguistics: University Of Hawai'I at Mânoa (2008)
17. Liu, H.: Research on Chinese quantitative syntactic based on dependency tree bank. Yangtze River Acad. 120–128 (2008)

A Dependency Structure Annotation for Modality in Chinese News Articles

Zhifu Liu[1](✉) and Nianwen Xue[2]

[1] School of Literature and Communication, China Three Gorges University, Yichang, China
zhifuliu1980@163.com
[2] Department of Computer Science, Brandeis University, Waltham, MA, USA
xuen@brandeis.edu

Abstract. This paper reports an effort to annotate modality in Chinese news articles. We introduce the annotation scheme for the modality that employs a dependency structure, which is based on Meagan Vigus (2019) and "UMR Aspect, Modal Strength, and Polarity Annotation Guidelines". We test the cross-linguistic adaptability of the schema we adopt, present the preliminary results of the first pass, and analyze the types of disagreement.

Keywords: Modality annotation · Dependency structure · Chinese text

1 Introduction

Modality characterizes the reality status of events, i.e. whether they occur in the real world, or any number of non-real 'worlds'. (Vigus et al., 2019) Together with tense, aspect, and temporal ordering information, the modality is fundamental to creating a complete representation of the meaning of a text. Based on Saurí and Pustejovsky's (2009) FactBank annotation scheme and Zhang and Xue (2018) temporal dependency structures, Vigus et al. (2019) develop an annotation scheme for the modality that employs a dependency structure. And it has been tested on six documents (containing 108 sentences with 377 identified events) with high levels of agreement. There are two main innovations to FactBank's annotation scheme, the first innovation is the interpretation of epistemic strength values in the domains of deontic and dynamic modality, that is, the epistemic modality was interpreted in the domain of deontic modality as the degree of predictability and within the domain of dynamic modality as the strength of a generalization over instances. The second innovation is the representation of modal annotation as a dependency structure, namely, events and sources (conceivers) are represented as nodes and epistemic strength relations characterize the edges in a modal super-structure. Following Vigus et al. (2019) and 'UMR Aspect, Modal Strength, and Polarity Annotation Guidelines', we developed the modal dependency annotation schema for Chinese and have annotated 305 texts (100 texts of CTB and 205 texts from the XINHUA net from May to August 2020). In this paper, we present the annotation scheme for Chinese news articles, the pilot annotation on 20 texts, and the errors that arose in this phrase.

Q. Su et al. (Eds.): CLSW 2022, LNAI 13496, pp. 143–157, 2023.
https://doi.org/10.1007/978-3-031-28956-9_12

The rest of the paper is organized as follows. In Sect. 2, we discuss the related work. In Sect. 3, we describe our annotation scheme in detail. We present the current implementation and the error analysis in Sect. 4, and conclude in Sect. 5.

2 Related Work

Modality annotation is a challenging work since it does not constitute a discrete linguistic system and it is expressed through a complex interaction of many different aspects of the overall linguistic expression (Roser Saurí, James Pustejovsky, 2009). In this section, we briefly survey the annotation schemes that are related to the identification of the events, the identification of the information source (conceivers), and the modal strength value.

Within linguistics, the studies that closed to events mainly concerned with event nominals (e.g., Lei Han, 2016; Dun Deng, 2021). There are many works like event extractions in Chinese texts done within the fields of NLP, they do not tag all events in the texts, but only a particular set of types and subtypes like the identification of the events in ACE. The works most close to ours are Jianfeng Fu (2010) and Mingyao Zhang (2013). The FactBank and Vigus et al. (2019) largely follow TimeML's event identification criteria, and we follow the guidelines of UMR's events identification since the criteria are specific and are applicable cross-linguistically.

As to the sources of information, the notion of nested sources was proposed by Wiebe et al. (2005) and was widely adopted, such as FactBank and Vigus et al. (2019) treat the sources(conceivers) as one kind of node in the dependency.

Modality is generally taken to encompass epistemic, deontic, and dynamic modality (e.g., Palmer 2001). And each type corresponds to particular markers in a particular language. Some annotation schemes presented the modality markers and annotated the modality type (Yanyan Cui et al., 2013; Ruppenhofer and Rehbein, 2012; Rubinstein et al., 2013) and reported a low inter-annotator agreement. Since the degree of modality is not a discrete system, different researchers have divided the modality degree into two, three, or four levels. Rubin (2007) divided the level of certainty into a four-way distinction (absolute, high, medium, and low), however, reported a low inter-annotator agreement. Roser Saurí and James Pustejovsky(2009) distinguish three levels of factuality: certain (CT), probable (PR), and possible (PS), and reached higher agreement scores. Vigus et al. (2019) and Van Gysel et al.(2021) Following Boye (2012), label their values FULL, PARTIAL, and NEUTRAL.

Kunli Zhang(2016)developed a Chinese modality annotation framework and annotated modal operators of a sentence. Zhong Qian et al. (2019) made the event factual annotation of the Chinese news text document level (document-level).

This paper mainly adopts the annotation concept of Meagan Vigus et al. (2019) and tests its applicability in a cross-language annotation.

3 Annotation Scheme

We created the first draft of annotation guidelines for modality in Chinese news articles based on Vigus et al. (2019) and "UMR Aspect, Modal Strength, and Polarity Annotation Guidelines". We illustrate the modal dependency structure and give the specific guidelines of events and conceivers identification and the annotation of modal strength value in this section.

3.1 Modal Dependency Structure

The dependency structure is a directed, acyclic graph. As be seen in Fig. 1, modified from "UMR Aspect, Modal Strength, and Polarity Annotation Guidelines". There are two types of nodes in the modal dependency structure: events and conceivers. The parents nodes of events may be conceivers or events, and conceivers only ever have other conceivers (or, ROOT) as parents. The edges between the nodes are labeled with epistemic strength values (the combination of epistemic strength and polarity values). The edge between ROOT and AUTH is annotated with MODAL. The conceivers often are mental-level entities whose perspective on events is modeled in the text, and the author conceiver node represents the perspective of the creator of the text, and each news article will automatically have one author conceiver node.

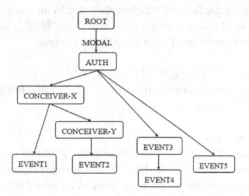

Fig. 1. Organization of nodes in the modal dependency structure

3.2 Annotation Procedure

In this section, we first provide the annotation procedure of the modal dependency structure for Chinese news articles and present the basic annotation guidelines for each pass.

To make the modal dependency structure feasible for manual annotation, we decomposed the annotation into three subtasks: event identification, conceiver identification, and the epistemic strength value annotation, that is, the annotation will proceed in three passes. In the first pass, the events in the news articles are identified. And the next pass involves finding the information sources (conceivers) for each event and setting up the modal 'superstructure' of the whole article. The third pass involves the annotation of the epistemic strength value.

3.2.1 The Guidelines for Event Annotation

Event annotation involves identifying event trigger words in the news articles, the trigger words can be verbs or adjectives, and sometimes even nouns in Chinese. Since the lack of morphological cues for part of speech in Chinese, we follow the criteria used to identify events in UMR. The criteria of event identification in the modal dependency structure are based on the combination of semantic type and information packaging. Semantic type is generally taken to encompass entities, states (or properties), and processes. Information packaging characterizes how a particular linguistic expression 'packages' semantic content, and it includes reference, modification, and predication. We identify a word or phrase as an event if it has either the semantic type of process or the information packaging of predication. Five types of combinations should be identified as events in Chinese, and the combinations are listed as follows:(Words that are identified as events will be shown in bold.)

A. *Processes in Predication*

The predicated process is the most prototypical for events, corresponding to verbs in Chinese. Regardless of whether they are in an independent clause, like '建'[jian](build) in (1), or a dependent clause, like '整治'[zhengzhi](renovate) in (1), predicated processes are always identified as events.

(1) 运河 整治 后, 苏钢 在 运河 对岸 建 了 新 厂区。

After the canal **renovation**, Suzhou Steel Group **built** a new plant on the other side of the canal.

B. *Process in Modification*

Process packaged as modifier should also be identified as an event, that is, the verb used in the modifier position, like '核准'[hezhun] (approve) in (2), should be annotated as the trigger for an event. It should be noted that there is a nominalization marker '的'[de] before the head of this noun phrase. The cases which do not have any aspect marker or the nominalization marker '的'[de], like '退休人员'[tuixiu renyuan](retired person), are always compound in Chinese, and the word '退休'[tuixiu](retired) is not an event trigger.

(2) 去年 经 台 当局 核准 的 台 商 投资 案。

The investment cases of Taiwan businessmen were **approved** by the Taiwan authorities last year.

C. *Processes in Reference*

Processes packaged as referents may take several morphosyntactic forms, such as events nominals, or the head of a noun phrase, for example, the word '整治'[zhengzhi](renovate) in (3).

(3) 大 运河 的 大规模 整治。

The massive **renovation** of the Grand Canal.

D. *States in Predication*

The adjectives that act as the predication are annotated as an event in Chinese, like '繁华'[fanhua](bustling) in (4).

(4) 京杭 运河 古来 繁华。

The Beijing-Hangzhou Canal was **bustling** in ancient times.

E. *Entities in Predication*

Entities packaged as predicates have two types of syntactic forms, the first one is that a nominal at as the predicate and without a copula between the subject and the predicate nominal, like (5).On the other hand, the second one has a copula between the subject and the predicate nominal, like '为'[wei](is) in (6). The phrase '4亿 美元'[si yi meiyuan]($400 million) in (5) and the copula '为'[wei](is) are will be annotated as the triggers of the sentence.

(5) 利税 **4** 亿 美元。

The profit and tax total **are $400 million**.

(6) 商务 代理 为 中国 进出口 公司。

The business agent **is** China National Import and Export Corporation.

Besides these five types of combinations of semantic type and information packaging, there are some special cases, like complex predicates and aspectual verbs, that require more specific annotation guidelines in Chinese. We did not give more details for the identification of events in the special cases but only emphasize that event identification is based on a combination of semantic type and information packaging in this article.

3.2.2 Identifying Conceivers

Conceiver refers to the information source of the event in the news article. Every text will have at least one author conceiver and all of the content in the text is ultimately from the author's perspective. The non-author conceivers in the text should be annotated when another entity's mental attitude or point of view towards an event is expressed in the text. In this section, we present how to identify a conceiver in a news article.

The conceiver is prototypically a mental-level entity, such as '专家们'[zhuanjia men](experts) and '保险界人士'[baoxianjie renshi](insurance people). So in the case '据海关总署提供的统计数据'[ju haiguan zongshu tigong de tongji shuju](according to statistics provided by the General Administration of Customs), the conceiver is ' 海关总署'[haiguan zongshu](the General Administration of Customs), but not '统计 数据'[tongji shuju](statistics). It can also be an inanimate entity when it metonymi-cally refers to volitional entities, for example, the government units '福建乡镇企业 局'[fujian xiangzhen qiye ju](Fujian Township Enterprise Bureau) and '台经济部'[tai jingjibu](Taiwan's economic ministry). We annotate the plan, like '浙江'九五'经贸发 展规划'[zhejiang jiuwu jingmao fazhan guihua](the ninth five-year plan for economic and trade development of Zhejiang province) for conceiver in the news article.

In the news text, the sources of information are often introduced by ' 据'[ju](according to), and form a construction such as "据'[ju](according to) + conceiver

+ verb', and '据'[ju](according to) can be considered as the marker of the conceiver. For example, in the construction '据福建乡镇企业局统计'[ju fujian xiangzhen qiye ju tongji](according to statistics of the township enterprise bureau of Fujian province), ' 福建乡镇企业局'[fujian xiangzhen qiye ju](the township enterprise bureau of Fujian province) is a conceiver. But in some cases, the author always left out the source of information, and the ellipsis construction is "据'[ju](according to) + verb', for instance, '据 称'[ju cheng](purportedly), '据悉'[ju xi](it is reported), '据了解'[ju liaojie](as we have learned), '据分析'[ju fenxi](according to the analysis), '据预测'[ju yuce](according to the forecast), '据统计'[ju tongji](according to the statistics), etc. For the solution to such cases, one is to find out the obvious source omitted in the text, and the other is to use AUTH as the source if there is no explicit source in the text.

It is important to point out that a conceiver should be annotated at the word or phrase level. When the conceiver is a phrase, the whole phrase should be annotated, for example, in the phrase '据江苏苏钢集团公司负责人介绍'[ju jiangsu sugang jituan gongsi fuzeren jieshao](according to the introduction of the responsible person of Suzhou Steel Group of Jiangsu province), the conceiver should be annotated is the whole phrase ' 江苏苏钢集团公司负责人'[jiangsu sugang jituan gongsi fuzeren](the responsible person of Suzhou Steel Group of Jiangsu province), not the modifier '江苏苏钢集团公司'[jiangsu sugang jituan](Suzhou Steel Group of Jiangsu province) or the head '负责 人'[fuze ren](the responsible person).

3.2.3 The Guidelines for Epistemic Strength Annotation

As mentioned above, the edges in the modal dependency structure correspond to modal strength values. The modal strength values are the combination of epistemic strength (Full, Partial, and Neutral) and polarity values(Positive and Negative). There are six values in total, and these values are shown in Table 1.

Table 1. Epistemic strength values

Label	Value
POS	Full positive
PRT	Partial positive
NEUT	Positive neutral
NEUTNEG	Negative neutral
PRTNEG	Partial negative
NEG	Full negative

These edge labels can be used at all levels of the dependency structure(the edge between the ROOT and AUTH node is annotated with Modal). The edges between two conceiver nodes represent the author or conceiver's certainty about another conceiver's mental content. For example, the epistemic strength values of the edges between the author and conceiver in (7) are annotated as follows.

(7) a. 小李认为小王在教室。(Mr. Li believes Mr. Wang is in the classroom.)
   PRT(小李, AUTH)
   b. 小李不认为小王在教室。(Mr. Li doesn't believe Mr. Wang is in the classroom.)
   NEG(小李, AUTH)
   c. 小李可能认为小王在教室。(Mr. Li might believe Mr. Wang is in the classroom.)
   NEUT(小李, AUTH)

As illustrated in 7c, the author is unsure whether or not '小李'[Xiaoli](Mr. Li) holds the belief about the *be-in* event. Therefore, there is a NEUT relation between the AUTH node and the '小李'[Xiaoli](Mr. Li) conceiver node.

The edge between a conceiver and an event represents the conceiver's certainty about the occurrence of an event in the real world. For example, the epistemic strength values of the events in (8) are annotated as follows.

(8) a. 小王在教室。(Mr. Wang is in the classroom.)
   POS(在, AUTH)
   b. 小王没在教室。(Mr. Wang is not in the classroom.)
   NEG(在, AUTH)
   c. 小王可能在教室。(Mr. Wang may be in the classroom.)
   NEUT(在, AUTH)

As can be seen in 8a, the AUTH is sure of the occurrence of the '在'[zai](be-in) event, and the edge between the AUTH and the *be-in* event is annotated for POS.

Note the modal dependency structure itself does not distinguish between episodic, deontic, or dynamic events, but annotates the epistemic strength. As mentioned above, in the modal dependency structure, the epistemic modality may be interpreted in the domain of deontic modality as the degree of predictability and within the domain of dynamic modality as the strength of a generalization over instances.

4 Annotation Evaluation and Error Analysis

Based on the modal dependency annotation guidelines for Chinese news articles, we have tested it on 20 news texts. This work was done by three postgraduates in linguistics independently on the MAE platform. Before the annotation, the annotators read the guideline and were trained to know how to use the MAE platform. As mentioned above, the annotation will proceed in three passes. Firstly, the annotators identified all of the events in the 20 texts. Secondly, they gave every event node a parent node (an event or conceiver). Thirdly, they labeled the edges with epistemic strength.

We measure the annotation quality with two metrics. First, we compare the annotation of three annotators with the annotation of an expert annotator and compute the precision, recall, and F-score. Second, we compute the agreement among annotators.

Table 2. Presents the agreement scores that were compared to the annotation of annotators with an expert. The first row shows precision, recall, and F-score for event identification. The middle row shows the same measures for the identification of the conceiver. And the bottom row shows these measures for the epistemic strength value annotation of each event.

Table 2. IAA for modal annotations(between annotators and an expert)

Pass	Measure	Annotator-A	Annotator-B	Annotator-C	Total
Event identification	Precision	85.46	84.20	82.73	84.13
	Recall	95.22	90.43	95.37	93.67
	F-score	90.08	87.20	88.60	88.63
Conceiver identification	Precision	92.21	89.27	85.67	89.05
	Recall	86.05	77.74	79.82	81.20
	F-score	89.02	83.11	82.64	84.92
Epistemic strength value	Precision	86.17	89.10	98.89	91.39
	Recall	80.42	77.60	92.14	83.37
	F-score	83.20	82.95	95.40	87.18

Vigus et al. (2019) annotated three different genres: news stories, narratives, and discussion forums, and reported the following F-scores for news: 0.94 for event ID, 0.86 for conceiver, and 0.93 for event space. Our F-scores are 0.8863 for event identification, 0.8492 for conceiver identification, and 0.8718 for epistemic strength value, and are slightly lower than F-scores reported by Vigus et al. (2019). Table 3. Shows the agreement among annotators for the event, the average F-score is 0.9393, and this score is identical to the F-scores for event ID of Vigus et al. (2019).

Table 3. IAA for event annotations(among the annotators)

	Annotator	Precision	Recall	F-score
Annotator-A	B	95.69	92.12	93.87
	C	91.43	94.47	92.93
Annotator-B	A	95.02	98.7	96.83
	C	91.97	98.7	95.22
Annotator-C	A	94.47	91.31	91.87
	B	96.26	89.69	92.86
Average		94.14	94.165	93.93

This suggests that annotators can consistently identify the events and conceivers and assess the epistemic strength values in Chinese news articles.

4.1 Event Identification Errors

As mentioned above, it is the combination of semantic type and information packaging that determines whether or not a particular word in a particular context is identified as an event, and there are five types of combination(process predication, process reference, process modification, entity predication, and states predication) should be identified as an event. We counted the errors in each type, and the proportion are listed as follow: process reference (23%), process predication (19%), process modification (18%), states predication (7%) and entity predication (4%). Besides the errors in these five types, complex predicates (21%) and aspectual verbs(4%) are the constructions that the disagreements arose between annotators.

The most common disagreement arose in the type of process reference. In Chinese, the process in the reference means that the verb is at the subject or object position of the sentence. There are three types of errors when the process is packaged as a reference. The first one is some abstract verbs that act as the subject or object of the sentence, just like 发展[fazhan](develop) in 9a. The second one is that a sentence has two or more syntactic analyses, for example, in 9b, the sentence can be equivalent to either the sentence 'the direct investment of the foreign tradesman is $5 billion.' or the sentence 'the foreign tradesman invest $5 billion directly.'. The third one is the annotators are confused with the 'state change verbs + object' construction, that is, they don't know whether the state change verbs or object should be identified as an event, just like 加强[jiaqiang](strengthen) and 合作[hezuo](cooperation) in 9c.

(9) a. 中国 闽 东南 乡镇 企业 发展 继续 领先。
     China's southern Fujian township enterprises continue to lead in the development.
     b. 外商 直接 投资 五十 亿 美元。
     The direct investment of the foreign tradesmen is $5 billion./the foreign tradesmen invest $5 billion directly.
     c. 加强 双边 经贸 合作。
     Strengthen bilateral economic and trade cooperation.

When the process was packaged as predication, the issues mainly arose in the 'V1 + V2' structure, such as '观光旅游'[guanguang lüyou](visit and travel), '出口创汇'[chukou chuanghui](earn foreign exchange through exports), '联合举办'[lianhe juban](jointly organized), '前来投资'[qianlai touzi](come to invest), etc. The annotators always ignore one of the two events.

When the process was packaged as modification, the issue mainly arose in the clause, for example, in the clause'新建的三个医院'[xinjian de san ge yiyuan](three hospitals that were built recently), '建'[jian](build) should be identified as an event, but the annotators tend to ignore it. The other issue arose in the 'V + N' compound, for example, in the compound '投资对象国'[touzi duixiang guo](investment target country), the lexical item '投资'[touzi](investment) is not an event, but the annotators tend to identify it as an event.

When the state packaged as predication, the issue mainly arose in the clause where there are adjectives act as the predicates and should be identified as an event, but the annotators tend to ignore it, for example, in the'一批科技含量较高的乡镇企业'[yi pi keji hanliang jiao gao de xiangzhen qiye](many township enterprises with higher scientific and technological content), the lexical item '高'[gao](high) should be identified as an event, but he annotators tend to ignore it.

When the entity was packaged as predication, the event that should be identified as an event is the copula '是'[shi](is), '为'[wei](is) in Chinese. But the noun phrase can be the predicate of the sentence independently without the help of a copula, for example, there is not a copula in the sentence '年进口贸易总额二亿美元'[nian jinkou maoyi zonge er yi meiyuan](The annual total import trade is $200 million), and the phrase '二亿美元'[er yi meiyuan] ($200 million)is the predicate, and the annotators always ignore it.

Complex predicates use multiple words to express a single event and are often a combination of 'verb + noun' in English. For example, the phrase 'take a walk' describes an act of walking, not an act of taking. The verb like 'take' in 'take a walk' is defined as a support verb in FrameNet's semantic guidelines. There are such words in Chinese, for example, '进行'[jinxing](carry out), '给予'[jiyu](give), etc., and they were called 'dummy verbs' (Zhu Dexi, 1985) or 'delexical verb'(Diao Yanbin, 2005). The issue here is that some verbs are not that typical and it is difficult for the annotators to decide whether a lexical item is an event or not, for example, in the phrase like '进入商品化生产'[jinru shangpinhua shengchan](enter the commercial production) or '投入使用'[touru shiyong](come into use), the event is '生产'[shengchan](production) or '使用'[shiyong](use), but '进入'[jinru](enter) or '投入'[touru](come into). The annotators are confused about this kind of case. The other kind of complex predicate is the cases like '转化为'[zhuanhua wei](change into), '建设成'[jianshe cheng](be constructed into), and '发展成为'[fazhan chengwei](develop into) in Chinese, and there is only one event in these phrases and they are '转化'[zhuanhua](change), '建设'[jianshe](construct) and '发展'[fazhan](develop), but the annotators tend to identify the phrase as two events.

Aspectual verbs refer to verbs that express inceptive, continuative, terminative, and completive phases of an event. The annotators sometimes identified the aspectual verb as an event, for example, in the phrase '继续优化投资环境'[jixu youhua touzi huanjing](continue to improve the investment environment) and '出口比重开始加大'[chukou bizhong kaishi jiada](the proportion of exports began to increase), the lexical items '继续'[jixu](continue) and '开始'[kaishi](begin) should not be identified as events, but the verbs '优化' [youhua](improve) and '加大' [jiada](increase) should be identified as events.

4.2 Conceivers Identification Errors

In this section, we discuss the disagreement that arose between annotators for the second pass. The conceivers of the events are identified in this pass and the errors and the proportion are listed as follows: the shared conceivers (37%), the boundary of the conceiver (25%), whether a conceiver should be introduced (22%) and the wrong annotation (16%).

The shared conceiver refers to several events shared by one conceiver. Because our annotation is a text-level work and not a sentence-level one. The annotator needs to find the conceiver of the event outside of the sentence. In most cases, it is not difficult for the annotators to decide whether an event node should be nested underneath the conceiver node. But when someone said several events and the author wrote these events in several sentences, the annotators may disagree on whether the events in each sentence share the same conceiver. For example, in 10, there are three sentences in this paragraph, and the '保险界人士'[baoxianjie renshi](insurance insiders) is the conceiver of the events '开放'[kaifang](opening), '发展' [fazhan](develop) and '重要'[zhongyao](important) in the second sentence. The annotators differ on whether the events in the third sentence share the same conceiver node with the events in the second sentence.

(10) 中国 现有 保险 公司 二十六 家, 境外 保险 公司 在 中国 设立 办事机构 的
有 一百 多 家。保险界 人士 表示, 随着 中国 保险 市场 的 逐步 对外 开放, 迅
速 发展 民族 保险 事业 十分 重要。这 次 批准 建立 的 五 家 保险 公司, 可以
说 是 由 此 推出 的 一 大 举措。

There are 26 insurance companies in China, and more than 100 overseas insurance companies have set up offices in China. Insurance insiders said that with the gradual opening of China's insurance market to the outside world, it is very important to rapidly develop the ethnic insurance industry. The approval of the five insurance companies can be said to be a big move.

There are two types of errors in the boundary of the conceiver. The first one is the annotators didn't identify the whole phrase as a conceiver but identified a part of the phrase as a conceiver. As mentioned above, the entities that identified as conceivers sometimes were expressed by phrases, when the annotators identify the conceivers in the text, they should take the whole phrase as a conceiver. For example, the phrase '江苏苏钢集团公司负责人'[jiangsu sugang jituan gongsi fuzeren](the responsible person of Suzhou Steel Group of Jiangsu province) should be identified as a conceiver, but sometimes, only the '苏钢集团公司负责人' [sugang jituan gongsi fuzeren](the responsible person of Suzhou Steel Group) was identified as conceiver. The second case is that the annotators consider all of the words after the marker '据'[ju](according to) as a conceiver. For example, in the phrase '据海关总署提供的统计数据'[ju haiguan zongshu tigong de tongji shuju](according to statistics provided by the General Administration of Customs), the organization '海关总署'[haiguan zongshu](the General Administration of Customs) is the source of '统计数据'[tongji shuju](statistics), and should be identified as a conceiver, but the whole phrase after the marker '据'[ju](according to) was identified as conceiver.

In some cases, the annotators do not know whether a conceiver should be introduced, that is, whether the author simply reports an event or ascribes mental content to a conceiver. For example, in 3, the predicate '提出'[tichu](put forward) invokes the mental content of its subject, here '经济专家'[jingji zhuanjia] (economic experts), and it should be identified as the conceiver of the event '扩大'[kuoda](expand), but the annotators think the author simply reporting an event, and it need not to introduce a conceiver, and link the event '扩大'[kuoda](expand) node to the author node.

(11) 经济 专家 提出 进一步 扩大 海南 对外 开放 的 系列 建议。

Economic experts put forward suggestions to further expand Hainan's opening-up.

There are two types of wrong annotation. The first one is the annotator didn't identify the source of an event and nested the event underneath the author. For example, in 5, the annotator nested the event node '超过'[chaoguo](more than) underneath the author node, but the conceiver node '缅甸官员'[Miandian guanyuan](Myanmar officials) didn't annotate. The second one is taking the subject as the parent node of the event which should be the child node of the author. For example, in 6, the event '分析'[fenxi](analyze) involves the conceiver, here the subject '国家统计局'[guojia tongji ju](Statistical Bureau of China), and it is the parent node of the event node '有'[you](have), and the event '分析' [fenxi](analyze) should be the child node of the author, and the annotator thinks it is the child node of the subject '国家统计局'[guojia tongji ju](National Bureau of Statistics).

(12) 据 缅甸 官员 透露, 1995 年, 缅泰 两 国 贸易 总额 超过 3亿 美元。
      According to Myanmar officials, trade between Myanmar and Thailand totaled more than $300 million.
(13) 国家 统计局 分析, 对 中国 经济 发展 十分 有利 的 条件 主要 有 两 方面。
      According to the National Bureau of Statistics, two main conditions are very favorable for China's economic development.

4.3 Epistemic Strength Value Errors

The disagreements mainly arose in the non-realistic events when annotated the epistemic strength values, especially when particular predicate and the modal auxiliary like '将'[jiang](will), '要'[yao](will), and '应'[ying](should) co-occur in the same sentence, both of them influence annotators to evaluate the epistemic value of the particular event. The most common situation is that a suggesting predicate and the modal auxiliary '应'[ying](should) co-occur in the same sentence, the proportion is 34%. And a forecasting predicate or a predicate of plan co-occurs with the modal auxiliary '将'[jiang](will) or '要'[yao](will) is almost as common as the case above, the proportion is 32%. Besides these two types of disagreements, the events in a purpose clause are also the cases in that disagreement often arises, the proportion is 15%. The annotators are confused about euphemistic expressions in Chinese, the proportion of disagreement is 7%. The proportion of the wrong annotation is 8% and the others are 4%.

In the case an event that was suggested co-occurs with the modal auxiliary '应'[ying](should), as in14, the event '采取'[caiqu](take) and the modal auxiliary '应'[ying](should) co-occur in the same sentence, the modal auxiliary '应'[ying](should) means that the event was modalized by it is more likely to occur, and should be annotated with partial. At the same time, the event '采取'[caiqu](take) was suggested by the conceiver, and it may or may not happen in the real world, therefore, the epistemic strength value is neutral. These make the annotator confused when annotating the strength value of the event '采取'[caiqu](take).

(14) 建议 提出 海南 应 在 近期 采取 以下 措施。

      It suggests that Hainan should take the following measures soon.

Since '将'[jiang](will) or '要'[yao](will) can be used to express that something will happen in the future objectively and subjectively, the annotators need to know the meaning of these two words in a particular sentence. For example, although the word '将'[jiang](will) is before the event '达到'[dadao](reach), it does not mean that the event '达到'[dadao](reach) has a positive strength value. It is very clear that all of the events in this paragraph are within the scope of the lexical item '预测'[yuce](forecast), and this means that all of the events should be annotated with neutral. And the word '可'[ke](may) before the event '高达' [gaoda](up to)in the next clause shows that the event has a neutral strength value. In 9, Although there is a marker '要'[yao](will) before the event '推进'[tuijian](promote), it should be annotated with partial.

(15) 据 预测, 今年 全球 经济 增长 幅度 可 达到 百分之 四 点 一。推动 经济 增长
的主要 因素 是 亚洲 经济 发展 依然 强劲 有力, 全 地区 经济 增长 速度 将
达到 百分之 七点九, 而 中国 增长 速度 可 高达 百分之 九 点 七。

The global economy is forecast to grow by 4.1 percent this year. The main factor driving economic growth is that Asia's economic development remains strong, with regional economic growth set at 7.9 percent and China as high as 9.7 percent.

(16) 浙江 "九五" 经贸 发展 规划 还 决定, 今后 要 把 全面 推进 对外 开放 向 高
层次、宽 领域、纵深化 发展 作为 重点。

The "ninth five-year" economic and trade development plan of Zhejiang province also decided that in the future to promote the comprehensive opening up to high-level, wide-field, in-depth development as the focus.

In Chinese, not all purpose clauses have the syntactic forms like '为了'[weile](in order to), as in 17, the events '运作'[yunzuo](operate), '领先'[lingxian](lead), and '成为'[chengwei](become) is the purpose of the subject '深圳市沙头角保税区'[Shenzhenshi Shatoujiao baoshuiqu](the Shatoujiao bonded zone of Shenzhen), but there is no signal for the purpose, and it is difficult for the annotators to mark the strength value for these events.

(17) 深圳市 沙头角 保税区 今后 五年 将 充分 发挥 保税区 的 区位 优势 和 政策
优势, 以 高新 技术 产业 为 先导, 实施 以 转口 贸易 和 仓储业 为 辅助 的 经
营 战略, 把 沙头角 保税区 建成 按 国际 惯例 运作, 国内 领先 的 特殊 综合
经济 区域, 使 其 成为 该 市 外向型 经济 的 快速 增长 点。

In the next five years, Shenzhen will give full play to the location advantages and policy advantages of the bonded zone, with high-tech industry as the guide, to implement the business strategy with entrepot trade and storage industry as the auxiliary, to build the bonded area according to the international practice, the domestic leading special comprehensive economic area, make it become the rapid growth point of the city's export-oriented economy.

In some cases, the author uses an indirect or euphemistic way to express the likelihood of the happening of events. When the annotators annotate the strength values for these events, they often do not know how to do it. For instance, since the author did not directly say the possibility of the happening of the event '控制' [kongzhi](control)in 12, it is difficult to decide whether the event should annotate with neutral or partial. And the annotators can not annotate the strength value for the event '参与'[canyu](participate) in 13 because the word '很难'[hennan](difficult) before the event is expressed euphemistically.

(18) 这 对 有效 地 控制 甲肝 流行 具有 重大 意义。
　　　This is of great significance for the effective control of the hepatitis A epidemic.
(19) 很难 在 海外 市场 参与 竞争。
　　　It is difficult to compete in overseas markets.

5 Conclusion

Based on Vigus et al. (2019) and 'UMR Aspect, Modal Strength, and Polarity Annotation Guidelines', we created the first draft of annotation guidelines for modality, and have a test annotation on Chinese news articles. We test the cross-linguistic adaptability of the schema we adopt, present the preliminary results of the first pass, and analyze the types of disagreement. The disagreements that arose in the annotation include the process packaged as a reference, complex predicates, the scope of the conceiver, and the epistemic strength value annotation under the situation where there are several markers. We updated the first version of the guidelines based on the first pass of annotation and completed 305 news articles. We will add conditional rode in the modal dependency structure and annotate the edge between author and conceiver for epistemic strength values.

References

Rubinstein, A., Harner, H., Krawczyk, E., Simonson, D., Katz, G., Portner, P.: Toward fine-grained annotation of modality in text. In: Proceedings of the IWCS 2013 Workshop on Annotation of Modal Meanings in Natural Language (WAMM), pp. 38–46 (2013)

Deng, D.: Definition and related problems of modern Chinese event nominals. Lexicographical Stud. **244**(04), 80–91 (2021)

Fu, J.: Event-oriented Knowledge Processing Research. Shanghai University (2010)

Palmer, F.R.: Mood and Modality. Cambridge University Press, Cambridge (2001)

Han, L.: Definition and system construction of Chinese event nominals. J. East China Normal Univ. (Humanit. Soc. Sci.) **48**(05), 161–175+196 (2016)

Wiebe, J., Wilson, T., Cardie, C.: Annotating expressions of opinions and emotions in language. Lang. Resour. Eval. **39**, 165–210 (2005)

Ruppenhofer, J., Rehbein, I.: Yes we can!? annotating the senses of English modal verbs. In: Proceedings of the Eighth International Conference on Language Resources and Evaluation (2012)

Vigus, M., Van Gysel, J.E. L., Croft, W.: A dependency structure annotation for modality. In: Proceedings of the First International Workshop on Designing Meaning Representations, pp. 182–198 (2019)

Saurí, R., Pustejovsky, J.: Factbank: a corpus annotated with event factuality. Lang. Resour. Eval. **43**, 227–268 (2009)

Van Gysel, J.E.L., et al.: Designing a Uniform meaning representation for natural language processing. Künstl Intell **35**, 343–360 (2021)

Rubin, V.L.: Stating with certainty or stating with doubt: Intercoder reliability results for manual annotation of epistemically modalized statements. In: NAACL 07: Human Language Technologies 2007: The Conference of the North American Chapter of the Association for Computational Linguistics; Companion Volume, Short Papers, pp. 141–144 (2007)

Zhang, Y., Xue, N.: Structured interpretation of temporal relations. In: Proceedings of the 11th Language Resources and Evaluation Conference (LREC-2018). Miyazaki, Japan (2018)

Zhang, M.: A Study on Discourse Coherence Based on Event Chain. WuHan University, (2013)

Z. Qian, P. Li, Q. Zhu, G. Zhou: Document-level event factuality identification via adversarial neural network. In: Proceedings of NAACL-HLT, pp. 2799–2809 (2019)

Zhu, D.: Dummy verbs and nominal verbs in modern written Chinese. J. Peking Univ. (Philos. Soc. Sci.) **05**, 3–8 (1985)

Diao, Y.: On Delexical Verb. Nankai University (2005)

How Do People React to COVID-19 Vaccination? A Corpus-Based Study of Macau Netizens' Online Comments

Xi Chen[1] , Vincent Xian Wang[1(✉)] , and Chu-Ren Huang[2,3]

[1] Department of English, University of Macau, Macau, China
{yb77703,vxwang}@um.edu.mo
[2] Department of Chinese and Bilingual Studies, The Hong Kong Polytechnic University, Hong Kong, China
churen.huang@polyu.edu.hk
[3] The Hong Kong Polytechnic University-Peking University Research Centre on Chinese Linguistics, The Hong Kong Polytechnic University, Hong Kong, China

Abstract. This study draws on corpus methodology to investigate people's reactions to COVID-19 vaccination using the data of Macau netizens' comments on a YouTube channel. Four main topics under discussion were identified based on the word lists. Meanwhile, people were concerned about the activity of vaccines and were also engaged in heated debates on both domestic and foreign vaccines according to the collocation of "疫苗" *yìmiáo* (vaccine). The discussion topics and concerns varied along with time, evidenced by the results of word lists and collocates of each month. It is also noticeable that some misinformation on vaccines burgeoned and faded before and after the mass vaccination of Macau residents. The supportive voices for the (Chinese) vaccines were building up their momentum over time. This phenomenon lends support to the effective persuasion of gain-framed messages in advocating safe behaviour based on Prospect Theory. Our research has revealed that the corpus-based study of online comments can be leveraged to uncover people's social behaviour in the pandemic context.

Keywords: COVID-19 · Vaccination · Corpus linguistics · Macau · Prospect Theory

1 Introduction

The COVID-19 pandemic has been sweeping the world since 2019. During this period, scientific literature has been burgeoning to meet this challenge in different disciplines, among which, data-based language studies also contribute to COVID-related research in domains, such as language use [1–3] and language processing [4–6]. As the cornerstone of linguistic data science, corpus and its related technologies have been intensively employed to tackle linguistic issues either in contemporary discourses [7–9] or from a diachronic dimension [10–12]. Resonating with these corpus- (and data-) based studies, this research utilises corpus tools to address the issues surrounding people's reactions

Q. Su et al. (Eds.): CLSW 2022, LNAI 13496, pp. 158–169, 2023.
https://doi.org/10.1007/978-3-031-28956-9_13

to vaccination from a linguistic perspective against the backdrop of the COVID-19 pandemic.

Taken as an effective measure to counter the epidemic by achieving herd immunity, mass vaccination has been launched globally. Endeavours have been made to study people's reactions to vaccination, however, vaccine hesitancy has been identified as a great threat to the vaccination process and even public health. Vaccine hesitancy can be further aggravated by social media [13–15], which has received particular attention in the stream of COVID-related studies [16–19]. It is therefore imperative to investigate the public responses to COVID-19 vaccination in social media. At this juncture, online comments have provided a valuable resource for monitoring netizens' perception of receiving COVID-19 vaccines. In this study, we examine online comments on COVID-19 vaccination on a YouTube channel based in Macau to reveal the topics under discussion and disclose netizens' concerns regarding COVID-19 vaccination by virtue of corpus methodology (word list and collocation analyses along with concordance). Our study aims to showcase that the corpus-based study of people's online comments can be leveraged to reveal their social behaviour in the pandemic context. Our research questions are:

- What are the topics discussed by Macau netizens and their concerns regarding COVID-19 vaccination?
- Did the topics and concerns vary with time?

2 Methodology

We crawled the comments (mostly in Chinese) under 41 videos related to COVID-19 vaccination on a Macau-based YouTube channel called "日更频道PLUS[1]" (Daily Update Channel PLUS) from December 2020 to June 2021. The ID information of each poster was removed, and the collected comments are for academic purposes only. We then sorted the comments by the time when they were posted. Subsequently, these comments were segmented by Jieba[2] in Python and then were loaded into LancsBox 6.0 [20] to compose the "Vaccination Comments Corpus" (VCC) with seven subcorpora of seven months (December 2020 to June 2021). The numbers of comments and words of each month are listed in Table 1. Starting from December 2020, netizens gathered to post their opinions and interact with each other under the relevant videos on vaccination on this YouTube channel. The numbers of comments and words culminated in March and began to decline (cf. Table 1). To investigate Macau netizens' responses to COVID-19 vaccination in terms of lexis, we made use of the word lists and collocates of "疫苗" (vaccine) based on the VCC corpus by the functions of "Words" and "GraphColl" in LancsBox. The Chinese instances (with our gloss translations in English) presented in the following sections are all from the VCC corpus.

---

[1] https://www.youtube.com/c/日更频道PLUS/videos.
[2] https://github.com/fxsjy/jieba.

Table 1. The numbers of comments and words of each month.

Month	Comments	Words
Dec. 2020	206	4,445
Jan. 2021	77	1,207
Feb. 2021	977	15,461
Mar. 2021	1,194	20,568
Apr. 2021	504	8,973
May 2021	498	9,435
Jun. 2021	386	6,301

3 Results

3.1 Word Lists

We made eight lists of the words that consist of two or more Chinese characters by the VCC corpus. They include a general word list of the whole corpus and seven word lists of each month (December 2020 to June 2021). The top words with their frequencies in each list are presented in Table 2. Since the number of words differs by month, the top words of each month are the ones with relatively high frequencies of that month. For the general word list, we selected the words with frequencies higher than 100.

According to the top words in the general word list and from our reading of their concordance lines in the VCC corpus, Macau netizens' discussions on COVID-19 vaccination are on four major topics: a) the concerns on vaccines, evidenced by the words, such as 疫苗 vaccine n = 965, 接种 inoculate n = 199, 病毒 virus n = 158, 科兴 Sinovac n = 134, 国药 Sinopharm n = 120, and even some misinformation on vaccination (问题 problem n = 118, 断子绝孙 cut off offspring n = 102); b) the trilateral relationship between Macau, Hong Kong and the Chinese mainland (澳门 Macau n = 624, 香港 Hong Kong n = 457, 大陆 Chinese mainland n = 165); c) the competition between China and the USA and their vaccines (中国 China n = 208, 美国 the USA n = 166); and d) the judgemental opinions of (Macau) government and its policies (政府 government n = 183).

On 6 February 2021, the first batch of 100,000 doses of inactivated vaccines produced by Sinopharm China National Biotec Group (Beijing) arrived in Macau, and an inoculation ceremony was held on the morning of 9 February. The Chief Executive of Macau, Ho Iat-seng was injected with the first vaccine at the inoculation ceremony, along with the key officials of the Macau government. The first phase of mass vaccination in Macau started at 9:00 am on 9 February. The priority groups for vaccination include front-line anti-epidemic personnel, high occupational exposure groups and those who need to travel to the epidemic areas. Against this backdrop, there is a demarcation line regarding the misinformation about vaccination manifested by the top words before and after February. Before February, the gossip on vaccines spread in the comments from the very beginning when the first video was posted (cf. Example 1). The rumours crested in

February with a cursing expression "断子绝孙" (n = 100 in February) to denote a side effect of sterilisation due to vaccination (cf. Example 2), which is definitely false. After February, people in Macau began to vaccinate orderly and the misinformation on vaccines decayed promptly, although it still reappeared from time to time in the following months, such as the discussions on Sinovac (科兴 n = 50 in April), which, however, is not one of the two types of vaccines that Macau has been using (cf. Example 3). In the three preceding months (December, January and February), people were also contrasting and debating on the Chinese and American vaccines (cf. Example 4). After that when Macau started the mass vaccination, people were comparing the conditions of vaccination in Macau and Hong Kong and discussing the policies of the (Macau) government, such as whether vaccination would affect cross-border travels between the mainland (Zhuhai) and Macau, and between Hong Kong and Macau (cf. Example 5).

Examples

1. 条命系自己的、打啲毒液在我身体里面、我冇病冇痛、睬你都戇鸠!万一
   打咗疫苗出咗事!谁负责? (2020/12/18).
   'My life is my own; the poisonous liquid is injected into my body; I'm not sick or in pain; only a fool will respond! In case something happens after injecting the vaccine! Who is responsible?'
2. 辉瑞疫苗被称作"断子绝孙针!"哈哈!(2021/2/8)
   'Pfizer's vaccine is called the "cut off the offspring shot!" Haha!'
3. 朋友, 搞清楚先喷啦, 澳门冇科兴啊!欧洲好多国家都停咗阿斯利康啦, 但系佢
   地都冇科兴, 唔通又关科兴事?(2021/4/17)
   'Friends, let's make sure before slandering; there is no Sinovac in Macau! Many countries in Europe have stopped using AstraZeneca, but there is no Sinovac anywhere in their countries; why does it have to do with Sinovac?'
4. 美国疫苗坚决不打, 因为没有经过动物实验, 直接人体, 面瘫, 晕过去……我还
   是选择大陆疫苗, 因为已经进行了动物实验, 还进行了三阶段的实验, 广东已经
   有18万人进行了注射, 没有出现比较大的副作用…… (2020/12/24)
   'The American vaccine is resolutely not injected, because it has not been tested on animals, directly on the human body, it will cause facial paralysis, fainting... I still choose the mainland vaccine, because animal experiments have been carried out, and three-stage experiments have been carried out; 180,000 people in Guangdong have already been injected, and no major side effects appeared...'
5. 香港市民已完成接种两齐疫苗澳门政府应该通关放行了。(2021/4/6)
   'Hong Kong citizens have completed two doses of vaccination, and the Macau government should let them cross the border.'

Table 2. Top words in the general list and the lists by month (with gloss in English).

General	May 2021	Jun. 2021
疫苗 Vaccine 965 澳门 Macau 624 香港 Hong Kong 457 可以 Can 246 自己 Self 210 中国 China 208 接种 Inoculate 199 频道 Channel 185 政府 Government 183 美国 The USA 166 大陆 Mainland 165 病毒 Virus 158 如果 If 147 所以 So 145 可能 May 136 科兴 Sinovac 134 国药 Sinopharm 120 问题 Problem 118 没有 No 115 不要 Not want 112 应该 Should 111 已经 Already 107 因为 Because 104 大家 Everyone 102 断子绝孙 Cut off offspring 102	疫苗 Vaccine 71 中国 China 41 美国 The USA 33	疫苗 Vaccine 29 澳门 Macau 15
Feb. 2021	Mar. 2021	Apr. 2021
疫苗 Vaccine 270 澳门 Macau 112 断子绝孙 Cut off offspring 100 美国 the USA 89 频道 Channel 59 国产 Domestic 59 不要 No 57 政府 Government 56 可以 Can 56 接种 Inoculate 50 所以 So 50 自己 Self 50	香港 Hong Kong 254 疫苗 Vaccine 245 澳门 Macau 218 可以 Can 84 中国 China 81 接种 Inoculate 61 病毒 Virus 61 自己 Self 53 可能 Can 50	疫苗 Vaccine 125 澳门 Macau 67 科兴 Sinovac 50 香港 Hong Kong 49 接种 Inoculate 37 自己 Self 34 频道 Channel 32

(continued)

3.2 Collocation

The "GraphColl" function of LancsBox [21] was employed to generate the collocates of "疫苗" (vaccine) and their visualisations (Figs. 1, 2, 3, 4, 5, 6, 7 and 8). We set the criteria as "MI > 5.0 and frequency > 5.0 in the L5-R5 range". In each figure, the strength of

Table 2. (*continued*)

General	May 2021	Jun. 2021
May 2021	Jun. 2021	
疫苗 Vaccine 174 澳门 Macau 66 香港 Hong Kong 48 可以 Can 42 接种 Inoculate 38 自己 Self 35 政府 Government 32 病毒 Virus 31	澳门 Macau 128 香港 Hong Kong 61 疫苗 Vaccine 51 通关 (Re)open the border 30	

collocation is indicated by the distance between the node (疫苗) and its collocates. The closer the distance is, the stronger the collocation is. The intensity of colour denotes the frequency of a collocate. A collocate in darker colour has a higher frequency. The relative position of a collocation is represented by L (left) and R (right).

In a general view of the collocates of "疫苗" (Fig. 1), the strongest collocate is "活性" (activity), which refers to the activity of vaccines that people are concerned about. The most frequent one is the word "国产" (domestic). By reading the concordance lines of "国产" and "疫苗", it was observed that netizens had heated debates on the efficacy of the domestic vaccines (cf. Example 6). The collocation of "疫苗" exhibited noticeable differences among the seven months (Figs. 2, 3, 4, 5, 6, 7 and 8). In December and January, the comments are small in quantity. People were comparing the Chinese vaccines (祖国 motherland, 中国 China) and the foreign vaccines (辉瑞 Pfizer) in December 2020 (cf. Example 7) and worried whether vaccines would protect them against COVID-19, even though (就算) they were vaccinated (接种) in January 2021 (cf. Example 8). In February, the rumours on vaccines (cf. Example 2) including the Chinese vaccines (国产 domestic, 中国 China) burgeoned. Some people groundlessly alleged that the domestic vaccines would lead to facial paralysis (面瘫) and incited people to resist (反对) them (cf. Example 9). At the same time, there were also voices supporting the Chinese vaccines and countering the misinformation in the concordance lines (cf. Example 10). After February when Macau people started to vaccinate in a large number and they could freely choose their desired types of vaccines, that is, between the inactivated vaccines by Sinopharm and mRNA vaccines by BioNTech, the misinformation faded, and the supportive voices built up their momentum (cf. Example 11). In the following months (March, April, May and June), people continued comparing the Chinese vaccines (祖国 motherland, 中国 China, 国产 domestic) and the foreign vaccines (辉瑞 Pfizer, mRNA).

Examples

6. 国产疫苗安全性我系相信架, 但打咗系咪一定有抗体?(2021/2/10).
    'I believe in the safety of domestic vaccines, but there must be antibodies after injecting the vaccine?'
7. 辉瑞、莫德纳的数据已公开, 科兴综合世界的测试数据也即将公开, 慢慢拣吧!(2020/12/24)
    'The data of Pfizer and Moderna have been made public, and the test data of Sinovac in the world will also be made public soon, please choose slowly!'
8. 全部打晒都没用, 以色列的疫苗接种经验告诉我们, 就算打了疫苗依然会有机率感染新冠肺炎。(2021/1/23)
    'It's useless after all finishing vaccination. Israel's vaccination experience tells us that even if you are vaccinated, there is still a chance of contracting the new crown pneumonia.'
9. 打国产疫苗会变鳄鱼, 会面瘫奥!(2021/2/8)
    'Injecting the domestic vaccines will turn into crocodiles and face paralysis!'
10. 强力支持接种国产疫苗! (2021/2/25)
    'Strong support for injecting the domestic vaccines!'
11. 中国疫苗外销90多个国家, 12个国家领导人带头接种, 接种人口上亿, 要对自己有信心, 不要相信假新闻和诽谤, 加油 👍 (2021/3/5)
    'China's vaccines are exported to more than 90 countries. Leaders of 12 countries have taken the lead in inoculating the vaccines. The number of inoculated people is over 100 million. You must have confidence in yourself, and don't believe in fake news and slander, cheers 👍'

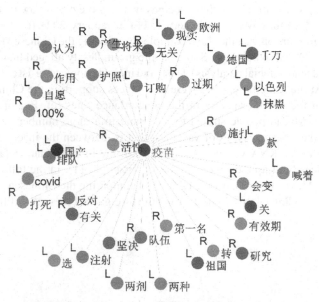

Fig. 1. Collocates of "疫苗" in the VCC corpus

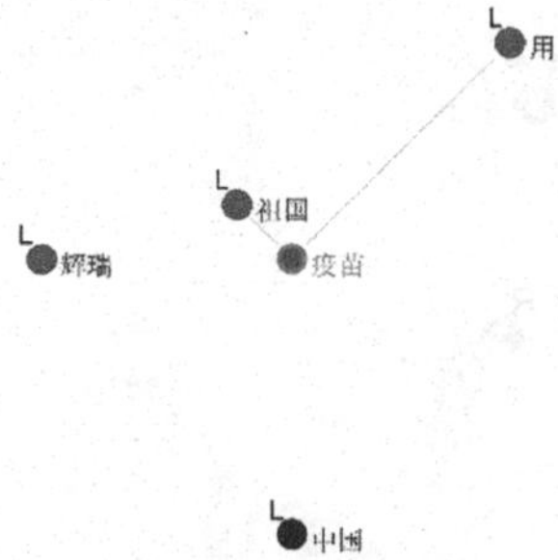

Fig. 2. Collocates of "疫苗" in December

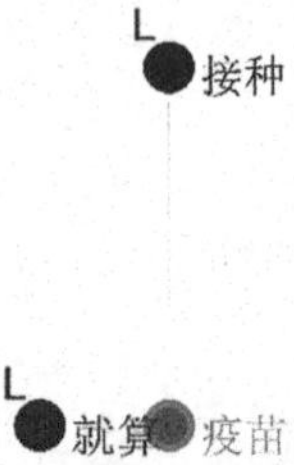

Fig. 3. Collocates of "疫苗" in January

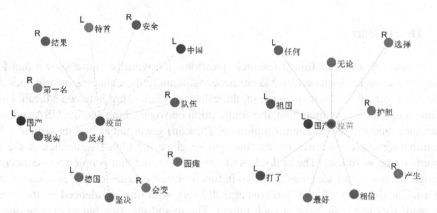

Fig. 4. Collocates of "疫苗" in February

Fig. 5. Collocates of "疫苗" in March

Fig. 6. Collocates of "疫苗" in April

Fig. 7. Collocates of "疫苗" in May

Fig. 8. Collocates of "疫苗" in June

4 Discussion

To answer the aforementioned research questions, the wordlists have shown that four main topics were discussed by Macau netizens, namely the concerns on vaccines and the misinformation about vaccination, the trilateral relationship between Macau, Hong Kong and the Chinese mainland, the competition between China and the USA and their vaccines, and the judgemental opinions of (Macau) government and its policies. The dominating concern centres on vaccines per se given the high frequencies of the top words in the word lists. The collocates of "疫苗" revealed that people were concerned about the activity of vaccines and also initiated heated debates on the efficacy of vaccines. The discussion topics and concerns did vary with time, evidenced by the results of word lists and collocates of each month. The misinformation burgeoned before the mass vaccination beginning in February 2021 and phased out following the event when more people received the injection. What we have observed in Macau netizens' attitudes towards vaccination lends support to the prediction of the persuasive power of gain- and loss-framed messages proposed by Meyerowitz and Chaiken [22] based on Tversky and Kahneman's Prospect Theory [23], which predicts that gain-framed messages are comparatively more effective in advocating safe behaviour. Since Macau presents a model of successfully containing the COVID-19 epidemic, it is a relatively safe place in the face of the pandemic. In addition, vaccination tends to be viewed as safe health behaviour to prevent the relevant illness. In the light of Prospect Theory, the supporting voices (gain-framed messages) for the (Chinese) vaccines eventually and overwhelmingly prevailed against the misinformation by virtue of the effective persuasiveness in promoting safe behaviour (vaccination), which is demonstrated by the voices building up to support the (Chinese) vaccines in the VCC corpus (cf. Examples 10–11). This phenomenon echoes Rothman and Salovey's study in health communication that disease prevention behaviour is more effectively promoted by gain frames [24], manifested in recent research on various psychological and sociological behaviours under COVID-19 [25, 26]. It, however, requires in-depth exploration in further studies.

5   Conclusion

The public comments investigated in this study revealed the primary topics and concerns when netizens discussed and perceived COVID-19 vaccination. As the mass vaccination event proceeded, the previous surge of misinformation faded in the face of the effective promotion of gain-framed messages. Assessing these discussions and understanding the concerns in the public comments can assist in devising public health communication and developing vaccination promotion schemes by policy-makers and health professionals, especially in major public health crises such as the pandemic. From our research that showcases the public opinions of Macau netizens, further studies are worth taking to examine the social behaviour changes in response to the COVID-19 pandemic [27], and Prospect Theory has shown much potential in public health communication.

Acknowledgements. The authors are thankful to the two anonymous reviewers of this paper. The authors would like to acknowledge the Higher Education Fund of the Macao SAR Government for financially supporting the FES project "HOPE and PAIN in the Time of a Pandemic: A corpus-based study of metaphor and synaesthesia in Macau"– reference no. HSS-UMAC-2020-10".

References

1. Lei, S., Yang, R., Huang, C.-R.: Emergent neologism: a study of an emerging meaning with competing forms based on the first six months of COVID-19. Lingua **258**, 103095 (2021). https://doi.org/10.1016/j.lingua.2021.103095
2. Wang, X., Ahrens, K., Huang, C.-R.: The distance between illocution and perlocution: a tale of different pragmemes to call for social distancing in two cities. Intercult. Pragmat. **19**(1), 1–33 (2022). https://doi.org/10.1515/ip-2022-0001
3. Wang, X., Huang, C.-R.: From contact prevention to social distancing: the co-evolution of bilingual neologisms and public health campaigns in two cities in the time of COVID-19. SAGE Open **11**(3), 1–17 (2021). https://doi.org/10.1177/21582440211031556
4. Chen, X., Wang, V.X., Huang, C.-R.: Themes and sentiments of online comments under COVID-19: a case study of Macau. In: Dong, M., Yanhui, G., Hong, J.-F. (eds.) Chinese Lexical Semantics: 22nd Workshop, CLSW 2021, Nanjing, China, May 15–16, 2021, Revised Selected Papers, Part I, pp. 494–503. Springer International Publishing, Cham (2022). https://doi.org/10.1007/978-3-031-06703-7_39
5. Gu, J., et al.: Multi-probe attention neural network for COVID-19 semantic indexing. BMC Bioinform. **23**(1), 259 (2022). https://doi.org/10.1186/s12859-022-04803-x
6. Wan, M., Su, Q., Xiang, R., Huang, C.-R.: Data-driven analytics of COVID-19 "infodemic." Int. J. Data Sci. Anal. (2022). https://doi.org/10.1007/s41060-022-00339-8
7. Wang, V.X., Chen, X., Quan, S., Huang, C.-R.: A parallel corpus-driven approach to bilingual oenology term banks: how culture differences influence wine tasting terms. In: 34th Pacific Asia Conference on Language, Information and Computation, pp. 318–328. Association for Computational Linguistics (2020)
8. Wang, V.X., Lim, L., Li, D. (eds.): New Perspectives on Corpus Translation Studies, Springer, Singapore (2021). https://doi.org/10.1007/978-981-16-4918-9
9. Wang, X., et al.: From complex emotion words to insomnia and mental health: a corpus-based analysis of the online psychological consultation discourse about insomnia problems in Chinese. In: Dong, M., Gu, Y., Hong, J.-F. (eds.) Chinese Lexical Semantics: 22nd Workshop, CLSW 2021, Nanjing, China, May 15–16, 2021, Revised Selected Papers, Part II,

pp. 221–232. Springer International Publishing, Cham (2022). https://doi.org/10.1007/978-3-031-06547-7_18

10. Chen, X., Wang, V.X., Huang, C.-R.: Sketching the English translations of Kumārajīva's *The Diamond Sutra*: a comparison of individual translators and translation teams. In: 34th Pacific Asia Conference on Language, Information and Computation, pp. 30–41. Association for Computational Linguistics (2020)

11. Li, L., Huang, C.-R., Wang, V.X.: Lexical competition and change: a corpus-assisted investigation of gambling and gaming in the past centuries. SAGE Open **10**(3), 1–14 (2020). https://doi.org/10.1177/2158244020951272

12. Li, L., Wang, V.X., Huang, C.-R.: Social changes manifested in the diachronic changes of reform-related Chinese near synonyms. In: Dong, M., Gu, Y., Hong, J.-F. (eds.) Chinese Lexical Semantics: 22nd Workshop, CLSW 2021, Nanjing, China, May 15–16, 2021, Revised Selected Papers, Part II, pp. 184–193. Springer International Publishing, Cham (2022). https://doi.org/10.1007/978-3-031-06547-7_15

13. Faasse, K., Chatman, C.J., Martin, L.R.: A comparison of language use in pro- and anti-vaccination comments in response to a high profile Facebook post. Vaccine **34**(47), 5808–5814 (2016). https://doi.org/10.1016/j.vaccine.2016.09.029

14. Puri, N., Coomes, E.A., Haghbayan, H., Gunaratne, K.: Social media and vaccine hesitancy: new updates for the era of COVID-19 and globalized infectious diseases. Hum. Vaccin. Immunother **16**(11), 2586–2593 (2020). https://doi.org/10.1080/21645515.2020.1780846

15. Wilson, S.L., Wiysonge, C.: Social media and vaccine hesitancy. BMJ Glob. Health **5**, e004206 (2020). https://doi.org/10.1136/bmjgh-2020-004206

16. Brailovskaia, J., Miragall, M., Margraf, J., Herrero, R., Baños, R.M.: The relationship between social media use, anxiety and burden caused by coronavirus (COVID-19) in Spain. Curr. Psychol. **41**, 7441–7447 (2021). https://doi.org/10.1007/s12144-021-01802-8

17. Schoultz, M., et al.: Mental health, information and being connected: qualitative experiences of social media use during the COVID-19 pandemic from a trans-national sample. Healthcare **9**(6), 735 (2021). https://doi.org/10.3390/healthcare9060735

18. Shi, W., et al.: Online public opinion during the first epidemic wave of COVID-19 in China based on Weibo data. Hum. Soc. Sci. Commun. **9**, 159 (2022). https://doi.org/10.1057/s41599-022-01181-w

19. Wicke, P., Bolognesi, M.M.: Framing COVID-19: how we conceptualize and discuss the pandemic on Twitter. PLoS ONE **15**(9), e0240010 (2020). https://doi.org/10.1371/journal.pone.0240010

20. Brezina, V., Weill-Tessier, P., McEnery, A.: #LancsBox v. 6.0. [software] (2021). http://corpora.lancs.ac.uk/lancsbox

21. Brezina, V.: Collocation graphs and networks: selected applications. In: Cantos-Gómez, P., Almela-Sánchez, M. (eds.) Lexical Collocation Analysis. QMHSS, pp. 59–83. Springer, Cham (2018). https://doi.org/10.1007/978-3-319-92582-0_4

22. Meyerowitz, B.E., Chaiken, S.: The effect of message framing on breast self-examination attitudes, intentions, and behavior. J. Pers. Soc. Psychol. **52**(3), 500–510 (1987). https://doi.org/10.1037/0022-3514.52.3.500

23. Tversky, A., Kahneman, D.: The framing of decisions and the psychology of choice. Science **211**(4481), 453–458 (1981). https://doi.org/10.1126/science.7455683

24. Rothman, A.J., Salovey, P.: Shaping perceptions to motivate healthy behavior: the role of message framing. Psychol. Bull. **121**(1), 3–19 (1997). https://doi.org/10.1037/0033-2909.121.1.3

25. Gantiva, C., Jiménez-Leal, W., Urriago-Rayo, J.: Framing messages to deal with the COVID-19 crisis: the role of loss/gain frames and content. Front. Psychol. **12**, 568212 (2021). https://doi.org/10.3389/fpsyg.2021.568212

26. Jiang, M., Dodoo, N.A.: Promoting mask-wearing in COVID-19 brand communications: effects of gain-loss frames, self- or other-interest appeals, and perceived risks. J. Advert. **50**(3), 271–279 (2021). https://doi.org/10.1080/00913367.2021.1925605
27. Bavel, J.J.V., et al.: Using social and behavioural science to support COVID-19 pandemic response. Nat. Hum. Behav. **4**, 460–471 (2020). https://doi.org/10.1038/s41562-020-0884-z

REFORM IS A JOURNEY: Conceptualizing China's Reform and Opening-Up in the Official News Discourse

Longxing Li[1,2]([envelope]) [iD], Vincent Xian Wang[2] [iD], and Lily Lim[3] [iD]

[1] Faculty of Languages and Translation, Macao Polytechnic University, Macao, China
lxli@mpu.edu.mo
[2] Faculty of Arts and Humanities, University of Macau, Macao, China
vxwang@um.edu.mo
[3] MPU-Bell Centre of English, Macao Polytechnic University, Macao, China
llim@mpu.edu.mo

Abstract. This study explores the conceptual metaphors used in the official news discourse of China's reform and opening-up. The BCC *People's Daily* Corpus is selected as the database from which concordances of the Chinese word *gaige* (reform) are retrieved and collected to build a reform-themed concordance corpus. The analysis of metaphors identified from the structure "*gaige + shi*" has revealed that journey is the predominant source domain of reform metaphors. The source, goal, path, and mode elements of the journey schema are also analyzed in detail. It is found that these elements are mobilized by the state media as important strategies in calling for more people in joining the reform and keeping it moving forward towards destinations one after another.

Keywords: Reform · *Gaige* · News Discourse · Conceptual Metaphor · Corpus

1 Introduction

Reform is a powerful driving force for social change and progress, and thus a topic studied intensively in social sciences. Although there have been some studies on reform from the perspective of linguistics, most of them either examine reform at the lexical level or focus on the English discourse of reform. Many lexical studies of reform are conducted from the perspective of keywords study. *Reform* has been investigated as a keyword of culture and society in English by many scholars [1–4]. While *reform* has been extensively studied in English, offering an intriguing linguistic perspective on Western cultures and societies, its Chinese equivalent – *gaige* – has received much less attention until recently. Since keywords are regarded as metadata produced socially and historically in relation to emerging practices and specific communities of users, the tremendous impact reforms have exerted on China as well as on its people strongly suggests that the word *gaige* must have carried rich and significant information about Chinese culture, history, and society. Zhang [5] investigated the origin of 改革开放 (*gaige kaifang, Reform and Opening-up*) and found that the phrase was used in 1984 at the earliest by Deng Xiaoping,

Q. Su et al. (Eds.): CLSW 2022, LNAI 13496, pp. 170–180, 2023.
https://doi.org/10.1007/978-3-031-28956-9_14

the recognized "general architect of Reform and Opening-up" and was popularized by *People's Daily* and the reports in the National Congress of the Communist Party of China. Li, Dong, and Wang [6] examined *gaige* and its English equivalent *reform* in their respective sociocultural contexts by adopting a historical semantics approach. Li and Wang [7] further compared *gaige* between the Chinese Mainland and Taiwan, finding the significance and impact of reforms in the two societies and revealing the social, cultural, and political factors underneath. Li, Wang, and Huang [8] studied nine reform-related Chinese near synonyms diachronically from the ancient dynasties to the recent century and further focused on the lexical competition and co-development of *geming* (revolution) and *gaige*. These studies on *gaige* are a good start for linguistic research on reform in China. More studies are expected to be conducted from the broader discourse level.

Metaphor is an important device in the construction and representation of important issues or phenomena. Flowerdew and Leong [9] found that four dominant themes (family, war, the body, and traitors) are used to construct identities and relationships between the Chinese Mainland and Hong Kong in Hong Kong's constitutional reform debate. Adopting the discourse dynamics approach, Yu [10] investigated how "leftover women" are represented metaphorically in English language news articles produced by the Chinese media and explained the potential ideologies behind the metaphor use. More recent metaphorical representation studies focus on multimodal discourse, such as the representation of depression, in short, wordless animation films [11]. So far, the important discourse and metaphorical representation of China's reform and opening-up have rarely been studied. Thus, this article examines China's reform and opening-up at the discourse level from the perspective of metaphor analysis. Two Research Questions are proposed:

1. How is reform conceptualized metaphorically in China's official reform discourse?
2. What is the predominant source domain and what does it reveal?

2 Methods

As there is no available corpus themed on China's reform, a specialized corpus of reform is built for this study. People's Daily (人民日报 *Renmin Ribao*) is an authoritative data source, speaking for the Communist Party of China and reflecting the position of the central government. Since reform is usually a top to bottom process, the information from the official state media is worthy of investigation in the first place. The BCC diachronic corpus provides year-by-year People's Daily news report data covering a long time span from 1946, the founding year of the newspaper, to 2015. The keyword 改革*gaige* is retrieved in the BCC diachronic corpus and the concordance lines containing around 60 Chinese characters with *gaige* as the KWIC (Key Word in Context) are collected. The recent years of data are complemented by CNKI People's Daily database. The two sources of data are uploaded to Sketch Engine [12] to build the Reform Corpus. Sketch Engine offers a wide range of functions such as Concordancing, Thesaurus, Word Sketch, and Sketch Difference and has been widely adopted in language teaching, discourse studies, translation studies, lexical studies, lexicography, and terminology [6, 7, 13, 14].

The well-established Metaphor Identification Procedure [15] is adopted to identify potential linguistic metaphors and the source domain verification procedure [16] is followed to address the issue of categorizing the identified metaphors into specific source domains. Four language resources and tools (Suggested Upper Merged Ontology, Word-Net, online dictionaries, and collocational patterns) are used alternatively or together to assist the source domain verification procedure.

Since metaphor identification and source domain determination is highly dependent on manual labor, it is impossible to annotate such a big corpus of China's reform and opening-up over the past four decades. Using signal words is one way to narrow down the data size. Linking verbs can serve as a connection between a subject and further information about that subject. Hou [17] examined the three-word Concgram "Chinese/dream/is" in his investigation of the media representations of the Chinese dream and found that this pattern strongly indicated a positive semantic preference. The interpretations or definitions introduced by the pattern provided the quality and value of the Chinese dream, which Hou claimed was a reformulation of the Chinese dream that echoes the elaboration of the Chinese dream by President Xi Jinping. Hou's research is an example of how the linking verb can be used to study representation.

Compared with English, the Chinese language has much fewer linking verbs. The equivalent of *be* in Chinese is 是 (*shi*), a verb that mainly plays the role of affirming or linking. According to Lv [18], *shi* is able to convey multiple relations and the structure "noun + *shi* + noun/…de/ …" usually expresses equality, categorization, characteristics, existence, description, explanation, reason, purpose, and so on. The sentences containing the structure could be very informative from which the metaphorical description of reform may be found. Therefore, the concordances of the structure "改革 + 是…" (*gaige + shi*…, reform is …) may tell how reform is verbalized, depicted, and conceptualized. Thus, 500 "*gaige + shi*" concordances are extracted from Sketch Engine as the sample to be annotated following the metaphor identification and source domain verification procedures introduced above.

3   Findings

3.1   Overview of the Conceptualization of Reform

A total of 115 linguistic metaphors about reform are identified from 108 of the 500 concordance lines, which indicates that the metaphorization ratio is higher than 20%. Nineteen source domains are sorted out. To measure and compare the productivity of particular source domains and indicate to which extent a source domain is found in this set of data, the resonance value of the source domain is used. The resonance value is calculated by multiplying the sum of the tokens (the number of times each form occurs) by the sum of the types (separate linguistic forms of metaphors or metaphorical keywords) of the metaphors from the same source domain [19].

Table 1 illustrates the distribution of the source domains with at least four instances in the sample data. The source domains which have less than four occurrences include ART, TIDE, FOOD, BODY, GAME, COURSE, DIVIDEND, LIQUOR- MAKING, ORGANISM, SPACE, ROOT, and SOUL. In terms of resonance value, the JOURNEY source domain, with the largest number of types and tokens and the highest resonance value, is the most productive and predominant. WAR and FORCE, with the second and the third highest resonance value, are much less productive. Considering its predominant role, the JOURNEY source domain will be the focus of the current metaphor analysis.

Table 1. Distribution of Major Source Domains of Reform Metaphors

Source domain	Tokens	Types	Resonance value
JOURNEY	31	19	589
FORCE	25	2	50
PROJECT	15	1	15
WAR	13	8	104
OBJECT	6	5	30
ARTICLE	4	3	12

3.2   Journey: The Predominant Source Domain of Reform

Journey metaphors are present in much political discourse [20]. JOURNEY is a potent source domain because of the availability of a clear schema that includes required elements – such as starting points and end points connected by paths and entities that move along the way. This is usually represented in cognitive linguistics as a source–path–goal schema. Besides, there are also optional elements in political speeches, including modes of travel, guides, and companions [21]. Table 2 presents four elements of the journey schema and their respective metaphorical keywords identified from the journey metaphors of reform. Among the four elements, the path and the mode elements are instantiated by rich metaphorical linguistic forms, while the source and the goal by only two and one metaphorical keyword respectively. The possible reasons are that reform is a process, which is a long 'path' with turns, barriers, and shortcuts, and the approaches to reform, which are 'modes' of travel along the 'path', are very diversified, whereas the source and goal do not have many alternatives.

Due to the limit of the current data, some common metaphorical keywords may not be found. To gain a full picture, other important metaphorical keywords based on the identified keywords and the present authors' native speaker intuition can be added to the retrieval in the larger corpus. The common word "起点" (starting point) which is absent from the sample data can be retrieved as an additional metaphorical keyword for the source element. Similarly, in addition to "落脚点", three other common words indicating the goal, "终点" (endpoint), "归宿" (a home to return to), and "彼岸" (the other shore), can be added to depict a more comprehensive picture of the goal element. By querying more metaphorical keywords and expanding the data source to the whole BCC People's Daily Corpus, more reliable and generalizable findings can be discovered. Therefore, the above-mentioned seven keywords are retrieved respectively with "改革" using the regular expressions such as "改革*出发", "改革*起步", "改革*起点", and "改革*终点" in the People's Daily Corpus to investigate the source and the goal elements

Table 2. Elements of the Journey Metaphor of Reform

Element	Metaphorical Keywords (Types)
Source	出发点starting point, 起步 start the first step
Path	途径path, 路子way, 出路way out, 道路way, 必由之路the only road, 坦途smooth road, 强国富民之路 the road to strengthen the country and enrich the people
Goal	落脚点foothold
Modes	不会一帆风顺will not be smooth sailing, 举足投步every single step, 前进或是倒退forward or backward, 踩着石头过河cross the river on stones, 探索中前进move forward while exploring, 一步one step, 不能止步不前cannot cease to advance, 走前人没有走过的路take the road no one has taken before, 行驶着的列车a moving train

of the journey metaphors of reform. The distribution of the source element and the goal element of the journey metaphors are shown in Fig. 1 and Fig. 2 respectively.

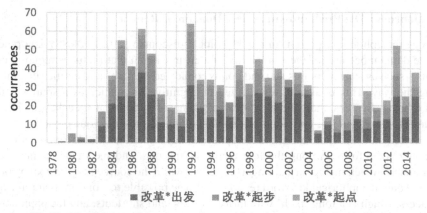

Fig. 1. Distribution of the source element of the journey metaphors of reform

According to Figs. 1 and 2, the total occurrence of the source element (1,090 times) is more than seven times that of the goal element (150 times) despite that one more keyword is retrieved for the goal element. It can be inferred that the source element of the journey metaphors of reform is much more prominent than the goal element. There are two interesting observations from Fig. 1. Firstly, the first 5 years of reform is a period with the least number of metaphorical keywords indicating the source element. Secondly, the source element, which is postulated to be prevalent at the beginning stage of the reform, occurred more frequently from 1983 to 1988 as well as in the middle and the more recent years (2008–2015).

Why did the keywords indicating the source element occur the least frequently in the initial five years of reform? In fact, the low occurrence of the source element of journey metaphors in the initial years is consistent with the low frequency of *gaige*

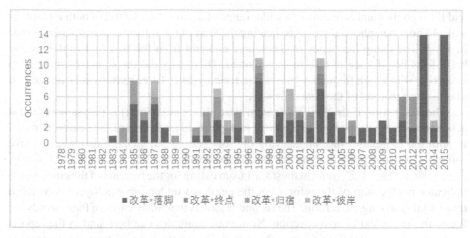

Fig. 2. Distribution of the goal element of the journey metaphors of reform

and the non-metaphorical expressions such as "改革*开始" (reform*start) and "开始*改革" (start*reform). The two non-metaphorical expressions occurred in the People's Daily Corpus 140 times in the first six years (1978–1983) and 623 times in the following five years (1984–1988). The reasons for the low occurrence of the source element in the first six years of reform are twofold. First, reform still faced strong opposition from the conservative forces, so it was not implemented immediately after the 1978 Third Plenary Session of the 11th CPC Central Committee which was held as the official starting point of China's Reform and Opening-up. Second, reforms during the first five to six years were not carried out nationwide nor in high-profile; instead, it was small in scale and restricted to some pilot sectors and areas such as the special economic zones of Shenzhen, Zhuhai, Xiamen, and Shantou which were established in 1979. The low frequency of the word *gaige* and the non-metaphorical expressions regarding the start of reform reinforce the fact that reform was not so actively promoted during that period. The main task of the early years seems more to "emancipate people's minds", mobilize the public, and accumulate experience through experiments and pilots. The latter half of the following Excerpt 1 illustrates that reforms were not so common in 1982 and thus even small and partial reforms needed to be urged and encouraged.

Excerpt 1
要有成效地进行改革, 首先必须有一个适合中国情况的战略性的总体规划。[...]但是, 小的、局部的改革, 现在就要起步, 不能等, 不能因为还没有一个总体规划而放弃了目前可以解决的问题。(1982)

To carry out reform effectively, there must first be a strategic master plan that suits China's situation…. However, small and partial reforms must start now without delay. We should not miss opportunities to solve problems that can be solved at present before the formulation of the master plan.

The CPC Central Committee's Decision on Economic Restructuring adopted in October 1984 marked the acceleration and expansion of reform from rural areas to the cities and from politics and economy to a wider range of sectors. So, the use of both metaphorical and non-metaphorical words indicating the start of the reform process began to soar in 1983. The rising frequency of the source element from the first half to the second half of the first decade of reform is explained. Then, why did the source element keep occurring with a high frequency later and in recent years? Three reasons are summarized after a close reading of the concordances.

The first reason is that "出发" (*chufa*, start off/set out/depart) is polysemous and it accounts for a big proportion of the three metaphorical keywords of the source element. In addition to the meaning of "starting off" or "setting out", *chufa* also means "have something or somebody in mind" or "see from the angle of". For example, "改革必须从关心职工利益出发" (reform must start from caring for the benefits of the employees) indicates not the start of the reform but the emphasis on having employees benefits in mind while carrying out reform. The second reason is that many cases of these words are found in the context of retrospection. Numerous examples can be found in the reports on the anniversaries of the reform or the significant events during the reform. Sentences such as "改革从农村起步, 走过20年光辉历程。" (The reform started in the rural areas and has undergone 20 years of splendid process.) and "35年前, 改革起步, ..." (Thirty-five years ago, the reform started...) found in 1998 and 2013 respectively are examples of the retrospection of and reflection on the reform. The third reason is that new and specific reforms turn out continuously in almost every sector of Chinese society and "new starts" of reform may be proposed when it enters new phases. Excerpt 2 is an example of restarting reform (改革再出发) in the sense of pushing reform from one sector to another or promoting another round of reform in the lasting process. By initiating "new starts", the continuous impetus is injected into the enduring cause of the Reform and Opening-up.

Excerpt 2
从收入分配到社会保障, 从行政体制改革到金融体制改革, 人们的改革期待涉及各个领域, 这也从一个侧面说明: 改革再出发, 必须树立"下好一盘棋"的整体思维。(2013)

From income distribution to social security, from reform of the administrative system to reform of the financial system, people's expectations for reform cover a wide range of fields, which also illustrates from one side that to start again with reform, we must establish holistic thinking of "playing a good game of chess".

Further to the discussion on the source element, interesting observations on the goal element are also made after retrieving representative phrases from the People's Daily Corpus (Fig. 2). Diachronically, none of the four metaphorical expressions for the goal element is found during the first five years of reform and the occurrence of these metaphorical expressions fluctuates significantly from period to period with occasional years such as 1985, 1987, 1997, 2003, 2013, and 2015 recorded high frequency. The expression "改革*落脚" is the most frequently occurred among the four retrieved expressions. Why do the metaphorical expressions for the goal element distribute in such a way? What do they reflect through the context in which they occur? These questions are also explored by examining the concordances.

The reason for the absence of the goal element in the first five years is similar to that for the low occurrence of the source element. Both are closely related to the low profile of reform in the early stage and the "delay" of the mass campaign. Similar to both metaphorical and non-metaphorical references to the source of reform, the metaphorical and non-metaphorical reference to the goal was also at the lowest during the first five years and only began to surge in 1983 (Fig. 2). The low frequency of *gaige* and the low occurrence of both metaphorical and non-metaphorical references to the reform source and goal during the first several years of the Reform and Opening-up reflect that reform is not much reported in the state newspaper and its influence is limited in the very beginning. It is a period of conception and pilot, preparing for promoting reform on a much larger scale and thorough manner in the later stage.

Then, what do these metaphorical expressions for the goal element reflect through their context? A close reading of the concordances of "改革*落脚", which is the dominant expression of goal, finds that more than 90% of them are instantiated by the phrase "出发点和落脚点" (starting point and ending point). One significant case in point comes from the *Decision of the CPC Central Committee on Major Issues Concerning Comprehensively Deepening Reform* which is adopted at the Third Plenary Session of the 18th CPC Central Committee and constitutes a framework document that guides China to refine the system of socialism with Chinese characteristics. Moreover, "出发点" and "落脚点" are regarded almost the same and are rendered into "the fundamental purpose" in the official translation. As Excerpt 3 shows, the fundamental purpose, i.e., the goal, of deepening reform is promoting social equity and justice and improving the people's well-being. Interestingly, "终点" (ending point) is often preceded by negation and is regarded as "起点" (starting point) in many cases as is exemplified by Excerpt 4. Equating the goal with the source and regarding the achieved goal as another point to start conceptualizes reform as an everlasting journey with continuous new starts on the basis of previous destinations arrived.

Excerpt 3 《决定》提出了全面深化改革的出发点和落脚点，体现了中国共产党人的崇高理念：全面深化改革必须以促进社会公平正义、增进人民福祉为出发点和落脚点。(2013)

The fundamental purpose of the initiatives to comprehensively deepen reform put forward by the *Decision* reflects the lofty ideal of the CPC members: we must regard promoting social equity and justice and improving the people's well-being as the fundamental purpose of our initiatives.

Excerpt 4. 但三年阶段性目标的实现，并不是国企改革的终点站，而应成为新的起点。(2001)

However, the realization of the three-year-phase objectives should not be the terminal station of state-owned enterprises reform but the new starting point.

After the investigation of the source and the goal elements, the path and the mode are also examined. To produce more data for analysis, "改革*路" (reform*road) and "改革*途" (reform*approach) are retrieved from the People's Daily Corpus. The two expressions are selected because the two core characters "路" and "途" are common in the seven metaphorical keywords identified in the path element (Table 2) and are believed to be able to elicit more results. Many new keywords are found in the corpus, including 路线 (route), 路线图 (route map), 路程 (distance), and 路径 (track). Figure 3 shows the number of occurrences of the two regular expressions for the path element of the journey metaphors.

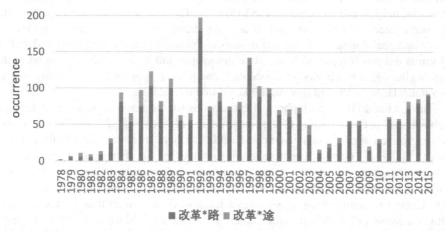

Fig. 3. Distribution of the path element of the journey metaphors of reform

Reading all the retrieved concordances reveals two main patterns: reform as a path and reform which has different paths. Reform is conceptualized as a path to solve various problems, improve social systems, and develop the nation. Among various expressions which regard reform as a path, "改革开放是强国之路" (reform and opening up are ways to make China powerful) is an important metaphorical statement put forward in 1989 in the Fourth Plenary Session of the Thirteenth CPC Central Committee (Excerpt 5). Besides 强国 (making the nation powerful), there are many other modifiers of the 'path', such as 繁荣 (prosperity), 复兴 (rejuvenation), 发展 (development), 富裕 (affluence) and 必由 (only). In addition to regarding reform as a path, reform itself has different paths to follow and the problems encountered in reform can also be solved via certain paths. For example, the central leadership of China may make a general roadmap for reform which will be regarded as the official and authoritative path and different sectors and departments may explore new approaches to reforms according to their specific situations.

Excerpt 5. 四中全会公报指出, 四项基本原则是立国之本, 改革开放是强国之路。 (1989)

The Communiqué of the Fourth Plenary Session of the Thirteenth CPC Central Committee pointed out that the Four Cardinal Principles are the very foundation on which we build our country and reform and opening up are ways to make China powerful.

In brief, the path element of journey metaphors of reform is seen from two perspectives. When reform is regarded as a path, metaphorical expressions are utilized to conceptualize reform as a promising and the only path for China and its people. When reform is seen from the traveler's perspective, they have the initiative and flexibility to explore different paths. The explorative nature of reform and its significant role and dominant position in China's development road is highlighted through the path element.

Lastly, the metaphorical expressions of modes in Table 2 reveal the characteristics of the reform journey from three perspectives. First, reform is explorative and risky as is demonstrated by saying that reform is crossing the river on stones (踩着石头过河) and taking the road no one has taken before (走前人没有走过的路). Second, reform is not a smooth journey (不会一帆风顺) and it can move forward or backward (前进或是倒退) in twists and turns. Third, the travelers on the journey are meticulous in every single step (举足投步, 重要一步) and are determined to keep moving forward (探索中前进, 不能止步不前, 行驶着的列车).

4 Conclusion

The journey metaphor is the most predominant source domain in the conceptualization of reform. The state newspaper has utilized various elements of the journey schema in depicting the image of reform. The source and the goal are well integrated and consistent in conceptualizing reform as a long-lasting journey with stopovers. The path and the mode elements depict reform as an explorative and uncertain, yet imperative and unstoppable journey. The use of the conceptual metaphor PURPOSEFUL ACTIVITY IS TRAVELING ALONG A PATH TOWARD A DESTINATION [22] thus becomes an important strategy for the state media in calling for more people in joining the reform and keeping it moving forward towards destinations one after another. The research has enriched current studies on reform discourse and has contributed a new perspective to research on China's reform and opening-up.

Acknowledgments. The authors would like to acknowledge the research project RP/FLT-04/2022 supported by the Macao Polytechnic University.

References

1. Williams, R.: Keywords: A Vocabulary of Culture and Society. Oxford University Press (1976, 1983, 2015)
2. Bennett, T., Grossberg, L., Morris, M.: New Keywords: A Revised Vocabulary of Culture and Society. Blackwell Publishing (2005)
3. Hindess, B.: Reform and revolution. In: Bennett, T., Grossberg, L., Morris, M. (eds.) New Keywords: A Revised Vocabulary of Culture and Society, pp. 300–304. Blackwell Publishing (2005)
4. Ryan, S.M.: Reform. In: Burgett, B., Hendler, G. (eds.) Keywords for American Cultural Studies. NYU Press, New York (2007)
5. Zhang, X.D.: An investigation of the origin of the concept of 'gaige kaifang'. Mao Zedong Thought Study 33(1), 126–129 (2016) (in Chinese)
6. Li, L., Dong, S., Wang, V.X.: Gaige and reform: a Chinese-English comparative keywords study. In: Su, Q., Zhan, W. (eds.) From Minimal Contrast to Meaning Construct. FCL, vol. 9, pp. 321–332. Springer, Singapore (2020). https://doi.org/10.1007/978-981-32-9240-6_22
7. Li, L., Wang, X.: Gaige (Reform) in Mandarin Chinese across the Taiwan Strait: a corpus-assisted comparative keywords study. In: Language and Culture Studies at Macao, pp. 104–113 (2019) (in Chinese)

8. Li, L., Wang, X., Huang, C.-R.: Social changes manifested in the diachronic changes of reform-related Chinese near synonyms. In: Dong, M., Gu, Y., Hong, JF. (eds) Chinese Lexical Semantics. CLSW 2021. Lecture Notes in Computer Science, vol. 13250, pp. 184–193. Springer, Cham (2022). https://doi.org/10.1007/978-3-031-06547-7_15

9. Flowerdew, J., Leong, S.: Metaphors in the discursive construction of patriotism: the case of Hong Kong's constitutional reform debate. Discourse Soc. **18**(3), 273–294 (2007). https://doi.org/10.1177/0957926507075476

10. Yu, Y.: Metaphorical representations of "leftover women": between traditional patriarchy and modern egalitarianism. Soc. Semiot. **31**(2), 248–265 (2021). https://doi.org/10.1080/103 50330.2019.1625515

11. Forceville, C., Paling, S.: The metaphorical representation of depression in short, wordless animation films. Vis. Commun. **20**(1), 100–120 (2021). https://doi.org/10.1177/147035721 8797994

12. Kilgarriff, A., Rychlý, P., Smrz, P., David, T.: The Sketch Engine. Paper presented at the Proceedings of the Eleventh EURALEX International Congress, Lorient, France (2004)

13. Li, L., Huang, C.-R., Gao, X.: A SkE-assisted comparison of three "prestige" near synonyms in Chinese. In: Hong, J.-F., Su, Q., Wu, J.-S. (eds.) CLSW 2018. LNCS (LNAI), vol. 11173, pp. 256–266. Springer, Cham (2018). https://doi.org/10.1007/978-3-030-04015-4_22

14. Li, L., Wang, Xian.: The development of COVID-19 word list from the perspective of emergency language services. China Terminol. **23**(2), 32–41 (2021). https://doi.org/10.3969/j.issn. 1673-8578.2021.02.005

15. Group, P: MIP: A method for identifying metaphorically used words in discourse. Metaphor. Symb. **22**(1), 1–39 (2007). https://doi.org/10.1080/10926480709336752

16. Ahrens, K., Jiang, M.: Source domain verification using corpus-based tools. Metaphor. Symb. **35**(1), 43–55 (2020). https://doi.org/10.1080/10926488.2020.1712783

17. Hou, Z.: A corpus-driven analysis of media representations of the Chinese Dream. Int. J. English Linguistics **6**(1), 142 (2016). https://doi.org/10.5539/ijel.v6n1p142

18. Lv, S.: Xiandai Hanyu Babai Ci. Commercial Press (1999) (in Chinese)

19. Charteris-Black, J.: Corpus Approaches to Critical Metaphor Analysis. Palgrave Macmillan UK, London (2004). https://doi.org/10.1057/9780230000612

20. Musolff, A.: Metaphor and Political Discourse. Analogical Reasoning in Debates about Europe. Basingstoke, p. 14 (2004)

21. Charteris-Black, J.: Politicians and Rhetoric: The Persuasive Power of Metaphor. Palgrave Macmillan, Basingstoke (2011)

22. Lakoff, G.: The Contemporary Theory of Metaphor. In: Ortony, A. (ed.) Metaphor and Thought, pp. 202–251. Cambridge University Press (1993). https://doi.org/10.1017/CBO978 1139173865.013

General Linguistics, Lexical Resources

The Emotion Code in Sensory Modalities

An Investigation of the Relationship Between Sensorimotor Dimensions and Emotional Valence-Arousal

Yin Zhong[1]([envelope])[iD] and Kathleen Ahrens[2][iD]

[1] Center for Language Education, The Hong Kong University of Science and Technology, Clear Water Bay, Hong Kong
lcyinzhong@ust.hk
[2] Department of English and Communication, The Hong Kong Polytechnic University, Hung Hom, Hong Kong
kathleen.ahrens@polyu.edu.hk

Abstract. Human sensations and emotions are our primary embodied feelings in experiencing the outside world. The two systems are closely intertwined and jointly contribute to cognitive processes such as language use. However, how the two systems interact as manifested in our languages is still not well understood. This paper utilizes perceptual strengths and affective ratings to delve into the interaction between specific sensory modalities and emotional valence-arousal in Chinese. We found that smell and interoception, considered the two sensations directly linked to emotional processing, are more emotional and can elicit higher arousal levels than words associated with other senses. This study demonstrates the relevance and significance of the relationship between sensorimotor and affective information. It further sheds light on the embodied effect and associated emotional implications in the Chinese language.

Keywords: sensorimotor norms · sensory modalities · valence · arousal · emotion

1 Introduction

Embodied cognition theories posit embodied experiences are encoded in the knowledge system and will be reactivated via cortical network simulation mechanisms in response to the original stimulus and/or its related stimuli (cf. [1–3]). For example, comprehending the word *cat* automatically simulates the sensorimotor, affection, and/or mental state that is associated with one's previous encounters with an actual cat, which includes but is not limited to what a cat looks like (via visual perception), what a cat sounds like (via auditory perception), what a cat feels like (via tactile perception), and what one's mental feeling is about a cat (e.g., via emotions). In general, our bodily physical interactions with the outside world ground cognitive processing and further influence our conceptual knowledge system.

To explore the fundamental position of the sensorimotor system in one of the most important cognitive processes, i.e., language comprehension, a proliferation of behavioral and neurological studies has tapped into the effects of sensorimotor and affective information on semantic processing (e.g., [4–6]). Recently, using the perceptual and action strengths assigned to lexical items, a series of perceptual strength norming studies (also known as modality exclusivity norms, or sensorimotor norms) has unraveled that specific sensory modalities (e.g., vision, hearing, smell, taste) and/or action effectors (e.g., head, mouth, leg, arm) exhibit varying levels of importance in different concepts across a variety of languages (see, e.g., [7–9]). Importantly, a sensation denoting internal bodily states, *interoception*, shares overlapping processing mechanisms with emotional experiences [10,11] and is thus suggested as a 'scaffolding' sense that associates physical sensations with mental representation as well as grounds abstract concepts [12,13].[1]

With regard to affective experiences, they were usually operationalized through a two-dimensional valence-arousal space (see Fig. 1 below). The dimension of valence denotes how positive or negative a concept is, whereas the dimension of arousal represents whether a concept is excited/tense (high-arousal) or calm/tired (low-arousal) (cf. [14]). Emotional valence or affective norms were normally collected via valence and arousal ratings in psychological studies (e.g., [15–17]). These studies focused mainly on correlations between valence and arousal values, with valence being recognized as the most powerful measure of the emotional nature of stimuli.

However, despite the considerable evidence of recruiting sensorimotor mechanisms in language comprehension that has been posed, the interaction between sensorimotor and affective systems coded in the semantic processing is still an underexplored topic. A direct linguistic attestation between specific sensory modalities and emotional valence is examined in [19], in which English gustatory- and olfactory-related lexical items were found to be more 'valenced' or 'emotion-laden' than words associated with other sensory modalities. Such emotional preference over gustatory and olfactory senses might be attributed to the neural base of the odors and flavors—they activate specific brain regions for emotional processing [20]. Winter [19] additionally proposed that olfaction contains more unpleasant and negative concepts than gustatory sense (for a similar idea, see [21]). Interestingly, the etymologies of the two adjectives in English describing a preferable flavor and an unpleasant odor, i.e., *tasty* and *smelly*, are originated in *to taste/taste* and *to smell/smell*, which denote an action of perceiving (or the perception of) a flavor and an action of perceiving (or the perception of) an odor, respectively.

Even though sensorimotor and emotional mechanisms are supposedly shared universally regardless of which language one speaks, social and cultural experiences might lexicalize inner bodily feelings, especially those related to emotions, distinctively across languages. This paper, thus, takes Chinese as a case in point to explore the reciprocal interaction of specific sensorimotor dimensions with emotional valence. More specifically, we will adopt the ratings collected in a

---

[1] Note that the five traditional sensory modalities, i.e., visual, auditory, gustatory, olfactory, and tactile senses, mainly detect signals from the external stimuli rather than from the inner body.

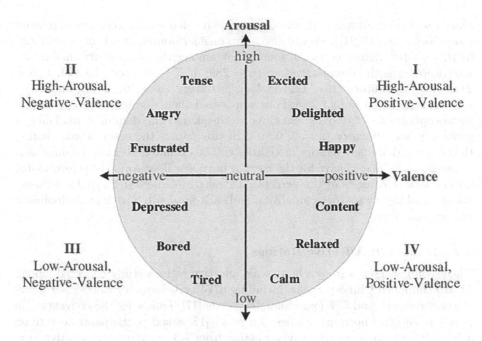

Fig. 1. Two-dimensional-valence-arousal space ([18], p.541)

study of sensorimotor norms of Chinese nouns [9] and another study of affective ratings in simplified Chinese words [17] to look for possible convergence between these two distinct yet affiliated systems. We ask two main research questions in this paper:

RQ1: Will sensory modalities influence affection (valence-arousal degree) in the Chinese language?

RQ2: Will affection (valence-arousal degree) differs in sensory modalities in the Chinese language?

2 Method

2.1 Dataset 1: Sensorimotor Norms

The dataset concerning sensorimotor strength was collected for 664 disyllabic Chinese nouns among native speakers of Mandarin Chinese [9]. This study asked participants to rate how much they experience each concept based on their six perceptual senses (i.e., vision, hearing, taste, smell, touch, and interoception) and the five action effectors from different parts of the body (i.e., foot/leg, hand/arm, head excluding mouth, mouth/throat, and torso), from 0 = no feelings at all, to 5 = very strong feelings. In order to identify which sensorimotor dimension is most associated with a word, "dominant sensory modality" as well as "dominant action effector" were assigned to each word according to the maximum perceptual and action strength across the six senses and the five effectors.

Since previous studies only discussed emotional valence in the context of sensory modalities (e.g., [19,21]), we will also only consider dominant sensory modalities in this study.[2] Zhong et al. [9] found that among the six sensory modalities, interoception is the dominant sense (n = 289; 43.5%), followed by visual (n = 211; 31.8%), auditory (n = 122; 18.4%), gustatory (n = 19; 2.9%), and olfactory and tactile (n = 8; 1.2%). Four words had their dominance in visual and interoception (n = 4; 0.6%), and three words shared the dominant modality in gustatory and olfactory (n = 3; 0.5%). In this paper, the seven words sharing the common dominant sensory modalities will be excluded because the dominant dimension will be exclusive for the current purpose. Therefore, the sensorimotor norms dataset consists of the perceptual strength of the 657 disyllabic Chinese nouns in all the six sensory modalities, and each word will have its sole dominant sensory modality.

2.2 Dataset 2: Affective Ratings

The second dataset is from a large-scale affective ratings study collected among 11,310 simplified Chinese words, including 9774 two-character words, 949 three-character words, and 587 four-character words [17]. Following the convention in previous affective norming studies, Xu et al. [17] asked participants to rate on a 7-point scale for valence ratings, ranging from −3 = extremely negative, 0 = neutral, to +3 = extremely positive. For the arousal ratings, participants were asked to rate on a 5-point scale, 0 = very low arousal to 4 = very high arousal.

To incorporate the sensorimotor norms into the affective ratings, we mapped the words in Dataset 1 to Dataset 2 and identified 649 two-character nouns as the data in this study.[3]

2.3 Data Analysis

We follow the "absolute valence" measurement in Winter [19] to calculate absolute valence values in addition to the valence ratings for the lexical items. Absolute valence removes the negative sign and entails whether a concept is "emotion-laden" irrespective of the actual valence value it receives.[4]

A simple linear model is fitted, with **valence**, **absolute valence**, and **arousal** analyzed separately as dependent variables. **Dominant sensory modality** (i.e., vision, hearing, touch, taste, smell, and interoception) is considered the categorical predictor. All the analyses were conducted with JASP [23].[5]

---

[2] Another reason for omitting dominant action effectors is because almost all the action effectors jointly shared a dominant place with other effectors in [9] since action strength is relatively low for noun concepts. Therefore, considering the statistical power, we will mainly focus on sensory modalities in this paper.

[3] Note the words in the two datasets were both from a Mega study of Lexical Decision in Simplified Chinese (MELD-SCH, Tsang et al. [22]).

[4] Absolute valence is achieved by subtracting the mean of all valence ratings from each rating and then taking the absolute value.

[5] JASP is a free and open-source program for statistical analysis.

3   Results

3.1   Valence and Absolute Valence

Table 1 shows the average (Mean), standard error (SE), and standard deviation (SD) of the valence and absolute valence across six dominant sensory modalities. On average, gustatory words had the highest valence score ($M = 0.56$, SD = 0.40), while olfactory words received the lowest rating ($M = 0.12$, SD = 1.36). However, the linear model for valence ratings was not well fitted (adjusted R^2 = $-.003$). Moreover, no effect of dominant sensory modality was suggested for the valence ratings, $F(5, 643) = 0.67$, $p = .646$.

Table 1. Mean, SE, and SD of the valence and absolute valence across dominant modalities.

	Dominant Modality	N	Mean	SE	SD
Valence	Auditory	122	0.283	0.0581	0.642
	Gustatory	19	0.555	0.0917	0.400
	Interoceptive	284	0.377	0.0593	0.999
	Olfactory	8	0.116	0.4824	1.364
	Tactile	8	0.226	0.0967	0.273
	Visual	208	0.334	0.0398	0.575
Absolute Valence	Auditory	122	0.445	0.0421	0.465
	Gustatory	19	0.254	0.0852	0.371
	Interoceptive	284	0.767	0.0379	0.639
	Olfactory	8	1.166	0.2142	0.606
	Tactile	8	0.237	0.0582	0.165
	Visual	208	0.366	0.0307	0.442

Considering the absolute valence, olfactory lexical items were the most "emotion laden" ($M = 1.17$, SD = 0.61), and the second highly emotional modality was interoception ($M = 0.77$, SD = 0.64). Tactile sense was seen the least emotion-laden modality among the six sensory modalities ($M = 0.24$, SD = 0.17). The model for the absolute valence fits, accounting for 12% of the variance in absolute valence ratings (adjusted $R^2 = .12$). There was a significant effect of dominant modality on the absolute valence ratings ($F(5, 643) = 18.62$, $p < .001$). A post hoc comparison showed that interoceptive words were more emotional than auditory ($t(643) = 5.51$, $p < .001$), gustatory ($t(643) = 4.00$, $p = .001$), and visual ($t(643) = 8.13$, $p = .001$) items. Olfactory words were also found more valenced than auditory ($t(643) = 3.66$, $p = .004$), gustatory ($t(643) = 4.01$, $p = .001$), and visual ($t(643) = 4.11$, $p = < .001$) words.

3.2   Arousal

Applying the same method as the valence and absolute valence, we provide the average (Mean), standard error (SE), and standard deviation (SD) of the arousal ratings across six dominant sensory modalities in Table 2.

Table 2. Mean, SE, and SD of the arousal across dominant modalities.

	Dominant Modality	N	Mean	SE	SD
Arousal	Auditory	122	2.02	0.0381	0.421
	Gustatory	19	2.06	0.1116	0.487
	Interoceptive	284	2.14	0.0284	0.479
	Olfactory	8	2.42	0.1178	0.333
	Tactile	8	1.75	0.0964	0.273
	Visual	208	1.93	0.0300	0.433

The overall results for arousal ratings replicated those for absolute valence, in which olfactory items were considered the highest arousal ($M = 2.42$, SD = 0.33), and the second-highest arousal modality was interoception ($M = 2.14$, SD = 0.48). Touch was seen as the lowest arousal sense ($M = 1.75$, SD = 0.27). In general, the model for the arousal fits, with 5% of the variance in arousal ratings (adjusted R^2 = .05). A significant effect of modality was likewise suggested on the arousal ratings ($F(5, 643) = 7.15$, $p < .001$). A post hoc comparison showed that interoceptive words had higher arousal than visual items ($t(643) = 5.15$, $p < .001$), and olfactory words also had higher arousal than visual words ($t(643) = 3.01$, $p = .041$).

4   Discussion and Conclusion

Consolidating Chinese sensorimotor norms and affective ratings, this paper explores how sensory modalities interact with emotional experiences—valence and arousal, in particular. First, we found evidence suggesting that dominant sensory modalities may affect the valence and arousal degree in the Chinese language, especially on absolute valence and arousal values. The reason for the null effect of dominant sensory modalities on valence might because the degree of valence has been "neutralized." Significant effect of dominant sensory modalities was suggested on absolute valence; that means, some sensory modalities are more "emotion laden" than others. Significant effect of dominant sensory modalities was likewise suggested on arousal – some sensory modalities are more "aroused" than others.

Concerning the second question on the differentiation of affection in the sensory modalities, our findings suggested that gustatory nouns elicited the most positive affection while olfactory words were the most negative. Other modalities are in between the two extremes. However, when positive or negative valence is discarded, interoception and olfaction are the two prominent "emotional" modalities that are more "emotion laden" than auditory, gustatory, and visual senses.

Arousal replicated the result for the absolute valence, in which interoceptive and olfactory lexical items evoked higher arousal levels than visual words. Some samples words that are dominant in olfactory and interoceptive senses are demonstrated in Fig. 2 and 3, respectively.

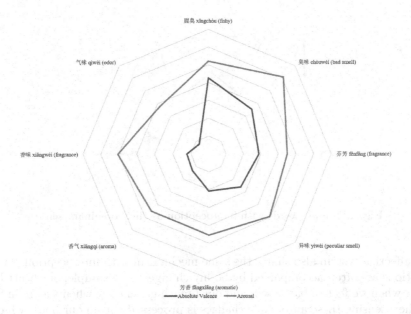

Fig. 2. Sample words with olfaction as their dominant sense

The findings mostly coincide with Winter's [19] study of affective loadings in the English lexicon. When considering actual valence values, gustatory words are the most positive while olfactory vocabulary is the most negative. For the case of Chinese, this is mainly because the nouns dominated by taste are mostly related to food items (e.g., 水果 shui3guo3 'fruit' and 蛋糕 dan4gao1 'cake'), which may largely elicit people's positive memories and experiences of the tastes and flavors of these foods, whereas the valence ratings for smell were possibly pulled low by two words that explicitly connote bad taste, i.e., 臭味 chou4wei4 'foul smell' and 腥臭 xing1chou4 'stinking smell.' Nevertheless, the model and the results were not capable of differentiating emotional valence across different sensory modalities.

However, the consistent findings of absolute valence and arousal suggest that smell and interoception are the two senses that are 'closest' to our affection. Note that the absolute valence only considers if a sensory modalities is emotional valenced regardless of the emotional strength. This finding is in line with neurological evidence because olfactory and interoceptive senses are directly connected with the emotional mechanism in our neural systems. There is evidence that different odors can elicit pleasant or unpleasant responses, influence cognition and emotion, and modulate psychological and physiological states [24].

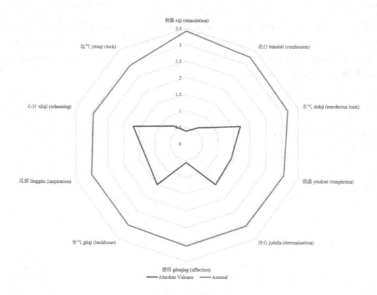

Fig. 3. Sample words with interoception as their dominant sense

The affective system also shares the same mechanism with interoception [25,26]. Emotions are often accompanied by bodily changes; for example, our heart beat faster when we feel embarrassed, and our breath go shallow when we are in fear. Further, sensing these autonomic changes is processed within our body, which is detected by the interoceptive sensation. Such intimate relatedness of the physiological and mental states possibly ground our cognitive processes and is further reflected in language representations. For example, those lexical items dominated by interoceptive sense mostly depict emotionally abstract concepts such as 胸怀 *xiong1huai2* 'heart; mind,' 苦海 *ku3hai3* 'abyss of misery,' and 悲叹 *bei1tan4* 'sigh mournfully' (for a discussion of the relationship between interoception and abstractness via the sensorimotor strength, see [13]).

It is worth noting that the present study may only reflect how emotional values are encoded in one type of part-of-speech, i.e., nouns; and the volume of dominant sensory modalities is considerably scarce for certain senses—for example, olfactory and tactile senses (only eight words are dominated by smell and/or touch). Another limitation is that we did not consider the context that the sensory lexicon appears. Provided that adjectives and contextual information (e.g., semantic prosody) predict emotional differences among sensory modalities [19], the association between these factors needs to be investigated in future studies.

Acknowledgement. This work is supported by the dean's reserve grant (1-ZVTL) from the Faculty of Humanities at The Hong Kong Polytechnic University.

References

1. Barsalou, L.W.: Situated simulation in the human conceptual system. Lang. Cogn. Process. **18**(5–6), 513–562 (2003)
2. Barsalou, L.W.: Grounded cognition: past, present, and future. Topics Cogn. Sci. **2**(4), 716–724 (2010)
3. Gallese, V., Lakoff, G.: The brain's concepts: the role of the sensory-motor system in conceptual knowledge. Cogn. Neuropsychol. **22**(3–4), 455–479 (2005)
4. Glenberg, A.M., Kaschak, M.P.: Grounding language in action. Psychon. Bull. Rev. **9**(3), 558–565 (2002)
5. Buccino, G., Riggio, L., Melli, G., Binkofski, F., Gallese, V., Rizzolatti, G.: Listening to action-related sentences modulates the activity of the motor system: a combined TMS and behavioral study. Cogn. Brain Res. **24**(3), 355–363 (2005)
6. Pulvermüller, F.: Brain mechanisms linking language and action. Nat. Rev. Neurosci. **6**(7), 576–582 (2005)
7. Chen, I.-H., Zhao, Q.Q., Long, Y.F., Lu, Q., Huang, C.-R.: Mandarin Chinese modality exclusivity norms. PLoS ONE **14**(2), e0211336 (2019)
8. Lynott, D., Connell, L., Brysbaert, M., Brand, J., Carney, J.: The Lancaster sensorimotor Norms: multidimensional measures of perceptual and action strength for 40,000 English words. Behav. Res. Methods **52**(3), 1271–1291 (2020)
9. Zhong, Y., Wan, M.Y., Ahrens, K., Huang, C.-R.: Sensorimotor norms for Chinese nouns and their relationship with orthographic and semantic variables. Lang. Cogn. Neurosci. **37**(8), 1000–1022 (2022)
10. Craig, A.D.: Emotional moments across time: a possible neural basis for time perception in the anterior insula. Philos. Trans. R. Soc. B: Biol. Sci. **364**(1525), 1933–1942 (2009)
11. Dunn, B.D., et al.: Listening to your heart: how interoception shapes emotion experience and intuitive decision making. Psychol. Sci. **21**(12), 1835–1844 (2010)
12. Connell, L., Lynott, D., Banks, B.: Interoception: the forgotten modality in perceptual grounding of abstract and concrete concepts. Philos. Trans. R. Soc. B: Biol. Sci. **373**(1752), 20170143 (2018)
13. Zhong, Y., Huang, C.-R., Ahrens, K.: Embodied grounding of concreteness/abstractness: a sensory-perceptual account of concrete and abstract concepts in Mandarin Chinese. Presented at the 22th Chinese Lexical Semantic Workshop (CLSW 2021), Nanjing Normal University, China, 15–16 May 2021
14. Russell, J.A.: A circumplex model of affect. J. Pers. Soc. Psychol. **39**(6), 1161–1178 (1980)
15. Bradley, M.M., Lang, P.J.: Affective norms for English words (ANEW): Instruction manual and affective ratings. Technical Report C-1, the Center for Research in Psychophysiology, University of Florida, vol. 30, no. 1, pp. 25–36 (1999)
16. Warriner, A.B., Kuperman, V., Brysbaert, M.: Norms of valence, arousal, and dominance for 13,915 English lemmas. Behav. Res. Methods **45**(4), 1191–1207 (2013). https://doi.org/10.3758/s13428-012-0314-x
17. Xu, X., Li, J.Y., Chen, H.L.: Valence and arousal ratings for 11,310 simplified Chinese words. Behav. Res. Methods **54**(1), 1–16 (2021)
18. Yu, L.C., et al.: Building Chinese affective resources in valence-arousal dimensions. In: Proceedings of the 2016 Conference of the North American Chapter of the Association for Computational Linguistics: Human Language Technologies, pp. 540–545 (2016)

19. Winter, B.: Taste and smell words form an affectively loaded and emotionally flexible part of the English lexicon. Lang. Cogn. Neurosci. **31**(8), 975–988 (2016)
20. Phillips, M.L., Heining, M.: Neural correlates of emotion perception: from faces to taste. In: Rouby, C., Schaal, B., Dubois, D., Gervais, R., Holley, A. (eds.) Olfaction, taste, and cogntion, pp. 196–208. Cambridge University Press, Cambridge (2002)
21. Krifka, M.: A note on an asymmetry in the hedonic implicatures of olfactory and gustatory terms. In: Fuchs, S., Hoole, P., Mooshammer, C., Zygis, M. (eds.) Between the regular and the particular in speech and language, pp. 235–245. Peter Lang, Frankfurt (2010)
22. Tsang, Y.-K., et al.: MELD-SCH: a megastudy of lexical decision in simplified Chinese. Behav. Res. Methods **50**(5), 1763–1777 (2018)
23. JASP Team: JASP (Version 0.16) [Computer software] (2021). https://jasp-stats.org/
24. Kadohisa, M.: Effects of odor on emotion, with implications. Front. Syst. Neuroscience **7**(66) (2013)
25. Critchley, H.D., Garfinkel, S.N.: Interoception and emotion. Curr. Opin. Psychol. **17**, 7–14 (2017)
26. Quadt, L., Critchley, H.D., Garfinkel, S.N.: Interoception and emotion: shared mechanisms and clinical implications. In: Tsakiris, M., De Preester, H. (eds.) The interoceptive mind: From Homeostasis to Awareness, pp. 123–143. Oxford University Press, Oxford, UK (2018)

From Genitive to Conjunctive: Coordinator li^{55} in Chongqing Mandarin

Yin Zhong[1] and Sicong Dong[2(✉)]

[1] Center for Language Education, The Hong Kong University of Science and Technology, Hong Kong, China
lcyinzhong@ust.hk

[2] School of Humanities and Social Sciences, Harbin Institute of Technology, Shenzhen, China
dongsicong@hit.edu.cn

Abstract. The genitive marker 的 li^{55} in Chongqing Mandarin can also function as a coordinating conjunction. This function develops from the usage of li^{55} to link numbers or quantities in calculations. Several restrictions are found on the coordinator li^{55}, e.g., conjuncts must be nominal and shall be all the members of a definite set; li^{55} must be used between every two conjuncts and can only be used in informal registers. Similar coordinate function of genitive markers can also be found in other Sinitic languages while rarely seen in other language families, which merits further typological investigations.

Keywords: Chongqing Mandarin · Coordinator · Genitive · Linguistic typology

1 Li^{55} as a Coordinator

Chongqing Mandarin 的 li^{55}, when used as a genitive marker, usually represents a possessive relation as well as an attributive relation when it appears between a modifier and a head noun, such as 我的钱 wo^{53} li^{55} $t\varphi^h ian^{21}$ I GEN money 'my money'. It can also mark a phrase as nominal, which is similar to the *de*-construction in Standard Mandarin, e.g., 没得吃的 $mei^{55}te^{21}$ $ts^h \gamma^{21}$ li^{55} have.not eat NMLZ 'there is nothing to eat'. Additionally, li^{55} can function as a coordinator that connects two conjuncts, as shown in the following two examples:[1]

---

[1] The districts and counties under the jurisdiction of Chongqing all use Southwestern Mandarin. Most of the Southwestern Mandarin varieties, including the dialect spoken in the Chongqing major urban area, belong to the Cheng-Yu branch according to the *Language Atlas of China (Second Edition)* [1]. The second author's native language is the dialect of Chongqing major urban area. The examples in this paper are all from the author's introspection and daily communication, and have been verified by other native speakers. Note that li^{55} can be written as 的 by native speakers, but its etymological character (本字) has yet to be confirmed. For example, Chen [2] argued that these types of structural particles used in Chongqing, Chengdu, Guiyang, and other Southwestern Mandarin varieties are likely to be derived from the locative morpheme 里 'inside'. However, whether 的 is the etymological character or the borrowing character (训读字) does not affect the discussion in this article. In addition, several borrowing characters are used in the examples without elaboration in order to keep the text intact.

© The Author(s), under exclusive license to Springer Nature Switzerland AG 2023
Q. Su et al. (Eds.): CLSW 2022, LNAI 13496, pp. 193–205, 2023.
https://doi.org/10.1007/978-3-031-28956-9_16

(1)

两	碗儿	的	两	碗儿,
liaŋ⁵³	wa˞⁵³	li⁵⁵	liaŋ⁵³	wa˞⁵³
two	bowl	and	two	bowl
总共	吃	了	四	碗儿。
tsoŋ⁵³koŋ²¹³	tsʰʅ²¹	lau⁵³	sʅ²¹³	wa˞⁵³
altogether	eat	PFV	four	bowl

'Two bowls plus two bowls, altogether had four bowls.'

(2)

三	米	的	四	米,
san⁵⁵	mi⁵³	li⁵⁵	sʅ²¹³	mi⁵³
three	metre	and	four	metre
就	是	十二	平米。	
təu²¹³	sʅ²¹³	sʅ²¹ə²¹³	pʰin²¹mi⁵³	
exactly	be	twelve	square.metre	

'Three metres multiplied by four metres is twelve square metres.'

The above examples showed that li^{55} indicates the addition and/or multiplication of the two quantities. Previous literature did not investigate such a phenomenon in Chongqing Mandarin. Yet, a genitive marker denoting addition and/or multiplication also exists in Chengdu Mandarin, a neighbouring dialect that also belongs to the Cheng-Yu branch of Southwestern Mandarin [1]. Liang and Huang [3] explained the similar usage of 的 ni^{55} in Chengdu Mandarin: "it is used between two numeral-quantifier phrases to express multiplication or addition" (p.29).

Although it seems that the above reading of ni^{55} in Chengdu Mandarin may also apply to Chongqing Mandarin, as shown in (1) and (2), li^{55} in Chongqing Mandarin has wider usage. Firstly, li^{55} can connect more than two quantitative components. As shown in (3), the three values of the length, width, and height of the box in the sentence can be connected by two li^{55}.[2] Secondly, li^{55} can not only be used in the middle of numeral-quantifier phrases but also in the middle of numerals, such as adding two numbers in the sentence (4). Finally, in specific contexts, apart from addition and multiplication, li^{55} also indicates subtraction and/or division, as shown in (5) and (6).

(3)

这	个	箱子	是	三	米
le²¹³	ko²¹³	ɕiaŋ⁵⁵tsʅ⁵³	sʅ²¹³	san⁵⁵	mi⁵³
this	CLF	box	be	three	metre
的	两	米	的	一	米。
li⁵⁵	liaŋ⁵³	mi⁵³	li⁵⁵	ji²¹	mi⁵³
and	two	metre	and	one	metre

'This box is three metres by two metres by one metre.'

---

[2] Strictly speaking, the interpretation of ni^{55} in Chengdu Mandarin in [3] does not exclude the condition that more than two numeral-quantifier phrases are involved, since ni^{55} can be used between any two items. We only would like to clarify that li^{55} in Chongqing Mandarin can connect more than two items.

(4)

二十七	的	二十三	等于	五十。
ə⁻²¹³sʅ²¹tɕʰi²¹	li⁵⁵	ə⁻²¹³sʅ²¹san⁵⁵	tən⁵³yi²¹	vu⁵³sʅ²¹
twenty.seven	and	twenty.three	equal	fifty

'Twenty-seven plus twenty-three equals fifty.'

(5) (When doing subtraction exercises, talking while doing)

九十	的	三十	等于	六十。
tɕiəu⁵³sʅ²¹	li⁵⁵	san⁵⁵sʅ²¹	tən⁵³yi²¹	lu²¹sʅ²¹
ninety	and	thirty	equal	sixty

'Ninety minus thirty equals sixty.'

(6) (When doing division exercises, talking while doing)

九十	的	三十	等于	三。
tɕiəu⁵³sʅ²¹	li⁵⁵	san⁵⁵sʅ²¹	tən⁵³yi²¹	san⁵⁵
ninety	and	thirty	equal	three

'Ninety divided by thirty equals three.'

In fact, *li*[55] is not merely used for mathematical operations; its essential function is acting as a coordinator. The addition, subtraction, multiplication, and division readings are only the different realizations from specific contexts. As shown in sentences (5) and (6), 九十的三十 *tɕiəu⁵³sʅ²¹ li⁵⁵ san⁵⁵ sʅ²¹* 'ninety and thirty' can represent both subtraction and division. If the context varies, *li*[55] can also indicate addition and multiplication. That is to say, *li*[55] is only responsible for connecting two values but does not entail any information about the operation method. Moreover, from examples (7)–(12), we can see that *li*[55] can be used beyond a mathematical environment but links multiple conjuncts to form a coordinate construction.

(7)

你	看	嘛,	我	包包儿	里头
li⁵³	kʰan²¹³	ma⁵³	wo⁵³	pau⁵⁵pa⁻⁵⁵	li⁵³tʰəu²¹
you	look	MOD	I	pocket	inside
只	得	三	张	钱,	五块
tsʅ⁵³	te²¹	san⁵⁵	tsaŋ⁵⁵	tɕʰian²¹	vu⁵³kʰuai⁵³
only	have	three	CLF	note	five.dollar
的	五块	的	一块。		
li⁵⁵	vu⁵³kʰuai⁵³	li⁵⁵	ji²¹kʰuai⁵³		
and	five.dollar	and	one.dollar		

'Look, I only have three notes in my pocket; two five-dollar and one one-dollar.'

(8)

他	有	两	个	女儿,	三
tʰa⁵⁵	jəu⁵³	liaŋ⁵³	ko²¹³	lyə⁵³	san⁵⁵
he	have	two	CLF	daughter	three

岁	的	五	岁,	都	还
suəi²¹³	li⁵⁵	vu⁵³	suəi²¹³	təu⁵⁵	xai²¹
year.of.age	and	five	year.of.age	both	yet

没有		上学。
mei⁵⁵jəu⁵⁵		saŋ²¹³ɕio²¹
NEG		go.to.school

'He has two daughters; one is three years old, and the other is five. Both have not yet reached school age.'

(9)

A:

那	桌	点	的	啥子?
la²¹³	tso²¹	tian⁵³	li⁵⁵	sa²¹³tsɿ⁵³
that	table	order	NMLZ	what

'What did that table order?'

B:

那	桌	点	的	牛肉
la²¹³	tso²¹	tian⁵³	li⁵⁵	liəu²¹zəu²¹³
that	table	order	NMLZ	beef

面	的	肥肠	面。
mian²¹³	li⁵⁵	fei²¹tsʰaŋ²¹	mian²¹³
noodle	and	fat.intestine	noodle

'That table ordered beef noodles and pork intestine noodles.'

(10)

A:

你	明天	考	啥子?
li⁵³	min²¹tʰian⁵⁵	kʰau⁵³	sa²¹³tsɿ⁵³
you	tomorrow	exam	what

'What are you going to test tomorrow?'

B:

考	语文	的	数学。
kʰau⁵³	y⁵³wən²¹	li⁵⁵	su²¹³ɕio²¹
exam	Chinese	and	Mathematics

'Chinese and Mathematics.'

(11)

A:

今天	晚上	是	哪	两
tɕin⁵⁵tʰian⁵⁵	wan⁵³saŋ²¹³	sɿ²¹³	la⁵³	liaŋ⁵³
today	night	be	which	two

个	队儿	踢	啊?
ko²¹³	tuə²¹³	tsua²¹	ja⁵⁵
CLF	team	kick	MOD

'Which two football teams are playing tonight?'

B:

英格兰	的	葡萄牙。
jin⁵⁵ke²¹lan²¹	li⁵⁵	pʰu²¹tʰau²¹ja²¹
England	and	Portugal

'England and Portugal.'

(12)

今天	要	发言	的	只	得
tɕin⁵⁵tʰian⁵⁵	jau²¹³	fa²¹jan²¹	li⁵⁵	tsŋ⁵³	te²¹
today	will	speak	NMLZ	only	have

两	个	人,	张红梅	的
lian⁵³	ko²¹³	zən²¹	tsaŋ⁵⁵xoŋ²¹mei²¹	li⁵⁵
two	CLF	people	ZHANG Hongmei	and

李国庆。
li⁵³kue²¹tɕʰiə²¹³
LI Guoqing
'There are only two people to speak today; ZHANG Hongmei and LI Guoqing.'

In the above example sentences, the conjuncts connected by *li*[55] meet the general requirements of a coordinate structure; that is, each conjunct shares a similar type in terms of its part-of-speech category, structural form, semantic category, and prosodic feature [4, 5]. On the contrary, the two items connected by *li*[55] in (13) and (14) belong to two categories in terms of their forms or semantic meanings; therefore, the two sentences are considered ungrammatical.

(13)

*他	有	两	个	女儿,	三
tʰa⁵⁵	jəu⁵³	lian⁵³	ko²¹³	lyə⁵³	san⁵⁵
he	have	two	CLF	daughter	three

岁	的	还	没	满月。	
suəi²¹³	li⁵⁵	xai²¹	mei⁵⁵	man⁵³jye²¹	
year.of.age	and	yet	NEG	full:month	

'He has two daughters; one is three years old, and the other is not yet one month old.'

(14)

*他	有	两	个	女儿,	三
tʰa⁵⁵	jəu⁵³	lian⁵³	ko²¹³	lyə⁵³,	san⁵⁵
he	have	two	CLF	daughter	three

岁	的	一	米	二。	
suəi²¹³	li⁵⁵	ji²¹	mi⁵³	ə²¹³	
year.of.age	and	one	metre	two	

'He has two daughters; one is three years old, and the other is 1.2 metres.'

2 Restrictions on *li*[55] as a Coordinator

The coordinate structure in Chongqing Mandarin mostly uses 和 *xo*[21] 'and' as the coordinator. Compared with 和 *xo*[21] 'and', the coordinate structure indicated by *li*[55] has more limitations or varieties.

Firstly, the conjuncts connected by *li*[55] can only be nominal components. Therefore, 和 *xo*[21] 'and' cannot be replaced by *li*[55] when it connects verbs or adjectives. For example, li^{55} is not able to be used in the phrases such as 调查和了解 $tiau^{213}ts^ha^{21}$ xo^{21} $liau^{53}t\varsigma ie^{53}$ 'to investigate and understand' and 雄伟和壮丽 $\varsigma io\eta^{21}wei^{53}$ xo^{21} $tsua\eta^{213}li^{213}$ 'majestic and magnificent'.

Secondly, li^{55} is mandatory between every two conjuncts. For example, the three items in (7) must use two li^{55} to connect every two of them; but 和 xo^{21} 'and' can only appear between the last two items.

Thirdly, like the genitive marker li^{55}, the coordinator li^{55} is phonetically attached to its left syllable. That is to say, if there is a pause within the phrase, the stop can only be seen between the li^{55} and the right conjunct, such as 三岁的，五岁 san^{55} $sua i^{213}$ li^{55}, vu^{53} $sua i^{213}$ 'three years old and five years old'. This is different from the coordinate structure denoted by 和 xo^{21} 'and' because the pause only appears between 和 xo^{21} 'and' and the left conjunct, namely, 三岁, 和五岁 san^{55} $sua i^{213}$, xo^{21} vu^{53} $sua i^{213}$ 'three years old and five years old'.

Fourthly, li^{55} can only be used in more informal registers. On formal and serious occasions, the coordinator li^{55} must be replaced with conjunctions such as 和 xo^{21} 'and', or a speech pause needs to be used to separate the conjuncts.

In addition, an important restriction that makes the use of li^{55} narrower in distribution than 和 xo^{21} 'and' is that li^{55} can only be used to enumerate all members in a definite set. Namely, li^{55} must exist in a context where all the members of a set shall be explicitly listed, or the listed items can deduce a definite set with explicit properties; for example, all the values in the operations of (1) – (6), the number of notes in (7), someone's daughters in (8), the dishes ordered in (9), the subjects to be examined in (10), the two sides of the football match in (11), and the speakers in (12). These elements constitute a definite set with exact members. However, consider (15). The condition of this sentence to be grammatical is that ZHANG Hongmei and LI Guoqing shall be the only two speakers in such an event. If there are other speakers, the two do not constitute a separate set in the above context, and the sentence (15) does not make sense anymore.

(15)	张红梅	的	李国庆	今天
	$tsa\eta^{55}xo\eta^{21}mei^{21}$	li^{55}	$li^{53}kue^{21}t\varsigma^hia^{213}$	$t\varsigma in^{55}t^hian^{55}$
	ZHANG Hongmei	and	LI Guoqing	today
	要	发言。		
	jau^{213}	$fa^{21}jan^{21}$		
	will	speak		
	'ZHANG Hongmei and LI Guoqing will speak today.'			

Moreover, the conjuncts connected by li^{55} must be all the members in the definite set, and the relationship among the members shall only be enumeration/listing but not other relationships such as selection. For example, the conjuncts connected by li^{55} in the above sentences (1) – (12) must be all the exact members in the relevant sets. For example, beef noodles and pork intestine noodles in the sentence (9) are both the dishes the table ordered; Chinese and Mathematics in the sentence (10) are both the subjects that will be tested. On the contrary, the following sentences (16)–(23) are either ungrammatical or weakly accepted because they violate this restriction on li^{55}. For instances, the coordinative members in (16) – (18) are not all the members in the set; in (19) and (20), the two items connected by *li*[55] are in selection relations; as for (21) – (23), the two items linked by *li*[55] do not constitute coordination in the strict sense, but rather a comitative or a comparative relationship. Moreover, sentences (21) – (23) are ungrammatical because they do not demonstrate simple enumeration. Therefore, the conjunction *li*[55] has to be replaced by a preposition (i.e., 和 *xo*[21] 'and') so as to make these sentences grammatical (see [6, 7]).

(16)	*他	有	三	个		女儿,	三
	tʰa⁵⁵	jəu⁵³	san⁵⁵	ko²¹³		lyə⁵³	san⁵⁵
	he	have	three	CLF		daughter	three
	岁	的	五	岁,		还	有
	suəi²¹³	li⁵⁵	vu⁵³	suəi²¹³		xai²¹	jəu⁵³
	year.of.age	and	five	year.of.age		also	have
	一	个	晓不得		有	好	大。
	ji²¹	ko²¹³	ɕiau⁵³-pu²¹-te²¹		jəu⁵³	xau⁵³	ta²¹³
	one	CLF	know-NEG-know		have	how	old

'He has three daughters. One is three years old, another is five, and the third one (I) do not know how old she is.'

(17)	?这	次	世界杯		的	八强	都
	le²¹³	tsʰ1²¹³	sʅ²¹³tɕie²¹³pei⁵⁵		li⁵⁵	pa²¹tɕʰiaŋ²¹	təu⁵⁵
	this	time	World.Cup		GEN	top.eight	all
	是	欧洲	的,	有	德国	的	
	sʅ²¹³	əu⁵⁵tsəu⁵⁵	li⁵⁵	jəu⁵³	te²¹kue²¹	li⁵⁵	
	be	Europe	GEN	have	Germany	and	
	法国	的	荷兰。				
	fa²¹kue²¹	li⁵⁵	xo²¹lan²¹				
	France	and	Netherlands				

'The teams for the quarterfinals of this time's World Cup are all from Europe, including Germany, France, and the Netherlands.'

(18)	?只有	双数		的	时候	才	可以
	tsʅ⁵³jəu⁵³	suaŋ⁵⁵su²¹³		li⁵⁵	sʅ²¹xəu²¹³	tsʰai²¹	kʰo⁵³ji⁵³
	only	even.number		GEN	time	then	can
	开车,	比如	二号		的	四号。	
	kʰai⁵⁵tsʰe⁵⁵	pi⁵³zu²¹	ə²¹³xau²¹³		li⁵⁵	sʅ²¹³xau²¹³	
	drive	such.as	two:date		and	four:date	

'You can only drive on an even day, such as on the second and the fourth day of the month.'

(19)

*不管	三	岁	的	五	岁,
pu²¹kuan⁵³	san⁵⁵	suəi²¹³	li⁵⁵	vu⁵³	suəi²¹³
no.matter	three	year.of.age	and	five	year.of.age

都	不	够	岁数	读	小学。
təu⁵⁵	pu²¹	kəu²¹³	suəi²¹³su²¹³	tu²¹	ɕiau⁵³ɕio²¹
both	NEG	enough	year.of.age	read	primary.school

'No matter three or five years old, they are not old enough to attend primary school.'

(20)

*不管	牛肉	面	的	肥肠	面,
pu²¹kuan⁵³	liəu²¹zəu²¹³	mian²¹³	li⁵⁵	fei²¹tsʰaŋ²¹	mian²¹³
no.matter	beef	noodle	and	fat.intestine	noodle

你	哪个	都	要	选	一	样。
li⁵³	laŋ²¹³ko⁵⁵	təu⁵⁵	jau²¹³	ɕyan⁵³	ji²¹	jaŋ²¹³
you	how	all	need	choose	one	CLF

'No matter the beef noodles or the pork intestine noodles, you have to choose one.'

(21)

*张红梅	的	李国庆	打
tsaŋ⁵⁵xoŋ²¹mei²¹	li⁵⁵	li⁵³kue²¹tɕʰiɚ²¹³	ta⁵³
ZHANG Hongmei	and	LI Guoqing	fight

起来	了。
tɕʰi⁵³lai²¹	lau⁵³
INC	PFV

'ZHANG Hongmei and LI Guoqing got into a fight.'

(22)

*英格兰	的	葡萄牙	说	的	话
jin⁵⁵ke²¹lan²¹	li⁵⁵	pʰu²¹tʰau²¹ja²¹	so²¹	li⁵⁵	xua²¹³
England	and	Portugal	speak	GEN	language

不	一样。
pu²¹	ji²¹jaŋ²¹³
NEG	same

'England and Portugal speak differently.'

(23)

*牛肉	面	的	肥肠	面
liəu²¹zəu²¹³	mian²¹³	li⁵⁵	fei²¹tsʰaŋ²¹	mian²¹³
beef	noodle	and	fat.intestine	noodle

价格	一样。
tɕia²¹³ke²¹	ji²¹jaŋ²¹³
price	same

'The price of the pork intestine noodles and the beef noodles is the same.'

This restriction on *li⁵⁵*, i.e., used to enumerate all members of a set, indicates that the usage of *li⁵⁵* connecting common noun components is likely to be derived from linking operands (or input values) in mathematics. A series of parallel features can be found in the two usages. In mathematical operations, operands are compulsory units to be manipulated regardless of addition, subtraction, multiplication, or division. Each value involved in the operation is essential; otherwise, the final output will be invalid. In the meantime, these values can be combined into a whole by the operation relationship and form one side of the equation. In other words, all the input values involved in the operation are all the members of a set and must appear at the same time. There is no selection relationship between them, nor is there a comparison relationship among the items. We can find the evidence in Liang and Huang [3], where ni^{55} in Chengdu Mandarin is treated as expressing an operational relationship. In addition, the obligatory requirement of li^{55} between every two conjuncts shares alike features as the compulsory position of the operators (e.g., +, -) in mathematical operations.

3 A Typological Discussion

As we noted above, li^{55} as a coordinator also exists in Chengdu Mandarin, but it is limited to expressing mathematical operations according to the dictionary definition. In fact, in Standard Mandarin/Putonghua and a large number of Sinitic languages or Chinese dialects, the genitive markers share a similar function to Chongqing Mandarin li^{55} and Chengdu Mandarin ni^{55}. Such function can be found in, for example, the varieties of Mandarin (官话) spoken in Wuhan [8], Liuzhou [9], Yinchuan [10], Xi'an [11], Lanzhou [12], Urumqi [13], Nanjing [14], Yangzhou [15], and Jinan [16], of Wu (吴语) spoken in Danyang [17] and Suzhou [18], as well as the varieties of Gan (赣语) spoken in Pingxiang [19] and Yudu [20].

The dictionary definitions of the genitive markers in the varieties mentioned above can be summarized as "used between two numerals or numeral-quantifier phrases to indicate addition (or multiplication)". Further investigations are needed to verify whether these genitive markers can be extended to function as coordinators as li^{55} in Chongqing Mandarin. Based on the dictionary sources, at least two of them can be identified as coordinators.

Liu [14] defined the 的 ·ti? in Nanjing Mandarin as "used between two *coordinate* [emphasis added] numeral-quantifier phrases, indicating addition". This definition shows that the Nanjing Mandarin ·ti?, though still limited to the function of mathematical operations, exhibits a coordinate structure of connecting items of equivalent syntactic status. Also, the structural particle 个 $k\mathfrak{d}^{11-1}$ in Pingxiang Gan has a similar usage: "used between two numeral-quantifier phrases, indicating a relationship of addition or *length and width* [emphasis added]" [19]. The relationship of "length and width" is, in fact, a coordinate relation. Therefore, at least in Nanjing Mandarin and Pingxiang Gan, the function of the genitive markers is not purely mathematical operations but coordination.

Although Sinitic languages seem mostly homogeneous in morphosyntax, they do show internal typological variations [21–25]. A follow-up big-scale investigation on Sinitic varieties can provide a detailed pattern of distribution. Moreover, such phenomena in Sinitic languages are typologically unique compared to other language families. Haspelmath [26] conducted a cross-linguistic survey of morphemes that function as coordinate markers, and he created a semantic map (see Fig. 1). The results in [26] show that coordinators often have other meanings or functions besides the function of conjunctive, including comitative, existence, instrumental, manner, comparison, etc., but no genitive, possessive, or attributive functions can be found in Fig. 1.

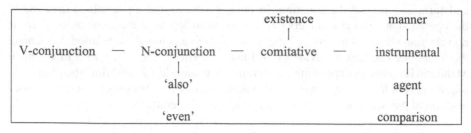

Fig. 1. A semantic map for conjunction and related notions in [26]

In addition, we also consulted the database of Cross-Linguistic Colexifications (CLICS) [27] to check the functions colexified with coordinators, namely, the same lexical form used for coordination and other functionally distinct meanings. As shown in Fig. 2, a total of 180 languages or dialects are found to colexify coordination and other meanings. More specifically, 131 varieties colexify the function of coordinate and comitative, as demonstrated by the line between AND and WITH in Fig. 2. Other colexified meanings include condition (IF), once more (AGAIN), alternative conjunction (OR), second person (THOU), affirmation (YES), and speaking (SAY). Again, no genitive function has been found to colexify with coordination in this database.

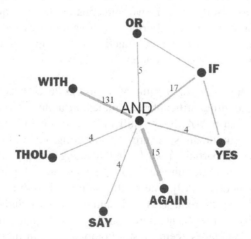

Fig. 2. Colexifications of coordinators in CLICS

To the best of our knowledge, no case in other language families has been recorded to show the evolution from genitive/attributive markers to coordinate markers. From this point of view, our data on Sinitic languages can provide another pathway to form coordinators. That is, genitive should be one of the source functions from which the coordinate function can develop. Consequently, the semantic map in [26] can be revised with an additional node of the genitive function. Since the Sinitic genitive markers only connect nominal components as discussed above, the added node is linked to the N-conjunction node as shown in Fig. 3.

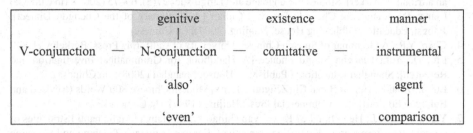

Fig. 3. A revised semantic map for conjunction and related notions

4 Conclusion

We have shown that li^{55} in Chongqing Mandarin has wider usage than the generalization in previous studies. Such usage can be well accounted for when li^{55} is considered as a coordinator. Its coordinating function develops from the usage of li^{55} to link numbers or quantities in calculations, which also leads to a series of restrictions on the coordinator li^{55} compared to other coordinating conjunctions. The diachronic development from genitive to conjunctive have been found in a number of Sinitic languages, but not in other language families. Our data thus provide another pathway to form coordinators for typological studies.

Abbreviations

CLF	Classifier
GEN	Genitive
INC	Inchoative
MOD	Modal particle
NEG	Negation, negative
NMLZ	Nominalizer, nominalization
PFV	Perfective

Acknowledgements. We would like to express our gratitude to Dr. Hongdi Ding and Dr. Yike Yang for their helpful comments. This work was partially funded by the National Social Science Fund of China (18ZDA291).

References

1. Li, L.: Xinan Guanhua de fenqu [Classification/distribution of Southwestern Mandarin]. Dialects **1**, 72–87 (2009). (in Chinese)
2. Chen, Y.: Lianxixiang yuanze yu li de dingyu biaoji zuoyong [Relator principle and li (里) as an attributive marker]. Studies in Language and Linguistics **27**(3), 69–75 (2007). (in Chinese)
3. Liang, D., Huang, S.: Chengdu Fangyan Cidian [A Dictionary of the Chengdu Dialect]. Jiangsu Education Publishing House, Nanjing (2007). (in Chinese)
4. Chao, Y.R.: A Grammar of Spoken Chinese. University of California Press, Berkeley (1968)
5. Liu, D.: Yufa Diaocha Yanjiu Shouce [A Handbook for Grammatical Investigation and Research]. Shanghai Educational Publishing House, Shanghai (2008). (in Chinese)
6. Lü, S.: Xiandai Hanyu Babai Ci (Zengding Ben) [Modern Chinese 800 Words (Revised and Enlarged Edition)]. The Commercial Press, Beijing (1999). (in Chinese)
7. Yang, M., Hu, J.: He yi binglie? Kua yuyan shijiao xia de Hanyu binglie nanti [Strategies of coordination from a cross-linguistic perspective]. Foreign Language Teaching and Research **49**(5), 719–731 (2017). (in Chinese)
8. Zhu, J.: Wuhan Fangyan Cidian [A Dictionary of the Wuhan Dialect]. Jiangsu Education Publishing House, Nanjing (1995). (in Chinese)
9. Liu, C.: Liuzhou Fangyan Cidian [A Dictionary of the Liuzhou Dialect]. Jiangsu Education Publishing House, Nanjing (1995). (in Chinese)
10. Li, S., Zhang, A.: Yinchuan Fangyan Cidian [A Dictionary of the Yinchuan Dialect]. Jiangsu Education Publishing House, Nanjing (1996). (in Chinese)
11. Wang, J.: Xi'an Fangyan Cidian [A Dictionary of the Xi'an Dialect]. Jiangsu Education Publishing House, Nanjing (1996). (in Chinese)
12. Zhang, W., Mo, C.: Lanzhou Fangyan Cidian [A Dictionary of the Lanzhou Dialect]. China Social Sciences Press, Beijing (2009). (in Chinese)
13. Zhou, L.: Wulumuqi Fangyan Cidian [A Dictionary of the Urumqi Dialect]. Jiangsu Education Publishing House, Nanjing (1995). (in Chinese)
14. Liu, D.: Nanjing Fangyan Cidian [A Dictionary of the Nanjing Dialect]. Jiangsu Education Publishing House, Nanjing (1995). (in Chinese)
15. Wang, S., Huang, J.: Yangzhou Fangyan Cidian [A Dictionary of the Yangzhou Dialect]. Jiangsu Education Publishing House, Nanjing (1996). (in Chinese)
16. Qian, Z.: Jinan Fangyan Cidian [A Dictionary of the Jinan Dialect]. Jiangsu Education Publishing House, Nanjing (1997). (in Chinese)
17. Cai, G.: Danyang Fangyan Cidian [A Dictionary of the Danyang Dialect]. Jiangsu Education Publishing House, Nanjing (1995). (in Chinese)
18. Ye, X.: Suzhou Fangyan Cidian [A Dictionary of the Suzhou Dialect]. Jiangsu Education Publishing House, Nanjing (1993). (in Chinese)
19. Qian, G.: Pingxiang Fangyan Cidian [A Dictionary of the Pingxiang Dialect]. Jiangsu Education Publishing House, Nanjing (1998). (in Chinese)
20. Xie, L.: Yudu Fangyan Cidian [A Dictionary of the Yudu Dialect]. Jiangsu Education Publishing House, Nanjing (1998). (in Chinese)
21. Dong, S., Yang, Y., Huang, C.-R., Ren, H.: Directionality and momentum of water in weather: a morphosemantic study of conceptualisation based on hantology. In: Hong, J.-F., Zhang, Y., Liu, P. (eds.) CLSW 2019. LNCS (LNAI), vol. 11831, pp. 575–584. Springer, Cham (2020). https://doi.org/10.1007/978-3-030-38189-9_59
22. Huang, C.-R., Dong, S.: From lexical semantics to traditional ecological knowledge: on precipitation, condensation and suspension expressions in Chinese. In: Hong, J.-F., Zhang, Y., Liu, P. (eds.) CLSW 2019. LNCS (LNAI), vol. 11831, pp. 255–264. Springer, Cham (2020). https://doi.org/10.1007/978-3-030-38189-9_27

23. Dong, S., Yang, Y., Ren, H., Huang, C.-R.: Directionality of atmospheric water in Chinese: a lexical semantic study based on linguistic ontology. SAGE Open **11**(1), 1–13 (2021)
24. Huang, C.-R., Dong, S., Yang, Y., Ren, H.: From language to meteorology: kinesis in weather events and weather verbs across Sinitic languages. Humanit. Soc. Sci. Commun. 8, 4 (2021)
25. Dong, S., Huang, C.-R.: From falling to hitting: diachronic change and synchronic distribution of frost verbs in Chinese. In: Dong, M., Gu, Y., Hong, J.-F. (eds.) CLSW 2021. LNCS (LNAI), vol. 13249, pp. 22–30. Springer, Cham (2022)
26. Haspelmath, M.: Coordinating constructions: an overview. In: Haspelmath, M. (ed.) Coordinating Constructions, pp. 3–39. John Benjamins Publishing Company, Amsterdam and Philadelphia (2004)
27. Rzymski, C., Tresoldi, T., Greenhill, S.J. et al.: The database of cross-linguistic colexifications, reproducible analysis of cross-linguistic polysemies. Scientific Data **7**, 13 (2020). Accessed at https://clics.clld.org/

The Prediction Function of Collocations on the Quality Assessment of Chinese Second Language Learners' Oral Production

Yuyan Zhang[1] and Meixiu Li[2(✉)]

[1] Department of Chinese International Education, Beijing Language and Culture University, Beijing, China
[2] School of Literature and Media, Yunnan Minzu University, Kunming, Yunnan, China
`lmxgrace@126.com`

Abstract. To test whether collocations play a key role in Chinese oral quality assessment, this study adopts correlation and multiple linear regression analyses to investigate the relationship between lexical collocations, grammatical collocations and Chinese oral production quality. Both lexical collocations and grammatical collocations are analysed using three indicators: collocation accuracy, collocation richness, and collocation transparency. The results show that the accuracy of lexical collocations can effectively predict the quality of oral production, and to a certain extent, grammatical collocation accuracy can also predict the quality of oral production. Specifically, the accuracy of lexical collocations has a significant impact on the oral production scores of advanced level learners while the transparency of lexical collocations plays an edge predictive role in the oral production quality of intermediate level learners. However, lexical collocation richness and all three grammar collocation indicators have no influence on the oral production quality at different levels.

Keywords: collocation accuracy · collocation richness · collocation transparency · oral production quality

1 Introduction

Lexical collocations are a key and difficult aspect for foreign students learning Chinese. If learners have good command of lexical collocations, they tend to speak out the sentences conforming to Chinese grammar in daily communication, achieving successful communication. Collocation knowledge is the key to second language lexical knowledge, and it is also the focus of Chinese teaching and research [1, 2]. However, regarding second language learners' oral production, the collocation is rarely studied as an indicator to evaluate the quality of Chinese oral production. Studies have shown that learners' speaking proficiency is moderately correlated with correct lexical collocations in quantity and variety [3, 4]. Wang and Zhou [5] found that for second language learners' spoken language, the usage of correct verb-noun collocations significantly and

Q. Su et al. (Eds.): CLSW 2022, LNAI 13496, pp. 206–220, 2023.
https://doi.org/10.1007/978-3-031-28956-9_17

positively correlates with the quality of oral production. Previous studies have examined several common indicators and types of collocations, but none have systematically explored whether collocation accuracy and transparency affects the quality of second language learners' oral production.

Research on the quality of second language learners' oral production has been a hot topic in psycholinguistics, cognitive linguistics and second language acquisition [6]. Oral test assessment is widely applied in English teaching. Guo and Wang et al. [7, 8] note that fluency is very important to evaluate oral proficiency and is also a necessary part of oral communication. Many studies have observed the effects of factors such as oral fluency, accuracy, complexity, from different perspectives on the quality of oral production [9–11]. Wu and Zhao [12] selected eight distinctive features belonging to language complexity, accuracy and fluency (type, token, lexical sophistication, pronunciation accuracy, lexical accuracy, grammar accuracy, speed and time ratio) to investigate their relationships with the spoken Chinese scores of second language learners at the low-intermediate level. They found that type, token and pronunciation accuracy can significantly predict spoken Chinese scores. However, can the collocation have an effect as fluency, accuracy, complexity and other indicators have had in realistic oral tests?

Shen [13] explored foreign students' Chinese oral expression at the advanced level, finding that they exhibited many problems. Foreign students in the process of learning Chinese can be generally divided into three levels: primary, intermediate and advanced. Each level has its own characteristics, and there are many differences in language expression. For primary level learners, the number of sentences they produced was limited [14]. Chen [15] found that the speech rate of advanced-level learners with Chinese as a second language was significantly quicker than that of intermediate-level learners. Learners' oral production quality was also examined from multiple dimensions and found that second language proficiency clearly affected fluency, accuracy and opinion complexity [16]. Based on the above findings, we can see that students at different levels make use of different lexical and grammatical collocations. Therefore, what are the specific effects of different collocational dimensions on students' oral production scores at different levels? No researchers have conducted a deep and extended discussion on this topic.

According to previous studies, learners' oral production quality is affected by many factors. In oral assessments, fluency, accuracy and complexity are often adopted as the measurement criteria for learners' oral production quality. However, collocational conditions affect learners' oral production of oral expression. To date, neither the subdimensions of collocation that interfere with learners' oral production quality nor the detailed effects of these dimensions on students' oral production scores at different levels have been identified. These two issues are still unsolved. Therefore, based on existing research, this study focuses on these two issues and explores the multiple dimensions of collocation. Using correlation analysis and multiple linear regression analysis in SPSS (IBM SPSS Statistics v 23), this study focuses on the influence of lexical and grammatical collocation accuracy, richness and transparency on the quality evaluation of Chinese oral production at different levels. We also seek to observe whether there are differences in the predictive effect on oral production quality from these two collocational types with different structures. We hypothesise that the predictive power of the various indicators of grammatical collocations on oral production quality may be smaller than that of lexical collocations.

2   Research Design

2.1   Collocational Structures

In this study, collocation refers to both lexical and grammatical collocations. Specifically, phrases that are combined by words belong to lexical collocations, while grammatical collocations are limited to the collocations of a dominant word and a preposition [1, 17–19]. Based on the relevant research, lexical collocation structures consisting of nouns, verbs, adjectives and adverbs were selected, and grammatical collocations will not be specified. Table 1 shows the specific collocational structures in this study, based on the division frameworks of lexical collocations by Shao [20] and Hu and Xiao [21].

Table 1. Structural type of collocations

Collocational range	Structure type	Structural form (sample)
Lexical collocations	Subject-predicate	N + N (今天星期三, today Wednesday); N + V (我想, I think); N + A (行为端正, correct behaviour); V + V (失恋引起, losing love caused)
	Verb-object	V + N (买东西, buy something); V + V (继续工作, continue to work); V + A (发现美, discover beautiful (things))
	Attribute-noun	A + N (美丽的学校, beautiful school); N + N (人的性格, people's personality); V + N (飘落的花, falling flowers)
	Adverb-predicate	Adv + V (已经结束, already over); Adv + A (很好, very good); A + V (兴奋地回答, answer excitedly); N + V (今天比赛, today compete); V + V (想要, want to possess)
	Predicate-complement	V + V (开回来, drive back); V + Adv (喜欢极了, like so much); A + Adv (好得很, very good); V + A (洗干净, make something clean); A + V (开心起来, become happy)
Grammatical collocations	Preposition-object	Pre + N (在中国, in China); N + Pre (我们跟, we follow); Pre + V (对劳动, for working); Pre + A (由弱小, from weak)

Notes: 'N' in this table includes nouns and pronouns.

2.2 Data Sources

For this study, 124 L2 learners' oral recordings were selected and transcribed. The students who participated in oral recordings are from Laos, Thailand, Pakistan, Myanmar, Cambodia, Vietnam, Bhutan, Japan and Mongolia. The average number of words per transcript was 150. Considering foreign learners' duration of learning Chinese and their Hanyu Shuiping Kaoshi (HSK) [22], all recordings were divided into three levels: primary (having learned Chinese for half to one year), intermediate (having learned Chinese for one and a half to two and a half years) and advanced (having learned Chinese for three to four years). If the intermediate learners did not pass HSK level 4, their data will belong to the primary level. Similarly, if the advanced learners did not pass their HSK level 6, their recording data will be placed in the intermediate level. Finally, the recording distributions were 39 at the primary level, 45 at the intermediate level and 40 at the advanced level.

For the recordings, students were asked to answer the following question within three minutes: What do you think are the advantages and disadvantages of studying abroad? Most learners at different levels can provide some oral production to this question. Before the oral recording, the foreign students were given approximately 10 min to prepare for answering on the spot, allowing them to write a simple outline; however, they are not allowed to read directly from their written content.

2.3 Definition of Dimensions in Collocation

Collocation Accuracy. Based on the analysis of the accuracy of collocation extraction by Zhou [23]. In this study, the collocations were manually extracted, individually, and evaluated to judge the correctness of the extracted lexical and grammatical collocations. Three students whose native language is Chinese served as judges. If two or three students judged a lexical or grammatical collocation as correct, we assumed that the collocation is correct. Finally, the following formula was used for all the evaluated results to assess the accuracy of lexical and grammatical collocations: accuracy = correct number/total collocation number.

Collocation Richness. Some studies [24–26] provide a definition of lexical variation and richness. Collocation richness is defined on the basis of lexical variation and richness. It refers to the size (sophistication) and range (variation) of the combination of multiple complex words in the text. The formula richness = type/token was employed to calculate the richness level of the lexical and grammatical collocations.

Collocation Transparency. Hong et al. [27] discussed semantic transparency, which refers to the predictable degree of the meaning of a compound word according to the meaning of its composite morpheme. Its operational definition refers to the degree of semantic correlation between each composite morpheme and the corresponding compound word. In reference to semantic transparency, Gao [28] states that if we see a compound word, we will understand its meaning. Collocational transparency is similar to semantic transparency. We focus on the specific meaning between the words constituting the collocation, hoping to acquire the meaning of the collocational phrase from that of the two composite words. Therefore, collocational transparency can also be called the semantic transparency of collocations.

Li [29] suggests that semantic transparency can be divided into three: semantic transparency, semi-transparency and non-transparency. Li [22] and Revier [30] divide the transparency of lexical and grammatical collocations into four levels: transparent, non-transparent, less transparent and semi-transparent collocations. Transparent collocation refers to whether the two composite words are used in their literal or core sense, and whether the overall meaning of the collocation can be obtained by adding the literal sense of the two words. Non-transparent collocation means that collocational meaning cannot be inferred through adding the literal sense of the two words. In the case of less transparent collocation, both words in the collocation make use of their non-literal or extended meanings. Semi-transparent collocation is defined as one word retaining its literal sense and the other using its non-literal or extended meaning. We adopt Li's classification of transparency as this study's framework. Furthermore, we make a quantitative value assignment on the transparency of each collocation through a four-level scale (non-, less-, semi- and transparent, coded as 1–4, respectively). Three native Chinese speakers (college students) assigned the transparencies of each lexical and grammatical collocation, according to their language sense. Thus, the transparency of each collocation is the average value of the transparencies judged by the three Chinese native speakers. Finally, the average value of all collocation transparency values in each recording text was calculated as the value of the collocation transparency index. Table 2 shows the detailed quantitative evaluation of transparency indicators.

Oral Production Quality Score. The quality of oral production was subjectively scored by 26 Chinese native speakers (Mandarin level ≥ 2), with a full score of 100. Based on the strength of the target language reference standard proposed by Xing [31], no specific scoring rules were set when scoring, and the graders gave a comprehensive score by virtue of their language sense.

The scoring criteria is not given in order to achieve an overall judgment on production quality for most native speakers, rather than a result judged by a set of standards for grading. This is because only when taking examinations can learners' production quality be judged according to a given grading criteria. However, in daily study, work and life, Chinese native speakers' evaluation of a speaker's production quality is a comprehensive judgment based on their own language senses. Thus far, we cannot precisely know how the judgment based on language sense is determined using an index system. Although many studies have found important indicators, these indicators cannot be regarded as a standard indicator system by most people's language sense judgment. If a grading criteria is set, the results will only be applicable to the evaluation of production quality in examinations rather than daily communication.

Finally, the average score was calculated based on the scores evaluated by each grader to obtain an average score of each recording text. The oral production score is the dependent variable in this study.

Table 2. Examples of the transparency evaluation of lexical and grammatical collocations

Lexical collocations or grammatical collocations	Transparency levels (quantised value)			
	Non-transparent (1)	Less-transparent (2)	Semi-transparent (3)	Transparent (4)
Go to learn (去学习)				4
Expensive school fees (学费贵)				4
Perform well in learning (学习好)				4
Relatively good (比较好)			3	
Understand culture (理解文化)				4
Communicate with... (跟……交流)			3	
In Yunnan province (在云南)				4

3 Result Analysis

3.1 Effects of Various Dimensions of Collocations on Oral Production Quality

In this study, collocation accuracy, richness and transparency were taken as the independent variables, and the oral production score was taken as the dependent variable. SPSS software (IBM SPSS Statistics v 23) was used for correlation analysis of the three independent variables and the dependent variable in lexical and grammatical collocations. Table 3 shows the correlation analysis results of the lexical collocations index and oral Chinese scores.

As shown in Table 3, only collocation accuracy has a significant positive correlation with the oral production score among the three indicators of lexical collocations. There is no significant correlation between the scores of lexical collocation richness and transparency. In addition, there are correlations between the various variables of lexical collocations. Lexical collocation transparency was significantly correlated ($p < 0.05$) with accuracy, while there was a negative correlation between lexical collocation richness and accuracy. No obvious correlation was found between lexical collocation transparency and richness.

Table 3. Correlation matrix between the related variables in lexical collocations and oral Chinese scores

	Scores	Lexical collocation accuracy	Lexical collocation richness	Lexical collocation transparency
Score	1			
Lexical collocation accuracy	$.256^{**}$	1		
Lexical collocation richness	$-.149$	$-.212^{*}$	1	
Lexical collocation transparency	$-.102$	$.181^{*}$	$-.098$	1

Notes: $**$ $P < 0.01$, $*$ $P < 0.05$

Table 4 shows the results of the correlation analysis between the indicators of grammatical collocations and oral Chinese scores.

Table 4. Correlation matrix between the related variables in grammatical collocations and oral Chinese scores

	Score	Grammatical collocation accuracy	Grammatical collocation richness	Grammatical collocation transparency
Score	1			
Grammatical collocation accuracy	$.260^{**}$	1		
Grammatical collocation richness	$.171$	$.773^{**}$	1	
Grammatical collocation transparency	$.213^{*}$	$.916^{**}$	$.782^{**}$	1

Notes: $**$ $P < 0.01$, $*$ $P < 0.05$

As can be seen, in addition to grammatical collocation richness, accuracy and transparency are significantly correlated with oral scores. When $p < 0.01$, the grammatical collocation accuracy is positively correlated with the oral production score. When $p < 0.05$, the grammatical collocation transparency significantly correlates with the oral production score. There is a higher correlation between the accuracy of grammatical collocation and the oral production quality score, followed by grammatical collocation transparency. Additionally, there are significant correlations among the three grammatical collocation variables. The correlation between grammatical collocation accuracy and transparency was the highest, followed by that between grammatical collocation richness and transparency. The correlation between grammatical collocation accuracy and richness was the lowest.

To further understand the specific effects of the various indicators of lexical and grammatical collocations on the oral production score, this study conducted multiple linear regression analyses on the three collocation indicators and oral scores in SPSS (IBM SPSS statistics v 23). The 'enter method' was used first to analyse. Table 5 shows the results of the lexical collocations analysis.

Table 5. Summary of the multiple regression analysis results of lexical collocations (n = 124)

Variables		Multiple linear direct regression				Hierarchical regression	
		B	Std. Error	Beta	Sig	R^2 change	Sig
Score	Lexical collocation accuracy	28.008	9.632	.261	.004	.063	.004
	Lexical collocation richness	−5.738	4.650	−.110	.220		
	Lexical collocation transparency	−5.903	3.265	−.160	.073		

As shown in Table 5, the three independent variables could explain 9.9% of total variation ($R^2 = 0.099$; F (3, 121) = 4.415; P = 0.006). Lexical collocation accuracy (p = 0.004 < 0.005) contributes greatly and has remarkable effects on the oral production scores, while lexical collocation richness and transparency have no significant effects.

Further hierarchical regression analysis indicated that lexical collocation accuracy had an independent contribution to the oral production score. That is, it could reach 6.3% when other variables remained unchanged.

The analysis results of the grammatical collocations are shown in Table 6.

Table 6. Summary of the multiple regression analysis results of grammatical collocations (n = 124)

Variables		Multiple linear direct regression			
		B	Std. Error	Beta	Sig
Score	Grammatical collocation accuracy	4.942	2.615	.424	.061
	Grammatical collocation richness	−.629	1.787	−.051	.725
	Grammatical collocation transparency	−.439	.738	−.136	.553

As shown in Table 6, the three independent variables could explain 7.3% of the total variation ($R^2 = 0.073$; F (3, 121) = 3.144; P = 0.028). However, there was marginal significant correlation between collocation accuracy and the oral production score among the three grammatical collocation variables, while grammatical collocation richness and transparency had no significant contributions.

3.2 The Influence of Collocation on the Quality of Oral Production at Different Levels

There are many differences in the oral expression of foreign students at different levels. In the oral evaluation, the scoring results are affected by numerous factors. In the process of grading, we often pay attention to students' mastery of the fluency, accuracy and complexity of collocation. However, it is hard to know the specific role of the various collocational dimensions on different levels of oral production scoring. Therefore, we investigated the accuracy, richness and transparency in both lexical and grammatical collocations at three levels. A multiple linear regression analysis was conducted in SPSS (IBM SPSS statistics v 23) to observe the three dimensions of collocations in lexical collocations and grammatical collocations on different levels of oral production score. The collocation dimensions scores for oral production at the primary level are shown in Table 7.

Table 7. Contribution of six collocation variables to the quality of oral production at the primary level

Variable		Multiple linear direct regression			
		B	Std. Error	Beta	Sig
Score	Lexical collocation accuracy	10.654	17.972	.107	.557
	Lexical collocation richness	−1.784	6.880	−.046	.797
	Lexical collocation transparency	−5.755	5.411	−.181	.295
	Grammatical collocation accuracy	4.734	3.145	.496	.142
	Grammatical collocation richness	−.005	2.816	.000	.999
	Grammatical collocation transparency	−.710	1.061	−.264	.508

As shown in Table 7, the three dimensions of collocations have no significant effect on the primary level oral production score in terms of lexical and grammatical collocations ($R^2 = 0.135$; F (6, 33) = 0.835; p = 0.552).

The results of the multiple linear regression at the intermediate level are shown in Table 8.

As shown in Table 8, the six variables explain 22.1% of the total variation ($R^2 = 0.221$; F (6, 39) = 1.801; p = 0.125). Only lexical collocation transparency has a marginal contribution to the score of oral production, while lexical collocation accuracy, richness and the three dimensions of grammatical collocation have no significant effect on the oral production score.

Table 8. Contributions of six collocation variables to the quality of oral production at the intermediate level

Variable		Multiple linear direct regression			
		B	Std. Error	Beta	Sig
Score	Lexical collocation accuracy	9.556	13.840	.104	.494
	Lexical collocation richness	−2.981	7.151	−.068	.679
	Lexical collocation transparency	−10.557	5.269	−.293	.052
	Grammatical collocation accuracy	−2.488	7.111	−.250	.728
	Grammatical collocation richness	3.206	3.122	.301	.311
	Grammatical collocation transparency	.832	1.631	.309	.613

The results of the multiple linear regression analysis at the advanced level are shown in Table 9.

Table 9. Contributions of six collocation variables to the quality of oral production at the advanced level

Variable		Multiple linear direct regression				Hierarchical regression	
		B	Std. Error	Beta	Sig	R^2 change	Sig
Score	Lexical collocation accuracy	43.417	17.073	.454	.016	.145	.016
	Lexical collocation richness	−3.659	10.417	−.056	.728		
	Lexical collocation transparency	−7.851	5.423	−.256	.157		
	Grammatical collocation accuracy	3.065	4.608	.268	.511		
	Grammatical collocation richness	−6.762	3.890	−.578	.091		
	Grammatical collocation transparency	1.845	1.314	.577	.170		

As shown in Table 9, the six variables explain 25.8% of the total variation (R^2 = 0.258; F (6, 34) = 1.917; p = 0.107). Among them, lexical collocation accuracy significantly affects the oral production score. However, lexical collocation richness, transparency, and the three dimensions of grammatical collocation have no significant effects on the oral production scores at the advanced level. Further hierarchical regression analysis shows that the independent contribution of lexical collocation accuracy to the oral production score reaches 14.5%.

4 Discussion

In this study, the relationship between the accuracy, richness and transparency of lexical and grammatical collocations and the quality of Chinese oral production were analysed by studying 124 L2 learners' oral recordings. The results show that lexical collocation accuracy can affect the oral production score. Grammatical collocation accuracy and transparency also impact the oral production score. Lexical collocation accuracy has an independent contribution to the oral production score, and grammatical collocation accuracy has a marginal contribution. In addition, lexical collocation accuracy has a stronger predictive effect on the advanced level oral production score. The transparency of lexical collocations has marginal contribution to the intermediate level oral production score, while other collocational dimensions have no specific contribution to the oral production scores at the intermediate and advanced levels. Meanwhile, collocation accuracy, richness and transparency have no significant influence on the primary level of oral production scores.

The statistical analysis indicates that there are strong positive correlations between the accuracy of both lexical and grammatical collocations and the oral production score, which is consistent with the findings of Wu and Zhao [12]. Therefore, if a foreign student can use as many correct collocations as possible in the process of oral expression, his or her oral score will be relatively high. Meanwhile, there is a positive correlation between lexical collocation accuracy and transparency. Collocation transparency is related to collocation semantics, and it is much easier and more accurate for students to use the more transparent collocations. From the perspective of the prediction effect of lexical and grammatical collocations on oral production quality, the prediction effect of lexical collocation accuracy is greater than that of grammatical collocation accuracy, further confirming our hypothesis. In the actual oral production of L2 learners, the semantics and usage of grammatical collocations are relatively difficult, thus the number of grammatical collocations used by L2 learners is expectedly less than that of lexical collocations. Therefore, grammatical collocations play a relatively small role in predicting oral scores in natural assessment.

When analysing the scores of different levels of oral production, the results differed from our expectations. At the primary and intermediate stages, the accuracy of both lexical and grammatical collocations had no predictive effect on the oral production score, and the accuracy of lexical collocations only contributed to the oral production score at the advanced level. A possible reason is that when foreign students orally express a given topic, primary and intermediate level students pause occasionally, and their sentences may be incoherent or illogical. When using collocations, they often use simple or repeated ones, and the accuracy and richness of the collocations are not high. In addition, some students may not know how to express themselves, saying some irrelevant sentences. In contrast, advanced level students have a certain oral expression ability with good fluency and accuracy. They may attempt to use different collocations to organise the language to enrich their expressions and enhance collocation accuracy.

There was no significant correlation between the richness of lexical and grammatical collocations and the oral production scores. There was a negative correlation between the richness of lexical collocations and their accuracy, while the richness of grammatical collocations was positively correlated with their accuracy. This shows that foreign students should fully understand the meaning and context of each collocation and should not blindly pursue collocation richness. For the use of grammatical collocations, learners can master some prepositional collocations with different structures, and pay attention to the accuracy of language expression, which can indirectly improve the complexity of language expression. Further study shows that the richness of lexical and grammatical collocations had no significant effect on the oral production score.

In addition, collocation richness had no predictive effect on the oral production score at different levels, which is consistent with existing research. Syntactic and lexical complexity have no significant effect on L2 oral proficiency [16]. A possible reason is that foreign students at different levels tend to avoid using complex collocations, especially grammatical ones, as they are difficult for them. They are afraid to make mistakes and lack a richness of grammatical collocations, thereby using repetitive ones.

Regarding collocation transparency, we found that lexical collocation transparency is unrelated to oral production score and is only correlated with lexical collocation accuracy, whereas grammatical collocation transparency has a significant correlation with oral production score. Moreover, the transparency of grammatical collocations is positively correlated with their accuracy and richness. This indicates that the more transparent the collocation, the higher its accuracy and richness will be. Further study on the contribution of collocation transparency to oral production score shows that the transparency of lexical and grammatical collocations have no specific predictive effect on oral production score, indicating that there is only a correlation between the transparency of grammatical collocations and oral production score but no obvious causal relationship. The results of the quality analysis at different levels of oral production are the same. The transparency of grammatical collocations had no significant effect on the scores of different levels of oral production. Only the transparency of lexical collocations can marginally predict the oral production score at the intermediate level, while it could not predict the oral production score at the primary and advanced levels. This result may be because the definition of the collocation transparency level itself includes the change of lexical meanings in the collocations. At the primary level, students are unable to understand the basic meaning of some non-transparent collocations, and they often choose some transparent collocations for expression. Thus, non-transparent collocations were seldom found in the oral recordings of primary-level foreign students. Students at the intermediate and advanced levels had a certain language foundation and expression ability. Thus, they used some complex words and collocations to improve their language, but there is a long way to realize collocation richness. Therefore, we can teach students to use different words and collocations to form sentences. They should master a certain amount of complex collocations and structures to enrich their language expression.

Oral production is influenced by many factors. Different dimensions of language indicators have different effects on the quality of language production. Through studying the impact of the three dimensions of collocations on oral assessment, we can identify problems in the specific use of collocations, and further understand the specific influence and role of collocations in foreign students' oral assessment. Collocations are restricted by lexical semantics, sentence context and pragmatics, and these factors directly affect foreign students' understanding and choice of collocations. The multiple dimensions of collocations can also indirectly reflect the influence of their mastery of syntax and semantic structure in discourse on the quality of oral production. Previous studies have also found that the quality of oral production is affected by other factors, such as personal emotional factors and anxiety [16]. These factors may also interfere with the choice and use of collocations in foreign students' oral expression. Therefore, based on the results of this study, we can further explore the possible collocational dimensions that may affect the quality of oral production, as well as the specific effects of different indicators.

Due to the limited research breadth, the oral recordings of foreign students from nine countries were selected for this study. The oral recordings of students from Europe and America were not included. Therefore, the research results are mainly applicable to students in Asia. In future research, we will expand the oral recording materials to further explore the predictive effect of collocations on oral production score.

5   Conclusions

In this study, the relationship between the accuracy, richness and transparency of lexical and grammatical collocations and Chinese oral production quality were studied. The results are as follows:

(1) Lexical collocation accuracy could effectively predict the quality of oral production, while grammatical collocation accuracy could also predict the quality of oral production to a certain extent. The prediction effect of grammatical collocation accuracy on oral production quality is relatively less than that of lexical collocation accuracy.

(2) At different levels of oral production, the accuracy of lexical collocations has an independent contribution to the quality of oral production at the advanced level, and the transparency of lexical collocations plays a marginal role in predicting the quality of oral production at the intermediate level. However, the accuracy, transparency and richness of grammatical collocations, and the richness of lexical collocations have no predictive effect on oral production scores at different levels.

Acknowledgments. We thank all reviewers for their constructive comments, and gratefully acknowledge the support of The Western and Frontier Project of the Humanities and Social Sciences Youth Fund of the Ministry of Education, "Research on the database construction of collocation knowledge and acquisition mechanism of Chinese as a second language" (No. 19XJC740002).

References

1. Xing, H.: Collocation knowledge and second language lexical acquisition. Appl. Linguist. **4**, 117–126 (2013). (in Chinese)
2. Shi, G., Yang, C., Xing, H.: A study on semantic features of antonymous verbs based on lexical knowledge system. In: Liu, M., Kit, C., Su, Q. (eds.) Chinese Lexical Semantics CLSW 2020 21st Workshop, CLSW 2020, Hong Kong, China, May 28–30, 2020, Revised Selected Papers. LNCS (LNAI), vol. 12278, pp. 421–431. Springer, Cham (2021). https://doi.org/10.1007/978-3-030-81197-6_35
3. Sung, J.: English Lexical Collocations and Their Relation to Spoken Fluency of Adult Non-Native Speakers. Doctoral Dissertation of Indiana University of Pennsylvania (2003)
4. Hu, Y.: Studies on the formulaic sequences in speech production: retrospect and prospect. Foreign Lang. Learn Theory. Pract. **2**, 55–63 (2011). (in Chinese)
5. Wang, W., Zhou, D.: The Use of V-N collocations in L2 oral production. Foreign Lang. Their Teach. (3), 54–63+147–148 (2020). (in Chinese)
6. Ma, J., Wang, H., Feng, Z.: Dynamic evaluation system construction of English majors' oral proficiency based on ZPD theory. J. Daqing Norm. Univ. **34**(6), 138–141 (2014). (in Chinese)
7. Guo, X.: The quantitative measure and scoring of fluency of spoken Chinese as a second language. J. Xiangtan Norm. Univ. (Soc. Sci. Ed.) **4**, 91–94 (2007). (in Chinese)
8. Wang, L., Wu, X.: Correlation between tolerance of ambiguity and the quality of oral output by gender. J. Chongqing Univ. Technol. (Soc. Sci.) **28**(3), 102–105 (2014). (in Chinese)
9. Lu, Y.: From Input to Output: An Analysis of the Cognitive Factors Affecting L2 Oral Production. Foreign. Stud. **4**(2), 37–42+105 (2016). (in Chinese)
10. Xu, J., Chen, C.: Effects of cognitive demands on learners' oral performance and attention allocation. foreign lang. Their Teach. (6), 42–52+144–145 (2018). (in Chinese)
11. Zhang, W., Ouyang, J.: The influence of topic cognitive difficulty on fluency, accuracy and complexity of oral production. J. Suzhou Univ. **27**(10), 98–101 (2012). (in Chinese)
12. Wu, J., Zhao, X.: On the quality assessment of spoken Chinese for low-intermediate level L2 LEARNERS. Appl. Linguist. **1**, 76–86 (2020). (in Chinese)
13. Shen, J.: A study on the advanced spoken Chinese discourse based on the corpus of the spoken test. Educ. Mod. **6**(70), 174–177 (2019). (in Chinese)
14. Mu, Y., Heseler, J., Xing, H.: The development of the semantic network of Chinese as second language learners' production: from the perspective of collocations. In: Liu, M., Kit, C., Su, Q. (eds.) Chinese Lexical Semantics CLSW 2020 21st Workshop, CLSW 2020, Hong Kong, China, May 28–30, 2020, Revised Selected Papers. LNCS (LNAI), vol. 12278, pp. 549–561. Springer, Cham (2021). https://doi.org/10.1007/978-3-030-81197-6_47
15. Chen, M.: Chinese oral fluency of CSL learners of American English speakers. Lang. Teach. Linguist. Stud. **2**, 17–24 (2012). (in Chinese)
16. Chen, C., Xu, J.: The influence of learners' L2 proficiency and anxiety on the quality of oral production. J. PLA Univ. Foreign Lang. **42**(1), 110–118 (2019). (in Chinese)
17. Zhen, T., Ren, Q., Yin, H.: The definition and overview of the word collocation. J. Qingdao Agric. Univ. (Soc Sci) **1**, 81–84 (2006). (in Chinese)
18. Benson, M.: A combinatory dictionary of english. dictionaries: J. Dictionary Soc. North America (7), 189–200 (1985)
19. Qian, X.: Automatic extraction of chinese V-N collocations. In: Ji, D., Xiao, G. (eds.) CLSW 2012. LNCS (LNAI), vol. 7717, pp. 230–241. Springer, Heidelberg (2013). https://doi.org/10.1007/978-3-642-36337-5_24
20. Shao, J.: General Modern Chinese, 3rd edn. Shanghai Education Publishing House, Shanghai (2016). (in Chinese)

21. Hu, R., Xiao, H.: The construction of Chinese collocation knowledge bases and their application in second language acquisition. Appl. Linguist. **1**, 135–144 (2019). (in Chinese)
22. Li, M.: A Research on Collocation Acquisition Mechanism in Chinese as a Second Language Based on Collocation Knowledge System. Doctoral Dissertation of Beijing Language and Culture University (2018). (in Chinese)
23. Zhou, Q.: The construction of a collocation list based on academic papers of teaching Chinese to speakers of other languages. In: Liu, M., Kit, C., Su, Q. (eds.) Chinese Lexical Semantics CLSW 2020 21st Workshop, CLSW 2020, Hong Kong, China, May 28–30, 2020, Revised Selected Papers. LNCS (LNAI), vol. 12278, pp. 576–592. Springer, Cham (2021). https://doi.org/10.1007/978-3-030-81197-6_49
24. Wen, Q.: A longitudinal study on the changes in speaking vocabulary by English majors in China. Foreign Lang. Teach. Res. (3), 189–195+240–241 (2006). (in Chinese)
25. Scott, J.: Capturing the diversity in lexical diversity. Lang. Learn. **63**, 87–106 (2013)
26. Ma, Q., Chai, X.: The relationship between lexical richness and the quality of CSL learners' oral narratives. In: Dong, M., Yanhui, G., Hong, J.-F. (eds.) Chinese Lexical Semantics: 22nd Workshop, CLSW 2021, Nanjing, China, May 15–16, 2021, Revised Selected Papers, Part II, pp. 95–105. Springer International Publishing, Cham (2022). https://doi.org/10.1007/978-3-031-06547-7_7
27. Hong, W., Feng, C., Zheng, Z.: Chinese L2 vocabulary learning: the influence of semantic transparency, contextual richness and number of encounters. Mod. Foreign Lang. **40**(4), 529–539+584–585 (2017). (in Chinese)
28. Gao, C.: Semantic transparency and the selection of entries in Chinese dictionaries. Stud. Chin. Lang. (5), 439–451+480 (2015). (in Chinese)
29. Li, L.: A study of the influence of semantic transparency on English learners' collocation acquisition. J. Dongguan Univ. Technol. **27**(2), 96–101 (2020). (in Chinese)
30. Revier, R.L.: Evaluating a new test of whole English collocations. In: Barfield, A., Gyllstad, H. (eds.) Researching Collocations in Another Language, pp. 125–138. Palgrave Macmillan UK, London (2009). https://doi.org/10.1057/9780230245327_10
31. Xing, H.: A preliminary study of the native-like attainment of second language production. J. Int. Chin. Teach. **1**, 52–62 (2020). (in Chinese)

Verb Raising and the Construction Mechanism of Synthetic Compounds

Zhang Chen[1], Rui Liu[2,3]([✉]), and Yi Tang[4]

[1] Department of Chinese Language and Literature, Faculty of Arts and Humanities, University of Macau, Macao SAR, China
[2] Department of Chinese Language and Literature, Faculty of Arts and Sciences, Beijing Normal University, Zhuhai, China
liu_rui@bnu.edu.cn
[3] Center for Linguistic Sciences, Beijing Normal University, Zhuhai, China
[4] Department of English, Faculty of Arts and Humanities, University of Macau, Macao SAR, China

Abstract. Synthetic compounds have received considerable research attention in linguistics, since they can provide important implications to explore the reciprocal relationship between syntax and morphology. It is suggested that synthetic compounds are generated by argument structure. For instance, the *zhǐzhāng* 'paper' and *jī* 'machine' in *zhǐzhāng-fěnsuì-jī* 'paper shredder' can be analyzed as the arguments of the verb *fěnsuì* 'shred'. Previous research on incorporation and adjunction analyses has demonstrated the syntactic-semantic relations in synthetic compounds but failed to explain the asymmetry between the actual linear order and the underlying argument structure. The current paper proposes and illustrates the analysis method of verb raising. The synthetic compounds are headed by a nominal affix *-n*, which selects a verb phrase as its complement leftwards. Then the [+affix] feature of *-n* triggers the verb to raise to the *-n* position to generate the surface linear order. This approach provides a solution to analyze Chinese synthetic compounds and can be supported by relevant facts in other languages such as English and Japanese.

Keywords: Synthetic Compounds · Verb Raising · Argument Structure · Lexical-Syntactic Interface

1 Introduction

The interaction between morphology and syntax has long been a premise research topic in linguistics. From the traditional point of view of Generative Grammar, Syntax and Lexicon are two separate systems. The Lexicon is responsible for word formation, while the syntactic operations should not intervene in this process, which is also known as the Lexical Integrity Hypothesis [1]. But synthetic compounds seem to be an exception. English synthetic compounds consist of two parts: a head derived from the verb, and a modifying element that is acted upon by the argument of the verb.

© The Author(s), under exclusive license to Springer Nature Switzerland AG 2023
Q. Su et al. (Eds.): CLSW 2022, LNAI 13496, pp. 221–231, 2023.
https://doi.org/10.1007/978-3-031-28956-9_18

(1) a. truck-driver   b. truck-driving

It is believed that there is a 'deverbal form' within the English synthetic compound. For instance, *driver/driving* in (1) is the head derived from the verb *drive*, and the modifying element *truck* also serves as an argument of *drive* [2]. Since the word formation combines both compounding and derivation, it is known as synthetic compounding.

Due to the lack of morphological changes in Chinese, research on synthetic compounds rarely involves de-verbalization, but emphasizes the verb-argument relations in the structure. He Yuanjian [3] emphasizes the presence of verbs, suggesting that synthetic compounds refer to compounds containing verbs, the lexicalized sentences. Gu and Shen [4] argue that synthetic compounds are a kind of attributive VP-N compounds, but a thematic relationship does exist between VP and N. For example, the *rén* 'person' in *jiēmù-zhǔchí-rén* 'host of the TV programme' has an AGENT-ACTION relationship with *zhǔchí* 'host', and the *zhǔchí* also has an ACTION-THEME relationship with *jiēmù* 'TV programme'.

In both English and Chinese, the internal elements of synthetic compounds can be analyzed as verbs and their arguments, which has demonstrated a high degree of similarity with the phrase structure. Therefore, many scholars hold the view that the formation of synthetic compounds can be deduced from syntactic rules [2–7, etc.]. However, as Cheng [5] points out that the syntactic analysis faces a serious challenge in terms of the internal order of synthetic compounds. For example, *zhǐzhāng-fěnsuì-jī* 'paper shredder' is a combination of the noun *zhǐzhāng* 'paper', *jī* 'machine', and the verb *fěnsuì* 'shred'. If we follow the syntactic rules for generating verb phrases, the underlying argument structure would be *jī-fěnsuì-zhǐzhāng*, which is inconsistent with the linear order of the synthetic compound. In addition, the typical order of synthetic compounds is $N_1 VN_2$ in English, Chinese, and Japanese, regardless of the basic syntactic order of that specific language:

(2) a. English (SVO) :   car drive -er $(N_1 VN_2)$

  b. Chinese (SVO) :   zhǐzhāng-fěnsuì-jī $(N_1 VN_2)$

         (paper shred machine)

  c Japanese (SOV) : shoseki-shuppan-kaisha $(N_1 VN_2)$

         (book publish company)

The abovementioned linguistic phenomena reflect the asymmetry between the underlying argument structure and the actual linear structure of synthetic compounds. It also involves relevant issues such as the inconsistency between the basic VP order and the order of synthetic compounds in different languages. Previous research has either been inadequate or inconsistent in providing explanations for these problems. Based on the analysis of some new types of synthetic compounds, this paper aims to demonstrate that synthetic compounds are generated by the operation of 'Verb Raising' of the underlying argument structures under the syntactic rules. This proposed analysis scheme can provide an effective explanation of the phenomenon of Chinese synthetic compound words, and also shed important implications on other languages, including Japanese and English.

2 Previous Analyses of Synthetic Compounds

Plenty of research efforts have been dedicated to explaining the correspondence of argument structure and linear order in synthetic compounds. Incorporation analysis is among one of the most common syntactic analysis schemes. There is an interesting linguistic phenomenon in Indian languages. It is found that the object noun can incorporate with the verb to form a new verb, and such process is known as Noun Incorporation (NI).

(3) a. Pet   wa?-ha-htu-?t-a? ne?   o -hwist -a?. [Onondaga]

Pat   PAST-3MS-lost-CAUS-ASP   the PRE-**money**-SUF

'Pat lost the money.'

b. Pet   wa? -ha - **hwist** -ahtu -?t   -a?.

Pat PAST-3MS- **money**-lost-CAUS-ASP

'Pat lost money.'

(Baker[6] pp.76-77)

There are two legitimate expressions in Onondaga: the verb and object are two separate words in (3a), whereas in (3b), the object noun is incorporated with the verb and the noun stem is moved to the front of the verb stem in accordance with the linear order. The phenomenon of noun incorporation and the synthetic compounds are both related to the reformation of the verb and its argument, except that the noun incorporation forms a new verb, and the synthetic compounding forms a new noun. Hence, Baker [6] suggested that the structure in (3b) is parallel to the English compound *money-loser* and considered the incorporation as a head movement operation. The new word formed by incorporation shares the same lexical category with the original word on the 'landing site', and the word order of the two components is also reversed. Based on these similarities, incorporation has become one of the most commonly adopted syntactic tools in analyzing synthetic compounds. More specifically, it can be divided into verb incorporation analysis and noun incorporation analysis.

2.1 Verb Incorporation Analysis

Gu and Shen [4] acknowledge that the formation of Chinese synthetic compounds follows syntactic rules. According to the Uniformity of Theta Assignment Hypothesis (UTAH), the Chinese synthetic compound *qìchē-xiūlǐ-gōng* 'car repair-man' has the underlying argument structure shown in Fig. (1a).

However, the argument structure in (1a) does not correspond to the actual linear order of the synthetic compound. It is structurally a verb phrase (VP) with *xiūlǐ* 'repair' as its head. In order to obtain the nominative phrase and the correct linear order, it needs to be transformed into a nominal construction with *gōng* 'worker' at its head. Gu and Shen

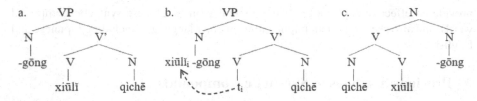

Fig. 1. Derivation of qìche-xiuli-gong 'car repair-man'

[4] claim that the verb *xiūlǐ* 'repair' is first incorporated into the external argument and forms a new noun *xiūlǐ-gōng* 'repair-man' (Fig. 1b). Then the internal argument *qìchē* 'car' is incorporated into V to form a new verb *qìchē-xiūlǐ* 'car repair' and achieve the correct linear structure '[[qìchē-xiūlǐ] -gōng]' (Fig. 1c).

This analysis maintains the argument-verb relationship in synthetic compounds and also partly explains the linear order issue. But it cannot be used to explain structures such as *jiāoshī-xiūxī-shì* 'teacher-rest-room', in which the first noun is the AGENT of the verb. Hong and Shen [7] state that the underlying structure of *jiāoshī-xiūxī-shì* is [nP *shì* [vP *(for)* [VP *jiāoshī* [V *xiūxī*]]]]. The verb *xiūxī* 'rest' is first raised to the position of the light verb *(for)* to get [nP *shì* [vP *[xiūxī* [VP *jiāoshī]]]*], and then *jiāoshī* 'teacher' is incorporated into the verb *xiūxī* 'rest', forming the structure of [nP *shì* [vP *jiāoshī-xiūxī]*]. Finally, *jiāoshī-xiūxī* 'teacher rest' is incorporated into the nominal head *shi* 'room' to obtain [nP *[jiāoshī-xiūxī]-shì*].

However, this new analysis method contradicts with the case of *qìchē-xiūlǐ-gōng* 'car repair-man', in which the verb *xiūlǐ* 'repair' is incorporated into the position of the external argument *gōng* 'worker'. On the contrary, in *jiāoshī-xiūxī-shì* 'teacher rest room', the external argument *jiāoshī* 'teacher' is somehow incorporated into the verb *xiūxī* 'rest'.

2.2 Noun Incorporation Analysis

Harley [8] also adopts the incorporation analysis to explain the formation of the English synthetic compounds based on Distributed Morphology, which claims that there is no divide between morphology and syntax. It is suggested that the underlying structure of *truck driver* is *-er drive truck*, but *truck* cannot be assigned an accusative case after merging with *drive*, so it must be incorporated into the verb and form a new stem *truck-drive* to escape from the 'Case Filter'. The new stem *truck-drive* is then incorporated into the affix *-er*, forming [[truck-driv] -er]. However, the stem will be separated from the affix through this analysis, which is contrary to our linguistic intuition (Fig. 2).

Based on Harvey's research, Cheng and Zhou [9] argue that the Chinese synthetic compound *yáoyán-zhìzào-zhě* 'rumor make-er' is generated by noun incorporation analysis. (see Fig. 3):

Verb *zhìzào* 'make' selects *yáoyán* 'rumor' as its internal argument and gets the structure *zhìzào yáoyán* 'make rumor'. The *yáoyán* 'rumor' here cannot be assigned an accusative case, so it must be incorporated into the verb to escape from the 'Case Filter', forming *yáoyán-zhìzào*. Finally, *yáoyán- zhìzào* is merged with nominal head -*zhě* 'person/-er' to obtain the noun *yáoyán-zhìzào-zhě*. Different from Harley [8], Cheng

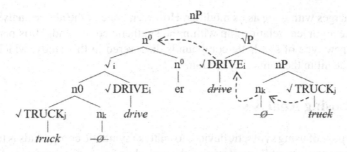

Fig. 2. Harley [8] 2008:136

Fig. 3. Cheng and Zhou [9] 2015:170

and Zhou [9] suggest that the structural head -*zhě* selects complement leftwards (Fig. 3c). However, this analysis still cannot explain structures such as *jiāoshī-xiūxī-shì* 'teacher-rest-room'. The initial position of the AGENT *jiāoshī* 'teacher' is above the verb *xiūxī* 'rest'. In accordance with the generative grammar theory, movement can only be done from the bottom up, so the external argument *jiāoshī* 'teacher' cannot be moved to the verb *xiūxī* 'rest'.

In order to explain the asymmetry between the underlying argument structure and the linear structure of synthetic compounds, previous studies have adopted incorporation analysis with the hope to achieve the transposition between the internal argument and the external argument. Those analyses can explain the case where N_1 is the object, like *zhǐzhāng-fěnsuì-jī*, the 'SVO' can be reversed to 'OVS' by incorporation. However, it does not work in some synthetic compounds with N_1 as the subject like *jiāoshī-xiūxī-shì*. Because the subject-predicate relationship between N_1 and V is in accordance with the argument structure, and further inversion would result in a wrong structure.

2.3 Attributive Analysis

Besides syntactic analyses, some studies hold the view that synthetic compounds are unrelated to syntactic rules. Wang Hongjun [10] argues that *fěnsuì* 'shred' and *jī* 'machine' form a modifier-head construction *fěnsuì-jī* 'shredder'. Then the words *zhǐzhāng* 'paper' and *fěnsuì-jī* 'shredder' again form a larger modifier-head compound *zhǐzhāng-fěnsuì-jī* 'paper shredder'. Shi Dingxu [11] suggests that in the compound word *xiūlǐ-gōng* 'repairman', the verb *xiūlǐ* 'repair' modifies the noun *gōng* 'worker'. In the structure of [[*qìchē xiūlǐ*] *gōng*], *qìchē* 'car' modifies *xiūlǐ*, forming *qìchē-xiūlǐ*, and then *qìchē-xiūlǐ* merges with *gōng* as its modifier. However, none of the above analysis methods reflect the argument relationship within the synthetic compounds. It is particularly evident in a new type of synthetic compounds discovered in this study, which will be discussed in detail in the following section.

3   Verb-Raising Analysis

The main purpose of using syntactic devices to analyze synthetic compounds is to explain the linear order correctly while maintaining the underlying argument structure. However, the analyses discussed in the last section do not provide an explanation for the synthetic compounds in which N_1 is AGENT. Some of them are self-contradictory, and the others generate counter-intuitive structures, like [[*truck-driv*] *-er*].

This paper argues that synthetic compound words do have internal argument structures, which need to be transformed by syntactic rules to obtain the final order. However, unlike the phrases, the formation of compound words also needs to follow the Right-Hand Head Rule [12, 13][1]. It suggests that the head of the compound word is on the right-hand side, which can be formalized as 'X → Y + X'. For instance, the *blackboard* has *board* on the right-hand as the structure head, and the head *-er* of *driver* is also on the right side. Based on the Right-Hand Head Rule, synthetic compounds can be generated by verb raising Analysis in different languages. The synthetic compound contains a VP corresponding to the argument structure. The VP merges with the nominative affix *-n* to form a noun, while V is raised to position *-n* through a head movement to generate the surface structure (e.g., Fig. 4).

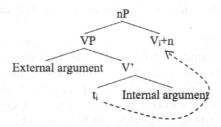

Fig. 4. Verb raising analysis of synthetic compounds

Verb raising analysis can provide an effective explanation for two different types of compound words in Chinese. Taking *yáoyán-zhìzào-zhě* 'rumor-maker' as an example, when N_1 is the THEME of the verb, the verb *zhìzào* selects *yáoyán* as its complement to get VP *zhìzào yáoyán*, which is then merged with the nominal affix *-zhě*. Since *-zhě* has the [+affix] feature and must be attached to a stem, it triggers the verb *zhìzào* to undergo

---

[1] Di Sciullo and Williams [12,13] use this term to summarize the situation in English and French, but Packard [14] points out that in Chinese the head of the noun is on the right and the head of the verb is on the left, and the head of the Japanese noun discussed below is also on the right. For the sake of convenience, the term "RRHR" is still used to summarize the situation in these languages.

a head movement and forms the surface structure [*yáoyán* [*zhìzào-zhě*]]. Similarly, when N_1 is the AGENT, it is generated in the Spec-VP position, then we get a VP *jiāoshī xiūxī* 'teacher rest'. When this VP merges with the nominal head *-shì* 'room', the [+affix] feature of *-shi* triggers the head V of VP to raise to *-n* position and forms the surface structure [*jiāoshī* [*xiūxī-shì*]] (e.g., Fig. 5).

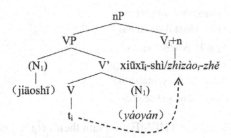

Fig. 5. Similar derivation of yáoyán-zhìzào-zhe and jiaoshi-xiuxi-shì

It is important to note that, according to the Right-Hand Head Rule, the head of a synthetic compound selects its complement leftwards and is usually filled by a (semi-) affix such as *-zhě/-shì/-jī/-rì*, which also takes on some of the thematic roles of the verb. As shown in Fig. (5), the nominal head *-zhě* 'person' is not in the VP but is still the AGENT of the verb semantically. On the other hand, these (semi-)affixes cannot enter the phonetic form (PF) on their own. It indicates that *-n* requires having a verb (not a VP) attached to it, so the [+affix] feature of *-n* triggers the closest V to raise to its position. Some scholars have suggested that N_1 in synthetic compounds undergoes incorporation because it does not receive a case. [8.9] The introduction of the 'Case Filter' provides a motivation for the movement of object nouns, but the movement can only take place from the bottom up. Such analysis cannot cope with the subject noun whose position is higher than the verb (4b), nor can it explain other thematic roles such as TIME and LOCATIVE that have a higher position. Thus, we argue that the Case Filte is not involved in the construction of synthetic compound words.

3.1 Tri-Argument Synthetic Compounds

We have identified a type of Chinese synthetic compound words that can strongly support the analysis of verb raising. Taking *értóng-yīngyǔ-xuéxí-jī* 'children-English-learn-machine' in (4a) as an example, there are three thematic roles in this structure. The *értóng* is AGENT, *yīngyǔ* is THEME, and *jī* is TOOL. We refer to this kind of phenomenon as 'Tri-argument synthetic compounds'.

(4) a. értóng-yīngyǔ-xuéxí-jī   'children-English-learn-machine'

jiāoshī-lǐlùn-yántǎo-bān   'teacher-theory-disscus-class'

lìnsèguǐ-yágāo-jǐchū-qì   'miser-toothpaste-squeeze-tool'

b. *értóng-xuéxí-yīngyǔ-jī

*jiāoshī-yántǎo-lǐlùn-bān

*lìnsèguǐ-jǐchū-yágāo-qì

c. *yīngyǔ-xuéxí-értóng-jī

*lǐlùn-yántǎo-jiāoshī-bān

*yágāo-jǐchū-lìnsèguǐ-qì

d. *yīngyǔ-értóng-xuéxí-jī

*lǐlùn-jiāoshī-yántǎo-bān

*yágāo-lìnsèguǐ-jǐchū-qì

In (4a), the AGENT and the THEME maintain their original positional relation. But there is no verb between them, suggesting that the verb has been moved. In addition, the N_3 in (4a) should be a non-core thematic role such as TIME or TOOL, which is generally considered to be outside the VP and guided by a preposition in the sentence. These phenomena support our structural analysis of synthetic compounds. The structure (4a) is formed by merging VP with a nominal head -n. The AGENT and the THEME are generated within the VP, and the non-core thematic roles such as TOOL and LOCATIVE are generated outside the VP and associated with the nominal head -n. After the VP is merged with -n, the [+affix] feature raises the verb to position -n and produces the correct linear order.

In the case of *értóng-yīngyǔ-xuéxí-jī* the nominal head -$jī$ takes the VP *értóng-xuéxí-yīngyǔ* as its complement leftwards. Then the V *xuéxí* raises to the -n position, forming *értóng-yīngyǔ-xuéxí-jī*. If the V *xuéxí* doesn't raise, it will result in an illegal form as shown in (4b) **értóng-xuéxí-yīngyǔ-jī*. If we adopt incorporation analysis to change the positions of internal and external arguments, it will lead to another ill-formed structure as demonstrated in (4c) **yīngyǔ-xuéxí-értóng-jī*. Finally, some studies have denied the existence of an argument-verb relationship in synthetic compounds, arguing that only a modifying relationship between the components exists. If the relationship between *értóng* 'children', *yīngyǔ* 'English', and *xuéxíjī* 'learning machine' were simply that of modifiers and head, the order of the two modifiers can be reversed. But only the AGENT-THEME form in (4a) is acceptable, and the THEME-AGENT structure in (4d) is illegitimate.

The constraints of arguments in synthetic compounds are not only related to the modifier N_1 but also involve the nominal head N_2 or N_3. We can summarize that Chinese synthetic compounds are constrained by the following rules: (1) N_1 can be either the THEME (*yáoyán-zhìzào-zhě* 'rumor make-er') or the AGENT (*jiāoshī-xiūxī-shì* '**teacher** rest room'), but it cannot be other thematic roles such as TIME, LOCATIVE, or TOOL that generated outside the VP; (2) N_2 can be either the AGENT (*qìchē-xiūlǐ-gōng* 'car repair **man**') or a non-core thematic role such as TIME (*yēsū-shòunán-rì* 'jesus sacrifice **day**/Good Friday'), LOCATIVE (*értóng-yóuyǒng-chí* 'children swimming **pool**'), or TOOL (*yīngyǔ-xuéxí-jī* 'English learning **machine**'), but cannot be THEME, which is generated under the verb; (3) When three nominal constituents are presented in the structure, the semantic relationship is 'AGENT + THEME + TOOL/ LOCATIVE/ TIME…'. All of these phenomena can be successfully predicted by UTAH and verb-raising analysis but cannot be explained with modifier-head analysis.

3.2 Cross-Linguistic Evidence

Though the discussion above focuses on Chinese, the verb-raising analysis is not only specific to Chinese. Based on a cross-linguistic perspective, verb-raising analysis can also be used to explain the construction mechanism of synthetic compounds in other languages, even in an SOV language.

Taking the *truck driver* in English as an example, when the VP *drive truck* merges with the nominal affix *-er*, the verb *drive* is attracted to the *-n* position, forming [*truck* [*driv-er*]]. According to Harley, the internal structure of *truck driver* is [[*truck driv*]-*er*], in which the stem and affix of *driver* are separated into two different syntactic hierarchies. The structure of analysis proposed in the current paper is more acceptable. Meanwhile, our new analysis denies Harley's [8] assumption of a 'Case Filter', suggesting that the movement is triggered by the [+affix] feature of the *-er* (Fig. 6).

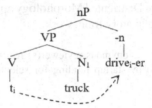

Fig. 6. Verb raising analysis of truck driver

We then test the applicability of the verb-raising analysis in Japanese, an SOV language. For instance, in *shoseki-shuppan-kaisha* 'book publish company', the verb *shuppan* is merged with its complement *shoseki*, forming a VP *shoseki shuppan*. If incorporation analysis is adopted here, it will lead to the transposition of *shoseki* and *shuppan*, forming a new stem **shuppan-shoseki* that does not correspond to the linear order of the synthetic compound. However, the correct linear structure [*shoseki*-[*shuppan-kaisha*]] can be deduced if we assume that the verb is raised to the *-n* position after the VP *shoseki shuppan* is merged with the nominal head *-n* (Fig. 7).

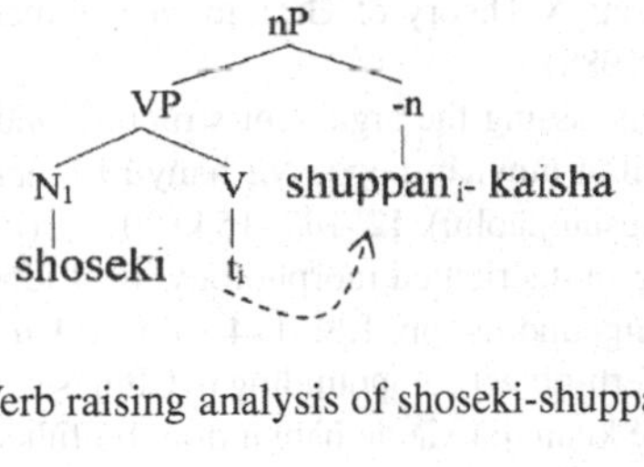

nP

VP   -n

N₁   V   shuppan ᵢ- kaisha

shoseki   tᵢ

Fig. 7. Verb raising analysis of shoseki-shuppan-kaisha

230 Z. Chen et al.

4 Conclusion

This paper proposes a verb-raising analysis scheme to explain the construction mechanism of synthetic compounds. The synthetic compound is headed by a nominal affix -n, which selects a VP as its complement leftwards. Then the [+affix] feature of -n triggers the V to raise to the -n position, forming the surface linear order. This analysis can explain the asymmetry between argument structure and linear structure in synthetic compound words and other relevant issues. It provides an effective explanation of different types of synthetic compounds in Chinese and is also supported by compound words in other languages such as English and Japanese.

The phenomenon of synthetic compounds is an important window for exploring the relationship between syntax and morphology. Some previous studies emphasize the independence of lexical formation [10, 11, etc.], while others argue that there is no divide between the construction mechanisms of synthetic compounds and phrases [8, 9, etc.]. This paper proposes that word formation and syntactic rule are parallel in some respects (e.g., UTAH and bottom-up movement). This approach is more beneficial in explaining the synthetic compound phenomenon. We acknowledge that word formation holds its own characteristics, such as following the Right-Hand Head Rule and not being subject to Case Filter. Compared with the Distributed Morphology approach, the proposed analysis provides a more powerful explanatory framework.

Acknowledgment. We thank the anonymous reviewer(s) for their helpful comments and suggestions. Rui Liu was supported by startup funding for scientific research of BNUZ (12900-310432118).

References

1. Lieber, R.: Deconstructing Morphology. University of Chicago Press, Chicago (1992)
2. Spencer, A.: Morphological Theory: An Introduction to Word Structure in Generative Grammar. Wiley Blackwell (1991)
3. He, Y.-J.: The loop theory in Chinese morphology (huíhuán lǐlùn yǔ hànyǔ gòucífǎ). Contemp. Ling. (dāngdài yǔyánxué) **3**, 223–235 (2004). (in Chinese)
4. Gu, Y., Shen, Y.: The derivation of synthetic compounds in Chinese (hànyǔ héchéngfùhécí de gòuzào guòchéng). Chin. Lang. (zhōngguó yǔwén) **2**, 122–133 (2001). (in Chinese)
5. Cheng, G.: *Zhe* (er) synthetic compounds in Chinese and their implications for UG (hànyǔ 'zhě' zì héchéngfùhécí jíqí duì pǔbiànyǔfǎ de qǐshì). Modern Foreign Languages (xiàndài wàiyǔ). **3**, 232–238 (2005). (in Chinese)
6. Baker, M.C.: Incorporation: A Theory of Grammatical Function Changing. University of Chicago Press, Chicago (1988)
7. Hong, S., Shen, Y.: Re-discussing the argument structure and the construction of Chinese synthetic compounds (zàilùn lùnyuán jiégòu yǔ hànyǔ héchéngfùhécí de gòuzào xíngshì). Academic Exchanges (xuéshù jiāoliú). **12**, 147–154 (2014). (in Chinese)
8. Harley, H.: Compounding in distributed morphology. In: Lieber, R., Stekauer, P. (eds.) The Oxford Handbook of Compounding, pp. 129–144. Oxford University Press, Oxford (2008)
9. Cheng, G., Zhou, G.-L.: Verb-object compounding in Chinese: A distributed morphology approach (fēnbùshìxíngtàixué kuàngjià xià de hànyǔ dòngbīnfùhécí yánjiū). Fore. Lang. Teach. Res. (wàiyǔ jiāoxué yánjiū) **47**(2), 163–175 (2015). (in Chinese)

10. Wang, H.-J.: The relations between the number of syllable, the tonal range of pitch and the grammatical structure in Chinese (yīnjiē dānshuāng, yīnyù zhǎnliǎn(zhòngyīn) yǔ yǔfǎjiégòulèixíng hé chéngfèn cìxù). Contemp. Ling. (dāngdài yǔyánxué) 3(4), 241–252 (2001). (in Chinese)
11. Shi, D.-X.: Chinese attributive V-N compounds (hànyǔ de dìngzhōng guānxì dòng-míng héchéngfùhécí). Chin. Lang. (zhōngguó yǔwén) 6, 483–495 (2003). (in Chinese)
12. Di Sciullo, A.M.: Williams, E.: On the Definition of Word, vol. 14. MIT Press, Cambridge, MA (1987)
13. Williams, E.: On the notions 'Lexically related' and 'Head of a word.' Linguist. Inquiry 12(2), 245–274 (1981)
14. Packard, J.L.: The morphology of Chinese: A linguistic and cognitive approach. Cambridge University Press, Cambridge (2000)

The Construction of Grammatical Synonym Resources of Disyllabic Verbs in Modern Chinese

Tian Shao[✉], Gaoqi Rao, and Endong Xun[✉]

Beijing Language and Culture University, Beijing, China
shaotian2017@163.com, edxun@126.com

Abstract. At present, there are about two shortcomings in the resources of Chinese synonyms. One is that there are no synonym resources specifically for verbs. The other is that scholars usually pay too much attention to the conceptual meaning of synonyms and ignore the grammatical meaning of synonyms. These two shortcomings may lead to inapplicability when applying synonym resources. Therefore, we are oriented toward verbs, consider conceptual and grammatical meanings, and construct grammatical synonym resources for verbs. Firstly, we formulated the *Grammatical Synonym Annotation specification for Modern Chinese Disyllabic Verbs*. Secondly, we constructed a collection of modern Chinese disyllabic verbs depending on the current research results. Finally, we took the annotation specification as the standard, referred to the related resources and the performance of verbs in the corpus, and built the grammatical synonym resources for modern Chinese disyllabic verbs. After forming the annotation team, it took us fourteen months to complete the annotation task. This paper provides high-quality data for natural language processing and dramatically improves the accuracy of sentence-level retelling.

Keywords: Annotation Specification · Disyllable Verb · Grammatical Synonym

1 Introduction

The verb is the core of a sentence. According to Lu, C. [1], the verb can connect other components within the sentence, such as the subject, object, adverbial, and complement. Therefore, sentence-level retelling can be achieved by replacing the core verb. However, sentence-level retelling is not only related to the conceptual meaning of the verb, but the grammatical meaning is also significant. In the retelling sentence obtained by replacing the core verb, if the two verbs are only similar in conceptual meaning but not similar in grammatical meaning, the retelling sentence may also be incorrect. For example:

(1) 建设社会主义文化强国的宏伟目标 鼓舞 人心。
     *Jiànshè shèhuì zhǔyì wénhuà qiángguó de hóngwěi mùbīao **gǔwǔ** rénxīn.*
     The grand goal of building a socialist cultural power is inspiring.

Q. Su et al. (Eds.): CLSW 2022, LNAI 13496, pp. 232–246, 2023.
https://doi.org/10.1007/978-3-031-28956-9_19

(2) *[1]建设社会主义文化强国的宏伟目标 鼓劲 人心。

    *Jiànshè shèhuì zhǔyì wénhuà qiángguó de hóngweǐ mùbīao **gǔjìn** rénxīn.

    *The grand goal of building a socialist cultural power rouses people's enthusiasm.

From examples 1–2 and the paraphrases of 鼓舞(gǔwǔ, inspire) and 鼓劲(gǔjìn, rouse one's enthusiasm) in *the Modern Chinese Dictionary* [2], we can know that both words have the conceptual meaning of 使振作起来(shǐ zhènzuò qǐlái, to cheer up). However, the grammatical meaning of the two is not the same. The difference in grammatical meaning between the two words is that 鼓舞(gǔwǔ, inspire) is a transitive verb that an object can follow. While 鼓劲(gǔjìn, rouse one's enthusiasm) is an intransitive verb that an object cannot follow. Although the two verbs have the same conceptual meaning, the grammatical meanings of the two words are different. Therefore, the retelling sentence obtained by replacing the core verb is incorrect.

(3) 国家 鼓励 企业开展个性化定制。

    *Guójiā **gǔlì** qǐyè kāizhǎn gèxìnghuà dìngzhì.

    The state encourages enterprises to carry out personalized customization.

(4) *国家 砥砺 企业开展个性化定制。

    *Guójiā **dǐlì** qǐyè kāizhǎn gèxìnghuà dìngzhì.

    *The state encourages enterprises to carry out personalized customization.

Similarly, as we can see from examples 3–4 and the paraphrases of 鼓励(gǔlì, encourage) and 砥砺(dǐlì, encourage) in *the Modern Chinese Dictionary* [2], both words have the conceptual meaning of 勉励(miǎnlì, encourage). Moreover, 鼓励(gǔlì, encourage) and 砥砺(dǐlì, encourage) are transitive verbs that an object can follow. However, they are used in different styles. This difference also results in the inaccurate retelling of sentences obtained by replacing the core verb.

From the above examples, we know that the reason for the inaccuracy of the retelling sentence is that scholars do not pay enough attention to the grammatical meaning of words during the construction of synonyms. Therefore, from the perspective of retelling, we focus on verbs and consider the conceptual and grammatical meanings to construct the grammatical synonym resources of modern Chinese disyllabic verbs. First, we formulate the *Grammatical Synonym Annotation specification for Modern Chinese Disyllabic Verbs* and set up a stable annotation team. Secondly, we synthesize the current research results to construct a collection of modern Chinese disyllabic verbs. Finally, the grammatical synonym resources of modern Chinese disyllabic verbs are constructed by referring to the resources such as *the Synonym Word Forest* [3], *HowNet* [4], *the Modern Chinese Classification Dictionary* [5–7], and *the Concise Chinese Dictionary of Meaningful Classes* [8], and the performance of verbs in the Beijing Language and Culture University Corpus Center (BCC) [9]. The obtained resources provide high-quality data for natural language processing and significantly improve the accuracy of sentence-level retelling.

---

[1] The symbol indicates that the accuracy of this sentence is not high.

234 T. Shao et al.

2 Related Research

In this section, we will introduce the related research from the perspectives of computational linguistics and linguistics.

In computational linguistics, many resources are related to the construction of semantic synonyms, such as *the Synonym Word Forest* [3], *HowNet* [4], and *ChineseSemanticKB* [10].

The Synonym Word Forest [3] is the first dictionary of Chinese words with similar meanings. "A dictionary of Chinese words with similar meanings is a repository of words that categorizes words within a language system according to the concept they represent, and words that represent the same concept are organized into a word group" [11]. *The Synonym Word Forest* [3] divides the collected units into twelve categories according to the logical and conceptual meanings of the words. However, *the Synonym Word Forest* [3] only considers the conceptual meaning between words but ignores the grammatical meaning. Therefore, it cannot meet the needs for the automatic generation of retelling sentences.

HowNet [4] contains the synonym set and the antonym label set. However, *HowNet* [4] does not distinguish the part of speech of words. Furthermore, it only contains a set of labels for antonyms, so it does not explicitly list which words have antonymous relations with each other. In addition, *HowNet* [4] also only considers the conceptual meaning between words.

ChineseSemanticKB [10] lists the synonyms and antonyms of words according to the senses of a word. However, in *ChineseSemanticKB* [10], the criteria for distinguishing the senses of words are uncertain. For example, 做事(*zuòshì*, doing things) has only one sense in *the Modern Chinese Dictionary* [2], however, it is listed 38 times in the synonym database of *ChineseSemanticKB* [10]. When the senses of the synonyms of verbs are not consistent with the senses of verbs in the dictionary, it will have a negative effect on the subsequent application.

In addition, the classification system, such as *the Modern Chinese Classification Dictionary* [5–7] and *the Concise Chinese Dictionary of Meaningful Classes* [8], is similar to *the Synonym Word Forest* [3]. Furthermore, Li, J. [12] investigates the near-synonyms discrimination resources, such as learning dictionaries, corpora, and online learning platforms. However, the lack of open electronic resources makes it highly inconvenient to use.

In linguistics, many scholars research the synonyms of one word or the semantic contrast between two words of similar meaning. For example, Wang, X [13] researches the discrimination of the synonyms of 引起(*yǐnqǐ*, cause), and Li, W. [14] researches the comparison and sense induction of temporal adverbs 仍(*réng*, still) and 还(*hái*, still). Moreover, Li, L. [15] researches the changes manifested in the diachronic changes of reform-related Chinese near-synonyms.

This paper considers the conceptual and grammatical meanings and constructs the grammatical synonym resources for verbs. Firstly, we integrate the current synonym resources. Then, we formulate the annotation specification, implement annotation tasks, and construct synonyms of conceptual and grammatical meanings of verbs.

3 Data Overview

The grammatical synonym resources of verbs constructed in this paper is based on the verbs in *the Modern Chinese Dictionary* [2]. In addition, we integrate the verbs and synonyms listed in *the Synonym Word Forest* [3], *HowNet* [4], and *ChineseSemanticKB* [10], as well as online resources such as *Chinese Dictionary* [16], *Baidu Chinese* [17], and *Online Word Forest* [18], as the initial resources of annotation tasks.

The *Modern Chinese Dictionary* [2] contains 18,209 verbs, including 1,805 monosyllabic verbs, 16,064 disyllabic verbs, 330 trisyllabic verbs, and 10 four-syllabic verbs. The number of verbs included in *the Modern Chinese Dictionary* [2] is compared with the number of verbs included in *the Synonym Word Forest* [3], *HowNet* [4], and *ChineseSemanticKB* [10]. Table 1 shows the comparison results of the number of verbs in the above dictionaries.

Table 1. The comparison results of the number of verbs in several dictionaries.

The name of the resource	The number of the verb	The same number of verbs	Number of verbs not listed in the dictionary
The Modern Chinese Dictionary	18209	–	–
The Synonym Word Forest	15970	9700	8509
HowNet	–	9750	8459
ChineseSemanticKB	–	10226	7983

The *Synonym Word Forest* [3] contains about 70,000 words, of which 15,970 are verbs. A comparison with the verbs in *the Modern Chinese Dictionary* [2] shows that only 9,700 verbs overlap between the two, and the remaining 8,509 verbs in *the Modern Chinese Dictionary* [2] are not listed in *the Synonym Word Forest* [3].

HowNet [4] includes 17,288 synonym sets and 492 antonym tag sets. However, *HowNet* [4] does not distinguish the part of speech of words, so the number of verbs it contains cannot be determined temporarily. A comparison with the verbs in *the Modern Chinese Dictionary* [2] shows that only 9,750 verbs overlap between the two, and the remaining 8,459 verbs in *the Modern Chinese Dictionary* [2] are not listed in *HowNet* [4].

ChineseSemanticKB [10] contains 424,826 pairs of words with synonyms and 34,380 pairs of words with antonyms. Similarly, it does not distinguish the part of speech of words. A comparison with the verbs in *the Modern Chinese Dictionary* [2] shows that 10,226 verbs overlap between the two, and the remaining 7,983 verbs in *the Modern Chinese Dictionary* [2] are not listed in *ChineseSemanticKB* [10].

After synthesizing the above verb resources, we get 23,712 verbs, of which 21,566 are disyllabic. Since disyllabic verbs occupy the majority of verbs, we take disyllabic verbs as the starting point and gradually expand to monosyllabic, trisyllabic, and four-syllabic verbs. In addition, the verb synonym resources listed in various resources are merged and used as the basic resources for this annotation task.

4 The Annotation Principles and the Specification for Grammatical Synonyms of Modern Chinese Disyllabic Verbs

Formulating the annotation specification is the most critical and challenging task in the process of annotation. A scientific and perfect annotation specification is essential for annotated data to meet the desired goals and ensure consistency and accuracy of the annotated data. At the same time, as the guiding ideology of formulating an annotation specification and implementing annotation tasks, annotation principles also play an essential role in the whole process of annotation.

4.1 The Annotation Principles

In order to keep the annotated results consistent with the desired goals, this annotation specification has one general principle and three main principles. The general principle is that the synonyms of the verb must be verbs. The three main principles are as follows. First, the verb and its synonyms are semantically similar. Second, the verb and its synonyms are grammatically replaceable. Third, the sentence's meaning after the replacement has not changed substantially.

The verb is the core of a sentence, and the grammatical meaning of the word in the same part of speech is similar. Therefore, this annotation specification limits the synonyms must be verbs. When judging the synonyms of verbs, the annotators should consider the conceptual meaning, grammatical meaning, emotional meaning, pragmatic environment, and other factors of verbs. Among them, conceptual meaning plays a dominant role. We also focus on grammatical meaning (whether two verbs can be replaced in the same position in the sentence) and consider the language environment and emotional meaning. Therefore, the main principle of this annotation task is to focus on whether synonyms can be replaced in the same syntactic position in a similar context without substantial semantic changes on the premise of similar conceptual meanings.

To construct relatively complete verb resources, we also construct the grammatical antonym resources of verbs.

4.2 The Annotation Specification

Formulating the annotation specification under the guidance of annotation principles, we need to focus on several questions: how to determine the part of speech of a word and the senses of a verb, and whether a word is a grammatical synonym or antonym of a verb. At the same time, these questions also reflect the process of labelling the grammatical synonyms and antonyms of verbs. The process of labelling the grammatical synonyms of the verb is shown in Fig. 1.

Firstly, according to the Modern Chinese Dictionary [2] and other dictionaries, we can determine whether a word is a verb. Secondly, the senses of a verb are also determined

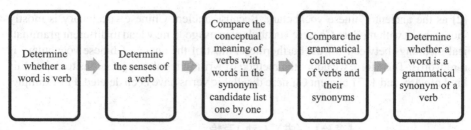

Fig. 1. The process of labeling the grammatical synonyms of the verb.

based on the dictionary. Thirdly, according to the paraphrase of *the Modern Chinese Dictionary* [2], we can compare the conceptual meaning of words. Then we go to BCC [9] to compare the grammatical collocation of the verb and synonym candidates, that is, whether they can be replaced in a similar context and whether the sentence semantics change substantially. Finally, according to the results of the above steps, we can determine whether the candidate word is a grammatical synonym of the verb. The labelling of grammatical antonyms of a verb is the same as the above steps. In the following, we will introduce the *Grammatical Synonym Annotation specification for Modern Chinese Disyllabic Verbs* from the above steps.

The Determination of Whether a Word is a Verb. In this paper, the verb is limited to the words marked as "{动(*dòng*, verb)}" in *the Modern Chinese Dictionary* [2]. At the same time, we also integrate the disyllabic verbs included in synonym resources such as *the Synonym Word Forest* [3], *HowNet* [4], and *ChineseSemanticKB* [10] for the supplement. However, there are unclear boundaries between words and phrases. Furthermore, verbs may be ancient Chinese vocabulary. Therefore, this annotation specification draws on some methods of distinguishing words and phrases. At the same time, since the current processing object of natural language processing is the modern language, ancient Chinese vocabulary is also deleted.

The Treatment of Phrases. Because the grammatical meaning of a phrase is inconsistent with that of a word, and the grammatical expression of the two in a sentence is also different. Therefore, it is necessary to distinguish between words and phrases.

We mainly refer to two classical methods in linguistics to distinguish between words and phrases. One is the case that the word meaning has integrity, and the overall meaning is not a simple addition of its morpheme meanings. However, the meaning of a phrase is a simple addition of its partial meanings. The other is whether there is a semantic change after inserting other components in the middle. In general, the semantic meaning of a word changes after inserting other elements into the middle of the word. In contrast, the semantic meaning of a phrase usually remains unchanged after inserting other components into the middle of the phrase.

In addition, two particular phrases are judged as words. First, idioms are not treated as phrases but are treated as words. Second, 不予(*bùyǔ*, refuse) is the structure of "word + non-morpheme", and this annotation specification treats similar structures as words.

The Treatment of Ancient Chinese Vocabulary. This annotation specification regards the verbs marked as "<书(*shū*, written language)>" in *the Modern Chinese Dictionary*

[2] as the ancient Chinese vocabulary. Because ancient Chinese vocabulary is mostly inconsistent with modern Chinese vocabulary in usage, it may lead to different grammatical meanings between words. Furthermore, most of the ancient Chinese vocabulary is rare words. Therefore, we adopt the method of writing regular expressions to delete this kind of verb, and 1171 ancient Chinese disyllabic verbs have been deleted. For example:

【哀矜】 〈书〉 { 动 }哀怜。

【*āijīn*】 〈*shū*〉 { *dòng* } *āilián*.

【Pity】 〈written language〉 { verb } pity.

The Determination of the Senses of a Verb. After determining that a word is a verb, the next step is determining the senses of a verb. This annotation specification takes the senses of the verb marked in *the Modern Chinese Dictionary* [2] as the standard, and individual verbs are slightly modified. In addition, if the verb is not included in *the Modern Chinese Dictionary* [2], the annotators need to check online resources such as *Chinese Dictionary* [16], *Baidu Chinese* [17], and *Online Word Forest* [18].

The Determination of the Number of Senses of a Verb. The senses of a verb listed in *the Modern Chinese Dictionary* [2] are the criterion for judging the number of senses of a verb in this annotation specification. However, if the senses of the verb cannot be distinguished in the context, the senses can be combined. For example, 传达(*chuándá*, convey) has two senses. The speakers not only do not distinguish the two senses in context, but the semantics expressed by the two senses are consistent in any context. Therefore, the senses ① and ② of 传达(*chuándá*, convey) are combined. At the same time, the verbs of the combined senses are recorded to provide a reference for lexicography.

【传达】①{动}把一方的意思告诉给另一方：传达命令 | 传达上级的指示②{动}在机关、学校、工厂的门口管理登记和引导来宾的工作：传达室|您在门口等着，我给您传达去。

【*chuándá*】 ①{ *dòng* } *bǎ yìfāng de yìsi gàosù gěi lìngyìfāng* : *chuándá mìnglìng* | *chuándá shàngjí de zhǐshì*.②{ *dòng* } *zài jīguān xuéxiào gōngchǎng de ménkǒu guǎnlǐ dēngjì hé yǐndǎo láibīn de gōngzuò*:*chuándáshì*| *nín zài ménkǒu děng zhe, wǒ gěi nín chuándá qù*.

【Convey】 ①{ verb} Tell one person's meaning to another: convey orders|convey the instructions of superiors. ②{ verb} the work of managing registrations and guiding guests at the entrance of institutions, schools, and factories: reception office| wait at the door, I will convey it to you.

The Treatment of Polysemous Verbs. If the verb is a polysemy verb, firstly, we use "[S1 S2... Sn]" to indicate the number of senses, and then use "Syn_1, Syn_2... Syn_n" to indicate the grammatical synonyms under each sense of the verb. For example, 找事(*zhǎoshì*, find a job and pick a quarrel) has two senses in *the Modern Chinese Dictionary* [2], so the grammatical synonyms of the two senses of 找事(*zhǎoshì*, find a job and pick a quarrel) are listed respectively.

【找事】{动}①寻找职业②故意挑毛病，引起争吵；寻衅。

【*zhǎoshì*】{ *dòng* }①*xúnzhǎo zhíyè* ②*gùyì tiáo miáobìng，yǐnqǐ zhēngchǎo；xúnxìn.*

【Find a job and pick a quarrel】{ verb }①find a job.②deliberately provoke problems, cause quarrels; provocation.

@找事(*zhǎoshì*, find a job and pick a quarrel)

.([S1 S2] {Sem})

.([求职 谋事 谋职 求业] {Syn_1})

.([*qiúzhí móushì móuzhí qiúyè*] {Syn_1})

.([find a job, find a job, find a job)] {Syn_1})

.([寻事 滋事 找碴儿 找茬 找碴 找茬儿 找麻烦] {Syn_2})

.([*xúnshì zīshì zhǎochaer zhǎochá zhǎochá zhǎochaer zhǎomáfán*] {Syn_2})

.([pick a quarrel, pick a quarrel, pick a quarrel, pick a quarrel, pick a quarrel, pick a quarrel, pick a quarrel)] {Syn_2})

Besides, if the synonym of a verb is a polysemous verb, we use serial number "① ②..." to indicate which sense of the polysemous verb is the grammatical synonym of the other verb. For example, "找事(*zhǎoshì*, find a job and pick a quarrel)①" is one of the grammatical synonyms of 求职(*qiúzhí*, find a job).

The Treatment of Polysyllabic Verbs. In the annotation specification, polysyllabic words are labelled as "word1 word2... wordn" according to the order in which they appear in the dictionary. At the same time, homophonous polysemy is also treated in the same way.

Therefore, if we need to locate a sense of a polysyllabic word or homophonous polysemy word, we can use the double serial number "word1①" to locate it. For example, we can use "透析(*tòuxī*, dialysis)2①" to locate the first sense in the second syllable of the homophonous polysemy word 透析(*tòuxī*, thoroughly analyze and dialysis).

【透析】1 {动}透彻分析。

【*tòuxī*】1 { *dòng* }*tòuchè fēnxī*.

【Thoroughly analyze】1 { verb } thoroughly analyze.

【透析】2 {动}①渗析 ②医学上指利用渗析技术把体液中的毒素和代谢产物排出体外。

【*tòuxī*】2 { *dòng* }①*shènxī* ②*yīxué shàng zhǐ lìyòng shènxī jìshù bǎ tǐyè zhōng de dúsù hé dàixiè chǎnwù páichū tǐwài*.

【Dialysis】2 { verb }①dialysis ②In medicine, it refers to the use of dialysis technology to expel toxins and metabolites from body fluids.

The Determination of Synonyms. In the annotation task, the most crucial step is how to determine the grammatical synonyms of verbs. This annotation specification is mainly based on the following standards.

The Relationship Between Conceptual Meaning and Word Meaning. Sometimes the conceptual meaning is not entirely equivalent to the word meaning, which may be more or less. Therefore, this should be taken into account in the process of annotation. For example, the primary meaning of 呐喊(*nàhǎn*, yell) is 大声喊叫(*dàshēng hǎjiào*, loud shouting) and 助威(*zhùwēi*, cheer) is an extensional meaning.

【呐喊】{动}大声喊叫助威。

【*nàhǎn*】{ *dòng* } *dàshēng hǎjiào zhùwēi*.

【Yell】{ verb } loud shouting to cheer.

Based on the Conceptual Meaning and Verified by Grammatical Meaning.
Based on the similar conceptual meaning, the candidate synonyms of the verb and their performance in the corpus are investigated in BCC [9]. We can use the comparative search function of the BCC [9] to examine the similarity of grammatical meaning between verbs and their synonym candidates in turn. For example, if we search for 鼓励(*gǔlì*, encourage) and 砥砺(*dǐlì*, encourage) followed by a noun, the comparison result is shown in Fig. 2.

The Auxiliary Judgment of the Internal Structure of Verbs. If the internal structure of the verb is verb-object, then in general, it cannot take an object again. Moreover, the structure of the listed synonyms should also be verb-object (only if the verb has synonyms). However, the decisive factor is whether the verb can take an object. For example, the internal structure of 爱国(*àiguó*, love one's country) is verb-object, and it can no longer take an object.

The Determination and Disposition of Hypernym. If the grammatical synonym of the verb is not found, we can expand the scope of the grammatical synonym of the verb and

Bcc | 单一来源中 ∨ | 报刊 ∨ | 鼓励n | 砥砺n | 对比

鼓励企业	2025	砥砺品质	36
鼓励社会	971	砥砺意志	18
鼓励群众	808	砥砺品德	13
鼓励学生	726	砥砺道德	9
鼓励职工	521	砥砺斗志	7
鼓励青年	488	砥砺作风	7
鼓励两国	395	砥砺青春	5

Fig. 2. BCC search example.

find the hypernym of the verb. However, we need to pay attention to two points. One is whether the hypernym of a verb can be replaced with the verb in a similar context and whether the semantic difference is significant. The other is that to find the hypernym of a verb, we usually delete the modifying elements from the paraphrase of the verb. For example:

【哀告(*āigào*, plead bitterly)】{动(*dòng*, verb) }苦苦央告(*kǔkǔ yānggào*, plead bitterly).

【央告(*yānggào*, plead)】{ 动(*dòng*, verb) }央求(*yāngqiú*, plead).

【求告(*qiúgào*, beg)】{ 动(*dòng*, verb) }央告(*yānggào*, plead).

Therefore, the hypernym 央告(*yānggào*, plead) and 求告(*qiúgào*, beg) of 哀告(*āigào*, plead bitterly) are in the grammatical synonym list of 哀告(*āigào*, plead bitterly).

The Determination of Antonyms. Determining the grammatical antonym of the verb is similar to that of a grammatical synonym. In addition, we can use the method of "不(*bù*, not) + verb" for auxiliary judgment, but we need to pay attention to the two points. One is the preference of the subject of the action. First, we prefer that the two actions are the same subject, such as 前进(*qiánjìn*, forward) and 后退(*hòutuì*, backward). Second, we prefer different actions involved in the same event, such as 教(*jiāo*, teach) and 学(*xué*, learn). The other is that antonyms may have multiple angles, and only one angle can be selected. If there is an intermediate state, both ends are preferred.

The Format of the Resources. This annotation specification also specifies the data format of the annotation result. Each verb corresponds to a series of grammatical synonyms according to different senses. The result is a linear sequence, which is different from the tree structure of *the Synonym Word Forest* [3] and the network structure of *HowNet* [4]. Take 找事(*zhǎoshì*, find a job and pick a quarrel) as an example.

@找事(*zhǎoshì*, find a job and pick a quarrel)

.([S1 S2] {Sem})

.([求职 谋事 谋职 求业] {Syn_1})

.([*qiúzhí móushì móuzhí qiúyè*] {Syn_1})

.([find a job, find a job, find a job)] {Syn_1})

.([寻事 滋事 找碴儿 找茬 找碴 找茬儿 找麻烦] {Syn_2})

.([*xúnshì zīshì zhǎochaer zhǎochá zhǎochá zhǎochaer zhǎomáfán*] {Syn_2})

.([pick a quarrel, pick a quarrel, pick a quarrel, pick a quarrel, pick a quarrel, pick a quarrel, pick a quarrel)] {Syn_2})

找事(*zhǎoshì*, find a job and pick a quarrel) has two senses in *the Modern Chinese Dictionary* [2]. The first sense is 寻找职业(*xúnzhǎo zhíyè*, find a job). The second sense is 故意挑毛病(*gùyì tiāo miáobìng*, deliberately provoke problems). The line of "Sem" attribute indicates that the word has two senses: S1 and S2. The followings are the grammatical synonyms listed for these two senses. Grammatical antonyms are also listed in the same format. However, we need to replace the "Sem" tag with the "Anto" tag. It is listed in the form of considering the paraphrase of verb meanings in the dictionary, which is easy to apply to natural language processing.

5   The Implementation of Annotation and the Comparative and Analysis of the Result

In this section, we briefly introduce the implementation process of the annotation task. At the same time, the annotation result of this annotation task is statistically analyzed and compared with *the Synonym Word Forest* [3] and *HowNet* [4].

5.1   The Implementation of Annotation

Balancing annotation quality and speed requires professional annotators, effective quality measurement and feedback mechanisms, and efficient management. The annotation of grammatical synonyms and antonyms of verbs involves semantic and grammatical knowledge of words, which requires professional annotators. Therefore, this annotation task has always maintained a relatively stable annotation team of linguistics majors, with eight people, all of whom are doctoral candidates or postgraduates majoring in linguistics. The annotation task starts in July 2020 and is completed in September 2021, lasting 14 months, with 53 periods calculated according to weeks.

In order to guarantee the quality of data and minimize the subjectivity caused by manual labelling, the grammatical synonyms and antonyms of each verb are respectively marked by two people. We take the week as the unit of calculation in the process of annotation. Weekly documents are randomly distributed to the annotators on the first four days of each week for the first annotation and the second three days for the second annotation and feedback. Two annotators of each period are randomly paired to enhance the authenticity of the first labelling result. In the second annotation, if the annotation opinions of both sides are inconsistent, it will be submitted to the annotation administrator, who will make the final decision. Only when the consistency rate reaches 100% after the second annotation can it be passed. The annotation flow chart is shown in Fig. 3.

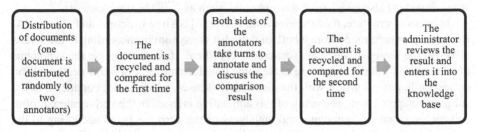

Fig. 3. Annotation flow chart.

The guiding ideology of the consistency comparison code used in this annotation specification is as follows. For each verb, the ratio of the same grammatical synonyms listed by both annotators to the number of all grammatical synonyms listed by both annotators, and sum all verbs and average them. Then, the consistency of the comparison document is obtained. Figure 4 is the dynamic change line chart of the first annotation consistency rate, which shows a dynamic growth trend.

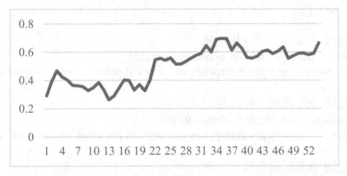

Fig. 4. Dynamic change diagram of consistency rate.

5.2 Comparison and Analysis of the Result

In this subsection, we compare the annotation result with *the Synonym Word Forest* [3] and *HowNet* [4] and analyze the distribution of the senses of the verb in the result.

The Comparison of Result. This annotation builds grammatical synonyms and antonyms for each disyllable verb in modern Chinese according to the senses of the verb. In the annotation results, there are 14,889 disyllable verbs with grammatical synonyms and 8,030 disyllable verbs with grammatical antonyms. However, 2,869 disyllable verbs have neither grammatical synonyms nor antonyms.

In terms of scale, compared with *the Synonym Word Forest* [3] and *HowNet* [4], this annotation result contains 18,430 disyllabic verbs, including 14,889 disyllabic verbs with grammatical synonyms. *HowNet* [4] includes 9,750 disyllabic verbs. However, *the Synonym Word Forest* [3] includes 15,970 disyllabic verbs, which is because *the Synonym Word Forest* [3] also consists of some phrases, such as 不能(*bùnéng*, cannot).

In terms of structure, *the Synonym Word Forest* [3] is a tree structure, and *HowNet* [4] is a network structure. Although both of them list the synonyms according to the senses of verbs, the senses of verbs are scattered everywhere. If we want to get the synonyms of all senses of a verb, we have to make some transformations. Furthermore, there is no corresponding relationship with the dictionary's senses, which is not conducive to the subsequent application. The result of this annotation is listed in the verb-centered form, and the grammatical synonyms and antonyms of the verb are listed according to the order of the dictionary's senses. Corresponding to the conceptual sense in the dictionary, it lays a good foundation for further research.

In addition, the most crucial point of this annotation is that we consider the conceptual and the grammatical meanings of the verb, which solves the problem that synonym resources are inapplicable in use to a certain extent. If we use the annotated list of the verb grammatical synonyms, the accuracy of sentence-level retelling can be significantly improved. For example, the grammatical synonyms of 鼓励(*gǔlì*, encourage) listed by the annotators are 激励(*jīlì*, encourage) and 勉励(*miǎnlì*, encourage). The following examples show that 激励(*jīlì*, encourage), 勉励(*miǎnlì*, encourage), and 鼓励(*gǔlì*, encourage) are inter-replaceable, and the meaning of the sentence does not change substantially.

(1) 国家 鼓励 企业开展个性化定制。
     *Guójiā **gǔlì** qǐyè kāizhǎn gèxìnghuà dìngzhì.*
     The state encourages enterprises to carry out personalized customization.

(2) 国家 激励 企业开展个性化定制。
     *Guójiā **jīlì** qǐyè kāizhǎn gèxìnghuà dìngzhì.*
     The state encourages enterprises to carry out personalized customization.

(3) 国家 勉励 企业开展个性化定制。
     *Guójiā **miǎnlì** qǐyè kāizhǎn gèxìnghuà dìngzhì.*
     The state encourages enterprises to carry out personalized customization.

The Analysis of Result. We also count senses of verbs with grammatical synonyms or antonyms. The result is shown in Fig. 5. Among the 14,889 disyllable verbs with grammatical synonyms, only one sense of 14,427 disyllable verbs has grammatical synonyms, accounting for 97%. Only two senses of 442 disyllable verbs have grammatical synonyms, accounting for 3%. However, only multiple senses of 40 disyllable verbs have grammatical synonyms, which is inconsistent with the senses of verbs in the dictionary. Meanwhile, the sense distribution of grammatical antonyms is not much different from that of grammatical synonyms.

It shows that most modern Chinese disyllabic verbs in usage have only one sense with grammatical synonyms or antonyms, and only very few have two or more senses with grammatical synonyms or antonyms. Therefore, it can be considered the result of grammatical filtering. At the same time, it also shows that although many verbs are polysemy in dictionaries, they tend to use a sense frequently; that is, the use of its meaning has a pronounced tendency.

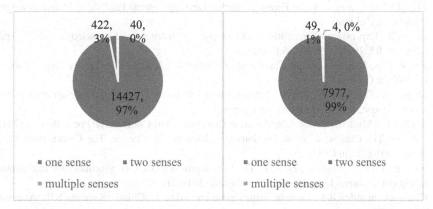

Fig. 5. Statistics of the number of senses of grammatical synonyms and antonyms.

6   Conclusion

Based on disyllabic verbs in *the Modern Chinese Dictionary* [2], we synthesize the resources of *the Synonym Word Forest* [3], *HowNet* [4], and *ChineseSemanticKB* [10] as the basic resources for the annotation tasks. Then we formulate an annotation specification and establish an annotation team. After fourteen months of labelling, the grammatical synonyms and antonyms resources of modern Chinese disyllabic verbs are constructed. Finally, we get 15,561 disyllabic verbs with grammatical synonyms or antonyms. It provides high-quality data resources for natural language processing and dramatically improves the accuracy of sentence-level retelling.

However, there are still several shortcomings in this paper. First, any annotation specification has imperfections. Second, it is challenging to avoid subjectivity in the manual annotation. Third, this annotation specification only distinguishes ancient words from modern Chinese words, and further distinctions can be made by the style. Fourth, verbs can be extended to monosyllabic verbs and polysyllabic verbs. Fifth, it is not rich enough to generate retelling sentences by replacing the core verb. The next step of this study is to improve the above shortcomings and to consider how to make grammatical synonym resources efficient for relevant applications.

Acknowledgments. This paper is supported by BLCU Supported Project for Young Researchers Program (supported by the Fundamental Research Funds for the Central Universities) (22YCX026) and the International Research Fund for Chinese Proficiency Test (CTI2022B03) and the National Natural Science Foundation of China, "Study on the Characterization and Generation Method of Chinese Parataxis Graph" (No.62076038).

References

1. Lu, C.: Chinese parataxis NetWork. Appl. Linguist. **02**, 84–90 (1998). (in Chinese)
2. Dictionary Editorial Office of Institute of Linguistics: The Modern Chinese Dictionary (Seventh Edition). The Commercial Press, Beijing (2016). (in Chinese)
3. Mei, J.: The Synonym Word Forest. Shanghai Lexicographical Publishing House, Shanghai (1983). (in Chinese)
4. Dong, Z.: Expression of semantic relationship and construction of knowledge system. Appl. Linguist. **03**, 79–85 (1998). (in Chinese)
5. Xu, W.: The Modern Chinese Classification Dictionary. Liaoning University Press, Liaoning (1984). (in Chinese)
6. Dong, D.: The Modern Chinese Classification Dictionary. Shanghai Lexicographical Publishing House, Shanghai (1998). (in Chinese)
7. Su, X.: The Modern Chinese Classification Dictionary. The Commercial Press, Beijing (2013)
8. Lin, X.: The Concise Chinese Dictionary of Meaningful Classes. The Commercial Press, Beijing (1987). (in Chinese)
9. Xun, E., Rao, G., Xiao, X., Zang, J.: The Development of BCC corpus under the background of big data. Corpus Linguist. **01**, 93–109+188 (2016). (in Chinese)
10. ChineseSemanticKB Homepage. https://gitee.com/xiaozha/ChineseSemanticKB/. Accessed 31 Sept 2021
11. Bao, K.: Exploration of Chinese Dictionary of similar meanings – after the compilation of the synonym word forest. Lexicographical Studies. **02**, 64–70+152 (1983). (in Chinese)
12. Li, J.: An overview of the construction of near-synonyms discrimination resources. In: Dong, M., Gu, Y., Hong, J.F. (eds.) CLSW 2021. LNCS (LNAI), vol. 13250, pp. 295–305. Springer, Cham (2021). https://doi.org/10.1007/978-3-031-06547-7_23
13. Wang, X., Wang, Y.: The discrimination of the synonyms of yǐnqǐ: a corpus-based study. In: Dong, M., Gu, Y., Hong, J.F. (eds.) CLSW 2021. LNCS (LNAI), vol. 13249, pp. 56–67. Springer, Cham (2021). https://doi.org/10.1007/978-3-031-06703-7_5
14. Li, W.: Comparison and sense induction of temporal adverbs Reng and Hai: a corpus-based study. In: Liu, M., Kit, C., Su, Q. (eds.) CLSW 2020. LNCS (LNAI), vol. 12278, pp. 371–385. Springer, Cham (2021). https://doi.org/10.1007/978-3-030-81197-6_31
15. Li, L., Wang, V.X., Huang, CR.: Social changes manifested in the diachronic changes of reform-related Chinese near synonyms. In: Dong, M., Gu, Y., Hong, J.F. (eds.) CLSW 2021. LNCS(LNAI), vol. 13250, pp. 184–193. Springer, Cham (2021). https://doi.org/10.1007/978-3-031-06547-7_15
16. Chinese Dictionary Homepage. https://www.zdic.net/. Accessed 31 Sept 2021
17. Baidu Chinese Homepage. https://hanyu.baidu.com/. Accessed 31 Sept 2021
18. Online Word Forest Homepage. https://www.cilin.org/jyc/. Accessed 31 Sept 2021

Extraction and Application of Verb Event Structure Based on Grammatical Knowledge-Base of Contemporary Chinese(GKB)

Mengxiang Wang[✉] and Bingxin Li

Teachers' College of Beijing, Union University, Beijing 100010, China
wmx1314-@126.com

Abstract. Although the semantic features of words are hidden deep-seated features, they can generally be shown through the grammatical combination of words. This paper mainly relies on the descriptions of some grammatical features of verbs in GKB, and then extracts the event structure of verbs by features' stacking and filtering. Finally, the authors use those features to construct semantic knowledge base of verbs. Experiments show that the event structure knowledge is useful for machine translation and semantic role labeling.

Keywords: Grammatical Knowledge-Base of Contemporary Chinese (GKB) · Event Structure · Semantic Knowledge Base · Semantic Role Labeling

1 Introduction

There are two common sentences:

(1) I have **had a cold** for 3 days. (This sentence expresses a state that lasts for a while and the durative verb "have" cannot be replaced by the instant verb "catch")
(2) Put on your coat, or you will **catch a cold**. (This is a temporary action, so the verb "catch" is used instead of "have")

Both of the two sentences above express the idea of "catching a cold". There are two different verbs in English to express the event of "catching a cold" in different time structures. However, Chinese use the same verb but often expresses different times structures by adding some additional components to verbs, such as the complement "shang" to indicate the time characteristics inside the two event structures. This shows that "catching a cold" implies two different internal semantic features. Compared with English, the formal representation of such semantic features in Chinese is not obvious, and how to study and extract the inherent semantic features implied by these expressions has always been a difficult subject in the academic.

There are two main ways to induct and extract such semantic characteristics hidden in the words [1, 2]. The one way is that people can use real corpus, to find syntax expression law of a certain semantic feature. Because the relation between syntax and semantics is like that of the appearance and the inherent qualities. The semantic characteristics of words, implied in the inherent qualities, highlight themselves through all sorts of complicated external grammatical combination forms [3]. On the other way, people can use the existing language knowledge database to select some syntactic combination features. For example, if you want to know whether a Chinese verb is "disposal", you can judge according to whether the verb can be put behind "ba". In Chinese, the verb following the preposition "ba" is usually "disposal". In fact, semantic features in words are implicit. If people completely rely on corpus, the extraction of semantic features may be limited due to the size of corpus. Moreover, some occasional or rare grammatical representations in the corpus may bring negative impact on the judgment of certain semantic features. For example, as mentioned above, verbs following the preposition word "ba" are generally disposal. So the verb "guang (walk)" in "ta dai wo ba beijing guang le ge bian (He took me around Beijing)" is connected with "ba", but the verb "guang(walk)" is not disposal. Therefore, a high-quality language knowledge database will be very useful to extract semantic features from words. Compared with several existing Chinese knowledge databases [4], the Grammatical Knowledge-Base of Contemporary Chinese (GKB) is chosen by us. The GKB makes a detailed description of the grammatical features of Chinese words, which is compiled by Yu Shiwen's group of Peking University as proposed in [5]. In GKB, the grammatical functions and grammatical features of the verb amount to as many as 50, which is of high quality and has been in use in several organizations that offer to feedback. It can be said that GKB is the most comprehensive dictionary to record Chinese grammatical features in the field of Chinese information processing.

Compared with the semantic features, the grammatical features of Chinese are more stable, and the change of grammatical representation is not obvious. Based on this, this paper chooses the grammatical information of some marked words in the GKB to generate the event structure features of the Chinese verbs through the superposition of grammatical combination features, and classifies the event structure of verbs. At the same time, this paper also aims to show the role of the GKB in semantic feature extraction, especially in natural language processing research, and to provide reference for the academic community to make better use of the GBK.

2   Relevant Theoretical Background

Event structure theory originated from the Western. Generally speaking, event structure mainly focuses on two things, one is the internal semantic features of words, the other is the syntactic features [6].

The early event structure theory focused on the aspect structure of predicates [7, 8]. The aspect structure of predicate is actually refer to a temporal structure of related verbs. Therefore, the structure of event was initially described as the temporal structure of verbs. It is generally admitted that the study of events structure began with Vendler [9, 10]. In 1957, Vendler divided English verbs into four categories according to their internal temporal characteristics and logical implications. They are: Status verbs (such as: love, know, care, etc.), Activity verbs (such as: swing, move, run, etc.), Accomplishment verbs (such as: die, appear, participate, etc.), and Achievement verbs (such as construct, produce, etc.). That was the earliest classifications of verbs' events and the most influential classification of verb modality types so far.

However, some scholars believe that the event structure theory comes from the American philosopher and logician Donald Davidson's event theory [11]. In 1967, Davidson described natural language in terms of first-order logic, formal symbols and computation. While the event of language is mainly a logic concept which contained the internal event structure with temporal meaning.

It can be seen that the event structure theory was related to temporal structure. The later event structure theory focused on the internal structure of individual verbs. For example, McCawley (1968) [12] decomposed the verb "kill" into four components: "Cause, Become, Not, and Alive". What is more, the event structure theory also used to pay attention to the external structure of verbs and syntactic components. Jackendoff [13, 14] and David Dowty [15] studied the deconstruction of lexical semantics within the framework of generative semantics, trying to make semantic representation with syntactic tree. The former was from verb to sentence to find the event structure features of verbs, while the latter was from sentence to verb to represent semantic facts. These two approaches complemented each other, and they were combined with syntactic research to form the modern event structure theory.

Pustejovsky first introduced the event structure theory into the field of computational linguistics [16–19]. According to the three categories of event structure, he tried to divide verbs into 3 types: Status (for example: "like"), Process (for example: "run") and Transition (for example: "build"), the corresponding event structure features of each verb are described in his "Generative Lexicon Theory (GLT)", which is also the idea of combining the internal structure of lexical items with syntactic research.

It should be noted that since the event structure theory is based on English and combined with the cognitive characteristics of westerners, it needs to be re-examined when it is applied to Chinese. Due to the cultural differences between the East and the West, people's cognitive psychology is different. When people use the English durative verbs and instant verbs, the English words will be changed according to the characteristics of time structure, while Chinese won't be changed. For example, "to catch a cold" in English is divided into "have a cold" and "catch a cold". One refers to a continuous state and the other refers to a temporary action. The corresponding English verb must be chosen according to the time structure characteristics.

Therefore, after the introduction of event structure theory into China, many scholars in the Field of Chinese have their own understanding of events in the syntactic and semantic category, taking the characteristics of Chinese itself into account. For example, Shen Jiaxuan [20] believes that a bounded action with internal termination point is an "event", while an unbounded action without internal termination point is an "activity". For example, "breaking" is an "event", and "beating" is an "activity".

Based on the above discussions of Chinese and foreign scholars on the event structure theory, it can be found that although there are still some disputes on the division of the internal semantic features of specific events, there are some consensus. For example, events are often related to verbs, they are not equal to verbs, but a semantic concept.

Then the features of event structure are all related to "situation"[1] [21]. Therefore, most Chinese scholars divide events and verbs according to their situations. Chen Ping [22] used three groups of distinguishing features [+static], [+ continuous] and [+ complete] to divide five types of situations: State, Activity, End, Univariant and Complex. Then, he classified verbs or sentences by integrating these modal features. In addition, although events and verbs are not at the same level, the characteristics of event structure can also be applied to the classification and study of verbs. For example, Guo Rui [23] used the event structure theory to highlight the temporal characteristics of verbs and divided them into: Status verbs, Action verbs and Inflective verbs. Some verbs can be divided into "stative verbs" and "dynamic verbs" according to whether they are static or moving, Dai Yaojing [24] being the representative of this classification. Ma Qingzhu [25, 26] holds that some verbs can be divided into "continuous verbs" and "non-continuous verbs", or "momentary verbs" and "non-momentary verbs" according to the characteristics of continuity. However, because there is no morphological change in Chinese, the time situation of some verbs can be revealed by some functional words or additional components, so there will be some cases in which instant verbs can represent continuous action. In this case, English usually replaces the original instant verb with a durative verb, while Chinese usually does not replace the verb. For example, the former "huan(to suffer)" can be used as a instant verb or as a durative verb, as long as the corresponding additional elements are added. For example, "huan gan mao le (have a cold)" and "huan shang gan mao (catch a cold, 'shang' is an additional element of 'huan')".

It can be seen that, for Chinese, a verb have a variety of event structure features. Therefore, it is necessary to build a relatively dynamic event structure feature database for Chinese verbs and list the event structure knowledge expressed by related verbs, which is also useful for Chinese language processing. The purpose of this paper is to enumerate and judge the event structure features of verbs exhaustively through the temporal situation representation of verbs, so as to generate semantic knowledge database of event structure of Chinese verbs and provide basic guarantee for the accurate processing of natural language.

3   Construction of the Description System of Verb Event Structure Features

Referring to the description of verb event structure by Pustejovsky [16], the feature database of verb event structure constructed in this paper includes four features: eventness, status, process and transition. Among them, status, process and transition are the

---

[1] Situation is a relatively abstract category, which firstly refers to the states and ways expressed by verbs in language. Whether the verb stands for stillness or activity, for duration or moment, with or without consequence, these are the conditions that the verb stands for. Circumstances, moreover, it is also possible that the sentence said state of time, for example, Deng Shouxin (1985) pointed out that there were different situations between the two sentences:"ta bing le san tian (He has been ill for three days)", "ta si le san tian(He has been dead for three days)". One kind was close to the starting point of a sentence, one kind was close to the end a sentence. But the differences in the situational characteristics of sentences were related to the predicate verbs.

narrow sense of event structure features divided from temporal features. The feature "eventness" mainly examines whether verbs have the ability to trigger Event or Verb Phrase (VP). That is, for a verb V to describe its event structure, there are at least two aspects in the description framework. One is whether it is an event verb, and the other is to describe the specific event structure. If it is an event verb or it is eventness, it should be described the following verb structure. In addition, it should be described that it belongs to a class or several classes in the status, process and transition in its specific application.

The specific 4 features are described as follows:

Eventness: This is not a type of event structure. It is a kind of ability, mainly to describe whether verbs can be followed by verb phrase (VP). If a verb have "eventness" feature, it usually cannot be an event on its own, but it can trigger or describe a complete event with the help of another verb or an implied verb. It is can also be called an Event Verb which means have the "eventness" feature and can trigger event. Generally, Event Verb can be followed by Verb Phrase (VP). For example, "kaishi (begin)" and "xue (learn)", both can be followed by verb "chang (sing)". Therefore, the verbs "kaishi (start)" and "xue (learn)" both have certain "Eventness" features and can also be regarded as event verbs.

Status Type: This type of event structure, usually represent the start or end of an event, and sometimes both. If people want to further subdivide, it can also be divided into three types: The first status is the starting point, indicating that event is the starting point, such as "kaishi (start)". The second is a final state, meaning that event is the ending point, such as "jiehun (marry)", and the third is a kind of instantaneous state, suggesting that there is no clear starting point, or no clear end point, the starting point or ending point are overlapping, such as "si (die)". Generally, the verbs corresponding to this kind of event structure can only appear once (e.g., si (die), jiesu (end), etc.) or can only appear again after a relatively long period of time (e.g., jiehun (marry), lihun (divorce), etc.). The third type of verbs generally can take "le" or not (such as "fachou (worry)"), but usually cannot take auxiliary word "zhe". Typical examples are "si (die), xihuan (love), panwang (hope), rezhong (crave), zhidao (know), zhuzhang (advocate), qiangdiao(emphasize), fangqi(give up)" and so on.

Process Type: This type of event structure usually represents the intermediate process of an action from its occurrence to its completion, usually excluding the beginning and end of time. The verbs expressing this kind of event structure are still instant verbs, and they are unbounded, can take the complement (e.g., shuaipo "crash down"), can last for a while. If it is in the form of double syllables, it can be in "dui + NP2 + de + V1" format (e.g., "dui jibing de yufang (prevention of diseases)"). It has more bounded feature than the preceding two classes, and it can be preceded by "zhengzai (-ing)" and followed by auxiliary words "zhe" or "le". Typical examples are "pao(Run), sha(kill), xue(learn), fangzhi(prevent), changshi(try)".

Transition Type: This type of event structure usually represents two sides. On the one hand, it can be in an ongoing state, and it has the character of "no boundary", so it can be preceded by "(zheng)zai", and sometimes followed by "zhe", such as "zhengzai jian fangzi/fangzi zheng jian zhe (The house is being built)". But on the other hand, it can be close to the final point in time, which is about to reach an end state, and generally cannot be used with "zhe", such as "jian le yi dong fangzi (built a house)". Typical examples are "jian(build), xie(write), zhiding(make), anpai(arrange), etc.".

If the number line is time, the internal time characteristics of these event structures can be abstracted as follows (Figs. 1, 2 and 3):

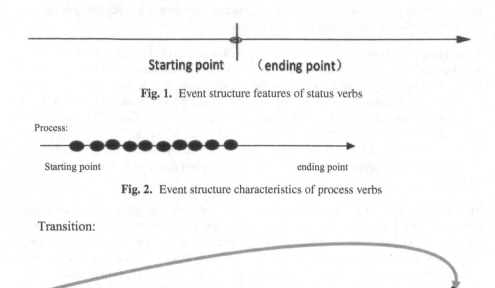

Fig. 1. Event structure features of status verbs

Fig. 2. Event structure characteristics of process verbs

Fig. 3. Event structure features of transition verbs

Although the internal classification of the event structure of the verb is relatively clear from the semantic point of view, in the actual judgment process, people cannot judge by the semantic dimension alone, and the formal means or grammatical function must be taken into consideration as well.

4 Extraction of Verb Event Structure Features

First of all, it should be made clear that Event structure does not exist in all verbs, because not all verbs can trigger events. For example, some linking verbs only represent the logical relationship between them, not the action, so they do not have "eventness" features and therefore, there is no event structure of it. So, event structure is for non-linking verbs.

As for the determination of whether a verb has the characteristics of event, this paper mainly focuses on whether the verb can trigger event. Generally, from the perspective of grammatical functions of verbs, it is based on whether the verb can be followed by Verb Phrase (VP). Formally, this paper believes that as long as either of the following two conditions is met, V_1 can be judged to be eventful and can be regarded as an event verb. The following rules are the two conditions that must be met to judge the event verb:

A. $NP_1 + V_1 + (V_2) + NP_2$
B. $NP_1 + V_1 + NP_2$的 V_2

For example:

(3)   xiao wang zhengzai xuexi xiuli qiche (Mr. Wang is learning repairing the car)
(4)   xiao wang zhengzai xuexi qiche de xiuli (Mr. Wang is learning car's repair)

The verb "xuexi (learn)" can be directly followed by a verb Phrase (VP) phrase " xiuli qiche(repair car)", or a noun structure with verb "qiche de xiuli(car's repair)". This article argues that the verb "learn" is "eventness", which can trigger event "xiu li qiche (repair the car)". Events are usually composed of verb phrases or we can say verbal groups. Constitute an events.

As for which verbs can be followed by verb phrases, people can directly count them based on massive corpus, or in context, or people can also make use of relevant language knowledge base. In fact, the "GKB" of Peking University contains some information about the grammatical functions of lexical items, and there are more than 50 grammatical features of verbs, including some information about the grammatical functions of verbs required by this study.

In this study, 1256 verbs were selected from 16,000 verbs based on the superposition of whether VP can be followed by an object and the features of the list of "aspect predicate accuracy" in the GKB, and then 1235 verbs were selected as event verbs through manual screening according to the relevant corpus.

In addition to the semantic concepts given above, this paper mainly starts from the formal representation and grammatical function of verbs in order to judge which verbs contain event structure features such as status, process and transition. At the same time this paper found that The GKB of Peking University has selected some grammatical features about the temporality of verbs, which also provides convenient conditions for us to judge the semantic feature of the structure of verb-related events. For example, the verbs of the structure characteristic of status events generally cannot be followed by "zhe", nor can they be preceded by "zhengzai". In the GKB, these kinds of grammatical features are actually described. In this paper, according to the characteristics of various verbs, some characteristics are selected as reference. The grammatical features of verbs in GKB specifically used to generate knowledge of event structure are shown in the following table (Table 1):

It should be noted that although the GKB has special statistics of grammatical information about verbs followed by temporal auxiliary words such as "zhe, le, guo" and these features can best reflect the temporality of verbs, but in fact, it is not accurate to determine whether a verb is a status or a process only by relying on auxiliary words "zhe, le, guo" features. Generally, it requires the superposition of multiple features to judge whether a verb can trigger status events.[2] For example, "die" can be followed by

---

[2] These features include whether the verbs can be preceded by "zhe, le, guo", whether it can be followed by a verb as an object, and whether it can be followed by a time quantifier or a momentum word. The reason why these features are selected is that they are all found in the GBK, and more importantly, they are all related to temporal situations. Generally, for example,

Table 1. Features Table of Verbs Event Structure

Event Structure Features	zhe 着	Le 了	guo 过	(zheng)zai (正) 在	dong jie 动结 Verb-Result	Hou shi liang 后时量 Times quantifier	Hou dongliang 后动量 Action quantifier	Example
Status	−	±	±	−	−	+	−	die, love
Process	±	+	±	+	±	−	+	run, learn
Transition	±	+	±	±	+	+	±	build, make

"le" (e.g., ta si le (He died)) and sometimes cannot be followed by "le" (e.g., ni gei wo qu si (You go to hell). At this time, we need to know whether it can be followed by a time quantifier. If so, we can basically assume that the verb can trigger status events. For example, "si san tian (die for three days)", "san tian" is time quantifier, and this phrase can be regarded as a status event.

What is more, the formal expression of Chinese does not completely correspond to its semantic connotation, and such formal extraction criteria will be more strict if these conditions are met simultaneously. However, the GKB is not completely correct in describing these information, and some features are short of statistical completeness, which tends to cause data sparsity. So, in fact, this paper selected some representative verbs with rich descriptive content to realize extraction in accordance with the GBK's verb characteristics. Then this paper aims to expand the semantic synonyms through semantic similarity. Finally, this paper proposes that the verb event structure characteristics of the corresponding data should be further confirmed through semi-artificial detection. This is based on the consensus that verbs with the same general semantics can have the same general event structure features, and also can guarantee the accuracy of data to some extent.

In addition, it should be noted that although each event structure has its corresponding verb, for a certain verb, the event structure it contains is not necessarily a specific one, and it may also have two different kinds of event structures. For example, "sha (kill)" should be a process verb in form, but it also includes the state of "death" in semantics, so its event structure can express both the process and the status. When Pustejovesky described the event structure of "kill", he believed that "kill" could convey two event structure types, one is "Process" and the other is "Status" [17]. Based on this, the method of this paper is to mark the word with two event structures, Process and Status, when describing words like "kill". Then, the synonyms of "kill" such as "tu sha (slaughter)" and "tu mie (annihilate)" are labeled in the same way. In this paper, the description of the event structure of "kill" is firstly to judge whether it can trigger event (that is, whether it is an event verb or can take the VP), and then to describe its event structure

anything that can be followed by "dongjie(verb-result mode)" can be understood as the end of an event.Therefore this kind of verbs have the characteristics of status event.

characteristics according to the grammatical features of "kill" such as the auxiliary words and quantifiers. Finally, the event characteristics of "kill" are as follows:

Kill shā
Event structure:
  Event verb: No
  Followed by VP: No
  Process: Yes
  Transition: No
  Status: No

Due to the fact that "kill" cannot be followed by the VP, so it's not an event verb, followed by the VP for an empty set. If a verb is an event verb, the knowledge base also describes the VP that follows it. For example, the event structure of "aiqiu (implore)" is described as follows:

Implore Āi qiu
Event structure:
  Event verb: Yes
  Followed by VP: Bang (help), jiu (save), juanxian (donate), na chu (take out), mai (buy), jie (lend), tingzhi (stop), da dianhua (call), bao jing (call the police).
  Process:Yes
  Transition: No
  Status: No

5   Application of Event Structure Description

5.1   Application in Machine Translation

Shen Yang [26] pointed out that most of Chinese sentences are double-action sentences, that is, double-event sentences including action, behavior and result state. For example, the action of "pao (run/escape)" is not only a temporary action, but also used together with some other components (such as "pao le (ran away)" and "pao bu(run)") to indicate a bounded event action with a certain result or termination point. Therefore, in the process of machine translation, people must pay attention to the fact that some verbs cannot be simply and directly translated. In this case, we should add some components to these verbs when translating, and these components should preferably form a complete event with the verb.

For example, "fan ren pao le (The prisoner has ran away)".

The verb "pao (run)" in the sentence is not "paobu", but "escape/run away".

So how to set rules for "pao (run/escape)" can help the computers know when to translate it into "run" and when to translate it into "escape"?

For this, this paper proposes to describe not only the event type of the verb, but also the replacement words of the corresponding event type when constructing the event knowledge database, and add the corresponding verbs of each event structure into the event structure knowledge. For example, "pao (run)" is generally used as a process verb, but it can often indicate an end state. Therefore, "pao (run)" also has two event structures, which are described in this paper as:

(A)   Process (running).
(B)   Status (escape).

When an actual sentence was describing a status event or result situation, the computer was asked to select a translation that was similar in meaning to the status event and the replacement word. While if the sentence is not status event, it will be translated as "running".

This paper takes the Chinese-English translation as an example. For the convenience of Chinese-English translation, this study adds the English corresponding words of each verb corresponding to the event structure type, taking the verb "chuan (wear)" as an example:

In Chinese, "chuan (wear)" consists of two event structures:

(A)   Process (put on);
(B)   Status (wear).

For general process events, people should choose "type A verbs" to describe it and for status events, people should choose "type B verbs" correspondingly. For example, when translating a process event such as "Ta zhengzai chuan maoyi (He is wearing a sweater)", "chuan(wear)" should be translated as "get on/put on", while when translating a status event such as "Ta chuan le yitian de maoyi (He has been wearing a sweater all day)", the verb "wear" should be chosen.

5.2 Application in Semantic Role Labeling

In fact, the semantic roles of verbs with different event structure characteristics also differ greatly. For example, a verb with transition event emphasizes an outcome, so a verb with transition event can be followed by a noun which expresses result. Such verbs as "make, build and write" are all transition events of expression, and the basic framework of their semantic role is mostly followed by "result role". In the process of dynamic semantic role labeling, the semantic relations between verbs-nouns are mostly determined by verbs' features. In fact, the event structures of verbs can also be used to improve the semantic role labeling.

In this paper, 1235 verbs describing the structural features of events are selected as the research objects. And the semantic role types of these arguments followed by these verbs are statistically analyzed.

The results of distribution of semantic role labeling with different kind of verbs are shown in the following table (Table 2):

Table 2. Distribution of Semantic Role Labeling

Verb types	Number	Patient role	Result role	Other roles
Status verbs	703	511	107	85
Transition verbs	156	32	98	26
Process verbs	376	263	83	30

Among the three kinds of verbs, status verbs and process verbs tend to be followed by "Patient role", while transition verbs tend to be followed by "Result role". Therefore, in the actual semantic role labeling process, people can refer to these features to set some semantic role labeling priorities, so as to improve the semantic role labeling.

Let's take the cooking verb "zhu (cook)" for example.

"zhu (cook)" contains two event structures, such as : (1) Process (cook); (2) Transition (cook into). When it comes to Process events, the following nouns tend to be labeled as "Patient". For example in "wo zai zhu yumi (I'm cooking corn)", the semantic relation between "zhu (cook)" and "yumi (corn)" is Patient; When referring to transition event, the argument that followed tend to be labeled as "Result role". But in another sentence "women yijing ba shengmi zhu cheng le shufan (We have cooked raw rice into cooked rice)", "mi (rice)" in this sentence should be labeled as "Result", while the "raw rice" should be labeled as "Patient".

From the above, the description of event structure can be useful to the semantic roles labeling.

6 Conclusion

Event structure is a concept about the verb's semantic feature. In general case, the semantic feature is a deep and implicit feature which is often hidden in words. People always can only generalize these characteristics through the grammatical information from the context or corpus.

This paper mainly introduces how to use the grammatical information of GKB to extract event structure features of verbs. For example, people can use the grammatical information marked for each verb in the GKB (such as if the verb get "zhe, le, guo", "Times quantifier" etc.) to judge whether the verb is an event verb and which type of event structure the verb can trigger.

The reason why GKB is chosen is not only for some components of verbs are classified and described in the GKB, but also the grammatical information of the verbs it describes is more comprehensive and high quality, which is useful and feedback by many organizations, so as to accurately summarize the various grammatical features of verbs. The development of this work benefits from the high-quality grammar information in GKB developed by Yu Shiwen. His painstaking efforts have provided a strong foundation for our natural language processing work. The GKB is not just a grammatical knowledge-base, it can be also useful for semantic feature extraction. This paper provide a reference for the academic community to make better use of the GBK.

These event structures knowledge extracted from GBK have been applied in machine translation and semantic roles labeling.

In addition, the description of verb event structure can not only be used in the field of natural language processing, but also solve some linguistic problems.

However, due to the space limitations, the authors will write another article to discuss those issues.

Acknowledgments. This paper is supported by Beijing Social Science Foundation (20YYC021).

References

1. Shui, C.: The bounded features of VP restrict the semantic constraints of temporal and quantitative phrases. Lang. Sci. **5**(6), 19–28 (2006). (in Chinese)
2. Wang, M., Liu, Y., Wang, H.: The processing of dummy verbs in semantic role labeling. In: Su, X., He, T. (eds.) CLSW 2014. LNCS (LNAI), vol. 8922, pp. 170–180. Springer, Cham (2014). https://doi.org/10.1007/978-3-319-14331-6_17
3. Xiao, G.: Syntactic events and semantic events – language research for artificial intelligence. Yangtze River Academ. **2**, 83–98 (2020). (in Chinese)
4. Meng, C., Zheng, H., et al.: The Dictionary of Chinese Verbs Usage. The Commercial Press, Beijing (1999). (in Chinese)
5. Yu, S., Zhu, X., et al.: The Grammatical Knowledge of Contemporary Chinese – A Complete Specification, 2nd edn. Tsinghua University, Beijing (2003). (in Chinese)
6. Zhu, H.: The origin and development of event structure theory. Foreign Lang. J. **6**, 82–85 (2011). (in Chinese)
7. Song, Z.: The Research of Event Forcing in Modern Chinese. Doctoral Dissertation, Peking University, Beijing (2009). (in Chinese)
8. Song, Z.: Light verbs, events and object coercion in Chinese. Stud. Chinese Lang. **3**, 205–217 (2011). (in Chinese)
9. Vendler, Z.: Verbs and times. J. Philosop. Rev. (1957)
10. Vendler, Z.: Linguistics in Philosophy. Cornell University Press, Ithaca N. Y. (1967)
11. Donald, D.: The Logic of Decision and Action. University of Pittsburgh Press, Pittsburgh (1967)
12. McCawley, J.: Lexical insertion in a transformation grammar without deep structure. In: Proceedings of Chicago Lingustic Society (1968)
13. Jackendoff, R.: Semantic Interpretation in Generative Grammar. MIT Press, Cambridge of MA (1972)
14. Jackendoff, R.: The Architecture of the Language Faculty. Cambridge of MIT Press (1997)
15. David, D.: Word Meaning and Montague Grammar: The Semantics of Verbs and Times in Generative Semantics and in Montague's Ptq. Springer press (1979)
16. Pustejovsky, J.: The Generative Lexicon. Computational Linguistics (1991)
17. Pustejovsky, J.: Generative Lexicon. MIT Press of Cambridge (1995)
18. Pustejovsky, J.: Type theory and lexical decomposition. J. Cogn. Sci. (2006)
19. Pustejovsky, J.: GLML: annotating argument selection and coercion. In: Proceedings of the 8th International Conference on Computational Semantics. Tilburg (2009)
20. Shen, J.: There are boundaries and there are no boundaries. Stud. Chin. Lang. **5**, 367–380 (1995). (in Chinese)
21. Deng, S.: The time structure of chinese verbs. Lang. Teach. Linguist. Stud. **4**, 7–17 (1985). (in Chinese)
22. Chen, P.: On the ternary structure of modern chinese time system. Stud. Chin. Lang. **6**, 401–422 (1988). (in Chinese)
23. Guo, R.: The process structure of chinese verbs. Stud. Chin. Lang. **6**, 410–419 (1993). (in Chinese)
24. Dai, Y.: A Systematic Study of Contemporary Chinese Tense and Aspect. ZheJiang Education Press, Hangzhou (1997). (in Chinese)
25. Ma, Q.: Chinese Verbs and Verbal Structures. Beijing Language and Culture University Press, Beijing (1992). (in Chinese)
26. Ma, Q.: The class of object and verbs. studies of the chinese language, vol. 2 (1981). (in Chinese)
27. Shen, Y.: The identification and analysis of CAUSE system in Chinese. In: The 7th International Conference on Teaching Chinese as a Foreign Language (2010). (in Chinese)

Semantic Classification of Adverbial Nouns Based on Syntactic Treebank and Construction of Collocation Database

Shaiquan Zhai, Tian Shao, Gaoqi Rao, and Endong Xun(✉)

Beijing Language and Culture University, Beijing, China
edxun@blcu.edu.cn

Abstract. Being an adverbial is a grammatical function of a small number of nouns. The nouns act as the adverbial and the subject are located before the predicate, and there is no formal mark, therefore, it is easy to cause syntax parsing mistakes. Meanwhile, there is a lack of semantic resources of adverbial nouns at this stage which makes it more difficult to do related semantic parsing. We extracted the "noun + verb/adjective" collocation corpora from a large-scale structure tree database. By writing code and manually proofreading, nouns that can act as the adverbial to directly modify verbs or adjectives which are also called the adverbial nouns are listed exhaustively. We conducted a comprehensive classification and quantitative analysis according to the semantics expressed by the adverbial nouns, and constructed an "adverbial noun-verb/adjective" collocation database based on this, so as to improve the accuracy of syntactic parsing and provide corresponding semantic information, and also to provide reference for the related research of linguistics.

Keywords: Adverbial Nouns · Semantic Classification · Collocation Database · Syntactic and Semantic Parsing

1 Introduction

Nouns are a class of words that represent the name of people, objects, time and places. Adverbial nouns refer to nouns that are in adverbial positions and modify verbs or adjectives alone without the help of function words such as prepositions. In terms of grammatical function, except for time words and location words, "general nouns and verbs that can directly modify verbs as adverbial words are few, and are limited to words that can be used to indicate the manner and state of an action" [1].

Formally, a general noun acts as the adverbial can be divided into two categories, that is, acting as the adverbial directly and with formal marks, such as 地 de, 似的 shide. The latter has formal marks indicating the combination relationship and can be located, extracted and analyzed pretty quickly and accurately, therefore, it is not included in this paper. As for the former, from the perspective of semantic structure, the relations between the noun and the head including agent-action, patient-action, scope-action, manner-action, instrument-action and so on. From the perspective of syntactic structure,

Q. Su et al. (Eds.): CLSW 2022, LNAI 13496, pp. 259–277, 2023.
https://doi.org/10.1007/978-3-031-28956-9_21

the relations including subject-predicate, adverbial-head or attributive-head. It is semantically complex and lacks formal marks which makes it difficult to correctly identify, segment and label in syntactic and semantic parsing.

[1] **学生学习**"空间与图形"**的知识。**
Xuéshēng xuéxí "kōngjiān yǔ túxíng" de zhīshì.
Students learn about "space and graphics".

[2] **树栽种**在田野里。
Shù zāizhòng zài tiányě lǐ.
Trees are planted in the field.

[3] 领导们正在观看**文艺演出**。
Lǐngdǎomen zhèngzài guānkàn wényì yǎnchū.
The leaders are watching a theatrical performance.

[4] 他们所唱的民歌都是师傅**口语相传**。
Tāmen suǒ chàng de míngē dōu shì shīfù kǒuyǔ xiāngchuán.
The folk songs they sing are handed down orally by their masters.

[5] 安桂香就不得不向儿子**电话求助**。
Ān guìxiāng jiù bùdé bù xiàng ér zǐ diànhuà qiúzhù.
An Guixiang had to call her son for help.

The part of speech sequences of the bold words in the above example sentences are all "N+V", however, 学生学习 *xuéshēng xuéxí* 'students learn' is a subject-predicate structure and the relation is agent-action; 树栽种 *shù zāizhòng* 'trees are planted' is a subject-predicate structure and the relation is patient-action; 文艺演出 *wényì yǎnchū* 'theatrical performance.' is an attributive-head structure and the relation is scope-action; 口语相传 *kǒuyǔ xiāngchuán* 'handed down orally' is an adverbial-head structure and the relation is manner-action; 电话求助 *diànhuà qiúzhù 'call for help'* is an adverbial-head structure and the relation is instrument-action. Take the parsing of 4 by the LTP-Cloud as an example, shown in Fig. 1, according to the annotation instruction given by the platform, 口语相传 *kǒuyǔ xiāngchuán* 'handed down orally' is a SBV, namely subject-predicate structure and the relation is EXP (experiencer)-action. The parsing is not correct both syntactically and semantically.

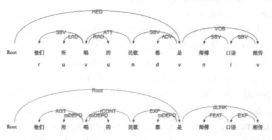

Fig. 1. The parsing of "The folk songs they sing are handed down orally by their masters."

"Collation" is a combination of words. An adverbial noun and the verb or adjective it modifies as a whole form an "adverbial noun + verb/adjective" collocation (hereinafter called "AdvN +V/A" collocation). Chen [2] pointed out that in syntactic research, the core of syntactic parsing is to illustrate the combination of words, and it can be described from two aspects: semantic structure relation and syntactic structure relation. Therefore, the construction of a collocation database containing syntactic and semantic information can contribute to the task of syntactic and semantic parsing in natural language processing.

To sum up, "adverbial nouns" in this paper specifically refers to general nouns that directly act as the adverbial to modify verbs or adjectives. The general nouns here are words labelled as "N(noun)" in the corpus and the *Xiandai Hanyu Cidian* [3] and have no time word or location word annotation. The proportion of adverbial nouns in large-scale corpus is small, which indicates that on one hand, the deep learning based syntactic and semantic parsing may have the problem of sparse data when dealing with the "AdvN +V/A" collocations, thereby reducing the accuracy of labelling. On the other hand, adverbial nouns are a relatively closed set, which can be exhaustively enumerated and semantically classified, and a corresponding collocation database can be constructed to improve the accuracy of syntactic segmentation and provide semantic information.

2 Related Work

The research on adverbial nouns in theoretical linguistics can be divided into two aspects: one is to discuss whether general nouns can act as the adverbial; and the other is the theoretical analysis of them on the premise that general nouns can act as the adverbial.

Regarding the question that whether general nouns can act as the adverbial, Mr. Lv Shuxiang [4] believed that this type of nouns act as the 加语 *jiā yǔ* of verbs, which is equivalent to the adverbial in a sense, and classified this phenomenon as the flexibility of parts of speech. Mr. Zhu Dexi [5] believed that a noun acts as the adverbial is actually a noun along with the adverb suffix 地/的 *de* converts into an adverb to act as the adverbial, such as 他的手本能的缩了回来 *tā de shǒu běnnéng de suōle huílái* 'his hand retracted instinctively' and 这个人物历史的落在了我们的肩上 *zhège rénwù lìshǐ de luò zàile wǒmen de jiān shàng* 'this character historically falls on our shoulders', both 本能 *běnnéng* instinctively and 历史 *lìshǐ* historically are converted into adverbs. Tu [6] denied the theories that "nouns are used as adverbs" and "nouns are flexibly used as verbs" but believed that nouns can act as the adverbial only when prepositions are added before them. Wen [7], on the basis of denying these two theories, believed that it should be recognized that general nouns can act as the adverbial. Yu Fangkui [8] specifically discussed whether general nouns can act as the adverbial. Looking at modern Chinese from Ancient Chinese, she affirmed this phenomenon. Facing the linguistic fact that a large number of "AdvN+V/A" collocations exist and are being used in communication, more and more scholars begin to admit the ability of general nouns acting as the adverbial, and describe and explain them. Huang and Liao [1] believed that there are very few general nouns that can act as the adverbial in Modern Chinese, such as 电话购票 *diànhuà gòu piào* 'purchasing tickets by phone', 笑脸迎人 *xiàoliǎn yíng rén* 'welcoming people with a smile', 公费出国留学 *gōngfèi chūguó liúxué* 'studying abroad at public expense' etc.

The analysis of general nouns act as the adverbial was first seen in "Adverbial nouns and verbs" [9], which pointed out that general nouns can act as the adverbial directly to indicate manner. Since the 1980s and 1990s, related researches have gradually increased, from example-oriented and heuristic ones to theoretical and multi-angle ones. The research perspectives are mainly on structure or form, pragmatics, prosody, and semantics.

From the perspective of structure or form, the main researches are: First, the way of distinguishing the adverbial noun phrase from the subject-predicate phrase. Li [10] proposed questioning method and expansion method. Second, whether it is necessary to act as the adverbial along with a preposition or a marker such as 地 de. Lu [11] proposed the "distance-marker correspondence law", which believes that the adverbial noun must be close to the verb it modifies, otherwise some markers must be added. From the perspective of pragmatics, the main researches are: First, the motivation or mechanism of general nouns directly acting as the adverbial. Dong, Yan [12] and Kang [13] believed that it is the interaction between the principle of iconicity and the economy principle. Zhou [14] believed that it is because of the parataxis of Chinese, the seek for balance beauty and rhythm beauty, and the analogy identification with idioms. Second, the expression effect of general nouns directly acting as the adverbial. Wang Li [15] pointed out its economy, generality, novelty and colloquial style. From the perspective of prosody, the main researches are: First, the prosodic effect of general nouns directly acting as the adverbial. Li Wenfang [16] believed that this expression is refined and can adjust syllables and enhance the sense of rhythm of sentences. Second, the syllable characteristics of adverbial nouns, mainly disyllabic, and there are few monosyllabic and polysyllabic. Third, researches on prosodic syntax. Huang Mei [17] discussed the grammatical properties and syntactic structure of general nouns acting as the adverbial from the perspective that prosody constrains syntax. Jia Linhua [18] combined the Case Theory and Light Verb Theory of contemporary Formal Syntax and Chinese prosodic syntax theory, pointed out that nouns acting as the adverbial is actually the result of the silentization of prepositions.

From the perspective of semantics, the main researches are: First, semantic features of adverbial nouns. Miao Yanyan [19] pointed out that adverbial nouns have the characteristics of nonreferentiality, weak spatiality and prominence of quality. Second, the semantics expressed by adverbial nouns. Wang Xiaoxi [20] divided them into ten categories, including manner, scope, according to, condition, tool and material, state, modality, nature, degree and figurative. Other classifications are similar. Liu Huiqing [21] pointed out that nouns acting as the adverbial generally expresses abnormal, non-default situations, or when special emphasis is needed. Third, illustrating the ability of different categories of general nouns acting directly as the adverbial. Zhang Wen [22] believed that nouns of space > nouns of abstract objects > nouns of objects > nouns of people.

In general, in theoretical linguistics, scholars mainly combine the three aspects including grammar, semantics and pragmatics, as well as methods or perspectives such as prosody, cognition and decategorization, and use qualitative analysis to study the phenomenon of general nouns acting as the adverbial. Although Sun Dejin [23], Wang Xiaoxi [20], Zhang Qian [24] and others comprehensively counted adverbial nouns according to the *Xiandai Hanyu Cidian* [3] or different graded word lists, they were limited to qualitative analysis, and when explaining the classification results, only common categories and typical words were listed, many of which were classified as "others" or roughly classified, which was not enough to reflect the internal characteristics of adverbial nouns. Therefore, the results are difficult to be applied to actual syntactic and semantic parsing. In computational linguistics, work on the syntactic and semantic parsing of nouns acting as the adverbial has not been found yet, and there are lots to be done. In this paper, we use a large-scale corpus to obtain adverbial nouns, classify them semantically and build a corresponding collocation database, in order to provide more syntactic and semantic knowledge for Chinese syntactic and semantic parsing, and also propose a classification system for reference in linguistics research.

3 Data and Method

In order to obtain as many adverbial nouns and their collocations as possible, meanwhile, considering that structural information can improve the accuracy of the extraction results to some extent, we adopt the syntactic structure treebank of Beijing Language and Culture University [25] which is a large-scale one with high accuracy, to extract and disambiguate on this basis.

3.1 Treebank Resource

The source of the corpora of this paper is the syntactic structure treebank of Beijing Language and Culture University. The treebank is a large-scale, multi-domain and high-quality treebank, in which sentences are analyzed into chunk sequences composed of syntactic components, cohesive components and auxiliary components, and represented by the chunk structure tree. The sentence skeleton is directly labelled according to the nature and function of each chunk and the head is highlighted. At present, a quality-assured shallow structure parsing treebank has been manually constructed, including more than 700,000 clauses, with a total of nearly 13 million words. The corpus includes more than 10,000 texts in application fields such as encyclopedia, news and patents, with an average Kappa value of 0.87. In addition, the treebank also includes corpora of 1.1 trillion words labelled by the model, with an F1 value of 94.3.

We only introduce the predicate and related annotations involved in this study. A predicate is the core of a sentence that states the subject and dominates the object. In this treebank, the predicate is a continuous predicate phrase with the maximum length including adverbial and complement. A verb (or a phrase with a verb as the head and a verb idiom), an adjective (or a phrase with an adjective as the head and an adjective idiom) and a subject-predicate phrase can act as the predicate. It's believed that there is only one core predicate in a predicate chunk, and there can be multiple predicates (serial verb construction and pivotal structure) in a single sentence. The predicate chunk as a whole is labelled with "()", and then the core predicate is labelled with another "()", that is, there are only two layers of "()", which can distinguish the core predicate from other components. For example:

[6] 旅客(可以提前(查询))车次。

Lǚkè (kěyǐ tíqián (cháxún)) chēcì.

Passengers (can in advance (check)) train times.

[7] 我们(电话(联系))。
 Wǒmen (diànhuà (liánxì)).
 We (by phone (contact)).

[8] 你(怎么(说)个没完没了)。
 Nǐ (zěnme (shuō) gè méiwán méiliǎo).
 You (why (say) endlessly).

 Among them, 可以提前查询 *kěyǐ tíqián cháxún* 'can check in advance', 电话联系 *diànhuà liánxì* 'contact by phone', and 怎么说个没完没了 *zěnme shuō gè méiwán méiliǎo* 'why say endlessly' are all predicate chunks, which are labelled with "()" as a whole, and the "VP-PRD" annotation is underlain to indicate the nature of the chunk. " 查询 *cháxún* 'inquire', 联系 *liánxì* 'contact' and 说 *shuō* 'say' are the core predicates, which are also labelled with "()", 可以提前 *kěyǐ tíqián* 'can be in advance', 电话 *diànhuà* 'phone' and 怎么 *zěnme* 'why' are the adverbials, and 个没完没了 *gè méiwán méiliǎo* 'endlessly' is the complement.

 Therefore, the treebank can be used to extract "AdvN+V/A" collocation corpora and obtain the adverbial noun word list on this basis.

3.2 Corpora Extraction and Disambiguation

For the purpose of classifying adverbial nouns semantically and constructing a corresponding collocation database, firstly, it is necessary to obtain adverbial nouns as many and as accurate as possible. In this section, we mainly introduce the extraction of "noun + verb/adjective" collocation (hereinafter referred to as "N+V/A" collocation) corpora from the treebank and the disambiguation of the corpora labelled by the model, and finally the process of obtaining "AdvN+V/A" corpora and the adverbial noun word list.

Instances Extraction. According to the features of the treebank that "()" is used to label the predicate and it includes part of speech and chunk information, combined with the grammatical fact that "AdvN+V/A" collocations generally act as the predicate in sentences, meanwhile, taking into account the need of analyzing the syllabic performance of adverbial nouns, we limit nouns and verbs or adjectives to be closely connected and appear in the predicate chunk when extracting. The structural retrieval formulas are divided into the following four categories according to the number of syllables:

1) Monosyllabic noun + monosyllabic verb/adjective: N1+V1/A1
2) Monosyllabic noun + disyllabic verb/adjective: N1+V2/A2
3) Disyllabic noun + monosyllabic verb/adjective: N2+V1/A1
4) Disyllabic noun + disyllabic verb/adjective: N2+V2/A2

 Take the extraction of " disyllabic noun + disyllabic verb" as an example, combined with the extraction results to explain the structural retrieval queries, see Fig. 2.
 First, the noun and the verb are limited to be disyllabic; second, the noun and the verb are limited to be contiguous with no other components in between; the third step is to locate a predicate chunk; the fourth step is that the contiguous noun and verb are limited to appear within the same predicate chunk, that is, the contiguous noun and verb

Fig. 2. The flowchart of the retrieval query.

act as the predicate of the sentence, and the sentence has only one core predicate; finally, obtain the instance and its context that meets the retrieval query.

Examples of structural retrieval results:

[9] 21489285267_ 她在网上查了一下,   <Q>邮轮</Q><Q>出行</Q>不仅浪漫
而且价格不贵。−1
21489285267_tā zài wǎngshàng chále yīxià, <Q>yóulún </Q><Q>chūxíng</Q>bùjǐn làngmàn, érqiě jiàgé bù guì. −1
21489285267_she checked online, <Q>cruise</Q><Q>travel</Q> is not only romantic, but also inexpensive. −1

[10] 51547552513_最高的楼是上海环球金融中心呢   <Q>手工</Q><Q>组装</Q>
不仅是对传统的一种尊重,同时也−1
51547552513_zuìgāo de lóu shì shànghǎi huánqiú jīnróng zhōngxīn ní! <Q>shǒugōng </Q><Q>zǔzhuāng </Q>bùjǐn shì duì chuántǒng de yī zhǒng zūnzhòng, tóngshí yě −1
51547552513_the tallest building is Shanghai World Financial Center! <Q>manully</Q><Q>assemble</Q> is not only a respect for tradition, but also −1

"21489285267_" and "51547552513_" are sentence numbers, and "−1" is the mark for outputting the entire sentence information. The words between " <Q>" and " </Q> " are the corresponding noun and verb or adjective. For example, 邮轮 *yóulún* 'cruise' and 出行 *chūxíng* 'travel' in 9 and 手工 *shǒugōng* 'manually' and 组装 *zǔzhuāng* 'assemble' in 10 are respectively the disyllabic nouns and disyllabic verbs corresponding to the retrieval query. 邮轮出行 *yóulún chūxíng* 'cruise travel' and 手工组装 *shǒugōng zǔzhuāng* 'manually assemble' are located within the predicate chunks, 邮轮 *yóulún* 'cruise' and 手工 *shǒugōng* 'manually' are the adverbials, and 出行 *chūxíng* 'travel' and 组装 *zǔzhuāng* 'assemble' are the core predicates.

Instances Labelling. Some of the results do not meet the requirements of this paper or the labelling is not accurate enough. In addition, the extraction ability of the structural retrieval query is limited, resulting in the following shortcomings:

1) Part of speech tagging errors and chunk parsing errors. For example, in <Q> 学 *xué* 'learn' </Q><Q> 起来 *qǐlái* 'begin' </Q>, the part of speech of 学 *xué* 'learn' is verb instead of noun; in 接受记者采访 *jiēshòu jìzhě cǎifǎng* 'interviewed by the reporter' <Q> 时 *shí* 'when' </Q> <Q> 表示 *biǎoshì* 'say' </Q>, 时 *shí* 'when' is actually a part of the time adverbial 接受记者采访时 *jiēshòu jìzhě cǎifǎng shí* 'when interviewed by the reporter'.

2) The "N+V/A" collocation can only be limited to be within the predicate chunk or be a part of it, but cannot be limited to be exactly the predicate chunk. Therefore, there are a large number of situations in which prepositional phrases act as the adverbial to modify verbs or adjectives. For example, 被 *bèi* 'by' <Q> 警方 *jǐngfāng* 'police' </Q><Q> 抓获 *zhuāhuò* 'captured' </Q>, 与 *yǔ* 'with' <Q> 大家 *dàjiā* 'everyone' </Q> <Q> 分享 *fēnxiǎng* 'share' </Q> and 据 *jù* 'according to' <Q> 记者 *jìzhě* 'reporter' </Q><Q> 了解 *liǎojiě* 'know' </Q> etc., although 警方抓获 *jǐngfāng zhuāhuò* 'captured by police', 大家分享 *dàjiā fēnxiǎng* 'everyone share' and 记者了解 *jìzhě liǎojiě* 'reporter know' are within the predicate chunks, however, 警方 *jǐngfāng* 'police', 大家 *dàjiā* 'everyone' and 记者 *jìzhě* 'reporter' are actually formed into prepositional phrases with prepositions like 被 *bèi* 'by', 与 *yǔ* 'with' and 据 *jù* 'according to' to act as the adverbial.

3) When the "N+V/A" collocation as a whole is the predicate chunk, the structural relationship between its internal components cannot be further limited. Therefore, there are a large number of situations in which the "N+V/A" collocations are head-complement phrases or subject-predicate phrases etc., instead of adverbial phrases to act as the predicate. Retrieval results such as <Q> 总结 *zǒngjie* 'summary' </Q><Q> 出 *chū* 'out' </Q> and <Q> 女孩 *nǚhái* 'girl' </Q><Q> 拍 *pāi* captures </Q> are not adverbial phrases.

In view of the above problems, considering that the extraction results are plain texts without part of speech and structural information for disambiguation, therefore, it is necessary to perform word segmentation, part of speech tagging and chunk dependency parsing on the extraction results. The chunk dependency labeling model which is trained on the chunk dependency graph database constructed by Qian Qingqing [26] based on the syntactic structure treebank of Beijing Language and Culture University meets the above requirements and has a high accuracy rate. Therefore, it is used in this paper to process the results. The chunk dependency graph database constructed by Qian Qingqing [26] is labelled by a professional labelling team pair to pair, producing high-quality corpora of about 3.55 million words and about 90,000 sentences and over 200,000 clauses. The concordance rate reaches 0.945. When labelling, 1–4 position marks are added to the core predicate, which represent subject, modifier, object and the relationship between predicates, so it can indicate the syntactic relationship between the core predicate and its related chunks to reduce ambiguity. The recall rate, accuracy rate and F1 value of the labeling model trained based on this are all above 0.85. The specific methods are as follows:

1) Model input: Considering that using the form of sentence as input can maximize the accuracy of word segmentation, part of speech tagging and chunking parsing of the model, some changes are made to the corpora. First, remove the irrelevant content before and after the punctuations that can segment sentences. Second, remove the "<Q> </Q>" tags before and after the retrieval query. Take 11 and 12 as examples:

[11] 邮轮出行不仅浪漫
[12] 手工组装不仅是对传统的一种尊重

2) Model output: The output includes sentence information (Sentence), word segmentation information, part of speech information, chunk segmentation information, chunk attribute information (POS) and chunk dependency information (Dep). Out of the need of this paper, we only describe word segmentation information, part of speech information and chunk segmentation information.

[13] {"Sentence": ["邮轮/n", ""出行/v"", ""不仅/c"", "浪漫/a"], "IP": [], "POS": ["NP", "VP", "NULL", "VP"], "Deps": [{"Head": 1, "Dep": [{"key": "sbj", "value": 0}]}, {"Head": 3, "Dep": [{"key": "sbj", "value": 1}]}]}}

[14] {"Sentence":   ["手工/n",   "   组装/v",   "   不仅/c", " 是/v", " 对/p 传统/n 的/u 一/m 种/q 尊重/vn"], "IP": [], "POS": ["NULL", "VP", "NULL", "VP", "NP"], "Deps": [{"Head": 1, "Dep": [{"key": "mod", "value": 0}]}, {"Head": 3, "Dep": [{"key": "sbj", "value": 1}, {"key": "obj", "value": 4}]}]}}

Each "," segments a chunk, corresponding to the attributes in "POS", each " " in the chunk segments a word, and "/" is followed by part of speech. Explanation: 邮轮 *yóulún* 'cruise' is a NP chunk, and the part of speech is n; 出行 *chūxíng* 'travel' is a VP chunk, and the part of speech is v. 手工 *shǒugōng* 'manually' is a NULL chunk, and the part of speech is n; 组装 *zǔzhuāng* 'assemble' is a VP chunk, and the part of speech is v; 对 传统的一种尊重 *duì chuántǒng de yī zhǒng zūnzhòng* 'a kind of respect for tradition' is a NP chunk, which is internally divided into 对 *duì* 'for', 传统 *chuántǒng* 'tradition', 的 *de*, 一 *yī* 'a', 种 *zhǒng* 'kind' and 尊重 *zūnzhòng* 'respect'.

3) Corpus restoration: retain word segmentation information, part of speech information and chunk segmentation information, use " " to divide chunks and restore the "<Q></Q>" tags before and after the query to ensure that the objects of subsequent processing is the original query instead of other ingredients in the context.

[15] <Q>邮轮/n</Q><Q>出行/v</Q>不仅/c 浪漫/a
[16] <Q>手工/n</Q><Q>组装/v</Q>不仅/c 是/v 对/p 传统/n 的/u 一/m 种/q 尊重/vn

Instances Disambiguation. The extraction results labelled by the model have part of speech information and structural information, which provides a basis for disambiguating and obtaining relatively accurate "AdvN+V/A" collocation corpora. The specific steps are as follows.

1) Remove the instances where the noun or the verb/adjective corresponding to the query is not a single chunk. For example:

[17]
    江苏/n 苏州/ns 市民/n 缪/nr 先生/n 近日/t 向/p<Q>媒体/n</Q> <Q>反映/v</Q>
[18] 夸德雷多/nr <Q>小/a 角度/n</Q> <Q>低射/v</Q>
[19] 争/v 得/v <Q>火花/n</Q> <Q>四/m 溅/v</Q>

In 17, 媒体 *méitǐ* 'media' and 向 *xiàng* 'to' together form a chunk, which is a prepositional phrase 向媒体 *xiàng méitǐ* 'to media' to modify 反映 *fǎnyìng* 'reflect'. In 18, 角度 *jiǎodù* 'angle' and 小 *xiǎo* 'small' together form a chunk, which is an attributive-head phrase 小角度 *xiǎo jiǎodù* 'small angle' to modify 低射 *dī shè* 'low shot'. In 19, 四溅 *sì jiàn* 'all directions splash' is divided into two chunks 四 *sì* 'all directions' and 溅 *jiàn* 'splash'.

2) Remove the instances where the chunk before the noun corresponding to the query is a preposition. Because under this circumstance, it is usually a prepositional phrase acts as the adverbial. For example:

[20]   据/p <Q>专家/n</Q> <Q>介绍/v</Q>
[21]   表示/v 网购/vn 消费者/n 可/c凭/p <Q>订单/n</Q> <Q>退/v</Q> 货/n

In 20, the chunk before 专家 *zhuānjiā* 'expert' is the preposition 据 *jù* 'according to', which constitutes the prepositional phrase 据专家 *jù zhuānjiā* 'according to the expert' to modify 介绍 *jièshào* 'introduction'. In 21, the chunk before 订单 *dìngdān* 'order' is the preposition 凭 *píng* 'by', which constitutes the prepositional phrase 凭订单 *píng dìngdān* 'by order' to modify 退 *tuì* 'return'.

3) Remove the instances where the parts of speech of the words corresponding to the query are not noun or verb/adjective. For example:

[22]   记者/n <Q>粗略/a</Q> <Q>统计/v</Q>
[23]   3000/m 3000/m 多/a 名/q 青年/n 农民工/n <Q>现场/s</Q> <Q>相亲/v</Q>
粗略 *cūlüè* 'roughly' and 现场 *xiànchǎng* 'on-the-spot' in 22 and 23 each is a single chunk, and the previous chunk is not a preposition, but the part of speech is not noun.
Extract the queries without the context from the corpora after the above three processing steps, remove duplication and count the frequency according to the syllables. Take the results of "N2+V2" as examples:
[24]   主场迎战 *zhǔchǎng yíngzhàn* 'home vs' 2875
[25]   全体出动 *quántǐ chūdòng* 'all out' 432

4) Compare the results with the *Xiandai Hanyu Cidian* [3], and remove the queries where the word is not a noun and a verb or an adjective, or does not exist in the dictionary. For example, in 王者归来 *wángzhě guīlái* 'the return of the king' and 头槌破门 *tóuchuí pòmén* 'head-hammer shot', 王者 *wángzhě* 'the king' and 头槌 *tóuchuí* 'head-hammer' do not exist in the dictionary.

From structural retrieval to model labelling, and then to the above steps, all are completed automatically through code or model to reduce labor costs as much as possible, but it still needs to be checked manually when judging whether the noun in the "N+V/A" collocation is used as the adverbial or whether the collocation as a whole is an adverbial phrase.

5) Remove the queries that are not adverbial phrases. The error rate of structural retrieval and model labelling leads to a batch of incorrect results. For example, 专家筛选 *zhuānjiā shāixuǎn* 'experts screen', 丈夫跟踪 *zhàngfū gēnzōng* 'husband tracks', and 上帝赐予 *shàngdì cìyǔ* 'God bestows' are all subject-predicate phrases. At this time, we have to manually judge whether all the collocations formed by a certain noun are qualified. We refer to the judgment standard of an adverbial phrase in the *Chinese Parts of Speech Classification Handbook* [27] which mainly go through a series of transforming, questioning, and inserting to check its eligibility.

6) Check the senses of concurrent words in the dictionary. The adverbial word may have other parts of speech rather than noun. For this type of word, we have to refer to the dictionary senses to judge whether it is a noun when it is used as the adverbial, and if not, remove the corresponding query. For example, 高度 *gāodù* 'highly' and 直线 *zhíxiàn* 'straight' in 高度注意 *gāodù zhùyì* 'pay highly attention to' and 直线 上升 *zhíxiàn shàngshēng* 'straight up' each is a single chunk in the model labelling, and both parts of speech are noun, but in the dictionary, 高度 *gāodù* 'highly' and 直 线 *zhíxiàn* 'straight' have two senses including noun and adjective. We found that it is an adjective when it acts as the adverbial.

After the above processes, a total of 809 adjective nouns are obtained, including 21 monosyllabic nouns and 788 disyllabic nouns.

4 Semantic Classification and Analysis

Based on the adverbial noun word list obtained above, this section is the semantic classification of the words in the list, involving classification standard, classification system, and analysis of the results.

4.1 Classification Standard and System

The first thing that needs to be determined for any classification is the classification standard. In linguistics, the classification standards generally include morphology, meanings and functions. Starting from the purpose of providing deep semantic information for syntactic and semantic parsing, we select meanings as the standard. Theoretically speaking, a good standard should be operable when judging and distinguishable in the results, and try to avoid too many cases of concurrent. Specifically, when classifying the adverbial nouns semantically, what is more important is the meanings shown in the "AdvN+V/A" collocations when they act as the adverbial rather than their word meanings. For example, in 手机上网 *shǒujī shàngwǎng* 'surf the internet by phone', what is more important is not the word meaning of 手机 *shǒujī* 'phone' which is the abbreviation of hand-held mobile phone, but the meaning of tool when it acts as an adverbial.

Therefore, the classification standard of the adverbial nouns is mainly based on the meanings shown in the collocations with reference to their word meanings. Combined with questions like "when", "where", "in what state", "how" and "what kind of tool" when judging.

In former researches, many scholars have classified the adverbial nouns semantically. The most detailed classification is Wang Xiaoxi [20] who divided them into ten categories, but no subcategories. In addition, although in a broad sense, many adverbial nouns can be seen to indicate a certain manner, in the classification results of Wang Xiaoxi [20], nearly half of the words were classified as manner, indicating that there is a possibility and necessity for further classification.

The second thing that needs to be determined is the classification system. Existing researches on nouns, such as Wang Jue [28], mainly classify nouns according to its word meanings, and have little reference to this paper. We believe that the semantic functions of adverbial nouns are similar to those of adverbial adverbs and adjectives, and they express similar semantic types and relationships in adverbial phrases. Therefore, we divide the meanings of adverbial nouns into major categories and subcategories with reference to the semantic classification system of adverbs by Jiang [29], Xing [30] and Zhang [31, 32].

According to the above classification standard and classification system, after several iterations by two people, the 809 nouns obtained in this paper are divided into 23 major categories and 47 subcategories. Compared with previous classification, our classification is more comprehensive and detailed, and generally, the words have the category it belongs to, and categories are distinguished from each other. The classification results are shown in Table 1. Because there are too many subcategories, only the major categories and representative subcategories, example words and example sentences are listed in the table.

Here, we want to explain a few questions that may cause confusion:

1) Regarding the division of subcategories, in addition to refer to the existing system, it is also necessary to make choices based on the words actually included in this category and their meanings. What's more, for subcategories with opposite properties, such as "deep degree" and "shallow degree" under the degree category, even if there is no corresponding word for "shallow degree", this subcategory is reserved to achieve the unity and completeness of the classification system, and prepare for the follow-up supplementary work.

2) There are few adverbial nouns in some major categories. For example, there are only 半路 *bànlù* 'halfway' and 中盘 *zhōng pán* 'middle process' under the process category. Or there are no obvious features for further classification. For example, the meanings of the words in the manner category are complex, so there is no subcategory.

3) When there is uncertainty between the manner category and other categories of a certain adverbial noun, we tend to classify it into other categories to avoid the situation of too many words in the manner category. For example, 电视 *diànshì* 'TV' in 电视告知 *diànshì gàozhī* 'notify by TV' can be regarded as a manner and also a tool, which is then classified into the tool category.

4) Regarding partial scope and abstract place, partial scope generally has other opposing or complementing words, semantically means to be within a certain scope. However, it is generally not the same for abstract place. For example, 局部 *júbù* 'part' that represents partial scope is opposed by 整体 *zhěngtǐ* 'whole', 政界 *zhèngjiè* 'political world' is complemented by 学界 *xuéjiè* 'academia'. However, 网站 *wǎngzhàn*

Table 1. Semantic classification of the adverbial nouns

Major category	Subcategory	Words	Sentences
Degree	Deep	极刑	遵旨将该二员极刑处死。
Time	Period	长假	长假出行已成为检验国民素质的重要途径。
Scope	Whole	全体	警员加民兵全体出动。
Tool	Appliance	电视	电视告知市民及各有关单位震情。
Location	Specific location	操场	山东某高校有人操场飙车。
Order	Sequence	先手	中国队先手进攻。
Process	Process	中盘	英超联赛进入中盘厮杀。
Tone	Strong	世纪	谢霆锋与王菲世纪复合。
Quantity	Absolute quantity	巨资	南宁市协和医院巨资引进该精密设备。
Speed	Fast	光速	这里还有上百种方法教你光速燃烧脂肪。
Position	Location	侧门	侧门逃生是最安全快捷的方式。
Result	Specific result	平局	是否能平局过关。
Companion	Companion	旅途	绝对适合旅途携带。
Reason	Disaster	车祸	临沂一老汉车祸昏迷入院多日。
Manner	Manner	手语	神十航天员手语告别天宫。
State	Body State	浓妆	奥运冠军刘璇浓妆出席。
Modality	Positive	笑脸	我们连忙笑脸迎接。
Limit	Limit	专线	最初网络购票还需专线入网。
Distance	Absolute distance	咫尺	与仙林新地王咫尺相隔。
Comment	Negative	套路	记者套路提问。
According	Abstract basis	惯例	法国老佛爷百货每周日惯例休息。
Origin	Identity	铁匠	那时我觉得我妈像是铁匠出身。
Parts	Body parts	拳头	学生插队打饭遭老师拳头制止。

'website' and 麾下 *huīxià* 'subordinate' that represent abstract place are independent expressions.

5) Regarding the location category and location in the position category, no matter words in the location category are concrete or abstract, they are absolute, such as 故乡 *gùxiāng* 'hometown', 人间 *rénjiān* 'human world', etc., and do not need other reference to indicate their existences. However, location in the position category is often relative, with reference of position words, such as 侧翼 *cèyì* 'flank', 后门 *hòumén* 'back door', etc., 侧 *cè* 'side' is opposed by 正 *zhèng* 'front', 后 *hòu* 'back' is opposed by 前 *qián* 'front', etc.

4.2 Results Analysis

After a comprehensive semantic classification of the adverbial nouns, in this section, we further analyze them from the perspectives of concurrency and quantitative performance.

Cross-Meaning Adverbial Nouns. In most cases, the meaning of an adverbial noun expressed in different collocations is the same, but there is also a case where an adverbial noun expresses different meanings in different collocations, that is, the case of concurrency. At this time, this adverbial noun has multiple meanings, which is called a cross-meaning adverbial noun in this paper. A total of 17 cross-meaning adverbial nouns are counted, of which 12 words express meanings which belong to two semantic categories, and 5 words express meanings which belong to three semantic categories. Table 2 shows the semantic categories and their example sentences of each cross-meaning adverbial noun.

Table 2. Cross-meaning adverbial nouns and their semantic categories

Cross-meaning adver-	Semantic categories	Example sentence
重炮	Degree-Deep degree	郝龙斌昨天在脸书重炮回击。
	Tool-Weapon	重炮攻击猫缆和捷运内湖线。
大学	Time-Period	你大学辍学创业、从投行转战游戏。
	Location-Specific location	高中毕业后的山田放弃了大学深造。
篝火	Tool-appliance	这些民兵 2 日晚篝火取暖。
	Companion	所以这些人主要还是篝火露营。
邮轮/地铁/飞机/游船/ 游艇/房车/公车/火车	Tool-Vehicle	地铁出行是老年人最好的选择。
	Location-Specific location	老外地铁劝架被打。
高层	Location-Specific location	高层逃生不要利用电梯。
	Manner	保持高层交往。
晚宴/宴席/家宴/酒宴/ 晚餐	Location-Abstract location	他刚刚晚宴归来。
	Time-Day	美国通用汽车公司总裁晚宴致辞。
	Manner	贾庆林晚宴接待访问团。

Among them, 晚宴致辞 *wǎnyàn zhìcí* 'make a speech at the dinner party' can be understood as make a speech when the dinner is going on or make a speech at the abstract place of the dinner party.

It can be seen that there are few cross-meaning adverbial nouns which is in line with the requirements of the classification standard. In addition, cross-meaning adverbial nouns have certain regularity. Words in the 邮轮 *yóulún* 'cruise' and 晚宴 *wǎnyàn* 'dinner party' categories often express multiple meanings, which is related to the word meanings and their collocations. The "cruise" category as a whole can be a tool of transportation when it is collocated with the "travel" category. Because it has internal space, it can be a specific place when it is collocated with the words of behavior. The dictionary definition of 晚宴 *wǎnyàn* 'dinner party' is "a banquet held in the evening", which includes the meaning of time, and the dinner party often occupies a certain space, so it can express the meaning of abstract place, and when it is collocated with the接待 *jiēdài* 'reception' category, it can express the meaning of manner.

Statistical Analysis. Based on the above semantic classification results, we carried out further statistical analysis. Figure 3 shows the proportion of the number of adverbial nouns in each major category. It can be seen that the location category has a total of 325 words, accounting for 39%, which is the most. The tool category is the second, with a total of 89 words, accounting for 11%, followed by the time category, with a total of 61 words, accounting for 7%, and the status category, manner category, modality category and scope category account for similar proportion.

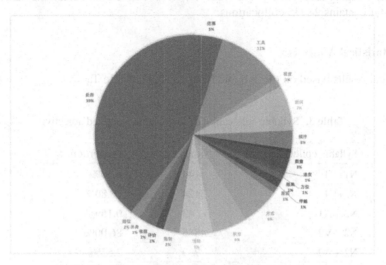

Fig. 3. The proportion of the semantic categories.

To sum up, the meanings expressed by the adverbial nouns are mainly location, time, tool, state, scope, manner, modality, quantity, frequency and order. Beyond this, although the semantic categories such as origin and companion account for a very low proportion, they express unique meanings, therefore, detailed classification of these words can give more accurate annotations during semantic parsing.

5   Collocation Database Construction and Analysis

Based on the disambiguated "AdvN+V/A" collocation corpora, according to the semantic classification results, in this section, we construct a syntactic and semantic collocation database of "adverbial noun + verb/adjective" and further analyze it from the perspectives of quantity proportion, syllabic and semantic features.

5.1   Collocation Database Construction

The results of semantic classification cannot be directly used in the actual syntactic and semantic parsing, because the collocations formed of the adverbial nouns and verbs or adjectives are not all adverbial phrases. Moreover, the same adverbial noun may express different meanings in different collocations. Constructing the "AdvN+V/A" collocation database can match the slots more accurately in subsequent applications. The construction of the collocation database is mainly carried out on the disambiguated "AdvN+V/A" collocation corpora, adding semantic classification information, and checking the situations of multi-meanings one by one. The results are as follows: "手剥 MOD = 部位 - 人体部位", 手剥 *shǒu bō* 'hand stripping' is the collocation, "MOD" is the adverbial semantic label, "=" means assignment, and before and after "−" are the major and sub semantic category respectively. The "AdvN + V/A" collocation database constructed in this paper contains 28935 collocations.

5.2   Statistical Analysis

Statistical results based on the syllabic features are shown in Table 3.

Table 3. Syllabic collocation distinguishing noun and adjective

Syllabic collocation	Number	Proportion
N1+V1	144	0.50%
N2+V1	3124	10.80%
N2 +A1	43	0.15%
N2 +V2	24885	86.00%
N2 +A2	739	2.55%

Although the corpora may be incomplete, some patterns can be seen from the statistical results: First, monosyllabic nouns generally do not modify disyllabic verbs or adjectives; Second, collocations are mainly disyllabic nouns modify disyllabic verbs or adjectives, accounting for nearly 90%. Both are two major prosodic features of Chinese.

According to the number of collocations under each major semantic category, considering the incompleteness of the collocation database, we use the ratio of the number of collocations in a semantic category to the number of words contained in this category as the indicator of collocation ability. The results are shown in Table 4.

It can be seen that from the perspective of the number of collocations, the scope category is the largest, with a total of 9923, accounting for 34.19%, followed by the place category, with a total of 5900, accounting for 20.33%. The total proportion of these two categories exceeds 50%, which shows that the overall distribution is relatively uneven. In terms of collocation ability, the scope type has the strongest collocation ability, with an average of 248.08 collocations per word, followed by the modality category and the process category. The origin category has the weakest collocation ability, because the only word that can be collocated with it is basically "born 出身".

Table 4. The proportion of numbers and collocation ability

Major category	Number	Proportion	Collocation ability
Scope	9923	34.19%	248.08
Location	5900	20.33%	18.15
Modality	3655	12.59%	81.22
Tool	1961	6.76%	22.03
Manner	1727	5.95%	33.86
Quantity	1288	4.44%	51.52
Time	977	3.37%	16.02
State	946	3.26%	19.71
Order	517	1.78%	22.48
Degree	340	1.17%	28.33
Result	279	0.96%	45.00
Limit	270	0.93%	15.00
Parts	218	0.75%	15.57
Comment	213	0.73%	19.36
Reason	166	0.57%	18.44
Process	140	0.48%	70.00
Tone	105	0.36%	26.25
Companion	103	0.35%	20.60
According to	102	0.35%	7.29
Speed	82	0.28%	13.67
Position	78	0.27%	9.75
Distance	20	0.07%	5.00
Origin	15	0.05%	1.36

6 Conclusion

In this paper, based on the syntactic structure treebank, we extracted the "noun + verb/adjective" collocation corpora through structural retrieval, further labelled the results using the chunk dependency graph database-based model, and disambiguated them by writing code, comparing to dictionary, and manually proofreading. We carried out a comprehensive and detailed semantic classification of the obtained 809 nouns, and obtained a total of 23 major categories and 47 subcategories, which are higher in quantity and fineness than the predecessors, and laid a classification standard and system for subsequent related work. In addition, we constructed an "AdvN+V/A" syntactic and semantic collocation database containing 28935 collocations, which can be used for syntactic and semantic parsing.

Acknowledgments. This paper is supported by BLCU Supported Project for Young Researchers Program (supported by the Fundamental Research Funds for the Central Universities) (22YCX069) and the National Natural Science Foundation of China, "Study on the Characterization and Generation Method of Chinese Parataxis Graph" (No. 62076038).

References

1. Huang, B., Liao, X.: The Modern Chinese. Higher Education Press, Beijing (2017)
2. Chen, B.: A study on the Methodology of Chinese Linguistics in the 20th Century. The Commercial Press, Beijing (2015). (in Chinese)
3. Dictionary Editorial Office of Institute of Linguistics: The Modern Chinese Dictionary 7th edn. The Commercial Press, Beijing (2016). (in Chinese)
4. Lv, S.: A Brief Introduction to Chinese Grammar. The Commercial Press, Beijing (1982)
5. Zhu, D.: Grammar Lectures. The Commercial Press, Beijing (1982). (in Chinese)
6. Tu, H.: A humble opinion on nouns as adverbial. J. Huzhou Teach. Coll. **03**, 47–51 (1986). (in Chinese)
7. Wen, L.: On nouns modifying verbs. J. Shanghai Norm. Univ. (Philos. Soc. Sci. Ed.) **03**, 96–99 (1994). (in Chinese)
8. Yu, F.: Can common nouns be adverbial. J. Nanchang Univ. (Hum. Soc. Sci.) **04**, 103–106+87 (1984). (in Chinese)
9. Hong, X.: Adverbial nouns and verbs. J. Fujian Norm. Univ. **01**, 151–159 (1963). (in Chinese)
10. Li, J.: On the use of non-temporal nouns as adverbial. Suzhou Univ. J. Med. Sci. **04**, 69–73 (1983). (in Chinese)
11. Lu, B.: The "distance-mark correspondence law" as a language commonality. Stud. Chin. Lang. **01**, 3–15+95(2004). (in Chinese)
12. Dong, S., Yan, Y.: A preliminary probe into the positive structure in the NV form in modern Chinese. J. Jianghan Univ. (Hum. Ed.) **03**, 87–90 (2003). (in Chinese)
13. Kang, Q.: An analysis of nouns as adverbial adverbs. J. Xinzhou Teach. Univ. **06**, 81–81+113 (2009). (in Chinese)
14. Zhou, X.: A brief analysis of the NV form in modern Chinese. Mod. Chin. (Acad. Compr. Ed.) **01**, 146–147 (2012). (in Chinese)
15. Wang. L.: A study of noun adverbs in modern Chinese. Huazhong Univ. Sci. Technol. Wuhan (2006). (in Chinese)
16. Li, W.: On adverbial nouns in modern Chinese. J. Chengde Teach. Coll. (Compr. Ed.) **03**, 89–91 (1989). (in Chinese)
17. Huang, M.: Research on the syntactic properties of common nouns as adverbial adverbs. Chin. Lang. Learn. **05**, 34–41 (2014). (in Chinese)
18. Jia, L.: Prosodic syntactic analysis of common nouns as adverbial. Linguist. Res. **04**, 33–38 (2014). (in Chinese)
19. Miao, Y.: A study on adverbial adverbial of non-temporal nouns. Capital Normal University, Beijing (2011). (in Chinese)
20. Wang, X.: A micro probe into the adverbial adverbial of non-temporal nouns in modern Chinese. J. Hebei Norm. Univ. (Philos. Soc. Sci.) **05**, 117–121 (2003). (in Chinese)
21. Liu, H.: Noun as adverbial and its related features. Lang.Teach. Linguist. Stud. **05**, 28–34 (2005). (in Chinese)
22. Zhang, W.: Research on Chinese Nouns as Adverbial Adverbs. Beijing Language and Culture University, Beijing (2009). (in Chinese)
23. Sun, D.: An investigation of modern Chinese nouns as adverbial adverbs. Lang. Teach. Linguist. Stud. **04**, 88–98 (1995). (in Chinese)

24. Zhang, Q.: Research on the Adverbial Adverbial of Common Nouns in Modern Chinese. Shanghai Normal University, Shanghai (2013). (in Chinese)
25. Lu, L., Jiao, H., Li, M., Xun, E.: The construction of chinese syntax structure tree library based on text. Acta Automatica Sinica, 1–12(2021). (in Chinese)
26. Qian, Q.: Block dependency grammar and library construction. Beijing Lang. Cult. Univ. Beijing (2021). (in Chinese)
27. Yuan, Y.: Handbook of Chinese Parts of Speech. Beijing Language and Culture University Press, Beijing (2009). (in Chinese)
28. Wang, J.: A Study of Nouns in Modern Chinese. East China Normal University Press, Shanghai (2000). (in Chinese)
29. Jiang, H., Xu, H.: A Practical Dictionary for Classification of Modern Chinese Adverbs. Foreign Trade Education Press, Beijing (1989). (in Chinese)
30. Xing, F.: The Modern Chinese. Higher Education Press, Beijing (1996). (in Chinese)
31. Zhang, Y.: The nature, scope and classification of modern Chinese adverbs. Stud. Lang. Linguist. 01, 51–63 (2000). (in Chinese)
32. Zhang, Y.: Research on Adverbs in Modern Chinese. Xuelin Press, Shanghai (2000). (in Chinese)

A Framework for Dictionary Development: Building Domain Dictionary for Legal Field

Jianying Zhu[1], Menglan Shen[2], and Nankai Lin[3(✉)]

[1] School of Law, Guangdong University of Foreign Studies, Guangzhou, Guangdong, China
[2] School of Software and Microelectronics, Peking University, Beijing, China
[3] School of Information Science and Technology, Guangdong University of Foreign Studies, Guangzhou, Guangdong, China
neakail@outlook.com

Abstract. The domain dictionary is a hotspot of research in natural language processing. Constructing a dictionary effectively for a specific field enables more precise labeling and classification of words. The development of legal domain dictionaries contributes to the advancement of artificial intelligence research. Despite extensive research on domain dictionaries, pre-trained models with high transcendental knowledge are underutilized, and legal domain dictionaries are scarce. To address these issues, this article is the first to employ the masked language model (MLM) to construct the legal domain dictionary. We verify the performance and effectiveness of the dictionary we construct. It will be available to the public to provide possible directions for future research. To facilitate related research in the community and benefit other researchers, we make our resource in this work publicly available on: https://github.com/GDUFS-Strawberry/Legal-Dictionary.

Keywords: Domain Dictionary · Legal Field · Masked Language Model

1 Introduction

Artificial intelligence is a new field of technical study that investigates and develops theories, methods, technologies, and systems for simulating, extending, and expanding human intelligence [1]. In recent years, both internationally and domestically, the application of artificial intelligence in judicial practice has advanced significantly and continues to deepen [2,3]. In terms of macros, "Smart Court", "Smart Prosecution", "Smart Police" and other platforms have emerged in China. And the whole process of criminal, civil, and administrative cases can rely on various judicial artificial intelligence, such as the online court, reference for sentencing with similar cases, intelligent execution, etc. On the micro-level, intelligent judicial innovation has been developed in different places in China, such as the "Judge Rui" Intelligent Research and Judgment System of

---

J. Zhu and M. Shen—Co-first authors. They have worked to-gether and contributed equally to the paper.

© The Author(s), under exclusive license to Springer Nature Switzerland AG 2023
Q. Su et al. (Eds.): CLSW 2022, LNAI 13496, pp. 278–290, 2023.
https://doi.org/10.1007/978-3-031-28956-9_22

The High People's Court of Beijing Municipality, the C2J Judge Intelligent Aid Case Handling System of The Second Intermediate People's Court of Shanghai Municipality, the "Jujing" financial cases online platform of The Primary People's Court of Yantian District of Shenzhen City of Guangdong, and the Cainiao intelligent delivery robot of The Railway Transportation Primary Court of Hangzhou, etc. Outside the territory of China, the development of judicial artificial intelligence has progressed from automated and intelligent retrieval of legal information to the establishment of legal artificial intelligence systems such as legal expert systems and judicial discretionary models. For example, the United States not only has famous legal information retrieval systems such as WESTLAW, which can intelligently retrieve, accurately identify and introduce similar cases in the databases but also has developed COMPAS, LSI-R, and other risk assessment software to assist in sentencing. Currently more than half of the states in the United States have utilized this software to assist judges in sentencing.

A domain dictionary is one sort of manifestation of domain knowledge that is used to store domain-specific terms and their relationships. It has a wide range of applications in a variety of fields. The development of high-quality legal domain dictionaries contributes to the advancement of artificial intelligence research in the legal field. Domain-specific terms refer to words or phrases that describe conceptual knowledge within certain domains, as well as vocabulary sets that denote domain definitions, perspectives, categories, and specific meanings. Lexical polysemy is the most frequent semantic phenomena in language, and Chinese includes a large number of polysemous terms. In different contexts, the same word can take on a variety of meanings. The establishment of domain dictionaries for various fields enables the resolution of the aforementioned issues.

At the present, domain-specific dictionaries have made extensive use of Machine learning and deep learning, leading to a wide range of important results. Point-wise Mutual Information (PMI) is an important metric that is frequently utilized to assess the interdependence of two variables in machine learning-based approaches. In order to make it easier to study the sentiment orientation analysis of a word, Li et al. [5] build a weighted Chinese sentiment lexicon with tendency, which gives sentiment information for words, using a machine translation system with bilingual resources. The label propagation algorithm and the PMI calculation of each word are used in the process to achieve good precision and efficiently cover domain information. Because the basic sentiment dictionary is insufficient for domain-specific sentiment analysis, Fan et al. [6] construct a catering domain sentiment lexicon by fusing a word vector and the SO-PMI algorithm. The word vector problem of sentiment words that are frequently contextually related but have the opposite sentiment polarity is solved. Zhou et al. [7] present an approach for deducing the polarity of sentiment terms and developing a dictionary of book domain sentiment from extremely short comments with a large-scale corpus of extremely short comments. They employ the PMI in conjunction with a user voting mechanism. Combining a word vector approach with a deep learning neural network classifier is what Hu et al. [8] do in order to produce a usable sentiment lexicon for the purpose of sentiment analysis in finance. This is done in the context of deep learning. Peng et al. [9] create a dictionary for defective products with the TF-IDF algorithm and a Convolutional Neural Network (CNN) model. Li et al. [10] develop a domain sentiment lexicon for online public opinion analysis using the Word2Vec model and the cosine similarity algorithm. A seed lexicon based on the large-scale public opinion corpus is constructed using the general sentiment dictionary, and emotional words are identified and corrected using the cosine similarity algorithm and the Word2Vec model. Using a large-scale online dataset, Xing and Zhu [11] construct a classical integrated Chinese dictionary that outperforms the general one in segmenting classical Chinese words.

While there is considerable research on the construction of domain dictionaries, much of it is rather traditional in nature, leaving pre-training models with a high degree of transcendent knowledge underutilized. Additionally, no dictionary has been constructed specifically for the legal field, thus the building of a law domain dictionary will have significant research implications and broad application potential. To this purpose, we propose a framework for domain dictionary building that encodes sentences based on the RoBERTa [12] model and utilizes a masked language model (MLM) strategy to evaluate the domain information contained in each token.

In summary, this article makes the following contributions:

(1) We present a framework for the construction of domain dictionaries.
(2) Our research indicates that we are the first to apply masked language model technology to dictionary construction.
(3) Following the framework we proposed, we have built a dictionary for the legal field that will eventually be made available to the public.

2   Methodology

Considering a sizable performance improvement for pretraining natural language processing (NLP), this paper proposes a framework for domain dictionaries that is based on the RoBERTa algorithm that builds on the language. Both a text classification system and an evaluation module for information about lexical domains are incorporated into the framework as part of its design. On the basis of a bidirectional attention mechanism and pretraining with a form of the masked language model, RoBERTa is an improved and robustly optimized recipe for training BERT models [13]. It demonstrates that training BERT on a more extensive dataset for an extended period of time results in a significant improvement in performance.

Our text classification module begins by encoding the text that is supported by the pre-trained model. After this step, domain classification is carried out, which refers to the process of determining the domain from which the legal text originates. Finally, the results are returned. In the lexical domain information metrics module, the mask operation and prediction are performed on each word in the sentence in turn. This module is based on the text classification model of the text classification module, and it also evaluates the domain information that is contained in each word.

2.1   Text Classification Module

RoBERTa [12] aims to fully exploit BERT architecture and training methodologies. This pre-trained language model will capture syntactical and semantic knowledge primarily from the pre-training task of masked language modeling [14] prior to fine-tuning the specific tasks on downstream datasets. For classification tasks, the input representation of a sentence is composed of its token, segment and position embeddings. In addition, we use a special token [CLS] to represent its sentence vector in general, and the previous BERT-based classification models mostly utilize it to classification. As a consequence, RoBERTa model is employed as the foundation for encoding linguistic characteristics and the first input token [CLS] is used to obtain the sentence vector representation in our proposed technique. Therefore, for the i-th sentence, the sentence vector is represented in the following manner., as shown in Fig. 1.

$$S_i = RoBERTa(a_i, b_i, c_i)$$

The token embeddings, segmentation embeddings, and position embeddings are denoted a_i, b_i, c_i, respectively.

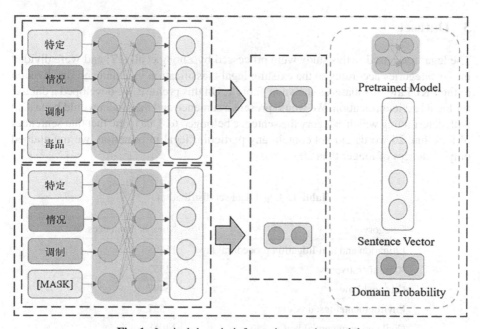

Fig. 1. Lexical domain information metrics module

2.2 Lexical Domain Information Metrics Module

Applications of the MLM model in natural language processing include multilingual sentiment categorization and Chinese word segmentation [15]. This multilingual sentiment categorization model is one that simultaneously trains contextual word embedding models across various languages, without the necessity for mapping to a common shared space in between [16]. The model performs differently depending on the language chosen, and even more so when the dataset is significantly skewed.

Under the direction of supervised fitting task representation, the model may learn and discriminate domain information in the lexical domain information metrics module. When the model predicts an output from a sample, the probability of the output prediction can be regarded as the proportion of domain information contained in the sample. In addition, as illustrated in Fig. 1, we employ this model and MLM approach to quantify the quantity of domain information of each word. Let $S = [x_1, x_2, x_3, \ldots, x_n]$ denote the input sentence, and $O_y(S)$ refers to the output prediction probability by the language recognition model RoBERTa for accurate label y. The domain information I_{w_i} of word w_i id defined as

$$I_{w_i} = O_y(S) - O_y\left(S_{\backslash w_i}\right)$$

where $S_{\backslash w_i} = [w_0, w_1, \ldots, [MASK], \ldots, w_n]$ is the sentence after replacing w_i as $[MASK]$.

3 Dataset

The legal texts used in this study were processed by Zhong et al. [17] and were divided into 9 categories according to the existing legal classification in China and the division of the PKULaw[1] database, as shown in Table 1. On this premise, we developed a dataset for legal text identification. We would present a sentence and the model would be tasked with determining which category the sentence belonged to. Due to the fact that sentences of less than 20 words did not contain any particular legal information, we maintained only sentences of longer than 20 words.

Table 1. Legal data set distribution.

Category	Num. of Sentences
Litigation and non-litigation procedural law	16493
Administrative law	2357
Criminal Law	6497
Environmental resources law	537
Civil and commercial law	14958
Constitution	2719
International law	8098
Social law	988
Economic law	2213

We collected 54860 samples in the dataset. The samples were classified in Table 1. All data were divided into five folds, with each fold containing a training set and a test

[1] http://www.pkulaw.cn/.

set. Each fold began with model training on the training set and ended with the model identifying vocabulary in the test set. The vocabulary was reviewed by legal scholars. During the review process, it was found that in order to maintain the dictionary's legal significance, certain useless words must be manually eliminated in accordance with the following regulations: 1. Non-conceptual texts such as year, date, serial number, etc.; 2. Non-conceptual individual Chinese characters texts. The resulting dictionary contained 2829 terms, each of which falled under one or more judicial categories, for example, "victim" falled into criminal law and litigation as well as non-litigation procedural law; "mortgage" belonged to civil and commercial law as well as economic law. Table 2 listed the terminology used in each judicial category.

Table 2. Legal dictionary distribution.

Category	Num. of Words
Litigation and non-litigation procedural law	924
Administrative law	317
Criminal Law	563
Environmental resources law	139
Civil and commercial law	999
Constitution	434
International law	760
Social law	91
Economic law	369

4 Experimental Settings

We implement our model based on HuggingFace's Transformers[2] with PyTorch[3] in one single NVIDIA Titan RTX GPU. Each model has 12 Transformer layers, 12 self-attention heads and 768 hidden units. Epochs, batch size, maximum sequence length, learning rate, and optimizer are set as 10, 32, 64, 5e−5, and AdamW [18] respectively.

5 Result

How to choose the base model affects the performance of text classification. For training, we use three different pre-training models BERT [19], MacBERT [20] and RoBERTa. Due to the imbalance of samples, Macro-F1 is regarded as the evaluation index. As shown in Table 1, all three pre-trained models perform well, and the Macro-F1 values

---

[2] https://github.com/huggingface/transformers.
[3] https://pytorch.org/.

are all greater than 92%, confirming the quality of the text classification dataset we produced. Furthermore, the RoBERTa model selected by our framework exhibits the best performance, with a Macro-F1 value of 92.46% (Table 3).

Table 3. Base model performance comparison results.

Model	Macro-F1
BERT	92.05%
MacBERT	92.21%
RoBERTa	**92.46%**

To compare, we select high-frequency words of the same scale as our dictionary, and train the three machine learning models based on the frequently-used dictionary and our domain dictionary respectively. The result reveals that the domain dictionary-based machine learning strategy outperforms the frequently-used dictionary-based one by an average of 3% (Table 4).

Table 4. Domain dictionary performance evaluation results

Method	Frequently-used Dictionary	Domain Dictionary
Decision Tree	74.03%	75.97%
KNeighbors	69.26%	75.26%
Random Forest	79.85%	80.69%
Average	74.38%	**77.31%**

6 Analysis

We list 20 domain words in each law as examples, as shown in Table 5. The domain dictionary we construct adapts to the actual features of legal text and serves as a reference for the development of judicial artificial intelligence in the legal field or other further studies in China:

1. The coverage of vocabulary is extensive and reasonable. The domain dictionary covers common words and highlights legal jargon. These terms are frequently used in the legal field. For example, "use" is a common term in criminal law, civil and commercial law, and environmental resources law, whereas "criminal" is a legal jargon in criminal law. However, legal jargon and common words have connections and differences. Firstly, legal jargon is a professional jargon of the legal field [21]. For example, the common word "gun" can refer to real guns, fake guns, toy guns,

pneumatic guns, etc., while the "gun" in criminal law generally refers to real guns, which is narrowed down by legislation. Secondly, there are many legal jargons, which are artificially created and not or rarely used in everyday speech. For example, the term "principal claim" in civil and commercial law. Therefore, the domain dictionary, which locates both legal jargon and common words, facilitates the flexible use and collocation of different terms by judicial artificial intelligence to construct more complex concepts.

2. The structure of vocabulary is well-structured and realistic. Table 2 manifests that civil and commercial law, as well as litigation and non-litigation procedure law, encompass the largest amount of legal language and have the most terms, 999 and 924 respectively. And the third-highest number of terms is in criminal law. Nowadays, according to the scope of cases, China's judicial artificial intelligence develops quickest in the civil and commercial field, with the Internet Court hearing many civil cases, and e-filing, collaborative enforcement, and other proceedings can be realized in judicial artificial intelligence [22]. In criminal cases, courts across the country at all levels begin to utilize judicial artificial intelligence to largely increase efficiency, such as online litigation and its auxiliary intelligent systems [23]. In addition, judicial collaboration in international law, such as international commercial arbitration, the collaboration of international criminal cases, etc., [24] is also one of the directions of judicial artificial intelligence in the future. In short, judicial artificial intelligence is increasingly used in practice, and obviously, the vocabulary structure constructed

Table 5. Examples of the domain dictionary

Litigation and non-litigation procedural law			
秩序 *(order)*	送达 *(delivery)*	申请 *(application)*	管辖权 *(jurisdiction)*
死亡 *(die)*	注明 *(mention)*	国家 *(nation)*	当事人 *(party)*
刑事 *(criminal)*	方法 *(method)*	法院 *(court)*	住所 *(residence)*
责任 *(responsibility)*	日期 *(date)*	受理 *(accept)*	中止 *(suspend)*
程序 *(procedure)*	裁决 *(decision)*	争议 *(dispute)*	履行 *(performance)*
Criminal Law			
受贿 *(bribery)*	侮辱罪 *(insult)*	刑期 *(jail term)*	紧急 *(emergency)*
利用 *(use)*	诽谤罪 *(libel)*	罪状 *(count)*	承诺 *(promise)*
威胁 *(threat)*	残币 *(mutilated currency)*	管制 *(regulation)*	骗取 *(defraud)*

(continued)

Table 5. (*continued*)

时期 (*period*)	危害性 (*hazardous*)	流产 (*abortion*)	嫌疑人 (*suspect*)
犯罪人 (*criminal*)	奸淫 (*rape*)	附加刑 (*punishment*)	检察院 (*procuratorate*)
Civil and commercial law			
折价 (*discount*)	公司 (*company*)	证券 (*security*)	管理人 (*manager*)
非营利 (*non-profit*)	股东 (*shareholder*)	发行人 (*publisher*)	主债权 (*principal claim*)
物权 (*property*)	董事 (*director*)	会计 (*accountant*)	包含 (*contain*)
赠与 (*gift*)	商标法 (*trademark law*)	受托人 (*trustee*)	利息 (*interest*)
劳动保险 (*labor insurance*)	少量 (*a small number of*)	承包 (*contract with*)	出借 (*lend*)
Environmental resources law			
保护 (*protect*)	损害 (*damage*)	海洋 (*ocean*)	经济区 (*economic zone*)
产权 (*property*)	污染者 (*polluter*)	水资源 (*water*)	造林 (*reforestation*)
节约 (*conservation*)	条例 (*rule*)	规划 (*program*)	育林 (*afforestation*)
质量 (*quality*)	多样性 (*diversity*)	污染 (*pollute*)	扶持 (*support*)
采矿 (*mining*)	气候 (*climate*)	公害 (*public nuisance*)	森林 (*forest*)
Administrative law			
起草 (*draft*)	治安 (*police*)	案卷 (*record*)	纳入 (*into*)
听证会 (*hearing*)	任期 (*term*)	任职 (*serve*)	国防 (*defense*)
公务员法 (*the civil service law*)	行政机关 (*administrative agency*)	吊销 (*revoke*)	精简 (*simplification*)
职位 (*position*)	论证 (*argument*)	发放 (*give out*)	公用 (*for public use*)
命令 (*command*)	废止 (*abolition*)	种类 (*type*)	裁定 (*rule*)
Constitution			
宪法性 (*constitutional*)	选民 (*voter*)	选区 (*district*)	政权 (*regime*)
界线 (*boundary*)	选举 (*election*)	主席 (*president*)	立法者 (*legislator*)

(*continued*)

Table 5. (*continued*)

国旗 (*flag*)	基本法 (*the Basic Law*)	总理 (*prime minister*)	民主性 (*democratic*)
国徽 (*emblem*)	附件 (*annexe*)	国务院 (*the State Council*)	政协 (*the Chinese People's Political Consultative Conference*)
华侨 (*overseas Chinese*)	广泛性 (*universality*)	政治权利 (*political right*)	阶级 (*class*)
International law			
内地 (*mainland*)	避税 (*tax avoidance*)	班轮 (*liner*)	海牙 (*Hague*)
认可 (*confirm*)	领土 (*territory*)	提单 (*bill of lading*)	承运人 (*carrier*)
当事方 (*party*)	军用 (*military*)	目的港 (*port of destination*)	雇员 (*employee*)
缔约国 (*contracting party*)	公海 (*the high seas*)	豁免 (*immunity*)	代理人 (*agent*)
最惠国 (*most-favoured-nation*)	磋商 (*consultation*)	待遇 (*treatment*)	要约人 (*offeror*)
Social law			
社会保险 (*social insurance*)	就业 (*employment*)	保障 (*security*)	劳动者 (*labor*)
企业 (*company*)	派遣 (*dispatch*)	服务 (*service*)	医疗 (*sanitation*)
失业 (*unemployment*)	福利 (*welfare*)	救助 (*assistance*)	关系 (*relationship*)
军人 (*soldier*)	工伤 (*occupational injury*)	报酬 (*payment*)	组织 (*organization*)
工会 (*union*)	期限 (*deadline*)	登记 (*register*)	险种 (*insurance*)
Economic law			
产业 (*industry*)	资金 (*capital*)	增值税 (*value-added tax*)	商品房 (*commodity houses*)
保修 (*warranty*)	贷款 (*loan*)	税额 (*tax*)	预售 (*pre-sale*)
诚信 (*integrity*)	商业 (*commerce*)	非居民 (*non-resident*)	收支 (*income and expenses*)

(*continued*)

Table 5. (*continued*)

核实 (*identify*)	竞争力 (*competitive*)	扣除 (*deduct*)	违约金 (*penalty*)
消费 (*consume*)	中介人 (*intermediary*)	船税 (*shipping tax*)	所得额 (*income*)

by the domain dictionary can conform to the scope of application basically. It is concentrated in litigation, civil, and criminal field, and with the development of judicial artificial intelligence, the application will also be extended to foreign-related judicial practice. Therefore, the existing reasonable structure of the domain dictionary can adapt to the needs of the judicial practice, and from the perspective of the development of judicial artificial intelligence, it will also meet the needs of future applications.

3. The composition of vocabulary is reasonable and foundational. The majority of the terms are content words while a few are function words. The function words include 11 categories of words, including linking verbs, prepositions, identifying words, quantifiers, conjunctions, relatives, adverbial conjunctions, conjunctive adverbs, intensifiers, auxiliary verbs, and pronouns [25]. For example, the terms "a small number of" and "contain" are function words in civil and commercial law. And few function words are in civil and commercial law, although this category contains the largest number of terms. The most common terms are "non-profit", "gift", "labor insurance" and other content words. This composition is following the essential feature of a domain dictionary. Although judicial artificial intelligence is sophisticated and specialized, as the basis of its learning, a domain dictionary cannot be constructed in isolation from the essence of dictionaries. Moreover, from the subsequent studies of the domain dictionary, although most function words, such as prepositions and quantifiers, etc., are necessary components of correct legal text, their inclusion in this dictionary will disproportionately increase the number of terms and so undermine the study of legal text and vocabulary.

4. The dictionary meets the needs of socialist rule of law with Chinese features. It includes a lot of terms with the Chinese features. For example, the terms "the Chinese People's Political Consultative Conference" in Constitution and "contract with" in civil and commercial law. The former is related to Chinese political system and the latter is related to Chinese farmers' land contract rights. The dictionary contains terms with Chinese features that will help judicial artificial intelligence to accurately match the context for selection. This is undoubtedly significant for the development of judicial artificial intelligence in the legal field or other further studies in China. Faced with the deepening of international artificial intelligence, the construction of a domain dictionary must take into account the needs of China's national conditions, otherwise, it is no different from copying other dictionaries.

7 Conclusion

This paper proposes a framework for dictionary construction and then demonstrates its application through the creation of a legal field-oriented domain dictionary. The domain dictionary we construct adapts to the actual features of legal text and serves as a reference for the development of artificial intelligence in the legal field in China. In the future, we will add additional legal texts to our domain dictionary.

References

1. Cheng, F.: Problems and responses of judicial artificial intelligence construction in China. Orient. Law **3**, 119–130 (2018)
2. Zuo, W.: From generalization to specialization: reflection on the application of judicial artificial intelligence in China. Legal Forum **35**(2), 17–23 (2020)
3. Ma, Z., Liu, B.: Jurisprudential analysis of application of judicial artificial intelligence: value, dilemma and path. Qinghai Soc. Sci. **5**, 135–141 (2018)
4. Fass, T.L., Heilbrun, K., DeMatteo, D., Fretz, R.: The LSI-R and the compas: validation data on two risk-needs tools. Crim. Justice Behav. **35**(9), 1095–1108 (2008)
5. Li, S., Li, Y., Huang, J., Su, Y.: Construction of Chinese sentiment lexicon using bilingual information and label propagation algorithm. J. Chin. Inf. Process. **27**(06), 75–81 (2013)
6. Fan, Q., Kuang, H., Xie, F.: Domain sentiment lexicon construction combining word embedding and pointwise mutual information. J. Fuyang Norm. Univ. (Nat. Sci.) **38**(3), 73–80 (2021)
7. Zhou, Z., Wang, C., Zhu, J.: Research on the construction of sentiment lexicon in book field based on extreme short reviews. Inf. Stud. Theory Appl. **44**(9), 183–189, 197 (2021)
8. Hu, J., Cen, Y., Wu, C.: Constructing sentiment dictionary with deep learning: case study of financial data. Data Anal. Knowl. Discov. **2**(10), 95–102 (2018)
9. Peng, C., Lv, X., Su, N., Zhang, L., Jiang, Z., Song, L.: Building phrase dictionary for defective products with convolutional neural network. Data Anal. Knowl. Discov. **4**(11), 112–120 (2020)
10. Li, C., Ji, X.: Construction of domain sentiment lexicon for online public opinion analysis in public emergencies. Digit. Libr. Forum **9**, 32–40 (2020)
11. Xing, F., Zhu, Y.: Large-scale online corpus based classical integrated Chinese dictionary construction and word segmentation. J. Chin. Inf. Process. **35**(7), 41–46 (2021)
12. Liu, Y., et al.: RoBERTa: a robustly optimized BERT pretraining approach. CORR (2019)
13. Dong, L., et al.: Unified language model pre-training for natural language understanding and generation. CORR (2019)
14. Zhou, W., et al.: Pre-training text-to-text transformers for concept-centric common sense. CORR (2020)
15. Wu, Z., Chen, Y., Kao, B., Liu, Q.: Perturbed masking: parameter-free probing for analyzing and interpreting BERT. In: Proceedings of the 58th Annual Meeting of the Association for Computational Linguistics, pp. 4166–4176 (2020)
16. Mutuvi, S., et al.: Multilingual epidemiological text classification: a comparative study. In: Proceedings of the 28th International Conference on Computational Linguistics, pp. 6172–6183 (2020)
17. Zhong, H., et al.: JEC-QA: a legal-domain question answering dataset. In: Proceedings of the AAAI Conference on Artificial Intelligence, pp. 9701–9708 (2020)
18. Loshchilov, I., Hutter, F.: Decoupled weight decay regularization. CoRR (2017)

19. Devlin, J., Chang, M.W., Lee K., Toutanova, K.: BERT: pre-training of deep bidirectional transformers for language understanding. In: Proceedings of NAACLHLT 2019, pp. 4171–4186 (2019)
20. Cui, Y., et al.: Revisiting pre-trained models for Chinese natural language processing. In: Proceedings of the 2020 Conference on Empirical Methods in Natural Language Processing: Findings, pp. 657–668 (2020)
21. Xiao, Y.: The Characteristics, etymology and translation of legal terms both in English and Chinese. Chin. Transl. J. **03**, 44–47 (2001)
22. Ji, W.: The change of judicial power in the age of artificial intelligence. Orient. Law **01**, 125–133 (2018)
23. Zuo, W.: Online litigation in China: empirical research and development prospect. J. Comp. Law **04**, 161–172 (2020)
24. Rudnev, V., Pechegin, D.: The impact of the leading digital technologies on criminal proceedings: a case of video conferencing. In: Proceedings of the 6th International Conference on Social, Economic, and Academic Leadership, pp. 323–329 (2020)
25. Gao, Y.: The study of function words since the 20th century. Foreign Lang. Teach. **05**, 20–22 (2001)

Computational Linguistics, Applications of Natural Language Processing

RoBERTa: An Efficient Dating Method of Ancient Chinese Texts

Meiwei Li[✉], Yunhui Qin, and Wei Huangfu

University of Science and Technology Beijing, Beijing, China
1393539093@qq.com, b20170317@xs.ustb.edu.cn, huangfuwei@ustb.edu.cn

Abstract. To address the dating problem of ancient Chinese texts, this paper proposes to model the text with RoBERTa(Robustly Optimized BERT Pretraining Approach) model, fully learn the contextual information of the text and combine with the ancient Chinese pre-training model for training. The experiments demonstrated the effectiveness of RoBERTa model for the chronological classification of ancient Chinese, and the accuracy of the classification reaches 93.98%. Our work can subsequently help researchers of ancient Chinese to perform automatic dating of ancient Chinese.

Keywords: Ancient Chinese · Dating · RoBERTa

1 Introduction

The evolution of language is a complex science that integrates the natural and human sciences. The evolution of language can contain features that reflect time, so linguistic evidence can be used to dating texts, especially in the absence of other archaeological evidence.

The historical development of the English language is usually divided into three stages: Old English, Middle English and Modern English. In the course of its use, English has adopted, absorbed and used the vocabulary and language usage of the places in which it was spoken. The changes have been gradual, with varying degrees and scope of compatibility with the vocabulary of other languages at each period of English's development.

Ancient Chinese is the language used by the people of ancient China. After thousands of years of historical evolution, the lexis and syntax of ancient Chinese have become very different from modern Chinese, and it is difficult to read and understand ancient Chinese without specialist knowledge of the language. The problem in this paper is to determine the dynasty which the ancient Chinese texts belong to. There are a huge number of ancient books in China, which contain the wisdom of many ancient people, and if we can read them, we can make use

---

Supported by Social Science Foundation Project of Beijing (Grant No. 18YYB003). The corresponding author is Prof. Wei Huangfu.

of the essence of them, and they are also important for historical research and discovery. On the one hand, the study of dating the ancient Chinese texts is a foundation for the construction of a corpus of ancient Chinese texts. On the other hand, it is the basis for the processing of information such as sentence segment, word segment, part-of-speech tagging and text classification. It is only when the period of the texts is clarified that research can be carried out in a more focused manner.

The established methods of dating ancient Chinese texts have all started from a linguistic perspective. Dobson [1] al. conducted an exhaustive study of all the dummy words in the ancient Chinese texts and determined the dynasty of the ancient texts by analysing the grammatical features of the dummy words. This exhaustive analysis is inefficient and the quality of the dating results is highly dependent on the level of knowledge of the researchers. How to efficiently and accurately dating ancient Chinese texts is a major issue at hand.

Natural Language Processing (NLP) refers to using computers to process the meaning of texts to achieve information exchange between humans and machines. Natural language processing techniques can perform tasks such as text classification, machine translation, sequence annotation, information extraction and automatic summarisation. The task of dating of ancient Chinese texts is a text classification task from the perspective of natural language processing.

In this paper, the RoBERTa model is introduced to realize the dating of ancient Chinese texts. The RoBERTa model is based on the self-attention mechanism to learn deep bidirectional linguistic representations through two tasks, masked language model and next sentence prediction, to accomplish the task of dating of ancient Chinese texts. In this paper, we simplify the original RoBERTa model by removing the segment embedding, and choose the median sentence length as the length of each sample because the length of each sentence varies greatly among ancient Chinese texts of different periods. Due to the specificity that language evolves gradually, the text of a certain dynasty may have similar features to the texts of its two neighbouring dynasties, so a new evaluation metric Acc@3 is proposed in this paper to evaluate the performance of the model. The experimental results demonstrate that the RoBERTa model achieves better results in dating of ancient Chinese texts.

2   Related Work

Previously, researchers have analyzed the dating of ancient Chinese mainly from a linguistic perspective, and these methods have been time-consuming and labor-intensive, relying on researchers to do so manually. In recent years, the combination of artificial intelligence and various fields continues to deepen, the use of computers and natural language processing techniques can be used to better investigate the dating of ancient Chinese texts. From the view of natural language processing tasks, the task of dating ancient Chinese texts is to input a text and output the period corresponding to this text, which belongs to the classification task in natural language processing.

Current text classification models can be broadly classified into three categories. The first category is rule-based text classification methods, the second category is traditional machine learning methods based on probability statistics, and the third category is deep learning methods based on neural networks and attention mechanisms.

The rule-based text classification method requires human knowledge to develop the rules. Yuqin [2] et al. implemented a text classification system by collaborating with experts in the field of classification, obtaining information on the subject terms of the classes through various classification dictionaries, and manually performing keyword screening to develop rules. The rules formed by this method are usually more accurate. However, when the rules change or are updated, the rules need to be manually re-summarized, and the maintenance cost is high. When there are more rules, there may be conflicts between the rules. And it is difficult to extend to other scenarios.

Traditional machine learning methods based on probabilistic statistics generally require manual feature selection in conjunction with scenes, and then the features are put into a machine learning classifier for training, including Naive Bayes [3], K-Nearest Neighbor (KNN) [4], Support Vector Machines (SVM) [5] and so on. McCallum [6] et al. conducted classification tests on five text corpora using multivariate Bernoulli Bayes networks as well as polynomial Bayes networks, and demonstrated better classification results using multivariate Bernoulli's Bayesian model. Bin [7] et al. used multi-level feature extraction methods and a kernel-based distance-weighted KNN algorithm to classify Chinese text, which better provides statistics on the distribution of documents while improving the classification accuracy of the text. Joachims [5] analyzed the suitability of SVMs for text classification tasks from the perspective of text attributes. Such statistical-based methods still require manual feature selection, are difficult to maintain and cannot be generalized to other scenarios.

Deep learning text classification methods based on neural networks and attention mechanisms are the trend in recent years to solve domain-specific text classification problems. These methods are mainly based on Convolutional Neural Networks (CNN) [8], Recurrent Neural Network (RNN) [9], Bidirectional Long Short-Term Memory (BiLSTM) [10], Self-Attention [11], Bidirectional Encoder Representations from Transformers (BERT) [12], RoBERTa [13] and so on. Kim [8] applied CNN to the field of natural language processing to improve the performance of text classification. Tang [9] applied RNN to text classification, but the memory of RNN is relatively short, and the network will forget the previous text information when the text is too long. BiLSTM [10]can remember longer-term information than RNN. Xuejin [14] applied the BiLSTM model to dating of ancient Chinese texts in 2019 and achieved good results. But there is a possibility of gradient disappearance or gradient explosion in the network. Transformer [11] is an attention-based model, which greatly solves the problem of short-term memory of RNN and can be processed in parallel. BERT [12] pre-trains the Encoder of the Transformer model on large-scale data by the two tasks of predicting the masked words and the next sentence prediction.

The state-of-the-art performance on many NLP tasks was achieved by fine-tuning BERT for specific tasks. Since then, the pre-training plus fine-tuning solution has become the paradigm of natural language processing. The RoBERTa [13] model uses the same model architecture as BERT, but improves the pre-training task of BERT by adopting a dynamic word masking strategy and eliminating the contextual coherence prediction task to train on a larger corpus. This approach eliminates the need for manual extraction of rules and features, and works well with more complex and larger data sets.

3   Experiments and Discuss

In this paper our raw data is a number of books downloaded from the open corpus of ancient Chinese available on the web. Each of these books has its own corresponding dynasty t. A sentence from each book is entered into the model as a sample, and the label corresponding to this sample is the label corresponding to this book. Let $S = \{s_1, s_2, ..., s_i, ..., s_n\}$ denote a sequence of input text, and s_i indicates a word in the input text sequence. We wish to construct a model M, so that model M can be used to solve the problem of determining the dynasty of input texts. The model is constructed as follows: $t = M(\{s_1, s_2, ..., s_i, ..., s_n\})$

We propose to use the RoBerta model for the dating of ancient Chinese texts. The RoBERTa model mainly consists of three parts: the embedding layer, the encoding layer and the output layer. The role of the embedding layer is to convert the input text into a vector, then the vector is sent to the coding layer for feature extraction to obtain the hidden vector, and finally the output layer calculates the prediction results based on the hidden vector containing the text features.

3.1   Data Set Introduction

The data used to conduct the experiments in this paper are ancient Chinese canonical texts downloaded from the open ancient Chinese corpus on the Internet. In order to make the time span of the dataset large enough for subsequent researchers to study the evolutionary process of language development in ancient Chinese on a continuous timeline, we selected ten time periods between Spring and Autumn and Qing dynasties as category labels and used T1, T2, T3, T4, T5, T6, T7, T8, T9 and T10 to represent them respectively, and the time labels and the corresponding years are shown in Table 1.

Table 1. Tags and corresponding year(Note: There are overlapping dynasties, the following table prevails.)

Tag	Dynasty	Year
T1	Spring and Autumn Period	770 B.C.—476 B.C
T2	The Warring States Period	475 B.C.—221 B.C
T3	Western Han period	206 B.C.—8 A.D
T4	Eastern Han period	25 A.D.—200 A.D
T5	Northern and Southern Dynasties	420 A.D.—581 A.D
T6	Tang Dynasty	618 A.D.—907 A.D
T7	Song Dynasty	960 A.D.—1279 A.D
T8	Yuan dynasty	1279 A.D.—1368 A.D
T9	Ming Dynasty	1368 A.D.—1644 A.D
T10	Qing Dynasty	1644 A.D.—1911 A.D

We selected ancient texts written in each period as training sets, and some of the selected books are shown in Table 2 below.

Table 2. Selected books and number of characters for each period

Tag	Book name	Characters
T1	*Guoyu, etc.*	346 k
T2	*Mozi, etc.*	362 k
T3	*Huainanzi, etc.*	341 k
T4	*A Comparative Study of Different Schools of Learning, etc.*	480 k
T5	*New Anecdotes of Social Talk, etc.*	209 k
T6	*The Biography of Yingying, etc.*	365 k
T7	*Dream Pool Essays, etc.*	630 k
T8	*The Romance of West Chamber, etc.*	276 k
T9	*Journey to the West, etc.*	332 k
T10	*Dream of the Red Chamber, etc.*	725 k

3.2   Evaluation Criteria

In order to evaluate the performance of the RoBERTa, we use the following four metrics: Accuracy (Acc), Precision (P), Recall (R), and F1 value.

The dating of ancient Chinese texts in this paper is a multiclassification problem, and because of the nature of languages that evolve gradually, a text from one dynasty may have similar characteristics to texts from two of its neighbours.

Therefore, this paper proposes a new evaluation metric Acc@3 to evaluate the performance of the model on the test set, that is to say the prediction result is ground truth and its two adjacent dynasties are considered as correct predictions, denoted by $N_{right}@3$. N_{all} is the number of all samples.

$$Acc@3 = \frac{N_{right}@3}{N_{all}} \tag{1}$$

Macro-averaging is used when evaluating multi-categorization problems, where the performance of the model under different categories needs to be evaluated comprehensively. Each category can be considered as a dichotomous problem, and the P, R, and F1 values can be obtained. Macro-averaging means the arithmetic mean of each evaluation index of all categories, that is, Macro-Precision (Macro-P), Macro-Recall (Macro-R), and Macro-F1 Score (Macro-F1). The calculation formula is as follows, where n denotes the number of categories of the classification problem and i denotes the i-th category.

$$Macro\text{-}P = \frac{1}{n}\sum_{i=1}^{n} P_i \tag{2}$$

$$Macro\text{-}R = \frac{1}{n}\sum_{i=1}^{n} R_i \tag{3}$$

$$Macro\text{-}F1 = \frac{2 * Macro\text{-}P * Macro\text{-}R}{Macro\text{-}P + Macro\text{-}R} \tag{4}$$

In order to verify the effectiveness of the model proposed in this paper for dating of ancient Chinese, experiments are conducted on the ancient Chinese canonical texts downloaded from the public ancient Chinese corpus on the Internet. This section will mainly introduce the data set used for the experiment, present the parameter settings for the experiment and introduce the three sets of experiments we have carried out. The first experiment aims to select the learning rate and batch size, the second experiment compares the performance of RoBERT, CNN, BiLSTM, and BERT, and the third experiment uses different dataset segmentation methods to compare the performance of the RoBERTa model.

3.3   Parameters Setting

The programming language used to write the code for this experiment is python, the deep learning framework used is pytorch, and the GPU of NVIDIA Tesla V100 is used for acceleration in this experiment. The software versions used for the experiments are python 3.8.8 and PyTorch 1.9.0.

The model parameters are set as shown in the following Table 3.

Table 3. Parameter setting

Parameter name	Parameter value
the hidden state dimension	768
the number of heads	12
the number of encoder layer	12
max sequence length	64
train epochs	30
weight decay	1e-3
batch size	64
learning rate	1e-5

3.4 Experiments and Analysis

In this section we conduct three experiments.

The first experiment is designed to select the optimal hyperparameters of the introduced RoBERTa, which include the batch size and the learning rate. The training batch size and learning rate are two important parameters in the model training process. We conducted multiple sets of experiments to select these two hyperparameters. We compared the performance of the model on the test set with different parameter combinations, We found that the highest classification accuracy of 93.98% was achieved on the test set when the training batch size was 64 and the learning rate was 1e-5, so we used this set of hyperparameters for all subsequent experiments.

Then, the second experiment is conducted to compare the introduced model and the baselines.

We compared a total of five models, TextCNN, BiLSTM, BERT based on bert-base-chinese pre-trained model, RoBERTa based on chinese-roberta-wwm-ext, and guwenBERT pre-trained model [15], respectively. The Chinese BERT model is bert-base-chinese provided by Google, the Chinese texts of RoBERTa pre-trained model is chinese-roberta-wwm-ext, and the ancient Chinese texts of RoBERTa pre-trained model is guwenBERT-base. Multiple sets of experiments were conducted on each model for hyperparameter selection, and the performance on the test set will be compared.

The accuracy of these five models during the training process is shown in Fig. 1, and it can be seen that the RoBERTa model based on ancient Chinese pre-training performs the best.

As shown in Table 4 below, the comparison shows that the guwenBERT-based model works better in the test set. The RoBERTa model based on ancient Chinese pre-trained guwenBERT has better results than the chinese-roberta-wwm-ext, which indicates that the semantics of modern Chinese and ancient Chinese have certain differences, and direct migration will affect the results to some extent. And pre-training based on data in the ancient Chinese domain can better learn the semantics and improve the performance of downstream tasks.

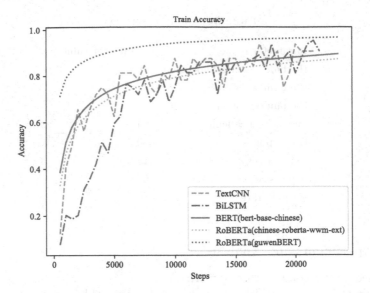

Fig. 1. The training accuracy of the five models

And the results show that the Roberta model is better in dating ancient Chinese texts than the BiLSTM model proposed by Xuejin [14].

Table 4. Performance of different models in the test set under optimal hyperparameters setting

Model	Acc(%)	Acc@3(%)	Macro-P(%)	Macro-R(%)	Macro-F1(%)
TextCNN	85.73	92.93	84.83	83.36	83.92
BiLSTM	83.37	92.32	82.44	81.24	81.44
BERT(bert-base-chinese)	85.20	93.20	83.75	83.95	83.85
RoBERTa(chinese-roberta-wwm-ext)	85.41	93.33	83.65	84.29	83.97
RoBERTa(guwenBERT)	93.98	97.49	92.05	93.07	92.56

4   Conclusion and Future Work

In this paper, we use RoBERTa for dating of ancient Chinese, and experimentally compare TextCNN, BiLSTM, BERT. We finally find that the performance of RoBERTa is better, which can be subsequently used to help ancient Chinese researchers to work on the dating of ancient books, and can also be used to build an ancient Chinese dating corpus to realize the retrieval and statistics of ancient books according to dynasties.

The next step of work can be considered to transform the classification problem into a regression problem of judging years to predict the specific years of ancient books, so as to achieve a finer temporal annotation and facilitate the study of more subtle changes in language by ancient Chinese language workers.

References

1. Dobson, W.A.C.H.: Authenticating and dating archaic Chinese texts. Toung Pao (Second Ser.) **53**(4–5), 233–242 (1967)
2. Lihua, S., Yuqin, L.: Rule-based automatic category application on text category. J. Chin. Inf. Process. **18**(4), 9–14 (2004)
3. Maron, M.E.: Automatic indexing: an experimental inquiry. J. ACM **8**(3), 404–417 (1961)
4. Cover, T., Hart, P.: Nearest neighbor pattern classification. IEEE Trans. Inf. Theory **13**(1), 21–27 (1967)
5. Joachims, T.: Text categorization with support vector machines: learning with many relevant features (1998)
6. McCallum, A., Nigam, K.: A comparison of event models for Naive Bayes text classification (1998)
7. Bin, L., Tiejun, H., Jun, C., Wen, G.: A new statistical-based method in automatic text classification. J. Chin. Inf. Process. **16**(6), 19 (2002)
8. Kim, Y.: Convolutional neural networks for sentence classification. In: Proceedings of the 2014 Conference on Empirical Methods in Natural Language Processing (EMNLP), pp. 1746–1751, Doha, Qatar, October 2014
9. Tang, D., Qin, B., Liu, T.: Document modeling with gated recurrent neural network for sentiment classification. In: Proceedings of the 2015 Conference on Empirical Methods in Natural Language Processing, pp. 1422–1432, Lisbon, Portugal, September 2015
10. Graves, A., Schmidhuber, J.: Framewise phoneme classification with bidirectional LSTM networks. In: Proceedings of the IEEE International Joint Conference on Neural Networks, vol. 4, pp. 2047–2052 (2005)
11. Vaswani, A., et al.: Attention is all you need. arXiv (2017)
12. Devlin, J., Chang, M., Lee, K., Toutanova, K.: BERT: pre-training of deep bidirectional transformers for language understanding. In: Proceedings of the 2019 Conference of the North American Chapter of the Association for Computational Linguistics: Human Language Technologies, Volume 1 (Long and Short Papers), pp. 4171–4186, Minneapolis, Minnesota, June 2019
13. Liu, Y., et al.: RoBERTa: a robustly optimized BERT pretraining approach (2019)
14. Xuejin, Y., Huangfu, W.: A machine learning model for the dating of ancient Chinese texts. In: Proceedings of the 2019 International Conference on Asian Language Processing, pp. 115–120 (2019)
15. Tan, Y.: GuwenBERT: a pre-trained language model for classical Chinese (literary Chinese). https://github.com/Ethan-yt/guwenbert(2021-07-06)

Building a Corpus for Chinese Causality Extraction in Futures Domain

Huiyong Sun, Yuxiang Jia[✉], Xiaojing Du, Shuai Cao, and Hongying Zan

School of Computer and Artificial Intelligence, Zhengzhou University, Zhengzhou, China
{ieyxjia,iehyzan}@zzu.edu.cn

Abstract. Causality extraction is to extract cause events and effect events from text, which is the basis for constructing causal event graphs and doing causal reasoning. The research on causality extraction needs the support of annotated causality corpus. In this paper, we construct an annotated causality corpus based on texts from Chinese futures domain. We annotate whether a sentence contains causality and for a causal sentence we further annotate spans of both cause and effect. Based on the 5557 cause and effect pairs, we analyze the distribution, categories of causal events and cases of causal chains in futures domain. Preliminary experiments on automatic causality extraction show an exact matching accuracy of 71.38%.

Keywords: Causality extraction · Corpus · Futures domain · Causal chain

1 Introduction

Causal relationship is one of the most important types of relationship between events. Causality extraction is a task to extract causal relationship from texts, which can support event inference, evolution analysis and other applications. Causality knowledge is especially important for tasks such as market analysis and risk prediction in the financial domain. However, the lack of publicly available annotated causality corpus hinders the research of causality extraction to some extent.

To alleviate the problem, we construct an annotated causality corpus based on texts from Chinese futures domain. Based on the corpus, we analyze causal events in futures domain and carry out preliminary experiments on causality extraction. The organization of this paper is as follows: Sect. 2 introduces related work. Section 3 describes in detail the corpus construction process. Section 4 analyzes the distribution of causal events in the corpus. Section 5 shows the experiments on causality extraction and Sect. 6 gives the conclusion.

2 Related Work

English corpora for causality extraction [1] include SemEval2010-task8 series [2], EventStoryLine [3], AltLex [4], Causal-TimeBank [5] and FinCausal [6]. SemEval2010-task8 is to determine the type of relationship between a pair of nouns in a sentence. There

Q. Su et al. (Eds.): CLSW 2022, LNAI 13496, pp. 302–314, 2023.
https://doi.org/10.1007/978-3-031-28956-9_24

are 9 types of relationships including causality. 1331 out of 10717 sentences in the corpus each contains a causal word pair. Based on the SemEval2010-task8 corpus, Li et al. [7] further annotates all related word or phrase pairs and their relationship types in each sentence, resulting in 1866 causal word pairs in 1270 sentences. The EventStoryLine corpus annotates stories with event relationships. In the 184 stories, 318 out of 7608 event pairs have causal relationship. The AltLex corpus is constructed based on PDTB and Wikipedia, and contains 4595 causal sentences. Causal-TimeBank enriches the TimeML corpus with causality. In the 258 documents, 1770 out of 7805 event pairs have causal relationship. FinCausal contains 29444 sentences in the domain of financial news, of which 2136 sentences contain 2388 causal event pairs.

Chinese corpora for causality extraction include CEC (Chinese Emergency Corpus) [8], the Chinese Discourse TreeBank [9] and Chinese legal corpus [10]. The CEC corpus is composed of 332 news texts of Internet emergencies, mainly including five types of emergencies such as earthquakes, fires, traffic accidents, terrorist attacks and food poisoning. 1575 pairs of causal events are annotated among other event relationships. The Chinese Discourse TreeBank is built based on the Chinese TreeBank [11]. 5534 event pairs are annotated with relation types in 164 documents, among which 261 event pairs have causal relationship. The Chinese legal corpus is annotated with causal events in texts of more than 30,000 cases of personal injury, violence, fraud, misappropriation of public funds, and abuse of power.

3   Construction of the Corpus

We crawl news texts in futures domain from websites like Sina.com, Sina Weibo, Toutiao, Sohu, NetEase, WeChat Official Accounts, Hexun.com, etc. The futures varieties we consider include Cotton, Red dates, Apple, Sugar, Glass and PTA. Finally, we obtain 64483 news texts between January 2020 and March 2021.

We clean the data by removing HTML tags, removing duplication, etc. Then we classify texts according to different futures varieties based on respective key words. We take an easy-to-hard approach for the annotation task and begin with simple cases by setting three constraints as shown in Table 1. Firstly, we choose texts about the most familiar futures variety, Cotton. Secondly, we segment the sentence by "comma" and only consider causality in sub-sentences. Thirdly, we only consider causality with explicit causal marker 导致/lead to.

Table 1. Constraints for simple causality cases

Futures varieties	Text unit	Causal marker
Cotton	sub-sentence	导致/lead to

3.1 Annotation Specification

In order to perform causality annotation more accurately and efficiently, we adopt a two-step strategy. The first step is causal sentence annotation task, annotating whether a sentence contains causality. The second step is causal component annotation task, annotating the scope of cause and effect.

Causal Sentence Annotation Rule: A causal sentence must and only contains a single pair of cause and effect. Example 1 is a causal sentence with a pair of cause, abundant supply of cotton, and effect, high commercial inventories of domestic cotton. However, Example 2 and 3 are not causal sentences as the former lacks cause while the latter has multi-causes.

Example 1: 棉花供应充足**导致**国内棉花的商业库存较高。

    *Abundant supply of cotton **leads to** high commercial inventories of domestic cotton.*

Example 2: 最终**导致**美印棉价差继续走高。

    *Eventually **lead to** the US-India cotton spread continues to rise.*

Example 3:
宏观经济增幅放缓、中美贸易摩擦**导致**粘胶短纤及下游服装需求减弱。

    *The slowdown of macroeconomic growth and the trade friction between China and the United States have **led to** weaker demand for viscose staple fiber and downstream apparel.*

Causal Component Annotation Rule: The cause and effect must be around the causal marker while express complete meaning and point to clear object or event. In example 4 to 6, the causal marker is 导致/lead to, while tag pairs (<cause>, </cause>) and (<effect>, </effect>) denote cause and effect respectively.

Example 4: 但 <cause>   过高的籽棉价格   < /cause>   依然导致   <effect> 轧花厂新花 皮棉成本抬升</effect>.

    However, <cause> excessive seed cotton prices </cause> still lead to <effect> the cost of new lint cotton in the ginning plant rising </effect>.

Example 5: 棕榈油生产国理事会表示因 <cause>   拉尼娜   </cause>   将导致 <effect>   东南亚持续出现强降雨 </effect>.

    *The Council of Palm Oil Producing Countries state that <cause> **La Nina** </cause> will lead to <effect> **continuous heavy rainfall in Southeast Asia** </effect>.*

Example 6: <cause>   棉花供应充足   </cause>   导致   <effect> 国内棉花的商业库存较高 </effect >.

    *<cause> **Abundant supply of cotton** </cause> leads to <effect> **high commercial inventories of domestic cotton** </effect>.*

3.2 Annotation Process

As shown in Fig. 1, the annotation process is divided into two stages, the causal sentence annotation stage and the causal component annotation stage. In each stage, a test annotation for the annotators to understand the specification is carried out in advance. 200 samples are randomly selected and all annotators try on these samples. Discussions are made on inconsistency and annotation specification is adjusted if necessary. If the inter-annotator agreement surpasses 80%, then we move onto the formal annotation stage.

In the formal annotation stage, each sample is annotated independently by two annotators. If inconsistency happens, the two annotators discuss and try to solve it. If agreement still cannot be reached, it will be put forward to the annotation supervisor for a decision. In the whole annotation process, the annotation specification can be updated if needed. Improper samples will be dropped during annotation.

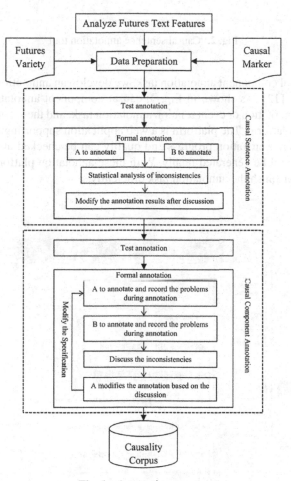

Fig. 1. Annotation process

3.3 Annotation Platforms

To assist the annotation process and ensure the annotation quality, we develop annotation platforms for annotators. Figure 2 shows the tool for the causal sentence annotation task. With the tool, the annotator can check sentence by sentence if causality exists therein. It is easy for the annotator to check the progress and jump to any target sentence.

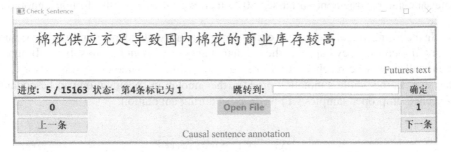

Fig. 2. Causal sentence annotation tool

For the causal component annotation task, we develop an annotation platform based on Zhang et al. [12]. As shown in Fig. 3, causal component annotation is similar to entity relation annotation or event relation annotation task, and these tasks can be solved using a unified platform. The platform is a web application supporting many annotators working together. Annotation progress and quality can be checked at any time and an analysis report will be generated finally. With these annotation platforms, 10 graduate students together finish the annotation task efficiently.

Fig. 3. Causal component annotation platform

3.4 Annotation Result

The Kappa value [13] and F1 score [14] are generally used as metrics to evaluate the inter-annotator agreement [15]. We use Kappa value to measure the inter-annotator agreement of causal sentence annotation task, and use F1 score to measure the inter-annotator agreement of causal component annotation task. For our corpus, the Kappa value is 94% and the F1 score is 85%, indicating a high quality annotation.

In total, 7470 sentences are annotated, 5871 of which are annotated as causal sentences, accounting for 78.5%. It shows that causal marker is a good signal of causality. After the causal component annotation, 5557 causal event pairs are annotated based on the 5871 causal sentences. It provides a data basis for causal event analysis in futures domain and automatic causality extraction.

4 Analysis of the Corpus

The annotated causal events are mainly about the futures variety Cotton. After word segmentation, the word clouds of cause events and effect events are drawn according to the word frequency. As shown in Fig. 4, " 疫情/Epidemic", " 新冠/New coronavirus" and " 肺炎/Pneumonia" appear more frequently in cause events, while " 棉花/Cotton", " 价格/Price" and " 需求/Demand" appear more frequently in effect events.

Cause   Effect

Fig. 4. Causal event word cloud

According to the annotated corpus, the cause events are roughly divided into six categories, namely Epidemic (1243), Supply and demand (1134), Weather (536), Policy (383), Emotion (98), and Others. The number in the brackets is the times such event happens. As shown in Table 2,

(1) Epidemic event: the outbreak of the new coronavirus since 2019.
(2) Supply and demand event: changes in the supply and demand of futures products.

(3) Weather event: natural conditions such as rain, snow, high temperature, pests and diseases.
(4) Policy event: the normal policy adjustments made by the government to stabilize the market.
(5) Emotion event: people's attitudes and views on the current market conditions.
(6) Others: events other than the above five types of events.

Table 2. Categories of cause events

Event Category	Specific Event
Epidemic event	新冠疫情/COVID-19, 疫情变化/epidemic changes, 海外疫情蔓延/overseas epidemic spread, 国内疫情爆发/domestic epidemic outbreak, etc.
Supply and demand event	需求减少/demand decrease, 需求增加/demand increase, 需求下滑/demand slump, 供给增加/supply increase, 供给收缩/supply contraction, 供需紧张/supply and demand tight, 供需错配/supply and demand mismatch, 供需双弱/supply and demand weaken, 高库存/high inventory, etc.
Weather event	寒流天气/cold weather, 干旱天气/drought weather, 暴雨天气/rainstorm weather, 雨水天气/rainy weather, 冰冻天气/freezing weather, 极寒天气/extremely cold weather, 高湿高温天气/high humidity and temperature weather, 阴雨天气/rainy weather, 潮湿天气/wet weather, 雨雪天气/rain and snow weather, 台风天气/typhoon weather, 大风天气/strong wind weather, 病虫害/pests, 拉尼娜/La Nina, etc.
Policy event	市场购买力的下降/decline of market purchasing power, 防疫措施/anti-epidemic measures, 市场缺乏流动性/lack of liquidity in the market, 市场大幅波动/large market volatility, 货币宽松/monetary easing, 中美贸易摩擦/Sino-US trade friction, 政策预期向好/better policy expectations, 政策的收严/stricter policy, 政策的滞后性/policy lag, etc.
Emotion event	恐慌情绪加剧/panic intensify, 看涨情绪提升/bullish emotion lift, 观望情绪升温/wait-and-see emotion heating up, 负面情绪增加/negative emotion increase, 避险情绪提高/risk-off emotion improve, 利空情绪增长/bearish emotion increase, etc.
Others	空头大幅减仓/significantly lighten up short positions, 空头资金/short funds, 多重利空/multiple bearish, etc.

According to the annotated corpus, the effect events are roughly divided into six categories, namely Price (882), Supply and demand (1496), Transportation (148), Enterprise (298), Emotion (189), and Others. The number in the brackets is the times such event happens. As shown in Table 3,

(1) Price event: price changes such as costs and profits of futures products.
(2) Supply and demand event: changes in the supply and demand of futures products.
(3) Transportation event: the delays in the transportation of futures products.
(4) Enterprise event: changes in business operations due to policies and epidemics.
(5) Emotion event: people's attitudes and views on current market conditions.
(6) Others: events other than the five categories above.

Table 3. Categories of effect events

Event Category	Specific Event
Price event	价格上涨/price rise, 价格下跌/price fall, 盘面价格下跌/market price fall, 成本上升/cost rise, 成本下降/cost fall, 利润反弹/profit rebound, 利润下降/profit fall, 国际棉下跌/international cotton price fall, etc.
Supply and demand event	需求回升/demand recovery, 需求下降/demand decline, 需求替代/demand substitution, 供应紧张/supply tight, 供应过剩/supply glut, 供需紧张/supply and demand tight, 供需错配/supply and demand mismatch, 供需双弱/supply and demand weaken, 国内库存回升/domestic inventory recovery, 产量下降/production decline, 产量增加/production increase, 产量持平/production flat, etc.
Transportation events	装运延迟/delayed shipment, 到港延迟/delayed arrival at port, 封路现象普遍/common road closures, 运输困难/difficult transportation, etc.
Enterprise event	企业经营困难/difficulty in enterprise operations, 企业倒闭/enterprise shutdown, 国内纺织企业延迟开工/domestic textile enterprises delayed the start of operation, 棉纺企业停工/cotton enterprises shutdown, etc.
Emotion event	恐慌情绪加剧/panic intensify, 看涨情绪提升/bullish emotion lift, 观望情绪升温/wait-and-see emotion heating up, 负面情绪增加/negative emotion increase, 避险情绪提高/risk-off emotion improve, 利空情绪增长/bearish emotion increase, 看涨情绪缓和/bullish emotion ease, 悲观情绪提升/pessimism rise, etc.
Others	行情快速拉升/rapid rise in market prices, 债务增长/debt growth, etc.

In the past three years, the emergence of the *Epidemic* has had a significant impact on our production and life. According to the annotated corpus, there are 1243 incidents caused by the *Epidemic*. From Fig. 5, it can be seen that the *Epidemic* has affected *Supply and demand, Price, Enterprise, Transportation*, and *Emotion* to varying degrees. *Supply and demand* event contains specific events like supply and demand weaken, and demand decline.

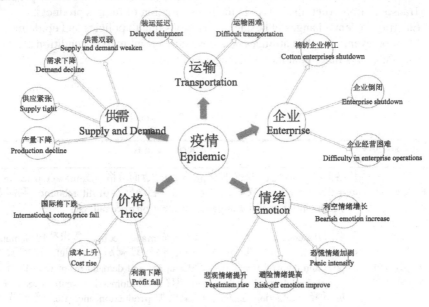

Fig. 5. Effects of the epidemic

The main purpose of analyzing futures texts is to predict the *Price* changes of futures varieties, so we analyze the influencing factors of *Price* according to the annotated corpus. It can be seen from Fig. 6 that *Supply and demand, Epidemic, Weather, Policy, and Emotion* events can all affect price changes. *Supply and demand* event includes specific events such as demand increase and demand slump.

The futures domain has intricate relationships, and it is a challenging task to clear up the relationships. Based on the causal events of this corpus, we illustrate the case of causal chains.

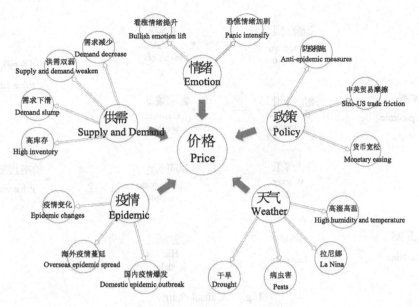

Fig. 6. Causes affecting price

A series of causal events can be seen from Fig. 7. The nodes represent causal events. These events are abstracted from specific events. The directed edges represent causality, which are from cause events to the effect events. For example *Epidemic → Economic downturn → Demand weaken → High inventory → Price fall*. We can also see one cause one effect, one cause multiple effects, and multiple cause one effect relationships exist, which supports causal event knowledge graph analysis and lays a foundation for causal inference.

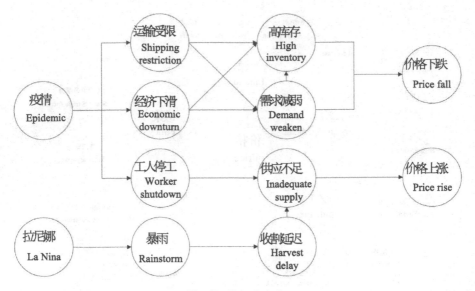

Fig. 7. Causal chains

5 Application of the Corpus

Based on the annotated corpus, we carry out experiments on causal sentence identification and causal component recognition. Causal sentence identification is regarded as a binary classification problem. We adopt BERT [16] as the classification model, which is fine-tuned on the basis of the BERT-base-Chinese pre-training model. The baseline model treats all sentences as causal sentences.

The corpus is randomly divided into training set, validation set, and test set with a ratio of 8:1:1. The experiments are run on NVIDIA RTX2080Ti for 10 epochs, and the learning rate is set to 5e−5. The evaluation metrics are Accuracy, Precision, Recall, and F1. Since we pay more attention to causal sentences, we mainly consider Causality-P, Causality-R, Causality-F1. The experimental results are shown in Table 4. We can see that the BERT model outperforms the baseline model by a large margin.

Table 4. The results of causal sentence identification

Model	Accuracy	Causality-P	Causality-R	Causality-F1
Baseline	78.59	78.59	**100**	88.01
BERT	**94.11**	**95.48**	97.10	**96.28**

Causal component recognition is to recognize the cause and effect from the causal sentence, which can be treated as a sequence labeling problem. We adopt BERT+CRF model, encoding the text with RoBERTa [17], and then outputting the last layer to CRF

[18]. The baseline model assumes that the text to the left of the causal marker is cause while the text to the right of the causal marker is effect.

The corpus is randomly divided into training set, validation set and test set with a ratio of 8:1:1. We run 30 epochs on NVIDIA RTX2080Ti with learning rate of 2e-5. The evaluation metrics [19] are Exact Match Accuracy (EMA), Weighted Precision (W-P), Weighted Recall (W-R), and Weighted F1 (W-F1). The experimental results of causal component recognition are shown in table 5. BERT+CRF (Gold) is based on gold standard causal sentences while BERT+CRF (Auto) is based on automatically identified causal sentences. We can see that the W-F1 scores are very close for the two models, which is an indication that the automatic causality extraction from the raw texts can perform well.

Table 5. The results of causal component recognition

Model	EMA	W-P	W-R	W-F1
Baseline	28.62	87.25	87.33	87.29
BERT+CRF (Gold)	**75.00**	**95.89**	**95.45**	**95.67**
BERT+CRF (Auto)	71.38	95.63	95.34	95.49

However, the EMA score still has room for improvement. On the one hand, the annotation quality of the corpus needs improvement. The current inter-annotator agreement is just 85%, which can be seen as a topline of EMA. On the other hand, the size of the corpus needs to be enlarged.

6 Conclusion

We annotate a corpus for Chinese causality extraction in futures domain, including causal sentence annotation and causal component annotation. Based on the annotated corpus, the taxonomy of causal events and cases of causal chains in the futures domain are analyzed. We also propose models for causal sentence identification and causal component recognition. The next step will be to extract causality from a larger-scale corpus, including different causal markers and different futures varieties, construct a knowledge graph of causal events, and conduct causal event inference research.

References

1. Xu, J., Zuo, W., Liang, S., Zuo, X.: A review of dataset and labeling methods for causality extraction. In: Proceedings of the 28th International Conference on Computational Linguistics, pp. 1519–1531 (2020)
2. Hendrickx, I.,et al.: Semeval-2010 task 8: multi-way classification of semantic relations between pairs of nominals. arXiv preprint arXiv:1911.10422 (2019)
3. Mirza, P., Sprugnoli, R., Tonelli, S., Speranza, M.: Annotating causality in the tempeval-3 corpus. In: Proceedings of the EACL 2014 Workshop on Computational Approaches to Causality in Language (CAtoCL), pp. 10–19 (2014)

4. Hidey, C., McKeown, K.: Identifying causal relations using parallel wikipedia articles. In: Proceedings of the 54th Annual Meeting of the Association for Computational Linguistics (Volume 1: Long Papers), pp. 1424–1433 (2016)
5. Caselli, T., Vossen, P.: The event storyline corpus: a new benchmark for causal and temporal relation extraction. In: Proceedings of the Events and Stories in the News Workshop, pp. 77–86 (2017)
6. Mariko, D., et al.: Financial document causality detection shared task (fincausal 2020). arXiv preprint arXiv:2012.02505 (2020)
7. Li, Z., Li, Q., Zou, X., Ren, J.: Causality extraction based on self-attentive BiLSTM-CRF with transferred embeddings. Neurocomputing **423**, 207–219 (2021)
8. Fu, J., Liu, Z., Liu, W., Zhou, W.: Event causal relation extraction based on cascaded conditional random fields. Pattern Recognit. Artif. Intell. **24**(4), 567–573 (2011)
9. Zhou, Y., Xue, N.: The Chinese discourse treebank: a Chinese corpus annotated with discourse relations. Lang. Resour. Eval. **49**(2), 397–431 (2015)
10. Liu, X., Yin, D., Feng, Y., Wu, Y., Zhao, D.: Everything has a cause: leveraging causal inference in legal text analysis. arXiv preprint arXiv:2104.09420 (2021)
11. Xue, N., Xia, F., dong Chiou, F., Palmer, M.: Building a large annotated Chinese corpus: the Penn Chinese treebank. J. Nat. Lang. Eng. **11**(2), 207–238 (2005)
12. Zhang, K., Yue, D., Zhuang, L.: Improving Chinese clinical named entity recognition based on BiLSTM-CRF by cross-domain transfer. In: Proceedings of the 2020 4th High Performance Computing and Cluster Technologies Conference & 2020 3rd International Conference on Big Data and Artificial Intelligence, pp. 251–256 (2020)
13. Leetaru, K., Schrodt, P.A.: GDELT: global data on events, location, and tone, 1979–2012. In: ISA Annual Convention, vol. 2, pp. 1–49. Citeseer (2013)
14. Hripcsak, G., Rothschild, A.S.: Agreement, the f-measure, and reliability in information retrieval. J. Am. Med. Inform. Assoc. **12**(3), 296–298 (2005)
15. Ogren, P., Savova, G., Chute, C.: Constructing evaluation corpora for automated clinical named entity recognition. In: Proceedings of the Sixth International Conference on Language Resources and Evaluation (LREC 2008) (2008)
16. Devlin, J., Chang, M.W., Lee, K., Toutanova, K.: BERT: pre-training of deep bidirectional transformers for language understanding. arXiv preprint arXiv:1810.04805 (2018)
17. Liu, Y., et al.: Roberta: a robustly optimized BERT pretraining approach. arXiv preprint arXiv: 1907.11692 (2019)
18. Lafferty, J., McCallum, A., Pereira, F.C.: Conditional random fields: probabilistic models for segmenting and labeling sequence data (2001)
19. Jia, Y., Kang, L., Sun, H., Du, X., Cao, S., Zan, H., Li, F.: Causality extraction in futures domain. In: 2021 International Conference on Asian Language Processing (IALP), pp. 111–116. IEEE (2021)

Research on Hotspots of Educational Application of Natural Language Processing Based on LDA Topic Model

Meng Wang(✉), Yuyang Xie, and Yu Tian

School of Humanities, Jiangnan University, Wuxi, Jiangsu, China
wangmengly@163.com

Abstract. As an important branch of artificial intelligence, natural language processing has become an effective tool to promote educational reform, improve educational quality and cultivate innovative talents. In order to comprehensively and systematically reveal the theme structure and evolution trend of educational application of natural language processing, this study takes the papers from the workshop "Innovative Use of NLP for Building Educational Applications" held by the NAACL conference from 2003 to 2021 as the data and uses LDA topic model for semantic analysis to identify the research topics automatically. Based on the results, this paper analyzes the topic intensity, topic novelty and topic evolution, so as to deeply explore the research hotspots of the educational application of natural language processing and provide reference and support for relevant scholars to grasp the research trends.

Keywords: Natural Language Processing · Educational Application · LDA Topic Model · Research Hotspots

1 Introduction

With the acceleration of a new round of scientific and technological revolution, the frontier technology represented by artificial intelligence has had a significant impact on people's life and has become an effective tool to promote educational reform, improve educational quality and cultivate innovative talents. The value and role of technology in promoting educational reform are becoming increasingly prominent. As an important branch of artificial intelligence, natural language processing is known as the "pearl on the crown of artificial intelligence", which has many research methods and application fields.

Natural language processing is a means for human-computer interaction through natural languages, which has a wide application space in the field of education [1]. The early application of natural language processing in education is grammar error detection. With the development of technology, automated writing evaluation system has been commercialized and is being used to evaluate the essays of millions of testers. Therefore, using bibliometric methods to deeply analyze the research findings of the

Q. Su et al. (Eds.): CLSW 2022, LNAI 13496, pp. 315–325, 2023.
https://doi.org/10.1007/978-3-031-28956-9_25

educational application of natural language processing is of great significance, which can comprehensively and systematically reveal the theme structure and evolution of the educational application of natural language processing.

At present, researchers mostly use citation-based and word-based quantitative methods to analyze the hotspots and frontiers of a particular field [2]. Word-based research is mainly using keywords to represent the research hotspots and frontiers by counting word frequency or co-occurrence frequency. However, this method lacks semantic information. Therefore, this paper uses the LDA topic model for semantic analysis to identify the topics automatically. Based on the results, this paper analyzes the topic intensity, topic novelty and topic evolution process, so as to deeply reveal the research hotspots of educational application of natural language processing and provide a reference for relevant scholars to grasp the research trends.

2   Research Data and Methods

2.1   Data

In order to achieve the most cutting-edge and comprehensive research trends in the field, this paper carries out research from an international perspective. NAACL (North American chapter of the Association for Computational Linguistics) is one of the top-ranking academic conferences in the field of natural language processing. With the increasing demand for natural language processing in the field of education, the conference has held special workshops "Innovative Use of NLP for Building Educational Applications (BEA)" since 2003, which aims to promote the innovative application of natural language processing technology in the field of education. The theme of the workshop is very consistent with the topic of this study. Therefore, we take BEA conference papers as the data, with a time span of 2003–2021. We delete conference notices, news and other non-academic documents, and finally keep 445 documents.

2.2   Methods

The LDA topic model, as an unsupervised model for extracting the hidden topics from large-scale document corpus [3], has a solid theoretical foundation, and has many advantages such as flexibility and easy expansion. It is widely used in various research fields. LDA model is a three-level Bayesian model of words, topics and documents. The basic principle of LDA is to consider each document as a probability distribution of potential topics, and each potential topic as a probability distribution over the words contained in the document set, shown as Eq. (1).

$$p(\text{words}|\text{documents}) = \sum_{\text{topics}} p(\text{words}|\text{topics}) * p(\text{topics}|\text{documents}) \qquad (1)$$

Through the chain of "documents → topics → words", two important probability distributions can be achieved: "documents → topics" distribution and "topics → words" distribution. The LDA model can well simulate the document generation process. The topic identification based on probability can accurately represent the semantic hierarchical relationship of words, and is very effective in topic analysis and topic prediction. In view of the advantages of the LDA model in semantic extraction and semantic expression, this study uses the LDA topic model to identify the research topics automatically. Based on the results, we analyze the topic intensity, topic novelty and topic evolution process, so as to deeply explore the research hotspots of the educational application of natural language processing. Figure 1 shows the overall research process.

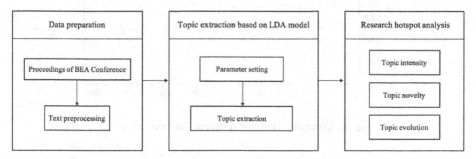

Fig. 1. Research process.

3 Topic Extraction Based on the LDA Model

3.1 Parameter Setting

In the LDA model, setting the number of topics is the first step of model construction, and the number of topics will directly affect the performance of the model. If the number of topics is too large, the training time of the model will be prolonged. If the number of topics is too small, the ability of the model to describe data will be limited. At present, the number of topics is mainly determined by three methods: experience, perplexity and coherence score [4]. Considering the semantic association between words in contexts, this study uses the coherence score to determine the optimal number of topics, as shown in Eq. (2):

$$coherence(W) = \Sigma_{(w_i, w_j) \in W} \log \frac{\left(P\left(w_i, w_j\right) + \varepsilon\right)}{P(w_i)P\left(w_j\right)} \tag{2}$$

In Eq. (2), W is a collection of words describing a topic, ε is the smooth factor (generally equals 1), w_i and w_j belong to the set W, $P(w_i)$ represents the occurrence probability of word w_i, and $P\left(w_i, w_j\right)$ represents the co-occurrence probability of word w_i and w_j. Normally, the higher the consistency score, the better the model performance. We set the number of topics from 2 to 40 respectively, and calculated the corresponding coherence score, as shown in Fig. 2. The number of topics with the highest coherence score (0.618) is 12. Therefore, we set the number of topics as 12. For each topic, the top 10 words with the highest probability are obtained based on the topic word probability distribution.

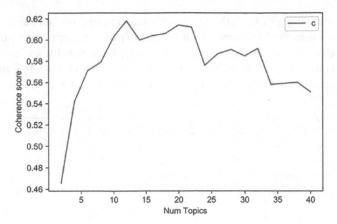

Fig. 2. Coherence scores of different numbers of topics.

3.2 Topic Extraction

As an unsupervised learning algorithm, the LDA model can extract the main semantic information of the documents. Each topic can be interpreted as the weight distribution of all words. By selecting the words with high weight in a topic and presenting them in the form of a topic-word probability distribution table, the topic semantic information can be visualized. According to the extracted keywords, we manually identified the 12 topics, and finally categorized them into 5 topics: intelligent tutoring system, reading support, grammatical error detection, native language identification and automated text evaluation. Table 1 shows the results of extracted topics, the top 10 words with the highest probability are listed for each topic.

Table 1. The results of topic extraction.

Topics	Topic number	Words and probability
Intelligent tutoring system	1	System (0.014) pedagogical roles (0.013) speech (0.012) teacher (0.012) classification (0.011) conversational agent (0.010) search terms (0.010) argument (0.010) phoneme (0.010) students (0.009)
	10	Sentence (0.012) tutorial dialogue (0.012) learning (0.009) summary (0.009) students (0.009) summaries (0.008) sentences (0.007) argument (0.007) writing (0.007) dialogue acts (0.007)
Reading support	3	Difficulty (0.027) shared task (0.017) sentence (0.015) approach (0.013) reading (0.011) reader (0.011) dialog (0.010) difficult (0.010) quality (0.010) active learning (0.009)

(continued)

Table 1. (*continued*)

Topics	Topic number	Words and probability
Grammatical error detection	4	Language (0.080) error (0.033) collocation (0.022) errors (0.020) model (0.019) shared task (0.017) words (0.016) translation (0.015) roman words (0.010) grammatical error correction (0.009)
	6	Grammatical error correction (0.014) target word (0.011) model (0.010) errors (0.010) responses (0.009) categories (0.009) method (0.008) blank (0.007) machine translation (0.007) correct (0.007)
Native language identification	7	Language (0.029) shared task (0.022) classifier (0.015) training data (0.015) native language (0.012) native language identification (0.010) model (0.008) test data (0.008) writing (0.007) sentence (0.007)
	12	Classifier (0.036) native language (0.022) native language identification (0.016) sentence (0.014) key point (0.012) language (0.012) translation (0.011) building educational applications (0.010) training data (0.010) shared task (0.010)
Automated text evaluation	9	Language model (0.020) concept (0.014) semantic distance (0.012) automated scoring (0.011) test item (0.011) target word (0.011) action (0.011) human score (0.009) results (0.009) context dependence (0.008)

4 Research Hotspots and Evolution Analysis

Research hotspots or frontiers are the latest literature collections or research topics with high attention, which mainly have three key characteristics: novelty, activity and attention [5]. In this paper, we analyze the research hotspots in the field of educational application of natural language processing by the indicators of topic intensity and topic novelty, using "topic intensity" to indicate the attention of the research topic and "topic novelty" to indicate the timeliness of the research topic. Then, we use the above statistics to represent the evolution of the topics in order to provide a comprehensive and systematic analysis of the research hotspots in the educational application of natural language processing.

4.1 Topic Intensity

Topic intensity represents the importance of the topic in literature. The higher the topic intensity, the more important the topic is. It is usually measured by the ratio of the sum of the topic weight over all documents to the total amount of documents [6], as shown in Eq. (3).

$$\theta_j = \frac{\Sigma_d \theta_j^{(d)}}{M} \tag{3}$$

M represents the total amount of documents, θ_j represents the overall strength of the j-th topic in all documents, $\theta_j^{(d)}$ represents the intensity (distribution probability) of the j-th topic in the d-th document set, $\sum_d \theta j^{(d)}$ is the sum of the intensity of the j-th topic in all documents [7], the sum of topic intensities of all topics equals 1. The intensity of each topic is calculated according to Eq. (3), and the results are shown in Fig. 3.

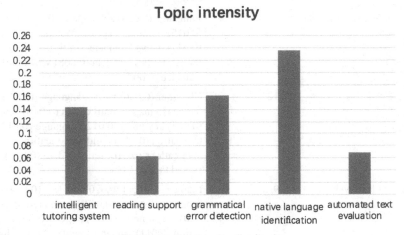

Fig. 3. Topic intensity distribution.

The five topics are ranked in descending order of intensity: native language identification (0.24), grammatical error detection (0.16), intelligent tutoring system (0.14), automated text evaluation (0.068), and reading support (0.063). This indicates that native language identification, grammatical error detection and intelligent tutoring system are concerned by researchers continuously.

It is worth noting that, in order to promote the application and development of natural language processing, the BEA conference has held many shared tasks, where the organizers released the task requirements and the training data, and participants submit their experiment results for evaluation by the organizers. The proposal of sharing tasks greatly aroused researchers' interest to the new topics. Six of the 16 conferences proposed the sharing tasks, and the "native language identification" sharing task was proposed in 2013 and 2017, which is also the reason for the high intensity of the "native language identification" topic. The intensity of "grammatical error detection" topic ranks the second, and the HOO (Helping Our Own, focusing on preposition and determiner error correction) sharing task in 2012 and the grammatical error correction sharing task in 2019 have played a great driving role.

4.2 Topic Novelty

Topic novelty represents the timeliness of a research topic, which is reflected by the average publishing time of documents supporting the topic. The more recent the average publishing time of a topic, the higher its novelty [8], as shown in Eq. (4).

$$Y_j = \frac{\Sigma_d y_j^{(d)}}{M} \tag{4}$$

Y_j denotes the novelty of a topic, that is, the average year of publication of the supporting documents on a topic, $y_j^{(d)}$ denotes the year of publication of the d-th document for the j-th topic, and M denotes the number of supporting documents for a topic [9]. In general, research hotspots and frontiers are mostly new scientific discoveries and problems in the field, and thus their novelty is high. In this study, the supporting documents for each topic are defined as those with a probability of distribution higher than 0.8 in all documents corresponding to the topic, and the distribution of their publication time was counted, as shown in Fig. 4.

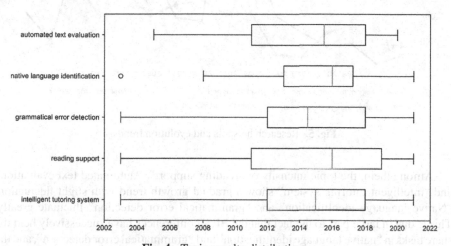

Fig. 4. Topic novelty distribution.

In Fig. 4, the left and right vertical lines represent the start and end year of relevant documents, the box represents the concentration year of relevant papers, the dotted line in the middle of the box represents the median of the publication time of relevant papers, and the circle represents outliers. Taking automated text evaluation as an example, the related papers began to appear in 2005 and continued to 2020. From 2011 to 2018, the papers appear in a centralized way. The median time of the papers related to this topic is 2015. The time span of this research paper is from 2003 to 2021. In general, Fig. 4 shows that the centralized publication interval of the five topics is from 2012 to 2018. Among them, the topic of native language identification appears the latest, and the concentrated development year starts from 2013 to 2017, but its topic intensity is the highest.

4.3 Topic Evolution

In order to analyze the evolution trends of each topic, we calculate the topic intensity of each topic according to the year and present its development trends, as shown in Fig. 5. We can see that the X-axis represents the year, and the Y-axis represents the topic intensity of the corresponding topic of the year.

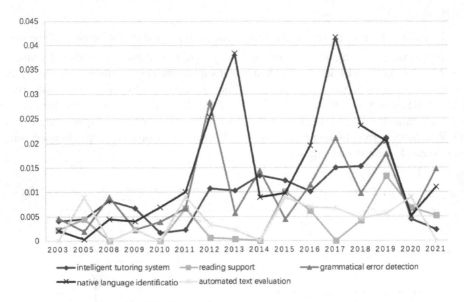

Fig. 5. Research hotspots and evolution trends.

Among them, the topic intensity of "reading support", "automated text evaluation" and "intelligent tutoring system" show a gradual growth trend with slight fluctuation. "Native language identification" and "grammatical error detection" fluctuate greatly. This is due in large part to the fact that the BEA conferences have successively held the share tasks in "native language identification" and "grammatical error detection", and the number of related papers increase significantly in those years, and the topic intensity will increase accordingly. It can be seen that the shared tasks on technology evaluation is not only an important means to promote the development of natural language processing, but also an important driving force for technology application. Researchers should make full use of the tasks on technology evaluation to promote the development and application of related technologies.

5   Conclusions and Future Work

Taking the papers of the BEA workshop from 2003 to 2021 as the research data, this paper uses the LDA topic model to analyze the data at the semantic level to identify the research topics automatically. Based on the results, the topic intensity, topic novelty and topic evolution process are analyzed to deeply explore the research hotspots and development trends of the educational application of natural language processing.

Based on the above analysis, there are the following trends for future developments that researchers can focus on.

(1) Enriching application scenarios to promote the development of natural language processing. The field of education provides rich application scenarios for the application of natural language processing. By setting up tasks on technology evaluation for educational applications, such as grammatical error detection [10, 11], native language identification and automated text evaluation [12], it can not only effectively promote the development of natural language processing technologies, but also play a vital role in improving the system performance of relevant educational applications. The technical problems involved in these evaluation tasks are of great significance and promotion for solving the bottleneck problems in the current educational field, such as students' intention understanding, emotional interaction, automated text evaluation, etc., and it is worthy of the attention of relevant researchers.

(2) Data-driven research on models and algorithms. Under the data-driven research paradigm, while researching various algorithms to improve the accuracy of models, we should pay more attention to the collection and annotation of learners' data and establish learner corpora to provide high-quality training data for machine learning models. The sharing of research data is a general trend. In addition, for some evaluation tasks that are difficult to obtain large-scale test data, small sample learning, transfer learning, reinforcement learning and other technologies have attracted the attention of researchers.

(3) Deep learning models and new text representation methods are widely used. In recent years, with the use of neural network models and word vector-based text representation, the performances of many tasks have been greatly improved, such as text classification [13], text emotion analysis, and text automatic evaluation [14]. It provides new research directions for the educational application of natural language processing technology.

Natural language processing is a typical interdisciplinary subject which involves many disciplines such as computer science, linguistics, mathematics, cognitive science, psychology and so on. The data in this study comes from the field of computer science, and we try to analyze the research hotspots of educational applications of natural language processing from the perspective of computer science, so as to provide a reference for related scholars to grasp the research trends. Next, we will expand the research data and collect papers from top-ranking journals and conferences on educational technology to provide a comprehensive and in-depth analysis of the research hotspots and development trends of educational applications of natural language processing with a muti-perspective view.

Acknowledgments. This work is funded by the following projects: Humanities and Social Science Research Project of Chinese Ministry of Education (No. 21YJA740037); Natural Social Science Foundation of China (No. 20BYY158); Chinese Central Government Guided Local Science and Technology Development Project (No. 2020L3024).

References

1. Wang, M., Yu, S.W., Zhu, X.F.: Natural language processing and its applications in education. Math. Pract. Theory **45**, 151–156 (2015). (in Chinese)
2. Chen, X.Y., Li, Y.: The hotspots and frontiers of Chinese educational technology research in the Latest 20 years—Based on the bibliometric analysis of 7 CSSCI journals. Mod. Educ. Technol. **30**, 12–19 (2020). (in Chinese)
3. Xie, T.: Recognition study on research fronts of artificial intelligence based on LDA model. Nanjing Uni. Aeronaut. Astronaut. (2019). (in Chinese)
4. Feng, J., Zhang, Y.Q.: Research on the method of detecting and analyzing scientific fronts based on LDA and ontology. Inf. Stud.: Theory Appl. **40**, 49–54 (2017). (in Chinese)
5. Han, Y., Zhong, M., Zhou, L., Zan, H.: Statistical analysis and automatic recognition of grammatical errors in teaching Chinese as a second language. In: Hong, J.-F., Zhang, Y., Liu, P. (eds.) CLSW 2019. LNCS (LNAI), vol. 11831, pp. 406–414. Springer, Cham (2020). https://doi.org/10.1007/978-3-030-38189-9_42
6. Sun, Y., Zhang, Y., Zhang, Y.: Chinese text proofreading model of integration of error detection and error correction. In: Dong, M., Lin, J., Tang, X. (eds.) CLSW 2016. LNCS, vol. 10085, pp. 376–386. Springer, Cham (2016). https://doi.org/10.1007/978-3-319-49508-8_35
7. Niu, G.: A corpus-based analysis of lexical bundles in English introductions of Chinese and international students' theses. In: Lu, Q., Gao, H. (eds.) CLSW 2015. LNCS, vol. 9332, pp. 486–493. Springer, Cham (2015). https://doi.org/10.1007/978-3-319-27194-1_49
8. Zhang, Q., Mu, L., Zhang, K., Zan, H., Li, Y.: Research on question classification based on Bi-LSTM. In: Hong, J.-F., Su, Q., Wu, J.-S. (eds.) CLSW 2018. LNCS (LNAI), vol. 11173, pp. 519–531. Springer, Cham (2018). https://doi.org/10.1007/978-3-030-04015-4_44
9. Lu, D., Qiu, X., Cai, Y.: Sentence-level readability assessment for L2 Chinese learning. In: Hong, J.-F., Zhang, Y., Liu, P. (eds.) CLSW 2019. LNCS (LNAI), vol. 11831, pp. 381–392. Springer, Cham (2020). https://doi.org/10.1007/978-3-030-38189-9_40
10. Gonzalez-Garduno, A.V., Søgaard, A.: Using gaze to predict text readability. In: Proceedings of the 12th Workshop on Innovative Use of NLP for Building Educational Applications, pp. 438–443 (2017)
11. Bingel, J., Barrett, M., Klerke, S.: Predicting misreadings from gaze in children with reading difficulties. In: Proceedings of the Thirteenth Workshop on Innovative Use of NLP for Building Educational Applications, pp. 24–34 (2018)
12. Deutsch, T., Jasbi, M., Shieber, S.: Linguistic features for readability assessment. In: Proceedings of the Fifteenth Workshop on Innovative Use of NLP for Building Educational Applications, pp. 1–17 (2020)
13. Wolska, M., Clausen, Y.: Simplifying metaphorical language for young readers: a corpus study on news text. In: Proceedings of the 12th Workshop on Innovative Use of NLP for Building Educational Applications, pp. 313–318 (2017)
14. Maamouri, M., Zaghouani, W., Cavalli-Sforza, V., Graff, D., Ciul, M.: Developing ARET: an NLP-based educational tool set for Arabic reading enhancement. In: Proceedings of the Seventh Workshop on Building Educational Applications Using NLP, pp. 127–135 (2012)
15. Liu, L., Liang, M.C.: A survey of automatic grammar error detection for English learners' writing. J. Chin. Inf. Process. 1–8 (2018). (in Chinese)

16. Rozovskaya, A., Roth, D.: Annotating ESL errors: challenges and rewards. In: Proceedings of the NAACL HLT 2010 Fifth Workshop on Innovative use of NLP for Building Educational Applications, pp. 28–36 (2010)
17. Liu, X., Lin, H., Li, Y., Ren, Y., Xu, B.: Generating dialogue responses with latent lexical meaning. In: Liu, M., Kit, C., Su, Q. (eds.) CLSW 2020. LNCS (LNAI), vol. 12278, pp. 482–490. Springer, Cham (2021). https://doi.org/10.1007/978-3-030-81197-6_41
18. Jeong, Y.H., Li, M.Y., Kang, S.M., Eum, Y.K., Kang, B.K.: Automatic prediction and linguistic interpretation of Chinese directional complements based on BERT model. In: Dong, M., Gu, Y., Hong, J.F. (eds.) CLSW 2021. LNCS, vol. 13249, pp. 405–416. Springer, Cham (2021). https://doi.org/10.1007/978-3-031-06703-7_31
19. Mao, T., Peng, Y., Jiang, Y., Zhang, Y.: A classification method for Chinese word semantic relations based on TF-IDF and CNN. In: Hong, J.-F., Su, Q., Wu, J.-S. (eds.) CLSW 2018. LNCS (LNAI), vol. 11173, pp. 509–518. Springer, Cham (2018). https://doi.org/10.1007/978-3-030-04015-4_43

A Metrological Study on the Spatial Narrative of *the Qishu Genre*: Take *A Dream of Red Mansions* and *Water Margin* as Examples

Xuemei Tang[1,2] and Qi Su[2,3,4](✉)

[1] Department of Information Management, Peking University, Bejing, China
tangxuemei@stu.pku.edu.cn
[2] Digital Humanities Center of Peking University, Bejing, China
[3] School of Foreign Languages, Peking University, Bejing, China
[4] MOE Key Lab of Computational Linguistics, School of EECS, Peking University, Bejing, China
sukia@pku.edu.cn

Abstract. *The Qishu genre* is Andrew H. Plaks's collective name for the *four great classic Chinese novels*, *The Golden Lotus*, and *The Scholars*. The reason is that these works represent a mature narrative style and a unique aesthetic structure of Ancient Chinese Novels. *The Qishu genre* is influenced by the concept of the "coexistence of fiction and reality" in Chinese historical narrative and the "non-narrative" of Chinese mythology, showing the characteristics of "spatialization". The previous works on the narrative space of *the Qishu genre* are mainly focused on qualitative research, and lack objective evidence to support conclusions. Therefore, in this paper, we take *A Dream of Red Mansions* and *Water Margin* as examples to analyze spatial narrative from the perspective of quantitative analysis. We use statistical analysis and visualization methods and combine them with the relevant theories of spatial narratology. Then we analyze and discuss from three perspectives: the narrative function of space, the performance of narrative rhythm in space, and the role of narrative time in the spatial narrative. This paper tries to provide a new research perspective for the spatial narrative research of *the Qishu genre*.

Keywords: The Qishu Genre · Spatial narrative · A Dream of Red Mansions · Water Margin

1 Introduction

American sinologist Andrew H. Plaks referred to *The Romance of the Three Kingdoms*, *Water Margin*, *Journey to the West*, *The Golden Lotus*, *A Dream of the Red Chamber*, and *The Scholars* in his book *Chinese narrative* as *the Qishu Genre*. The reason is that these six novels can serve as a milestone, as they represent the mature narrative paradigm of the 16_{th}-century Chinese novel. On the one hand, it is an innovation and surpassing of the traditional literary narrative pattern of its predecessors. On the other hand, it also has an inherited relationship with the past literary narrative tradition [16]. To distinguish it from other traditional Chinese chapter novels of the same period, Plaks specially named this type of genre as *the Qishu Genre*. The "Qi (peculiar)" of *the Qishu Genre* refers to the wonder of thought and content and peculiar writing.

The Qishu genre is influenced by the "non-narrative" and "spatialization" of Chinese history books narratives and Chinese mythology narratives, presenting the narrative feature of "spatialization" [9].

The main reason for this phenomenon is that space in narratives is often dynamic, ambiguous, and imprecise [8]. Since the 21st century, spatial narrative in China has gradually attracted some attention. The writings and essays represented by Long [4] *A Study of Spatial Narrative* have provided new ideas for the study of narratology, taking space as the core of interpretation.

At present, the mainstream space analysis in novels is the qualitative analysis [15, 18, 19], which depends on the subjective experience and literary accomplishment of researchers in the study process. With the increasing maturity of natural language processing (NLP) technology, some intelligent analysis approaches have assisted literature research and provided' new perspectives for literature analysis, such as the analysis of personal characters [17], visualization of narrative structure [1].

Encouraged by these efforts, we selected *A Dream of the Red Chamber* and *Water Margin* as the raw corpus and then used the NER toolkit to automatically annotate entities and manually proofread the annotated texts. Finally, we use these annotated texts to study the spatial narrative of *the Qishu Genre*. We attempt to interpret the spatial narrative *the Qishu Genre* from a new quantitative perspective, revealing the importance of the spatial factors and the impacts of spaces on the narrative rhythm of *the Qishu Genre*.

2 Related Work

2.1 The Spatial Narrative of *the Qishu Genre*

Regarding the spatial narrative of the novels of *the Qishu Genre*, there have been many studies on the spatial narration of *A Dream of Red Mansions* and *Water Margin*. Among these works, some of them focused on the relationship between spaces and characters. Li [13] took the chapter "Grandma Liu's Second Entry into the Daguan Garden" as an example to analyze the role of space transformation in shaping the characters' image in the novel and reveal the relationship between the characters. Yan [15] studied the spatial layout, furnishings and style of residences in *A Dream of Red Mansions* from the perspective of spatial narrative, and analyzed the main relationships among the characters in Rongguo Mansion based. Some specific spaces often imply special meanings. For example, Sun [11] analyzed the natural landscape, architectural space, dream space, and the four typical spaces represented by "doors" and "sedans" in *A Dream of Red Mansions*, and explored the cultural and symbolic meanings.

Space arrangement is usually related to narrative rhythm and narrative method. Zhang [18] called the pause and transition of the narrative space scene in the novel as articulation, which has effect on expanding the tension of space description and promoting the development of the plot. Lin [3] summarized the methods of spatial narrative in *A Dream of Red Mansions*, such as the borrowing method, borrowing some ideas from Buddhist and Taoist concepts, folk beliefs, and classic literary works; the mutual occurrence method, which corresponds to the spatial description before and after; the rendering method, repeated depiction, highlighting space characteristics. Xie [14] discussed the transformation of the narrative space, the connection method, and the narrative rhythm of *Water Margin* from the three aspects of mysterious space, display space and book space.

2.2 Intelligent Toolkits to Assist Literature Analysis

Some automatic extraction of entities and sentiment algorithms are proposed, and most researchers leveraged these methods to help literature analysis. Character analysis is a research hotspot. Bilenko [1] visualized dynamic character relationships and the emotional path of each character in three books: *The Glass Menagerie* by Tennessee Williams, *Kafka on the Shore* by Haruki Murakami, and *The Hobbit* by J.R.R. Tolkien. Viehhauser [12] applied named entity recognition and manual annotation to extract space and character name in *Around the world in Eighty Days*. Then they analyzed main characters by character and place markers co-occurrence network. Yuan [17] analyzed the big five personality prediction scores of the characters in *Ordinary World* by processing the language of the characters in the novel with the Chinese psychological analysis system.

Narrative analysis and visualization also attract much attention. Hu [2] took *Never Let Me Go* as an example, then they utilized nonlinear adaptive filtering and fractal analysis to analyze the narrative coherence and dynamic evolution of this novel. Segel [10] identified salient dimensions of visual story-telling, including how graphical techniques and interactivity can enforce various levels of structure and narrative flow.

In summary, this spatial narrative research of *the Qishu genre* mainly focused on qualitative analysis and lacked objective evidence to support them. Encouraged by the development of NLP technologies, we try to use intelligent toolkits to assist spatial narrative analysis for *the Qishu genre*.

Table 1. Statistics for two novel entities.

	Space	General Space	Time	General Time	Total
A Dream of Red Mansions	1219	1207	440	4665	7531
Water Margin	5354	3035	450	3710	12549

3 Datatsets

We choose 120 chapters of *A Dream of Red Mansions* and *Water Margin* published by the Chinese People's Literature Publishing House as the raw texts.

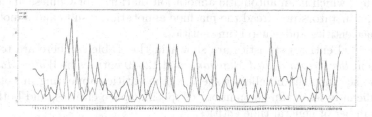

(a) The number of time entities and space entities in each chapter of *A Dream of Red Mansions*.

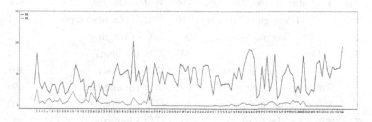

(b) The number of time entities and space entities in each chapter of *Water Margin*.

Fig. 1. The change trend in the number of time entities and space entities that appear in each chapter of two novels.

We apply the automatic annotation platform and manual annotation to recognize space and time in two novels.

According to Long [5], writing about a particular space in a narrative work can be a good way to express the personality traits of a character. When the "external space" is insufficient to build the character and portray the character image, a solution is to depict the "inner space", such as decorations, arrangement of the character's residence. Therefore, we divide the space into two types: definite space, general space. General space refers to words that don't represent specific location, but contain spatial elements. They usually include the part of the building, such as "卧室 (bedroom)", "屋里 (inside house)", and "垂花门 (weeping flower door)" , and these belong to a kind of "inner space"; definite spaces refer to a specific identifiable space or a space with a name, such as "荣国府 (Rongguo Mansion)", "大观园 (Daguan Garden)", "梨香院 (Lixiang courtyard)". We also divide time into general time and definite time. General time refers to words with time meaning but imprecise, including seasons, morning and twilight, such as "昨日 (yesterday)", "前儿 (before)", "八月初五 (this moment)"; definite time refers to a specific year month and day may be converted into specific time, including festivals and hours, such as "中秋 (the fifth of August)", "中秋 (Mid-Autumn Festival)" and so on.

First, we clean the raw texts by removing the special symbols, spaces, etc. Then we annotate definite entities using the "Wu Yu Dian" Intelligent Annotation

Platform[1], which is an automatic annotation platform for Chinese ancient text. Finally, annotators proofread the machine annotation results and annotate general space entities and general time entities.

The final entities statistics are shown in the Table 1. There are total 7531 entities in *the Dream of Red Mansions*, and 12549 entities in *Water Margin*. We can also see that the number of specific time entities appearing in both novels is significantly less than the number of specific space entities, and both have a large number of general time entities.

Table 2. High-frequency definite spaces in two novels.

No.	A Dream of Red Mansions	Fre.	Water Margin	Fre.
1	荣国府 (Rongguo Mansion)	106	梁山泊 (Liangshanpo)	537
2	宁国府 (Ningguo Mansion)	96	东京 (Dongjing)	252
3	京 (Jing)	93	北京 (Beijing)	112
4	怡红院 (Yihong courtyard)	82	济州 (Jizhou)	108
5	潇湘馆 (Xiaoxiang pavilion)	69	山东 (Shandong)	102
6	大观园 (Daguan Garden)	48	蓟州 (Jizhou)	100
7	贾府 (Jia Mansion)	33	江州 (Jiangzhou)	98
8	铁槛寺 Tiekan temple)	23	京师 (Jingshi)	94
9	梨香院 (Lixiang courtyard)	22	祝家庄 (Zhujia village)	79
10	金陵 (Jingling)	22	大辽 (Daliao)	77
11	水月庵 (Shuiyue temple)	21	郓城县 (Yuncheng County)	74
12	栊翠庵 (Longcui temple)	21	睦州 (Muzhou)	67

4 Analysis

4.1 The Narrative Function of Space in *the Qishu Genre*

In *A Dream of Red Mansions*, there are about 230 specific spaces and about 300 general spaces after removing duplication. In *Water Margin*, there are about 640 deduplicated spaces and about 530 general spaces. The high-frequency spaces are shown in the Table 2.

In *Water Margin*, "梁山泊 (Liangshanpo)" is the main gathering place for the characters. As different characters walk up to Liangshan (梁山) on different journeys, a series of spaces are connected in series. For example, "岳庙还香愿结识鲁智深 (meet Lu Zhishen in the temple)", "冲撞高衙内 (conflict with Gaoya Nei)", "误入白虎堂 (mistaken entry the White Tiger Hall)", "刺配沧州 (exile to Cangzhou)", "大闹野猪林 (make a big fuss in the wild boar forest)", "棒打洪教头 (beat Hongjiaotou)", "风雪山神庙 (Shanshen Temple in wind and snow), "雪夜上梁山 (go up Liangshan in the snowy night)", and above story scenes changing and shifting constitute a narrative space with Lin Chong as the

---

[1] http://wyd.pkudh.xyz/.

core. Seeing "Beijing", we can remember the plot of Liangshan heroes attacking Beijing, so each location more or less carries the task of plot development.

In addition to creating some large spaces (e.g., 贾府 (Jia Mansion), 荣国府 (Rongguo Mansion), and 大观园 (Daguan Garden)), *A Dream of Red Mansions* also creates "small spaces" closely related to characters, (e.g., 大观园 (Xiaoxiang Pavilion), 怡红院 (Yihong courtyard), and 蘅芜苑 (Hengwu courtyard)). At the same time there are some dream spaces, like "大荒山 (Great Barren Mountain)", and "太虚幻境 (Taixu Realm)". And there are also some high-frequency Buddhism and Taoism spaces, such as "铁槛寺 (Tiekan Temple)", "水月庵 (Shuiyue Temple)", and "栊翠庵 (Longcui Temple)". These spaces highlight the religion topic in *A Dream of Red Mansions*.

We can see that the frequent places in both novels are also important spaces for the characters' behavior and activities, closely linked to the fate of the characters, the plot and the themes of the novels.

The large space expresses the commonality and collective temperament of the group, while the description of the "space in a space", the aforementioned small space, is used to highlight the particular personalities of the characters. "忠义堂 (Loyalty Hall)", and "聚义厅 (Gather righteousness Hall)" they are consistent with the collective character of Liangshan heroes.

4.2 The Space Embodiment of the Narrative Rhythm of *the Qishu Genre*

There are generally four types of relationships between narrative time and story time. A narrative with near zero narrative time and infinitely long story time is an omission; a narrative with longer story time than narrative time is a summary; a narrative with equal story time and narrative time is a scene; a narrative with infinitely long narrative time than story time is a pause [6]. According to Miao [7] and Xie [14], two novels both use an omission narrative approach in begin chapters, and authors prefer to use scene and pause narrative methods in later chapters. The latter two methods are reflected in the novel as the specific time entities rarely appear, and the space entities appear intensively.

We count the number of definite time entities and space entities that appear in each chapter of the two *"the Qishu"* genre novels, and their changing trends are shown in Fig. 1. In these two novels, spaces entities are more than time entities. In *Water Margin*, there is a large gap between the numbers of the two types of entities, and there are even several chapters without definite time entities. It indicates that "space" is a significant part of the two novels, reflecting the characteristics of "spatialization" mentioned by Andrew H. Plaks. When there are no definite time terms and the concept of time is vague, the story plots can be driven mainly through the spatial shifting. As we can see in Fig. 1(a), the number of specific spaces entities will peak every few chapters, which shows the pattern of "movement and static" phase contrast.

Vernacular popular novels are classified into two main types based on the narrative rhythm: one is a fast-paced type of work represented by historical novels, heroic novels, and gods and demons novels. The other is a slow-paced type of work represented by novels about worldly novels and genius and beauty novels. They respectively represent the two narrative rhythm traditions of ancient Chinese popular novels. *A Dream of Red Mansions* is a slow-paced worldly novel, while *Water Margin* is a fast-paced heroic novel. The narrative rhythm of these two types of novels is also reflected in their spatial transformation. We draw a color-changing bar to represent the space transformation in each chapter. As shown in Fig. 2, Fig. 2(a) shows the space shifting from the 41_{st} chapter to the 50_{th} chapter in *A Dream of Red Mansions*, and the Fig. 2(b) shows this change in *Water Margin*. To distinguish the two types of spaces, we use the two relatively dark colors to represent definite entities, and the two lighter colors represent general entities.

Comparing the two figures, we find that the space density of each chapter of the *Water Margin* is higher than that of *The Dream of Red Mansions*. There are two possible reasons for this phenomenon. According to Zhou Ruchang, the first 80 chapters of *Dream of Red Mansions* cover 15 years, with an average of five chapters describing the events of each year. The narrative period of the 120 chapters of the Water Margin is 67 years, and the ratio of the story time to the text is 1:1.5. Therefore, the 67-year narrative can be completed by moving characters or space conversion more quickly. The second reason is that Dream of Red Mansions belongs to ancient family narrative novels. The space is mainly concentrated in the courtyard and day after day banquet scene. Hence there are often only a few spaces in one chapter, and there is also a high repetitiveness of space transformation and the physical spaces are not rich. However, *the Water Margin* belongs to the hero and legend novel. From the point of view of writing, there is no limit to spatial transformation, which is relatively free.

Both works show a pattern of alternating internal and external spaces, which shows the harmony between the internal and the external spaces.

4.3   The Role of Narrative Time in Spatial Narrative

The spatial form of the novel must be established based on time logic to establish the narrative order [5]. In this paper, we focus on the spatial narrative of *the Qishu Genre* as the main research object, but we cannot ignore the role of time in the spatial narrative. In both novels, relatively accurate time and vague time entities both appeared. When the author was writing, clear time markers appeared in the work to increase the authenticity of the story. Counting the specific time entities that appeared in the two novels, there are about 160 specific time markers in *Water Margin*. The distribution of each chapter is shown by the yellow solid line in Fig. 1(b). We can see that there is hardly any specific time marker in the middle part of the novel and the last 10 chapters. There are probably more than 190 definite time entities in *A Dream of Red Mansions*. The distribution is shown in the yellow solid line in Fig. 1(a). As can be seen, there are 11 chapters from the 80_{th} chapter to the 91_{st} chapter, with almost no time entities available for calculating specific years. Maybe it's because the author who continues to write *A Dream of Red Mansions* can't arrange the narrative time reasonably, so vague time entities are often used. Although there are relatively

(a) *A Dream of Red Mansions*   (b) *Water Margin*

Fig. 2. Spaces shifting in each chapter form the 41_{st} chapter to the 50_{th} chapter in two Qishu novels, including definite spaces and general spaces. A color bar represents a chapter, each color bar is composed of color blocks of four colors, each color block represents a entity, the two relatively dark colors represent definite entities, and the two lighter colors represent general entities. The number at bottom represent the number of space entities.

few definite time markers, they serve as nails to fix the entire story on the canvas from beginning to end and determine the length of the entire story.

At the same time, a large number of general time entities appear in both novels. For example, "当日 (the day)", "以往 (the past)", "一日 (one day)", "冬初 (early winter)", and these time points are rather vague, and they cannot give readers a clear concept of time like "宣和四年三月日 (March Xuanhe Fourth Year)". If a clear time marker can determine the horizontal length of the story, then general time words continue to reappear with the development of the story, and their main function is to expand the vertical width of the story. The "episodic" structure adopted in *the Qishu Genre*, that is, namely the "interspersed" structure, has the effect of enriching the narrative content and increasing the length of the work. In *Poetics*, Aristotle wrote that " As for the story, whether the poet takes it ready made or constructs it for himself, he should first sketch its general outline, and then fill in the episodes and amplify in detail.", There are a lot of "interspersed" narratives in Homeric. Vague time terms, as a kind of time that can be flexibly reused, play an important role in the "interspersed" structure. For example, in *A Dream of Red Mansions*, another incident often started with "一日 (one day)". In the 16_{th} chapter, "贾元春才选凤藻宫，秦鲸卿夭逝黄泉路 (Jia Yuanchun is, on account of her talents, selected to enter the Feng Ts'ao Palace. Qin Jingqing died at a young age)". At this chapter's beginning, the author continued to write content associated with the last chapter "凤姐弄权 (Wang Xifeng engages power)", and then "一日正是贾政生日 (One day is Jia Zheng's birthday)" turns to the "元春晋封 (Yuanchun was promoted)" event. Vague time words such as "饭后 (after a meal)", "那日 (that day)", "黄昏时 (dusk)", and "今夜 (tonight)" can connect the events of a day. Words such as "昨日 (yesterday)" and "五年前 (five years ago)" can

Table 3. The chapters and frequencies of the three festivals in two novels. "24_{th} chapter(2)" represents the festival appears two times in the 24_{th} chatper

Festival	A Dream of Red Mansions	Water Margin
Mid-Autumn Festival	1_{st} chapter(3), 3_{rd} chapter(1), 11_{th} chapter(1), 72_{nd} chapter(1), 73_{rd} chapter(1), 74_{th}chapter , 75_{th} chapter(3), 76_{th} chapter (2), 77_{th} chapter(2)	2_{nd} chapter(5), 30_{th} chapter(2), 31_{st} chapter(1)
Lantern Festival	1_{st} chapter(1), 17_{th} chapter(1), 18_{th} chapter(2), 20_{th} chapter(1), 22_{nd} chapter(2), 53_{rd} chapter(2), 54_{th} chapter(1), 55_{th} chapter(2), 62_{nd} chapter(1), 96_{th} chapter(1)	33_{rd} chapter(3)
Dragon Boat Festival	24_{th} chapter(2), 28_{th} chapter(1), 29_{th} chapter(1), 30_{th} chapter(1), 31_{st} chapter(1), 48_{th} chapter(1), 50_{th} chapter(1)	

introduce past events into the current narrative. These vague time words make the interspersed narrative more flexible.

In addition to enriching the story narrative with general time words, both works like to use festivals to expand the breadth of the narrative. According to rough statistics, as shown in Table 3, the Mid-Autumn Festival in *A Dream of Red Mansions* appeared 14 times, the Lantern Festival appeared 11 times, and Dragon Boat Festival appeared five times. The "Lantern Festival" and "Mid-Autumn Festival" also appeared in *Water Margin* several times. For example, "宋江清风寨被擒 (Songjiang was captured in Qingfengzhai)", "大名府救石秀 (rescue Shixiu in Daming Mansion)", "李逵闹东京 (Li Kui disturbs in Dongjing)" and other key scenes took place during the Lantern Festival. "张监督陷害武松 (Zhang Jiandu frames Wu Song)" and "鲁智深圆寂 (Lu Zhishen passed away)" both took place on the Mid-Autumn Festival.

In summary, the specific time marker determines the horizontal length of the story, and the general time markers and birthday festival broaden the vertical width of the story. The repetition of the general time markers provides opportunities for the transition of scenes and the advancement of the plot in spatial narratives.

5   Conclusion

In this paper, we first use NLP technology to annotate the entities in the two novels and then perform a statistical and visual analysis of time and space entities. Different spaces have different narrative functions, but they are all closely related to character building and plot development. At the same time, the narrative rhythm of *the Qishu genre* novels is also reflected in the arrangement of spaces. For example, heroic novels are fast-paced, so locations are dense, while worldly novels are slow-paced, so locations shift very slowly. Finally, in the narrative time, the vague time provides an opportunity to arrange more spatial changes in the novel.

Acknowledgement. This research is supported by the NSFC project "the Construction of the Knowledge Graph for the History of Chinese Confucianism" (Grant No. 72010107003)

References

1. Bilenko, N.Y., Miyakawa, A.: Visualization of narrative structure analysis of sentiments and character interaction in fiction (2013)
2. Hu, Q., Liu, B., Thomsen, M.R., Gao, J., Nielbo, K.L.: Dynamic evolution of sentiments in never let me go: insights from multifractal theory and its implications for literary analysis. Digital Sch. Humanit. **36**(2), 322–332 (2021). https://doi.org/10.1093/llc/fqz092
3. Lin, C.: The cultural implications of space narration in a dream of red mansions. Southeast Acad. Res. **03**, 178–184 (2016)
4. Long, D.: Spatial narratology: a new field of narratology research. J. Tianjin Normal Univ.(Soc. Sci.) **06**, 54–60 (2008)
5. Long, D.: A study of Spatial Narrative. SDX Joint Pubisheing Company, Hong Kong (2015)
6. Luo, G.: Introduction to Narratology. Yunnan People's Publishing House, Kunming (1994)
7. Miao, H.: The narrative rhythm and regulation mechanism of a dream of red mansions. Caoxueqin Stud. **01**, 61–71 (2017)
8. Piatti, B., Bär, H.R., Reuschel, A.K., Hurni, L., Cartwright, W.: Mapping literature: Towards a geography of fiction. In: Cartography and art, pp. 1–16. Springer, Berlin (2009). https://doi.org/10.1007/978-3-540-68569-2_15
9. Plaks, A.H.: Chinese Narrative: Critical and Theoretical Essays, vol. 2460. Princeton University Press, Princeton (2014)
10. Segel, E., Heer, J.: Narrative visualization: telling stories with data. IEEE Trans. Vis. Comput. Graph. **16**(6), 1139–1148 (2010). https://doi.org/10.1109/TVCG.2010.179
11. Sun, S.: The dream of red mansions is a study of space imagery. Ph.D. thesis, China: Harbin Normal University (2017)
12. Viehhauser-Mery, G., Barth, F.: Towards a digital narratology of space. In: DH (2017)
13. Wei, L., Lu, X.: An interpretation of the space narrative function of a dream of red mansions - taking grandma Liu's second entry into the daguan garden as an example. Times Lit. **06**, 118–119 (2011)
14. Xie, L.: A study of space narration in water margin. Ph.D. thesis, China: Capital Normal University (2004)
15. Yan, Y.: Analysis of the relationship between characters in a dream of red mansions by space narration. Youth Literator **23**, 14 (2012)

16. Yang, Y.: Si Da Qi Shu from the perspective of new hermeneutics. Seeker **05**, 147–154 (2002)
17. Yuan, Y.: The intelligence analysis of personal characters about ordinary world. Digital Scholarship in the Humanities, fqz050 (2019). https://doi.org/10.1093/llc/fqz050
18. Zhang, S.: The articulation of space narration in a dream of red mansions. Jinan J.(Philos. Soc. Sci.) **06**, 36–44 (1999)
19. Zhang, Y.: The narrative function of spaces in the novel's chapter-a case study of magic novel Xiu Yun Ge in qing dynasty. J. Xi'an Shiyou Univ. (Soc. Sci. Edn.) **30**(02), 99–107 (2021)

Chinese Argument Identification Based on Bert

Yi Zhang[1][(✉)], Guirong Wang[2], Ye Xiao[1,2], and Endong Xun[1,2]

[1] Institute for Language Intelligence, Beijing, China
yizhyi12@gmail.com, edxun@126.com
[2] Beijing Language and Culture University, Beijing, China

Abstract. Traditional semantic role labeling is mostly based on the results of syntactic analysis. On the basis of syntactic analysis, argument identification and argument classification are carried out in two steps. Due to the problem of error cascade, the effect of argument identification directly determines the quality of semantic role labeling. However, converting the semantic role labeling into a sequence labeling task tries to ignore syntactic information, which increases the difficulty of the model and relies on limited labeling data. Therefore, this paper focuses on improving the accuracy of Chinese argument identification, that is, identify all candidate arguments given a predicate. Specifically, based on the results of Chinese chunk dependency parsing, an argument identification model is built based on the pretrained language model BERT (bidirectional encoder representations from transformers). The AUC of the model reaches 97.18% and the accuracy reaches 98.10%, which provides a reliable data for subsequent argument classification task. At the same time, large-scale pretrained language model can overcome the problem of sequence dependency, and perform well in argument identification of complex sentences.

Keywords: Argument identification · semantic role labeling · chunk dependency · BERT

1 Introduction

Semantic role labeling (SRL), also known as shallow semantic analysis, aims to recognize the predicate-argument structure of each predicate in a sentence, which is usually described by answering the question "Who did what to whom?". Specifically, SRL seeks to identify arguments and label their semantic roles given a predicate. SRL is an important method for obtaining semantic information which is beneficial to a wide range of natural language processing (NLP) tasks, including machine translation [19], question answering [2, 28] and discourse relation sense classification [13] and relation extraction [10]. The example below presents one sentence with SRL.

$$a. [Tom]_{A_0}[ate][some][fruit]_{A_1}[at][home]_{AM-LOC}[this][morning]_{AM-TMP}$$

This sentence includes the predicate "ate", the agent "Tom", the patient "fruit", the time "morning" and the place "home". Semantic role labeling is to

Q. Su et al. (Eds.): CLSW 2022, LNAI 13496, pp. 337–350, 2023.
https://doi.org/10.1007/978-3-031-28956-9_27

determine the arguments and label their semantic roles given a predicate. The standard semantic role task is generally divided into four sub-tasks: predicate identification, predicate disambiguation, argument identification and argument classification.

Traditional semantic role labeling relies on domain knowledge and feature engineering, such as "predicate", "path", "phrase type", "position", "head word", "affiliation" and other features. Moreover, argument identification and argument classification are carried out in two steps, errors in argument identification will be propagated to argument classification. With the introduction of deep learning, a series of neural SRL models have been proposed, SRL has been more and more formulized into standard sequence labeling task. This simplifies the task on the surface, but in fact, it requires higher model performance, increases the complexity of the model, and relies on limited human-annotated data for supervised training, which cannot effectively overcome the problems of domain adaption and poor interpretability.

Therefore, this paper focuses on the step of argument identification. We trained a transition-based dependency graph parser on the manually annotated Chinese chunk dependency treebank, and obtained millions of Chinese chunk dependency data. Then introduced syntactic rules to obtain candidate predicate-argument pairs from chunk dependency data. We use the pretrained model BERT to build a Chinese argument identification model, all arguments of the predicate can be identified when a sentence and predicates in the sentence are given. And the accuracy reaches 98.10%, which optimizes the argument identification in the semantic role labeling task, and 500,000 high-quality data based on Chinese chunk dependency and argument identification are obtained, which provides reliable data for natural language processing and language theory research. The processing of data is shown in Fig. 1.

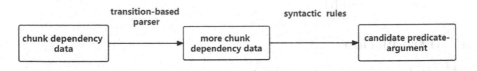

Fig. 1. Data processing.

2 Related Work

2.1 Semantic Role Labeling

The traditional SRL were mostly about designing hand-crafted feature templates and then employed linear classifiers [16,17,30]. For example, Liu [11] proposed a semantic role labeling system based on maximum entropy classifier. Hacioglu [7] first used the method based on dependency analysis and SVM classifier to realize semantic role labeling. Wang [23] proposed a semantic role recognition method based on dependency tree distance, and extracted the best candidate argument set of the target verb by formulating rules, which requires a lot of expert knowledge and syntactic rules.

With the introduction of deep learning, a series of neural SRL models have been proposed [3,8,9,14]. For example, Foland [6] used convolutional and time-domain neural networks to form a semantic role label system. Marcheggianiet [12] leveraged the graph convolutional network to incorporate syntax into a neural SRL model. Recently, Strubell [21] presented a multi-task neural model to incorporate auxiliary syntactic information for SRL. Zhou and Xu [31] proposed the first syntax-agnostic model for SRL using LSTM sequence labeling. Jimmy Lin [20] used the pretrained language model BERT to encode the semantic information of sentences, and proposed an argument recognition and classification model to dependency SRL task. The deep learning method recognizes the text as sequence data, so the semantic information in the tree structure cannot be considered, and relies on the labeled data. The quality of the labeled data has a great impact on the model performance. Chinese has a variety of forms and rich syntactic and semantic features. Recurrent neural networks and convolutional neural networks have good performance in acquiring short text features. However, when faced with long texts, most neural network models can't capture the semantics between long sequences.

2.2 Corpus Resources

Semantic role labeling requires high-quality corpus. At present, FrameNet [1] and PropBank [15] are well-known semantic role labeling resources in English, while Chinese Proposition Bank (CPB) [27] is the most widely used SRL data in Chinese. The Chinese Proposition Bank adds a layer of semantic annotation to the Chinese Treebank(CTB) [26]. This layer of semantic annotation mainly deals with the predicate-argument structure of Chinese verbs. The Chinese Treebank, started at University of Pennsylvania, is a segmented, part-of-speech tagged, and fully bracketed corpus . The sources of this corpus are mostly Xinhua newswire, Sinorama news magazine and Hong Kong News. CPB contains more than 20 semantic roles. The core semantic roles are Arg0-5.

High-quality Chinese semantic role labeling data is very limited, and the CPB mentioned above comes from texts in normalized fields such as news and newspapers. Therefore, models built based on these limited public datasets are poor in domain adaption. In recent years, the basic technologies of natural language processing such as word segmentation and part-of-speech tagging have become more and more mature, which has effectively improved the data quality of syntactic analysis. Therefore, compared with the sequence tagging method that ignores syntactic information, semantic role labeling based on syntactic analysis can alleviate the problems of data sparseness and domain adaption to a certain extent. At the same time, it is more conducive to optimize each step in the semantic role labeling task.

2.3 BERT

The pretrained BERT model [5] is a multi-layer bidirectional transformer encoder [22]. The model is pretrained on a large of unlabeled data for two tasks: MLM (Mask Language Model) and NSP (Next Sentence Prediction) and then fine-tuned on downstream NLP tasks. It has achieved excellent performance.

In the field of deep learning, RNN and its improved models LSTM, GRU are suitable for modeling sequences, but there are problems of catastrophic forgetting and slow calculation speed. CNN is fast in calculation, but in fact can only obtain local information. Google's model based on multi-head self-attention mechanism can well resolve parallel computing and sequence dependency problem. BERT is actually the encoder of the multi-layer bidirectional model. Most of the practice of text classification based on BERT has achieved good results. Xie [25] used BERT to extract emotional features and achieved good results in sentiment classification. Zhang [29] combined with entity information also showed that BERT can obtain the semantic information of the text.

3 Methodology

Based on previous work, we transform argument identification into binary classification task, construct training data based on chunk dependency treebank. Argument identification aims to identify the arguments corresponding to the given predicates. We use BERT as a semantic encoder to obtain the vectors of predicates and arguments.

3.1 Model Architecture

Figure 2 shows the architecture of our approach. For a sentence S, we add '[CLS]' and '[SEP]' at the beginning and end of the sentence respectively. Given a sentence with predicate(P) and argument(A), suppose its final hidden state output from BERT module is H. Suppose vectors H_x to H_y are the final hidden state vectors from BERT for P, and H_m to H_n are the final hidden state vectors from BERT for A. We apply the average operation to get a vector representation for predicate and argument. Then after an activation operation (i.e. $relu$), we add a fully connected layer to each of the two vectors, and the output for P and A are P' and A' respectively. This process can be mathematically formalized as Equation (1).

$$P' = W_1 * [relu(\frac{1}{y - x + 1} \sum_{s=x}^{y} H_s)] + b_1 \qquad (1)$$

$$A' = W_2 * [relu(\frac{1}{n - m + 1} \sum_{s=m}^{n} H_s)] + b_2 \qquad (2)$$

We make W_1 and W_2, b_1 and b_2 share the same parameters. We use bert as a semantic encoder to concatenate the word vectors of the predicate and argument

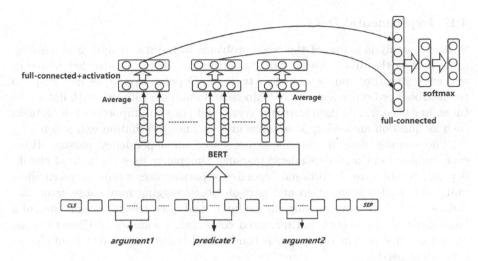

Fig. 2. Model architecture.

as a positive example. Randomly select 15% of the non-argument words in the sentence, and combine them with the predicate as negative examples in the same way. when predicting, it will output the probability of each word in the sentence as an argument. We concatenate $P^{'}$ and $A^{'}$ then add a fully connected layer and a softmax layer, which can be expressed as Equation (2).

$$h^{'} = W_3 * [concat(P^{'}, A^{'})] + b_3 \qquad (3)$$

$$p = softmax(h^{'}) \qquad (4)$$

b_1, b_2, b_3 are bias vectors. We use cross entropy as the loss function. For the combination of predicates and argument vectors, we tried the following five methods to compare the semantic representation effects of different combinations.

1. Addition of dimensions of predicates and arguments vectors.
2. Mean of each dimension of predicates and arguments vectors.
3. Maximum of each dimension of predicates and arguments vectors.
4. Concatenation of predicates and arguments vectors.
5. Concatenation of predicates and arguments and $H_{[cls]}$ vectors.

4 Experimence

All of the experiments mentioned in this paper were done on Linux, using four NVIDIA GeForce1080Ti graphics cards, and python3.6 under the deep learning framework pytorch 1.9.1.

4.1   Experimental Data

Syntactic analysis is one of the basic problems in natural language processing, according to the difference of syntactic structure, it can be divided into constituency structure and dependency structure. Dependency parser can adapt to the flexible word order features of Chinese and analyze sentences with flat structures, has been widely used in recent years, and plays an important role in tasks such as question answering, knowledge graphs, and information extraction.

The training data in this paper are based on dependency parsing. However, unlike traditional dependency parsing, this paper uses the data of chunk-dependent structure. Traditional dependency parsing uses words as the smallest unit, and word segmentation and part-of-speech tagging may cause error cascade. Chunk-dependent parsing can be further adapted to the phenomenon of a large number of inflected and increased contextual meanings in Chinese texts. Therefore, the data in this paper is constructed based on the results of chunk-dependent parsing.

Based on the chunk dependency analysis proposed by Qian [18], it took six months to manually label the Chinese chunk dependency treebank. The treebank contains 127,367 sentences of text, including 83.67% of encyclopedic text, 13.28% of news text and the remaining 3.13% of data in the fields of law, patents and primary school students' compositions. Table 1 shows the statistics of labeled data.

Table 1. Statistics of labeled data.

Field	Num	Prop	Field	Num	Prop
Encyclopedia	106,450	83.57%	Patent	1,387	1.08%
News	16,916	13.28%	Composition	436	0.34%
Law	2,178	1.71%	Sum	127,367	100%

The difficulty of syntactic labeling is much higher than other labeling tasks, and it requires annotator with professional knowledge. Our annotators are graduate students majoring in linguistics. We annotate the same text in pairs, and finally calculate the concordance rate between the two annotators for the same text. The concordance rate is calculated by the Kappa value. If it is greater than 0.9, the text will be reserved, and if it is less than 0.9, it will be re-marked.

Wang [24] proposed a neural transition-based parser, using a variant of list-based arc-eager transition algorithm for dependency graph parsing. We use Wang's algorithm to train a transition-based dependency graph analysis model on the labeled data mentioned above. And the F1 score reaches 94.29% (the specific experiment will be introduced in another paper). We applied the dependency model to the data of news field and obtained millions of chunk dependency data. Based on these chunk dependency data, the core predicate in the sentence and the dependency relationship between the predicate and the chunk can be obtained.

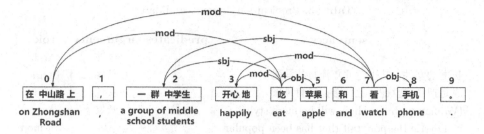

Fig. 3. Model architecture.

Figure 3 shows that each sentence is divided into chunks, and the predicate chunks and argument chunks are connected by dependency arcs and marked the syntactic relationship between them. For example in the Fig. 3, there are two core predicates "eat" and "watch", and the corresponding chunk indexes are 4 and 7. The subject ("sbj") of the predicate ("eat") is "middle school students", its chunk index is 2. The object ("obj") is "apple", whose chunk index is 5, and the location is "ZhongShan Road", whose chunk index is 0.

Based on the chunk dependency data introduced above, we extract candidate predicate-argument pairs by regular grammar and syntactic rules. On the one hand, the dependency model provides a syntactic structure, while the semantic role labeling data is a semantic structure. On the other hand, the chunk dependency data gives the dependency relationship between chunks, while the semantic role focuses on the argument role at the word level. So, it is necessary to extract the predicate-argument dependency semantic relationship from the chunk dependency data.

Although dependency parsing provides syntactic relations, there is a certain consistency between syntax and semantics: 1) The subject and object of syntactic are often the subject and object of semantic; 2) The argument in modifier component of predicate always follows a preposition; 3) Chinese is a right-centered language, that is, the core words of a substantive chunk are generally non-punctuation words located at the rightmost side of the chunk.

This paper designs a series of rules based on these three characteristics to extract the predicate-argument candidates and their semantic relationship. Table 2 shows the specific rules, and the final extracted predicate-argument candidates is shown in Table 3.

Table 2. Syntactic rules for predicate-argument candidates.

Dep_role	Chunk label	Content
None	VP	First verb that appears from left to right in a predicate chunk
Arg0	NP-SBJ	Last head word in the subject chunk
Arg1	NP-OBJ	Last head word in the object chunk
Arg-mod	NULL-MOD	Head word that follows a preposition in a modifier chunk

Table 3. Predicate-argument candidates.

sentences	predicates	arguments	role
长发的女性，扎上近几年流行的马尾，或是把长发盘在头上，会比较有风采。(Women with long hair will be more stylish if they tie the ponytail that has been popular in recent years, or wear long hair on the head.)	扎	女性	Arg0
		马尾	Arg1
	盘	女性	Arg0
		长发	Arg1
		头	Arg-mod
	有	女性	Arg0
		风采	Arg1

4.2 Parameter Setting

The training set contains 400,000 data, and the validation set contains 1,000 data. Validation set and test set are mixed data of multiple predicates and single predicate. The model is evaluated on five different test sets with a total of 5,000 data.

Table 4. Main parameters used in our experiments.

Model	Chinese_Bert_WWM
Sentence Length Function	512
Sentence Length	5e–5
Batch Size	96
Optimizer	BERTAdam
Dropout	0.1

For the pretrained BERT model, we use the full word coverage (Whole Word Masking) Chinese BERT pretrained model [4] released by the Harbin Institute of Technology Xunfei Joint Laboratory, and the main parameters in our experiment are in Table 4.

4.3 Evaluation Criteria

Argument identification is a binary classification task, the precision, recall and F1-score are usually used as evaluation criteria, but this paper uses the AUC (Area Under ROC Curve) as evaluation criteria. AUC (Area Under Curve) is defined as the area under the ROC curve, where the ROC curve is called the receiver operating characteristic curve, which is based on a series of different binary classification methods (cutoff value or threshold), a curve drawn with the true positive rate (sensitivity) as the ordinate and the false positive rate (1-specificity) as the abscissa. AUC can be obtained by summing the area of each part under the ROC curve, and the classifier with a larger AUC has higher accuracy. To a certain extent, AUC can describe the probability that positive examples are ranked ahead of negative examples in the prediction results, so that it can well describe the overall performance of the model. Therefore, this paper adopts AUC, and calculates the accuracy together as the evaluation criteria of the model.

4.4   Experimental Results and Analysis

As for the combination of predicates and arguments vectors, this paper tries the following five fusion methods to compare the impact of different combinations on the performance of classifiers. The final experimental results are as follows.

Table 5. Results of different combinations.

Model	AUC	Accuracy
Addition of dimensions of vectors of predicates and arguments	95.91%	97.41%
Mean of each dimension of vectors of predicates and arguments	96.45%	97.45%
Maximum value of each dimension of vectors of predicates and arguments	96.40%	97.58%
Concatenation of vectors of predicates and arguments and $H_{[cls]}$	95.51%	97.09%
Concatenation of vectors of predicates and arguments	97.18%	98.10%

According to Table 5, concatenation of vectors of predicates and arguments has the best semantic representation and the highest accuracy.

Most of the semantic role labeling data are simple sentences, that is, there is only one predicate in a sentence, while the model in this paper can effectively deal with difficult sentences, that is, a sentence contains multiple predicates. The performance of the model was tested on two types of datasets: single-predicate sentences and multi-predicate sentences. The results are shown in Table 6. The ACU can reach more than 97% in the two types of datasets, and the accuracy is more prominent in the multi-predicate dataset, which can reach more than 98%, while in the single-predicate dataset. The accuracy is also higher than 97%, which fully shows that the model can effectively identify the arguments of complex sentences.

Table 6. Results on single-predicate and multiple-predicate.

Dataset	AUC	Accuracy
Single-predicate dataset	97.70%	97.67%
Multi-predicate dataset	97.03%	98.04%

At the same time, in order to verify that BERT can effectively encode text semantic information, we set up two comparative experiments, which are based on Bi-LSTM (Bi-directional Long Short-Term Memory) and the Bi-LSTM with an attention mechanism (Att-BiLSTM). The results are shown in Table 7. As a text encoder, BERT has obvious advantages compared with LSTM. This stems from the fact that BERT is a large-scale pretrained model trained on rich news corpora based on the transformer structure, and the self-attention mechanism can effectively deal with long texts.

At the same time, the results show that Att-BiLSTM are better than Bi-LSTM, which proves that the attention mechanism can alleviate the sequence dependency problem, and it also further confirms that BERT with the self-attention mechanism can better encode the semantics of text.

Table 7. Results of comparison experiments.

Model	AUC
Bert	97.18%
BiLSTM	91.11%
Att-BiLSTM	91.88%

The model is trained based on chunk-dependent data in the news domain. In order to prove that the model can also perform well on data in other fields, we conducted experiments on manually annotated data covering encyclopedias, law, patent and other fields, and the results are shown in Table 8. It can be seen that in other fields, the AUC can reach more than 90%, indicating that the argument identification model has good domain adaption ability.

Table 8. Field migration experiment results.

Field	AUC	Accuracy
News(training)	97.18%	98.04%
Encyclopedia	90.60%	94.06%
Law	92.55%	96.23%
Patent	92.21%	96.27%

4.5 Example Analysis

Table 9 shows the probability of the model's prediction of arguments in multi-predicate and single-predicate sentences. It can be seen the score for correct arguments is far greater than 0.5, and the score for non-arguments is far less

Table 9. Predicate-argument candidates.

Sentence	Field	Predicate	Argument _ score
由此，胶黏剂成本低，工艺流程简单，耐水性好，粘合强度高，便于储存。(As a result, the adhesive has low cost, simple process flow, good water resistance, high bonding strength and easy storage.)	专利(patent)	低	成本_0.9602
			粘合_0.0042
		简单	工艺流程_0.8646
			强度_0.0065
		好	耐水性_0.8105
			粘合_0.0452
		高	强度_0.9514
			便于_0.0471
		便于	储存_0.9359
			成本_0.1203
它的解粗略地描述了人造地球卫星、月球卫星、人造行星的运动，成为研究航天器运动的基础。(Its solution roughly describes the motion of artificial earth satellites, lunar satellites, and artificial planets, and becomes the basis for studying the motion of spacecraft.)	百科(Encyclopedia)	描述	解_0.8782
			运动_0.8503
			卫星_0.0322
		成为	基础_0.9016
			解_0.8590
			月球_0.0102
针对这起系列案件，市、区两级刑侦部门随即组织精干力量，合力展开侦破工作。(In response to this series of cases, the criminal investigation departments at the city and district levels immediately organized capable forces to jointly carry out detection work.)	法律(law)	针对	案件_0.9411
			部门_0.7971
			系列_0.0447
		组织	部门_0.9113
			力量_0.8837
			工作_0.0100
		合力	部门_0.8350
			展开_0.4937
			组织_0.1783
		展开	工作_0.8950
			部门_0.8662
			案件_0.0233
长发的女性，扎上近几年流行的马尾，或是把长发盘在头上，会比较有风采。(Women with long hair will be more stylish if they tie the ponytail that has been popular in recent years, or wear long hair on the head.)	新闻(news)	扎	马尾_0.9157
			女性_0.9119
			长发_0.0373
		盘	头_0.8732
			长发_0.8212
			女性_0.7591
		有	风采_0.9251
			女性_0.8218
			头_0.0424

than 0.5, which fully shows that the classifier can effectively distinguish between arguments and non-arguments. And it can still maintain good accuracy in different fields.

In order to verify that the model can also perform well in difficult sentences, that is, multi-predicate sentences, we selected a complex sentence containing 6 predicates, and the model can still give the corresponding arguments for each predicate in this sentence, the result is shown in Table 10.

Table 10. Predicate-argument candidates.

Sentence	Predicate	Argument_score
现在美国一般是以大学和研究机构为中心，建立横向联系的风险企业网络，使科研与生产相结合，发挥群体优势，在经济杠杆的作用下，成为经济社会发展中相当活跃的一支力量。(At present, the United States generally centers on universities and research institutions, and establishes a horizontally connected venture enterprise network, combining scientific research and production, giving play to group advantages, and under the effect of economic leverage, it has become a fairly active force in economic and social development.)	为	美国_0.8326
		机构_0.82945
		中心_0.81163
	建立	美国_0.8976
		网络_0.8900
	使	科研_0.9276
		美国_0.7691
	结合	生产_0.9327
		科研_0.8915
	发挥	优势_0.9027
		美国_0.7830
	成为	作用_0.8560
		力量_0.8494
		美国_0.6295

5 Conclusion

Based on the chunk dependency data introduced above, we extract candidate predicate-argument pairs by regular grammar and syntactic rules. Use BERT to encode the input text, build an argument identification model, and identify all the arguments in the sentence when predicates are given, the AUC reaches 97.18%, and the accuracy reaches 98.10%, which optimizes the argument identification in the semantic role labeling task, and 500,000 high-quality data based on chunk dependency and argument identification were obtained, which provided reliable data for natural language processing. At the same time large-scale pretrained language models are able to overcome the sequence dependency problem and perform well in complex sentences and other fields.

By analyzing the existing systems and in-depth understanding of the semantic role labeling, we believe that the model can also be improved by appropriate class promotion of words with some external knowledge such as hownet, which is a common-sense knowledge base that takes the concepts represented by Chinese and English words as the description objects, and reveals the relationship between concepts and the attributes of concepts as the basic content. Hownet can generalize words to the greatest extent. For example, "apple" and "banana" in "I like apples" and "I like bananas" are objects of "eat", and they all belong to the category of "fruit". Hownet contains information such as hyponyms and the relationship between the attributes of concepts, which can well establish the connection between things with the same attributes, so as to effectively generalize individual cases. Furthermore, this paper will proceed with the argument classification task based on the obtained argument labeling data.

Acknowledgements. BLCU supported project for young researchers program (supported by the Fundamental Research Funds for the Central Universities) (22YCX147).

References

1. Baker, C.F., Fillmore, C.J., Lowe, J.B.: The berkeley framenet project. In: COLING 1998 Volume 1: The 17th International Conference on Computational Linguistics (1998)
2. Berant, J., Chou, A., Frostig, R., Liang, P.: Semantic parsing on freebase from question-answer pairs. In: Proceedings of the 2013 Conference on Empirical Methods in Natural Language Processing, pp. 1533–1544 (2013)
3. Che, W., Zhang, M., Aw, A., Tan, C., Liu, T., Li, S.: Using a hybrid convolution tree kernel for semantic role labeling. ACM Trans. Asian Lang. Inf. Process. (TALIP) **7**(4), 1–23 (2008)
4. Cui, Y., et al.: Pre-training with whole word masking for Chinese bert. IEEE/ACM Trans. Audio Speech Lang. Process. **29**, 3504–3514 (2019)
5. Devlin, J., Chang, M.W., Lee, K., Toutanova, K.: Bert: pre-training of deep bidirectional transformers for language understanding (2018)
6. Foland, W., Martin, J.: Dependency-based semantic role labeling using convolutional neural networks. In: Joint Conference on Lexical and Computational Semantics (2015)
7. Hacioglu, K.: Semantic role labeling using dependency trees. In: COLING 2004: Proceedings of the 20th International Conference on Computational Linguistics, pp. 1273–1276 (2004)
8. He, S., Li, Z., Zhao, H.: Syntax-aware multilingual semantic role labeling. arXiv preprint arXiv:1909.00310 (2019)
9. Li, Z., Guan, C., Zhao, H., Wang, R., Parnow, K., Zhang, Z.: Memory network for linguistic structure parsing. IEEE/ACM Trans. Audio Speech Lang. Process. **28**, 2743–2755 (2020)
10. Lin, Y., Liu, Z., Sun, M.: Neural relation extraction with multi-lingual attention. In: Proceedings of the 55th Annual Meeting of the Association for Computational Linguistics (Volume 1: Long Papers), pp. 34–43 (2017)
11. Liu, Che, Li: Semantic role labeling based on maximum entropy classifier. Ph.D. thesis, Citeseer (2007)
12. Marcheggiani, D., Titov, I.: Encoding sentences with graph convolutional networks for semantic role labeling. empirical methods in natural language processing (2017)
13. Mihaylov, T., Frank, A.: Discourse relation sense classification using cross-argument semantic similarity based on word embeddings. In: Proceedings of the CoNLL-16 Shared Task, pp. 100–107 (2016)
14. Munir, K., Zhao, H., Li, Z.: Adaptive convolution for semantic role labeling. Speech, and Language Processing. IEEE Trans. Audio (2020)
15. Palmer, M., Gildea, D., Kingsbury, P.: The proposition bank: an annotated corpus of semantic roles. Comput. Linguist. **31**(1), 71–106 (2005)
16. Pradhan, S., Ward, W., Hacioglu, K., Martin, J.H., Jurafsky, D.: Semantic role labeling using different syntactic views. In: Proceedings of the 43rd Annual Meeting of the Association for Computational Linguistics (ACL 2005), pp. 581–588 (2005)
17. Punyakanok, V., Roth, D., Yih, W.t.: The importance of syntactic parsing and inference in semantic role labeling. Comput. Linguist. **34**(2), 257–287 (2008)

18. Qian, Q., Wang, C., Rao, G., Xun, E.: Chinese chunk-based dependency grammar. In: Proceedings of the 19th Chinese National Conference on Computational Linguistics (2020)
19. Shi, C., et al.: Knowledge-based semantic embedding for machine translation. In: Proceedings of the 54th Annual Meeting of the Association for Computational Linguistics (Volume 1: Long Papers), pp. 2245–2254 (2016)
20. Shi, P., Lin, J.: Simple bert models for relation extraction and semantic role labeling. In: Computation and Language (2019)
21. Strubell, E., Verga, P., Andor, D., Weiss, D.J., McCallum, A.: Linguistically-informed self-attention for semantic role labeling. empirical methods in natural language processing (2018)
22. Vaswani, A., et al.: Attention is all you need. neural information processing systems (2017)
23. Wang, S.: A semantic role recognition method based on dependency tree distance. In: Research Frontiers of Computational Linguistics in China (2009–2011) (2011)
24. Wang, Y., Che, W., Guo, J., Liu, T.: A neural transition-based approach for semantic dependency graph parsing. In: Proceedings of the AAAI Conference on Artificial Intelligence, vol. 32 (2018)
25. Xie, L.: Text sentiment classification model based on bert and two-channel attention. Data Collect. Process. **35**(4), 642–652 (2020)
26. Xue, N., Xia, F., Chiou, F.D., Palmer, M.: The penn chinese treebank: Phrase structure annotation of a large corpus. Nat. Lang. Eng. **11**(2), 207–238 (2005)
27. Xue, N., Palmer, M.: Adding semantic roles to the Chinese treebank. Nat. Lang. Eng. **15**(1), 143–172 (2009)
28. Yih, W.t., Richardson, M., Meek, C., Chang, M.W., Suh, J.: The value of semantic parse labeling for knowledge base question answering. In: Proceedings of the 54th Annual Meeting of the Association for Computational Linguistics (Volume 2: Short Papers), pp. 201–206 (2016)
29. Zhang, P.: Ent-bert: entity-relational classification model combining bert and entity information. Small Microcomput. Syst. **41**(12), 2557–2562 (2020)
30. Zhao, H., Chen, W., Uchimoto, K., Torisawa, K., et al.: Multilingual dependency learning: exploiting rich features for tagging syntactic and semantic dependencies. In: Proceedings of the Thirteenth Conference on Computational Natural Language Learning (CoNLL 2009): Shared Task, pp. 61–66 (2009)
31. Zhou, J., Xu, W.: End-to-end learning of semantic role labeling using recurrent neural networks. In: International Joint Conference on Natural Language Processing (2015)

Irony Recognition in Chinese Text Based on Linguistic Features and Attention Mechanism

Xiaofeng Qiu[✉] (iD)

Peking University, Beijing, China
qiuxiaofeng@pku.edu.cn

Abstract. As a rhetorical means of expressing emotional tendency, irony is challenging to identify and analyze because of the contrast between its actual semantics and literal expression. To improve the accuracy of sentiment analysis and increase the understanding of the phenomenon of irony, this paper conducts a study on Chinese irony recognition. By analyzing the characteristics of irony in Chinese social media texts, we refine irony linguistic features and integrate them into a deep learning model through the attention mechanism to construct a new Chinese irony recognition model. The experimental results indicate that the proposed method has certain advantages over classical purely data-driven deep learning models in terms of both performance and interpretability.

Keywords: sentiment analysis · irony recognition · attention mechanism

1 Introduction

Irony has become a common way of language expression with the rise of social networks. Users normally use irony to express strong negative emotional tendencies including the ridicule and criticism for trending and controversial issues, and the situation poses a challenge to correct analysis of users' emotions in social media. The calculable research on irony recognition has also become a hot topic for researchers and delivers important significance: on the one hand, it can enrich the research results related to irony, and then promote the understandings of the essential significance, cognitive process and differentiation mechanism of irony; on the other hand, the accuracy of natural language processing tasks involving sentiment analysis and man-machine dialogue are supported to be improved.

The studies on irony recognition are mainly English oriented presently. The language structure of Chinese is complex, and the ways to realize irony are extremely abundant. Consequently, the studies on Chinese irony recognition are scarce and challenging. Based on relevant studies, this paper analyzes Chinese irony by combining the characteristics of social media and Chinese irony corpus examples, generalizes and acquires some explicit linguistic features highly related to irony, and proposes a method of integrating linguistic features into deep learning model for irony recognition. Experiments show that the new model can capture deep semantics of the text more effectively and exhibits better interpretability than previous data-driven deep learning models.

Q. Su et al. (Eds.): CLSW 2022, LNAI 13496, pp. 351–363, 2023.
https://doi.org/10.1007/978-3-031-28956-9_28

2 Related Work

There have been many studies on irony ontology from different perspectives. Based on Grice's cooperative principle [1], the substitution theory considered that irony is substituting implicit meaning for literal meaning by violating the principle. Sperber and Wilson [2] proposed the relevance theory and pointed out that irony is always or at least partly determined by the speaker's attitude to the view. Clark and Gerrig [3] put forward the pretense theory. This theory held that the ironic speaker S, in order to cater to a specific listener H, pretends to be $S1$ to speak to an imaginary listener $H1$, S is critical of what $S1$ says, $H1$ may only understand the literal meaning of the words, but the real listener H can recognize the disguised intent from $S1$'s ignorance, ill-consideration, etc. and derive the intended irony. Utsumi [4] defined irony as implicit display of ironic environment and suggested ironic environment contains three states (suppose there are time points t_0 and t_1 before the utterance): (1) the speaker has a certain expectation at t_0; ; (2) the speaker's expectation is inconsistent with reality at t_1; (3) the speaker has a negative emotion towards this inconsistency.

Irony recognition mainly looks at the feature construction and classification learning methods for irony recognition from the perspective of calculability. The traditional machine learning models [5–8] classifies based on statistical situation of features, it is difficult to mine deep semantic information, and it normally suffers from serious problem of cross domain effect degradation. As deep learning evolves, Ghosh [9] first applied convolutional neural network (CNN) and long short-term memory network (LSTM) models to irony recognition. Considering that it was difficult to precisely capture the characteristics of long-term dependence in the text and opposite emotional polarity of word pairs with the existing models, Yi et al. [10] applied self-attention mechanism to extract the information between word pairs and proposed a context-free irony recognition model. Hazarika et al. [11] considered the combination of context information involving users and topics with text information and proposed a complex model combining context to identify irony. Deep learning models have higher recognition accuracy compared to traditional machine learning models except complex network structure, abundant parameters and poor interpretability.

Presently, studies on Chinese irony recognition are still in the exploratory stage. Tang [12] constructed an irony corpus of traditional Chinese characters and analyzed some common sentence patterns of irony without mentioning recognition features and classification algorithms. Deng et al. [13] marked 300 irony and 28,545 non-irony corpora from Sina Microblog to build an experimental data set and set up six features including basic vocabulary emotion and homophonic words with an accuracy of 76.74% to the maximum extent in the traditional machine learning model. Xing [14] summarized the features of the deviation between the implicit meaning and literal meaning, tension of emotional changes, etc. in Chinese texts, and achieved the highest recall rate of 71.2% and accuracy rate of 60.3% on the logistic model. Sun et al. [15] set up a data set of $1,000$ ironic and non-ironic corpora, and proposed a neural network model for CNN and LSTM based on collocation rules and emotional semantics. Lu et al. [16] inputted emotional words, homonyms, network words and collocation feature as additional information into CNN model, achieving relatively high recognition effects.

3 Feature Analysis

3.1 Linguistic Features of Irony in Chinese Social Media

Based on the existing studies, our research describes the irony as a rhetorical way of expressing negative implicit meaning by means of non-negative literal meaning. The most typical formal feature of ironic language is the positive-negative opposition, that is, both component P of which the literal meaning is non-negative and component N of that the literal meaning is negative are included. A special expression effect is achieved through the semantic contrast between P and N: the component P of which the literal meaning is non-negative delivers implicit meaning that also expresses negative meaning. In a nutshell, it is "expressing the opposite of what is right" or "secretly belittling while openly praising".

The realization of formal features depends on more specific features in language, which are greatly correlated with ironies. By combining with linguistic features of Chinese social media, ironic linguistic features constructed in our paper are shown as follows:

(1) Skip-n words. A sentence with a length of n after word segmentation, is supported to construct n^2 compound words. Some co-occurrence phrases can connect syntactic components and express specific syntactic relations including progressive relation and adversative relation, and the phrases are eligible to inspire listeners to understand the implicit meanings of sentences. For example, "很好, 我又写错作业了。" (*Awesome, I wrote my homework incorrect again.*) "很好…又…" (*Awesome… Again…*) is a common combination in ironies.

(2) Adverbs marking intense emotional intensity. Adverbs are frequently used in Chinese ironies, which are mainly degree adverbs that modify the degree of emotional intensity and modal adverbs that express strong tone. For example, "这帮人正事不会干, 贩卖焦虑最在行!" (*the guys fail to handle better things, and they are the best at mongering fear!*), the degree adverb "最"(*most*) modifies the emotional word "在行" (*best*) with positive evaluation meaning, is capable of expressing strong emotional tendency, forming a striking contrast with the negative semantics expressed by the preceding components of the sentence.

(3) "被 + X" (*be + X*) construction. The conventional passive usage of the preposition "被" (*be*) is followed by the agent (normally supported to be omitted) and then the transitive verb to form the conventional "被 + VP" construction. However, in Chinese social media language environment, the "被" (*be*) is allowed to be followed by intransitive verb, adjective, noun, etc. For example, "乱收费的最高境界就是被自愿。" (*the highest state of arbitrary charge is allowed to be voluntary.*), "自愿" (*voluntary*) is originally a self-executing behavior so it is [+ controllable] in semantic features. In the routine "被 + VP", the occurrence of VP for the object is normally uncontrollable, namely [- controllable]. Consequently, the existence of "被" makes "被 + X" form a controllable and uncontrollable conflict in semantic features, succinctly and concisely reflecting the irony of unreasonable social problems through semantic contradictions.

(4) Specific punctuation marks mainly indicate exclamation mark, question mark, ellipsis and quotation marks. Exclamation marks and question marks in Chinese social

media can enhance the tone to express users' strong emotional tendencies. Ellipsis and quotation marks can imply the implicit meanings of readers to realize ironic expression. For example, "别忘了这些战疫英雄: '居里夫人'王某、'通稿复读机'某君、'好院长'蔡某……" (*don't forget these anti-epidemic heroes: 'Madame Curie' Mrs. Wang, 'manuscript repeater' some guy, 'great director', Cai…*)

(5) Specific cyber words. Social media language is characterized with concise, colloquial and creative features, and has formed abundant emerging cyber words dominated in the form of words. Some cyber words are eligible to play hinting irony effects thanks to that they are normally related with ironies, and even some cyber words themselves have negative implicit meanings, such as the "公知" (*the public intellectual*), "键盘侠" (*keyboard man*), "废青" (*useless teenager*), and so on.

3.2 Selection Method for Linguistic Features

χ^2 statistics is a classical and effective feature selection method. By targeting at Chinese irony microblogs, we calculated the combined χ^2 value of skip-n words, and then manually selected 15 combinations with higher χ^2 value as ironic combinations. See Table 1 for some statistical results. The χ^2 values of all words are calculated after removing the stop words from the microblog corpus, and then the first 15 adverbs marking emotional intensity and specific cyber words are selected respectively, and results are shown as follows:

Adverbs marking emotional intensity include "很" (*very*), "真是" (*really*), "太" (*too*), "有点" (*slightly*), "挺" (*quietly*), "完全" (*completely*), "非常" (*awfully*), "那么" (*so*), "超" (*super*), "过于" (*excessively*), "最" (*most*), "满" (*fully*), "却" (*yet*), "反倒" (*instead*), "偏偏" (*just*).

Specific cyber words include keyboard "键盘侠" (*keyboard man*), "毒鸡汤" (*motivation porn*), "五毛" (*troll*), "公知" (*the public intellectual*), "尼玛" (*asshole*), "作死" (*dramatic*), "废青" (*useless teenager*), "醉了" (*inconceivable*), "人设" (*persona*), "圣母" (*social justice warrior*), "战狼" (*brainless fans*), "沙雕" (*stupid ass*), "奇葩" (*weirdo*), "屌丝" (*loser*), "河蟹" (*yes-man*).

Table 1. Statistical values of skip-n words combinations

Number	Skip-n words combination	χ^2	Number	Skip-n words combination	χ^2
1	…这…很… (…*this…very…*)	3.54	4	…可以…再… (…*could…further…*)	2.79
2	…连…都… (…*even…unexpectedly…*)	3.44	5	…又…真是… (…*and…really…*)	2.78
3	…很好…又… (…*pretty great…and…*)	3.25	6	…再…一点… (…*further…a bit/little…*)	2.69

4 Model

4.1 Word Embedding

Mikolov [17] presented the word2vec model to train word embedding vector in a specific field, and the Skip-gram model predicts the word vectors of contextual words through the word vectors of the target words. A sequence of words is supposed to be $w_1, w_2, \ldots, w_n$, and the goal of the model is to maximize the value of Eq. 1.

$$E = \frac{1}{N} \sum_{n=1}^{N} \sum_{-a \leq i \leq a, i \neq 0} -\log p(w_{n+i}|w_n) \tag{1}$$

where a is the window size centered on the current word, denoting that the first a words and the next a words of the current word w_n are selected. $p\,(w_{n+i}\,|w_n)$ denotes the probability of occurrence of the word w_{n+i} when the word w_n has appeared, and it is normally calculated based on Eq. 2 in the Skip-gram model.

$$p(w_{n+i}|w_n) = \frac{exp\left(v_{w_{n+i}}^{T} v_{w_n}\right)}{\sum_{t=1}^{|V|} exp\left(v_t^{T} v_{w_n}\right)} \tag{2}$$

v_t and v_t' denote the input vector and output vector of word w_t respectively, and $|V|$ denotes the lexicon size. Skip-gram model is applied in this paper to train the word vector. The dimension is set to 300, and the sliding window is sized in 10. The training process is shown below.

4.2 Irony Feature Enhanced Attention Network (IEAN)

For purpose of combining intrinsic linguistic features of irony with deep learning method in a better way, a new irony recognition model is set up in this paper. Word embedding is applied to set up the context word matrix and feature word matrix as model inputs. The attention layer is applied to enhance the ironic features of sentences to achieve the attention representation of features. To expand sentence semantics, we build our representation by concatenating the attention representation and the sentence compositional representation at the fully connected layer. Finally, the spliced embedding vector is input into softmax classifier to realize irony recognition of sentences. The overall framework of our model is shown in Fig. 1.

Input Layer. The input layer of the model contains word embedding matrices including the context word matrix and feature word matrix. PKUSeg[1], an open-source word segmentation tool of Peking University, is applied to segment all sentences in the dataset. The sentence S is supposed to contain t words, and then the outcome is expressed in word order as shown in Formula 3.

$$S : \{w_1, w_2, \ldots, w_t\} \tag{3}$$

---

[1] https://github.com/lancopku/PKUSeg-python.

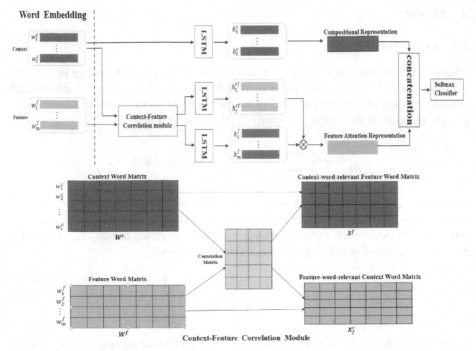

Fig. 1. Framework for irony recognition model integrating linguistic features.

The vector of word w_i is acquired and represented from the trained word embedding, whose dimension is supposed to be d. w_i is expressed as shown in Eq. 4.

$$w_i = (c_{i1}, c_{i2}, ..., c_{id})i \in [1, t] \tag{4}$$

The context word matrix is to arrange each word vector of S in word order, as shown in Eq. 5.

$$S = w_1 \oplus w_2 \oplus ... \oplus w_t \tag{5}$$

Accordingly, the sentence S is transformed into the appropriate vector matrix W^c, as shown in Eq. 6. Similarly, let the number of extracted feature words be m, and the feature word matrix W^f is shown in Eq. 7.

$$W^c = \begin{bmatrix} c_{11} & c_{12} & \dots & c_{1d} \\ c_{21} & c_{22} & \dots & c_{2d} \\ \vdots & \vdots & & \vdots \\ c_{t1} & c_{t2} & \dots & c_{td} \end{bmatrix} \in \mathbb{R}^{t \times d} \tag{6}$$

$$W^f = \begin{bmatrix} f_{11} & f_{12} & \dots & f_{1d} \\ f_{21} & f_{22} & \dots & f_{2d} \\ \vdots & \vdots & & \vdots \\ f_{m1} & f_{m2} & \dots & f_{md} \end{bmatrix} \in \mathbb{R}^{m \times d} \tag{7}$$

Attention Module Integrating Linguistic Features. The core of this module is the context-feature correlation module. Inspired by Xiong [18], this paper defined the correlation matrix M^f of context words and feature words by dot products to express the correlation degree between feature words and context words, as shown in Formula 8.

$$M^f = \left(W^c\right)^T \cdot W^f \in \mathbb{R}^{m \times t} \tag{8}$$

The text-related feature representation matrix X^f is defined and shown in Formula 9, representing the vectors of feature words for the context words.

$$X^f = M^f \cdot W^c \in \mathbb{R}^{m \times d} \tag{9}$$

The feature-related context representation matrix X_f^c is defined as Formula 10, and it represents the vectors of context words for the feature words.

$$X_f^c = \left(M^f\right)^T \cdot W^f \in \mathbb{R}^{t \times d} \tag{10}$$

Next, the hidden state matrixes H^c, H^f and H_f^c are encoded by three independent LSTM layers, as shown in Formula 11–13.

$$H^c = LSTM\left(X^c\right) \tag{11}$$

$$H^f = LSTM\left(X^f\right) \tag{12}$$

$$H_f^c = LSTM\left(X_f^c\right) \tag{13}$$

After obtaining the hidden state matrixes, the semantic representation r_a of the sentence enhanced by ironic features is calculated as in Formula 14–17. Where q_f is the average pooling of H^f to reduce parameters and prevent overfitting. [;] denotes the concatenation operation. s denotes the attention function to calculate the importance of the ith word of the sentence to the task. The calculation results of s are normalized through softmax to acquire the attention weights α_i of each word in the sentences. Finally, the weighted average output representing the sentence semantics with enhanced ironic features is denoted as r_a, and u_s^T and W_s are parameters to be learned.

$$r_a = \sum_{i=1}^{t} a_i h_{if}^c \tag{14}$$

$$q_f = \sum_{i=1}^{m} h_i^f / m \tag{15}$$

$$s\left(\left[h_{if}^c; q_f\right]\right) = u_s^T \tanh\left(W_s\left[h_{if}^c; q_f\right]\right) \tag{16}$$

$$\alpha_i = \frac{exp(s\left(\left[h_{if}^c; q_f\right]\right))}{\sum_{i=1}^{t} exp(s\left(\left[h_{if}^c; q_f\right]\right))} \tag{17}$$

Fully Connected Layer and Softmax Layer. Splice the serialized modeling of regular context h^c with the intra-context attention representation r_a, and the acquired representation h downstream of the model serves as the input of the classifier, as shown in Eq. 18. The sentence representation h is fed into a softmax layer to predict the distribution of ironic category labels for the sentence, as shown in Eq. 19.

$$h = h^c \oplus r_a \tag{18}$$

$$\hat{y} = \frac{exp\left(\tilde{w}_o^T h + \tilde{b}_o\right)}{\sum_{i=1}^{C} exp\left(\tilde{w}_o^T h + \tilde{b}_o\right)} \tag{19}$$

where $\hat{y}$ denotes the predicted distribution of ironic category labels, C denotes the number of categories of labels, $\tilde{w}_o^T$ and $\tilde{b}_o$ are parameters required to be learned. In the process of model training, our goal is to minimize the cross entropy of truth class labels and prediction class labels. Moreover, the dropout strategy is applied to randomly omit some parameters in all training samples for purpose of preventing overfitting.

4.3   Chinese Irony Data Set

Presently, few studies on Chinese irony are conducted, and there is also a lack of open and authoritative irony corpus. Most of the existing studies are mainly expanded based on traditional Chinese character corpus constructed by Tang [12], which exhibits relatively single corpus mode. For example, over 58% of the corpus is "很好" (*very stunning*) or "太好" (*too stunning*) followed by negative emotion contents, and over 35% of the corpus is "可以再" (*can be further*) followed by adjectives expressing negative emotion. If the expansion fails to be handled properly, as a data set of irony recognition, the classifier is at high risk of overfitting.

In terms of sectors including the sports, movie, news, entertainment, etc., 10,000 items of microblog data are collected in this paper for manual tagging. Since the implicit display theory [4] has better revealed the manner of distinguish irony and non-irony in existing irony ontology studies, we use it as a labeling guide during manual tagging. More specifically, if the precondition of irony —— ironic environment exits, then the sentence is considered to be ironic. For sentence "这帮人正事不会干, 贩卖焦虑最在行!" (*the guys fail to handle better things, and they are the best at mongering fear!*), "贩卖焦虑" (*mongering fear*) is an act against social norms and the general expectation of speakers is "not to monger fear", but the fact "贩卖焦虑最在行" (*they are the best at mongering fear*) goes against the general expectation, so it is reasonable to assume that "最在行" (*best at*) implies negative attitude of speakers towards this inconsistency. So far, all three states of ironic environment have been realized, then the sentence should be tagged as ironic. In the labeling setting, the irony labeling is regarded as a binary classification problem, and we use the label 1 for irony and 0 for non-irony. Sentiment labeling is also human-based, labeling sentence sentiment categories as positive, negative, or neutral. In order to reduce the judgment bias caused by subjective factors in manual tagging, cross-checking is adopted in the process, and inconsistent labeling opinions are discussed and unified. Finally, a total of 19,268 emotional sentences are tagged, including 1291 sentences with ironies which account for 6.58% of the total number of emotional sentences. The data categories are subject to balancing treatment, and 1, 291 sentences are extracted from the non-irony data set to have the positive-negative sample ratio of the Chinese irony data set become 1:1.

4.4 Model Parameters

The longest sentence in the experimental data set contains 72 words with the word vector dimension is 300, the objective function in the model training is the cross entropy loss function with the learning rate of 0.001 and the forgetting rate of 0.5. The size of LSTM hidden layer is 256, and the number of iterations amounts to 20. The training set and test set are divided by 4:1.

5   Experiments and Analysis

The effectiveness of methods set out in this paper is validated by the following groups of experiments.

5.1   Validation on Ironic Linguistic Features

The effects of two types of language modeling involving Bag-of-Words (BOW) model and BOW model combined with ironic language features (BOW + Feature) on different classifiers are compared in the experiment. Naive bayes (NB), support vector machines (SVM) and random forests (RF) are used as classifier. The experimental results are shown in Table 2.

The BOW model combined with ironic language features is significantly improved in terms of precision, recall and F1-score, proving that the manually selected language features are effective. Semantic studies of irony [19] refer to these features as lexical-level linguistic cues which are the additional information left by the speaker intentionally and become a breakthrough for the listener to recognize irony. It is difficult to identify irony simply through word co-occurrence information, while the selected ironic language features are significantly related to irony, alleviating the above problems to a certain extent.

5.2   Validation on Attention Network Model Based on Linguistic Features

To comprehensively evaluate the performance of models in this paper, several sentence-level irony recognition models are compared.

It can be found from Table 3 that LSTM model has the worst result and does not reflect the advantages of deep learning models compared with traditional machine learning models above. The main reason might be the size of the ironic data set in this paper is relatively small, which cannot give full play to the learning ability of LSTM. Comparing 1 and 2 in Table 3, the effect of bidirectional LSTM model has been improved (F1≈ +

Table 2. Experimental results of the first group

Method	BOW			BOW + Feature		
Classifier	NB	SVM	RF	NB	SVM	RF
Precision	0.6971	0.7500	0.8125	0.7786	0.8182	**0.8361**
Recall	0.6682	0.7058	0.6259	0.6994	**0.7578**	0.693
F1-score	0.6823	0.7272	0.7071	0.7368	**0.7868**	0.7578

2.2%) after splicing the contextual information of the sentence, indicating the importance of word order information in ironic language modeling, especially whether irony is used in interpreting a literal non-negative sentence component depends on components of the sentence before and after. In comparison 2 and 3, the effect of the model is further improved (F1$\approx$ + 2.4%) after self-attention mechanism is added, indicating self-attention model dynamically focuses on which words are more conducive to irony recognition by comparing the relationship between word pairs within the sentence.

Table 3. Experimental results of the second group

Number	Method	Precision	Recall	F1-score
1	LSTM	0.7679	0.7396	0.7535
2	Bi_LSTM	0.7858	0.7656	0.7756
3	Self_Attention[2]	0.8125	0.7864	0.7993
4	CNN	0.8404	0.7907	0.8148
5	IEAN(our model)	**0.8527**	**0.8269**	**0.8390**
6	IEAN w/o pretrained wv	0.7806	0.7380	0.7587

Compared to CNN which performs best in the benchmark model, the model proposed in this paper exhibits slight increase in the precision and significant increase in both recall (R$\approx$ + 3.6%) and F1-score (F1$\approx$ + 2.4%), proving that it makes for acquiring the overall semantics of sentences to further identify irony more effectively. Besides, this paper also verifies the effectiveness of word embeddings, compares with the method of discarding pre-trained word embeddings and applying randomly initialized word embeddings (marked as w/o pretrained wv), the performance of the model is significantly improved by using pre-trained word embeddings. This is because the domain-based pre-trained word embeddings support capturing the correlation between words and describing the word distribution in the language in a better manner. This is equivalent to indirect introduction of external data, which alleviates the overfitting problem to a certain degree.

---

[2] Implemented based on LSTM by referring to the model in [6].

5.3 Model Analysis Based on Attention Matrix Visualization

The attention matrixes are extracted from two models including self-attention model and IEAN model for normalization, and the visualization results are shown in Table 4 (the darker the color, the greater the weight). In quite a few sentences, self-attention will focus on the end element of the sentence that is insignificant for irony recognition, probably because that LSTM combines the information of different time nodes in self-attention model to acquire the sentence representation. When the text is short, the representations of the n-1th and n^{th} hidden states may be very similar, and the attention will be concentrated on the last one or several hidden state representations. Overall, the attention of IEAN to a series of feature words significantly related to ironies is completely appropriate, which is similar to the process human use to acquire hints from language features and then identify implicate meanings of ironies, and it also helps the model identify irony more effectively. The visualization of attention matrix for IEAN measures the contribution of specific concept representation of a neural network model to the task goal, which is an improvement over traditional models in terms of the interpretability.

Table 4. Visualization of attention matrixes for two models

Category	Model	Sentence
Ironic	Self_Attention	社会 可以 再 肮脏 一点 吗 ?
		(*Can the community be a little more immoral?*)
	IEAN	社会 可以 再 肮脏 一点 吗 ?
		(*Can the community be a little more immoral?*)
	Self_Attention	公知 们 为了 他们 的 洋爹 真的 够 忍辱负重 了 。
		(*Public intellectuals are really sufficient to endure humiliation for their foreign masters.*)
	IEAN	公知 们 为了 他们 的 洋爹 真的 够 忍辱负重 了 。
		(*Public intellectuals are really sufficient to endure humiliation for their foreign masters.*)
Non-Ironic	Self_Attention	别 把 某些 东西 看 的 太 重要 。
		(*Don't take something too serious.*)
	IEAN	别 把 某些 东西 看 的 太 重要 。
		(*Don't take something too serious.*)
	Self_Attention	前 七 集 真的 是 太 压抑 了 !
		(The first seven episodes are really too stifling!)
	IEAN	前 七 集 真的 是 太 压抑 了 !
		(The first seven episodes are really too stifling!)

5.4 Error Analysis

We selected the results of one experiment from the five cross-validations and used it as an example to analyze the recognition errors. Table 5 shows the recognition results of this experiment.

Table 5. Recognition result of one experiment

Reality	Prediction	
	Ironic	No-Ironic
Ironic	222	38
Non-Ironic	40	220

14 of the 40 sentences predicted to be ironic and actually non-ironic contained at least one of the feature words selected in Sect. 3.2, for example, "我个人很喜欢肖战在这部戏里的人设" (*I personally like the persona of Xiao Zhan in this play*). This is also consistent with the phenomenon we observed in the third set of experiments. Linguistic features that are strongly correlated with the phenomenon of irony can also appear in non-ironic texts, when the sentence representation obtained by focusing attention may not help or even interfere with the goal of identifying non-ironic texts. Among the 38 sentences predicted to be non-ironic and actually ironic, we found that the determination of some ironic sentences relied heavily on extra-sentential information including background knowledge and overall contextualization. The linguistic features selected in this paper are actually the same form of information that has a positional relationship with the text to be recognized in a long text, that is, the narrowly defined contexts. The broader context should also include the speaker's voice, tone, expression, status, or social media retweets, replies, comments, and the background knowledge mentioned above. Therefore, in theory, adding contextual information can make irony recognition more accurate.

6 Conclusion and Prospect

The irony phenomenon is analyzed in this paper, and the effectiveness on ironic features in terms of statistical significance supported by linguistic theories is verified. Based on this, we propose an irony recognition model (IEAN) combining linguistic features and attention mechanism. Experiments show that IEAN demonstrates certain advantages over traditional data-driven deep learning models in terms of both performance and interpretability.

The linguistic features selected in this paper mainly come from lexical level, and although this brings some convenience for combining attention mechanism, it also lacks the mining and utilization of deeper sentence information such as grammar. Besides, our research integrates some linguistic features through attention mechanism, and attempts to combine linguistic knowledge with computational models to solve the sentiment analysis task in the field of natural language processing by means of a better manner. People have accumulated extensive language resources in studies on sentiment analysis for quite a long time, and it will be an interesting and rewarding study on how to input high quality linguistic knowledge into deep learning models.

Acknowledgements. This paper is supported by Major Project of the New Generation of Artificial Intelligence funded by Ministry of Science and Technology (project no. 2020AAA0106701) and by NSFC (project no.62076008).

References

1. Grice, H.P.: Logic and conversation. In: Cole, P., Morgan, J. (Eds.) Syntax and Semantics, vol. 3. Speech Acts: 41–58. Academic Press, London (1975)
2. Sperber, D., Wilson, D.: Relevance: Communication and Cognition. Blackwell, Oxford (1986)
3. Clark, H.H., Gerrig, R.J.: On the pretense theory of irony. J. Exp. Psychol.: General **113**(1), 121–126 (1984)
4. Utsumi, A.: Verbal irony as implicit display of ironic environment: distinguishing ironic utterances from nonirony. J. Pragmat. **32**, 1777–1806 (2000)
5. Reyes, A., Rosso, P., Veale, T.: A multidimensional approach for detecting irony in Twitter. Lang. Res. Eval. **47**(1), 239–268 (2013)
6. Buschmeier, K., Cimiano, P., Klinger, K.: An impact analysis of features in a classification approach to irony detection in product reviews. In: Proceedings of the 5th Workshop on Computational Approaches to Subjectivity, Sentiment and Social Analysis, pp. 42–49 (2014)
7. Lunando, E, Purwarianti, A.: Indonesian social media sentiment analysis with sarcasm detection. In: Proceedings of the Advanced Computer Science and Information Systems (ICACSIS), International Conference on IEEE, pp. 195–198 (2013)
8. Bamman, D, Smith, N.: Contextualized sarcasm detection on Twitter. In: Proceedings of the 9th International AAAI Conference on Web and Social Media, pp. 574–577 (2015)
9. Ghosh, A., Veale, T.: Fracking sarcasm using neural network. In: Proceedings of NAACLHLT, pp.161–169 (2016)
10. Yi, T., Luu, A.T., Siu, C.H., Jian, S.: Reasoning with sarcasm by reading in-between. In: Proceedings of the 56th Annual Meeting of the Association for Computer Linguistics (2018)
11. Hazarika, D., Poria, S., Gorantla, S., Cambria, E., Zimmermann, R., Mihalcea, R.: CASCADE: contextual sarcasm detection in online discussion forums. In: Proceedings of the 27th International Conference on Computational Linguistics (2018)
12. Tang, Y.J., Chen, H.: Chinese irony corpus construction and ironic structure analysis. In: Proceedings of the 25th International Conference on Computational Linguistics, pp. 1269–1278 (2014)
13. Deng, Z., Jia, X.Y., Chen, J.J.: Research on Chinese irony recognition for microblogs. Comput. Eng. Sci. **37**(12), 2312–2317 (2015)
14. Xing, Z.T., Xu, Y.: A study of Chinese irony rhetoric recognition method for online texts. J. Shanxi Univ. (Nat. Sci. Ed.) **38**(3), 385–391 (2015)
15. Sun, X., He, J.J., Ren, F.J.: Pragmatic analysis of irony based on hybrid neural network model with multi-future. J. Chin. Inf. Process. **30**(6), 215–233 (2016)
16. Lu, X., Li, Y., Wang, S.G.: Linguistic features enhanced convolutional neural networks for irony recognition. J. Chin. Inf. Process. **33**(5), 31–38 (2019)
17. Mikolov, T., Chen, K., Corrado, G., Dean, J.: Efficient estimation of word representations in vector space. Comput. Sci. (2013). https://doi.org/10.48550/arXiv.1301.3781
18. Xiong, C.M., Zhong, V., Socher, R.: Dynamic coattention networks for question answering. In: Proceedings of the International Conference on Learning Representations (2017)
19. Roy, M.A.: Irony in Conversation. University of Michigan dissertation, Ann Arbor (1978)

A Phrase Disambiguation Method
of "Quanbu V de N" Based on SBERT Model
and Syntactic Rule

Siqi Xie and Quan Yang[✉]

School of International Chinese Language Education, Beijing Normal University, Beijing, China
201922090058@mail.bnu.edu.cn, yangquan@bnu.edu.cn

Abstract. A method combining syntactic rule and semantic preference in resolving ambiguous structures "全部V的N (*Quanbu V de N*)" is proposed in this paper. First, a rule base is constructed, and the rules of ambiguity division are described in accordance with the syntactic structural constraints and semantic representation function. Secondly, the homomorphic and heterogeneous phrase is converted into two heteromorphic phrases "全部都V的N (*Quanbu dou V de N*)" and "全部的V 的N (*Quanbu de V de N*)". We use the SBERT model to calculate the semantic similarity between the original sentence and the two candidate sentences so that the optimal phrase segmentation is obtained. The experiment was conducted on 646 texts with ambiguous phrases "Quanbu V de N" as the object for testing. The disambiguation accuracy and the F1 value are both over 95%, which proves that this method can effectively disambiguate this phrase in natural language.

Keywords: Structural ambiguity · Disambiguation · Syntactic restriction · Semantic preference · SBERT

1 Introduction

Structural ambiguity, also known as "isomorphic" ambiguity, refers to the different syntactic structures that occur when a sentence or a larger component of a sentence is decomposed into several smaller components [1]. For example, the phrase "全部V 的N" (*Quanbu V de N*) is a typical ambiguous phrase, which is very common in modern Chinese. According to the self-built corpus[1] data, the number of ambiguities formed by "全部V的N" accounts for 45.69% of the total corpus.

In the early days, Chinese scholars explored the methods of disambiguation of structural ambiguity mainly on the basis of linguistics, proposing means of disambiguation in terms of syntax, semantics, and context, such as synonym substitution, the addition of

---

This research is sponsored by the National Social Science Fund of China, No. 21BYY205.

[1] The self-built corpus is composed of *Quanbu V de N* phrase structures extracted from BCC corpus, CCL corpus and the parallel Corpus of Modern Chinese of the National Language Commission. There are 1714 items in the whole corpus, and the ambiguity is manually marked, among which 646 items are marked with ambiguity.

Q. Su et al. (Eds.): CLSW 2022, LNAI 13496, pp. 364–374, 2023.
https://doi.org/10.1007/978-3-031-28956-9_29

empty words, syntactic conversion, semantic orientation, or semantic role differentiation [2, 3].

After the 1980s, with the advancement of information technology, researchers gradually turned to the use of computer analysis to deal with ambiguity problems, and the approach of computational linguistics was proposed. The focus is on three main aspects: 1) the rule-based rationalist approach [4–6], which is constrained by the limited rule base and the disambiguation effect is not outstanding; 2) the statistical empiricist approach, an approach generally relies on large-scale treebanks [7, 1], which has advantages in terms of data scale and has improved disambiguation effects compared to the previous approach; 3) the combined approach: machine learning or neural network models are used on the basis of structured knowledge bases or language rule bases, the disambiguation effect can be significantly optimized, with an optimal rate of 94. 8% correct rate [8].

All in all, theoretical linguistics and computational linguistics approach need to make full use of the contextual information of structure to achieve disambiguation. Although structural ambiguity seems a problem at the level of syntactic structure, its essence is still semantic inconsistency. The study can not only focus on the syntactic relationship judgment and neglect the issue of deep representation of semantics. Besides that, even though the methods of structural ambiguity resolution based on machine learning or neural network models are effective, there are still some key problems that remain to be explored: 1) since the neural network method is a simple empiricism method, the machine cannot learn the methodology of structure division and the semantic information behind it, but only know why; 2) the existing neural network-based methods rely on large-scale corpora in model training tasks, but the validity of the model in small tasks has yet to be verified.

Therefore, this paper proposes a method of disambiguation that integrates syntactic and semantic information, simulates the cognitive process of disambiguation, and combines disambiguation based on syntactic constraints with semantic preference, rule-based matching and semantic similarity calculation are used to resolve structural ambiguity. The rule base is established by the regular expression, and the semantic preference is based on similarity calculation, with the Sentence-Bert (SBERT) model [9], whose parameters are fine-tuned according to the experiment.

2 Relative Research

2.1 An Analysis of the Ambiguity Structure of "全部V的N"

Firstly, the research object of this paper——the ambiguous structure "全部V的N" should be clarified. "V" in this structure is the verb extracted from corpora and does not involve verb phrases. In addition, this study only discusses the resolution method of the true ambiguity structure, not including word segmentation and lexical ambiguity.

In modern Chinese, the relationship between structures consisting of two or more words is uncertain, and different relations correspond to different meanings. Among many ambiguity structures, "全部V的N" is a typical ambiguity caused by differences in surface syntactic structure, which has two ways of segmentation, as shown in Fig. 1 and Fig. 2:

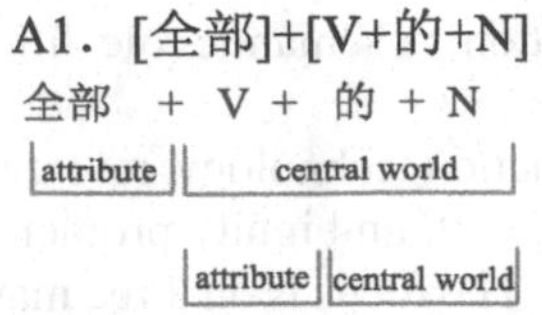

A1. [全部]+[V+的+N]

全部 + V + 的 + N

| attribute || central world |

| attribute || central world |

Fig. 1. Schematic diagram of structure segmentation of [全部] + [V + 的 + N]

B1. [全部+V+的]+[N]

全部 + V + 的 + N

| attribute | central world |

| adverbial | central world |

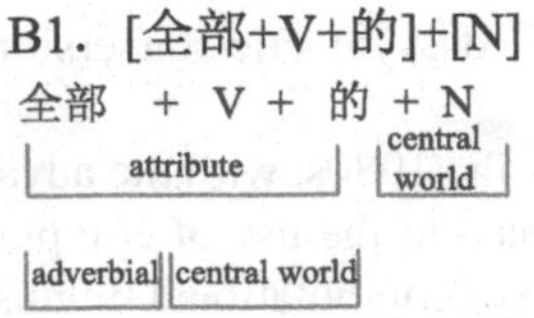

Fig. 2. Schematic diagram of structure segmentation of [全部 + V + 的] + [N]

This kind of ambiguity mainly results from the difference of the syntactic function of 全部 in the structure, which in turn leads to the difference in semantic orientation and semantic expression function. As mentioned above, 全部 can be used as an attributive or an adverbial. If the segmentation model is A1, 全部 is the modifier of the definite structure V的N, and the semantic direction can only be right, pointing to "N", and does not adhere to the verb.

If the segmentation mode is B1, "全部" is the modifier of the structure "全部V" in the form, and the semantic orientation can be either right or left, but it must adhere to the verb. In this case, "全部" is a complete kernel mark of the verb, and the semantic category of the structure "全部V的N" is uncertain.

2.2 Principle of Ambiguity Resolution

Two main ways to resolve structural ambiguity is context restriction, followed by transformation restriction. Context restriction means that the configuration of ambiguous structures is constrained by context [12], which is mandatory whether "全部" is oriented to "V" or "N" in the "全部 V的N" structure. Taking "从阿富汗全部撤军的军队" (troops full withdrawal from Afghanistan) as an example, the preposition "从(from)" limits the word "撤军[Chejun] (withdrawal)" only as a predicate in the sentence, namely "全部" can only be used as a universal quantification mark to modify verb "撤军".

As for transformation restriction, it differentiates ambiguity by adding, omitting, shifting, and replacing, etc. If we transform "homomorphic" structures to "heteromorphic" structures according to the semantic expression function of "全部", the meaning of this structure can be simplified. In A1 case, "全部" is a noun modifier, which is almost equivalent to "全部的" in terms of grammatical and semantic functions. Therefore, in A2 case, the auxiliary word "的" is added to "全部" as "全部的". In B1 case, referential "都" is a whole-quantity marker that attaches to the main verb, which is head-marking in nature [11]. Besides that, "dou" is a traditional qualitative scope adverb. And in terms of semantic function, it is a reinforcing word, that is, the use of "都" can enhance sentence tone. Therefore, in B2 case, "dou" is attached to the adverb "全部", replacing "全部" with "全部都". At this point, ambiguity is differentiated, and the two.

phrase segmentation methods after differentiation are shown in Fig. 3 and Fig. 4:

Since the above disambiguation principle is based on linguistics, how can the machine learn the judgment basis, and achieve better disambiguation results? We might as well regard the computer as a language learner. As mentioned above, people disambiguate mainly through context stipulation and transformation restriction. Context stipulation relies on syntactic restriction rules, while transformation restriction is the differentiation

A2. [全部的]+[V+的+N]

全部的 ＋ V ＋ 的 ＋ N

| attribute | | central world |

| attribute | central world |

B2. [全部都+V+的] + [N]

全部都 ＋ V ＋ 的 ＋ N

| attribute | central world |

| adverbial | central world |

Fig. 3. Schematic diagram of segmentation of [全部的] + [V + 的 + N]

Fig. 4. Schematic diagram of segmentation of [全部都 + V + 的] + [N]

of ambiguity, which divides heterogeneous phrases into heteromorphic phrases, and puts them into the original text to compare which of the two phrases is more consistent with the original meaning of the sentence. The process is shown in Fig. 5

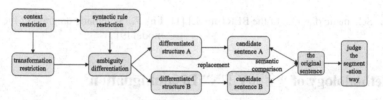

Fig. 5. Schematic diagram of ambiguity resolution process

The restricted rules can be converted into regular expressions. If they cannot be matched by the machine, the principle of transformation restriction should be used to resolve ambiguity. After transforming the heterogeneous structure of "全部V的N" into "全部都V的N" and "全部的V的N", the computer can distinguish them in text form, and the grammatical function and semantic expression function of *Quanbu* are differentiated. The brain relies on knowledge of the world and native language proficiency to infer the right segmentation way. As for machines, semantic preference is an effective way to realize semantic simplification, which means selecting an optimal solution between the two potential outcomes based on the semantic similarity of the candidate and the original sentences of semantic similarity. The SBERT model, which has produced great results in the calculation of semantic similarity, will be used in this paper.

2.3 Sentence Semantic Similarity Calculation Based on SBERT Model

The SBERT model is an improved model based on the BERT model [1], which uses the Siamese network for model training, especially suitable for text similarity calculation tasks. BERT no longer predicts a word from above, as traditional language models do, but in two innovative ways: MLM (Masked Language Model) and NSP (Next Sentence Prediction) are used for training, which is a two-way Language Model that can more accurately obtain contextual semantic information in sentences. The Model is shown in Fig. 6. However, in the task of semantic similarity calculation, the BERT model has a huge overhead. It takes about 50 million inference calculations to find the most similar sentence-pair from 10,000 sentence sets. Therefore, researchers proposed the SBERT model to modify the BERT of pre-training: Sentence embedding is obtained by using twin (Siamese) and three-level (Triplet) network structures to obtain fixed-length sentence vector representations. Semantically similar sentences are found by comparison using cosine similarity or Manhattan distance [9], as shown in Fig. 7.

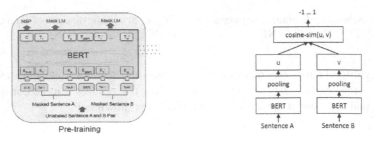

Fig. 6. Schematic diagram of the BERT model [1]   **Fig. 7.** Schematic diagram of the SBERT model [9]

3   Methodology of "全部V的N" Disambiguation

3.1   Syntactic Constraint Method Based on the Rule Base

Ambiguity resolution is not only dependent on probabilistic analysis of data, but also depends on the rules of language itself [15]. Combining language data with language knowledge can give full play to the value of language data. Therefore, after analyzing 646 instances of ambiguous structure "全部V的N" in the self-built corpus, this paper constructs the rule base according to the syntactic constraints of contexts of "全部V的N" structure. Taking "全部撤军的迹象" [*Quanbu chejun de jixiang*](*signs of complete withdrawal*) as an example, we conclude the main restrictions as follows:

到目前为止，我没有看到苏联准备从阿富汗[全部撤军的迹象]。(*So far, I see no sign that the Soviets are ready to withdraw from Afghanistan.*)

The preposition "从 (*from*)" appears before "全部撤军的迹象", which restricts "撤军 (*withdrawal*)" only as the central word. The whole structure should be divided into [全部撤军/的迹象], thus the ambiguity is eliminated.

After the syntactic restriction rule is obtained, the pos tagging specification of jieba word segmentation in the Python module is used as the standard to convert it into regular expression:

Pattern = r '从/p + (.*?)/n + 全部/n + (.*?)/v + 的/uj + (.*?)/n'.

The regular expression is imported to match the input sentences, if successfully matched, the right structure segmentation way is directly output.

3.2   Semantic Optimization Method Based on Similarity Preference

This method uses the SBERT model to present sentence pairs as vectors and then uses the cosine distance to calculate similarity.

Take the case of "全部在押的罪犯 [*Quanbu Zaiya de Zuifan*]":

S1: 监狱特赦释放了全部在押的罪犯。(*The prison amnesty set the prisoners fully in detention/ all the prisoners in detention free*).
S2: 监狱特赦释放了全部都在押的罪犯。(*The prison amnesty set the prisoners fully in detention free.*)
S3: 监狱特赦释放了全部的在押的罪犯。(*The prison amnesty set all the prisoners in detention free.*)

The model is used to vectorize sentences, and then the cosine value between two sentence vectors is calculated to obtain the semantic similarity between two sentences.

$$\text{sim}\,(S1,\ Si) = \cos\theta = \frac{S_1 \cdot S_i}{|S_1| \cdot |S_i|} \tag{1}$$

S is the text vector, and Si is the text vector of the ith sentence. Sim1 and sim2 are used to represent the text similarity between S1 and S2 and S1 and S3 respectively. The SBERT model is used to carry out sentence vectorization respectively, and the calculation process is shown in Fig. 8:

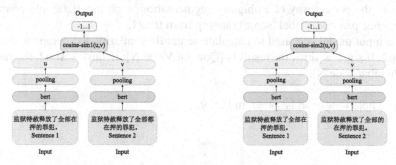

Fig. 8. Schematic diagram of similarity calculated by the SBERT model

The cosine similarity results obtained are shown in Table 1:

Table 1. Calculation results of cosine similarity

Value	Similarity
Sim1 = Sim (S1, S2)	0.9798
Sim2 = Sim (S1, S3)	0.9888

It can be concluded from the table that sim2 > sim1, which means that S1 and S3 are more similar, so the structure should be divided into [全部/在押的罪犯].

4 Experiment

4.1 Design and Process

The experiment is mainly divided into two parts: In the first part, regular expression formalization rule base was used to match the corpus one by one. If the matching is successful, the segmentation method is output directly, and if the matching is unsuccessful, the next step is taken. The second part is semantic similarity calculation. The SBERT model is used to calculate the similarity between sentence pairs, and the segmentation way is determined by the size of the similarity value. The specific experimental steps are described as follows:

1) Use regular expressions to build rule libraries. The whole corpus is matched one by one according to the regular expression of the syntactic rule base.
2) Output segmentation results after manual proofreading. Due to the long span and other reasons, regular matching cannot exactly match the corpus, so the segmentation results of the matched corpus should be output after manual proofreading.
3) Fine-tuning of the SBERT model. In this experiment, the model is fine-tuned according to the correct way of ambiguity segmentation, each InputExample contains a sentence pair and a label (score) ranging from 0 to 1.
4) The input model was used to calculate semantic similarity and compare sim1 and sim2. If sim1 > sim2, the result is [Quanbu V/ de N]; if sim1 < sim2, the result is [Quanbu/ V de N].

The whole flow chart is shown in Fig. 9:

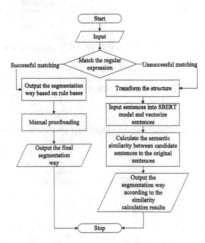

Fig. 9. Experimental flow chart

5　Result

This experiment aims at the phrase "全部V的N" and uses a self-built corpus as the test set. After screening out the repeated, semantically unqualified, and structurally unambiguous texts, there are 646 items in the experimental corpus.

In the first part of regular matching, 276 pieces of text were successfully matched, and the remaining 370 pieces entered the second semantic similarity calculation step. Accuracy, Precision, Recall and F1 values are mainly used as measurement indexes to evaluate the overall disambiguation effect of this experiment.

Take "全部V/的N" as the positive class and "全部/V的N" as the negative class, and calculate the following confusion matrix according to whether the predicted results of the model are correct or not in Table 2:

Table 2. Segmentation Judgment of "全部V的N"

	Is the class	Negative class
Prediction is class	558 (TP)	21 (FP)
Prediction is negative class	11 (FN)	46 (TN)

Through the confusion matrix, the accuracy, precision, recall and F1 values are calculated, and the final calculation results are shown in Table 3:

Table 3. Ambiguity Resolution Results of "全部V的N"

	Accuracy	Precision	Recall rate	F1 value
The percentage	95.05%	96.37%	98.07%	97.21%

As can be seen from Table 3, the overall accuracy rate of the experiment is 95.05%, the accuracy rate is 96.37%, the recall rate is 98.07%, and the F1 value is 97.21%. The accuracy, precision, recall rate and F1 values are all above 95%, which indicates that the experimental method has a significant effect on resolving the ambiguity of "全部V的N" phrase.

6　Discussion

The accuracy, precision, recall rate and F1 values were examined in the experiment, and the results showed that all the values were more than 95%, indicating that although the SBERT model is a large-scale model with large parameters, the effect of its application to small samples of structural ambiguity resolution is still very significant. Of course, there is several limitations to this method. For example, regular expressions are prone to inaccurate matching due to the span problem, which requires manual proofreading. In the future, more accurate regular expressions should be adopted to express rules. In addition, from the part of semantic similarity calculation, the text feature extraction ability of the SBERT pre-training model, especially the feature recognition ability of grammar nodes, needs to be strengthened.

After the statistics and investigation of all the examples, it is found that the disambiguation strategy proposed in this paper is not effective for some verbs. In the similarity calculation part, there are some results with wrong judgment, and typical examples are listed in Table 4:

Table 4. Examples of Verbs with Incorrect Judgment of "全部V的N" Segmentation

V	Number	Accuracy	Examples
起义 (*uprising*)	2	50%	1) 赵博生说明了全部起义的条件。 Zhao Bosheng explained all the conditions for the uprising
倒下 (*fall down*)	2	50%	2) 赛门气愤地指着里头全部倒下的人。 Sai men angrily points to the inside of all the people who fall down
收回 (*take back*)	7	71.43%	3) 债权人要承担本息到期无法收回或不能全部收回的风险。 The creditor must bear the risk that the principal and interest cannot be recovered or cannot be fully recovered when it is due
社会化 (*socialize*)	1	0	4) 一切生产资料全部社会化的前提是…… The premise of all means of production was wholly socialized on was that…

1) Some sentences in the corpus lack context hints and have unclear semantics. In case 1, "赵博生说明了全部起义的条件 (*Zhao Bosheng explained the conditions for all uprisings*)", here "the conditions for all uprisings" can be understood as both "the conditions for all uprisings" and "the conditions for all uprisings". Without context information, it is difficult to accurately judge the segmentation method of the phrase. The irrationality of natural language and the limited contextual information will hinder the realization of effective disambiguation. In future research, the length of the text can be increased in corpus collection to make the sentence form a complete context as much as possible.

2) The ambiguity of natural language can't be eliminated. Such as case 2, "全部/倒下的人all the people of the fallen" or "全部倒下/的人 (*body completely fallen man*)" can both make sense. We cannot determine which phrase segmentation way is semantically correct, only according to the text messages. Therefore, this kind of circumstance also can't be completely disambiguated. The improved method may start from expanding the corpus of the original text, restoring the original meaning as

far as possible, and analyzing it from syntactic, semantic, and pragmatic perspectives combined with the overall context.

3) It is difficult to accurately identify the semantic orientation. In case 3, "Bear the risk that principal and interest cannot be collected at maturity or cannot be collected in full". Here, "全部收回 (*take back completely*)" refers to "本息 (*principal and interest*)" rather than the "风险 (*risk*)" following the verb. Therefore, if the text is replaced with "承担本息到期无法收回或不能全部的收回的风险 (*bear the risk that principal and interest cannot be collected at maturity or cannot be collected in full*)", the grammar is not qualified. In this part, the experiment adopts the method of screening out the grammatically unqualified corpus manual. The scale of the test corpus is small, nevertheless, it needs a large amount of manpower if we make large-scale disambiguation tasks. Therefore, further research can add semantic representation information annotations, such as semantic role and semantic pointing annotations, add syntactic restriction rules in the matching link of the rule base, and try to integrate semantically pointing structured information into the language model.

4) The judgment accuracy of phrase segmentation containing technical term phrases and low-frequency words is relatively low. For example, "全部社会化的前提 (*The premise of total socialization*)", based on the knowledge of political science, one can easily judge that "全部社会化 (*total socialization*)" is a fixed expression, and that the phrase has a specific meaning. However, there are few combinations of "全部" and "社会化 (*socialize*)", and it is difficult to determine the correct structure segmentation method because computers lack the corresponding world knowledge when learning. In the future, we can use the language model that integrates world knowledge and domain knowledge to get through the heterogeneous data by combining the knowledge graph, and then fine-tune the downstream task according to our own experimental data to achieve a better ambiguity resolution effect.

7 Conclusion

Structural ambiguity resolution is a key problem to solve syntactic semantic relation judgment and improve the efficiency of natural language processing. Aiming at "全部V的N", this paper proposes a method of ambiguity resolution based on syntactic restriction and semantic preference. Experimental results show that this method can effectively judge the relationship of phrase structure, and its effect is still significant on small sample data. Compared to the pure syntactic parsing based on neural network, this ambiguity disambiguation method is based on the criterion of the human brain cognitive process, with a better explanatory system, playing a double advantage of rationalism and empiricism. Additionally, it provides some reference of disambiguation for other phrases like "部分V的N (*Bufen V de N*)" and "V + V", "N + N" phrase. In the next research process, we will attempt to integrate prior syntactic knowledge and rules as well as world knowledge and domain knowledge into model training to enhance the ability of semantic feature recognition, generalization ability, and reasoning ability.

With the rapid development of modern computer science, the arrival of the era of large models has promoted the transformation of the research paradigm to "pre-training-fine-tuning". However, if ambiguity resolution only relies on deep-learning models to improve the effect of probability calculation and ignores the deep knowledge of grammar and semantics, the interpretability of the method is not strong. To make artificial intelligence truly understand human language, computers should also truly understand the meaning of language itself and have the ability of independent learning and knowledge reasoning. So, we need to follow the new paradigm which combines the rationalism method based on linguistics and the empirical method based on large data, which can stimulate the longer vitality of the discipline development.

References

1. Yang, X.F., Li, T.Q., Hong, Q.Y.: Example-based Chinese syntactic structure disambiguation. J. Chin. Inf. Process. **3**, 22–28 (2001). (in Chinese)
2. Shao, J.M: Discussion on the method of ambiguity differentiation. Lang. Teach. Linguist. Stud. **1**, 38–50+37 (1991). (in Chinese)
3. Xu, L.J.: Reference, Sequence and Semantic Interpretation. The Commercial Press, Beijing (2009). (in Chinese)
4. Li, G.C., Zhang, K.Y., Zhang, Y.K.: Segmentating Chinese word and processing different meanings structure. J. Chin. Inf. Process. **03**, 27–33 (1988). (in Chinese)
5. Yang, Q.: Research on Ambiguity of Chinese Phrases with the Same POS for Information Processing. China Social Science Press, Beijing (2019). (in Chinese)
6. Zhan, W.D.: The characteristics of "NP+ +VP" deviation structure in sentence planning. Linguist. Res. **1**, 18–25 (1998). (in Chinese)
7. Peng, W., Song, J., Sui, Z., Guo, D.: Formal schema of diagrammatic chinese syntactic analysis. In: Lu, Q., Gao, H. (eds.) Chinese Lexical Semantics. CLSW 2015. Lecture Notes in Computer Science, vol. 9332. Springer, Cham (2015). https://doi.org/10.1007/978-3-319-27194-1_68
8. Yang, Q.: Research on judging method of N1 + N2 structure grammatical relation based on random forest. J. Chongqing Univ. Technol. (Nat. Sci.) **35**(07), 125–130 (2021). (in Chinese)
9. Reimers, N., Gurevych, I.: Sentence-BERT: sentence embeddings using siamese BERT-networks. arXiv preprint arXiv:1908.10084 (2019). https://doi.org/10.48550/arXiv.1908.10084
10. Devlin, J., Chang, M.-W., Lee, K., et al.: BERT: pre-training of deep bidirectional transformers for language understanding. arXiv preprint arXiv:1810.04805 (2018). https://doi.org/10.48550/arXiv.1810.04805
11. Dong, X.F.: On Targets of *dou* and some related issues. Stud. Chin. Lang. **6**, 495–507+574 (2002).(董秀芳. "都"的指向目标及相关问题[J]. 中国语文, 06, 495–507+574 (2002)). (in Chinese)
12. Feng, Z.W.: On potential nature of ambiguous construction. J. Chin. Inf. Process. **04**, 14–24 (1995). (冯志伟. 论歧义结构的潜在性[J]. 中文信息学报 **04**, 14–24 (1995)). (in Chinese)
13. Mikolov, T., Sutskever, I., Chen, K., et al.: Distributed representations of words and phrases and their compositionality. arXiv preprint arXiv:1310.4546 (2013). https://doi.org/10.48550/arXiv.1310.4546
14. Le, Q., Mikolov, T..: distributed representations of sentences and documents. In: Proceedings of the 31st International Conference on Machine Learning, PMLR, vol. 32, no. 2,pp. 1188–1196 (2014)
15. Yu, S.W.: Ambiguity of natural language and the approaches of machine translation. J. Chin. Inf. Process. **2**, 59–66 (1989). (俞士汶. 自然语言的歧义与机器翻译的对策. 中文信息学报, **02**, 59–66 (1989). (in Chinese)

Automatic Recognition of Verb-Complement Separable Words Based on BCC

Yuxin Peng[1] and Jian Wu[2]($\boxtimes$)

[1] College of Media and International Culture, Zhejiang University, Hangzhou, China
22123017@zju.edu.cn
[2] International College, Zhejiang University, Hangzhou, China
wujian0823@zju.edu.cn

Abstract. This research is aimed to summarize rules to automatically recognize verb-complement separable words from the perspective of information processing. First, the research based on the BLCU Corpus Center (Abbreviated BCC throughout), uses its retrieval function for verb-complement separable words to perform an exhaustive search for all of them in *The Contemporary Chinese Dictionary*, and calculate their Positive Rate of identification. Second, summarize and count the internal insertion components of verb-complement separable words in tens of thousands of corpus, observe the before and after components, and conclude them into the corresponding separated form. Research points out the reasons why the corpus recognizes them as verb-complement separable words incorrectly: the result of the machine's segmentation is wrong, the separated form of verb-object separable words is recognized as a separated form of verb-complement separable words, a morpheme in a compound directional verb is fetched alone, two independent verbs are seen as a separated form, the overlapping usage of verb-complement separable words can't be recognized accurately, and the ability to deal with polysemous and polysyllabic words is not strong. Finally, transform the separated form from the perspective of linguistics into the corresponding rules that can be recognized by the computer, and write the program for experimentation. This program can make further judgments based on the separable word retrieval of the corpus itself, and realize that the recognition accuracy of these separated words can be increased to more than 90%.

Keywords: Verb-complement Separable Words · Separated Form · Verb-direction Separable Words · Verb-result Separable words · BCC

1 Introduction

The phenomenon of separable words refers to the fact that in a compound word, two or three adjoined morphemes can be split or reversed in practice, either "combined" into a single word or "separated" into individual morphemes, with other components split or reversed in the middle, with less structural stereotypes. The structure is less definite. As a result of the diphthongization of Chinese, the emergence of new words, the derivation of old words, and the addition of separate meanings, the number of separate words

Q. Su et al. (Eds.): CLSW 2022, LNAI 13496, pp. 375–389, 2023.
https://doi.org/10.1007/978-3-031-28956-9_30

identified with the double-slash symbol '//' in The Contemporary Chinese Dictionary (the Seventh Edition) has reached 4,044, with a total of 55 new separate words and separate meanings compared to The Contemporary Chinese Dictionary (the Sixth Edition). The development of separable words has become a trend.

With the rapid development of linguistic information processing, the fields of automatic word division, machine translation, lexical annotation, and information retrieval have to face the complex grammatical phenomena of Chinese. In recent years, several scholars have made remarkable contributions to Chinese information processing in the areas of automatic word separation and automatic recognition. Hongying *et al.* (2021) [1] under the guidance of the Chinese word segmentation and named entity labeling, the specifications for pediatric medical texts have been constructed. Duanzhu *et al.* (2021) [2] propose a neural network architecture for Tibetan Word Segmentation, which can produce a promising performance on the test set. Wang *et al.* (2022) [3] propose a data storage solution using the InfluxDB time series database, and utilizing the phrase mining technology for quality scoring and filtering of buzzword candidates. Separable words have gradually become an inescapable topic. The types of separable words in modern Chinese are complex, but most scholars classify the verb-object type and the verb-complement type as the two indispensable types of separable words. Among them, the verb-complement type is the second most important type after the verb-object type, but the current research focuses mainly on the verb-object type, neglecting the study of the verb-complement type in comparison. Zang & Xun (2017) [4], based on BCC, formally expressed the separated forms of each separable word and summarized them into automatic recognition rules for the design of subsequent automatic recognition algorithms, but their algorithms were mainly used for verb-object type, and the team still proposed that the next step would be to extend the research to all types in separable words. Therefore, this paper focuses on verb-complement separable words in the light of the current situation in the academic community and based on the research results of Zang & Xun (2017) [4].

1.1 An Overview of Verb-Complement Separable Words

Since the 1980s, scholars represented by Li (1983) [5] have conducted a lot of research on the classification and grammatical features of verb-complement separable words, and many studies have elaborated on the classification of verb-complement separable words based on their complements' features.

Li (1983) [5] proposed to classify separable words into verb-object and verb-complement structures, arguing that separable words with verb-complement structures were more often composed of monophthong verbal morphemes plus monophthong complements and that this monophthong complement was mostly a verb or adjective. Liu (1999) [6] divided the verb-complement separable words into two categories, the first being the verb-result type, such as "líkāi dǎdǎo jiēchuān", and the second being the verb-direction type, such as "shànglái xiàqù jìnlái". He argued that "the common feature of these types of separable words is that they have the unity of meaning, and at the same time they can all be inserted in the middle of the constituent morphemes, and generally *de* or *bù* can be inserted to indicate the possibility, and no other component other than these two can be inserted easily". Wang (1999) [7] classified verb-complement separable words into two categories according to the nature of the complement, the first being verb-complement separable words in which the complement was an adjectival morpheme, such as "dǎbài bágāo dǎtōng", and the second was also verb-complement separable words in which the complement was a verbal morpheme, such as "kànjiàn gàndiào", and illustrated the expansion and functions of the verb-complement separable words. Cao & Feng (2003) [8] also argued that verb-complement separable words could be divided into "verb-direction type" and "verb-result type", of which "verb-direction type" was divided into two cases. One could only insert *de* and *bù* to form a "verb-complement phrase", such as "bāndedòng", and the other in addition to *de* and *bù*, other components could be inserted, e.g. "jiàngdebùdī".

The development of natural language processing has led to a gradual shift from ontological to applied research on separable words. Current applications and specifically verb-complement separable words in Chinese information processing include automatic identification and processing strategies for separable words in machine translation, design of linguistic knowledge bases for separable words' disambiguation rules, determination of whether the disambiguation forms meet the requirements, and automatic error correction. Fu (1999) [9] proposed to set up common rules for the restricted extended forms of verb-complement separable words. The conditional part of the rules described each extended form, in which the extended parameters were represented by morphological parameters, the set of insertable components was determined as real parameters, the base form was substituted into the rules during recognition, and the morphological parameters were replaced by real parameters to achieve the recognition of separable words. Wang *et al.* (1999) [10] applied two methods to deal with separated structures, the first one was to recombine the constituent elements of separable words into words while keeping the basic semantics unchanged, adjusting the whole separated structure into a structure without separation, e.g. "tā xǐguòzǎo le" to "tā xǐzǎo le". The second was to recombine the constituent elements of the disjunction into a word and gave a semantically correct and common translation, e.g. "xià le yītiān yǔ" was recombined as "xiàyǔ+for+yītiān". Liu *et al.* (2001) [11] set up two processing rules for verb-complement separable words, "A+*de*/*bù*+B" and "A+(object)+(modifier)+B", as a knowledge base to design an intelligent input system for Chinese. Yang (2011) [12] designed an automatic error correction system based on the HSK dynamic Composition Corpus by annotating the features shown when each separable word co-occurred with other words so that each feature of each separable word would have a feature value corresponding to it, and determining whether the composition written by international students conformed to the rules according to the feature value. Xiao *et al.* (2014) [13] examined the dependency parsing on the legal separated forms of separable words trigger words in sentences using dependency analysis and converted this dependency parsing into rules, using those rules to determine whether any sentence containing a separable word is a regular separated form of a separable word.

1.2 An Focus on Verb-Complement Separable Words in Chinese Information Processing

In the past three decades, in addition to the fast development of ontological research on separable words, the scope of them have also been gradually extended to include second language acquisition, text linguistics, semantic analysis, valence grammar, information processing, and other aspects. In the area of information processing, many scholars have focused their research on the automatic recognition of separable words, and nowadays, a shift from proposing ideas or making small-scale attempts to conducting large-scale application research has been achieved. Automatic recognition of separable words is the basis for automatic segmentation and subsequent applications. Only when the machine can read separable words can it serve functions such as Chinese-English translation, information retrieval, or text modification.

Wang (2001) [14] designed a set of algorithms combining statistics and rules and conducted both closed and open tests, but the experimental results were not very good on the whole due to the lack of in-depth knowledge of separable words and the lack of full use of various materials. Zhou (2007) [15] used rules to generalize each separable word to form a lexicon so that the extended forms of separable words could be marked in automatic word division and lexical annotation. However, their study defined separable words narrowly, and therefore only the two structural types cover, verb-object type and parallel type, and didn't examine special categories such as verb-complement type. Liu (2015) [16] designed an automatic recognition system for the extended forms of separable words and kept optimizing it through experiments, but the focus was mainly on the recognition of the extended forms of verb-object separable words, and the recognition effect of the 3,376 separable words included in his automatic recognition system as a whole was not shown. Zhao (2019) [17] studied the automatic recognition of separable words based on rules, traditional machine recognition methods, and neural networks, and finally constructed three cascade models for the automatic recognition of separable words in a large-scale corpus, with the shortcoming that the corpus in this research was selected from the Xinhua News Agency news corpus from 1991–2004, and the recognition effect on separable words in other fields was not known yet. Wang *et al.* (2022) [18] described an empirical approach to the study of the interaction between verbs and chunks, but they didn't focus on the verb-complement separable words.

This study will design a set of rules for verb-complement separable word recognition based on the BCC, and translate them into a corresponding algorithm written in a computer programming language. The accuracy of the algorithm for verb-complement separable word recognition will be further investigated and optimized to further improve the automatic recognition of verb-complement separable words in our study.

2 Statistics and Analysis of Verb-Complement Separated Forms

2.1 Determination of Verb-Complement Separable Words' Word-List and Corpus Sources

To make the word list adopted in this paper representative and authoritative, this study uses the separable words identified with the double-slash symbol '//' in *The Contemporary Chinese Dictionary (the Sixth Edition)* and *The Contemporary Chinese Dictionary (the Seventh Edition)* as the main reference. The double-slash symbol '*//*' generally appears between the notes of multi-character entries, indicating that other components can be inserted in between, e.g. "[married] jié//hūn" can be inserted as "got married once". At the same time, using *The Dictionary of Modern Chinese Separable Words Usage* (Yang, 1995) [19] and *The Dictionary of Modern Chinese Separable Words Learning* (Wang *et al.*, 2013) [20] as auxiliary references, and following the definitions and classifications of verb-complement separable words by Liu (1999) [6] and Cao & Feng (2003) [8], we have collated 92 verb-complement separable words that appear together in the two editions of *The Contemporary Chinese Dictionary*, among which they can be further divided into 79 verb-result separable words and 13 verb-direction separable words. Among the verb-result separable words, "chāisǎn" and "chāisàn", which are polysyllabic words, and these two words were deleted because computer recognition of polysyllabic words was not considered in this study. And the word "zhǎo píng" was not retrieved from the BCC, so it was also deleted. In the end, leftover 89 verb-complement separable words were used as the subject of this study (see Appendix).

The BCC is a large-scale corpus developed by the Institute of Big Data and Educational Technology, School of Information Science, Beijing Language and Culture University, covering a total of 15 billion words in various fields such as newspapers, literature, microblogs, science and technology and ancient Chinese, which can comprehensively reflect the current situation of language life in today's society. As a special grammatical phenomenon arising from the trend of Chinese syllabification, the principle of language simplification, and the proliferation of new words, separable words are widely used in various fields. Therefore, this study uses the "multi-domain" search channel in the BCC to conduct a comprehensive examination of the occurrence of separable words in various domains.

2.2 Determination of Train and Test Sets for Verb-Complement Separable Words

Manual Annotation and Pre-processing
By entering the retrieval formula "A*B", we were able to identify and retrieve the separable words in the BCC. Firstly, an exhaustive search of 89 verb-complement separable was conducted and there were correctly identified and incorrectly identified were found. To calculate the current positive and negative recognition rates of the BCC for verb-complement separable words, we manually marked the retrieved separable words with a '+' for correct recognition and a '−' for incorrect recognition. For example:

Wǒ xiǎng tā zhǎo yějī, wǒ zhǎo cǎigòuyuán, chědepíng.+ (*Brother Jiu Is a Piece of Scenery*).

Zài yīshēng luó xiǎng, chěqǐ jìngpíng báiqí, liǎngxià zhòngguān méi yīgè gǎn zǒudòng húyán shuōhuà, jìngjìng de lìzhe. - (*Water Margin*).

After human annotation, the corpus is pre-processed with automatic word segmentation and parts of speech tagging, in preparation for subsequent rule design and experimental analysis. After that, we also need to do the word segmentation on the corpus, because only the preceding and following morphemes of a separable word co-occurring in the same utterance can be called a separable word, and it makes no sense to judge two morphemes that co-occur in different utterances and formally happen to constitute a certain separable word as a separable word. Therefore, based on the punctuation code 'x' in the lexical annotation system of Peking University, we used the program to split the corpus into sentences.

Positive and Negative Case Rates for Separated Forms of Verb-Complement Separable Words

The results of the human annotation were counted to calculate the positive and negative case rates for each separated form. The positive case rate of a separable word refers to the percentage of correctly annotated sentences in the total number of sentences, while the incorrect case rate refers to the percentage of incorrectly annotated sentences in the total number of sentences. The formula (1) and (2) are as follows:

$$positive\ case\ rate = \frac{correctly\ annotated\ sentences}{total\ number\ of\ sentences} \tag{1}$$

$$negative\ case\ rate = \frac{incorrectly\ annotated\ sentences}{total\ number\ of\ sentences} \tag{2}$$

Following the formula, we calculated the positive case rates of the 89 verb-complement separable words. Table 1 shows the distributions of the results for the 89 separable words.

Table 1 shows that the overall recognition of the BCC for the verb-complement separable words is not very good. Some of them, including "bùzú, dǎpò, dédào", have positive case rates of less than 1%, and "dǎzhù, jiàozhǔn, jiéduàn" are even 0%. Overall, none of the verb-complement separable words' positive case rates are greater than 90%. The fact that more cases are incorrectly identified as separated forms, while the correct separated forms are not captured by the systematic search, is the main reason for the low correct rate of verb-complement separable words. In the statistical results, the positive case rates of the words such as "tígāo xiāngzhōng yùjiàn" are less than 10%, accounting for 64.0%; the positive case rates of the words such as "bǎipíng kàntòu pǎopiān" ranging from 10% to 20%, accounting for 12.4%; the positive case rates of the words such as "gǎodìng yādī xiàlái" range from 20% to 30%, accounting for 5.6%; the positive case rates of the words such as "táigāo jìnqù guòqù" range from 30% to 40%, accounting for 4.5%; the positive case rates of the words such as "lāozháo miáozhǔn guòlái" range from 40% to 50%, with the same percentage of 4.5%; the positive case rates of the words such as "bódǎo chūlái" range from 50% to 60%, with the same percentage of 2.2%; the positive case rates of the words such as "bāndǎo chàdiǎnr" range from 60% to 70%, accounting for 3.4%; the positive case rates of the words such as "tíxǐng" range from 70% to 80%, accounting for 1.1%; the positive case rates of the words such as "jùqí qǐlái" range from 80% to 90%, accounting for 2.2%.

In determining the test and train sets, the 11 words "dǎzhù, jiàozhǔn, jiéduàn, pèngjiàn, pīzhǔn, shípò, shuōfú, tuīfān yādǎo yùjiàn zhǎoqí" all had a positive rate of 0%, so they could only be placed in the train set. At the same time, 1/3 of the number of verb-complement separable words used in this study, i.e. 30 words, were used as the test set, and 22 verb-result separable words and 8 verb-direction separable words were adopted proportionally. The test set was generated using Random by Python. The test set consisted of "kànzhòng xiāngzhòng dédào luòhòu yuèguò tígāo dǎtōng chīzhǔn wàngdiào luòkōng fēnqīng zhànzhù kàntòu chěpíng cāntòu yādī táigāo lāozháo pūmiè dǎkuǎ chàbuduō tíxǐng dǎkāi xiǎngkāi huíqù shàngqù jìnqù guòqù gǎnshàng qǐlái", and the other 59 verb-complement separable words were grouped into the train set.

Table 1. Distribution of positive case rates for the 89 verb-complement separable

Positive case rates [a,b)	Number	Percentage/% (one decimal place retained)
0%–10%	57	64.0
10%–20%	11	12.4
20%–30%	5	5.6
30%–40%	4	4.5
40%–50%	4	4.5
50%–60%	2	2.2
60%–70%	3	3.4
70%–80%	1	1.1
80%–90%	2	2.2
90%–100%	0	0.0

2.3 Analysis of Separated Components of Verb-complement Separable Words

Summary of Separated Forms of Verb-Complement Separable Words
We summarized the insertion components of the separated forms of separable words in the train set and found that they were mainly divided into the following types. Among them, A and B denote the two morphemes before and after a certain word in the verb-complement separable words respectively.

The Common Separated Forms of Verb-Complement Separable Words

(1) The possibility of inserting the complement *de* or *bù* alone to indicate whether the action or behavior can be achieved.

Most of the verb-complement separable words can insert the possible complement *de* or *bù* on their own and are used very frequently. However, there are several uses of the verb-complement separable words with the insertion of *de* or *bù* alone that were not retrieved from the BCC, such as "chàdediǎnr jiǎodehún jiǎobùhún". And a secondary search in the corpus Center Chinese Linguistics PKU confirmed that no relevant usage examples were retrieved. However, based on the probability of the use of the words *de* and *bù*, we can still take them as one of the important conditions for determining whether a word is a verb-complement separable word.

(2) A small number of verb-complement separable words can form the structure "A *bù* A *de* B", which indicates the questioning of an action or behavior.

By counting the examples of each verb-complement separable word, we find that the structure "A *bù* A *de* B" is also very common in the use of some verb-complement separable words, such as "dǔ nǐ diànhuà dǎbùdǎ*de*tōng", "bùguǎn wàngbùwàng*de*diào", "kàn wǒ qiáobùqiáo*de*jiàn" and so on, meaning the "néng*bù*néng+AB (the prototype of separable words)".

The Separated Form of Verb-Result Separable Words

The verb is usually used as a complement to the adjective, e.g. "bágāo bǔzú", and to a lesser extent as a complement to the verb, e.g. "tīngjiàn shōuhuí".

(1) Regardless of the lexical nature of the complement, as long as the complement can express a sustainable state, it is possible to insert *de*, *bù* followed by an adverb of degree, and in a small part, *le* followed by an adverb of degree.

   Due to the common use of degree adverbs and the complexity of collocations, there is a wide variety of verb-result separated forms that satisfy this rule. The specific forms are *de*+ "zài/ tài/ hǎo/ hěn/ gèng/ jí/ zhēn/ bǐjiào/ yuè/ guò/ zhème/ nàme/ bèir/ yǒudiǎntài/ fēicháng/tàiguò", *bù*+"zhème/ nàme/ duō/ tài/ dà/ zhēn" and other degree adverbs. In addition to the collocation of "*de*", "*bù*" with degree adverbs, "*de*" can be followed by a negative adverb or a noun phrase, and "*bù*" can also be preceded by a personal pronoun. The corpus also covers examples of the use of dialects or Internet neologisms, such as the Cantonese 'ńg' and the Internet colloquialism '8' (both meaning "*bù*" in Mandarin). They are usually inserted separately. Examples of their use are "bá*de*tàigāo", "bǎ*de*bùláo", "zhì *de* zhèděng è'rén fú".

(2) When adjectival morphemes are used as complements, the adjectival morphemes can overlap with the "BB+*de*"structure.

   The adjectival morphemes overlap with the "BB+*de*" structure, indicating a sufficient amount of description of a thing or action. The phrases "bǎ xiǎoqū dàmén bǎ de láoláo*de*", "zhè xiàwǔjiào bǔ de zúzú*de*" are similarly used.

(3) When the adjectival morpheme is used as a complement, "bǐ" can be inserted to form a comparative structure.

   The comparative structure generally consists of "A+*de*+bǐ+other components+B", and an adverb of degree can be inserted before and after the adjectival morpheme. For example, "bǎ jiàgé yā *de* bǐ biérén dī hěnduō", etc.

(4) When the adjectival morpheme is used as a complement, the auxiliary words "*zhe, le, guò, de*" and their related extended structures can be inserted in the middle.

   Generally, when the adjectival morpheme can have a part of speech of noun or assume a noun semantic meaning, the tense auxiliary "*zhe, le, guò*" and the structural auxiliary "*de*" can be inserted in the middle, often in combination with individual quantifiers or quantity phrase. For example, the words "chà *zhe* diǎnr", "luò *le* yīgè kōng", "ti *guò* xíng", etc. Some of the separated forms of the separable words have their own fixed collocations when expressing the perfect tense, e.g. "miáo hǎo *le* zhǔn", "luò chéng *le* kōng". It is worth noting that some morphemes such as "hé", "xǐng" do not have a full meaning when used alone, which can't be the words, but can assume the semantic meaning of a noun and be used as an object in these separated forms.

(5) When the adjectival morpheme is used as a complement, the "AAB" structure can be used for a small number of verb-result separable words.

   The "AAB" structure is used in both written and spoken language, for example, "jí súhuà suǒshuō*de* liǎngbiān bǎibǎipíng", etc.

(6) A small number of verb-result separable words have given rise to fixed collocations.

The fixed collocations are such as "pūwúbùmiè *de* xiāofángduì", "pūérmièzhī", "pūzhīmiè". These come from literature and the press but are used very infrequently.

The Separated Forms of Verb-Direction Separable Words
The verb-direction separable words by directional verbs "lái qù" as complements, such as "shànglái xiàqù", etc.

(1) When the verb-direction separable word is separated and the preceding and follow-ing morphemes can still be used as lexical verbs, "*de*", "*bù*" and their extensions or noun components can be inserted.

The insertion of "*de*" or "*bù*" alone, such as "shàng*de*qù", "shàng*bù*qù", "shàng", and "qù" are both lexical verbs, and colloquial usage with emphatic seman-tic overtones also occur, such as "xià*bùde*qù", it is also possible to insert a nominal in the middle, with the latter followed by a verb, e.g. "shàng wǒmen *de* píngtái lái zhùcè", with the word "lái" dividing the phrase, the former indicating the method, direction or attitude of the latter, the latter indicating the purpose of the former.

(2) The verb-direction separable words can insert a nominal between two of their morphemes.

The main components are location words, pronouns, "pronoun+noun", and "numeral+location words" phrases, which indicate that the action is taking place towards a certain place. For example, "huíjiālái", "shàng zhèr qù", etc.

(3) When the verb-direction separated words are separated, both elements of the delexical directional verbs act as complementary components, and the phrase "verb+A+other components+B" can be formed.

The first element of the verb-direction separable word can often be put together with some verbs to form a composite tendency verb, e.g. "hē shàng yīhú jiǔ qù", "tiào xià shuǐ qù". In this case, "shàngqù xiàqù qǐlái" are all used as complementary elements, playing a certain grammatical role. Often the meaning of the latter element is more delexical, as in the case of "tiào xià shuǐ qù", the meaning of which is equivalent to "tiào xià shuǐ", and "qù" in the phrase hardly indicates a substantive semantic meaning.

2.4 Causes and Countermeasures of Errors in Separated Form

(1) Errors in machine word splitting. The error in the division of words can lead to many inherent nouns being recognized as separated forms of separated words, such as "shàngyīcì qù" being recognized as separated forms of "shàngqù". In fact, "shàngyīcì" should be seen as fixed collocations, if "shàng" is separated from "yīcì", it increases the recognition error probabilities of the separated form of "shàngqù".

(2) The inaccuracy of machine recognition of verb-object separable words can also have an impact on the recognition of verb-complement separable words. For example, "luò *le* suǒ hòu" is recognized as the separated form of "luòhòu", but it should be the separated form of the verb-object separable word "luòsuǒ", while the word "hòu" is used here as a localizer, indicating the time after an action.

(3) A morpheme in a non-compound directional verb is presented separately and identified as one of the morphemes of the verb-complement separable words. For example, "băinòng píngbăndiànnăo" is identified as separated forms of "băipíng". In fact, "băinòng" as a compound word that doesn't belong to the compound directional verb, should be excluded from consideration as a certain morpheme of the verb-complement separable word and is supposed to be treated as a verb to use. In similar cases, therefore, the machine should no longer retrieve forward or backward to match a separated form of a verb-complement separable word.

(4) Identification of two independent verbs as separated constructions. For example, the phrase "chǒu bàntiān méi jiànzháo Xīnjīngbào" is identified as a separated form of "chǒujiàn", while the verbs "chǒu" and "jiàn" are both lexical verbs in this sentence.

(5) Inaccurate machine recognition of four characters words made up of two overlapping adjectives can lead to errors. For example, if "zhì de fúfútiētiē" is recognized as a separated form of "zhìfú", the semantics of a four-letter word like "fúfútiētiē" will become broken.

(6) There is still room for improvement in the machine's handling of Chinese polysyllabic words and words with multiple meanings. There are many polysyllabic and polyphonic words in Chinese. Multiple-meaning situations such as "niánzēngsù kě dá 6% dào 8%", "dá" in this sentence means "reach" broadly, while "dào" means "reach a range", so that it is inappropriately labeled as a separated form of "dádào". Polysyllabic characters situation such as "děi" means "need" in the sentence "huǒchē wòpù 800 duō érqiě děi 40 gè xiǎoshí néng dào". And in the sentence "nǐ de rúyìsuànpán dǎ de dàoshì tǐng xiǎng de ma", the word "dào" here indicates a negative, reproachful tone.

(7) Writing errors in the corpus itself. In the microblog crawled by the BCC, there are some simple writing errors that cause misspellings to be identified as other separated words.

3 Automatic Recognition of Separated Forms Based on BCC

3.1 Summary of the Rules for Separated Form of Verb-Complement Separable Words

After discussing and summarizing the separated forms of verb-complement separable words, they need to be converted into a language recognizable by the computer. Taking into account that different verb-complement separable words have their separated forms, we summarize them to their common rules, the specific rules for verb-result separable words, and verb-direction separable words.

The rules use the set of lexical annotation markers of Jieba, which involve the following markers (d: adverb, n: noun, v: verb, r: pronoun, m: numeral, q: quantifier, s: location, t: time, u: auxiliary, and y: mood particle). Although not every verb-complement separable word has a corresponding use case in the following rules, they are seen as common situations to ensure the correctness and completeness of the rules for most verb-complement separable words' separated forms as far as possible.

Common Rules for Verb-Complement Separable Words

Based on the statistics of the separated forms of most verb-complement separable words, the following two common rules can be summarized.

(1) A+*de/bù*+B, e.g. "kàn*de*jiàn", "kàn*bù*jiàn".
(2) A+*bù*+A+*de*+B, with the former morpheme forming an overlapping form, e.g. "kàn*bù*kàn*de*jiàn".

Rules of Verb-Result Separable Words

The corresponding rules for verb-result separable words are as follows. Because of the simplicity of the separated form of the verb-result separable words, (...) indicates the insertion of more than one word and no more than three words.

(1) A+*u*+B (*u*=a collection of Chinese characters), *u* includes the Chinese characters "*de bù zhe le guò*", e.g. "chà *zhe* diǎnr", "luò *le* hòu".
(2) A+*de*+d/n+B, where an adverb or noun is inserted after the word "*de*" between the preceding and following morphemes, e.g. "bá *de* hěngāo", "xiǎng *de* bèir kāi".
(3) A+*de*+(...)+d/n+B, inserting various components between the preceding and following morphemes, if the component closest to the morpheme B is a pronoun or a noun, then this form is most likely to be a separated form of a verb-result separable word. For example, "kàn *de* bù zhème tòu", "zhì *de* zhèděng è'rén fú".
(4) A+*de*+BB+*de*, with the latter morpheme forming an overlapping form, e.g. "bǔ *de* zúzúde".
(5) A+*de*+比+r/n/t/d+B, e.g. "jiàgé yā *de* bǐ shìchǎng dī", "bá *de* bǐ jiǎ háigāo".
(6) A+q+B, inserting a quantifier, e.g. "bá gè gāo", "tí gè xǐng".
(7) A+*le/r*+mq/q+B, inserting "*le*" or a "numeral and classifier" or a measure word, e.g. "luò *le* yīchǎng kōng", "luò *le* chǎng kōng", "tí nǐ yīgè xǐng", "tí nǐ gè xǐng".
(8) AAB, the former morpheme forming an overlapping form, e.g. "bǎibǎipíng".

Rules for Verb-Direction Separable Words

The (...) in the rules for verb-direction separable words is greater than one word, with no upper limit on the number of words.

(1) A+*bùde*+B, which is a special collocation, e.g. "xià *bù de* qù".
(2) A+m+n+B, inserting a "number+noun" phrase, e.g. "shàng sānlóu qù".
(3) A+n/r+B, inserting noun or pronoun, e.g. "shàng lóu qù", "shàng nǎr qù".
(4) A+r+n/s+B, inserting a "pronoun+noun/location" phrase, e.g. "shàng tājiā qù".
(5) v+A+a/r+B+v/u/d/y, an adjective or pronoun can be inserted between A and B when "v+A" is a compound directional verb. If the morpheme B can be followed by a verb, a modality particle "*le*" and "*de*", an adverb, a mood particle, or no component at all, then this form is most likely a possible separated form of verb-direction separable words, e.g. "chuàngzào chū shénme lái ne", "huì gàn chū shén me lái a".
(6) v+A+(...)+n+B+v/u/d/y, when "v+A" is forming a compound directional verb, it can insert multiple components between A and B. If the nearest component before the morpheme B is a noun, and if it can be followed by a verb, a modality particle

"*le*" and "*de*", an adverb, a mood particle, or no component at all, then this form is most likely a separated form of verb-direction separable words, e.g. "ménwài shǎnjìn yīgè yātou lái", "diàojìn yīgè gǔlǎo de quāntàolǐ qù le".

3.2 Specific Process of Automatic Recognition for Separable Words

Once the rules have been designed, the automatic recognition process is elaborated as follows. First, based on BCC, the 89 identified separable words were performed automatic word separation and parts of speech tagging and divided into a single sentence by punctuation, and the pre-processed corpus was stored in a text file, and word lists were respectively created for the verb-result separable words and verb-direction separable words. Secondly, the corpus in the text file was read into the program for retrieval by line, and if two characters in the same sentence were retrieved as belonging to a verb-result separable word or a verb-direction separable word, it is judged whether they satisfy one of these rules. Finally, if two characters are judged to satisfy the rule, they are judged to be the separated form and marked with a '+' at the end of the sentence; if not, they are marked with a '−' at the end of the sentence, and the results will be written to a new file.

For some rare special cases, to ensure the overall correctness, no new rules are created for them, but a word list can be created as a criterion, e.g. if there is "chà *le* yīxiǎodiǎnr" in the word list, then the program will also determine it a separated form.

4 Experimental Conclusions and Analysis

The study uses Python to automatically label and calculate the corresponding correct rate. The calculation formula (3) is as follows.

$$correct\ rate = \frac{number\ of\ messages\ automatically\ marked\ correctly}{number\ of\ messages\ extracted} \tag{3}$$

Table 2 shows the correct rates for the partial separable words.

Through testing, we have found that the correct rates of verb-complement separable words are generally high. In particular, the correct rates are very high for inserting just "*de*", and "*bù*" and simple separated forms of adverb of degree. Other factors affecting the correct rate are as follows and require further optimization.

Firstly, the recognition rules are too broad, which can lead to some incorrect cases being recognized. The most frequent problem is the recognition of two unrelated morphemes as separated forms, e.g. "qiáo/v zhè/r zhāng/q rénjiànrén'ài/l jùn/nr liǎnfèn/n" is incorrectly identified as a separated form of "qiáojiàn" because it satisfies the rule "A+r+q+B", but in this case "jiàn" is a predicate component of the idiomatic phrase "rénjiànrén'ài".

Secondly, the correct recognition rate is very much dependent on the correctness of the participle and parts of speech tagging. Since the results returned by Jieba are based on the statistical probability of each word, words of the same separated form will return different results. This has a significant impact on verb-complement separable words with complex interjections, especially verb-direction type, as exemplified by "shàngqù": in

Table 2. Positive case rates for partial verb-complement separable words

Separable words	Number of messages automatically marked correctly	Number of messages extracted	Correct rate/%
fúzhèng	5013	4970	99.1%
qiáojiàn	915	907	99.1%
chīzhǔn	6745	6670	98.9%
jiàozhǔn	2139	2116	98.9%
yùjiàn	2243	2206	98.4%
shípò	216	212	98.1%
pūmiè	503	491	97.6%
dǎkuǎ	1286	1223	95.1%
gàndiào	5315	5027	94.6%
bágāo	949	878	92.5%

"hē/vg shàng/f yīhújiǔ/i qù/v", "pá/v shànglóuqù/i", "shàng" and "qù" as complementary components sometimes can be labeled separately as localizers or verbs, sometimes they need to be marked together with the object component, and sometimes only the verb "qù" can be marked separately, which can cause problems with the rules not achieving an exact match.

5 Conclusions and Outlooks

Based on tens of thousands of sentences from the BCC, this study has written separated forms and rules for 89 verb-complement separable words from a linguistic and information processing perspective and attempts to solve the problems caused by automatic segmentation errors, misidentification of a morpheme in the verb-object form as a morpheme in the verb-complement form, and identification of an independent morpheme as a morpheme in the separable word and achieves a correct rate of 90% for partial separable words. It has implications for both the ontological study of separable words and for research in Chinese information processing. Due to the overly broad recognition rules and the high dependence of the correct recognition rate on the correctness of automatic segmentation and parts of speech tagging, the function of the program needs to be further optimized. Future work will hopefully address the two problems reported in the experimental analysis, refine the rules and design an algorithm with a higher overall correctness rate.

Acknowledgments. This paper is supported by the The National Social Science Fund of China (20BYY001). The anonymous reviewers of CLSW2022 put forward many valuable comments. Here, please allow us to express our sincere thanks!

Appendix

Verb-Result Separable Words

bágāo bāndǎo bǎláo bǎipíng bódǎo bǔzú chàdiǎnr cāntòu chěpíng chīzhǔn chǒujiàn dádào dǎdǎo dǎkuǎ dǎpò dǎtōng dǎzhù dédào fēnqīng fúzhèng gàndiào gǎodìng géduàn huàqīng huìqí jiǎnghé jiǎohún jiàozhǔn jiéduàn jùqí kànchuān kànjiàn kànpò kàntòu kànzhōng lāpíng lāozhá0 luòhòu luòkōng miáozhǔn pǎopiān pèngjiàn pīzhǔn pūmiè qiáojiàn shípò shōuhuí shuōfú táigāo tígāo tíxǐng tīngjiàn tuīdǎo tuīdòng tuīfān wánchéng wàngdiào xiāngzhōng yādǎo yādī yāfú yùjiàn yuèguò zhǎoqí zhànzhù zhìfú zhìfú líkāi xiǎngkāi kànkāi piěkāi zhǎnkāi dǎkāi fēnkāi kànshàng gǎnshàng.

Verb-Direction Separable Words

chūlái chūqù guòlái guòqù huílái huíqù jìnlái jìnqù qǐlái shànglái shàngqù xiàlái xiàqù.

References

1. Hongying, Z., Wenxin, L., Kunli, Z., Yajuan, Ye., Baobao, C., Zhifang, S.: Building a pediatric medical corpus: word segmentation and named entity annotation. In: Liu, M., Kit, C., Su, Qi. (eds.) CLSW 2020. LNCS (LNAI), vol. 12278, pp. 652–664. Springer, Cham (2021). https://doi.org/10.1007/978-3-030-81197-6_55
2. Duanzhu, S., Jiacuo, C., Jia, C.: Revisiting Tibetan word segmentation with neural networks. In: Liu, M., Kit, C., Su, Q. (eds.) CLSW 2020. LNCS (LNAI), vol. 12278, pp. 515–524. Springer, Cham (2021). https://doi.org/10.1007/978-3-030-81197-6_44
3. Wang, Y., Liu, H., Yang, E., Jiang, Y.: Research and implementation of Buzzword detection technology based on the dynamic circulation corpus. In: Dong, M., Gu, Y., Hong, J.F. (eds.) CLSW 2021. LNCS, vol. 13249, pp. 518–530. Springer, Cham (2022). https://doi.org/10.1007/978-3-031-06703-7_41
4. Zang, J.-J., Xun, E.-D.: Automatic recognition of separable words based on BCC. J. Chin. Inf. Process. **31**(1), 75–83 (2017). (in Chinese)
5. Li, Q.-H.: About the characteristics and usage of separable words. Lang. Teach. Linguist. Stud. **3**, 91–100 (1983). (in Chinese)
6. Liu, S.: The modern Chinese word for "Separable Words". J. Qiqihar Univ. (Philos. Soc. Sci. Ed.). (5), 46–48 (1999). (in Chinese)
7. Wang, S.-M.: On the structure, expansion and usage of the bisyllabic separable words. J. Shenyang Normal Univ. (Soc. Sci. Ed.) (4), 62–66 (1999). (in Chinese)
8. Cao, B.-P., Feng, G.-H.: Forming type of separable word and its separating rule. J. Radio TV Univ. (Philos. Soc. Sci.) (4), 95–97 (2003). (in Chinese)
9. Fu, A.-P.: Chinese sentence tokenization in a Chinese-English MT system. J. Chin. Inf. Process. **5**, 7–13 (1999). (in Chinese)
10. Wang, H.-F., Li, S., Zhao, T.-J., Yang, M.-Y.: Processing of separable word in Chinese-English machine translation. J. China Soc. Sci. Tech. Inf. **4**, 301–305 (1999). (in Chinese)
11. Liu, L.-Y., Qu, Y.-L., Fan, X.-Z.: Design of an intelligent Chinese language input system. Trans. Beijing Inst. Technol. **3**, 342–344 (2001). (in Chinese)
12. Yang, Q.: A computer automatic correcting system for separable verbs based on the HSK composition corpus. Appl. Linguist. **2**, 116–124 (2011). (in Chinese)
13. Xiao, S., Li, Y.-F., He, Y.-X.: Decision on legal separation form of separable triggers based on dependency parsing. Comput. Eng. Appl. **50**(10), 11–17 (2014). (in Chinese)

14. Wang, C.-X.: A Corpus-based Study of Separable Words. Beijing Language & Culture University, Beijing (2001). (in Chinese)
15. Zhou, W.-H.: Information Processing Oriented Researches on the Semantic Collocation Between the Verbs and Objects in Modern Chinese Language. Central China Normal University, Wuhan (2007). (in Chinese)
16. Liu, B.: Research on Automatic Recognition of Separable Words Based on Corpus. HeBei University, Baoding (2015). (in Chinese)
17. Zhao, Y.-X: Application Oriented Chinese Separable Words Recognition. Nanjing Normal University, Nanjing (2019). (in Chinese)
18. Wang, C., Rao, G., Xun, E., Sui, Z.: Chunk extraction and analysis based on frame-verbs. In: Dong, M., Gu, Y., Hong, J.F. (eds.) CLSW 2021. LNCS, vol. 13249, pp. 417–425. Springer, Cham (2022). https://doi.org/10.1007/978-3-031-06703-7_32
19. Yang, Q.-H.: The Dictionary of Modern Chinese Separable Words Usage. Beijing Normal University Press, Beijing (1995). (in Chinese)
20. Wang, H.-F., Xue, J.-J., Wang, J.-P.: The Dictionary of Modern Chinese Separable Words Learning. Peking University Press, Beijing (2013). (in Chinese)

Author Index

Q. Su et al. (Eds.): CLSW 2022, LNAI 13496, pp. 391–393, 2023.
https://doi.org/10.1007/978-3-031-28956-9

Printed in the United States
by Baker & Taylor Publisher Services